A Companion to Racial and Ethnic Studies

Blackwell Companions in Cultural Studies

Advisory editor: David Theo Goldberg, University of California, Irvine

This series aims to provide theoretically ambitious but accessible volumes devoted to the major fields and subfields within cultural studies, whether as single disciplines (film studies) inspired and reconfigured by interventionist cultural studies approaches, or from broad interdisciplinary and multidisciplinary perspectives (gender studies, race and ethnic studies, postcolonial studies). Each volume sets out to ground and orientate the student through a broad range of specially commissioned articles and also to provide the more experienced scholar and teacher with a convenient and comprehensive overview of the latest trends and critical directions. An overarching *Companion to Cultural Studies* will map the territory as a whole.

A Companion to Racial
and Ethnic Studies

Edited by

David Theo Goldberg and John Solomos

BLACKWELL
Publishers

Copyright © Blackwell Publishers Ltd 2002

First published 2002

2 4 6 8 10 9 7 5 3 1

Blackwell Publishers Inc.
350 Main Street
Malden, Massachusetts 02148
USA

Blackwell Publishers Ltd
108 Cowley Road
Oxford OX4 1JF
UK

Library of Congress Cataloging-in-Publication Data has been applied for.

ISBN 0-631-20616-7 (hardback)

British Library Cataloguing in Publication Data

A CIP catalogue record for this book is available from the British Library.

Typeset in 10/12pt Ehrhardt
by Kolam Information Services Pvt. Ltd, Pondicherry, India

Printed in Great Britain by T.J. International, Padstow, Cornwall

This book is printed on acid-free paper.

Contents

Contents

Contents

List of Contributors

Bill Ashcroft is Associate Professor in the School of English, New South Wales University, Sydney.

Les Back is Reader in Sociology, Goldsmiths College, University of London.

Michael Banton is Professor Emeritus of Sociology, University of Bristol.

Zygmunt Bauman is Professor Emeritus of Sociology, University of Leeds.

Robert Bernasconi is the Lillian and Morrie Moss Professor of Philosophy at the University of Memphis.

Gargi Bhattacharyya is a Lecturer in the Department of Cultural Studies and Sociology, University of Birmingham.

Charles Briggs is Professor of Ethnic Studies, University of California, San Diego.

Stephen Castles is Director of the Refugee Studies Centre, University of Oxford.

Phil Cohen is Professor of Sociology at the University of East London.

Frank Dikötter is Lecturer in Chinese History at the School of Oriental and African Studies, University of London.

Philomena Essed is Senior Researcher at the University of Amsterdam and Visiting Professor at the University of California, Irvine.

Peter Fitzpatrick is Anniversary Professor of Law at Birkbeck College, University of London.

Henry A. Giroux is Waterbury Chair in Secondary Education at Penn State University.

Pandeli Glavanis is Deputy Dean of the Faculty of Social Sciences, University of Northumbria, Newcastle upon Tyne.

David Theo Goldberg is Director, University of California Humanities Research Institute and Professor of African American Studies and Criminology, Law, and Society at the University of California, Irvine.

Sandra Harding is Professor of Education and Philosophy, UCLA.

Douglas Hartmann is Assistant Professor of Sociology at the University of Minnesota, Twin Cities.

Percy C. Hintzen is Associate Professor of African American Studies at the University of California, Berkeley.

Jennifer Hochschild is Professor of Government and Afro-American Studies, Harvard University.

Michael Keith is Professor of Sociology, Goldsmiths College, University of London.

Tony Kushner is Professor of History, University of Southampton.

Marco Martiniello is Senior Research Associate at the National Fund for Scientific Research (FNRS) and Lecturer in Politics at the University of Liège and director of the Centre d'Études de l'Ethnicité et des Migrations (CEDEM).

Douglas S. Massey is Dorothy Swaine Thomas Professor and Department Chair of Sociology, University of Pennsylvania.

Stephen May is Lecturer in Sociology, University of Bristol.

Claudia M. Milian Arias is Mellon Postdoctoral Fellow in Humanities at Haverford College, Pennsylvania.

Jan Nederveen Pieterse is Associate Professor of Sociology at the Institute of Social Studies in The Hague, Netherlands.

Deborah Posel is Professor of Sociology and Director of Wits Institute for Social and Economic Research (WISER), University of Witwatersrand.

Liza Schuster is T. H. Marshall Fellow, Department of Sociology, London School of Economics, University of London.

Stephen Small is Associate Professor of African American Studies at the University of California, Berkeley.

Werner Sollors is Henry B. and Anne M. Cabot Professor of English Literature and Professor of Afro-American Studies, Harvard University.

John Solomos is Professor of Sociology, Department of Sociology, City University, London.

France Winddance Twine is an Associate Professor of Sociology at the University of California at Santa Barbara.

Teun A. van Dijk is Professor of Discourse Analysis at the University of Amsterdam and Visiting Professor at the Universidad Tat Pompeu Fabra, Barcelona.

Vron Ware is Lecturer in Sociology, Yale University.

Jonathan W. Warren is an Assistant Professor of Latin American Studies at the University of Washington, Seattle and Assistant Professor of African and African American Studies and Cultural Anthropology at Duke University.

Michel Wieviorka is Professor at the École des Hautes Études en Sciences Sociales and Director of the Centre D'Analyse et d'Intervention Sociologiques (CADIS) in Paris.

Adrien Katherine Wing is Professor of Law, University of Iowa.

Elvan Zabunyan is a Lecturer in the History of Art Department of the Université de Rennes, Brittany.

Preface

As the twenty-first century dawns, questions about race, racism, and ethnic conflict remain at the heart of both public debate and academic discourse. In academic and everyday discourses it is now almost impossible to ignore the preoccupation with different facets of racial or ethnic conflict in various parts of the globe. Yet it is also clear that there is a lack of clarity about both the substance and the boundaries of race and ethnicity as related fields of study, about their scope, social conditions and formations, the relations and implications they signal and signify. Given the upheavals of at least the past two decades, it seems clear that this is an area that is rapidly changing, both in terms of its focus and in terms of its disciplinary location. In this environment there is a need for rethinking the ways in which race and ethnicity have been studied. At the heart of this rethinking we need to ask what it is that we mean when we use terms such as race, racism, ethnicity, and ethnocentrism. There is also a need to review the current theoretical and research agendas around these concepts in order to situate recent trends against a wider historical perspective.

It is because we would like to encourage more open debate about what it is that we do when we study race and ethnicity that we have put together this volume, with an eye both on key historical trends and on more contemporary developments. The Blackwell *Companion to Racial and Ethnic Studies* brings together both more established scholars and younger researchers to discuss some of the most important conceptual and political issues that are at the core of contemporary debates about race and racism. Our primary concern has been to bring together a collection of essays responding to the need for students and scholars of race and ethnicity to have access in one volume to the whole spectrum of theoretical debates and empirical research reshaping the field at present. We have intentionally sought for the *Companion* a cross-disciplinary feel. This strikes us as far more compelling than limiting the focus to a prevailing discipline such as sociology. In recent years there has been a rapid expansion in the number of courses offered on racial matters at all levels of higher education, in a variety of disciplines. At the same time there has been a proliferation of new research agendas and theoretical debates. We have attempted as far as possible to reflect key facets of the new debates and research agendas around race and ethnicity; and we have been concerned to convey the vibrancy of the current work about race and racism.

In assembling a volume such as this one we have inevitably accumulated numerous debts to colleagues and friends. Our first debt is to all the contributors who have made this volume possible. As seems to happen inevitably with complex projects, there were delays in bringing together the final version and we are grateful for the patience of those contributors who produced their contributions in a timely fashion. We also thank the editorial staff at Blackwell Publishers for their support throughout the long process of production, and their patience at the inevitable delays, especially our copy-editor Jenny Roberts. Andrew McNeillie and Jayne Fargnoli rolled with our rolling deadlines, quietly confident always that we would deliver in the end. We are convinced that the quality of their editorial leadership and patience is a function of the quality of the jazz they have shared with us throughout. Our respective academic institutions and colleagues have helped us to devote time to complete this project, and we greatly appreciate this.

We have also gained much from the support of friends and collaborators who encouraged us along the way. Our special thanks to Claire Alexander, Les Back, Chetan Bhatt, Martin Bulmer, Lewis Gordon, Harry Goulbourne, Randy Hanson, Clive Harris, Barnor Hesse, Michael Keith, Marco Martiniello, Karim Murji, Michael Musheno, and Liza Schuster.

David Theo Goldberg could not have completed his work on this volume without the selfless assistance of Kim Furumoto and Kay Korman at Arizona State University, and Doug Feremenga, Jocelyn Pacleb, and Susan Feighn at the University of California Humanities Research Institute. The book took shape through daily conversations with Philomena, each productive moment shared in ways large and small. Gabriel lightened the intellectual intensity with boyish interventions and calls to "keep it real."

John Solomos is grateful to Chris, Nikolas, and Daniel for putting up with his fixation with writing or editing books such as this one, the seemingly endless research projects, and the numerous trips involved in following the fortunes of West Bromwich Albion.

David Theo Goldberg
June 2001
Irvine
John Solomos
June 2001
London

General Introduction

David Theo Goldberg and John Solomos

One of the most notable features of recent developments in the field of racial and ethnic studies has been the search for an adequate theoretical analysis of what we mean by notions such as race, racism, and ethnicity. In a growing number of advanced industrial societies, questions about race and ethnicity have moved to the center of scholarly debate, to a considerable degree displacing preoccupation with class and other forms of social inequality. This is evident in the massive increase in scholarly texts regarding race and ethnicity, and the growing number of specialized journals in a variety of disciplines across the social sciences and humanities focusing on theoretical and empirical research on race. This is in marked contrast to the earlier study of race and ethnic relations as largely a sociological or anthropological concern. The crumbling of these disciplinary boundaries in research around race has meant that it is no longer possible or desirable to approach the study of race and/or ethnicity from a single disciplinary perspective.

It is against this background that we started to produce this volume towards the end of the 1990s. In a very real sense, then, this is a volume that could only have been produced at the present time. In putting together the Blackwell *Companion to Racial and Ethnic Studies* we had two key objectives in mind. First, to bring together in an integrated fashion a series of synoptic chapters to provide an overview of the key debates and issues in current research concerning race, ethnicity, and racism. In structuring the volume, we have therefore sought to reflect the changing dynamics of scholarly debate in a field that has transformed tremendously over the past two decades. All six parts of the *Companion* are structured to provide an overview of specific areas of scholarship and debate. Second, we have sought to signal relatively new areas of scholarship that have emerged in recent times. Rather than remain within the boundaries of race and ethnic studies as they have been defined historically, we have sought to include contributions that are suggestive of new avenues of scholarship and research. In the latter sense, we set out to commission essays, for example, on race and cyberspace, on fashion, and on sports.

Bearing these two overarching objectives in mind, we have sought to produce a volume reflecting significant differences in theoretical and empirical research agendas. We have included contributions from both established and emerging scholars whose work has helped to shape recent analysis of race, racism, and ethnicity. This volume offers accessible accounts written by experts in their specific areas of interest. It therefore serves as useful and authoritative starting points for students taking courses in racial and ethnic studies.

In addition, we have drawn on a variety of historical and disciplinary perspectives. The contributions reveal in dynamic ways how race and ethnicity are socially fashioned in particular social and political environments. The meanings of race and racism are located within particular fields of discourse and these fields, in turn, are contextualized within the social relations giving rise to them. A clear point of reference in this regard is the situation in Eastern Europe since the early 1990s, where the collapse of the Soviet bloc set in train processes of questioning and re-evaluation, especially of categories of national and ethnic identity but also concerns over regenerated expressions of racism (Miles, 1994). At the same time, developments within Western Europe – in particular, the emergence of new immigration patterns and refugee movements as key political questions – have centralized the politics of drawing Europe's boundaries, external and internal. These processes of social and political transformation are taking place inter-actively with economic and political restructuring that contributes to a sense of insecurity and anxiety, refueling politics of ethnoracial conflict and exclusion.

Beyond Disciplinary Boundaries

Over the past two decades or so, the shifting boundaries of race and ethnicity as categories of social analysis have become increasingly evident. Despite a history that can be traced back to the 1920s and 1930s, explicit critical study of race and ethnicity remained a relatively small subfield in disciplines such as sociology and anthropology until late into the twentieth century. Yet there can be little doubt that in the past 20 years work on race and ethnicity has flourished, becoming one of the most intense areas of academic and political debate across a whole range of societies (Back and Solomos, 2000; Cohen, 2000). Perhaps the most notable feature of this new work is that it can no longer be reducible to any single discipline in assumption or methodology, scope or content. The multidimensionalities of ethnoracial definition and experience as well as of racist expression have prompted the multidisciplinary and interdisciplinary nature of the analytic work necessary to understand them.

One of the considerations at issue here concerns the role of racial and ethnic categor-ization in the making and remaking of social and political identities. A clear case in point is the intense debate about "immigration" and "minorities" that has raged across Europe over the past decade (Wrench and Solomos, 1993; Joppke, 1999; Castles and Davidson, 2000). At the heart of contemporary discourses about migrants, minorities, and citizen-ship are to be found anxieties about what it means to "belong" or to be excluded from particular national collectivities. These concerns inform debates about the changing nature of citizenship in an era of increased transnational mobility. Citizenship and migration form part of a matrix with questions of identity, nationality, and ethnicity. Within both popular and academic discourse there is growing concern about how this matrix of questions can be reconceptualized in the context of multicultural societies (Ford, 1992; Tully, 1995; Kymlicka, 1996; Kymlicka and Norman, 2000; Schuster and Solomos, 2001). In contemporary European societies, governments of various kinds are trying to come to terms with the conditions indexed by these categories. At issue are the political rights of minorities, including representation in both local and national politics, and the position of minority religious and cultural rights in societies becoming more diverse. Underlying all of these concerns is the thorny issue of what, if anything, can be done to protect the rights of minorities and to develop extensive notions of citizenship and democracy that incorporate those minorities hitherto excluded on racial and ethnic criteria (Solomos and Back, 1995, 1996; Castles and Miller, 1998; Papastergiadis, 2000).

Despite the growing political and social importance of race and ethnicity, however, there is still much confusion about what it is that we mean by these notions, as evidenced by the range of terminological debates that have tended to dominate much discussion in recent years. The considerable body of work now notwithstanding, there do remain significant questions that have not been adequately addressed. Why is it, for instance, that race and ethnicity retain their considerable hold over individual and collective action? What factors explain the mobilizing power of ideas about *race* and *ethnicity* in the contemporary environment? What countervalues and ideas can be developed to undermine the general appeal of racist ideas and movements? Is it possible for communities that are socially defined by differences of race, ethnicity, religion, or other social signifiers to live together in societies that are able to ensure equality, justice, and mutually respectful consideration?

Conceptualizing Race and Ethnicity

A guiding theme in much recent scholarship, which is discussed from a variety of perspectives, concerns the claim that race and ethnicity are not *natural* categories, even though both concepts are often represented as if they were (Stoler, 1995; Smaje, 2000). Their boundaries are not fixed, nor is their membership uncontested. Race and ethnic groups, like nations, are now quite widely considered to be "imagined communities" (Anderson, 1991), socially conceived and considered, manufactured and inflected group formations (Mosse, 1985; Peterson, 1995). They are discursively fashioned or ideologically produced, made and changed in relation to, and molded by, social conditions, relations, clashes, and struggles. They signal a language in and through which differences are accorded social significance and may be named and explained (Goldberg, 1993, 1997). But what is of importance for social researchers studying race and ethnicity is that such ideas also carry with them material consequences for those who are included within their parameters or excluded in terms of their extension.

As Sandra Harding shows in her powerfully revealing contribution to this volume, efforts to divide human beings into groups on the basis of alleged genetic or phenotypical differences have proved to be spurious and misleading, even in some cases politically and humanly disastrous (Gilman, 1985; Gilroy, 2000). Rather, it is best to see race as always a medium by which difference is represented and otherness produced, so that contingent attributes such as skin color are transformed into supposedly essential bases for identities, group belonging and exclusion, social privileges and burdens, political rights and disenfranchisements. We do not mean to deny, therefore, that race remains, at the level of everyday experience and social representation, a potent political and social category around which individuals and groups organize their identity and construct a politics. We are pointing to the fact that race is fabricated, socially made and politically manipulated (Giroux, 1993; Sears, Sidanius, and Bobo, 2000). Blackness and whiteness, "colored" or "mestizaje" accordingly are not essential characteristics of human beings but defined by sociohistorical conditions and political struggles over their valence and meaning, referents and extension.

So categories such as race and ethnicity are best conceived as political resources. They are used by both dominant and subordinate groups for the purposes of legitimizing and furthering their own social identities and interests, claims and powers. In this context it is important to remember that identities based on race and ethnicity are not only imposed, even though they often are, but they also can be formulated and fashioned through resistance. Here racially constituted minorities play a key and active role. It is more accurate as a consequence to speak of a racially fashioned or created (or more commonly, if awkwardly, of a "racialized") group than of a racial group since race is a product of racism and not vice versa. It is also and relatedly important to note that the now popular if overused notion of "racialization" and its cognates ("racialize," "racialized") are ambiguous. They fail in their often facile usage to distinguish descriptive context from normative critique, analysis from dismissal, processes of race-making from critical rejection of racist implications.

Racism, by extension, is an expression of racially predicated or manifested social and political relations of domination, subordination, and privilege. Racism operates by positioning subjects old and new to exclusionary or demeaning purposes. Race is about the representation of difference. Sites of difference are also sites of power, a power in terms and by means of which the dominated come to see and experience themselves as "Other," as alien and strange.

The rise of extreme right-wing and neofascist movements and parties in the past decade in both Western and Eastern Europe has resulted in the emergence of new forms of racist politics, a surge in popular racism, and violence against migrant communities. At the same time, we have seen a noticeable rise in antisemitism in many European countries, East and West, evident equally in physical and symbolic threats to Jewish and Roma/Sinti communities. It is not surprising, then, that questions about immigration and race have assumed new salience, both politically and socially. This has contributed to creating an environment in which the future of settled migrant communities as well as of new groups of migrants and refugees is very much at the heart of public debate.

These developments, among others, show why it is impossible in the present political and social climate to ignore the impact of race and ethnicity on the social and political institutions of those states drawn into the global sphere of modernity's influence. As late as the 1980s it was still relatively common to treat questions about racism, ethnicity, and nationalism as relatively marginal to the agenda of social scientists and policy makers. By contrast, it is hardly an exaggeration now to say that these issues have invaded the core of public debate. It is therefore imperative to develop an historically based view of the role played by racially fashioned social relations and implications in contemporary societies.

Racism and Social Change

The various components of this volume highlight the fact that the terms of official and popular discourses about race and racism are in constant flux. Trends and processes in the United States and in European societies most clearly exemplify this conceptual volatility. The volatility is a product of the development of new racist political movements as well as of intense official debate about the kinds of policies that should be pursued to deal with immigration, the political and social rights of migrants, and so on. This changing politics of migration worldwide illustrates the complex variety of factors that has helped to construct political understandings of the position of migrant communities in disparate geographical and social contexts.

Racist ideas and movements thus are continuing variously to impact a range of contemporary societies (Winant, 1994; Wieviorka, 1995; Bulmer and Solomos, 1999; Marable, 2000). Racial and ethnic forms continue to structure modern societies, giving rise recently to numerous excesses in different parts of the globe, including most notably in parts of Africa, a surge in neo-Nazi sympathies in North America as well as throughout Europe, East and West. It is almost impossible to read a newspaper or watch television news coverage without seeing the contemporary expressions of racist ideas and practices. These expressions now commonly include examples of neofascist movements or occasionally the implementation of policies of genocide and what euphemistically is called "ethnic cleansing."

These trends need to be situated within the changing socioeconomic environment of contemporary societies. It is also important to situate them within processes of cultural and social change. We should not, in other words, lose sight of the complex social, political, and cultural determinants shaping contemporary racist discourses and movements. Recent accounts of the growth of new forms of cultural racism reveal two pertinent considerations vested in the language of contemporary racist movements. On one hand, there is a certain flexibility about what is meant by race. On the other hand, an attempt is made by racist movements to reconstitute themselves as concerned with defending their "nation" rather than attacking others as such. It is not surprising in this context that one finds within the contemporary languages of race a combination of arguments favoring cultural difference along with negative images of the *other* as a racial threat and as representing an *impure* culture.

Given the embedded nature of racial processes in the contemporary environment, it is unsurprising that subordinate groups may invoke difference to mystify, to deny knowledge of themselves to the dominant groups, to confuse and neutralize those who attempt to control or "help" them, or to reduce them to research objects. They may use difference to stress their own separateness, and to authorize their own representations. They may seek to legitimize their own definitions of cultural difference, including those against others from within their own collectivity. They may seize the category, claim it for their own and invert it, attaching positive value where before it was totalizingly negative (Goldberg, 1993). This can lead at times, as we shall see later, to a strange convergence in the language of the racist right and of black or ethnic nationalists, as both infuse the racial or ethnic category with essentialist, and supposedly naturally inherited, characteristics.

Questioning Identities

Race and ethnicity are intrinsically forms of collective social identity. The subject of identity consequently has been at the heart of both historical and contemporary discussions about ethnoracial issues. The question of identity has become a keyword in contemporary politics and it has taken on so many different connotations that sometimes it is obvious that people are not talking about the same phenomena. One thing at least is clear: identity becomes hotly contested when it is in crisis, when something assumed to be fixed, coherent, and stable is placed in question, and subjected to doubt and uncertainty.

The preoccupation with identity in scholarship concerning race and ethnicity can be taken as one outcome of concerns about where minorities in "Western" societies actually belong (Castles and Davidson, 2000; Hesse, 2000). At a basic level, after all, identity is about belonging, about what we have in common with some people and what differentiates us from others. Identity gives one a sense of personal location, and provides a stable core for one's individuality; but it is also about one's social relationships, one's complex involvement with others, and in the modern world these have become even more complex and confusing. Each of us lives with a variety of potentially contradictory identities, which battle within us for allegiance: as men or women, black, brown, or white, straight or gay, able-bodied or disabled. The list is open-ended, and so too are our possible belongings or identifications.

So identity is not simply imposed. It is also chosen, and actively used, albeit within particular social contexts and constraints. Against dominant representations of "others" there is resistance. Within structures of dominance, there is agency. Analyzing resistance and agency repoliticizes relations between collectivities and draws attention to the central constituting factor of power in social relations. But it is possible to overemphasize resistance; to validate others through validating the lives of the colonized and exploited. Valorizing resistance may also have the unintended effect of belittling the enormous costs exacted in situations of unequal power, exclusion, and discrimination. While political legitimacy, gaining access or a hearing, may depend on being able to "call up" a constituency and authorize representations through appeals to authenticity, it provides the basis for policing the boundaries of authenticity. Here, some "insiders" may find themselves excluded because they are not considered to be authentic enough.

For example, stressing racial and ethnic differences can obscure the experiences and interests women may share as women. We therefore need to ask: Who is constructing the categories and defining the boundaries? Who is resisting these imposed identity creations and definitions? What are the consequences being written into or out of particular categories? What happens when subordinate groups seek to mobilize along boundaries drawn for the purposes of domination? What happens to individuals whose multiple identities may be fragmented and segmented by category politics?

A central concern with the contemporary discussion around "identity politics" is that the dilemmas and questions outlined here are not adequately addressed. This is largely because much discussion is underpinned by the presumption that one's identity necessarily defines one's politics and that there can be no politics until the subject has excavated or laid claim to his or her social identity. Inherent in such positions is the failure to understand the way in which identity grows out of, and is transformed by, action and struggle. This is one of the dangers of the preoccupation with exactly who is covered by the category "black" in contemporary British society. The usage of the notion of black to cover a variety of diverse communities has been rejected by some scholars in favor of other categories such as Asian, Muslim, or African-Caribbean. Yet others have sought to argue for a notion of "black" grounded in "racial" particularity. But the danger with these approaches is that one is presented with no more than a strategy of simple inversion. Here, the old bad black essentialist subject is replaced by a new good black essentialist subject whose identity necessarily guarantees a correct politics.

Culture and Politics

Part of the dilemma we face is that collective identities are not things with which we are born. Rather, they are formed and transformed within and in relation to representation. We only know what it is to be English or French because of the way Englishness and Frenchness has come to be represented, as a set of meanings within a national culture. It follows that a nation is not only a political entity but something which produces meanings – a system of cultural representation. People are legal citizens of a state; but they also participate and are implicated in the idea of the nation as represented in national culture. A nation is a symbolic community and it is this which accounts for its power to generate a sense of identity and allegiance.

National cultures, then, are composed not only of cultural institutions, but in addition of symbols and representations. A national culture is a discourse. It is a way of constructing meanings which influences and organizes both our actions and our conceptions of our selves. National cultures construct identities by producing meanings about "the nation" with which we can identify: these are contained in the stories which are told about it, memories which connect its present with its past, and images which are constructed of it. Differences between nations lie in the different ways in which they are imagined, that is, conceived, comprehended, represented, and critically considered.

But how is the modern nation imagined? What representational strategies are deployed to construct our commonsense views of national belonging or identity? What are the representations of, say, England, which win the identifications and define the identities of English people? Collective identity is based on the (selective) process of memory, so that a given group recognizes itself through its recollection of a common past. From this perspective national identity is a specific form of collective identity, a belonging, which is both a way of being, of social existence, and a longing. Identity thus conceived fluctuates between two poles, "romantic longing" and "terror." "Romantic longing" involves a hungering for identification with common members, those one takes to be like oneself because social representation has suggested they are. "Terror," by contrast, is prompted by the inevitable failure to fulfill the membership drive (Goldberg, Musheno, and Bower, 2001). This is the fear at the heart of the question of identity, whether posed at the level of the individual or nation. Driven by such fears, the defense of a cherished cultural identity easily slips into the most hackneyed nationalism, or often enough racism, and the nationalist affirmation of the superiority of one group over another. The question is not abstract; it is a matter of the relative power of different groups to define their own identities, and the ability to mobilize these definitions through their control of cultural institutions. Tradition is not a matter of a fixed and given set of beliefs or practices which are handed down or accepted passively.

The growth of identity politics has been seen by some as challenging cultural homogeneity and providing spaces for marginal groups to assert the legacy and importance of their respective voices and experiences. At the same time, however, identity politics has often failed to move beyond a notion of difference structured in polarizing binarisms and an uncritical appeal to a discourse of authenticity. It has allowed many formerly silenced and displaced groups to emerge from the margins of power and dominant culture to reassert and reclaim suppressed identities and experiences. But in doing so, these groups have often substituted one master narrative or theory for another, invoking a politics of separatism, and they have suppressed differences within their own "liberatory" narratives (Bhatt, 1997).

This is a point made succinctly by Stuart Hall in his critique of black essentialism. Hall argues that essentialist forms of political and cultural discourse naturalize and dehistoricize difference, and therefore mistake what is historical and cultural for what is natural, biological, and genetic. The moment we tear the signifier "black" from its historical, cultural, and political embedding and lodge it in a biologically constituted racial category, Hall insists, we valorize, by inversion, the very ground of the racism we are trying to deconstruct. We fix the signifier outside of history, outside of change, outside of political intervention. This is exemplified by the tendency to see the term "black" as sufficient in itself to guarantee the progressive character of the politics articulated under that banner. It is evident, nevertheless, that we need to analyze precisely the content of these political strategies and how they construct specific "racial" meanings through politics.

We have arrived, Hall argues, at an encounter, the "end of innocence," and so the end of the innocent notion of the essential black subject. What is at issue here is the recognition of the extraordinary diversity of subject positions, social experiences, and cultural identities which compose the category *black*. This involves the recognition that *black* is essentially a politically and culturally constructed category, one that cannot be grounded in a set of fixed transcultural or transcendental racial categories and which therefore has no guarantees. This brings into play the recognition of the immense diversity and differentiation of the historical and cultural experiences of minority communities in societies that throughout modernity have traded on their claim to, and acted to "protect" their projected homogeneity. This inevitably entails a weakening or fading of the notion that race or some composite notion of race around the term "black" will either guarantee the effectiveness of any cultural practice or determine in any final sense its aesthetic value (Hall, 2000).

While writers such as Hall have been attempting to question essentialist notions of black identity, it is interesting to note that new right political discourses have become increasingly preoccupied with defending the importance of ever more fixed notions of culture and nation. They have sought to reconstruct primordial notions of ethnic exclusivity which celebrate national identity and patriotism in the face of criticism from multiculturalists and antiracists.

Central to such discourses is the attempt to fuse culture within a tidy formation that equates nation, citizenship, and patriotism with a racially exclusive notion of difference. Conservatives have given enormous prominence to waging a cultural struggle over the control and use of the popular media and other modes of representation. They have done so in order to articulate contemporary racial meanings and identities in new ways, to link race with more comprehensive political and cultural agendas, to interpret social structural phenomena (such as inequality or social policy) in terms of "race." For the new right, the appeal by and large is no longer to racial supremacy but to cultural uniformity parading under the politics of nationalism and patriotism. This emphasis on heritage concerns the valorization of an elitist view of self and social development, the call to define civilization as synonymous with selected aspects of Western tradition, matched by a fervent attempt to reduce pedagogy to the old transmission model of teaching and learning. This repositioning of national culture seeks to recode it around consecrated relics, shrines, and tradition, for instance, in the syllabus of English culture.

In this case, difference is removed from under the language of biologism and firmly established as a cultural creation only to be reworked within a language that concretizes race and nation through the elimination of any claim that structural and cultural inequality persists.

Between Borders

The various contributions in Part VI underline the fact that issues of race and ethnicity are implicated in global arrangements. It is more evident now than during the last century that ethnoracial considerations are part of global processes of social and political order and change.

In their analysis of the politics of citizenship under the conditions of increasing globalization, Castles and Davidson (2000) reveal the range of research questions concerning the changing morphology of ethnoracial politics in various parts of the world. Writing from a comparative perspective, they link questions about the shifting boundaries of citizenship to the socioeconomic and political realities of the migration process. Drawing on their research in Europe and Australasia, Castles and Davidson argue that migrant communities cannot simply be incorporated into society as discrete individuals. In particular, ethnically or racially positioned migrants in practice may need to mobilize in these terms in order to deal with the consequences of racism and marginalization in their specific environments. States, in turn, may have to develop policies that can respond to marginalized populations as collectivities with specific demands concerning their social and political positions rather than as individuals.

There are quite divergent perspectives in the present political environment about how best to deal with this range of concerns. There is, for example, a wealth of discussion about what kind of measures are necessary to tackle the inequalities and exclusions confronting marginalized groups. At the same time there is clear evidence that existing initiatives are severely restricted in their impact. Many commentators have pointed to the limitations of legislation and public policy interventions in bringing about major improvements to the sociopolitical positions of marginalized groups.

This raises a number of questions. First, what kind of policies could tackle discrimination and inequality more effectively? Second, what links could be made between policies on immigration and policies on social and economic issues? What kind of productive social policy agenda can be developed to deal with the positions of established communities, groups within the society long marginalized, and new (im)migrants? These questions are at the heart of contemporary debates and have given rise to quite divergent policy prescriptions. In particular, policies promoted in response to one set of issues or one group are quite often at odds or inconsistent with those addressed to other concerns. Little attention has been paid to thinking through the global and interactive considerations of those concerns. It is quite clear that in the present political environment it is unlikely that any sort of agreement about how to develop global policies regarding these matters will be easy to achieve.

Nevertheless, it is clear that some key issues are evident in public debate. A case in point concerns the pressing question of citizenship in relation to race and ethnicity. Responses to the question have varied widely across different societies. Policy debates in Britain, unlike other European societies, have often not taken seriously the issues of political and citizenship rights regarding migrants and their descendants. However, ethnic minorities in Britain and elsewhere have questioned vigorously whether they are fully included in and represented through political institutions. There is growing awareness of the gap between formal citizenship and the *de facto* restriction of the economic and social rights of traditionally or newly marginalized groups as a result of discrimination, economic restructuring, and the decline of the welfare state.

The relationship between identity, difference, and culture needs to be located within a broader reconceptualization of substantive democracy that addresses the rights of minorities and the racially marginalized. The value of such a politics is that it foregrounds the complicated issues of difference in the discourse of substantive citizenship. Moreover, it centers the conflict over relations of power, identity, and culture in the broader struggles to advance the critical imperatives of a democratic society. Primary in such struggles is a rethinking and rewriting of difference in relation to wider considerations of membership, community, and social responsibility.

In the present environment, then, it has become clear that patterns of exclusion are often interlinked. Thus political, social, and economic exclusion can culminate in physical exclusion. This occurs most obviously at the border, either with a refusal of permission to enter, as is frequently the case, or deportation. The importance of not being physically included can be seen in the high price that some pay to enter or remain in wealthier states. The narratives in the press of those frozen to death in the undercarriages of aircraft, asphyxiated while being forcibly deported, or committing suicide while in detention awaiting deportation are increasing. Often these are socially invisible populations. Often physically excluded within the territory of nation-states, asylum seekers and refugees repeatedly find themselves confined for indefinite periods of time, without full explanation of the reasons for their detention in a language they can understand, and too many times without legal representation.

Not all migrants suffer these extremes, however. The trends identified by some commentators towards globalization of labor and the emergence of transnational citizenship are real enough. It is also clear, however, that for everyone who can claim to enjoy global or flexible citizenships (Ong, 1999), there are many more who are shut out from every aspect of citizenship, local and global (Goldberg, 2001). These different forms of exclusion emanate from the restrictions of the nation-state. They stunt the development and impede the advancement of sizeable population groups within societies. They are the reason it is important to develop an analysis of contemporary trends and developments sensitive to what is happening at the level of nation-states, localities, and regions as well as transregionally. It is only through such an analysis that we can begin to understand the nature of political debates about (im)migration, the tensions between those newly arriving and the settled if long marginalized groups within the society, and the difficulties and dangers that lie ahead.

Taken together, then, the papers in the *Companion* touch on key dilemmas we face today in thinking about race and racism, and the changing politics of racial and ethnic identity. At the most general level the six component parts of this volume pose questions about the boundaries of "race" and "ethnicity" as modes of identification, organization, exclusion, and experience, as well as fields of study.

References

Anderson, B. (1991) *Imagined Communities: Reflections on the Origin and Spread of Nationalism*. London: Verso.

Back, L. and Solomos, J. (eds.) (2000) *Theories of Race and Racism: A Reader*. London: Routledge.

Bhatt, C. (1997) *Liberation and Purity*. London: UCL Press.

Bulmer, M. and Solomos, J. (eds.) (1999) *Racism*. Oxford: Oxford University Press.

Castles, S. and Davidson, A. (2000) *Citizenship and Migration: Globalization and the Politics of Belonging*. Basingstoke, UK: Macmillan.

Castles, S. and Miller, M. J. (1998) *The Age of Migration*, 2nd edn. London: Macmillan.

Cohen, P. (ed.) (2000) *New Ethnicities, Old Racisms?* London: Zed Books.

Ford, G. (1992) *Fascist Europe: The Rise of Racism and Xenophobia*. London: Pluto Press.

Gilman, S. L. (1985) *Difference and Pathology: Stereotypes of Sexuality, Race and Madness*. Ithaca, NY: Cornell University Press.

Gilroy, P. (2000) *Between Camps: Nations, Cultures and the Allure of Race*. London: Allen Lane.

Giroux, H. (1993) "Living dangerously. Identity politics and the new cultural racism: Towards a critical pedagogy of representation." *Cultural Studies* 7,1:1–27.

Goldberg, D. T. (1993) *Racist Culture: Philosophy and the Politics of Meaning*. Oxford: Blackwell.

Goldberg, D. T. (1997) *Racial Subjects: Writing on Race in America*. New York: Routledge.

Goldberg, D. T. (2001) *The Racial State*. Oxford: Blackwell.

Goldberg, D. T., Musheno, M., and Bower, L. C. (2001) "Shake yo' paradigm: Romantic longing and terror in contemporary socio-legal Studies," in D. T. Goldberg, M. Musheno, and L. C. Bower (eds.) *Between Law and Culture: Relocating Legal Studies*. Minnesota: University of Minnesota Press, pp.ix–xxix.

Hall, S. (2000) "Conclusion: the multicultural question," in B. Hesse (ed.) *Un/Settled Multiculturalisms: Diasporas, Entanglements, "Transruptions."* London: Zed Books, pp.209–41.

Hesse, B. (ed.) (2000) *Un/Settled Multiculturalisms: Diasporas, Entanglements, "Transruptions."* London: Zed Books.

Joppke, C. (1999) *Immigration and the Nation State: The United States, Germany and Great Britain*. Oxford: Oxford University Press.

Kymlicka, W. (1996) *Multicultural Citizenship: A Liberal Theory of Minority Rights*. Oxford. Oxford University Press.

Kymlicka, W. and Norman, W. (eds.) (2000) *Citizenship in Diverse Societies*. Oxford: Oxford University Press.

Marable, M. (ed.) (2000) *Dispatches from the Ebony Tower: Intellectuals Confront the African American Experience*. New York: Columbia University Press.

Miles, R. (1994) "A rise of racism in contemporary Europe?: Some sceptical reflections on its nature and extent." *New Community* 20,4:547–62.

Mosse, G. (1985) *Toward the Final Solution: A History of European Racism*. Madison: University of Wisconsin Press.

Ong, A. (1999) *Flexible Citizenship: The Cultural Logics of Transnationality*. Durham, NC: Duke University Press.

Papastergiadis, N. (2000) *The Turbulence of Migration: Globalization, Deterritorialization and Hybridity*. Cambridge, UK: Polity Press.

Peterson, P. E. (ed.) (1995) *Classifying by Race*. Princeton, NJ: Princeton University Press.

Schuster, L. and Solomos, J. (eds.) (2001) "New perspectives on multiculturalism and citizenship." Special Issue of *Patterns of Prejudice* 35, 1.

Sears, D. O., Sidanius, J., and Bobo, L. (eds.) (2000) *Racialized Politics: The Debate About Racism in America*. Chicago: University of Chicago Press.

Smaje, C. (2000) *Natural Hierarchies: The Historical Sociology of Race and Caste*. Oxford: Blackwell.

Solomos, J. and Back, L. (1995) *Race, Politics and Social Change*. London: Routledge.

Solomos, J. and Back, L. (1996) *Racism and Society*. Basingstoke, UK: Macmillan.

Stoler, A. L. (1995) *Race and the Education of Desire: Foucault's History of Sexuality and the Colonial Order of Things*. Durham, NC: Duke University Press.

Tully, J. (1995) *Strange Multiplicity: Constitutionalism in an Age of Diversity*. Cambridge, UK: Cambridge University Press.

Wieviorka, M. (1995) *The Arena of Racism*. London: Sage.

Winant, H. (1994) *Racial Conditions: Politics, Theory, Comparisons*. Minneapolis: University of Minnesota Press.

Wrench, J. and Solomos, J. (eds) (1993) *Racism and Migration in Western Europe*. Oxford: Berg.

PART I

History

Introduction to Part I

David Theo Goldberg and John Solomos

The complex social histories of racial and ethnic formations is a recurrent theme in this volume. This is partly because it seems impossible to discuss the present state of race and ethnicity without contextualizing current trends against the background of historically specific economic, social, and political processes. In Part I of the *Companion*, accordingly, we have chosen to bring together papers focused in one way or another on the complex range of processes shaping our understanding of the role of race and racism in contemporary social formations. This is partly because we feel it is important to question the tendency in much contemporary theorizing either to ignore the historical background or to oversimplify complex historical trends and processes.

It is with this concern in mind that we begin the *Companion* with six papers that reflect on the history of key ideas and processes that helped to shape the role of race and ethnicity in specific historical environments. The first two papers focus on the relationship between "Europe and its Others." Jan Nederveen Pieterse's exploration of this theme provides insight into the ways in which the "idea of Europe" is predicated constitutively on processes that have created the "other," those who fail to belong, both within and outside Europe. Focusing on the ways in which markers of "difference" became a mechanism for the development of images of religious, cultural, and racial difference, Pieterse's account serves to remind us of the complex role of internal and external "boundaries" in shaping modern-day ideas about European cultures and societies. Pieterse's analysis is complemented by Peter Fitzpatrick's insightful exploration of the meanings that have been attached over time to the "doctrine of discovery." Taking his starting point as the encounter between Europe and other lands that followed Columbus's "discovery" of the Americas, Fitzpatrick helps to situate the ways in which versions of this doctrine served to establish racial, ethnic, and religious boundaries. By highlighting the long-term impact of ideas of discovery on racial and racist doctrines, Fitzpatrick links contemporary processes to the underlying historical patterns of European expansion and domination.

Charles Briggs connects these histories of racial thinking and racist practice to their most extreme manifestations in genocidal expression. Thus Briggs shows how the extreme manifestations of ethnoracially expressed genocides are deeply entangled in daily practices and "ordinary," socially acceptable racist expression. In this, Briggs's deeply insightful account should be read alongside not only the following articles by Zygmunt Bauman on the Holocaust and Tony Kushner on antisemitism, but also

15

Philomena Essed's analysis of "everyday racism" in Part II and David Theo Goldberg's reading of racial states in Part III. For, as Briggs shows, genocides are implications in a deep sense, of the exclusions reproduced through everyday exclusionary practice undergirded by the institutional apparatuses of deeply structured racial states.

If the first three papers focus on a rather wide-ranging historical overview, the following two are more tightly organized around the racial framing of a particular group, namely Jews. Zygmunt Bauman's characterizes the Holocaust as the ultimate expression of the genocidal tendency in racial and ethnic hatred. Bauman's analysis of the Holocaust has been an important point of reference in discussions concerning the Holocaust over the past decade or so, reflecting a wider literature that has grown up in sociology and other disciplines. Bauman's account begins from a seemingly simple question: How modern is the Holocaust? The parameters of Bauman's response to this question are framed around his concern to show that the Holocaust is very much the product of quintessentially modern social and political conditions, forces, and relations.

The complex history of antisemitism has been the subject of much scholarly debate, although within the mainstream of racial and ethnic studies there is surprisingly little discussion of the historical processes by which antisemitism becomes a form of racism. Tony Kushner provides a wide-ranging overview of the origins and usages of the notion of antisemitism. Kushner's analysis can be seen as a critical reassessment of the limits and contradictions in some popular understandings of antisemitism, particularly those focused on the Holocaust. He suggests that there is a need for clearer analytical thinking about the relationship between antisemitism and racism, ethnic hatreds, and persecution as a whole. A recurrent theme throughout Kushner's analysis relates to the limitations of recent trends to the Holocaust's supposed exceptionalism, to see it as a unique and incomparable phenomenon. In contrast, he suggests, there is a need to contextualize antisemitism within a wider conceptual and historical framework of analysis.

The final paper in Part I, by Deborah Posel, looks at another important expression of racism in the twentieth century, namely, the apartheid regime in South Africa. In the second half of that century apartheid became an almost universal reference point for discussions about racism. This is perhaps unsurprising, given the extreme and largely visible nature of the political, social, and economic structures of the apartheid regime and the centrality of race in shaping its development. Posel's account provides both a detailed critical analysis of various explanations of the emergence and development of apartheid and an account of the processes that shaped its emergence and eventual decline. Her account is suggestive also of the need to rethink the way in which understandings of apartheid and their explanatory limitations have developed.

Chapter 1

Europe and its Others

Jan Nederveen Pieterse

From time immemorial, peoples have considered themselves as "the people" and all the rest as "others." Familiar examples are the Greeks and the *barbaroi*, the Jews and the *goyim*, the Japanese and the *gajjin*, and China as the Middle Kingdom. Throughout, designating others and emphasizing their "otherness" have been fundamental to the construction of boundaries of identity and community, between and within societies. Over time, otherness has had many different meanings, as many as identity. It has referred to cultural differences along the lines of language, religion, civilization, "race," ethnicity, region, nationality, gender, age, and to class, development, ideology, and so forth.

"Europe and its others" is a sprawling theme that involves a variety of historically changing boundaries that share an element of "difference." "Europe" can be taken in two ways: within Europe, that is, within what is now considered Europe, and in relation to Europe, that is, problematizing the identity of Europe. Both are considered here. While "Europe" is an old concept it did not gain currency until the seventeenth century and, by and large, only became an active boundary as such in the course of the nineteenth century and particularly from the beginning of the twentieth century. This treatment opens with a discussion of the different meanings of otherness in relation to Europe over time, including the role of Islam, and concludes with a brief theoretical reflection on otherness.

Europe

"Otherness" has many faces. Table 1.1 is a schema of the different ways "Europe and its others" has been viewed over time and what kind of notions of difference and otherness it has given rise to. Several of these markers of difference have been around in one form or other for quite a long time. Obviously over time they have changed meaning and gone through several stages. Also they overlap and interact in several ways. In this schema differences outside Europe are juxtaposed to differences within Europe, considering that differences between Europe and others outside have not necessarily been more important than differences within Europe.

In medieval Europe, Christianity was the major marker of difference, internally and externally. The distinction between Christians and heathens and nonbelievers served as

Table 1.1 Europe and its others over time

Time	Boundaries	External differences	Internal differences
CE–present	Religion	Pagans, nonbelievers. Christianity vs. Islam and other religions	Heathens. Heretics, witchcraft. Roman vs. Orthodox Christianity, Catholicism, Protestantism, etc.
1790–1950	Race	Race, language	Class, status. Nation, national character. Ranking among and within European countries
1800–1970	Imperialism, colonialism, neocolonialism	Civilization and savagery, evolution. Colonizer and colonized. Orientalism. Eurocentrism	"Backward areas" within Europe (e.g., Celtic fringe, "urban jungle")
1950–present	Development, North and South	Developed/advanced and underdeveloped/less developed or developing countries	Uneven development within Europe and within countries (under-developed and deindustrializing regions)
1900–present	Europe	European civilization, identity, boundaries, Europeanness	Europe of multiple speeds. Tension between deepening and widening of European Union
1960–present	Cultural difference	Cultural difference	Multiculturalism; cultural difference in lifestyle, sexual preference, age
1980–present	Citizenship, legal status	"Fortress Europe." Illegal immigrants, asylum seekers	Citizens, denizens

the main boundary between self and others. One of the root meanings of "pagan" is peasant (*paysan* in French). This suggests that Christianity was the umbrella for a wider set of meanings and that the original difference between Christians and heathens ran *within* Europe. The distinction between Christians and Muslims and other faiths came later. Campaigns of conversion within Europe – first aimed at the countryside and then at Ireland, the Frisians, Saxons, Slavs, and so forth – set the framework for the campaigns that were directed outward, such as the *Reconquista* of the Iberian Peninsula and the Crusades overseas. While the Crusades were directed against Islam, there were also Crusades within Europe. Internal Crusades were directed against dissident faiths – such as the Cathars and the Bogomils – and later against "heretics" and witches (Cohn, 1975). The onset of the Crusades overseas also coincided with the persecution of Jews within Europe. Within Christendom there were also different centers of power: Greek Christianity was centered in Constantinople and Latin Christianity in Rome. Later a rift developed between Roman Catholicism and the Holy Roman Empire in Germany: the medieval power struggle between the Pope and the Emperor, which involved Cologne as a rival center of faith and power. The subsequent divide between Catholicism and

Protestantism (and further differences within Protestantism – Calvinism, Lutheranism, Anabaptism, etc.) built on the old lines of demarcation that ran between the Roman Empire and the "savage tribes" outside the empire. In the North, the dividing line was the Rhine. During the Renaissance, the distinction between "Ancients" and "Moderns" overlaid these differences.

This shows that "Europe's others" were located primarily within Europe. The contemporary perspective of "others" as being located outside Europe, also retroactively, is a recent development of the last two hundred years, if only because the consciousness of Europeanness is recent. Second, otherness outside Europe was not necessarily as important as otherness within Europe, and was generally conceived along lines first developed in relation to Europe's internal others. Third, "otherness" refers to a complex layer or web of differences that ramifies multidimensionally in many directions. If it is coded in cultural terms (in terms of religion, language, or ethnicity) it also signifies geographical, historical, political, class and status, urban and rural differences, all mingling within a fluid mosaic. Fourth, therefore it is not possible to produce a clear cognitive map of "others" because there is no stable or fixed notion of "self" that could inform this. There is no fixed point or "view from nowhere" from which this can be conceptualized. The longer the period and the wider the geographical space taken into account the more difficult this becomes. Collective identities are stable enough to generate clear boundaries of difference only over brief periods. The mosaic of difference seems stable enough only in, say, 50-year segments. Some differences may seem to be of longer duration, but if we examine them closely it turns out that over time their meaning or function changes radically, so that continuity is a superficial impression only. Let us develop some of these considerations further.

"Europe's others" were located primarily within Europe. Medieval Christianity was part of the foundation of the feudal estates of nobles, clerics, and peasants, each occupying their God-given place, like the caste system in India founded in Hinduism. Differences between Christians and heathens overlaid earlier lines of distinction that ran between the Roman Empire and its peripheries: the *Pax Romana* and the world outside. Regional differences in language, food, costume, and customs were significant. In the hierarchy of estates, "others" were primarily those who did not fit in – Jews, Gypsies, travelers, regional minorities such as the Marranos in southern Spain, heathens and nonbelievers. The real Other in the Christian world was the Devil – represented by the "Bogey," the "Bugaboo," the "Black Man." Thus, the main difference was a metaphysical difference with moral ramifications, and other differences were mirrored in this central difference – identity and otherness were essentially measured in relation to God and the Devil. Gradually the emergence of burghers, merchants, and towns with rights began to undermine the feudal hierarchy and so did the development of monarchy and absolutist states.

Otherness outside Europe was not necessarily as important as otherness within Europe. Tales of strange beings outside Europe – such as Herodotus' tales of monstrous beings overseas – were matched by tales of others within Europe, such as the "Wild Man" and the "Green Man." These figures were real enough considering that Europe until the eleventh century mostly consisted of forest and uncleared land, so much of Europe was unknown and mysterious. Pagan practices continued locally long after the imposition of Christianity. Crusader stories, Marco Polo's tales of far-off civilizations, Montaigne's observations on American Indians served as a backdrop of exotic differences in addition to those that were lived close by. The invasions of the Huns and Mongols into

19

Europe and the siege of Vienna by the Ottoman Turks were experienced as major threats, but if we compare the casualties of these conflicts with those of the Thirty Years War in Germany, they pale into insignificance. Even in later times of imperialism and colonialism, for all the talk of others – racism, Orientalism, the White Man's Burden, and so forth – the main conflicts took place within Europe. The major wars – the Napoleonic wars, the Franco-German war, the two world wars – were largely European wars. Imperialism itself, at any rate the "new imperialism" of the late nineteenth century, can be understood as the extension of the European balance of power on the world map. Overseas conquests were a way of settling accounts or keeping other European powers from gaining control – the Dutch against the Spanish and the Portuguese, the French against the English, the English against Russia, and so forth. If we compare the numbers of casualties in the two world wars with those of the wars of colonialism and imperialism, then where were Europe's others?

Otherness outside Europe was generally conceived along lines first developed in relation to or patterned by Europe's internal others. Thus, "savages" were discussed with quite different emphases by Montaigne (the noble savage), Thomas Hobbes (in the state of nature life is brutish and short), Locke (all men are endowed with reason), Daniel Defoe (cannibals), Rousseau (the good savage) or the Romantic poets (paradise lost). In each instance these views were articulated with dramatically different domestic preoccupations and led to profoundly different conclusions (discussed in Nederveen Pieterse 1992:30–9).

The direct contact between Europe and Asia and the Americas set the stage for much of the vocabulary of difference that occupied the next centuries. In relation to Asia, the theme of civilization came to the foreground: here were "ancient civilizations" that, so it appeared to nineteenth-century Europeans, had stagnated or declined to the level of barbarism. The way this was understood was modeled on the rise and decline of classical civilizations – Greece, Rome and, further in the distance, Egypt and Mesopotamia. Gibbon's account of the rise and decline of the Roman empire followed Tacitus, who had attributed the decline of the Romans to their mixing with different peoples and customs, whereas the Teutonic tribes had remained "pure." This view later contributed to "race" thinking. If European civilization was not to succumb to decadence and decay, and undergo the same fate as the classical and Asian civilizations, Europeans had to be on guard against mixing with different races and lower elements, for in any combination, the lower element would predominate. This applied primarily to aristocracies in Europe who had to keep their distance from the peasantry and lower classes. Thus in many ways, "race" thinking started out as status anxiety on the part of aristocracies and upper classes in Europe, who at the time felt threatened and insecure because of the revolutionary changes at the turn of the eighteenth century.

In relation to the Americas, different tropes emerged. Cannibalism (a theme in Daniel Defoe's *Robinson Crusoe* and stories about Captain Cook in the Pacific) was the flipside of the romantic paradise-lost image of life among the savages. During colonialism the accusation of cannibalism often served as a justification of conquest. Recently it has been argued that cannibalism is basically a myth: while ritual cannibalism (eating a small part of an enemy's body for magical purposes) does occur, gustatory cannibalism (eating humans as food) has nowhere been observed (Arens, 1979; Barker, Hulme, and Iversen, 1998).

With the Enlightenment and its concern with scientific classification came attempts to classify humans based on "race" and language. In the wake of the French Revolution, *nationhood* became a defining element of identity. Through the nineteenth century, the notions of "race," language, and nationality mingled: nations were thought of as races (as in "Irish race" or "German race") and races were viewed as language groups. All along, otherness has been an ambivalent notion, a combination of attraction (paradise lost, the appeal of the exotic) and repulsion. Romantic preoccupation with the past and the unknown was yet another face of the Enlightenment. The pathos of the wild, the remote, and the unknown may be interpreted as a secular version of pantheism or of the "hidden God" (*deus absconditus*). "Others" were embodiments of ideals (the noble or good savage), objects of desire, windows of mystery, or embodiments of fear (monsters, cannibals) and targets of hatred – scapegoats, as in antisemitism and the pogroms. "Nothing but otherness killed the Jews." Genocides of indigenous peoples – native Americans, Tasmanians, Armenians – and dehumanizing treatment of slaves and "natives" – are part of the history of otherness. In nineteenth-century Orientalism and exoticism, all these attitudes are reflected, within a general setting of Western expansion, imperialism, and colonialism.

For centuries, Europe's main other has been the world of Islam. Defining episodes in European history – Muslim domination of the Mediterranean during the early Middle Ages, the conquest of Spain, the Crusades, the fall of Constantinople, the siege of Vienna – refer to Islam. No threat has compared to the threat of Islam and no civilization has been as close by either. Nowadays political Islam is often presented as the major outside challenge to Western hegemony. The world of Islam, unlike other challenges, encompasses a worldview, a way of life, a historical formation as well as a geographical space, stretching from Morocco to Southeast Asia. Its scope includes Islamic politics and law (*sharia*), Islamic geopolitics, Islamic economics and social policy, Islamic science, and Islamic identity and culture. To a varying extent these owe their present salience to government-sponsored initiatives, which are made possible by rentier oil economies. Although perceptions and realities are difficult to disentangle, Islamism is a significant movement, which is at times presented as the most significant challenge to the hegemony of the West as Euro-America. The challenge of political Islam stems from civilizational legacies, anticolonialism, anger and frustration about Western double standards, and cultural disaffection. Ever since the *Nahda* (the nineteenth-century awakening or Renaissance in the Arab world), Islam has been repeatedly held up as an alternative to Western hegemony, at times under the heading of Arab unity. Benjamin Barber captured this under the heading of *Jihad vs. McWorld* (1996). It forms part of Samuel Huntington's (1996) *Clash of Civilizations*.

But from here on the story unravels. The real world of Islam is internally fractured; the *umma* is a delta of many streams – Sunni and Shiite, clerical Islam, Sufism and folk Islam. The different forms of Islam in the Arab world, Iran and Turkey, South and Southeast Asia, Africa and Europe, are each historically and culturally articulated. "Like other religions, Islam is not a generic essence, but a nominal entity that conjoins, by means of a name, a variety of societies, cultures, histories and polities" (Al-Azmeh, 1993:60). In addition, the distinctive character of Islamic institutions may be more a claim than a reality: what is "Islamic" in Islamic science may be a matter of packaging rather than content. Just as Europe ignored or downplayed its dependence on Islamic and Arabic influences in earlier times, the current dependency of Islamic modernization on Western technologies and examples tends to be downplayed in the Islamic world. Without a common opposition to the West, there might not be any umma politics, and what is there is largely political fiction. Part of political Islam is a critique of capitalism, which it shares with Roman Catholicism. Both Islam and Catholicism reflect the ethos of an older, medieval political economy, in which "community" values prevail over merely commerical and economic interests.

Development is another boundary of difference. This derives from earlier ideas of progress, viewed as a single-track path with less and more advanced peoples and civilizations. The eighteenth-century Scottish Enlightenment set forth a schema of evolutionary stages, from primitivism, savagery, and barbarism to civilization. These were combined with modes of production: hunters and gatherers, agriculture and crafts, and industrial society. The development gap only arose when the difference in techno-logical capacity between Europe and non-Western countries became significant – from the turn of the eighteenth century onward, with the onset of industrialization. Prior to that time, Europeans had looked up to other civilizations and been inspired by their example (see Nederveen Pieterse, 1994). European chauvinism only dates from that period.

The difference between less developed, underdeveloped, or backward societies and developed or advanced societies further corresponded with notions of "tradition" and "modernity," the "Third World," and later the difference between North and South. The imagery of backwardness or underdevelopment also applied to peripheral regions or slum areas within Europe. Initially development was looked at solely through Western eyes and modernization was held to be the same as Westernization. This biased view was subsequently identified as Eurocentrism, in which Europe stands for Euro-America (Amin, 1989; Nederveen Pieterse and Parekh, 1995).

In the course of time, Europe itself also began to function as a boundary of difference, first in the context of the turn-of-the-century "Pan" movements (Pan-Arabism, Pan-Turkism, Pan-Europe, etc.), and later after World War II, in the context of the making of the European market. Which is more "European," Northwest Europe or "Central Europe"? Are Turkey and Russia part of Europe? Is Europe part of Eurasia? The current tension between the deepening (further integration) or the widening (including East European countries and Turkey) of the European Union involves not only econo-mic and security issues but also questions of identity and what constitutes "European-ness."

In the European context, cultural difference is the latest boundary of difference. In the course of the 1960s, racism gradually changed to the "new racism" that focuses on cultural difference instead of phenotypical differences. In the context of globalization with increasing communication, migration, and travel, and as societies became increas-ingly mixed, the older ideas of race and civilization became increasingly quaint. Within societies, there are many streams and flows of difference, such as differences in lifestyle, sexual preference, age, and class. Arguably two major differences remain. One is the gap between less and more developed countries. The other significant boundary of difference is the question of citizenship or legal status. Whether immigrants, refugees, and asylum seekers obtain citizenship rights or whether they are clandestine and deprived from legal rights and social entitlements, is a major dividing line. This relates to the image of "Fortress Europe" and the realities of the Schengen and Dublin Accords. Through all these changes, ideas of others and what constitutes otherness have changed.

Otherness

"Otherness" has been discussed under many headings, such as prejudice, ethnocentrism, and racism. The terminology of otherness derives from phenomenology and structuralist anthropology. The theme originates in philosophical queries about the nature of identity. Wherein lies the identity of a thing? Is the difference between same and other a matter of essence or existence? With Hegel, identity and difference refers to the antinomy of being and nothingness, which in turn refers to spirit and matter unfolding in history. What Hegel calls the life and death struggle with the other, for instance between master and slave, is a relationship that changes dialectically over time. Schopenhauer speaks of will and representation, Heidegger of being and time, Sartre of being and nothingness. Different queries yield various notions of otherness, such as the unthought, the implicit (Husserl), the virtual or unfulfilled possibilities (Herbert Marcuse). Psychoanalysis and the idea of the unconscious as ego's other led to the theme of oneself as an other, which had also figured in Dostoevsky's story of "The Double" and came back in Jung's notion of the "shadow." In his book *I and Thou*, Martin Buber addresses the other as a potential partner in dialogue. In a similar way, in the work of the philosopher Emmanuel Levinas, "alterity" becomes a relational concept.

After World War II, at the time of decolonization when imperial identities were decentered, "the question of the Other" became a critical and prominent theme. In structuralist anthropology, cultures were understood as a system of systems, a structural ensemble on the model of language. This approach uses binary schemas, such as naked and clothed, raw and cooked, and self and other. Claude Lévi-Strauss, the foremost representative of this approach, influenced Albert Memmi, Tzvetan Todorov (1984), Jean-Paul Sartre and others. A different approach came with Michel Foucault's work on knowledge and discourse as the foundation of relations of power and domination (e.g., 1965). Foucault concentrated on those classified as deviant, criminal, heretic, insane, or diseased in French society, who were subjected to regimes of "normalization" in medical and penal discourses and in prisons, hospitals, or asylums. In *Orientalism*, Edward Said (1978) applied Foucault's method of discourse analysis to the texts produced by European orientalists about the "Orient," the colonized world. In this view, the way others are represented in talk or discourse reflects prevailing regimes of knowledge and their truth claims, and in the process representation itself becomes a form of power. Foucault's post-structuralism broke with the idea of cultures as systemic structures and shifted attention to structures of knowledge within and across cultures instead. Jacques Derrida (1978) rephrases the question of otherness in terms of identity and difference, thereby returning it to the wider terrain of philosophical questioning where it had originated. In Derrida's method of the deconstruction of texts, the dissembly of structures continues infinitesimally.

These influences – idealist philosophy, phenomenology, structuralism, hermeneutics, post-structuralism, deconstruction – are part of the broad stream of cultural and post-colonial studies that now examines how others are represented in discourse and images. The major axis of difference is the "Big Three" of race, class, and gender. Historically representations of racial (ethnic, national) others often overlap with those of women, children, and lower-class people. Representations of others have been analyzed in relation to Europe (Barker et al., 1985) and in the context of colonialism (Gidley, 1992; Thomas, 1994) and race (Sardar et al., 1993), but the terms of analysis have been changing. "The

Other" is increasingly left behind as too narrow and static a notion. There are so many different kinds of "others" that there is little point in generalizing about them. Besides, the "Self" no longer represents a fixed identity: witness postmodern understandings of multiple identity and the "decentering of the subject." As the typical Enlightenment subject (who was white, male, middle-aged, rational) is no longer being taken for granted as the center and yardstick of the human universe, also its "other" loses relevance and meaning. In sociology, cultural and gender studies, the terminology of *difference* increasingly takes the place of otherness. This terminology is more neutral and matter-of-fact and less historically burdened than that of otherness. Difference, of course, comes in many forms: as ontological difference, metaphysical difference, the difference of God, gender, class, geography, development, legal status, and cultural diversity. So cultural difference is but one type of difference among several and not necessarily the most salient or important difference. Another theme is the growing concern with hybridity, mixing, *métissage*. As societies become more diverse, intermarriage also increases, cultural differences criss-cross and in the process generate new identities, and new differences. Cultural differences erode over time, due to globalization, changing identities, and consumption patterns, while local and regional reactions to globalization generate new identities and differences. Amidst this flux, the old notions of otherness are increasingly outdated.

References

Al-Azmeh, A. (1993) *Islams and Modernities*. London: Verso.

Amin, S. (1989) *Eurocentrism*. London: Zed.

Arens, W. (1979) *The Man-Eating Myth: Anthropology and Anthropophagy*. New York: Oxford University Press.

Barber, B. J. (1996) *Jihad vs. McWorld*. New York: Ballantine Books.

Barker, F. et al. (eds.) (1985) *Europe and its Others*. Colchester, UK: Essex University.

Barker, F., Hulme, P., and Iversen M. (eds.) (1998) *Cannibalism and the Colonial World*. Cambridge, UK: Cambridge University Press.

Cohn, N. (1975) *Europe's Inner Demons*. New York: Basic Books.

Derrida, J. (1978) *Writing and Difference*. Chicago: Chicago University Press.

Foucault, M. (1965) *Madness and Civilization: A History of Insanity in the Age of Reason*. New York: Random House.

Gidley, M. (ed.) (1992) *Representing Others: White Views of Indigenous Peoples*. Exeter, UK: University of Exeter Press.

Huntington, S. P. (1996) *The Clash of Civilizations and the Remaking of World Order*. New York: Simon and Schuster.

Nederveen Pieterse, J. (1992) *White on Black: Images of Africa and Blacks in Western Popular Culture*. New Haven, CT: Yale University Press.

Nederveen Pieterse, J. (1994) "Unpacking the West: How European is Europe?," in A. Rattansi and S. Westwood (eds.) *Racism, Modernity, Identity: On the Western Front*. Cambridge, UK: Polity, pp.129–49.

Nederveen Pieterse, J. and Parekh, B. (1995) *The Decolonization of Imagination*. London: Zed.

Said, E. (1978) *Orientalism*. Harmondsworth, UK: Penguin.

Sardar, Z., Nandy, A. Davies, M. W. (1993) *Barbaric Others*. London: Pluto Press.

Thomas, N. (1994) *Colonialism's Culture: Anthropology, Travel and Government*. Cambridge, UK: Polity Press.

Todorov, T. (1984) *The Conquest of America: The Question of the Other*. New York: Harper and Row.

Chapter 2

Doctrine of Discovery

Peter Fitzpatrick

Whilst the racial, and racist, basis of the doctrine of discovery is a modern innovation, the doctrine owes much to its premodern forms and ethos. The finding and settlement of putatively unknown lands has long been attended with mythic and religious justification and with rituals of appropriation, all of which strikingly resemble modern practice. Similarity in this case, however, serves to dramatize difference. What marks modern discovery of the occidental variety, the subject of this present paper, is the displacement of the mythic and religious by a combination of racism and legalism. The story of that displacement is told here along with an analysis of the poverty, not to say vacuity, of the doctrine of discovery as a justification for imperial appropriation. Since the story is told in broadly historical terms, its conception of the modern relies on the temporal "depth" which historians usually attribute to this term, the discoveries of Columbus here providing something of a benchmark. But this account of the doctrine of discovery is not an antiquarian exercise, not a tale told in a now entirely discovered world, the unfolding of which may have had its reasons for regret but is now decidedly done with. Rather, this account is modern also in the sense of having current significance, of discovery's still being an impelling force in the treatment of peoples supposedly once discovered, and in the self-identity of those who would claim to have once discovered them.

Perhaps the most compendious point to be made about discovery in this present setting is that it involves something specifically more than the word's ordinary meaning. What the word normally imports is the uncovering or the disclosure of what is already there. In this sense, the word is contrasted to invention, to the creation or inauguration of what was not already there. However, the prefix "dis-" does have a privative force with its connotations of actively denying or undoing a previous condition. What this intimates for discovery is that the thing discovered is now different for having been discovered. It is now denied its "cover" and put in a new scene, one pertaining to the discoverer. If this discoverer claims to be the repository of universal truth, a claim which modern discoverers invariably do make, then discovery in this extended sense can join with its primal meaning and the discovered be now revealed as what they should, in truth, be.

This stretching of the semantic is given a more explicative force by the mythic renditions of discovery. With these, the act of discovery is equated with the deific creation, with a "transformation" of what is discovered by endowing it with "forms and norms" (Eliade, 1965:9–11). This mythic charge was encapsulated and made effective in possessory rituals. So, the almost paradigm planting of the Christian cross

25

"was equivalent to a justification and to the consecration of the new country, to a 'new birth,' thus repeating baptism (act of Creation)" (Eliade, 1965:11). What is more, the prior "undiscovered" condition was comprehensively subordinated to this new dimension, a dimension in which the condition had now "become real" (Eliade, 1965:11). The seeming secular equivalent is captured in Diderot's aptly fanciful account of Bougainville's discovery of Tahiti (Diderot, 1972). Here the French envelop a Tahiti that is but "a remote recess of our globe." For Tahiti to be brought into the ambit of the Occident, for it to be quite overwhelmed by this "contact" with the French, it is enough for Bougainville to have touched the island and to have enacted there a ritual of appropriation – the erection of a plaque asserting "this land is ours," described by Diderot's ever-perspicacious Tahitian sage as the title "of our future slavery." The encompassing, transforming effect of imperial discovery was then reassuringly confirmed by the ease with which savage cultures were supposedly subverted by it. Thus Bougainville's visit brings about "the eclipse" of a Tahitian society left in heavy expectation of what is to come (Diderot, 1972:147–8, 175, 178). This putative effect, along with the quasi-redemption of "contact," echoed a prior religious doctrine conferring title to lands populated by infidels or pagans on their first Christian discoverer (Williams, 1990, part I).

The transformation of discovery from a religious doctrine brought together hugely significant forces in the making of the modern Occident. Intriguing similarities with religious forms and justifications remained, but the search for a legitimating basis of discovery shifted from the papal and universal to the monarchical and national. A pointed significance attached to the technique of enquiry adopted by the Church for its government and taken over, as it were, by monarchical government through law: such enquiry extended to "a technique of traveling – a political enterprise of exercising power and an enterprise of curiosity and acquisition of knowledge – that ultimately led to the discovery of the Americas" (Foucault, 1996:340). Thus Columbus relied on papal authority, religious rituals of appropriation, and redemptive invocation, but his claims to the land in the name of the Spanish Crown were taken to be valid only when legally authorized by that sovereign power. Furthermore, Columbus usually insisted on some legalistic recording of discovery by a notary. The rituals of appropriation themselves came to adopt a legal aspect. Thus, a contemporary royal instruction of Spanish origin directed that "acts of possession" be made "before a notary public and the greatest possible number of witnesses"; also, "you shall make a gallows there, and have somebody bring a complaint before you, and as our captain and judge you shall pronounce upon and determine it" (see Greenblatt, 1991:56). There was yet another momentous force at work, one intimated in the notorious distinction which Columbus drew between some of the peoples discovered, between those who were quite virtuous and those who were utterly degraded. For the considerable refinement of this division and its implanting in the modern doctrine of discovery, however, we have to move on just a few years to the contribution of Francisco de Vitoria.

The ambivalence of Vitoria could hardly be more pronounced. He is almost invariably received as the benign humanist who erected a basic defence of Indian sovereignty and title to their lands and fathered international law. Yet in doing both these things he provided a consummate legitimation for one of the more spectacularly rapacious of imperial acquisitions. In his meditation *On The Indians Recently Discovered*, delivered as lectures in 1539, Vitoria went so far in elevating the Indian interest as to deny the validity of the title which

Columbus claimed (Vitoria, 1934 – first published 1557). He reached this result by finding that natural law, in the form of a universalized "law of nations," would only support title acquired by discovery where the lands discovered were deserted. This was not the case with any of the Spanish claims to the Americas. Indeed, for Vitoria the Indians already had that *dominium* – a combination of sovereign and proprietary title – which in natural law attached to all "men." They were even similar to the Spanish in having families, hierarchical government, legal institutions, and something like religion. In all, the Indians had the accoutrements of natural law and were participating subjects in that law.

Vitoria also managed, however, to arrive at a contrary conclusion by relying on that same natural law. This infinitely amenable law also provided that the rights of the Indian peoples had to adjust to the expansive rights of all other people, including the Spanish, to travel, trade, "sojourn" and, in the cause of Christianity, to proselytize. There was also something of a right to enforce natural law. These rights could not be aggressively asserted unless they were resisted by the Indians. When so resisted, however, they could be asserted to the full extent of conquest and dispossession. And so they were. This process was greatly facilitated by Vitoria's deeming the Indians to be inherently recalcitrant. Although included initially within its universal embrace, Vitoria also found the Indian to be outside the range of natural law. The details of their utter deviance was even then quite standard, ranging from the instantly egregious, such as cannibalism and sexual perversion, to more picayune affronts to European taboos of diet and dress – nudity, consuming food raw, eating reptiles, and so on.

This conflicting constitution of non-European peoples persisted in international law and eventually negated Vitoria's ascribing *dominium* to them. What happened, in broad outline, was that international law became a matter of relations between sovereign states, and such sovereignty was intrinsically contrasted to certain uncivilized others excluded from participation in international law. From at least the late eighteenth century, the doctrine of discovery, now a tenet of international law, provided that full title was conferred on the sovereign state on whose behalf the discovery was made, and this was so even where the lands discovered were manifestly inhabited. The old doctrine that discovery conferred title only on deserted lands now segued with the new through the latter's equating the chronic inadequacy of non-European occupation with the virtually deserted (Green, 1989:75). Reference to the *doctrine* of discovery now became one of an indulgent exactitude. Apart from the hardly veiled racial ascription, the doctrine now lacked any palpable criterion of application. The civilized occidental discoverer assumed title on discovery of land occupied by the uncivilized, by those whose "uncertain occupancy" cannot be "a real and lawful taking of possession," as one leading authority put it with unabashed clarity (Vattel, 1971:44). The discovery still had to be marked and evidenced but the marking and the evidence were of discovery, not of adequate occupation. Although the discoverers' justifications often advanced the superiority of their agriculture over nomadism or over inadequate cultivation, the quality of superiority attached to them and not to a more effective working of the lands discovered. But having discovered lands of allegedly "uncertain occupancy," it was then "entirely lawful" to occupy them (Vattel, 1971:44–5).

In this blank apotheosis, the doctrine of discovery acquired its definitive version in the judgment of Chief Justice Marshall delivering the decision of the Supreme Court of the United States in the case of *Johnson v. M'Intosh* (1823). As well as legally settling the doctrine and its effects for the United States, Marshall's judgment became "accepted as the settled law on indigenous peoples' rights and status in all the European-derived settler-colonialist states of the West" (Williams, 1990:289). Despite the range of its influence, the issues in this case, as Williams goes on to indicate, were quite specific to the settlement of the United States (Williams, 1990:289). But the case did basically pose a poignant issue which concentrated the whole history of the doctrine of discovery. The contest giving rise to it concerned title to certain frontier lands. On one side were settlers who, doubtless more out of convenience than conviction, asserted the rights of the Indians from whom they had derived the titles which they claimed. The Indians, just like those championed by Vitoria, were said to have had full transferable title to the lands acquired from them. Such a line of argument evoked, with excusable confidence, the credo of natural rights which inspired the revolution in the United States. These were rights intrinsic to all "men" – the equivalent here of Vitoria's natural law. The other side in the case argued that the fullest possible title to the lands had, on the contrary, vested in the government of the United States as the successor to the British Crown, and the Crown in turn had acquired this title on discovery. It would follow from this that the Indians would not have had a transferable title. In an extended declamation, one of obscene eloquence, Marshall accepted that argument.

The resonant confidence of Marshall's judgment was more a compensation for the intractability of the issues in dispute than a reflection of felt certitude. From a sweeping survey of the practices of imperial states, from "the history of America, from its discovery to the present day," and from the remarkable consistency of the claims of its various colonizers, Marshall derived the view that discovery by the British had conferred on them an "absolute" and "exclusive" title, one which not only "gave to the nation making the discovery the sole right of acquiring the soil from natives and establishing settlements upon it," but one which also conferred on that nation the "right" of consequent conquest (*Johnson v. M'Intosh*, 1823:573, 586, 590–1, 595). Without wishing to impugn the Court's delicate impartiality in the matter, it could be added that to have held otherwise may well have proved disastrous for the fledgling union of the United States, and it could also be added that the Court's position in that scheme of things was itself far from secure (see Williams, 1990:231, 306–8). There was, however, the inconvenience, not to say embarrassment, that such a decision ran counter to the impelling ideology of the "American" revolution and its trumpeting of natural rights. Pre-eminent among these was the right to property. Appropriately, then, Marshall did recognize that Indian people had "natural rights" in their land, and that this would include the right to transfer ownership (*Johnson v. M'Intosh*, 1823:563).

Marshall sought to negate this right, and to resolve the conflict, by defaming the Indian people who held it. He initiates this exercise somewhat tentatively by saying that the "principles which Europeans have applied to Indian title" may be indefensible but "they may, we think, find some excuse, if not justification, in the character and habits of the people whose rights have been wrested from them" (*Johnson v. M'Intosh*, 1823:588). There follows an unexceptional catalog. The "actual condition" of the Indian people was savage, degraded, and recalcitrant, "the condition of a people with whom it was impossible to mix, and who could not be governed as a distinct entity" (p. 590). In that stunning synopsis, it was, then, the Indians' own irresolute condition that led to the truncation and eventual elimination of the rights to their land. They could not be "mixed" with, could not become the same and have the same rights as everyone else, but neither could they remain distinct and different, retaining their own natural and integral rights to the land. So, this was initially Marshall's "excuse." Later in the judgment it becomes "justification." In the climax of the judgment, Marshall writes of the denial of the Indians' right to transfer that:

> However this restriction may be opposed to natural right, and to the usages of civilized nations, yet if it be indispensable to that system under which the country has been settled, and be adapted to the actual condition of the two people, it may perhaps be supported by reason, and certainly cannot be rejected by courts of justice. (*Johnson v. M'Intosh*, 591–2)

It "cannot be rejected" because the settlers' property originates in it, and that "becomes the law of the land and cannot be questioned" (p. 591). Hence there emerges the "ground" of Marshall's opening contention that the Court must ultimately bow to the government which has laid down the law of property, bow to what is "given us as the rule for our decision" (p. 572). The "actual condition" of the Indian people and of their suppression becomes indistinguishable from the primal assertion of legal sovereignty.

It is this sovereign assertion which, more than anything else, distinguishes occidental title and makes manifest the racial basis of the doctrine of discovery. Bluntly, the discoverers were the kind of people who had sovereignty and title, and the discovered were the kind of people who had neither. Not only did the discoverers acquire "absolute" and "exclusive" title to the land, not only did discovery thence give them "the exclusive right ... to appropriate the lands occupied by the Indians," they also "asserted the ultimate dominion to be in themselves" (p. 574). Unlike Vitoria's involving natural law which recognized something like sovereignty vested in them, the Indians were now utterly subordinate to a sovereign power and were "excluded ... from intercourse with any European potentate than the first discoverer" (p. 573). The doctrine of discovery becomes one in which the discovered are no longer actors but merely acted upon. They are excluded from operative participation in the doctrine as a mode of legal determination and its constituent purpose becomes "to avoid conflicting settlements, and consequent war" between "European potentates" (p. 573).

That purpose produced a telling hiatus in the doctrine of discovery itself. This is intimated in a disparity barely hidden within Marshall's statement of the "principle" of discovery in this setting of interimperial rivalry:

> This principle was that discovery gave title to the government by whose subjects, or by whose authority, it was made, against all other European governments, which title might be consummated by possession. (*Johnson v. M'Intosh*, 1823:573)

But this title, as we have just seen, was one of an ultimate and absolute kind and hardly required "consummation." It could also be added that sovereignty, national sovereignty, was at the core of modern, civilized "European" being, as was property (Kelley, 1984:129–33). Here these qualities of being are revealed as integral only in their opposition to uncivilized "others." When, however, there are contrary claims to discovered territory between the exemplars of transcendent sovereignty and property, such elevated attributes degenerate to a drab "effectiveness," the test of effectiveness having been promoted in international law to decide between such competing claims, among other things (Shearer, 1994:145–8). Effectiveness here is equivalent to Marshall's "possession" and connotes the ability to "hold down" territory, to deal with disruption from within or from without. In a feat of legal legerdemain, this requirement came in the nineteenth century to be reconciled *sotto voce* with instant and full title as against the discovered by the invention of "inchoate title." As against other civilized "European" sovereign powers, the initial title had to be, in Marshall's term, "consummated" by effective occupation (*Re Island of Palmas Arbitration*, 1928).

And so the doctrine of discovery forms finally around a gaping disparity, one reconciled only in the ascription of a subordinate racial status. Its effect in these terms persists to this day (e.g., Motha, 1999; Shattuck and Norgren, 1991).

References

Diderot, D. (1972) *Supplément au voyage de Bougainville, Pensées philosophiques, Lettre sur les aveugles.* (*Supplement to the voyage of Bourgainville.*) Paris: Garnier Flammarion.

Eliade, M. (1965) *The Myth of the Eternal Return, or Cosmos and History.* Princeton, NJ: Princeton University Press.

Foucault, M. (1996) "Truth and juridical forms." *Social Identities* 2:327–41.

Green, L. C. (1989) "Claims to territory in colonial America," in L. C. Green and O. P. Dickason *The Law of Nations and the New World.* The University of Edmonton: Alberta Press.

Greenblatt, S. (1991) *Marvelous Possessions: The Wonder of the New World.* Oxford: Clarendon Press.

Johnson v. M'Intosh (1823) *United States Reports* 21:543–603.

Kelley, D. R. (1984) *History, Law and the Human Sciences: Medieval and Renaissance Perspectives.* London: Variorum Reprints.

Motha, S. (1999) "Mabo: encountering the epistemic limit of the recognition of 'difference.'" *Griffith Law Review* 7:79–96.

Re Island of Palmas Arbitration (1928) *American Journal of International Law* 22:867–912.

Shattuck, P. T. and Norgren, J. (1991) *Partial Justice: Federal Indian Law in a Liberal Constitutional System.* Oxford: Berg.

Shearer, I. A. (1994) *Starke's International Law,* 11th edn. London: Butterworths.

Vattel, E. de (1971) "Emer de Vattel on the occupation of territory," in P. D. Curtin *Imperialism.* London: Macmillan, pp.42–5.

Vitoria, F. de (1934) "*De Indis,*" in J. B. Scott *The Spanish Origin of International Law: Francisco de Vitoria and his Law of Nations.* Oxford: Clarendon Press.

Williams, R. (1990) *The American Indian in Western Legal Thought: The Discourses of Conquest.* New York: Oxford University Press.

Chapter 3

Genocide

Charles Briggs

At first glance, an essay on genocide would seem to bear only a marginal relationship to racial and ethnic studies. After all, the gap between everyday acts of housing discrimination; race-based differentials in searches, prosecutions, sentencing, and access to health care; the appearance of denigrating media images, and the like are far removed from the Holocaust or the massive killings that have taken place recently in Bosnia, Kosovo, Rwanda, and East Timor. This essay suggests that the relationship is well worth a second look. Genocide fundamentally informs racial constructions, their political effects, and the political contours and costs of efforts to resist them. Just as racialization and the production of other schemes of social difference play a key role in making such acts of mass and systematic killing possible, genocides constitute key sites in which the nature and limits of racialization and efforts to resist and punish it are constructed.

Aggrieved populations frequently use cries of genocide in attempting to secure larger audiences for protests regarding everyday racism and racializing practices. If scholars of race and ethnicity disconnect the two phenomena by deeming such accusations simply unimportant or illegitimate, they run the risk of placing themselves on the side of racial states and dominant sectors of populations, and at the same time they may miss the epistemological value of the situated theorizing from which such protests can emerge. Convincing specialists on genocide that they should study practices of everyday racializations will help them understand the sorts of events on which they focus, particularly the possibility of including racially targeted violations of medical or legal rights. This takes us into the heart of battles over the definition of genocide and efforts to expand it. I do not argue here that all racially shaped violence should be deemed to be genocide and treated identically to the Holocaust. Nevertheless, I hope that this essay will help reveal the way that the construction of strict limits of what types of violence can be placed within this frame are – like genocide accusations in general – inextricable from processes of racialization and liable to their political effects.

A crucial issue revolves around the relationship of genocide and its study to modernity. For some, the Holocaust demonstrates the horrifying persistence of premodern irrational tendencies, even in the heart of European modernity. In his contribution to this volume Zygmunt Bauman challenges such efforts to exoticize and historicize the

Short sections of this essay are adapted from material that appeared in Briggs (1997) and Briggs and Mantini-Briggs (1997).

Holocaust; he argues that they fail to interrogate the way that the Shoah or Holocaust reveals the violent underpinnings of the desire for order and control that lies at the heart of modern society and its thirst for order and control (see also Bauman, 1990). While Bauman is certainly correct, the question for me is less one of whether the Holocaust is modern than it is the status of it and other genocides during the past half century as a key locus for *debating* metanarratives of modernity. As the killings in Bosnia, Kosovo, Rwanda, East Timor, and elsewhere marked the century's close, genocide provided a crucial arena for questioning linear narratives of progress, modernity, democracy, and the "rule of law" versus the politics of force. The complexity of these issues is increased by the way that recent scholarship has produced new understandings regarding how concepts of race, ethnicity, nation, and group are constructed; the many ways that nation-states inflict violence on citizens and those excluded from citizenship; and on the way that transnational corporations, international organizations, and new social movements shape "local" situations. I focus in this essay on how post-structuralist and postmodern perspectives have shifted the grounds of debates about genocide and efforts to resist these epistemological transformations.

Defining Genocide

New conceptions require new terms. By "genocide" we mean the destruction of a nation or of an ethnic group. This new word, coined by the author to denote an old practice in its modern development, is made from the ancient Greek word *genos* (race, tribe) and the Latin *cide* (killing) (Raphael Lemkin, 1944:79)

This statement continues to inform twentieth-century constructions of genocide. Here Lemkin displaces genocide into the past as "an old practice" at the same time that he makes it an essential part of our definition of high modernity. One of the marks of the modern, for Lemkin, is "a long period of evolution in civilized society" from wars of extermination against populations to wars against nation-states and armies (p. 80). For him, as for many writers, the Holocaust was so exceptional as to challenge the foundations of modernity by uniting "barbarous practices reminiscent of the darkest pages of history" with "an elaborate, almost scientific system" for creating death (p. 90). Both political theory and international law had *tout à coup* become obsolete; naming genocide and criminalizing it in every nation-state was a prerequisite to restoring the promise of modernity.

Subsequent writers adopted Lemkin's term and expanded its power for mapping the nature and limits of modernity. Habermas (1989) followed Lemkin in his exceptionalism, characterizing the Holocaust as a betrayal of Enlightenment rationality. Critics counter that Habermas's characterization covers up the way that talk about rationality and human nature has supplied Western elites with a key tool for legitimating the annihilation of people who supposedly lack these "universal" human traits. In her influential account of the trial of Adolf Eichmann, subtitled *A Report on the Banality of Evil*, Hannah Arendt (1964) ties modern genocide to the way that nation-states place themselves above the rules they impose on their citizens; states can thus legally commit crimes in order to preserve the rule of law – and their own existence (Arendt, 1964:288, 291). When this political order is linked to bureaucratic organization, the hegemony of dominant groups, and an impersonal economic order, both bureaucrats and surplus populations may be sufficiently dehumanized that the former gains the right to exterminate the latter. As I noted above, a leading student of modernity, Zygmunt Bauman, argues that the Holocaust stands as the essence of modern bureaucratic rationality. Writer Edwin Black (2001) has recently argued that the Holocaust could not have assumed its systematic and mechanical shape without the card punch and sorting devices that were manufactured for the Third Reich by IBM and its European affiliates and adapted for use in tracking death camp populations. Dominick LaCapra (1994, 1998) suggests that the mechanized death of Nazi concentration camps reveals the way that bureaucratic and scientific rationality remains deeply joined to the ritual spheres that it was supposed to displace. Michael Taussig (1997) characterizes the foundations of the nation-state as magical; state hegemony ultimately rests, he argues, on the circulation of ritual means for invoking the dead. In referring to the twentieth century as "an age of genocide," Rogers Smith (1987) seems to suggest that these events are not isolated, accidental, or atypical but shape the very core of high modernity.

In recent decades, the epistemological foundations of debates regarding the nature of genocide have been shaken by post-structuralist and postmodern critiques. Some writers now locate the Holocaust in relation to the postmodern era. Commentators have disagreed vehemently over whether the Holocaust lies within, outside of, or beyond representation, meaning, explanation, comparison, and even history. Until recently, however, the existence and importance of these categories were largely taken for granted. Post-structuralist and postmodern writers have challenged these assumptions, asserting that such categories are constructed, shifting, and problematic and that their deployment is contingent on the positionality and interests of those who use them. What happens to the search for the "truth" about a genocide if truth is, as Michel Foucault (1980:131) has argued, a question of "the types of discourse which [each society] accepts and makes function as true"? For Jean-François Lyotard (1984, 1988, 1990), "the Jews" become the clearest example of a postmodern people; Auschwitz thus provides the most unimpeachable sign of the failure of any single, totalizing discourse to encompass history and politics. Life now confronts us with heterogeneous and often unintelligible signs – rather than facts that can be verified and systematized. Deborah Lipstadt (1993) blames the proliferation in recent decades of attempts to deny that the Holocaust took place and the public attention they have generated on post-structuralist and postmodern scholarship. She argues that a "relativistic approach to the truth," which she pins on Stanley Fish, has made it impossible to fix meanings and make critical judgments about the comparative value of texts, thereby destroying the value of rationality in deciding which statements can vie for legitimacy in the public sphere.[1]

Questions of historical methodology similarly have been debated. New forms of academic writing, film, and literature have opened up the Holocaust and other genocides to a wider range of styles and genres, as well as to critical reflexive accounts. Some reject these innovations. Saul Friedlander asserts that "there are limits to representation *which should not be but can easily be transgressed*" (1992:3; emphasis in original). Berel Lang (1990:151) argues that only literal representationalist narratives can bear the test of "authenticity and truthfulness." Hayden White, who pioneered our understanding of how realist historical narratives are produced (White, 1978), counters that such realism springs from the same modernist order as the Holocaust itself; more critical, reflexive, and experimental techniques are thus needed to reveal this relationship (White, 1992).

The responses that were published in the same volume in which White's paper appeared provide a measure of the political complexities surrounding representations of genocide. Friedlander (1992:7) accuses White of an "extreme relativism" that undermines efforts to assess the truth and the significance of the Holocaust, and Carlo Ginzburg (1992) chides that White's relativism refuses to confront fascism. On the other hand, Martin Jay (1992) suggests that White's attempt to avoid the charge of relativism leads him to contradict his rhetorical view of history.

Similar problems emerge with the concept of "intent." Lemkin (1944:79) stated that the term he coined was intended "to signify a coordinated plan of different actions aiming at the destruction of essential foundations of the life of national groups, with the aim of annihilating the groups themselves." The UN Convention also stressed intent in its definition. Nevertheless, Wallimann and Dobkowski (1987:xvi) argue that intentionality is currently hard to demonstrate, given "the anonymous and amorphous structural forces that dictate the character of our world." Tony Barta (1987:239) asserts that intentionality is also rooted in a subjective perspective that attempts "to explain everything from the will of the persons acting." Rather than challenge the implications of using definitions to pre-empt consideration of particular cases as genocide, he presses for a more scientific and "objective" definition based on "the objective nature of the relationships" that underlie political conditions. Barta's statement points to the way that competing claims to authority advanced by academic disciplines helps shape these debates.

Again, post-structuralist and postmodern criticism presents an even more radical challenge as it reveals the philosophical and linguistic problems embedded in the concept of intent and stresses the difficulty of mapping out "intentions." Michel Foucault (1970), Jacques Derrida (1974), Judith Butler (1997), and other scholars have exploded notions of a bounded and sovereign subject and of singular and stable meanings and intentions. Michelle Rosaldo (1982), Marilyn Strathern (1988), and other anthropologists have suggested that perceiving action as the externalization of intentions by active human agents is a key facet of the Western imagination. We might add that the right to discover, classify, and judge intentions, as invested in many legal systems, is a crucial means of exerting social and political control. LaCapra (1994) and White (1992) both note that discussions of genocide rely heavily on binary oppositions; recent scholarship has suggested that oppositions and systems of classification involve processes of social construction, the imposition of rhetorical constraints, and, in Derrida's (1974) terms, discursive violence.

Post-structuralist and postmodern scholarship regarding the notions of "group," "nation," "ethnicity," "race," gender, and sexuality that are used in defining and bounding populations would seem to have equally serious implications for studies of genocide and efforts to prosecute violations. Lemkin (1944:79) sought to embed the notion of a bounded and clearly defined group deeply in the term itself through use of the Greek *genos* (race, tribe). Indeed, one of the arguments that bolstered efforts to exclude "political groups" from the UN Convention was that "racial or national groups" – being distinct, stable, bounded communities – could provide a scientific and objective basis for defining genocide (see Kuper, 1981:25). Benedict Anderson ([1983] 1991) and others have argued, however, that national identities are "imagined," not primordial, and that they are part of modernist political projects. James Clifford (1988), George Marcus and Michael Fischer (1986; also see Clifford and Marcus, 1986) have questioned the rhetorical practices by which ethnographers construct cultures as bounded, homogeneous, totalizing, and knowable – by anthropologists. Pursuing Eric Hobsbawm's (1983) work on the "invention of tradition," Richard Handler (1984, 1988) characterizes the sense that particular social groups are discrete, distinct, bounded, and relatively stable over time as a politically positioned and interested invention. Some activists charge, however, that scholarly studies of such "inventions" can be used in undermining challenges to racial oppression (Briggs, 1996). Werner Sollors (1989) similarly suggests that ethnicity is invented.

"Identity" and "culture," which are often used in discussions of genocide, have been characterized as complex, shifting constructions that serve a variety of political functions, including racist ones (see, e.g., Balibar, 1991, 1995). Stuart Hall (1985, 1988) has argued that cultural identity is "not an essence but a positioning," a complex, contradictory, and shifting arena in which racial and ethnic categories become both the dominant way that hegemony and exploitation are experienced, and sites of hybridization and resistance (see also Lowe, 1996). By treating "a national, ethnical, racial or religious group" as a real, bounded, and stable natural entity, do scholars and prosecutors of genocide run the risk of reinforcing the hegemonic reifications that were used in catalyzing and attempting to legitimate genocide? It would certainly seem to be necessary to see the way that racial and ethnic imaginations are created and naturalized, including the material components of both processes, if we are to document adequately how genocide becomes possible. Since everyday racism places a crucial role in producing social categories and converting them into social and institutional practices (see the essay in this volume by Philomena Essed), linking genocide to less visible and more pervasive forms of violence would seem to be necessary.

Starting with the Genocide Convention and the Nuremberg Trials, key institutional sites have been vested with the authority to define genocide and to determine which actions fall within its aegis. As the debate over Hannah Arendt's (1964) famous *Eichmann in Jerusalem* attests, however, trials do not necessarily generate consensus regarding how genocide should be defined, described, explained, and punished, particularly as they become topics of debate worldwide. More recently, in the wake of the genocides in the former Yugoslavian republics and Rwanda, two different kinds of judicial bodies are applying legal definitions of genocide: the International Court of Justice, which primarily focuses on the responsibility of states, and the International Criminal Tribunals for the Balkan republics and Rwanda, which process accusations against individuals (see Ball, 1999; Fisher Damrosch, 1998). One problem, as Martha Minow (1998:9) suggests, is that "prosecutions are slow, partial, and narrow," providing forums that favor the telling of only some stories, generally in fragmented and simplified form and within hierarchical and relatively rigid participatory roles. As Veena Das (1995) argues in the case of litigation that focused on Union Carbide's culpability in the Bhopal disaster, prosecutions marginalize the narratives of individuals who have suffered directly, particularly when they are poor. The South African Truth and Reconciliation Commission and similar forums, on the other hand, are able to investigate broader social and political issues and to explore more complex relationships and forms of responsibility, and they permit a wider range of actors and narrative modes of depicting genocide (see Minow, 1998).

Expanding definitions of genocide

The question of definitions is an object of intense scrutiny in genocide scholarship. Following its adoption by the General Assembly in 1948, the definition embedded in the

United Nations Convention on Genocide has provided a crucial point of reference: "Genocide means any of the following acts committed with intent to destroy, in whole or in part, a national, ethnical, racial or religious group" (United Nations, GAOR Resolution 260A (III) 9 December 1948, Article II). Strong arguments have been made in ensuing decades to broaden this definition. The resolution passed by the General Assembly in 1946 included "political" groups, but this category was deleted from the Convention itself. Kuper (1981) and others have continued to call for inclusion of the systematic extermination of political opponents in legal definitions of genocide.

As LaCapra (1994:45–7) observes, the Holocaust or Shoah has become the quintessential embodiment of the oldest opposition in historical thinking: the unique versus the universal. Recently, several writers have suggested that the Holocaust is both unique *and* universal, standing as a "generic term" (Bauer, 1990:154) for a type of genocide that could be repeated (Rosenberg, 1987). In spite of their differences, these positions place the Holocaust at the center of discourses of genocide; insofar as it becomes the prototype of genocide, all other events are evaluated in relation to it (see Goekjian, 1991), seemingly occupying a more marginal relationship to the category. Efforts to compare the Holocaust to the Armenian genocide (see Dadrian, 1996) or to the "American Indian Holocaust" (see Churchill, 1997; Stannard, 1992; Thornton 1987) have thus been deemed to trivialize it.[2] In 1951, the Civil Rights Congress petitioned the UN to consider charges under the Convention against the US government for the oppression of African-Americans (see James, 1996:46–7). Barta (1987) goes so far as to attempt to reverse the Holocaust as the *locus classicus* of genocide, suggesting that Australia has been, "during the whole 200 years of its existence, a genocidal society" while Germany has not. David Stannard (1996:167) claims that by attempting to characterize the Holocaust as unique, and thus limit the use of "Holocaust" and "genocide" drawing attention to other situations, the "hegemonic" perspective promoted by "a handful of Jewish scholars and writers ... willingly provides a screen behind which opportunistic governments today attempt to conceal their own past and ongoing genocidal actions." Stannard (1996:165) refers to efforts by members of the U.S. Senate to cut funding for the Smithsonian Institution over a film that characterized the history of violence against Native Americans as genocide, citing it as an example of how an "exclusivist" perspective can be used by the state to suppress memory of racialized violence.[3]

Ironically, it would seem as if arguments for the uniqueness of the Holocaust and for its pre-eminent claim on the category of genocide enhance the rhetorical value of Holocaust denials. If the Holocaust is construed as the prototype for genocide, and genocide provides a model for the violence of racialization, interest on the part of white supremacist and other racist organizations in promoting efforts to deny the reality of the Holocaust makes excellent discursive and political sense. If the Shoah can be erased and its representations discredited, then the violence of racialization in general can be more successfully denied, and blame-the-victim rhetorics can be promoted with even greater success.

Some influential writers have resisted efforts to widen the definition of genocide or shift the criteria on which it rests. In spite of his efforts to include politically based killing as genocide, Kuper warns against using the term in a "loose and exaggerated way" (Kuper, 1981:59); he creates a category of "genocidal massacres," which are excluded from the formal crime of "genocide," to cover instances in which there is no clear intent to destroy the group. R. J. Rummel similarly complains that "genocide" has become tainted by the inclusion of violence that is not conducted intentionally by governments;

he accordingly creates a new term, "democide," "that covers and is *limited to* intentional government murder" (1994:34; emphasis in original). Frank Chalk argues that deeming massacres to be genocide when intent is not present bears "an enormous cost in the rigour of the analysis" and deprives the concept of its practical political value (1989:156).

At the same time, scholars have argued for inclusion of quite different types of violence under the aegis of genocide. Nancy Scheper-Hughes (1992) uses a notion of "small wars and invisible genocides" in focusing on the killing of older children and young adults. She argues that the targeting of "street children" in Brazil and the use of violence against – and by – politicized youth in South Africa are key features of emerging political and ideological orders. Her article poses a challenge to those who would use genocide, as does Rummel (1994), to extol the virtues of democracy over "totalitarian communist governments" and raises perplexing questions regarding the nature of both democracy and genocide.

In other cases, however, populations constructed as racial, national, or sexual minorities themselves expand the notion of genocide in order to embrace the forms of oppression they face. Charles Briggs and Clara Mantini-Briggs (1997) document a cholera epidemic that killed some 500 people in a rain forest region in eastern Venezuela. Public health officials classified most of the people who were infected by and died from cholera as "Warao," that is, members of an *étnia*, an "indigenous ethnic group." In combating the threat to the legitimacy of public health institutions posed by alarmingly high rates of mortality, officials often characterized "indigenous culture" as the key "risk factor" in shaping patterns of morbidity and mortality. Many members of communities in which cases were concentrated cited national and transnational patterns of land expropriation and environmental degradation in charging that the epidemic constituted an act of genocide. This rhetoric provided them with a means of challenging stigmatizing images, regaining a sense of agency, and calling attention to the conditions in which they were living (in which infant mortality stands at 36 percent in some areas).

Steven Epstein (1996) traces the use and subsequent disavowal of genocide rhetoric by HIV/AIDS activists in the United States. When epidemiologists, politicians, and the media identified AIDS with gays, lesbians, Haitians, intravenous drug users, and hemophiliacs (see Farmer, 1992), activists charged the government, drug companies, and scientists with genocide. Once activists achieved their goal of gaining "a seat at the table" in decisions regarding research treatment, however, "genocide" began to fade from their vocabulary. Epstein suggests that this rhetoric defined the limits of discourse regarding HIV/AIDS during the 1980s and reconfigured how the public thought about the disease and the people it killed. AIDS activism also helped make more room for considerations of effect rather than intent in definitions of genocide. Dorothy Roberts (1997) describes how African Americans have used genocide accusations in protesting the role of judicial, prison, and public health institutions and the media in scapegoating women for the violence they face in their daily lives. The image of excessive fertility, a long-standing dimension of stereotypes of African-American women, helped rationalize efforts to criminalize drug-involved pregnant women and to force poor women to use even potentially dangerous methods of contraception. Charging genocide reconfigured the situation as violence deliberately directed at a racialized group, thereby refuting the idea that black reproduction is the cause of demeaning social conditions. Roberts argues that framing the issue as genocide construes social justice rather than individual rights as the standard for judicial decisions regarding reproductive policies. Troy Duster (1990)

37

argues that new genetics research can afford new spaces for old biologically based racisms in public debate and policy, thereby providing a back door to genocide through the promotion of new eugenic schemes. Emily Martin (1994) suggests that intersections between globalization and reconceptualizations of the body are leading to new fusions of biological and cultural notions of difference.

The Right to Cry Genocide

Henry Huttenbach (1988:297) argues that if "genocide" is used "simply for the emotional effect or to make a political point," the "original" or "explicit" meaning of the term will be "lost" or "eroded." Such statements seem to construe violence as revolving exclusively around acts of killing, thereby drawing attention away from the political underpinnings and effects of debates regarding genocide. As such, they often erase two crucial concerns, ones that, I would argue, lie at the heart of relationships between work on genocide and racial and ethnic studies.

First, debates about genocide are themselves political events that bear powerfully on creating, legitimating, and challenging violence shaped by racial, sexual, and gender inequality. As LaCapra (1994) has pointed out, discourse about genocide provides a powerful example of the performativity of language. Actions generally come to be referred to as genocides – and as "events" – *post facto*. The labeling shapes how they are perceived and remembered and their implications for the future.[4] Constructing an event as genocide places it in relationship to other acts and creates conduits for the circulation of accusations. The architects of genocide are often as concerned with suppressing discourse about the event as with the killing itself. Drawing on a term proposed by Pierre Bourdieu (1991), LaCapra (1994) argues that discourses of genocide constitute symbolic capital. They can accordingly be used not only in constructing, legitimizing, and challenging racializing schemes but also in promoting political agendas. Charles Maier (1988) argues that recent debates in Germany regarding the uniqueness or comparability of the Holocaust have provided opposing sides with capital that has been used in shaping political programs and questions of identity. Such writers as Rummel use discussions of genocide to support sweeping judgments regarding the value of political systems: "At the extremes of Power, totalitarian communist governments slaughter their people by the tens of *millions*; in contrast, many democracies can barely bring themselves to execute even serial murderers" (Rummel, 1994:2; emphasis in original).

A modernist, strictly referential view of language that construes discourses of genocide as the application of strictly defined terms that transparently represent language-external events erases awareness of their broader political significance. Symbolic capital is not used exclusively in the *aftermath* of genocide. Bette Denich (1994) relates the way that Serbian nationalists have drawn on images of the massacre of Serbs in World War II in inciting Serbs to conduct campaigns of "ethnic cleansing" against Muslims and Croatians. Liisa Malkki (1995) argues that a crucial dimension of the construction of historical memory by refugees and by the Burundi and Rwandan states revolved around not just who inaugurated genocides, and at whom they were directed, but the concept of "genocide" itself. The military has repeatedly justified mass killings by constructing the prospect of victims as the perpetrators of genocide (see Des Forges,

1999). Depicting some genocide accusations as "emotional," "political," "rhetorical," or the like limits the ability of scholars to grasp the political power of their own work and the debates in which they engage, thwarting the possibility of finding ways to keep discourses of genocide from becoming means of motivating and legitimizing violence.

Second, efforts to hold onto narrow definitions of genocide and to disqualify accusations that approximate accepted juridical and historical models erase the differential access that communities enjoy to educational, legal, political, and media institutions – in short, their access to symbolic capital in general. Images of criminality and sexual perversion are much more useful than discourses of genocide and social justice in helping state institutions to dominate the way that institutions respond to growing social inequality and the HIV/AIDS epidemic. Epstein (1996) argues that gays were able to use their efforts to characterize HIV/AIDS as genocide in gaining access to decisions regarding research and treatment questions at the same time that African Americans, women, and low-income communities were much more effectively shut out. He argues that many gay HIV/AIDS activists dropped genocide in favor of more conciliatory rhetorics, while other besieged populations continued to use the notion of genocide to draw attention to their efforts.

Herein lies a telling contrast with Venezuelan identifications of cholera and genocide. In spite of homophobic oppression, white, middle-class (and often professional) men in the United States were much more effective in using accusations of genocide in calling attention to their suffering and legitimating their protests than were poor rural Venezuelans; they also enjoyed greater access to other rhetorical resources, such as the language of medical science. In eastern Venezuela, on the other hand, public health authorities officialized their narratives of the cultural intractability of "indigenous persons," while accounts that placed cholera within a wider frame of deplorable health conditions, economic exploitation, transnational capital, and racism seldom made their way into the press or policy forums.

These cases indicate a point of convergence between the way such events are discussed in transnational, elite forums, such as scholarly journals or international tribunals, and the rhetorical confrontations that are woven into situations of death and suffering. In both contexts, "genocide" and related concepts constitute powerful rhetorical devices for highlighting images of violence, drawing attention to questions of agency, requiring assessments of culpability, and occasioning debates regarding potential consequences. Charges of genocide thus create transnational audiences and invite international intervention aimed at stopping the violence and punishing its perpetrators to a much greater extent than do other rhetorical frameworks. They similarly avoid the individualization that often accompanies efforts to challenge violence through rhetorics of human rights. Accordingly, it seems inevitable that questions of genocide will be raised when pronounced social inequality is connected with widespread death and suffering.

Transnational discussions of genocide enter directly into these contestations. Narrow, legalistic assertions regarding how "genocide" should be defined, and when it is appropriate to use the term, regulate access to the means by which discourses of genocide are legitimated. Discussions of genocide are not confined to international forums, nor do they take place only after suffering and death has ended. In suggesting that discussions of genocide should be guided exclusively by the application of narrow, strictly defined semantic criteria to nondiscursive acts, scholars and activists fail to appreciate the way that discourses of genocide are themselves part of the practices through which violence is produced, legitimized, and challenged and the question of differential access to both the media and public cultural debates as well as institutions of the nation-state.

When international authorities and activists on issues of genocide and human rights fail to recognize (in both senses of the term) the links between elite discussions of genocide and those that emerge in circumstances of suffering and violence, and when they decree that the deployment of genocide accusations must be contingent on the strict application of legalistic frameworks, they intervene profoundly in the discursive con-testations that shape such situations and their effects. They require, in essence, that some of the most oppressed groups must exert the very sorts of symbolic capital from which they have been systematically deprived. Maintaining such a position amounts to asserting a monopoly over discourses of genocide by reserving the right to grant or deny access to them as modes of depicting particular cases of violence and death. Since the members of dominated communities suffer from inequalities in access to the educa-tional opportunities that enable individuals to construct these sorts of arguments, as well as to publications and venues (such as international conferences) where these issues are discussed, "narrow" or "strict" definitions of genocide greatly restrict the ability of people suffering from violence to imbue their representations with authority. This weakness, in turn, renders genocide accusations less effective in creating international audiences and advancing calls for intervention and redress. Such restrictions are pro-posed without examining the rights of members of affected communities to determine which modes of representation will be authorized, and without ascertaining what other discursive practices may be available to them. Withholding international recognition from attempts to invoke discourses of genocide reinforces the hegemonic position of elites in Europe and the United States; furthermore it can easily strengthen the hand of already powerful national and transnational institutions. The failure to challenge repre-sentations that may be implicated in occasioning violence and loss of life exacerbates the social inequality that facilitates genocide and its discursive erasure. The creation by international elites of monopolies over the circulation of legitimate discussions of genocide bears an uncanny resemblance to the centralization of the production and transmission of statistics on disease, poverty, and crime by nation-states and inter-national agencies.

By being excessively concerned with restricting the use of rhetorics of genocide, the arbiters of these discourses ironically thwart the ability of dominated communities not only to communicate with them but to have greater say in how their suffering is defined in public and institutional forums and what sorts of responses it evokes. At the same time that genocide scholars often proclaim the need to listen to the voices of "victims," narrow definitions of genocide widen the gap between elite forums and those positioned within or fleeing from the sites of conflict. When the victims' narratives are replayed in international discussions, they emerge as displaced fragments of "local" discourses or as anecdotes that exemplify the positions adopted by international authorities, rather than as substantive interventions into the process of deciding when and how discourses of genocide are to be deployed. Donna Haraway's (1992) discussion of the dangers of ventriloquism is particularly pertinent here.

A Crucial Dialogue

I hope that this brief excursion into – rather than survey of – genocide scholarship points to the value of linking it with racial and ethnic studies. Postmodernism and post-structuralism have critically engaged definitions of genocide, techniques of representation, and understandings of the place of genocide in history. Students of the Nazi Holocaust in particular have often challenged efforts to rethink and rewrite genocide as part of efforts to desecrate the memory of Holocaust victims and survivors and undermine the use of historical memory in challenging antisemitism and preventing future Holocausts. Racial and ethnic studies have an important contribution to make in getting students of genocide beyond this debilitating polemic. As I discuss above, many writers have argued that scholars should not reproduce the reified and essentialist notions of homogenous and bounded communities defined by race, ethnicity, gender, sexuality, class, and nation. Recent work stresses the need to connect cultural and material dimensions, to view the creation of difference in relational rather than exclusionary terms, and to analyze relations of domination within racialized and sexualized communities. Essentialisms that take for granted received categories and relations of difference – and particularly the practices used in defining and naturalizing them – run the risk of being appropriated by states, institutions, elites, and other parties that seek to sustain or extend relations of social inequality and domination. Scholars, activists, and jurists who endeavor to challenge racialized violence do not stand above or apart from the politics of the situations they study; they play in particular key roles in interpellating violence, creating intertextual relations between the accounts of "victims," "perpetrators," journalists, jurists, and mass audiences. In doing so, they help determine the success or failure of other parties who attempt to effect these discursive and political transformations. Specialists on genocide thus have a great deal to gain, I would argue, in learning from recent work in racial and ethnic studies which maintain that only by critically rethinking categories, ideologies, practices, and strategies of writing can scholars hope to help challenge racialist violence.

By paying close attention to the way that regulation and criminalization of African American reproduction, state complicity in the massacre of street children and youths, and the role of public health authorities in naturalizing the burden of infectious disease borne by members of racial or sexual minorities, are framed as genocide, we enter productive sites to rethink the relationship between everyday racism and genocide. Dismissing such situations out of hand deprives genocide specialists of important tools for understanding the way that everyday racisms can be used in analyzing the key tools used in creating a space in which genocide is possible and in dealing with the thorny issue of intent. By examining minutely the dynamic changes that racializing ideologies and practices exhibit, scholars can better assist in identifying explosive situations and in suggesting the sorts of interventions that might be useful in countering their cultural and material bases. At the same time, I hope that students of racial and ethnic studies will pay closer attention to the importance of the notion of genocide in shaping how oppressed communities conceptualize the violence of race and the strategies they use in challenging it. As genocide continues to be a focus of media, scholarly, and public debate, and racialized death remains a common feature of contemporary society, efforts to relegate interrogations of everyday racism and genocide to nonoverlapping forums and groups of

41

specialists can only benefit those who are content with business-as-usual social inequality and its increasingly violent effects.

Notes

1 Interestingly, Lipstadt (1993:240, n.67) does not cite Fish's work but rather Peter Novick's characterization of it, a rhetorical move that does not seem to jibe with her concern for scholarly canons of textual authority.

2 See Churchill (1997) for an in-depth examination of the relationship between the Nazi Holocaust and Native American genocide.

3 At the same time that he accuses Holocaust scholars of narrow and reductionist interpretations of other cases, Stannard (1996) reads Holocaust scholarship in this fashion. For example, Stannard places Zygmunt Bauman in the "exclusivist" camp by virtue of the latter's efforts to characterize the Holocaust as "modern." Stannard fails to realize that Bauman's argument counters the tendency to place the Holocaust outside of history and modernity, to characterize it as a unique example of antimodern brutality. Remarkably, Stannard seems to believe Bauman's concept of "modernity" refers exclusively to the twentieth century, thereby overlooking the latter's many contributions to our understanding of how modernity has used constructions of knowledge to create and enforce schemes of social inequality since the seventeenth century (see Bauman, 1987).

4 Jay (1992:103) suggests that the Holocaust is "a post facto conceptual entity not in use at the time"; its power as a set of historical events is thus inseparable from discourses about it. James Young (1993:viii) argues that the construction of the Holocaust in memory "varies from land to land, political regime to regime and is mediated by the memorials and museums."

References

Anderson, B. ([1983] 1991) *Imagined Communities: Reflections on the Origin and Spread of Nationalism*, revised edn. London: Verso.

Arendt, H. (1964) *Eichmann in Jerusalem: A Report on the Banality of Evil*. Harmondsworth, UK: Penguin.

Balibar, E. (1991) "Is there a 'neo-racism'?" in Etienne Balibar and Immanuel Wallerstein *Race, Nation, Class: Ambiguous Identities*. London: Verso, pp.17–28.

Balibar, E. (1995) "Culture and identity (working notes)," in John Rajchman (ed.) *The Identity in Question*. New York: Routledge, pp.173–96.

Ball, H. (1999) *Prosecuting War Crimes and Genocide: The Twentieth-Century Experience*. Lawrence: University Press of Kansas.

Barta, T. (1987) "Relations of genocide: Land and lives in the colonization of Australia," in Isidor Wallimann and Michael N. Dobkowski (eds.) *Genocide and the Modern Age: Etiology and Case Studies of Mass Death*. New York: Greenwood Press, pp.237–51.

Bauer, Y. (1990) "Is the Holocaust explicable?" *Holocaust and Genocide Studies* 5,2:145–55.

Bauman, Z. (1987) *Legislators and Interpreters: On Modernity, Postmodernity and Intellectuals*. Ithaca, NY: Cornell University Press.

Bauman, Z. (1990) *Modernity and the Holocaust*. Cambridge, MA: Blackwell.

Black, E. (2001) *IBM and the Holocaust: The Strategic Alliance between Nazi Germany and America's Most Powerful Corporation*. New York: Crown.

Bourdieu, P. (1977) *Outline of a Theory of Practice*, trans. R. Nice. Cambridge: Cambridge University Press.

Bourdieu, P. (1991) *Language and Symbolic Power*, trans. G. Raymond and M. Adamson. Cambridge, MA: Harvard University Press.

Briggs, C. L. (1996) "The politics of discursive authority in research on the 'Invention of Tradition.'" *Cultural Anthropology* 11,4:435–69.

Briggs, C. L. (1997) "Introduction: The power of discourse in (re)creating genocide." *Social Identities* 3,3:407–13.

Briggs, C. L. and Mantini-Briggs, C. (1997) "'The Indians accept death as a normal, natural event'; Institutional authority, cultural reasoning, and discourses of genocide in a Venezuelan cholera epidemic." *Social Identities* 3,3:439–69.

Butler, J. (1997) *Excitable Speech: A Politics of the Performative*. New York: Routledge.

Chakrabarty, D. (1992) "Postcoloniality and the artifice of history: Who speaks for Indian pasts." *Representations* 37:1–26.

Chalk, F. (1989) "'Genocide in the 20th century': Definitions of genocide and their implications for prediction and prevention." *Holocaust and Genocide Studies* 4,2:149–60.

Chatterjee, P. (1993) *The Nation and Its Fragments: Colonial and Postcolonial Histories*. Princeton, NJ: Princeton University Press.

Churchill, W. (1997) *A Little Matter of Genocide. Holocaust and Denial in the Americas, 1492 to the Present*. San Francisco: City Lights.

Clifford, J. (1988) *The Predicament of Culture: Twentieth-Century Ethnography, Literature, and Art*. Cambridge, MA: Harvard University Press.

Clifford, J. and Marcus, G. E. (eds.) (1986) *Writing Culture: The Poetics and Politics of Ethnography*. Berkeley: University of California Press.

Dadrian, V. N. (1996) "The comparative aspects of the Armenian and Jewish cases of genocide: A sociohistorical perspective," in A. S. Rosenbaum (ed.) *Is the Holocaust Unique? Perspectives on Comparative Genocide*. Boulder, CO: Westview Press, pp.101–35.

Das, V. (1995) "Suffering, legitimacy and healing: The Bhopal case," in *Critical Events: An Anthropological Perspective on Contemporary India*. Delhi: Oxford University Press, pp.137–74.

Denich, B. (1994) "Dismembering Yugoslavia: Nationalist ideologies and the symbolic revival of genocide." *American Ethnologist* 21,2:367–90.

Derrida, J. (1974) *Of Grammatology*. Baltimore, MD: Johns Hopkins University Press.

Des Forges, A. (1999) *"Leave None to Tell the Story": Genocide in Rwanda*. New York: Human Rights Watch.

Duster, T. (1990) *Backdoor to Eugenics*. New York: Routledge.

Eckardt, A. R. (1979) "Is the Holocaust unique?" *Worldview* September: 31–5.

Epstein, S. (1996) *Impure Science: AIDS, Activism, and the Politics of Knowledge*. Berkeley: University of California.

Epstein, S. (1997) "Aids activism and the retreat from the 'genocide' frame." *Social Identities* 3,3:415–38.

Farmer, P. (1992) *AIDS and Accusation: Haiti and the Geography of Blame*. Berkeley: University of California Press.

Fisher Damrosch, Lori (ed.) (1998) *The International Court of Justice at a Crossroads*. Dobbs Ferry, NY: Transnational.

Foucault, M. (1970) *The Order of Things: An Archaeology of the Human Sciences*. New York: Vintage.

Foucault, M. (1980) *Power/Knowledge: Selected Interviews and Other Writings, 1972–1977*, trans. Colin Gordon et al. New York: Pantheon.

Friedlander, S. (1992) "Introduction," in S. Friedlander (ed.) *Probing the Limits of Representation: Nazism and the Final Solution*. Cambridge, MA: Harvard University Press, pp.1–21.

Ginzburg, C. (1992) "Just one witness," in S. Friedlander (ed.) *Probing the Limits of Representation: Nazism and the Final Solution*. Cambridge, MA: Harvard University Press, pp.82–96.

Goekjian, G. F. (1991) "Genocide and historical desire." *Semiotica* 83,3/4:211–25.

Gramsci, A. (1971) *Selections from the Prison Notebooks of Antonio Gramsci*, trans. Q. Hoare and G. Nowell Smith. New York: International Publishers.

Habermas, J. (1989) *The New Conservatism: Cultural Criticism and the Historians' Debate*. Cambridge, MA: Harvard University Press.

Hall, S. (1985) "Signification, representation, ideology: Althusser and the poststructuralist debates." *Critical Studies In Mass Communication* 2,2:91–114.

Hall, S. (1988) "New ethnicities." *ICA Documents* 7:27–31.

Handler, R. (1984) "On sociocultural discontinuity: Nationalism and cultural objectification in Quebec." *Current Anthropology* 25:55–71.

Handler, R. (1988) *Nationalism and the Politics of Culture in Quebec*. Madison: University of Wisconsin Press.

Haraway, D. (1992) "Promises of monsters," in L. Grossberg, C. Nelson, and P. Teichler (eds.) *Cultural Studies*. New York: Routledge, pp.295–337.

Hobsbawm, E. (1983) "Introduction," in E. Hobsbawm and T. Ranger (eds.) *The Invention of Tradition*. Cambridge: Cambridge University Press, pp.1–14.

Huttenbach, H. (1988) "Locating the Holocaust in the genocide spectrum: Towards a methodology of definition and categorization." *Holocaust and Genocide Studies* 3,3:289–303.

James, J. (1996) *Resisting State Violence: Radicalism, Gender, and Race in U.S. Culture*. Minneapolis: University of Minnesota Press.

Jay, M. (1992) "Of plots, witnesses, and judgments," in S. Friedlander (ed.) *Probing the Limits of Representation: Nazism and the Final Solution*. Cambridge, MA: Harvard University Press, pp.97–107.

Kuper, L. (1981) *Genocide*. Harmondsworth, UK: Penguin.

LaCapra, D. (1994) *Representing the Holocaust: History, Theory, Trauma*. Ithaca, NY: Cornell University Press.

LaCapra, D. (1998) *History and Memory after Auschwitz*. Ithaca, NY: Cornell University Press.

Lang, B. (1990) *Act and Idea in the Nazi Genocide*. Chicago: University of Chicago Press.

Lemkin, R. (1944) *Axis Rule in Occupied Europe: Laws of Occupation, Analysis of Government, Proposals for Redress*. Washington, D.C.: Carnegie Endowment for International Peace, Division of International Law.

Lipstadt, D. E. (1993) *Denying the Holocaust: The Growth in Assault on Truth and Memory*. New York: Free Press.

Lowe, L. (1996) *Immigrant Acts: On Asian American Cultural Politics*. Durham, NC: Duke University Press.

Lyotard, J.-F. (1984) *The Postmodern Condition: A Report on Knowledge*. Minneapolis: University of Minnesota Press.

Lyotard, J.-F. (1988) *The Differend: Phrases in Dispute*, trans. G. Van Den Abbeele. Minneapolis: University of Minnesota Press.

Lyotard, J.-F. (1990) *Heidegger and "the Jews,"* trans. Michel and M. S. Roberts. Minneapolis: University of Minnesota Press.

Maier, C. S. (1988) *The Unmasterable Past: History, Holocaust, and German National Identity*. Cambridge, MA: Harvard University Press.

Malkki, L. H. (1995) *Purity and Exile: Violence, Memory, and National Cosmology among Hutu Refugees in Tanzania*. Chicago: University of Chicago Press.

Marcus, G. E. and Fischer, M. M. J. (1986) *Anthropology as Cultural Critique: An Experimental Moment in the Human Sciences*. Chicago: University of Chicago Press.

Martin, E. (1994) *Flexible Bodies: Tracking Immunity in American Culture from the Days of Polio to the Age of AIDS*. Boston: Beacon Press.

Minow, M. (1998) *Between Vengeance and Forgiveness: Facing History after Genocide and Mass Violence*. Boston: Beacon.

Roberts, D. (1997) *Killing the Black Body: Race, Reproduction, and the Meaning of Liberty*. New York: Vintage.

Rosaldo, M. Z. (1982) "The things we do with words: Ilongot speech acts and speech act theory in philosophy." *Language in Society* 11:203–35.

Rosenberg, A. (1987) "Was the Holocaust unique?: A peculiar question," in I. Wallimann and M. N. Dobkowski (eds.) *Genocide and the Modern Age: Etiology and Case Studies of Mass Death*. New York: Greenwood Press, pp.145–61.

Rummel, R. J. (1994) *Death by Government*. New Brunswick, NJ: Transaction.

Scheper-Hughes, N. (1992) *Death Without Weeping: The Violence of Everyday Life in Brazil*. Berkeley: University of California Press.

Smith, R. (1987) "Human destructiveness and politics: The twentieth century as an age of genocide," in I. Walliman and M. Dobkowski (eds.) *Genocide and the Modern Age*. Westport, CN: Greenwood Press, pp.21–39.

Smith, R., Markusen, E., and Lifton, R. J. (1995) "Professional ethics and the denial of Armenian genocide." *Holocaust and Genocide Studies* 9:1–22.

Sollors, W. (1989) "Introduction: The invention of ethnicity," in W. Sollors (ed.) *The Invention of Ethnicity*. New York: Oxford University Press, pp.ix–xx.

Stannard, D. E. (1992) *American Holocaust: Columbus and the Conquest of the New World*. New York: Oxford University Press.

Stannard, D. E. (1996) "Uniqueness as denial. The politics of genocide scholarship," in A. S. Rosenbaum (ed.) *Is the Holocaust Unique? Perspective on Comparative Genocide*. Boulder, CO: Westview Press, pp.163–208.

Strathern, M. (1988) *The Gender of the Gift: Problems with Women and Problems with Society in Melanesia*. Berkeley: University of California Press.

Taussig, M. (1997) *The Magic of the State*. New York: Routledge.

Thornton, R. (1987) *American Indian Holocaust and Survival: A Population History Since 1492*. Norman: University of Oklahoma Press.

United Nations (1948) *Convention on Genocide*. GAOR Resolution 260A (III) 9 December 1948, Article II. Geneva: United Nations.

Wallimann, I. and Dobkowski, M. N. (1987) "Introduction," in *Genocide and the Modern Age: Etiology and Case Studies of Mass Death*. New York: Greenwood Press, pp.xi–xviii.

White, H. (1978) *Tropics of Discourse: Essays in Cultural Criticism*. Baltimore, MD: Johns Hopkins University Press.

White, H. (1992) "Historical emplotment and the problem of truth," in S. Friedlander (ed.) *Probing the Limits of Representation: Nazism and the Final Solution*. Cambridge, MA: Harvard University Press, pp.37–53.

Young, J. E. (1993) *The Texture of Memory: Holocaust Memorials and Meaning*. New Haven, CT: Yale University Press.

Chapter 4

Holocaust

Zygmunt Bauman

The Holocaust – the murder of about six million European Jews by Nazi Germany and its allies, committed during World War II – was an ultimate expression of genocidal tendency present in race and ethnic hatred. It was also a peculiar case of genocide to an extent which prompts many historians to present it as unique. What was peculiar or unique was the systematic and methodical fashion in which the extermination of men, women, and children classified as members of a particular – undesirable – race was conducted over many years, and the enormous number of people involved in the perpetration of the murder in their various professional capacities. It is this peculiarity that renders insufficient the routine explanations of the Holocaust as another, even if extreme, case of racial and ethnic genocide. It is true that the Holocaust is a most dramatic demonstration of the murderous potential of race or ethnic hatred; this is, however, not the only, and neither a particularly novel nor the most seminal of lessons which could be derived from its experience. Another lesson, drawing on the peculiarity of the Holocaust among other cases of genocide, seems to be as unique as the Holocaust itself and eminently important because of its bearing directly on the nature of the society in which this particular genocide was conceived and committed. That other lesson is addressed directly to the possible link between the holocaust-style genocide and certain attributes of modern society. If the first lesson sends us back to the familiar issue of racial prejudice and its morbid consequences, the second prompts us to rethink the routine, confident, and often self-congratulatory opinion of the essentially antiprejudicial impact of modernization.

How Modern is the Holocaust?

Understandably, resistance to accepting *this* lesson of the Holocaust is widespread. It manifests itself primarily in the manifold attempts to *exoticize* or *marginalize* the Holocaust as an episode confined to peculiar circumstances, marginal and untypical as far as modern society in general is concerned, and so of little or no consequence for the opinions held of the nature of modern living.

The most common among such attempts is the interpretation of the Holocaust as a specifically *Jewish* affair: as the culmination of the long history of Judeophobia reaching far into antiquity, and at best as the outcome of its modern form, antisemitism in its racist variety. This interpretation overlooks the essential discontinuity between even the most violent outbursts of premodern Judeophobia and the meticulously planned and executed operation called the Holocaust. It also glosses over the fact that – as Hannah Arendt pointed out long ago – only the choice of victims, not the nature of the crime, can be derived (if at all) from the history of antisemitism; indeed, it replaces the crucial issues of the nature of crime with the question of the unique features of Jews or Jewish–Gentile relations.

"Exoticization" is also achieved through the deployment of another strategy – attempts to interpret the Holocaust as a specifically *German* affair (at best, also an affair of some other, still more distant and bizarre, nations, whose concealed yet innate murderous tendencies had been released and set loose by German overlords). One hears of the unfinished business of civilization, of the liberalizing process that went awry, of a particularly morbid brand of national philosophy that poisoned the minds of citizens, of frustrating vicissitudes of recent history, even of the peculiar perfidy and shrewdness of a bunch of conspirators. Hardly ever, though, of what made the editors of *The Times, Le Figaro,* and other highly respected organs of enlightened opinion wax lyrical when they wistfully described Germany of the 1930s as the paragon of a civilized state, of prosperity, of social peace, of obedient and cooperative workers' unions, of absence of street crime, of security and safety, of law and order; indeed, as an example for the wan and ineffective European democracies to follow.

The paramount strategy, aimed at simultaneously marginalizing the crime and exonerating modernity, is the interpretation of the Holocaust as a singular eruption of premodern (barbaric, irrational) passions, as yet insufficiently tamed or ineffectively supressed by (presumably weak or faulty) German modernization. One would expect this strategy to be modernity's favorite form of self-defense: after all, it obliquely reaffirms and reinforces the etiological myth of modern civilization as a triumph of reason over passions, as well as its corollary: the belief that this triumph has marked an unambiguously progressive step in historical development of public morality – has made the world safe for humanity. This strategy is also easy to pursue. It neatly fits the well-established habit (forcefully supported by modern scientific culture, but rooted primarily in the protracted military, economic, and political domination of the modern part of the globe over the rest) of automatically defining all alternative modes of life, and particularly all critique of the modern virtues, as stemming from premodern, irrational, barbaric positions, and hence unworthy of serious consideration: as a specimen of the selfsame class of phenomena which modern civilization vowed to confine and exterminate. As Ernst Gellner put it with his usual brevity and straightforwardness, "if a doctrine conflicts with the acceptance of the superiority of scientific-industrial societies over others, then it really is out" (Gellner, 1968:405).

In more ingenuous times, when tyrants razed cities for their own greater glory, when the slave chained to the conqueror's chariot was dragged through the rejoicing streets, when enemies were thrown to wild animals in front of the assembled people, before such naked crimes consciousness could be steady and judgment unclouded. But slave camps under the flag of freedom, massacres justified by philanthropy or the taste of the superhuman, cripple judgment. On the day when crime puts on the apparel of innocence, through a curious reversal peculiar to our age, it is innocence that is called on to justify itself. (Camus [1951] 1971:11–12)

That much Albert Camus made clear in 1951, before Hannah Arendt's book *Eichmann in Jerusalem* (1964) first appeared in New York and before Eichmann, its hero, appeared in Jerusalem. The possibility that crime is logical, that "murder has rational foundations," is "the question put to us by the blood and strife of our century," Camus insisted. "We are being interrogated." We may refuse to listen to the question and to console ourselves with the eternity of evil and perpetuity of murder only at our peril; and first and foremost peril to our humanity, which is, in its innermost essence, our nonanimality, the *ethicality* of our being.

Camus recalls that Heathcliff of *Wuthering Heights* would be ready to kill everybody to win Cathy – but he would never think of saying that murder is reasonable or theoretically defensible. Heathcliff had no makings of a theorist: he did not theorize, nor did he need a theory. He loved Cathy, he wanted Cathy, and that was the only reason he needed in order to kill – that is, if reason he needed. Murder, were Heathcliff to commit it, would have been a *crime of passion*, and acting out of passion means putting reason to sleep; passion is, by definition, the unreason. When we speak of passion, we also speak of the nonbeing of reason. Passion and reason are at loggerheads: one wilts and fades in the face of the other.

Modernity declared war on passion and inscribed Reason, in the boldest of letters, on its banners: *in hoc signo vinces*. Modern mind shuns passion, denigrates and disdains passion, and in every manifestation of passion sniffs evidence of its own failure. By doing so, it refuses, not unjustly, to bear responsibility for crimes of passion. Whoever kills for love or hatred is out of modern bounds. There is indeed nothing particularly modern about the crime of passion. And it is hardly the fault of modern ambition that some men and women refuse or fail to listen to the voice of reason and remain slaves to their passions. Modernity has no need to apologize for crimes of passion. And if it does apologize it could only be for slackness, for negligence, for not doing its modernizing job thoroughly enough.

As long as one can ascribe crimes to the passions of their perpetrators, crime may be condemned without awkward questions about the nature of modern life being asked.

Neither Hitler nor Stalin were yet born, *Arbeit macht frei* was not yet written above the gates of Auschwitz, nor were large sections of the population murdered wholesale for the love of mankind, but modern life was already in full swing when Nietzsche noted down the baffling and horrifying paradox of our civilization:

> The same men who are held so sternly in check *inter pares* by custom, respect, usage, gratitude, and even more by mutual suspicion and jealousy, and who on the other hand in their relations with one another show themselves so resourceful – in consideration, self-control, delicacy, loyalty, pride, and friendship – once they go outside, where the strange, the *stranger* is found . . . [they] emerge from a disgusting procession of murder, arson, rape, and torture, exhilarated and undisturbed of soul, as if it were no more than a student's prank, convinced that they have provided the poets with a lot more material for song and praise. (Nietzsche, 1968:476)

The paradox is as much terrifying as defiant to all easy explanation. What is the case here? The beasts of prey relishing their escape from the stuffy and stifling cage called civilization and falling back, with a deafening sigh of relief, on their true nature, as Nietzsche seems to suggest? Or, rather, the once resourceful, now hapless humans, thrown out of their element, their understanding and wits, cast into the eerie world where their habits can guide them no more and the rules by which they played their games have been officially declared null and void or simply are no longer applicable? Both answers are as plausible as they are unprovable, and there is little point in arguing their substantive (as distinct from instrumental) merits. One conclusion, though, seems to be beyond reasonable doubt. It has been recently spelled out with exemplary clarity by Roberto Toscano:

> [W]hat is at stake here is not an attempt to explain individual violence that finds its roots in personal passions, desires, hate, greed. On the contrary, it is significant that the mechanisms of the two kinds of violent action (individual and group) are different and manifest themselves differently in the same individuals, who may have a radically different propensity to have recourse to group versus individual violence. (Toscano, 1998:67)

And Toscano spells out what makes the two situations, and so also the deceptively similar acts of violence that occur in their contexts, so radically different, and the reason why they call for altogether different explanations. Unlike individual violence, "group violence is by definition abstract"; "real individual neighbors are not necessarily loved, but they are loved or hated for concrete, not abstract reasons . . . On the contrary, in order to apply group violence to the neighbor as belonging to a category, the concrete individual's face has to be erased: the person must become an abstraction."

The Ordering Ambitions and Practices of the Modern State

At the threshold of the modern era Frederick the Great, admittedly the monarch most closely approximating the model of "enlightened despot" sketched by the philosophers of the Enlightenment, and indeed the favorite address of their projects, set the tone for the social-engineering ambitions of the new – modern – state:

> It annoys me to see how much trouble is taken to cultivate pineapples, bananas and other exotic plants in this rough climate, when so little care is given to the human race. Whatever people say, a human being is more valuable than all the pineapples in the world. He is the plant we must breed, he deserves all our trouble and care, for he is the ornament and the glory of the Fatherland.

While Frederick the Great merely demonstrated how eagerly he wished to absorb the Enlightenment lesson, at least some of his successors did their best to "make philosophy into a material force" and thus treat humans as one does bananas and pineapples, using for this purpose the unprecedented technological resources and managerial capacities offered by the modern state. And they understood literally the precept of breeding, which Frederick the Great could treat as no more than a wistful metaphor. In 1930, R. W. Darré, later to become the Nazi Minister of Agriculture, wrote:

> He who leaves the plants in a garden to themselves will soon find to his surprise that the garden is overgrown by weeds and that even the basic character of the plants has changed. If therefore the garden is to remain the breeding ground for the plants, if, in other words, it is to lift itself above the harsh rule of natural forces, then the forming will of a gardener is

necessary, a gardener who, by providing suitable conditions for growing, or by keeping harmful influences away, or by both together, carefully tends what needs tending, and ruthlessly eliminates the weeds which would deprive the better plants of nutrition, air, light and sun ... Thus we are facing the realization that questions of breeding are not trivial for political thought, but that they have to be at the center of all considerations ... We must even assert that a people can only reach spiritual and moral equilibrium if a well-conceived breeding plan stands at the very *center* of its culture. ...[1]

In 1934, the world-famous biologist Erwin Bauer, holder of many scholarly distinctions, then the director of the Kaiser Wilhelm Institute for Breeding Research, was more specific yet:

Every farmer knows that should he slaughter the best specimens of his domestic animals without letting them procreate and should instead continue breeding inferior individuals, his breeds would degenerate hopelessly. This mistake, which no farmer would commit with his animals and cultivated plants, we permit to go on in our midst to a large extent. As a recompense for our humanness of today, we must see to it that these inferior people do not procreate. A simple operation to be executed in a few minutes makes this possible without farther delay ... No one approves of the new sterilization laws more than I do, but I must repeat over and over that they constitute only a beginning.

Similarly, his learned colleague, Martin Stämmler, said in 1935:

Extinction and selection are the two poles around which the whole race cultivation rotates ... Extinction is the biological destruction of the hereditary inferior through sterilization, then quantitative repression of the unhealthy and undesirable ... The ... task consists of safeguarding the people from an overgrowth of the weeds. (Weinreich, 1946:30–4)

To underline the ambitions of the state now firmly set on substituting a designed and state-monitored plan for uncontrolled and spontaneous mechanisms of society, the medical metaphor soon joined forces with the traditional gardening one. Thus one of the most prominent and acclaimed zoologists of world-wide fame and the 1973 Nobel Prize winner Professor Konrad Lorenz declared in June 1940:

There is a certain similarity between the measures which need to be taken when we draw a broad biological analogy between bodies and malignant tumors, on the one hand, and a nation and individuals within it who have become asocial because of their defective constitution, on the other hand ... Any attempt at reconstruction using elements which have lost their proper nature and characteristics is doomed to failure. Fortunately, the elimination of such elements is easier for the public health physician and less dangerous for the supraindividual organism, than such an operation by a surgeon would be for the individual organism. (Müller-Hill, 1988:14)

None of the above statements was motivated by racist or ethnic animosity. In particular, none of them aimed specifically at the Jews, or stemmed predominantly from antisemitic sentiments. (As a matter of fact, there were quite a few Jews among the most vociferous scholarly preachers of gardening and medical techniques in social engineering. For instance, as late as in 1935, and shortly before his dismissal for reason of Jewish origin, noted psychiatrist Dr. F. Kallmann advised compulsory sterilization even of the healthy, yet heterozygous carriers of the "abnormal gene of schizophrenia." As Kallmann's plan would require sterilizing no less than 18 percent of the total population, the author's zeal had to be held back by his Gentile colleagues.) The quoted scientists were guided solely by the commonly accepted understanding of the role and mission of science and by feelings of duty towards the vision of a good, healthy, and orderly society. In particular, they were guided by the typically modern and not in the least idiosyncratic conviction that the road to such a society leads through the ultimate taming of the inherently chaotic natural forces and by systematic, and ruthless if need be, execution of a scientifically conceived, rational plan. As was to transpire later, the admittedly unruly and anarchistic Jewry was one of the many weeds which inhabited the plot marked for the carefully designed garden of the future. But there were other weeds as well – carriers of congenital diseases, the mentally inferior, the bodily deformed. And there were also plants which turned into weeds simply because a superior reason required that the land they occupy should be transformed into someone else's garden.

The most extreme and well documented cases of "social engineering" in modern history, all their attendant atrocities notwithstanding, were neither outbursts of barbarism, not yet fully extinguished by the new rational order of civilization, nor the price paid for utopias alien to the spirit of modernity. On the contrary, they were legitimate offspring of the modern spirit, of that urge to assist and speed up the progress of mankind toward perfection that was throughout the most prominent hallmark of the modern age – of that "optimistic view, that scientific and industrial progress in principle removed all restrictions on the possible application of planning, education and social reform in everyday life," of that "belief that social problems can be finally solved." Nazi vision of harmonious, orderly, deviation-free society drew its legitimacy and attractiveness from such views and beliefs already firmly entrenched in the public mind through the century and a half of post-Enlightenment history, filled with scientistic propaganda and the visual display of the wondrous potency of modern technology. The Nazi vision did not jar with the audacious self-confidence and the hubris of modernity. It merely offered to do better what other modern powers dreamed of, perhaps even tried but failed to accomplish:

> What should not be forgotten is that fascist realism provided a model for a new order in society, a new internal alignment. Its basis was the racialist elimination of all elements that deviated from the norm: refractory youth, "idlers," the "asocial," prostitutes, homosexuals, the disabled, people who were incompetents or failures in their work. Nazi eugenics – that is, the classification and selection of people on the basis of supposed genetic "value" – was not confined only to sterilization and euthanasia for the "valueless" and the encouragement of fertility for the "valuable"; it laid down criteria of assessment, categories of classification and norms of efficiency that were applicable to the population as a whole.

Indeed, one must agree with Detlev Peukert that National Socialism merely "pushed the utopian belief in all-embracing 'scientific' final solutions of social problems to the ultimate logical extreme".[2] The determination and the freedom to go "all the way" and reach the ultimate was Hitler's, yet the logic was construed, legitimized, and supplied by modernity.

It is vital also to remember that the gardening-breeding- surgical ambitions were in no way specifically German; rather, German scholars and social engineers tried desperately to "catch up" with, and if possible to overtake, the "most advanced" ideas of contemporary science. Even the retrospectively most sinister among the expressions of grand social-engineering ambitions – eugenics, that "science of human heredity and art of human breeding" – was born outside Germany. It basked in the international prestige and deference that an advanced and resourceful science would expect to achieve long before Hitler and his companions patched together their vision of the Thousand Years Reich. It was none other than the distinguished head of the Cold Spring Harbor Laboratory, Professor C. B. Davenport, who gave the public accolade and blessing to the top German expert-breeder of human animals, Professor E. Fischer, by nominating him his successor as President of the International Federation of Eugenic Organizations.[3] The grandiose German plan to rest the reproduction of society on a scientific basis and eliminate the heretofore unharnessed (and hence haphazard) forces of heredity and selection was simply the most radical expression of the universal ambitions inherent in the modern mentality. It was, indeed, a relatively small part of a much wider totality. It earned its terrifying fame not because of its uniqueness, but because – unlike most similar sentiments elsewhere – it did reach its purpose: it was put into practice, with the help of technological and organizational resources available to a modern society fully mobilized by the unchallenged might of a centralized state.

Eugenics was pioneered simultaneously in several European countries; as in many other areas of modern intellect, English scholars vied for pride of place with their German colleagues. The Eugenics Education Society was founded in Britain in the nineteenth century (Galton established the highly successful journal *Eugenics* in 1883) and was given a tremendous boost by the panic caused by the poor physical and mental quality of army recruits discovered during the Boer war. British eugenists were not short of engineering ambitions. They posited in front of the educated public a truly breathtaking vista:

> Would it not be possible to "breed out" certain grave hereditary ailments in the way that Mendelian geneticists had learned to breed "rustiness" out of wheat, and perhaps also to develop mental or physical faculties in men that were generally regarded as desirable? . . . Eugenics would then stand to genetics in rather the same relationship that engineering does to mathematics.

The prospect of scientifically managing the presently defective human stock was seriously debated in the most enlightened and distinguished circles. Biologists and medical experts were, of course, in the forefront of the debate; but they were joined by famous people from other areas, like the psychologists Cyril Burt and William McDougall, politicians Balfour and Neville Chamberlain, the whole of the infant British sociology, and on various occasions by J. B. S. Haldane, J. M. Keynes, and Harold Laski. Concepts like "rabid and wilted stock" (coined by Wheethams in 1911), "degenerate stock," "submen," "low-grade types," "biologically unfit" became staple figures of intelligent debate, while the tremendously influential Karl Pearson sounded in 1909 the alarm that shook the reading and debating public: "the survival of the unfit is a marked characteristic of modern town life." (He only expressed already widespread concerns; here as elsewhere, British scholars were well attuned to the intellectual climate of the day. Six years before Pearson, Wilhelm Schalimayer stated in an award-winning essay that civilized man is threatened by physical degeneration, and that natural selection could not be depended upon as the basis for the social progress and perfectibility of man; it had to be guided by some form of *social* selection. In her entry of 16 January, 1903, gentle and humane Beatrice Webb noted in her diary that human breeding "is the most important of all questions, this breeding of the right sort of man . . .") (See Searle, 1976:8, 13, 29, 75).

English liberal, socialist, and gallant fighter against narrow nationalism, religion, and everything which smacked of a prescientific age – H. G. Wells – pondered throughout his long life and relentlessly preached to his numerous avid readers ("I doubt whether anyone who was writing books between 1900 and 1920, at any rate in the English language, influenced the young so much" – testified George Orwell on Wells' impact on the minds of the English educated classes) the urgency of "replacing disorder by order" and of placing scientifically informed, planning agencies at the control desk of social development (see Wells, 1984). To Wells, the crowning argument in favor of a planned, socialist society was its affinity (indeed, synonymity) with recognition of the fundamental idea on which all true science is founded: "the denial that chance impulse and individual will and happenings constitute the only possible methods by which things may be done in the world." Like the scientist, the socialist wants "a complete organization for all these human affairs that are of collective importance . . . In place of disorderly individual effort, each man doing what he pleases, the socialist wants organized effort, and a plan." And here, of course, the by now familiar garden metaphor is summoned to assist in making the case persuasive: the Socialist, like the scientist,

> seeks to make a plan as one designs and lays out a garden, so that sweet and seemly things may grow, wide and beautiful vistas open, and weeds and foulness disappear . . . [What makes all its graciousness and beauty possible, is the scheme and the persistent intention, the watching and the waiting, the digging and burning, the weeder clips and the hoe. (Orwell, 1961:164)

It was his love of wide vistas and straight paths which made Wells dislike the Jews: Jews were "firmly on the side of reaction and disorder" (Cheyette, 1988:23) and as such spoiled the landscape and thwarted the efforts of the planner. There was but a short step from this verdict to the application of the weeder. As it happens, the step was never taken. But there was little in Wells' declaration, and in the scientific ambitions in the name of which he wrote it down (though arguably not in some other segments of his profuse legacy) to prevent it from being taken.

On the face of it, conservative and romantic T. S. Eliot would occupy an opposite pole on many a continuum on which the liberal and progressive H. G. Wells could be also plotted. Indeed, Wells' brash, all-stops-pulled bravery fed by scientific hubris would jar stridently with T. S. Eliot's worldview; but the desire of a harmonious, aesthetically pleasing and "clean" society was common to both thinkers, as was the conviction that society would not become clean or harmonious if guided solely by its natural inclinations.

> The population should be homogenous; where two or more cultures exist in the same place, they are likely either to be fiercely self-conscious or both to become adulterate. What is still more important is unity of religious background; and reasons of race and religion combine to make any large number of freethinking Jews undesirable. There must be a proper balance between urban and rural, industrial and agricultural development. And a spirit of excessive tolerance is to be deprecated.

All too often Eliot's ugly and sinister sentence about the undesirability of free-thinking Jews is cut out of its context, deemed to provide by itself the complete and sufficient insight into the structure of Eliot's antisemitic prejudice. This is a mistake, and a dangerous mistake at that, as Christopher Ricks (1988) convincingly argues in his profound study of Eliot's antisemitism. However repulsive the quoted sentence may sound, "it is importantly less objectionable than the sequence of sentences within which it is deployed." The sequence, Ricks points out, "is a more insidious incitement to prejudice than any single sentence." Prejudice is most powerfully itself when expressed in "plausible processes of corrupted reasoning, by the disguising of a *non-sequitur*" (Ricks, 1988:41). Indeed, it is only when anti-Jewish sentiments are riveted in an enticing vision of a total, harmonious design, which the Jews allegedly disturb and prevent from implementation, that old Judeophobia turns – at least potentially – into modern genocide. It is only the admixing of resentment of "the other" to the gardener's self-confidence that is truly explosive.

The praise of weeders and trimming shears was not sung solely by intellectual dreamers and self-appointed spokesmen of science. It permeated modern society and remained arguably the most salient feature of its collective spirit. Politicians and practitioners of economic progress joined in the chorus. Scientific studies in eugenics conducted by Terman, Yerkes, and Goddard, and the fashionable Binet's IQ test were used in the US Johnson Immigration Act of 1924 to separate the "dangerous classes" who were "destroying American democracy," while Calvin Coolidge argued in 1922 that "the laws of biology had demonstrated that Nordic peoples deteriorate when mixing with other races." According to John R. Rockefeller's expression of faith, that preceded both events by about a generation,

> [t]he American Beauty rose can be produced in the splendor and fragrance which bring cheer to its beholder only by sacrificing the early buds which grow up around it. This is not an evil tendency in business. It is merely the working-out of a law of nature and a law of God. (Ghent, 1902:29)

Genetical deficiency, manifested in crime and idiocy, became – following the scientists' lobbying or advice – the legitimate reason for compulsory sterilization in the states of Indiana, New Jersey, and Iowa (where the state law covered "criminals, rapists, idiots, feeble-minded, imbeciles, lunatics, drunkards, drug fiends, epileptics, syphilitics, moral and sexual perverts, and diseased and degenerate persons"). Altogether 21 states of the USA enacted eugenic sterilization laws between 1907 and 1928 (Chorover 1979:42). Quite recently, after decades of silence and whitewashing, we have heard of the policy of compulsive sterilization conducted (by right-wing and left-wing governments alike) for many years (and well after the defeat of Nazi Germany) towards the "inferior," "unreliable," and otherwise undesirable categories of the population. This was revealed thanks to the curiosity and dedication of one investigative journalist. How many other dark secrets still wait for their discoverers?

Modern Genocide as Categorial Murder

Abstraction is one of the modern mind's principal powers. When applied to human beings, that power means effacing the face: whatever individual marks of the face are left to remain serve as badges of membership, the signs of belonging to a category, and the fate meted out to the owner of the face is nothing more and nothing less than the treatment reserved for the *category* of which the owner of the face is but a *specimen*. The overall effect of abstraction is that rules routinely followed in personal interaction, ethical rules most prominent among them, do not interfere when handling of a category is concerned and every entity is classified into that category just for the circumstance of having been so classified.

Nazi legislation, propaganda, and management of social setting went out of their way to separate the one and only "abstract Jew" from the many concrete Jews known to the Germans as neighbors or workmates; and to cast all "concrete Jews," through exclusion, deportation, and confinement, into the position of abstract ones. Genocide differs from other murders in having a category for its object. Only the abstract Jews could be subjected to genocide – the kind of murder oblivious to differences of age, sex, personal quality, or character. For genocide to be possible, personal differences must be first obliterated and faces must be melted in the uniform mass of the abstract category. Julius Streicher, the infamous editor-in-chief of the equally infamous *Der Stürmer*, had a hard time trying to stick the exceedingly popular stereotype of the "Jew as such," which his paper forged and disseminated, to the concrete Jews the readers knew from their daily intercourse; while Himmler found it necessary to reprimand even the selected and tested elite of his SS henchmen:

> "The Jewish people is to be exterminated," says every party member. "That's clear, it's part of our programme, elimination of the Jews, extermination, right, we'll do it." And then they all come along, the eight million good Germans, and each one has his decent Jew. Of course the others are swine, but this one is a first class Jew (quoted in Bauman, 1989:187).

Decent Germans were forbidden to have their own decent Jews – decent *because* "their own": the next-door neighbors, caring doctors, or friendly shopkeepers. Up to six million Jews were murdered wholesale not for what any of them had done but for how they had all been classified – just like, quite recently, in another hour of ultimate triumph of all-defining, all-classifying, modern bureaucracy, the armed gangs of Hutus and Tutsis of Rwanda set off their victims from the others of the same appearance, language, and religion as their killers, but meant to kill rather than be killed, simply *according to the entries in their passports*.

Jock Young coined the term *essentialization* for the tendency to "categorize" the others – the tendency perhaps extemporal as far as the human species goes, but most certainly aided and abetted, as Georg Simmel already noted, by the modern powers' knack for abstraction, and practiced with particular zeal and put to the widest range of uses in modern times. "Essentialism," Jock Young writes, "is a paramount strategy of exclusionism: it separates out human groups in terms of their culture or their nature. The advantages have always been there throughout human history but there are obvious reasons why the above strategies should appeal as we enter the late modern period" (Young, 1999:104). Among the reasons for essentialization becoming a favorite modern strategy, Young lists the provision of otherwise sorely missing ontological security, legitimation of privilege and deference otherwise jarring with the modern promise of universality and equality, proffering the facility to shift the blame onto the other and to project onto the other the inner fears and suspicions about one's own ability to match the standards of adequacy and decency one professed. Treating others as separate beings endowed with personal virtues or vices would fail to serve such purposes: essentialization is indispensable, and the modern power of abstraction comes in handy. The abstracting powers simultaneously underlie and overtop the other accoutrements of modernity without which the Holocaust, that exquisitely modern form of genocide, would have been inconceivable.

Some of those other necessary conditions available solely in the modern setting are by now well known and have been repeatedly discussed. Technological tools, as necessary for mass murder as they are indispensable for mass industrial production, are perhaps most frequently mentioned. Scientific management as embodied in the bureaucratic organization – the ability to coordinate the actions of a great number of people and make the overall result independent from the personal idiosyncrasies, convictions, beliefs, and emotions of individual performers – comes a close second. These two traits of modernity supply the *possibility* for genocide, if and when it occurs, to be conducted with a cold and ethically indifferent efficiency and on a scale akin to that which set the Holocaust apart from all past, however cruel and gory, cases of mass murder.

What may lift that possibility to the level of reality is, however, the characteristically modern order-making zeal; the kind of posture which casts extant human reality as a perpetually unfinished project, in need of critical scrutiny, constant revision, and improvement. When confronted with that stance, nothing has the right to exist just because it happens to be around. To be granted the right of survival, every element of reality must justify itself in terms of its utility for the kind of order envisaged in the project. This is, as I have suggested elsewhere (in Bauman 1987), an ambition which can be grasped best with the help of the "gardening" metaphor (uprooting the weeds to enable useful plants to grow and preserve the elegance of overall design). Medicine (cutting out the diseased parts to secure the health of the organism) and architecture (eliminating from the design everything out of place and redundant) offer equally useful metaphors.

What is to be Learned from the Holocaust?

This last point needs particularly strong emphasis, when the affinity between modern life and Holocaust-type murder is pondered. Indeed, this point is crucial if one wishes to comprehend the true nature of modernity *as modality of being*, rather than any particular, concrete state of affairs already constructed, projected, or adumbrated. Modern modality of being is characterized first and foremost by its endemic unfinishedness; by its orientation towards a state of affairs not yet in existence. To speak of modernity as an unfinished project is to commit a tautology. Modernity is by definition forever in the running, always (and incurably) not yet accomplished. What is "modern" about any project is precisely its being a step, or two, or a hundred steps, ahead of reality; what is "modern" about modernity is its built-in capacity to self-transcend, to push back the finishing line in the course of running, and so to bar itself from ever reaching it.

Modernity is an inherently *transgressive* mode of being-in-the-world. Visions of order are born out of disaffection with the existing state of affairs; while attempts to make such visions into flesh give birth to new disaffections and new, revised, and so deemed to be improved, visions. Modernity rolls and blends into one the act of drawing a frontier and the resolve to transgress it. All orders constructed under the aegis of modernity are therefore, even if only unintentionally, local, temporal, until further notice – bound to be reshaped before reaching fulfillment. "Modernization" is not a road leading to the station called "modernity." Modernization – the continuous, unstoppable, compulsive, obsessive, and in many ways self-propelling, modernization – is the very human condition the concept of "modernity" stands for; the permanent urge to modernize is modernity. Were the modernizing thrust ever to grind to a halt, this would not augur the completion of modernity, but its demise or bankruptcy. Ulrich Beck has captured that state of affairs splendidly in his portrayal of our times as a process of constant modernization of modernity or rationalizing rationality (see e.g., Beck, 1998).

Because of the endemically precocious and precarious nature of all partial, local, and temporary order-making efforts, Ulrich Beck thought it fit to describe modern society as *Risikogesellschaft*: ours is a kind of society in which the order-making urge results in generating ever new series of disorders, imbuing all order-making endeavors with risks which one can perhaps roughly calculate in probability terms, but would never avoid. What is especially relevant to our topic is that living in a *Risikogesellschaft* is, and is bound to remain, a *Risikoleben*.

Life full of risks, the incurably risky life without reliable knowledge of what the future may bring and without the possibility to control the outcomes of one's own actions (that *conditio sine qua non* of all rational choice), is an unnerving, disturbing, anxiety-generating condition. Perhaps modern life started, as Sigmund Freud suggested, from surrendering a large slice of individual freedom in exchange for collectively endorsed security. In its present-day phase, though, the offer of social guarantees of individual security has been withdrawn or is no longer trusted. This state of affairs is a recipe for a life of insecurity and anguish; and also for the desperate search for a genuine or putative, but trustworthy-looking, promise of a great simplification of a world too complex to walk safely through.

We may say that the modern order-making urge is self-perpetuating and self-propelling: the state of affairs to be brought into order is as a rule the leftover (the waste, the unanticipated and unwanted consequence) of past ordering bustle. Since the substance of modernity is a *compulsive modernization*, there is no end to tension saturating society and desperately seeking unloading and an outlet through which to unload. The constantly replenished supplies of anxiety and the pent-up aggression it generates are channeled into concerns with "law and order": into fighting crime and rounding up the criminals, or into control over the suspicious, unreliable, and thus feared elements – mostly foreigners, people of another race or ethnicity, of different or opaque customs and lifestyle, the very epitome of instability, of the ground shaking under one's feet, of the porousness of the thickest and ostensibly secure fortress walls. A growing section of law-and-order concerns focuses on the figures of the prowler, stalker, traveler, and of course the "migrant," on whom the diffuse fears of increasingly alien, wayward, and erratic *Umwelt* converge; and on tough police forces, long prison sentences, high security prisons, and capital punishment, as well as isolation and deportation of "undesirables" – these and other deemed remedies for the novel, off-putting and disturbing, experience of the fluidity of space.

There is a lot of political capital lodged in the modern safety obsession. And there is hardly ever a shortage of political players eager to deploy that capital in the power game. From the Alps to the northernmost parts of Scandinavia, the influence of the fiercely anti-immigrant parties and movements demanding "cleaning up" the country of "foreign elements" is felt. The recent success of Jörg Heider's party in Austria, of the *Front National* and the *indépendantiste* "Savoignard League" of Patrice Abelle in France, the Association for Independent Switzerland of Christoph Blocher, the Republicans of Franz Schönhuber in Bavaria, Pia Kjersgaard's movement in Denmark, and other similar one-issue "antialiens" populist movements, forces the hands of right-of-center, and increasingly also of left-of-center, parties in charge of nationality and immigration policies.

To be sure, thanks to the late-modern or postmodern surfeit of mutually canceling authorities, and due to the irredeemable polyvocality which goes together with political democracy and the weakening grip of the state powers, the chances of such political players gaining an upper hand and deploying the absolute powers of the state to set Holocaust-style "solutions" in motion are slim and remote. Yet to say with any degree of self-assurance that the forces eager for an *Endlösung* (final solution) type of action, and either the necessary or sufficient conditions of their acting in that way are no longer present today, would be equally premature and imprudent. Over fifty years after the military rout of Hitler's Germany, evidence continues to arrive of the tendency of the endemic tensions of *Risikoleben* and endemic modernization to condense in the projects of "cleaning-up" operations, of ethnic and/or racial purity, of transparent order with nothing to obscure or cloud the harmonious and homogenous native unity.

What follows is that with all the uniqueness of the Holocaust, the processes pregnant with genocidal potential are far from unique; on the contrary, they seem to accompany modern life at all times and places. The specifically modern tensions may not be the only causes of genocide, but when the roots of genocide are analyzed they certainly cannot be left out of account.

This aspect of the Holocaust – its intimate link with universal attributes of modernity – has been recently denied in the new spate of "revisionist" debate triggered by Daniel Goldhagen's *Hitler's Willing Executioners* (1996). The message of that book was quite straightforward: "with regard to the motivational cause of the Holocaust, for the vast majority of the perpetrators, a monocausal explanation does suffice" – that is, "a demonological antisemitism." Historians who wished to acknowledge more complex aspects of the Holocaust's mechanism were, in Goldhagen's view, wrong: they should get rid of the idea that Germans (of Hitler Germany at least) were "more or less like us," that "their sensibilities had remotely approximated our own" (Goldhagen, 1996:416, 279, 269). The reader would easily conclude that it was precisely because the Germans were *not* "more or less like us" that the Holocaust happened. And since "being unlike" is a symmetrical relation, the next conclusion is equally easy: because all the rest of us are not "more or less like Germans," nothing "remotely approximating" the Holocaust-style genocide can be perpetrated by anybody else and nowhere else. Holocaust was, is, and will remain the *German problem*, and so the rest of the world has nothing to fear, put conscience to rest and stop the vexing soul-searching. In other words: nothing that we can possibly learn from the event called "the Holocaust" can teach us anything about ourselves, the world we live in, or indeed anything else – except German guilt.

It is tremendously difficult to square with the one-dimensional worldview the fact that in the course of Hitler's war against the Jews many declared antisemites stoutly refused to cooperate with the perpetrators of the Holocaust; and that, on the other hand, the ranks of the executors were full of law-abiding citizens and disciplined functionaries who happened to be free of any peculiar resentment against the Jews as such and in particular bore no grudge whatsoever against the concrete Jews they shot *or* gassed (Nechama Tec, the indefatigable and remarkably perceptive student of the "ordinary humans" cast in inhuman conditions, reports that according to a witness of one mass execution, among 13 policemen one stood out for his bestial cruelty, three did not participate in the Jewish action, and the rest saw the operation as "unclean" and refused to talk about it). It is similarly hard to come to grips with the fact that "the deportation of the Jews" (as the annihilation of European Jewry was officially defined), derived its meaning in Nazi thinking from the overall, audacious plan of wholesale *Umsiedlung* – the vision of a European continent in which well nigh everyone will be transported from their present, contingent site to the place where reason orders them to be (see Aly and Heim's (1991) penetrating and thoroughly researched study). Or to accept that the extermination of the Jews (and Gypsies) was conceived in the framework of a total "cleansing operation" (which included also the mentally deficient, physically handicapped, ideologically deviant, and sexually unorthodox) by a state powerful enough, and sufficiently protected and immune against all opposition, to afford such total plans and to execute them without fear of effective dissent. Finally, to comprehend that the Nazis behind the Holocaust, whatever creatures they must have been otherwise, were *also* "Bürgers," who like all *Bürgers* then as much as now, here as much as there, had their "problems" which they dearly wished to resolve (as Klaus Dörner (1998:12ff.) convincingly argues).

Christopher R. Browning, whose eye-opening findings Goldhagen borrowed only to twist them and stretch them beyond their capacity in order to sustain his verdicts, charges Goldhagen with:

> inventing an artificial dichotomy between actions motivated by allegedly "internal" factors permitting moral judgments (namely beliefs and values, which in effect Goldhagen limits to antisemitics or racist convictions) and actions "compelled" by what he terms "external" factors that, because of the compulsion, are devoid of a moral dimension involving choice. In reality, of course, there are numerous "values and beliefs" that motivate people other than racist ones, such as perceptions of authority, duty, legitimacy, and loyalty to one's unit and country in wartime. And there are other personality traits such as ambition, greed, and lack of empathy that shape people's behavior without absolving them of individual responsibility. (Browning, 1999:58)

This is precisely the point: it took quite a few formidable modern inventions, the "rational bureaucracy" prominent among them, to render certain murders and other acts of cruelty exempt from moral judgments and so, in the eyes of the perpetrators, "morally neutral," and to deploy a wide range of human "values and beliefs" in the service of murder. But one would search Goldhagen's book in vain to find any sign that the author is aware of this and prepared to see the complexity of the modern predicament of the moral person beyond the most crude of dichotomies.

That some of the participants of mass murder did enjoy their part in crime, either because of their sadistic inclinations or for their hatred of the Jews or for both reasons simultaneously, is not, of course, Goldhagen's fantasy; though it is not his discovery either. Taking that fact, however, as the explanation of the Holocaust, as its central point or the deepest meaning, turns the attention away from what is the most sinister truth of that genocide and what is still the most salutary lesson which our own world could learn –

should learn, has the moral obligation to learn – from its recent history which contains the Holocaust as its major event.

Social Production of Killers

For every villain of Goldhagen's book, for every German and non-German who killed his victims with pleasure and enthusiasm, there were dozens and hundreds of Germans and non-Germans who contributed to the mass murder no less effectively without feeling either way about their victims and about the nature of the actions involved. While we know quite well that prejudice threatens humanity, and we know a little how to fight and constrain the ill intentions of people tainted with prejudice, we know next to nothing of how to stave off the threat of a murder which masquerades as the routine and unemotional function of orderly society. However, the other kind of knowledge – how to deploy people free of any inborn or acquired murderous instincts in the service of "legitimate killing," and the skills and technology needed to apply such knowledge in practice – is by now, thanks to the united efforts of psychologists, technologists, and experts in scientific management, considerable and continually growing.

Modernity would not get where it has got were it to rely on forces as erratic, whimsical, and thoroughly unmodern as human passions. Instead, it relied on the division of labor, on science, technology, scientific management, and the power of the rational calculation of costs and effects – all thoroughly unemotional. In his recent study of the American practice of capital punishment Stephen Trombley (1993) has shown beyond reasonable doubt that the setting which in modern society renders mass or regular killing possible is indistinguishable from that which makes mass production and unstoppable technological rationalization possible. Gotz Aly and Susanne Heim (1991) documented the crucial role played by the thousands of high-class experts – engineers, architects, constructors, medics, psychologists, and countless others – in making mass extermination on a heretofore unheard-of scale feasible. From the carefully documented history of the electric chair written by Trombley, we read that the first electrocution (of William Kemmler, held on 6 August, 1890 in New York's Auburn State Prison) "excited a great deal of medical interest, and of the twenty five witnesses who watched Kemmler killed by electricity, fourteen were doctors." We also learn that the invention of the electric chair became an occasion of thorough scientific debate about the respective advantages of alternating and direct currents, and caused a heated public argument between such supreme luminaries of modern technology as Thomas Edison and George Westinghouse. We learn in addition that the distinguished members of Governor Hill's commission set to find the proper methods of execution fell for the arguments carrying the authority of science and progress: what convinced them was that electricity, "the invisible and imperfectly understood form of energy was quintessentially modern"; it was also clean and promised to be cheap – and the members of the commission were duly impressed.

As Enzo Traverso (1996) put it recently in reference to France, the causes of the Holocaust in general, and that "wall of indifference" which surrounded the mass slaughter of the French Jews, need to be sought not in the "Jewish question," as Jean-Paul Sartre saw fit, not even in the circumstances of the genocide itself, but in French pre-Vichy society. There are unwanted strangers in any society, and in any society there are some people who wish such strangers not to be there; but in no society can a genocide of the unwanted strangers take place. The presence of a quantity of Jew-haters is not the only, not even the necessary, and certainly not a sufficient condition which needs to be met to make that genocide a possibility.

Hannah Arendt pointed out long ago that in the phenomenon of the Holocaust antisemitism may explain at most the choice of the victims, but not the nature of the crime. Nothing has happened since then to invalidate Arendt's verdict, while the monumental memoirs of Primo Levi, the monumental historical research of Raoul Hilberg, and the monumental documentary of Claude Lanzmann, to mention but a few landmarks, did a lot to confirm and reinforce it.

Recently another important voice has been added – that of the Italian philosopher Giorgio Agamben – to the attempts to pierce through the mystery of genocide. Agamben (1997) recalled the legal concept of the "*homo sacer*," coined in the archaic Roman Law: the concept of a human being who could be killed without punishment, but at the same time – being absolutely Other, alien, indeed inhuman – a kind of being that could not be used in ritualistic religious sacrifices and whose murder had no religious significance. "*Homo Sacer*" was totally "useless" – completely outside human society and exempt from all obligations and other considerations due to other humans on account of their humanity. *Homo Sacer*'s life was "nude" – that is, stripped of all social quality and political rights, and as such unprotected, made into a sitting target for every frustrated sadist or murderer, but also a recommended target for everyone seeking to conform and exercise their civic duty.

"*Homo sacer*" was a legal construction. As a legal construct, it was addressed to the loyalty and *discipline* of law-abiding subjects, not to their beliefs and senti-ments. Like all legal constructs it bypassed or suspended feelings and personal beliefs, also moral emotions, and as far as the required action was concerned cast them into irrelevance. The point about law is that it is expected to be obeyed *whether or not* the law-abiding person likes it, dislikes it, or has no feelings about it. That particular legal construct of *homo sacer* was in Roman legal practice an exceptional, marginal, and almost empty category. It is different in the modern state, Agamben points out.

True, the concept of "*homo sacer*" is absent from the modern law and largely forgotten. But having appropriated the monopoly over means of enforcement and violence as well as over the means and the prerogatives to offer or to refuse the right to live, over the entitlement to control the bodies of the subjects including the right to inflict pain, the state has expanded what used to be an extraordinary category into a potentially universal aspect of its subjects' existential status: it has thus no need to resort to a special exceptional category to sustain what has now become a routine prerogative. Concentration camps, also a gruesome invention of the modern world, were a space where what in other parts of the state realm is but a potential was made into the norm and practical rule.

The invisible presence of the "*homo sacer*" as the potential of the modern state – the potential which can be made into reality once "the conditions are right" – brings into relief once more the most terrifying, and still most topical, aspect of the "Holocaust experience": that even in our modern society people who are neither morally corrupt nor prejudiced may still partake with vigor and dedication in the destruction of targeted categories of human beings; and that their participation, far from calling for the mobilization of their moral or any other convictions, demands on the contrary their suspension, obliteration, and irrelevance.

Notes

1   Darré (1978:115). In *L'homme régénéré* Mona Ozouf suggested that the French Revolution, itself the high point in the history of Enlightenment, focused its intentions on the "formation" of *un nouveau peuple*, by the same token positing the "new breed of men" as *a task* (p. 119). The intended "regenerated" society, composed of "new people," was to be, among other things, *"une société purgée de ces membres douteux"* (p. 143). In this way, according to Ozouf, the French Revolution was in a sense a "premonition" of times to come; it anticipated the course of later exercises in "society building"; temptingly, it left unfulfilled the *"projet de visibilité absolue où l'indetermination est insupportable"* and just started on the way leading to *"des Lumières au Goulag"* (p. 120).

2   Peukert (1987:248). The modern dream of a uniform, harmonious order of society, and the equally modern conviction that the imposition of such order upon recalcitrant reality is a progressive move, promotion of the common interests and by the same token legitimate whatever the "transitional costs," can be found behind every case of modern genocide. Thus the builders of the modern Turkish state murdered the bulk of the "harmony-spoiling" Armenian population because "they sought to convert the society from its heterogenous makeup into a homogenous unit. Here genocide became a means for the end of a radical structural change in the system." The vision of state-administered progress removed all moral compunctions that the bestiality of the mass murder might have caused. The architect of the Armenian genocide, the Minister of Internal Affairs Taleat, explained: "I have the conviction that as long as a nation does the best for its interest and succeeds, the world admires it and thinks it moral" (Dadrian, 1974:133, 131). As the later turn of events abundantly demonstrated, Taleat, it must be admitted, was not wide of the mark.

3   Müller-Hill (1988:28–9). The experimental station at Cold Spring Harbor, led by Charles Benedict Davenport from 1904 on, was founded by the Carnegie Institution of Washington, with the brief to identify individuals who carried "defective germ plasm" (see Chorover, 1979). Indeed, in many respects eugenic and other demographic regulatory practices recommended by American scientists and implemented by American politicians served as a source of inspiration for the German planners of genocide. German "racial hygienists drew upon the examples of American immigration, sterilization and miscegenation laws to formulate their own politics in these areas" (Proctor, 1988:286).

References

Agamben, Georgio (1997) *Homo Sace: Le pouvoir souverain et la vie nue*. Paris: Seuil.

Aly, Gotz and Heim, Susanne (1991) *Vordenker der Vernichtung: Auschwitz und die deutschen Plane für eine neue europaische Ordnung*. Hamburg: Hoffman and Campe.

Arendt, Hannah (1964) *Eichmann in Jerusalem: A Report on the Banality of Evil*. Harmondsworth, UK: Penguin.

Bauman, Zygmunt (1987) *Legislators and Interpreters*. Cambridge, UK: Polity Press.

Bauman, Zygmunt (1989) *Modernity and the Holocaust*. Cambridge, UK: Polity Press.

Beck, Ulrich (1998) "What comes after postmodernity? The conflict of two modernities," in *Democracy Without Enemies*. Cambridge, UK: Polity Press, pp.19–31.

Browning, Christopher R. (1999) "Victims Testimony . . . ," *Tikkun* 14,1:56–8.

Camus, Albert ([1951] 1971) *The Rebel*, trans. Anthony Bower. Harmondsworth, UK: Penguin.

Cheyette, Bryan (1988) "H. G. Wells and the Jews: Antisemitism, socialism, and English culture." *Patterns of Prejudice* 22,3:22–35.

Chorover, Stephan L. (1979) *From Genesis to Genocide: The Meaning of Human Nature and the Power of Behavior Control*. Cambridge, MA: MIT Press.

Dadrian, Vahakn N. (1974) "The structural-functional components of genocide: A victimological approach to the Armenian case," in Israel Drapkin and Emilio Viano (eds.) *Victimology*. Lexington, MA: Lexington Books, pp.123–36.

Darré, R. W. (1978) "Marriage laws and the principles of breeding," in Barbara Miller Lane and Leila J. Rupp (eds.) *Nazi Ideology Before 1933*. Manchester, UK: Manchester University Press, pp.111–18.

Dörner, Klaus (1988) *Tödliches Mitleid: Zur Frage der Unerträglichkeit des Lebens, oder: Die Soziale Frage: Entstehung, Medizinisierung, NS-Endlösung, heute, morgen*. Gütersloh, Germany: Verlag Jakob van Hoddis.

Gellner, Ernest (1968) "The new idealism," in I. Lakatos and A. Musgrave (eds.) *Problems in the Philosophy of Science*. Amsterdam: Van Nostrand, pp.377–406.

Ghent, William J. (1902) *Our Benevolent Feudalism*. New York: Macmillan.

Goldhagen, Daniel (1996) *Hitler's Willing Executioners*. London: Little, Brown.

Müller-Hill, Benno (1988) *Murderous Science, Elimination by Scientific Selection of Jews, Gypsies and Others, Germany 1933–1945*, trans. George R. Fraser. Oxford: Oxford University Press.

Nietzsche, Friedrich (1968) "On the geneology of morals," in *Basic Writings*, ed. Walter Kaufmann. New York: Modern Library, pp.460–92.

Orwell, George (1961) "Wells, Hitler, and the world state," in *Collected Essays*. London: Secker and Warburg.

Ozouf, Mona (1989) *L'homme régénéré*. Paris: Gallimard.

Peukert, Detlev J. K. (1987) *Inside Nazi Germany: Conformity, Opposition and Racism in Everyday Life*, trans. Richard Deveson. New Haven, CT: Yale University Press.

Proctor, Robert (1988) *Racial Hygiene: Medicine Under the Nazis*. Cambridge, MA: Harvard University Press.

Ricks, Christopher (1988) *T. S. Eliot and Prejudice*. London: Faber and Faber.

Searle, J. R. (1976) *Eugenics and Politics in Britain 1900–1914*. Leyden, Netherlands: Noordhoff.

Toscano, Roberto (1998) "The face of the other: Ethics and intergroup conflict," in Eugene Weiner (ed.) *The Handbook of Interethnic Coexistence*. New York: Continuum, pp.63–81.

Traverso, Enzo (1996) *L'histoire déchirée*, Paris, Cerf.

Trombley, S. (1993) *The Execution Protocol: Inside America's Capital Punishment Industry*. New York: Anchor Books.

Weinreich, Max (1946) *Hitler's Professors*. New York: Yiddish Scientific Institute.

Wells, H. G. (1984) "Socialism and the new world order," in *Journalism and Prophecy 1893–1946*. London: Bodley Head.

Young, Jock (1999) "Essentialising the Other: Demonisation and the creation of monstrosity," in *The Exclusive Society: Social Exclusion, Crime and Difference in Late Modernity*. London: Sage.

Chapter 5

Antisemitism

Tony Kushner

General Explanations and Issues

Antisemitism has been labeled "the longest hatred" (Wistrich, 1992) and "the persisting question" (Fein, 1987). Nevertheless, academic analysis of antisemitism is relatively recent, as is the term itself which was coined in Germany during the 1870s by one of the founders of its politicized and racialized form, Wilhelm Marr, to differentiate it from earlier, Christian anti-Judaism. In terms of explanations, with only a few exceptions, until the Nazi era, it was assumed in the non-Jewish world that the Jews had brought on their own misfortune. In Christian tradition, the accusation of deicide, followed by Jewish "stubbornness" in not recognizing Jesus as the messiah, explained and justified the continuing pariah status and persecution of the Jews, typified by the construction in popular culture of the "wandering Jew," forever doomed to live in miserable exile. The Enlightenment and the growth of secular thought did not necessarily lead to a reassessment of the tendency to blame the victim. The continuation of Jewish particularity after the granting of political emancipation in the wake of the French Revolution was perceived across a range of Western and Central European countries as further evidence of Jewish obstinacy, and therefore the explanation of why antisemitism persisted. Moreover, the growth of scientific racism and race-influenced nationalism from the nineteenth century gave added weight to the idea that antisemitism was a rational and natural reaction to the essential difference of the Jew.

There were exceptions to this general, dominant trend. First, there was a strand of Christian philosemitism from the seventeenth century that argued that past persecution of the Jews had itself been responsible for the refusal of Jews to embrace the "true" faith. By recognizing the mistakes of the past and by treating the Jews sympathetically in the present, they hoped that Jews would convert *en masse* and thereby hasten the coming of the messianic age. In addition, the growth of Jewish secular thought after the *Haskalah*, or Jewish Enlightenment, also enabled an analysis, albeit one with little wider impact, of persecution as a human phenomenon rather than as part of divine punishment. For Jews anxious to embrace forms of acculturation and assimilation, the persistence of antisemitism was regarded as the continuation of dark forces of medieval reaction fighting against the benign influence of modern progress. But for many Zionist intellectuals, antisemitism in the past and present was the inevitable result of Jewish minority status which could be solved only through the creation or recreation of a Jewish state and not through emancipation within other nations.

By the beginning of the twentieth century, even in liberal democracies such as Britain and the USA, while the excesses of violent antisemitism, as typified by the increasingly murderous pogroms and state-sponsored discrimination of Eastern Europe, was condemned, there was still a widespread tendency to see antisemitism at its root cause as the reaction to the Jewish presence. The interwar period saw a greater reassessment as the coming to power of Nazism forced a questioning of the tenets of scientific racism, especially in left-liberal circles, although the attention given to the Nazi state's policies gave a certain credibility to eugenics and race thinking in general. Indeed, there was still a tendency until well after 1945 to argue that while the treatment of the Jews by the Nazis could not be justified, there still had been a Jewish "problem" that had to be confronted (Kushner, 1994). James Parkes, an Anglican clergyman and historian, was almost alone during the 1930s in arguing that not only was antisemitism a "problem for non-Jews" to face but that its origins were not to be found in Jewish behavior or difference, racial or other, but in Christianity itself (Parkes, 1934), or what the French Jewish historian, Jules Isaac, later described as the "teaching of contempt" (Isaac, 1964).

What would, by the late 1950s, be known as the Holocaust, did not initially stimulate much interest in the history and nature of antisemitism outside small sections of the Jewish intellectual world. Indeed, the current obsession with the Holocaust in popular culture as well as Western academia is of very recent origin. It did, however, stimulate some, such as the scholar Gavin Langmuir (1990), to look towards the medieval period as the origins of antisemitism, and others, more narrowly, to see it as a specifically German problem "from Luther to Hitler." Rather than being a chronologically specific response to anti-German revulsion following the revelations of the liberated concentration camps in the last stages of the war, the popular success of Daniel Goldhagen's (1996) *Hitler's Willing Executioners* suggests that the desire to see antisemitism as someone else's problem – belonging to a particular time or a particular place – was still very much alive at the end of the twentieth century.

Another development from the late 1930s was, especially in the USA, sociological and psychological research into ethnic and racial prejudice. Work sponsored by the American Jewish Committee, culminating in *The Authoritarian Personality* (Adorno et al., 1950), suggested that those who were prejudiced against Jews were likely to be also hostile to those of color and other minority outgroups. This research had its limitations – it tended to lack a wider sense of historical or political context – but it did at least connect antisemitism to other forms of ethnic and racial hatreds. Unfortunately, the potential for such comparisons was not fully exploited beyond the work of social psychologists whose work on the prejudices of individuals generally failed to connect to scholarship in other disciplines. Furthermore, it tended to locate racism only among the minority who were maladjusted or disaffected, rather than being a general problem throughout mainstream society, politics, and culture. Thereafter, until the very late twentieth century, the study of antisemitism and of other forms of ethnic and racial prejudice largely went along separate paths, with the former occupying a rather marginal status. Histories of racism, for example, tend to consider antisemitism only with reference to the case of the Holocaust, ignoring many other types and manifestations of hostility towards Jews and Jewishness. As work on antisemitism, whether on past and present, or in liberal and illiberal societies and cultures, has become ever more sophisticated, the relative lack of dialogue has been particularly inopportune.

Ultimately, if not immediately, the Holocaust acted as a stimulus to the reassessment of attitudes to the Jews in the past and present. Its influence on research, however, was not unambiguous. On the one hand, it led to much fresh research with a wide geographical and chronological scope, as scholars moved beyond the Nazi era and the case of Germany. On the other, there was sometimes a tendency to view past hostility as "a rehearsal for destruction" rather than to put it in specific context reflecting the anxieties of a particular age and the particular impact on the Jewish minority. Continuity has been emphasized at the cost of looking at periods in history which were marked by an absence of persecution or when responses were more complex than outright rejection. Furthermore, the sheer enormity of the Holocaust has often acted as a barrier to meaningful comparisons, even within the other racisms and general persecutions carried out by the Nazi state and its collaborators.

To summarize this overview: although the study of antisemitism beyond the assumption that it was a natural reaction to Jews and Jewish behavior is a recent development, two particular questions or issues have emerged in the historiography. First, is there a history of antisemitism? That is, is there anything to connect the persecution of the Jews before and after the Christian era or indeed between one part of the latter and another? Second, is antisemitism a unique phenomenon or should it be studied as part of an analysis of racisms, ethnic hatreds, and indeed persecutions as a whole? It will be argued below that the greater attention paid to the first question in scholarship since the Nazi era has been at the expense of the second.

Continuity or Discontinuity

The Imperial War Museum's Holocaust Gallery in London, opened in the summer of 2000, provides a now commonly held but rather simplistic and misleading interpretation in which to contextualize and explain the Nazis' "Final Solution": "Antisemitism – 'the longest hatred' – developed over nearly two thousand years, as Europe found ways to blame the Jews for more and more of society's ills." There are some who would go back even earlier, exploring what they see as evidence of pagan antisemitism in the pre-Christian era. The evidence for such hostility, however, is limited, and needs to be set alongside positive comments about Jews and Judaism by Greek and other pagan writers. Equally importantly, Jews were rarely if ever singled out for particular animosity – Greeks, Romans, Egyptians and the Jews themselves tended to view all other groups as culturally inferior. Moreover, Jews were not an insignificant force in the ancient world, and some conflict between Jews and non-Jews was based on real tension over political and other power (Gager, 1983).

It is possible that some hostile pagan accusations against the Jews were utilized by some Christians at a later time and in a very different context. Nevertheless, in the absence of a clear animus against the Jews *per se*, the case for continuity from pagan to Christian antisemitism is a weak one. It is further undermined in the light of more recent scholarship in relation to antisemitism and the founding fathers of Christianity. On the surface, the books of the New Testament appear to provide strong evidence of early Christian antisemitism. In the gospel of John, for example, Jews are identified with the devil and his works. Yet again, however, context is all important. If these writings are regarded as coming from within a Jewish sect aimed at a Jewish audience (and thus relating to an internal conflict about the future direction of Judaism), they have a totally different meaning than if they were intended for an external audience. Yet what is beyond doubt is how key quotations from the founding documents were used by later Christians and non-Christians to justify and stimulate hatred and persecution of the Jews in both medieval and modern times (Dunn, 1992).

The absence of systematic persecution of the Jews or widespread antisemitic writings in the first 10 centuries of Christianity would also weaken the argument that the new religion was inherently and consistently opposed to the Jews *per se*. Hostile figures such as St. John Chrysostom (347–407) wrote of the Jews as the source of all evil on earth, but such writings were not common and were often aimed indirectly as a way of attacking fellow Christians rather than the Jews themselves, who generally were not subject to sustained violence or particular discrimination. Indeed, admiration of Jews and Judaism continued, including amongst Christians. The evidence at least until the tenth century if not later, therefore, is against a continuous history of persecution, even if older charges against the Jews were revived and recontextualized at particular moments and by particular individuals, both Christian and other.

A strong case can be made, therefore, that the first widespread and sustained animosity against the Jews as Jews occurred during the medieval period. If persecution was at most sporadic and rarely murderous before then, the question is: why the radical change in attitudes and responses? It has been argued by Moore that "In the early middle ages as in the later, persecution began as a weapon in the competition for political influence, and was turned by the victors into an instrument for consolidating their power over society at large." The twelfth century renaissance led to "the tremendous extension of the power and influence of the literate" and, alongside the "emergence of a bureaucratic regime," enabled the formation of a persecuting society as well as the positive achievements of this age within Western Europe. Moore points out that it was not only Jews who were persecuted in the early middle ages but also those constructed as heretics, lepers, and sodomites who "for all imaginative purposes . . . were interchangeable . . . [and] presented the same threat: through them the Devil was at work to subvert the Christian order and bring the world to chaos" (Moore, 1987:65,140,146,153). Later in the early modern period the witch-hunting craze would fulfill the same function.

Moore, by placing the legislation against and treatment of Jews in the Middle Ages alongside those of other groups defined as a threat to Christian society, helps to provide a general context for the persecution experienced by the Jewish minority across Western Europe and more widely through the mass bloodshed of the Crusades. Langmuir and others, however, argue that in the twelfth and thirteenth centuries Jews became "the target of an unusual kind of hostility in northern Europe," unusual because it was "completely irrational" (Langmuir, 1990:17) The "Jew," unlike other persecuted minorities at this time, was constructed in these centuries in a totally unreal manner, culminating in the ritual murder and then "blood libel" accusations. In these the Jews were first alleged to have murdered Christian children and then to have carried out acts of cannibalism (the drinking of the murdered children's blood) essential to their diabolical nature. Langmuir argues that what had been anti-Judaism – an opposition to a religion that was viewed as invalid as it had been superseded by Christianity and was also tainted because of the alleged Jewish responsibility for killing Jesus – was transformed, because of its irrationality, into antisemitism, a hatred that would lead ultimately to Auschwitz. Norman Cohn argues similarly, suggesting that "The myth of the Jewish world-conspiracy represents a modern adaptation of this ancient demonological tradition" (Cohn [1967] 1996:26) For Langumuir and Cohn, the absence of a clear racist ideology behind medieval hatred of Jews is not crucial in showing continuity with modern antisemitism – it is the construction of the "Jew" as a satanic, conspiratorial world power that links the persecutions of the Middle Ages with the Nazi death camps. Their argument needs to be qualified by the continuation of more "traditional" anti-Judaism alongside the "new" antisemitism, and often a complex intermingling of the two. Moreover, the fantastical nature of the new medieval allegations against the Jews should not disguise the fact that many in positions of power, or seeking power, exploited animosity against the Jews for their own practical purposes (Cohen, 1982).

In theory, if not always in practice, Jews could escape persecution in the medieval period by conversion (although the suspicion and later persecution of the *conversos* in Spain from the fourteenth century indicates the existence of a protoracist ideology). It is also dangerous, in spite of widespread pogroms, to talk of an undifferentiated and unrelenting "popular" antisemitism. In York in 1190 at the time of the Third Crusade, local nobles in debt to the Jews were largely responsible for the massacre of the community. Yet several years later Jews returned to the town and lived in relative peace amongst their non-Jewish neighbors. But the diabolical image of the Jews coming out of the Middle Ages, alongside their new association with money lending and finance (a result of the Jews being excluded from other economic activities), proved to have massive endurance in Western culture even when Jews were expelled and absent for many centuries.

The particular nature of medieval antisemitism, especially its irrationality, does not imply that it had no parallels in the future – Langmuir points to the witch hunting of the early modern period and anti-black racism in colonial and slave societies as other examples of what he calls chimerical hostility, that is, when the construction of the "other" is totally unreal (Langmuir, 1990:341–2). Moreover, while persecution was not absent in the early modern period – it was particularly marked around the time of the Thirty Years War in the seventeenth century – there was also a growing toleration of the Jews' presence in Western Europe. Even when there was mass destruction, as in the Chmielnicki uprising in 1648, the violence against Jews, where between 40,000 and 100,000 Jews were murdered, was also aimed at others in what was at heart an attempt to assert Ukrainian identity in the Polish kingdom. The majority of the Jews now lived within Poland where, at a local level, although the Church continued to portray Jews as Christ killers, Jewish culture and religion flourished often in relative peace if not total harmony with the Christian population.

Many scholars, while acknowledging the Christian influence in separating out the Jews as different and problematic, nevertheless argue that antisemitism proper came only with the development of scientific racism in the mid-nineteenth century and the beginning of an organized political movement against Jewish power in Germany from the 1870s (including the foundation by Wilhelm Marr of the Antisemitic League) (Katz, 1980). Only then, they suggest, could antisemitism become a total ideology with genocidal potential. It is true that some of the new political antisemites such as Marr (and later Hitler) rejected religious opposition to Jews because it missed the racial threat posed by the minority. Yet other political antisemites were more Christian-influenced but all were agreed on the conspiratorial power possessed by the Jews, suggesting both a link between earlier antisemitism/anti-Judaism and a plurality of approaches, embracing *volkisch* racial mysticism with a profound antimodernity alongside those who embraced elements of modernity in their Jew-hatred.

Moreover, not all racial thinkers in the nineteenth century saw Jews as inferior, or believed that their "race" made them unsuitable to entry into the nation-state. In the German example in particular, if continuity is sought, it should be remembered that the antisemitic parties faded very quickly, even if elements of antisemitism entered mainstream political parties. Many Jews became ardent German nationalists and the treatment and status of Jews still differed immensely in the various German states. It was, before 1914, French rather than German society that was riven by the question of antisemitism through the Dreyfus affair, an episode that divided France not between those who were pro- and anti-Jewish, but between broadly conservative and liberal camps. Both sides harbored negative views about the Jews, although it was of course the anti-Dreyfusards who launched the violent and murderous attacks on the Jews across the country and into Algiers. Context is again crucial, and the Dreyfus affair was not just about whether the Jews could be loyal French citizens or not, but about the future direction of the nation.

If it is true that the Dreyfus affair was about much more than antisemitism, was this also the case with the Holocaust? Attempts have been made to explain the number of Jews murdered in each country occupied by the Nazis by the level of domestic antisemitism. Yet ultimately the number of Polish Jews murdered by the Nazis, for example, had more to do with the Nazis' control over the country and their animus against Eastern Jews than Polish antipathy to the Jewish minority. As was the case in other countries in the Nazi era, personal antisemitism was not necessarily incompatible with rescue and help towards the persecuted Jews. Where the Nazis were particularly successful in stirring up sections of the local population, such as in Lithuania in 1941, it was not necessarily based on past traditions (Lithuania had largely avoided pogroms in the late czarist era) but as a result of the brutality of the previous Soviet occupation and the ability of the Nazis and local extreme nationalists to blame Bolshevism on the Jews. Alternatively, those countries that helped to save the Jews, such as Denmark, Italy, and Romania in the latter part of the war did not do it necessarily out of pro-Jewish sentiment but more as a way of asserting their own national dignity, having in other ways been humiliated by Nazi Germany.

Recent scholarship explaining the Holocaust has tended to downplay antisemitic ideology as a factor on its own. Bauman has stressed the forces of modernity and the need within the nation-state to tidy away, by whatever means, those sections that do not "fit" (Bauman, 1989). More detailed work on the Third Reich has emphasized its wider function as a "racial state," attempting and indeed partly succeeding in reordering the geopolitical map of Europe with huge forced movements of population, genocidal impulses, and the weeding out of the "unfit" (Burleigh and Wippermann, 1991). Such work corresponds to the sheer destructive capacity of the Third Reich, although it perhaps understates the ideological animus against the Jews and what Hitler and other leading Nazis perceived as the battle of survival between the Aryans and their ultimate racial enemy. It was, harking back to the work of Langmuir on the medieval period, the absolute irrationality of Nazi antisemitism and its construction of the all-powerful, conspiratorial Jew that singled out their hatred in contrast to their equally murderous assault on the Sinti and Roma, the Slavs and the physically and mentally "unfit."

The Nazis' attempted destruction of European Jewry was thus a part of, and apart from, its murderous racial reordering of Europe. Its unique elements, however, in no way mean that it should be seen as incomparable. The placing of the Holocaust within a history of twentieth century genocide, starting often with the Armenian genocide carried out by the Turkish state during World War I, has been one fruitful area of comparative research. As the awareness of examples of genocide in the past and in the present grows, the Holocaust becomes less exceptional (Levene and Roberts, 1999). It is a process that could be taken much further, following the work of Gilroy, if it can be extended to include the genocidal impulses of the European powers in carrying out colonialism and slavery (Gilroy, 2000).

The Nazi state, however, in its total hatred and mass murder of the Jews, should not act as a paradigm of antisemitism as a whole. Whether continuity, at least from the medieval period, is emphasized or not, no previous example of Jew-hatred had been genocidal: it was in no way the only logical culmination of many centuries of animosity and persecution even if, without that previous history, such mass murder would have been hard, if not impossible, to explain. The example of the Holocaust disguises the fact that attitudes to Jews, both in history and in the modern period, have been complex and avoid easy labeling such as antisemitism, or its equally imaginery construction of "the Jew," philosemitism. Moreover, focusing attention on more general relations between Jews and non-Jews enables an exploration of ordinary day-to-day life and the more subtle pressures faced by minority groups (Bering, 1992).

Ambivalence and the Need for Wider Contextualization

Recent work on the representation, attitudes towards, and responses to Jews in liberal cultures has emphasized that the concept of antisemitism is limited as an analytical tool. Instead, scholars such as Cheyette, building on much earlier theoretical work (Sartre, 1948; Fanon [1952] 1986), argue that the terms "ambivalence" and "ambiguity" are more helpful in explaining the way in which Jews have been constructed at any one time and place (Cheyette, 1993). The construction of the "Jew" as "other" may involve positive and negative elements representing both the anxieties and desires of the majority society and culture. It is the exception (although clearly in the case of the twentieth century, not one that can be in any way dismissed as unimportant) for the Jew to be seen as the unambiguous source of all evil. Indeed, what the hard core Nazi antisemites exploited was not so much the indifference of those both under their control and outside it (as was the case with the Western Allies) towards the Jews, but their fundamental ambivalence, enabling the victims to be seen somehow as "other," as not fully belonging in the construction of place identity, and therefore beyond the universe of moral obligation.

Such processes of "othering" so that the minority fulfills the role projected onto it, revealing the concerns and hopes of the majority, link the construction of the Jews to those of other minorities, ethnic/racial or otherwise. It is indeed in the world of cultural and literary studies that connections are at long last being made between discourses about Jews and other groups. Such work takes us away from the study of the minority and to the majority society and culture in explaining the treatment of the former (although the responses of the minorities themselves to such processes are of equal importance).

Returning to the medieval period, it is remarkable how the tendency to approach ritual murder and blood libel accusations through attempts to prove or disprove them lasted throughout the twentieth century. Only recently have scholars attempted to understand the worldview of contemporaries that led to the holding of such phenomenal beliefs, even if there has been a recent revival in some academic works relating to Jews, those of color, and other minorities to blame the victims. Aside from this worrying tendency, the starting point for most contemporary scholarship is a desire to contextualize why particular allegations were made about Jews and other minorities, or why some allegations made in an earlier period (but not all) could be successfully revived and remolded, rather than to see the continuity of such imagery as an explanation in itself. Anxiety about the place and security of children, for example, continue in the modern world, but the construction of the Jew as child murderer can no longer be utilized successfully to articulate and displace such fears. Ambivalence is now the norm, and violence and exclusion the exception in responses to Jews in the contemporary world.

Jews are not exempt from the physical attacks that mar the experiences of other ethnic and racial minorities in the Western world but they are no longer its major victims. Nevertheless, the experience of Jews and the pressure they have felt within the liberal democratic and other frameworks to conform and to assimilate, or what Williams has called "the antisemitism of toleration" (Williams, 1985), offers an indication of other dangers that minorities can face aside from outright rejection. Jews are not unduly part of an economic underclass anymore. But as the analysis of the position of ethnic minorities broadens to consider their place also in the culture and everyday life of dominant societies, there is again much to be gained by placing the history of the Jews and responses to them in the broader perspective of the minority experience as a whole. Extreme racism, as well as the construction of minority identities by majority culture, links the Jewish case to many others. Ultimately, the study of antisemitism, and the recent questioning of the utility of this concept, has much to offer those interested in racial and ethnic studies.

Acknowledgment

My thanks to David Cesarani and Sarah Pearce for their helpful comments on an earlier version of this entry.

References

Adorno, T. W., Frenkel-Brunswick, E., Levinson, D. J., and Sanford, R. N. (1950). *The Authoritarian Personality*. New York: Harper and Row.

Almog, S. (ed.) (1988) *Antisemitism Through the Ages*. Oxford: Pergamon.

Bauman, Z. (1989) *Modernity and the Holocaust*. Cambridge, UK: Polity.

Bering, D. (1992) *The Stigma of Names. Antisemitism in German Daily Life, 1812–1933*. Cambridge, UK: Polity.

Burleigh, M. and Wippermann, W. (1991) *The Racial State: Germany 1933–1945*. Cambridge, UK: Cambridge University Press.

Cheyette, B. (1993) *Constructions of "the Jew" in English Literature and Society. Racial Representations, 1875–1945*. Cambridge, UK: Cambridge University Press.

Cohen, J. (1982) *The Friars and the Jews. The Evolution of Medieval Anti-Judaism*. Ithaca, NY: Cornell University Press.

Cohn, N. ([1967] 1996) *Warrant for Genocide*, 2nd edn. London: Serif.

Dunn, J. (1992) "The question of anti-semitism in the New Testament writings of the period," in J. Dunn (ed.) *Jews and Christians*. Tübingen, Germany: J. C. B. Mohr, pp.177–211.

Fanon, F. ([1952] 1986) *Black Skins, White Masks*. London: Pluto.

Fein, H. (ed.) (1987) *The Persisting Question: Sociological Perspectives and Social Contexts of Modern Antisemitism*. Berlin: de Gruyter.

Gager, J. (1983) *The Origins of Anti-Semitism: Attitudes Toward Judaism in Pagan and Christian Antiquity*. Oxford: Oxford University Press.

Gilman, S. and Katz, S. (eds.) (1991) *Anti-Semitism in Times of Crisis*. New York: New York University Press.

Gilroy, P. (2000) *Between Camps*. London: Allen Lane.

Goldhagen, D. (1996) *Hitler's Willing Executioners*. London: Little, Brown.

Isaac, J. (1964) *The Teaching of Contempt: Christian Roots of Anti-Semitism*. New York: Holt, Rinehart, and Winston.

Katz, J. (1980) *From Prejudice to Destruction. Anti-Semitism, 1700–1933*. Cambridge, MA.: Harvard University Press.

Kushner, T. (1994) *The Holocaust and the Liberal Imagination*. Oxford: Blackwell.

Langmuir, G. (1990) *Toward a Definition of Antisemitism*. Los Angeles: University of California Press.

Levene, M. and Roberts, P. (eds.) (1999) *The Massacre in History*. New York: Berghahn.

Moore, R. (1987) *The Formation of a Persecuting Society*. Oxford: Blackwell.

Parkes, J. (1934) *The Conflict of the Church and the Synagogue: A Study in the Origins of Antisemitism*. London: Soncino Press.

Poliakov, L. (1974, 1975) *The History of Anti-Semitism*, vols. 1–3. London: Routledge & Kegan Paul.

Poliakov, L. (1985) *The History of Anti-Semitism*, vol. 4. Oxford: Oxford University Press.

Sartre, J. (1948) *Anti-Semite and Jew*. New York: Schocken Books.

Steiman, L. (1998) *Paths to Genocide. Antisemitism in Western History*. New York: St. Martin's Press.

Williams, B. (1985) "The anti-Semitism of tolerance," in A. Kidd and K. Roberts (eds.) *City, Class and Culture*. Manchester, UK: Manchester University Press, pp.74–102.

Wistrich, R. (1992) *Antisemitism. The Longest Hatred*. London: Thames.

Chapter 6

Apartheid and Race[1]

Deborah Posel

Apartheid is the state and the condition of being apart. It is the no man's land between peoples. But this gap is not a neutral space. It is the artificially created distance necessary to attenuate, for the practitioners, the very raw reality of racial, economic, social and cultural discrimination and exploitation. Apartheid is the White man's night, the darkness which blurs his consciousness and his conscience. What one does not see doesn't exist. (Breytenbach, 1972:137)

Perhaps the one thing everyone knows about apartheid in South Africa is the ubiquity of race within that system: all social, political, economic, and cultural processes and experiences were racialized. Various academic commentators have made similar sorts of points. As Pierre van den Berghe put it in 1967:"of all contemporary multiracial societies, South Africa is the most complexly and rigidly stratified on the basis of race, the one in which race has greatest salience *vis à vis* other structural principles" (Van den Berghe, 1969:319). More recently, Jacques Derrida went so far as to treat apartheid as "the unique appellation for the ultimate racism in the world" (Derrida, 1985:330). It is highly paradoxical then, that for many scholars surveying the academic literature on apartheid, one of its biggest gaps is an engagement with the nature of race itself: "there must be very few places in the academic community which has actively neglected the study of race to the same extent as in South Africa" (Greenstein, 1996:5).

In some respects, this judgment is unduly harsh: precisely because the effects of race under apartheid were ubiquitous, pretty much any of the academic literature on apartheid encompasses the subject of race in some way. So, lots has been written about the nature of racial discrimination in a range of spheres, institutionally and legally; experiences of so-called "ordinary people" – particularly black – have been documented; the growth, ideologies, and politics of black resistance movements have attracted academic interest, and some of the ambiguities and complexities of racialized modes of power have been explored (even if the manner of that racialization was not itself the focus of discussion). Much of this work has made an enormous contribution in debunking official myths about apartheid propagated by the apartheid regime itself, as well as in stimulating further research and animating debate on many fronts. Yet, if race is everywhere in these literatures, there are also some lingering silences on the subject – as both the focus and the context of academic study. With some significant exceptions, there has been relatively little research into the social meanings of race under apartheid. Again with some

73

noteworthy exceptions, much more could have been written about the politics of race on the left, where an ideology of "nonracialism" became hegemonic. Nor have racial discourses as sources of power attracted much research interest. And very few apartheid scholars have grappled with the theoretical issue of what "race" is, so that long-standing themes in the American literature on race, for example – debates about biological essentialism and its social constructionist critiques – have not been mainstream fare in the apartheid literature. Another powerful silence within the apartheid literature concerns the epistemology and academic politics of race, and their effects on the character of historical explanation and modes of evidence. Academic communities (largely white) have been loath to confront the sense in which apartheid was not only the object of study but, in some uncomfortable respects, also the medium of it.

Why, in a society that has been so thoroughly steeped in the effects of race, has the issue been so frequently unspoken amongst scholars writing about apartheid itself? The central purpose of this article is to examine the academic "repression" of race, by locating theoretical and historiographical debates about race in apartheid in the context of the politics of intellectual production during the apartheid era.

Mainstream Scholarship on Race in Apartheid

The National Party came to power in South Africa in 1948, with the promise of restoring "order" to South African society under the auspices of *die apartheidgedagte* (the apartheid-idea) – an affirmation of the principle of white supremacy; as the basis for a more thorough-going racialization of the country's laws and institutions than had previously existed. At a time when other African colonial societies were encountering the first shock waves of decolonization, white South Africans voted in a government which promised to contain the threat of black militancy, heighten the physical, social, and cultural distance between races, and preserve the principle of racial purity. In 1948, the National Party's margin of victory was slight; indeed, it was only in 1961 that the party secured a majority of election votes. With the party's hold over the white polity then firmly in place, the 1960s and early 1970s saw the apartheid state strengthen its grip on power even further. A wave of strikes in 1972 and 1973, however, marked the onset of worsening political and economic instability during which apartheid was reconfigured as a combination of intensifying repression on one hand, and efforts at reformist accommodation on the other. But as these dual strategies of stabilization failed, the National Party entered into a period of negotiations with the African National Congress, which culminated in the transition to constitutional democracy in 1994. Apartheid, then, spans a period of over 40 years – a history shaped in complex ways by the shifting interactions of long-standing ideological principles and political imperatives, *ad hoc* strategies and decisions of the political moment, the pressures of popular resistance, the opportunities and constraints created by the global economy, the unintended consequences of existing policies, together with the uneven capacities of an increasingly ambitious state.

The academic literature on apartheid, which spans debates on many facets of this history, is considerable and wide-ranging. Since it is impossible to produce anything like a comprehensive survey within a short article, my purpose is rather to offer an interpretative, highly selective reading of mainstream academic debates which have tried to make sense of race, as a factor in the origins, stabilization, and decline of apartheid. This makes for a commentary using broad brush-strokes, rather than attending to the details of any one text or body of writing.

The "race–class debate"

Students of apartheid are typically introduced to the academic literature on this subject by way of the so-called "race–class debate," which dominated the historiography of apartheid throughout the 1970s and 1980s. It seems a promising route to go: the way the debate was construed suggests a head-on critical encounter with "race." Yet one of the most striking features of this debate is the way in which it deflected attention from "race."

The debate was constructed by Marxist historians and sociologists, as a critical rejection of the then dominant approach to apartheid, which they named as "liberal." The immediate focus of contention was an empirical issue, about the relationship between apartheid and capitalism; but this was theoretically overlaid with a debate about the relative analytical salience of "race" or "class" in making sense of apartheid's origins, character, and future.

The idea of a single, homogenous "liberal" position on apartheid is to some extent an artifice of the debate, which tends to ignore a range of differences within the allegedly "liberal" camp (Wright, 1977:7). Nevertheless, a series of central themes emerges with sufficient regularity and consistency to warrant the use of the label. The ideologues of apartheid presented their preoccupation with racial purity as a divinely ordained mission undertaken by the Afrikaner nationalists on behalf of all their white brethren. Liberal scholars of apartheid were primarily concerned to debunk these ideas as nationalist myth-making, by exposing the politics of racial discrimination. The liberal critique of apartheid emphasized the connection between racial discrimination and political power, invoking an understanding of power as a party political project (launched by the National Party) to use the apartheid state as an instrument for promoting Afrikaner interests within the framework of white supremacy (de Villiers, 1971). According to Heribert Adam, "this project ought to have included a sociological...analysis of racialism [which]...probes into the historical dimensions of racial attitudes, thereby explaining and elucidating racialism in its entanglement with the social structure" (Adam, 1971:20). But in the main, liberal scholarship dealt less with the sociology of race and racism than with an analysis of the politics of Afrikaner nationalism, showing how the ideology of apartheid served as a tool of what Heribert Adam and Herman Giliomee (1979) called "ethnic mobilization."

This interest in exposing the *realpolitik* of race rapidly homed in on the relationship between apartheid and capitalism, as the nub of the issue. Like their Marxist critics, liberal scholars regarded the intersection of political and economic factors as the crucial vantage point from which to understand the apartheid system and assess its future prospects. For liberals, apartheid systematized and institutionalized racial discrimination to the point of economic irrationality (De Kiewiet, 1956:47, 65). In their eyes, apartheid had created a "contradiction between the economy and polity" (Wright, 1977:12). Intent on exposing the effects of this contradiction, liberal scholars tended therefore to concentrate their research and analysis on the problems of African labor in the country, which they saw as the nub of the contradiction. In their eyes, it was the efforts by the apartheid state to keep African labor "cheap" – by imposing statutory job reservation for white

75

workers and inhibiting African workers' access to skills – which lay at the root of apartheid's economic "irrationalities" (Lipton, 1985; Horwitz, 1967). Apartheid's "racist labour policies," argued Ralph Horwitz, were instruments of "industrial retrogression, decay and atrophy" (Horwitz, 1957:12), since their inevitable consequence would be increasingly crippling skills shortages, coupled with artificially constricted domestic markets for locally produced goods (given the limited purchasing power of those paid artificially low wages).

If apartheid and capitalism had inverse logics, for these liberal writers it was the power of the market which would ultimately prevail, bringing the apartheid state to its knees. John Lonsdale points out that while the earlier cohort of liberal scholars writing about segregation in South Africa (pre-1948) were more concerned with issues of "political morality than economic efficiency," much of the liberal writing on apartheid was profoundly shaped by the principles of modernization theory gaining intellectual prominence globally at the time (Lonsdale, 1983:69), in terms of which the racist fetters imposed by apartheid on the country's labor markets would be eroded by the "color-blind" logic of economic growth. Exactly *how* this was expected to happen was not clearly specified; much of the liberal analysis of apartheid was more an expression of faith in the "modernization" thesis than a demonstration of these forces at work within the society at that time.

The Marxist critique of liberal scholarship took varying forms, depending on the particular version of Marxism being espoused; but there was little variation in the approach to questions of "race." In much the same vein as Harold and Ray Simons' (1983) book on *Class and Colour in South Africa* (first published in 1969) a group of white political exiles studying in England initiated a new wave of Marxist scholarship intent on exposing apartheid's chief *raison d'être* as to serve the interests of capital (understood generically). Whereas the first phase of liberal analysis took place against the backdrop of mixed economic performance in South Africa during the 1950s, this new surge of interest in a Marxist approach must be seen in the context of the exceptional economic growth rates sustained during the late 1960s, in tandem with the intensification of apartheid repression – a combination which seemed *prima facie* evidence of the falsity of the liberal case.

"Cheap black labor," argued Rick Johnstone (1970), Harold Wolpe (1972), and Martin Legassick (1974), was the lynchpin of apartheid, the point of effective fusion of political and economic interests. Where liberals saw a "contradiction" between apartheid and capitalism, these Marxist scholars saw an essential complementarity, a unity of purpose. The mechanisms of racial discrimination then, were to be understood as instruments of class domination – designed, promulgated, and monitored with that basic purpose. Wolpe thus characterized apartheid's distinguishing and defining feature as the fact that it "provides the specific mechanism for maintaining labour power cheap through the elaboration of the entire system of domination and control and the transformation of the function of pre-capitalist society" (Wolpe, 1972:425).

As Marxist theories came increasingly to dominate scholarship on apartheid during the 1970s and early 1980s, the primary focus of debate shifted somewhat. With the liberal position pretty well flogged to death – at least within the "radical" camp – the principal points of contention now corresponded to controversies within Western Marxism, particularly the contest between structuralist and humanist readings of Marx (Bozzoli and Delius, 1990; Deacon, 1991). Structuralist versions of Marxism attempted to produce more nuanced accounts of the workings of capitalism, emphasizing, *à la* Poulantzas, the differentiated, fractured nature of capital itself (Davies et al., 1976; O'Meara, 1983). But the instrumentalist treatment of apartheid's race policies as a tool of class interests remained unchanged. Social historians, inspired by E. P. Thompson's study of the English working class, disputed the version of "class" embedded in these structuralist accounts, proposing to analyze "class" as a set of social relations which were more actively crafted, in ways which already exhibited the traces of political, cultural, and ideological factors (Bozzoli and Delius, 1990:21). "Race" – its meaning unspecified – was *de facto* included in this mix; but without unpacking its place in the range of noneconomic processes.

As waves of resistance broke over the apartheid state during the 1970s, Gramscian notions of "an organic crisis" besetting the society were invoked (Saul and Gelb, 1981), to produce a Marxist version of the idea of the contradictory effects of apartheid. While the applicability of a Gramscian conception to the South African case can be disputed (Posel, 1983), this line of argument did draw attention to the shifting racial strategies of the apartheid state. But, as was the case in other "radical" writings, the politics of race were understood as an essentially class-based set of processes.

As the "race–class debate" lingered and the issues seemed to grow stale, it became increasingly fashionable to pronounce its epitaph. But its imprint remained clearly visible within the conventional wisdom of the 1980s, in the conviction that apartheid was essentially a system of "racial capitalism" – capitalism of a particular ("racial") type. With "race" thoroughly infused in the trajectory of economic development, it seemed that research at the coalface of class would simultaneously serve to illuminate the workings of "race."

This assumption is not without some merit; a reading of the "radical" literature on apartheid would retrieve a lot about the effects of racial discrimination and surveillance in the workplace and in the economy at large. Yet, the "race–class debate" also produced a series of theoretical and empirical closures on the subject of race, as a focus of research interest and analysis in itself.

The focus on the relationship between apartheid and capitalism signaled the consensus that lay at the heart of the debate, that the key to understanding apartheid lay at the interface of political and economic processes. So the research generated by this debate tended to say little, if anything, about racist institutions and practices which seemed more remote from the capitalist nexus. Even if the "relative autonomy of race" was acknowledged (and at times, stressed), there was little interest or effort made to unpack it. Due note was taken of the formidable battery of apartheid laws and regulations concerned directly with the official construction and surveillance of racial differentiation and segregation: the Population Registration Act (1950), the Group Areas Act (1950), which created residentially segregated "group areas" along racial lines, the Immorality Act (1950), which prohibited sex across racial lines, the Reservation of Separate Amenities Act (1953), which segregated access to a range of public facilities. But these mechanisms of control were regarded as descriptive features of the political landscape, the backdrop against which analysis took place, rather than a focus of research interest in themselves (e.g., Greenberg, 1980; Lipton, 1985).

The theoretical terms of debate created other forms of closure. Constructed in essentially "either–or" terms, the analytical choice to be made was whether class trumped race as the fundamental category of historical explanation, or *vice versa*.

Choosing class meant dumping race. The possibility of a more complex notion of social causation – premised on multiple and contingent versions of the interconnections between race and class – was excluded by theoretical fiat (Posel, 1983).

Perhaps the most remarkable theoretical feature of this debate was the failure to engage the question of what "race" actually is, either in general theoretical terms or as an historical reality under apartheid. On the Marxist side, the concept of race was never explicitly defined; but tacitly, it became the signifier of all that was "not class," in a debate which in fact confined itself – both empirically and theoretically – to a cluster of concerns about "class." On the liberal side, scholars of apartheid tended overwhelmingly to take the realities of race and racism as given, the burden of analysis falling on showing how these features of the apartheid system supported Afrikaner nationalist political causes and ambitions. In these ways, the historiography of apartheid tended to sidestep what became one of the most significant issues in literatures on race elsewhere in the world: the critique of biological essentialism by way of different varieties of social constructionism.

If partly the product of a theoretical disinterest, these silences were also associated with a discursively demonstrable discomfort with the issue of race. Many a preface to an historical or sociological study of apartheid (my own included) comments on the use of racial "nomenclature." Announcing a distaste for official apartheid racial categories, yet recognizing the impossibility of dispensing with them, many scholars have resorted to inverted commas to deal with this dilemma. But within the space of these inverted commas, the raw nerve of "race" is exposed and then sealed: on one hand, the association of racial categories with the discourse of apartheid, imposed on the country by a repressive regime, rendered them aberrant; on the other hand, these categories could not be erased since they were also (somehow) constitutive of the lived experiences of South African people.

The discomfort with the issue of "race" was also closely bound up with the politics of intellectual production during the apartheid era. Research and scholarship is surely never wholly politically or ideologically neutral; but this is particularly striking in the case of the apartheid literature. Theoretical emphases and priorities have been thoroughly embedded in political and ideological concerns. As Norman Etherington points out, the "efflorescence of scholarship" on South Africa from the 1960s to the 1980s was directly related to the intensification of apartheid oppression: "in the years between the tragedy of Sharpeville and Mandela's triumphant emergence from prison, historians of many different tendencies saw their research as a useful political tool in the fight against injustice" (Etherington, 1996:10)

Academic modes of analysis have therefore been closely aligned with the politics and discourses of opposition to apartheid. If the power of the apartheid state derived in large measure from its capacities to "normalize" race in the discourses and experiences of South Africans, Marxist theories which displaced race with class as the most fundamental cleavage in apartheid became instruments of intellectual and political subversion. The experiential ubiquity of race became exactly the reason to shift the primary focus of analysis to its material underpinnings.

The tendency to steer clear of the subject of race was also intertwined with the politics of nonracialism on the left. With the language of race being the language of the apartheid state, the dominant tendency amongst apartheid's critics was to position themselves as advocates of nonracialism. Theoretically, of course, an academic interest in questions of race does not preclude a political or ideological commitment to the principles of non-racialism; but in a context in which nonracialism was as much the dominant "etiquette of power relations" (Scott, 1990:8) on the left as an ideological doctrine, this seems to have been a difficult position for most academics (predominantly white) to entertain. Given the realities of apartheid oppression, the issue of race was politically highly charged, and therefore often the subject of intense conflict. Perhaps for this very reason, the ideological commitment to nonracialism was also a tool of organizational discipline to prevent the emergence of deep racial fault lines on the left. Within the Congress movement (of which the African National Congress was part) and the nonracial trade union movement, these strategies were largely effective: one of the most striking features of opposition ideology and politics in South Africa has been the resilience of its commitment to nonracialism. Yet, along with this has been a tendency within opposition movements and the intellectuals associated with them to speak relatively rarely on the subject of race, at least in the domain of public debate and discussion, barring the occasionally open and heated exchanges when the issue was more directly exposed, such as in the conflicts on the left triggered by the emergence of the Black Consciousness Movement in the early 1970s (Hemson, 1995:188).

Indeed, an engagement with the issue of race confronted white intellectuals on the left with "an essential dilemma," which was perhaps most clearly articulated within the left-wing student movement, in the aftermath of the breakaway of the Black Consciousness-aligned South African Students Organisation (SASO) from the nonracial National Students Union of South Africa (NUSAS) in 1969. As soon as the realities of race were confronted, the fragility of nonracialism became painfully clear. As student leader Clive Nettleton put it,

> the major problem facing NUSAS as a nonracial Organisation existing in a society based on discrimination and racialism is that, while preaching the ideal of nonracialism, the members of the Organisation are unable to live out their ideals...The fact is that, while it is possible for white and black students to hold joint congresses and to meet occasionally at social events, *they live in different worlds.* (Nettleton, 1972:125; my emphasis)

He acknowledged that for this reason, SASO "realistically rejected...the nonracial concept on which NUSAS's ideal rested" (p. 129). Yet, racial separatism was simultaneously deeply problematic, particularly for whites on the left, because it reproduced the political and intellectual logic of apartheid: "in a racially sensitive country like ours, provision for racially exclusive bodies tends to widen the gap that already exists between races ... " (p. 129).

The politics of black consciousness, particularly the mutual suspicion between the exponents of black consciousness and "white leftists" (Nolutshungu, 1983:158) in turn resonated in academic circles, the political rift being mirrored in theoretical terms. As David Hemson points out,

> there [was] a curious disjuncture between the flowering of class analysis – a peculiarly creative intellectual epoch among white intellectuals building common cause with African workers – and the theoretical explorations of black consciousness. Black consciousness never attempted to appropriate this line of theory and the proletarian resistance it espoused. The lines of departure were absolute, and the theoretical gulf very broad. (Hemson, 1995:204)

79

Sam Nolutshungu's book *Changing South Africa* (1983) was rare in engaging with the liberal-radical debate through the lens of an analysis of the black consciousness movement.

Other Voices, New Trends

The debate about apartheid and capitalism wound down from the late 1980s, with the publication of works which challenged the terms of debate, producing more nuanced versions of the nature and effects of class together with more complex and uneven versions of the relationship between apartheid and capitalism (e.g., Greenberg, 1987; Wolpe, 1988; Posel, 1991; O'Meara, 1996). This period also saw the fruits of a more diverse research agenda, with a more explicit interest in the subject of race beginning to feature more prominently (e.g., Bozzoli, 1991; Dubow, 1995; Mamdani, 1996; Marks, 1994; Norval, 1996; van Onselen, 1996).

This trend is set to accelerate further, as mainstream international debates about race seem more likely to infuse research on South Africa. During the apartheid era, international opposition to apartheid included an academic boycott of exchange between local and foreign scholars, which tended to keep South Africans isolated and inhibited foreign scholars from visiting and researching in the country. With the cessation of the boycott in the early 1990s, research and writing on South Africa seem to be becoming more common within international disciplinary and interdisciplinary journals, not simply within the sphere of African Studies – a development which is likely to foreground an interest in race through the prism of other theoretical and historical literatures.

The more assertive and controversial interventions on the subject of race, however, have tended to come from a new cohort of young scholars, many of whom are black, who have drawn attention to the racialized politics of intellectual production in South Africa. In the wake of postmodern and postcolonial preoccupations with the effects of a researcher's/writer's positionality in the production of knowledge, Windsor Leroke, Tshidiso Maloka, Christine Qunta (1987) and others have questioned the extent to which white scholars can effectively and legitimately document the experiences of black peoples. Maloka, for example, accuses "radical" social historians of reproducing stereotypes of black people as

> Other, in their less politically organised and sophisticated form – an approach which is tacitly informed by a Eurocentric sense of superiority. Of course, Africans do feature as workers or peasants (or as "class"), as well as women (or as "gender"); but they are generally "crowds", "rebels", "gangs", runaway wives or prostitutes. In as far as their level of development is concerned, Africans feature in the "formative", never as organised and sophisticated actors ... as the unsophisticated many. Not only is the history of Africans subdued, neocolonised and appropriated in this way, but 'radicals' also want to position themselves as the spokespersons and representatives of these 'many' on the front of History. (Maloka, n.d.:7)

This suppressed epistemology of race is seen as inextricably linked to the structure of academic production within South Africa, in which whites have shaped the historical research agenda and enjoyed preferential access to research skills and resources (Evans, 1990). One of the effects of racially segregated education under apartheid was the "virtual absence" (Maloka, n.d.:1) of black scholars in an academy dominated by white scholars

(Evans, 1990). That this trend is changing very slowly is itself the subject of fierce debate, as academically powerful communities are accused of having failed to promote effectively the development of black academic scholarship (Saunders, 1991; Worger, 1991).

This is not the place to debate the merits and demerits of these arguments; the point, rather, is to underscore their importance in opening up the subject of race, bringing to the surface a series of concerns which have tended to remain subterranean in the past.

Conclusion: Retrieving Race and Class

Research which takes race as its immediate and explicit focus is a relatively recent feature in the apartheid literature, which means that there are many new research areas inviting more extensive study. For example, we need to know much more about the ways in which racial identities were forged (including the social meanings of whiteness); how changing racial discourses under apartheid operated as modes of power/knowledge; the differences between what James Scott would call "public" as compared to "hidden transcripts" (Scott, 1990) of race within social movements committed to an ideology of nonracialism.

As always, the emergence of a new research agenda cannot be separated from the political moment: it seems no accident that the subject of race in apartheid should be more extensively researched in the wake of its defeat than during its ascendancy. But there are also theoretical factors at play here, deriving from the influence of theoretical critiques of Marxism, particularly postmodern and postcolonial modes of theorizing, closely attuned to issues of identity, discourse, and the intersections of the two. Even for those of us who remain sceptical about the overall merits of these bodies of theory, the controversies which they have generated have had a profound impact in foregrounding new sorts of questions and animating more diverse research areas. However in retrieving the subject of race, we should not throw the proverbial baby out with the bathwater: whatever the economistic excesses of the past, the central concern should surely be to root racial discourses in their material contexts, so as to understand the complex and shifting interconnectedness of race and class, along with the other processes that criss-cross our lives, such as gender and ethnicity.

Note

1 This chapter was written in 1998. Since then scholarship on race in South Africa has begun to accelerate, but in ways which obviously elude the scope of discussion here.

References

Adam, H. (1971) *Modemizing Racial Domination*. Los Angeles: University of California Press.
Adam, H. and Giliomee, H. (1979) *Ethic Power Mobilized*. New Haven, CT: Yale University Press.
Beinart, W. and Dubow, S. (eds.) (1995) *Segregation and Apartheid in Twentieth Century South Africa*. London: Routledge.
Biko, S. (1978) *I Write What I Like*. London: Heinemann.
Bonner, P., Delius, P., Posel, D. (eds.) (1994) *Apartheid's Genesis*. Johannesburg: Ravan and Wits University Press.

Bozzoli, B. and Delius, P. (eds.) (1990) *History from South Africa*. New York: Radical History Review.

Bozzoli, B. (1991) *Women of Phokeng*. Johannesburg: Ravan Press.

Breytenbach, B. (1972) "Vulture culture: The alienation of white South Africa," in A. la Guma (ed.) *Apartheid: A Collection of Writing on South African Racism by South Africans*. London: Lawrence & Wishart, pp.137–48.

Cooper, F. (1994) "Conflict and connection: Rethinking colonial African history." *American Historical Review* 99,5:1516–45.

Davies, R., Kaplan, D., Morris, M., and O'Meara, D. (1976) "Class struggle and the periodisation of the state in South Africa." *Review of African Political Economy* 7:4–30.

Deacon, R. (1991) "Hegemony, essentialism and radical history." *South African Historical Journal* 24:145–53.

De Kiewiet, C.W. (1956) *The Anatomy of South African Misery*. London: Oxford University Press.

Derrida, J. (1985) "Racism's last word," in H. L. Gates (ed.) *"Race," Writing and Difference*. Chicago: University of Chicago Press, pp.329–38.

de Villiers, R. (1971). "Afrikaner nationalism," in L. Thompson and M. Wilson (eds.) *The Oxford History of South Africa*. Oxford: Oxford University Press, pp.365–423.

Dubow, S. (1995) *Scientific Racism in Modern South Africa*. Johannesburg: Wits University Press.

Etherington, N. (1996) "Po-mo and South African history." *South African Review of Books*, July/August: 10–12.

Evans, I. (1990) "The racial question and intellectual production in South Africa." *Perspectives in Education* 1,1/2:21–35.

Gerhardt, G. (1978) *Black Power in South Africa: The Evolution of an Ideology*. Berkeley: University of California Press.

Goldin, I. (1987) *Making Race: The Politics and Economics of Coloured Identity in South Africa*. Cape Town: Maskew Miller Longman.

Greenberg, S. (1980) *Race and State in Capitalist Development*. Johannesburg: Ravan Press.

Greenberg, S. (1987) *Legitimating the Illegitimate*. New Haven, CT: Yale University Press.

Greenstein, R. (1995) "History, historiography and the production of knowledge." *South African Historical Journal* 32:217–32.

Greenstein, R. (1996). "Identity, race, history: South Africa and the Pan-African context," Seminar Paper no. 405, Institute for Advanced Social Research, University of Witwatersrand.

Hemson, D. (1995) "The antinomies of black rage," *Alter*nation, 2,2:184–206.

Horwitz, R. (1957) *Expand or Explode: Apartheid's Threat to South African Industry*. Cape Town: Bookman.

Horwitz, R. (1967) *The Political Economy of South Africa*. London: Weidenfeld & Nicholson.

Jansen, J. (ed.) (1991a). *Knowledge and Power in South Africa: Critical Perspectives across the Disciplines*. Johannesburg: Skotaville.

Jansen, J. (1991b). "The racial question and intellectual production in South Africa": A critical response to Ivan Evans." *Perspectives in Education* 12,2:107–10.

Jewsiewicki, B. and Newbury, D. (eds) (1986) *African Historiographies: What History, for which Africa?* London: Sage.

Johnstone, F. (1970) "White supremacy and white prosperity in South Africa." *African Affairs* 275:124–40.

Legassick, M. (1974) "Legislation, ideology and economy in post-1948 South Africa." *Journal of Southern African Studies* 1,1:5–35.

Leroke, W. (1996) "Historiography, or knowledge of the African other: The possibility of reflexive history." Paper presented at conference on *The Future of the Past*, University of Western Cape, 10–12 July.

Lipton, M. (1985) *Capitalism and Apartheid: South Africa, 1910–1986*. Aldershot, UK: Wildwood House.

Lonsdale, J. (1983) "From colony to industrial state: South African historiography as seen from England." *Social Dynamics* 9,1:67–83.

Maloka, T. (n.d.) " 'Radical' historiography and African historians in South Africa: A preliminary reflection." Unpublished mimeo, Princeton University.

Mamdani, M. (1996) *Citizen and Subject.* Cape Town: David Philip.

Marks, S. (1994) *Divided Sisterhood: Race, Class and Gender in the South African Nursing Profession.* Johannesburg: Wits University Press.

Marks, S. and Trapido, S. (eds.) *The Politics of Race. Class and Nationalism in Twentieth Century South Africa.* London: Longman.

Moodie, D. (1975) *The Rise of Afrikanerdom.* Berkeley: University of California Press.

Nettleton, C. (1972) "Racial cleavages on the student left" in H. van der Merwe and D. Welsh (eds.) *Student Perspectives* on *South Africa.* Cape Town: David Philip.

Nolutshungu, S. (1983) *Changing South Africa.* Cape Town: David Philip.

Norval, A. (1996) *Deconstructing Apartheid Discourse.* London: Verso.

O'Meara, D. (1983) *Volkskapitalisme.* Cambridge: UK: Cambridge University Press.

O'Meara, D. (1996) *Forty Lost Years.* Johannesburg: Ravan Press.

Posel, D. (1983) "Rethinking the 'race–class debate' in South African historiography." *Social Dynamics* 9,1:50–66.

Posel, D. (1991) *The Making of Apartheid, 1948–1961: Conflict and Compromise.* Oxford: Clarendon Press.

Qunta, C. (ed) (1987) *Women in Southern Africa.* London: Allison and Busby.

Saul, J. and Gelb, S. (1981) *The Crisis in South Africa – Class Defense, Class Revolution.* New York and London: Monthly Review Press.

Saunders, C. (1988) *The Making of the South African Past: Major Historians on Race and Class.* Cape Town: David Philip.

Saunders, C. (1991) "Radical history – the Wits workshop version – reviewed." *South African Historical Journal* 24:160–5.

Schlemmer, L. and Webster, E. (1977) *Change, Reform and Economic Growth in South Africa.* Johannesburg: Ravan Press.

Scott, J. (1990) *Domination and the Arts of Resistance.* New Haven, CT: Yale University Press.

Simons, H. and Simons, R. ([1969] 1983). *Class and Colour in South Africa 1850–1950.* London: International Defence and Aid.

Sizwe, N. (1979) *One Azania, One Nation.* London: Zed Press.

Thompson, L. (1985) *The Political Mythology of Apartheid.* New Haven, CT: Yale University Press.

van den Berghe, P. (1969) *Race and Racism in South Africa.* Harmondsworth, UK: Penguin.

Van der Merwe, H., Charton, N., Kotze, D., Magnusson, A. (eds.) (1978) *African Perspectives on South Africa.* Cape Town: David Philip.

Van der Merwe, H. and Welsh, D. (eds.) *Student Perspectives on South Africa.* Cape Town: David Philip.

van Onselen, C. (1996) *The Seed is Mine: The Life of Kas Maine, a South African Sharecropper.* Cape Town: David Philip.

Vaughan, M. (1994) "Colonial discourse theory and African history, or has postmodernism passed us by?" *Social Dynamics* 20,2:1–23.

Wolpe, H. (1972) "Capitalism and cheap labour-power in South Africa." *Economy and Society* 1,4:425–56.

Wolpe, H. (1988) *Race, Class and the Apartheid State.* London: James Currey.

Worger, W. (1991) "White radical history in South Africa." *South African Historical Journal* 24:145–53.

Wright, H. M. (1977) *The Burden of the Present: Liberal-radical Controversy over South African History.* Cape Town: David Philip.

PART II

Theory

Introduction to Part II

David Theo Goldberg and John Solomos

Recent scholarship on race and ethnicity has been marked by the multiplicity of theoretical paradigms shaping the field. This multiplicity has been prompted both by a notable growth in the range of disciplines in the humanities and social sciences contributing to the critical study of race and ethnicity, and to the consequent range of concepts circulated in intense debate. Part II of the *Companion* focuses on some of the key theoretical and conceptual considerations in contemporary ethnoracial analysis.

The first paper by Michael Banton takes up an approach that has been at the heart of social scientific debates about race and ethnicity, namely, race relations. Banton's account traces the emergence of this commitment and its implications. He shows that the various meanings associated with the notion of "race relations" order not only academic but political and policy agendas as well. Banton's account necessitates that we pay attention to how race and ethnicity are spoken about in everyday language. Here, the contrasting experiences of countries such as Britain, the United States, and Germany are especially revealing, for their differentiated modes of reference order how racial and ethnic matters are referenced in each society, and what can be achieved or what is silenced politically and at the level of policy.

Banton's analysis is followed by Werner Sollors' insightful account of the evolution of the concept of ethnicity. Sollors traces the ambiguities and overlaps between ideas of race and ethnicity, highlighting the ways in which ethnicity as a conceptual tool has been differentiated from race and how, in turn, issues of race and racism have been seen as separate from ethnic and cultural identity. He argues forcefully that there is a need for a more nuanced and contextualized understanding of the interrelationships between race and ethnicity.

An important feature of much of the historical and contemporary discussions of race and ethnicity has been that its field of vision has been limited by and large to racial and ethnic minorities. In the Western context, this has meant that much of the literature on race and ethnicity remains silent on issues of whiteness. It is only in recent years that a substantial body of work has begun to emerge on the social inventions, meanings, and implications of whiteness. Vron Ware's paper traces the emergence of studies of whiteness, and the impact of this body of work on the analysis of race and ethnicity. Although much of the literature on whiteness has a particular focus on historical conditions in the United States, Ware broadens the frame of reference, offering a more rounded and complex analysis of whiteness (and hence of ethnoracial considerations) in comparative perspective. In particular, she highlights the role of tacit notions of whiteness as a prevailing norm in structuring conceptions of self and other in societies bounded by discourses of race and ethnicity.

What does citizenship mean in societies shaped by social relations based on race and ethnicity? Is it possible for increasingly multiethnic states that are demographically and culturally heterogeneous to evolve more inclusive conceptions of citizenship and structures of belonging? These questions are especially salient for those societies marked not just by ethnic, religious, and cultural difference but more deeply by racially predicated and prompted inequalities. Marco Martiniello and Stephen May address these issues, though from rather different angles. Martiniello's account is organized around the need to rethink the boundaries of citizenship in societies that are not only multicultural but have evolved beyond the everyday notions of citizenship framing the well-known work of T. H. Marshall, among others. Drawing extensively on academic and policy debates in North America and Europe, Martiniello insists on the need to see citizenship as evolving in directions that take us beyond the narrow boundaries of the nation-state.

May's paper moves the discussion more centrally onto questions about the ways in which ethnic, cultural, religious, and linguistic minorities are afforded recognition and representation in liberal democratic nation-states. His underlying aim is to untangle the various meanings attached to the notion of multiculturalism over time with the view to developing a "critical multicultural paradigm." In developing the key elements of this critique, May engages with key conceptual debates about the nature of racial and ethnic identities in contemporary societies as well as policy debates about what can be done to develop strategies for the social and cultural integration of minority communities. A clear implication of this analysis is that much of the current preoccupation with multiculturalism remains rather limited in scope and fails to address key concerns about the nature of inequality in society as well as the forms that racial and ethnic divisions assume in the present environment.

Teun A. van Dijk follows the discussion of multiculturalism with a masterful overview of developments regarding the role played by various forms of discourse in reproducing everyday as well as political understandings of race and racism. For van Dijk discourse involves a whole range of texts in addition to talk. This includes parliamentary debates, news reports, advertising, textbooks, films, and talk shows. Van Dijk is particularly concerned to subject "elite racism" to discourse analysis with a view to assessing what can be done to counter forms of racist discourse. As one of the main contributors to the development of discourse analysis and its contribution to understanding racism, van Dijk offers an overview of current research agendas on racism, and a discussion of key research findings.

Adrien Katherine Wing's contribution is more tightly focused, and deals with the development of "critical race feminism." This is a trend of thought that emerged particularly out of the traditions and critical interactions of critical legal studies, critical race theory, and feminist jurisprudence in the United States. Wing traces the development of critical race feminism from these influences. From critical legal studies it assumed the challenge to common assumptions within the dominating paradigm of liberal legalism that law is objective, neutral (regarding class, race, or gender), and therefore fair, and that proper application of law will produce determinate and fixed outcomes. From critical race theory, critical race feminism adopted the conception that race is invented and elaborated in good part through and by the law. And feminist jurisprudence made critical race feminists deeply conscious of the gender biases that continue to mark liberal legalism. Thus Wing is concerned to show how law perpetuates unjust class, race, and gender hierarchies. She indicates how such injustices cannot simply be added discretely one to another but serve to exacerbate – to multiply – the force of exclusions through their mutual constitution and expression. She is especially concerned to show that critical race feminism has a more global motivation and reach than has been the case for critical race theory.

The next two papers take up issues that have moved from the margins of scholarly research on race to become the focus of considerable research and controversy in recent years. Phil Cohen's paper is a richly textured analysis of the ways in which a psychoanalytic perspective can contribute to the analysis of racism. Cohen's account starts from a brief engagement with how psychoanalysis can help to reframe conceptualizing issues such as racist violence or hatred. He then provides a detailed overview of classical attempts to link the analysis of racism to psychoanalysis, particularly through an account of Frantz Fanon's work. Cohen turns to examine the influence of more contemporary authors such as Žižek, particularly in light of what current debates can add to an understanding of racist practices as well as wider social processes.

Philomena Essed's paper is concerned with another facet of racism that has recently emerged as an important point of reference in shaping research agendas, namely, "everyday racism." Drawing on her own extensive empirical research and experiences, Essed's account is framed around a concern to situate the importance of everyday events and experiences in telling us something about the nature of race and ethnicity in specific situations. She also seeks to show how dominant scholarly focuses on race and racism often ignore or give minimal attention to the everyday experiences of racism and individual or collective responses.

The concluding paper in Part II, by Sandra Harding, focuses on a simple enough question: is science racist? This is a question that has been much debated throughout the history of the sociology of race, and particularly in relation to both classical forms of scientific racism and twentieth century forms of racial science such as Nazi eugenics. Harding's account takes a wide-ranging look at the core components of debates about the relation between science and racism. She provides examples of the role of science in reproducing forms of "race thinking" by exploring the interaction between science and racist ideologies and the role of science in relation to European expansion and the establishment of forms of imperial domination and colonialism. In doing so, Harding also maps out an agenda for a mode of scientific inquiry that goes beyond the boundaries of race.

Chapter 7

Race Relations

Michael Banton

The first recorded use of the expression *race relations* was in the title of a study of the economic status of "Negroes" in various counties of Georgia in the United States that was published in 1911. The article compared the status of blacks and whites as groups but had nothing to say about the relations between individual blacks and whites. It simply assumed that the two groups were properly designated *races* (Brooks, 1911). This assumption brought with it a series of highly questionable beliefs about the nature of racial differences in the human species which made the expression potentially misleading.

In the mid-nineteenth century United States it was customary to refer to the three main sections of the population as "whites," "negroes," and "Indians" (a capital letter for Negro came later), and to call them *races*. This nomenclature was made official by the Civil Rights Act of 1866 which spoke of "citizens of every race and color." Four years later the Fifteenth Amendment to the Constitution provided that the right to vote should not be denied "on account of race."

In European countries at this time there was active discussion of theories of racial superiority, and of whether biological differences might explain differences in cultural development, but (as in the United States) the organizing idea was usually that of "the race problem," or "the race question." Since groups were not often designated as *races* there was no consideration of racial relations as interpersonal relations. In the decades following World War I (as was illustrated by the name *Commission on Race Relations* given to the body appointed to investigate the Chicago riot of 1919), the expression came into more frequent use in the USA and was taken up elsewhere. The South African Institute of Race Relations was founded in 1929, at a time when Afrikaans-speaking and English-speaking whites were often referred to as *races*, but it concerned itself primarily with black–white relations.

The expression *race relations* was misleading because it implied that relations between blacks and whites, blacks and Native Americans, Native Americans and whites, together shared a quality absent from, say, Catholic–Jewish, Catholic–Protestant, and Jewish–Protestant relations. In both cases the relations in question could be either the relative social positions of the groups or the personal relations between individuals belonging to different groups. It would therefore have been more correct to speak of racial relations instead of race relations. Using the noun *race* instead of the adjective *racial* strengthened the assumption that what made black–Indian, black–white, and Native American–white relations resemble one another and differ from Catholic–Jewish, Catholic–Protestant, and Jewish–Protestant relations, was the distinctive biological nature of blacks, Native Americans, and whites.

Research during the 1920s and 1930s assembled more evidence that biological inheritance explained only a small portion of the differences between blacks, Native Americans, and whites in countries like the United States. The culture and history of the groups explained much more of the variation between them and of their relative positions in US society. Vehemently opposed to any such conclusion was the Nazi ideology in Germany, which at this time was preaching white superiority and calling Jews subhuman. Attempting to set the record straight, Huxley and Haddon (1935:220) argued that the groups which were commonly called races were genetically mixed, and that mixture was a matter of nationality, class, and social status; "the word *race* should be banished, and the descriptive and noncommittal term *ethnic group* should be substituted." The relations between blacks, Native Americans, and whites in the US were ethnic relations because social and cultural factors occasioned their differences. This was a proposed correction of the first word in the expression.

Racial Consciousness

The first writer to give a deeper meaning to the second word in the expression was the Chicago sociologist Robert E. Park, who in 1939 maintained that race relations were not so much the relations that existed between individuals of different races as between individuals conscious of these differences (Park, 1950). He thought that there were no race relations in Brazil because there was nothing in that country corresponding to what a North American recognized as racial consciousness. Park believed that racial prejudice had existed from the earliest periods of history and he described it as a defense-reaction, a defense of privilege. This provoked the dissent of his principal critic, the black Trinidad-born sociologist Oliver Cromwell Cox, who insisted that racial prejudice as it was known in the twentieth century had not existed before the European colonization of the Americas. It developed concomitantly with Western capitalism so that "race relations . . . are labor-capital-profits relationships" (Cox, 1948:336). Nevertheless, he agreed with Park that interpersonal relations could be racial only if the parties were conscious of their differences as being racial. He made this explicit when he wrote that "two people of different 'race' could have a relation that was not racial." Cox stated that in Brazil "colored-and-white amalgamation is far advanced," implying that this was because it had no white ruling class.

There was very little teaching of sociology in Britain until the 1950s, so there were few scholars to reflect on the arguments of Park and Cox. British ideas about racial relations derived substantially from South Africa and from experience in the colonial empire. When an Institute of Race Relations was established in London in 1958, the expression was taken to denote relations between physically distinguishable populations, but the prime focus was still on the different positions of groups rather than the relations between persons.

This had to be expanded when a new Labour government decided to introduce legislation against racial discrimination. Immigration into Britain from New Commonwealth countries in the Caribbean and the Indian subcontinent had been unrestricted because the immigrants were British citizens and not subject to the controls that regulated alien immigration. The government acted to put New Commonwealth immigration on a basis similar to that for alien immigration. At the same time it introduced measures to facilitate the integration of immigrants who were already settled, notably the Race Relations Act of 1965. Why it should have been given this name instead of being called a Racial Discrimination Act was never explained. Nor was the selection of this name queried; it seems to have been taken for granted that the relations within which such discrimination could occur must be racial relations. The name was repeated in later acts of Parliament passed in 1968 and 1976 and in similar acts adopted in Australia and New Zealand. This has reinforced the assumption that "race relations" was the correct name to use.

Other countries did not follow this example. In 1965 the United Nations General Assembly adopted the International Convention Against All Forms of Racial Discrimination. This is a treaty to which 157 states are now parties and in fulfillment of their obligations under the treaty most have enacted laws against racial discrimination (Banton, 1996). No other states use the expression "race relations" as a name for their laws or policies.

In the mid-1960s sociologists usually regarded race relations (or racial relations) as the *general name* comprehending racism, prejudice, and discrimination. A textbook published at this time distinguished, first, an approach from ideology which had *racism* as its basic concept; secondly, an approach from *attitude*, with *prejudice* as its basic concept; and thirdly, an approach from *social relationships* based upon the concept of *discrimination* (Banton, 1967:7–8)

The academic consensus on this conceptual framework was broken in the late 1960s by the effects of the Civil Rights Movement in the United States and particularly by sympathy for the doctrines advanced by the protagonists of Black Power. The debate in the USA took place within the framework of US constitutional law. In order properly to appreciate how this differs from the frameworks employed in Britain and other countries, it can be helpful to distinguish three ways in which states prohibit racial discrimination. The first starts from *human rights*; it sees these as existing prior to the creation of states and asserts that states are under an obligation to protect the rights (including the enjoyment of rights without discrimination of everyone within their jurisdiction). As part of the human rights movement, conventions have been adopted which states are expected to incorporate into their national law. The second approach starts from *parliamentary sovereignty*; a legislature, as in Britain, may enact a statute providing specific protections against discrimination. The third approach, as in the USA, starts from a *constitution* which recognizes the rights of citizens; any discrimination which infringes these rights is unlawful. Other laws may protect the rights of resident noncitizens.

Both sociologists and political activists in the United States have seen questions of racial relations within this third framework. They have highlighted the conflict between the experience of blacks and the manner in which the US Constitution was supposed to be given effect in everyday life. This conflict also lay behind the assertion of two of the leaders of the Black Power movement that "By *racism* we mean the predication of decisions and policies on considerations of race for the purpose of *subordinating* a racial group and maintaining control over that group." They went on to distinguish between individual and institutional racism (see Carmichael and Hamilton, 1967:19–21). They expanded the concept of racism to comprehend cultural assumptions, motives, institutions, attitudes, and beliefs about superiority, substituting it for race relations as a general name for the entire field of study. Whereas the social scientists were increasingly uncomfortable with the use of the words "race" and "racial" to designate relations that were social and political rather than biological, and thought it might be better to speak instead of *ethnic relations*, the activists were opposed to any expression which seemed to equate the harsh black experience in the New World with the milder experience of immigrant groups from Europe. They therefore preferred to retain the idiom of "race," which they found empowering. It gave them a moral advantage in any debate with persons who sought to excuse the prevailing state of affairs.

There are differences between US and British universities in the structuring of the undergraduate curriculum in sociology. In the United States a teacher may have considerable freedom to choose the title of a course of lectures. In Britain there is a stronger expectation that the subject shall be taught in a standard fashion, and therefore more concern about how a course shall be fitted into the curriculum. This helps explain why there has been a more animated debate in Britain about the appropriateness of the expression *race relations* as a general name for a field of study.

One of the main sociological problems in defining such a field has been that of consciousness. If people were conscious of racial differences in the United States but not in Brazil, just what was it they were conscious of? Should evidence about Brazil be used only as a negative example, as Park implied? Cox outlined a more general approach. He viewed *race* as a political idea which was generated by particular sorts of social situation and identified seven as being of special relevance. This scheme was elaborated by John Rex (1970:9) who emphasized the dependence of belief systems on underlying structures. Rex maintained that the necessary and sufficient conditions for the identification of a race relations situation were the presence of exploitation and oppression, role ascription, and a deterministic theory of social groups. He identified nine historical situations in which relations were likely to be conceived in terms of race, those: (1) at frontiers where peoples at different technological levels were in competition; (2) in which one group supplied unfree labor, or (3) supplied it under unusually harsh and exploitative terms; (4) of inequality in estate or caste systems; (5) of inequality along a continuum; (6) of cultural pluralism; (7) of urban stratification with migrants forming an underclass; (8) in which members of an outsider group perform pariah roles, or (9) in which they become scapegoats (Rex, 1973:203–4). This was later expanded (Rex, 1986:20–6) to incorporate situations of ethnic relations.

According to Robert Miles, schemes like those of Cox and Rex oversimplified the relation between social structures and the ways in which people thought of the social relations in which they were involved. Racism was an ideology which could be relatively autonomous, rather than simply the product of a structured situation. Building on the view that medical science could not have progressed had doctors accepted the patient's conception of his or her complaint as an identification of the disorder from which he or she was suffering, Miles went on to deploy Marx's distinction between phenomenal form and essential relations. Phenomenal form could be equated with the patient's conception of what was wrong. The essential relations could be equated with the real causes of the disorder (Miles, 1982:31–42). Calling attention to the conclusions of geneticists, Miles insisted that sociology must start from a recognition that the popular consciousness of race was false because "there is no scientific basis for categorising *Homo sapiens* into discrete races." To use *race relations* as a general name for a field of study was a false problematic; it misrepresented the reality, which was that of white racism evoked as a result of the appearance of a new source of labor. This presented capitalists with an opportunity for exploitation, while their employees saw it as threatening. (By a problematic Miles meant a set of research questions and of opinions about the best ways to answer them; others may call this a paradigm.)

Miles's criticism of previous writing has great force. It can be accepted without agreeing to his claim that the essential relations responsible for the phenomenal form are those of class formation within a capitalist order. Nor need it be assumed that social science concepts must seek to represent reality in the way he implied. Miles aligned himself with the realist school of philosophical thought, according to which a definition should grasp the essence of the things to be defined. In opposition the nominalist school has contended that a definition should distinguish the thing being defined from other things with which it might be confused. A favorite illustration is to say that while a realist (or essentialist) might define *Homo sapiens* as a rational animal, a nominalist would define *Homo* as a featherless biped! Realists seek the true nature of the relations that are called racial; nominalists assume that these relations are too complex to be grasped in this way and elaborate concepts that will facilitate analysis of the different component parts or aspects of the relations in question. Since these relations change over time, realists claim to distinguish new racisms. Nominalists believe that instability of definitions leads to confusion; instead of talking of new expressions of some underlying essence it is better to identify the component elements of social processes.

A Social Construct

There is now general agreement that when in English-speaking countries reference is made to *race*, as, for example, in instances of racial discrimination, the reference is to race as a *social construct* and not a biological category. The social nature of the category can be demonstrated by considering the position of persons of mixed origin. In the United States a person of 90 percent African and 10 percent European ancestry may consider himself or herself, and be considered by others, to be black, or African-American. It is social practice and not genetics which decides that person's position. If social scientists take over the popular terminology to talk of race relations they are legitimating a misrepresentation when they should be addressing the problems posed by racism. This argument – which was synthesized by Miles – has been paralleled in France. To classify black–white relations as race relations seems, to French people, to be itself racist. Like Carmichael and Hamilton, French writers take racism to be the general name for the field of study. Pierre-André Taguieff (1988:228), for example, turns round Banton's scheme of 1967 to write of racism as ideology, racism as prejudice, and racism as discrimination.

Germans see these matters differently. For them the word *Rassismus* recalls the doctrines and practices of the Nazi era, features of their past which they cannot forget but insist have no place in their present society. There are expressions of hostility towards Turkish and other foreign workers, but then there is also hostility towards immigrants of German ancestry returning several generations after their forebears settled in Russia. They call it *Fremdenfeindlichkeit*, or hostility towards the foreign. (This is usually translated as xenophobia though this is not an exact equivalent since a phobia is an irrational fear and attitudes towards foreigners have rational as well as irrational sources.) In Sweden, where first and second generation immigrants constitute 18 percent of the total population, most immigrants are from other parts of Europe and therefore are not very distinctive in appearance. This may explain why the Swedish government has legislated against *ethnic* discrimination, while defining the scope of its law to cover what would elsewhere be called racial discrimination.

In many European countries there has been much uncertainty about what to call the various aspects of relations associated with immigration. The names chosen have often reflected the political pressure brought to bear by particular groups. Thus the European Parliament in 1984 established a Committee of Inquiry into the Rise of Fascism and Racism in Europe. This was followed five years later by a Committee of Inquiry into Racism and Xenophobia. The Council of Europe in 1993 agreed to set up a Commission on Racism and Intolerance, while the European Union declared 1997 the European Year against Racism without defining what it meant by racism.

In debates at the United Nations it is widely assumed that race relations have come about because of the colonization of other regions by Europeans, and by the propagation of ideas of white superiority. Yet in Asia and elsewhere members of the majority population often regard the indigenous inhabitants of the country as inferior. There are forms of intergroup discrimination just like those in the West. The parties may not think of their relations as racial, but the outside observer may nevertheless conclude that they should be counted as ethnic or racial relations. The institution of democratic government in South Africa in 1994 brought an aspiration for a "nonracial" society, but group differences persist, there and elsewhere, and so long as it is necessary to use words like race and racial in the prohibition of incitement to hatred and in penalizing racial discrimination, it will not be possible to eliminate all use of the idiom of race in either law or popular speech. Can other words be employed to get round the difficulties that derive from the dubious status of the race concept?

In Britain during the 1970s and 1980s some argued for antiracism in education and opposed this philosophy to that of multiculturalism, but by the latter they did not necessarily mean the same as those who used this expression in the United States, Canada, or Australia. Others preferred to speak of interculturalism, to take the ideal of equal treatment as a better expression of what they were aiming at, or to argue for the goal of equal participation in society since this implied that ethnic minorities had obligations as well as rights. While not disputing that social scientists might learn from legal reasoning about the nature of discrimination, Miles (1993:5–6) has insisted that the law only validates popular misconceptions. He contends that academic analysis should develop its own vocabulary starting from the concept of racism. One of the problems with this alternative can be brought to the fore by contrasting the two approaches in the light of Durkheim's famous argument ([1895] 1950:65–73) that crime is a normal, and not a pathological, social form. Even in a society of saints, he wrote, some forms of behavior would be considered scandalous. There can be no society without norms, and no norms without deviance, so deviance is a normal phenomenon. Racial discrimination is likewise a normal, if deplorable, form of behavior, whereas racism is frequently described as a cancer, a virus, or with the use of some other medical metaphor to make it appear a pathology that would not be found in a healthy society. People are not blamed if they are afflicted by a cancer, but for every act of discrimination someone is responsible and should be brought to account (though, of course, there will be varying degrees of responsibility). The racism problematic too easily evades the question of responsibility and its central concept is inadequately defined.

Racial discrimination is just one form of discrimination, and shares many common features with discrimination on the basis of age, disability, gender, religion, social status, and so on. Many forms of discrimination are now prohibited under United Nations human rights conventions so it may be that in the future both the racial discrimination and the racism problematics will be incorporated within a human rights problematic. When in 1994 the United States of America ratified the International Convention on the Elimination of All Forms of Racial Discrimination it undertook to report to the United Nations every two years on what it had been doing to fulfill its obligations under the Convention. Once it starts to report periodically there will be a regular review, from an international perspective, of so-called race relations within the USA, as there already is of other countries. This will help promote a common perspective on the practical problems.

Social scientists will nevertheless continue to maintain that any analysis of events that is grounded in popular consciousness and everyday language will never be sufficient to identify the underlying causes of social trends. These causes, and the complex interrelations between them, will be uncovered only by formulating theories that provide more powerful explanations of the phenomena. The presently available conceptions of race relations, whether they start from discrimination, from racism, or from some other key concept, will have to be subsumed within some more powerful sociological theory, such as, perhaps, the theory of collective action (Banton, 1998:196–235), which will explain the special features of race relations within a framework that also explains other kinds of group relations.

The twentieth century started confident about the use of race to designate certain kinds of group; it ended very doubtful whether any relations can properly be named racial relations, but from discussion of the difficulties much has been learned.

References

Banton, Michael (1967) *Race Relations*. London: Tavistock and New York: Basic Books.

Banton, Michael (1996) *International Action Against Racial Discrimination*. Oxford: Clarendon Press.

Banton, Michael (1998) *Racial Theories*, 2nd edn. Cambridge, UK: Cambridge University Press.

Brooks, R. P. (1911) "A local study of the race problem: Race relations in the Eastern Piedmont region of Georgia." *Political Science Quarterly* 26:193–221.

Carmichael, Stokely and Hamilton, Charles V. (1967) *Black Power. The Politics of Liberation in America*. Harmondsworth, UK: Penguin.

Cox, Oliver C. (1948) *Caste, Class, and Race: A Study in Social Dynamics*. New York: Monthly Review Press.

Durkheim, Emile ([1895] 1950) *Les Regles de la methode sociologique*. Paris: Presses Universitaires de France.

Huxley, Julian S. and Haddon, A. C. (1935) *We Europeans. A Survey of Racial Problems*. London: Jonathan Cape.

Miles, Robert (1982) *Racism and Migrant Labour*. London: Routledge.

Miles, Robert (1993) *Racism After "Race Relations."* London: Routledge.

Park, Robert Ezra (1950) *Race and Culture*. New York: The Free Press.

Rex, John ([1970] 1983) *Race Relations in Sociological Theory*, 2nd edn. London: Routledge.

Rex, John (1973) *Race, Colonialism and the City*. London: Routledge.

Rex, John (1986) *Race and Ethnicity*. Milton Keynes, UK: Open University Press.

Taguieff, Pierre-André (1988) *La Force du préjugé. Essais sur le racisme et ses doubles*. Paris: La Découverte.

Chapter 8

Ethnicity and Race

Werner Sollors

Origins of "Race"

The *Oxford English Dictionary* dates the first English equivalent for Italian *razza*, Spanish and Castilian *raza*, and Portuguese *raca* in the sixteenth century. An example from 1570 reads: "Thus was the outward race & stocke of Abraham after flesh refused." This instance supports the theory that the obscure roots of "race" may lie in the word "generation," and "race" and "generation" remained synonyms for some time in such languages as English or French.[1] Sir Thomas Browne wrote in 1646 that "complexion was first acquired, it is evidently maintained by generation," and Le Cat made a similar argument in 1765 that even at the poles of the earth Moors "keep their black skins without any change from generation to generation" ("*de race en race*"). The development from "generation" to "race" slowly resolved the ambiguity in genealogies against family connectedness and in favor of human divisions. Verena Stolcke has stressed that the word "race" could mean "the succession of generations (*de raza en raza*) as well as all the members of a given generation"; that it often had a close connection with "quality" and "nobility of blood" (inserting an aristocratic dimension to its legacy); yet that it was also "confused in the middle of the fifteenth century with the old Castilian raza which meant 'a patch of threadbare or defective cloth,' or, simply, 'defect, guilt,'" obtaining a meaning exactly opposite to "nobility," namely, "taint" and "contamination," which is why the word appeared in Castilian, with a negative meaning, in connection with the doctrine of purity of blood (*limpieza de sangre*), "understood as the quality of having no admixture of the races of Moors, Jews, heretics, or penitenciados (those condemned by the Inquisition)" (Stolcke, 1994:276–7). With its legacy from fifteenth-century Spain, "race" can thus evoke both the generational pride of a "nobility" and the "taint" of those descended from socially ostracized groups and their descendants.

Origins of "Ethnicity"

The word "ethnicity" is once recorded in 1772, in an instance listed as "obsolete and rare" in the *Oxford English Dictionary*: "From the curling spume of Egean waves fabulous

Examples and arguments presented here have been drawn from my introduction to *Theories of Ethnicity: A Classical Reader* (Sollors, 1997).

97

ethnicity feigned Venus their idolatress conceived." The word was revived only during World War II, at a time when "race" had become compromised by its fascist abusers. W. Lloyd Warner reintroduced "ethnicity" as a social category, parallel to sex and age, by which human beings can be differentiated from each other. Like "race," which it set out to replace, "ethnicity" contains a doubleness. Derived from the Greek root *ethnikos*, the word refers both to people in general and to people who are different from the speakers, making "ethnic" applicable to self-description and to ascription.

Racism, and from Race to Ethnicity

"Racism" is a word that came into general usage only in the 1930s. It was at first a positive term launched by fascists to describe the importance they assigned to race, and then became the central term to express intellectual critiques of fascism. Magnus Hirschfeld's still remarkable antifascist book *Racism* (1938) marked the turning point, according to Robert Miles (1989:42). Race was affected by the vicinity to racism. In scholarly language, after World War II "race" slowly began to be displaced by "ethnicity" so that Irish-Americans, for example, did not remain a "race" but became an "ethnic group" (a term that enjoyed wider circulation than "ethnicity").

"Ethnicity" as Exclusive of "Race"

While the word "race" never completely disappeared from the field of ethnic studies, it became common practice to define "racial" as a part of "ethnic" phenomena. John Higharn's collection *Ethnic Leadership in America* (1978), for example, includes entries on Afro-Americans and Native Americans. A journal devoted to "American ethnic literature," *MELUS: The Journal for the Society of Multi-Ethnic Literature of the United States*, similarly offered (and still offers) criticism of literature from many ethnic groups, white and nonwhite; and many anthologies of ethnic literature followed the pattern of interspersing writings by African-Americans, Asian-Americans, Latinos, and Native Americans with texts written by "white ethnics" (e.g., Blicksilver, 1978; Faderman and Bradshaw, 1975; Newman, 1975; Simon, 1972). In fact, the very term "white ethnic" implies that the word "ethnic" is still not, in common usage, considered to be limited to whites; and many "Ethnic Studies" programs in the United States are devoted to the study of "racial" minorities.

The view of the intimate interrelationship of race and ethnicity is not just a matter of common usage: it has been argued in scholarship. Milton M. Gordon (1988) argued that "the term 'ethnic group' is broad enough to include racial groups." The inclusive quality of the term "ethnic group" becomes apparent in usage, for "all races, whatever cautious and flexible term we shall give to the term, are ethnic groups. But all ethnic groups, as conventionally defined, are not races" (1988:119). Ironically, it is thus the more inclusive quality of "ethnicity" that separates it somewhat from "race." Gordon specifically states it: "The larger phenomenon, then, is not race but ethnicity which, as a sociological concept, includes race" (p. 131). Hence he speaks of "races and many other types of ethnic groups" (p. 130). Yet their difference should not be exaggerated, as it is "a matter of degree rather than of kind." Most importantly, scholars should not be led to believe that conflicts based on "racial" difference are inevitably more serious than those based on "ethnic" distinctions.

> [T]he most momentous and catastrophic forms of ethnic conflict in some cases rest on the perception of differences that are physical and externally visible, and in other cases on differences that are cultural and ideological, no matter how the latter differences are phrased by the participants or perpetrators. (Gordon, 1988:131)

For Gordon, both the "physical" differences (often associated with "race") and the "cultural" differences (of "ethnicity") rest not on objective criteria but on "perception."

Race Differentiated from Ethnicity

In *Racial Formation in the United States* (1986) Michael Omi and Howard Winant take the view that the inclusive view of ethnicity tends to ignore different historical experiences, leading to the possibility of lending support to the strategy of "blaming the victim." A conceptual differentiation between race and ethnicity would, by contrast, help to explain why, because of race, group distinctiveness is not altered by long-standing adoption of majority norms and culture. Finally, the distinction would open up more scholarly interest in, for example, ethnicity among blacks (Omi and Winant, 1986:21ff.) This argument marks a particular counterpoint to Gordon's maxim that "all races are ethnic groups," which could be misunderstood as inviting a method of regarding all blacks as only one ethnic group, because they are also a "race." Races may be, and often are, ethnically differentiated (African Americans and Jamaicans in the United States), just as ethnic groups may be racially differentiated (Hispanics – who "may be of any race," as census takers know). Omi and Winant's argument supports the need for a careful examination of the relationships of "visible" and "cultural" modes of group construction in specific cases, but not the assumption that there is an absolute dualism between "race" and "ethnicity," and a deep rift between them.

Benjamin B. Ringer and Elinor R. Lawless (1989) make a stronger claim:

> The they-ness imputed to racial minorities by the dominant American society has been qualitatively different from the they-ness imputed to white ethnic minorities. . . . So imprinted has this differential treatment [of racial minorities in the United States] been onto the very foundations of the American society from the colonial period onward that we have constructed a theory of duality to account for this differential treatment. (Ringer and Lawless, 1989:27)

Ringer and Lawless add a very important qualification: "Accordingly we shall keep the two terms separate, although on occasion when we shall be looking at matters common to both racial and ethnic groups we may for the sake of simplicity use the term 'ethnicity' only." The language rule they apply could have been written by Milton Gordon, as it effectively makes ethnicity the superordinate category.

Race Unlike Ethnicity

The most systematic brief in favor of a sharper distinction between "race" and "ethnicity" may be the one advanced by Pierre L. van den Berghe in *Race and Racism* (1967), a work comparing the United States and South Africa. Van den Berghe argues that four principal connotations of "race" make it confusing. First, there is the dated and no longer tenable context of physical anthropology that once classified all human beings into customarily three to five races, that is evoked when scholars now speak of "race." Second, the term has been and still is applied to numerous groups such as the "French race" or the "Jewish race" – and in these cases, van den Berghe recommends the use of the terms "ethnicity" or "ethnic groups" as synonyms for only this meaning of "race." Third, the polysemous word is also synonymous with "species" when one says, "the human race." Only the fourth sense of "race" is the one van den Berghe proposes we should use; it refers, as defined by social scientists, to a "human group that defines itself and/or is defined by other groups as different from other groups by virtue of innate and immutable physical characteristics" (van den Berghe, 1967:9).

This differentiation leaves two meanings of "race" to be discarded, one to be replaced by "ethnicity," and the remaining instance of "race" defined on the ground of the distinction Gordon also suggested between "visible," "physical" (for van den Berghe also "innate" and "immutable") distinctions and "cultural" ones. (Schermerhorn's definition of ethnicity was broad enough to include cultural *and* physical – he says "phenotypal" – features). This brings us back, however, to the point made by Gordon that "physical" distinctions are also a matter of "perception," an issue addressed by van den Berghe's point that "physical" distinctions depend on external or internal definitions – which sets up a tension. The terms "physical," "phenotypal," "innate," and "immutable" suggest a fixed, objectively measurable difference; the notion of "visibility" (which could be complemented by Hannah Arendt's point that there are "audible" ethnic groups as well as visible ones, and by the fact that the olfactory sense is also often invoked in setting up ethnic boundaries) rests on culturally shaped sensory "perception," hence not on "objective" factors. In fact, van den Berghe acknowledges this problem to the extent that he feels compelled to add a qualification to his distinction between "race" and "ethnicity":

> In practice, the distinction between a racial and an ethnic group is sometimes blurred by several facts. Cultural traits are often regarded as genetic and inherited (e.g., body odor, which is a function of diet, cosmetics, and other cultural items); physical appearance can be culturally changed (by scarification, surgery, and cosmetics); and the sensory perception of physical differences is affected by cultural perceptions of race (e.g. a rich Negro may be seen as lighter than an equally dark poor Negro, as suggested by the Brazilian proverb: "Money bleaches"). However, the distinction between race and ethnicity remains analytically useful. (van den Berghe, 1967:10)

In other words, van den Berghe's demarcation between race and ethnicity may rest on what is really a blurry and dynamic line at best. It is a matter of a relationship and of a difference in degree, of "perception" more than of "objective" difference.

David Theo Goldberg (1993) extends these reflections and complicates them even more. He writes: "The influential distinction drawn by Pierre van den Berghe between an ethnic group as 'socially defined on the basis of cultural criteria' and a race as 'socially defined but on the basis of physical criteria' collapses in favor of the former." This is so, Goldberg says, because that assignation of significance to "physical" criteria is in itself the result of a "cultural" choice that has been made differently in different countries and times. Goldberg reminds us that what he terms "ethnoraces" (echoing Gordon's "eth-classes") may also be formed "by consent or domination by others." Goldberg concludes: "Ethnicity ... tends to emphasize a rhetoric of cultural consent, whereas race tends to resort to rhetoric of descent" (Goldberg, 1993:75–6). Yet it is a matter of a "tendency," not of an absolute distinction.

Mixed-race in Relationship to Race and Ethnicity

One area in which one can see this tendential divergence in operation in the United States is in the different rules of self-definition for ethnically mixed and for racially mixed individuals that has been the subject of Mary Waters' (1990) fascinating research. She found that not all persons from dual backgrounds have the same options for identification:

> Certain ancestries take precedence over others in the societal rules on descent and ancestry reckoning. If one believes one is part English and part German and identifies as German, one is not in danger of being accused of trying to "pass" as non-English and of being "redefined" English.... But if one were part African and part German, one's self-identification as German would be highly suspect and probably not accepted if one "looked" black according to the prevailing social norms. (Waters, 1990:18–19)

The Afrocentrist scholar Molefi Kete Asante took an example quite similar to the one Mary Waters analyzed in order to argue against a racially mixed identity in America: to claim, for example, a partly German heritage for black Americans, he writes, may be "a correct statement of biological history but is of no practical value in the American political and social context. There is neither a political nor a social definition within the American society for such a masquerade" (Asante, 1993:142). What Waters describes as a social norm, Asante tries to enforce by considering a person's real ancestry "of no practical value" for identification, and the claiming of a parent's ethnicity merely a "masquerade." Those types of ancestry that are colloquially associated in the United States with the term "race" rather than "ethnicity" may deny a descendant the legitimate possibility of identifying with certain other forms of his or her ancestry (even though "ancestry" may mean one parent, three grandparents, or an even higher proportion of ancestors further removed). The social phenomenon of "passing" also throws into question the notion that "race" rests on "physical" features or that such features are visible – since "passing" implies that people who "look white" may be considered to be "really" black (see Davis, 1991). From a stronger theoretical probing of the issue of "mixed race" the concept of "race" as a "physically based" ethnic distinction may be fundamentally questioned, as Naomi Zack (1993) demonstrates. Naomi Zack has subjected the dualistic racial axioms to logical scrutiny and delineated the following schema:

> An individual, Jay, is black if Jay has one black forebear, any number of generations back. An individual, Kay, is white if Kay has no black forebears, any number of generations back.

> There is no other condition for racial blackness that applies to every black individual; there is no other condition for racial whiteness that applies to every white individual.
>
> This schema is asymmetrical as to black and white inheritance. It logically precludes the possibility of mixed race because cases of mixed race, in which individuals have both black and white forebears, are automatically designated as cases of black race. (Zack, 1993:5)

In an unsystematic fashion, the U.S. Census adheres to the principal of dividing Americans into four categories that are identical with nineteenth-century "races" (Caucasians, Africans, Asians, and Indians and a fifth, Hispanics, who can be of any race). And while the Census has found a simple method of counting multiethnic citizens, the government bureaucracy finds it difficult to acknowledge the existence of biracial citizens and, as Joel Perlmann (1997) has stressed, is unable to consider the possibility, in its statistical forecasts, that children may in fact be born from the unions of members of different races. In short, the U.S. Census predicts population growth only within (and not crossing) the five categories that David Hollinger (1995) polemically refers to as "the ethnoracial pentagon."

Conclusion

Some contemporary scholars would like to consider "race" a special "objective" category that cannot be meaningfully discussed as a part of "ethnicity."[2] Yet it seems that, upon closer scrutiny, the belief in a deep divide between race and ethnicity that justifies a dualistic procedure runs against the problem that the distinction between ethnicity and race is simply not a distinction between culture and nature. Few if any scholars manage to sustain a completely dualistic procedure, and even fewer advocate abstaining from any comparisons between "racial" and "ethnic" groups. What seems to be the case then is that in a society in which ethnic differentiation along racial lines has historical depth and is supported by governmental bureaucracies, certain ethnic conflicts will come to be understood as "racial."

If the Spanish origin of the term is true, then the problem with "race" goes back to its beginnings. It was used to expel from Spain people "tainted" by Jewish and Moorish blood – hence "race" in the "physical" and "visible" sense, we might think. Yet the list of people to which the doctrine of purity of blood (*limpieza de sangre*) was applied went on and included descendants of heretics and of "*penitenciados* (those condemned by the Inquisition)" (Stolcke, 1994:276–7). Thus at this terrible beginning, "race" was hardly based on the perception of phenotypal difference but on a religiously and politically, hence "culturally," defined distinction that was legislated to be hereditary, innate, and immutable. It was what we would now call an "ethnic" distinction, as defined by Nathan Glazer as well as by Pierre van den Berghe. Stuart Hall (1994) said memorably that race and ethnicity play hide-and-seek with each other. A categorical refusal to find any possible relationship between ethnicity and race – even if that relationship should turn out to make "race" an aspect of "ethnicity" – does not seem promising as a program of scholarship.

Notes

1 Other contenders are "ratio," "natio," and "radix" to Spanish and Castilian *raza*, Italian *razza*, and Old French *haraz*.
2 See, for example, Smith (1982). Ronald Takaki (1993:10) argued more subtly that race "has been a social construction that has historically set apart racial minorities from European immigrant groups. Contrary to the notions of scholars like Nathan Glazer and Thomas Sowell, race in America has not been the same as ethnicity." Yet he does not draw the conclusion from this assessment that "race" and "ethnicity" should not be compared. Most page references to what is indexed as "ethnicity" in Takaki's book actually refer to discussions of Jewish immigration.

References

Asante, Molefi Kete (1993) "Racism, consciousness, and Afrocentricity," in Gerald Early (ed.) *Lure and Loathing: Essays on Race, Identity, and the Ambivalence of Assimilation*. New York: Allen Lane, The Penguin Press.

Blicksilver, Edith (1978) *The Ethnic American Woman: Problems, Protests, Lifestyles*. Dubuque, IA: Kendall/Hunt.

Davis, F. James (1991) *Who Is Black? One Nation's Definition*. University Park: Pennsylvania State University Press.

Faderman, Lillian and Bradshaw, Barbara (1975) *Speaking for Ourselves: American Ethnic Writing*. Glenview, IL: Scott/Foresman.

Goldberg, David Theo (1993) *Racist Culture Philosophy and the Politics of Meaning*. Oxford: Blackwell.

Gordon, Milton M. (1988) *The Scope of Sociology*. New York: Oxford University Press.

Hall, Stuart (1994) "Ethnicity." W. E. B. Du Bois lecture, Harvard University.

Higharn, John (1978) *Ethnic Leadership in America*. Baltimore: Johns Hopkins University Press.

Hirschfeld, Magnus (1938) *Racism*. London: Victor Gollancz.

Hollinger, David (1995) *Postethnic America: Beyond Multiculturalism*. New York: Basic Books.

Miles, Robert (1989) *Racism*. London: Routledge.

Newman, Katharine D. (1975) *Ethnic American Short Stories*. New York: Washington Square Press.

Omi, Michael and Winant, Howard (1986) *Racial Formation in the United States: From the '60s to the '80s*. London and New York: Routledge.

Perlmann, Joel (1997) "'Multiracials,' racial classification, and American intermarriage – the public's interest." Working Paper No. 195 of Jerome Levy Economics Institute, Bard College.

Ringer, Benjamin, B. and Lawless, Elinor, R. (1989) *Race-Ethnicity and Society*. London and New York: Routledge.

Schermerhorn, Richard Alonzo (1970) *Comparative Ethnic Relations: A Framework for Theory and Research*. New York: Random House.

Simon, Myron (1972) *Ethnic Writers in America*. New York: Harcourt Brace Janovich.

Smith, M. G. (1982) "Ethnicity and ethnic groups in America: The view from Harvard," *Ethnic and Racial Studies* 5:, 1–22.

Sollors, Werner (1997) *Theories of Ethnicity: A Classical Reader*. Basingstoke, UK: Macmillan and New York: New York University Press.

Stolcke, Verena (1994) "Invaded women: Gender, race, and class in the formation of colonial society," in Margo Hendricks and Patricia Parker (eds.) *Women, "Race," and Writing in the Early Modern Period*. London: Routledge, pp.272–86.

Takaki, Ronald (1993) *A Different Mirror: A History of Multicultural America*. Boston: Little Brown.

van den Berghe, Pierre L. (1967) *Race and Racism: A Comparative Perspective*. New York: Wiley.

Waters, Mary C. (1990) *Ethnic Options: Choosing Identities in America*. Berkeley: University of California Press.

Zack, Naomi (1993) *Race and Mixed Race*. Philadelphia: Temple University Press.

Chapter 9

The Parameters of "White Critique"

Vron Ware

Peering Into the Dark

...walk around the silent swelling of *When I am Pregnant*. Trace the shape as it grows obliquely out of the wall and then suddenly when you stand in front of it, face to face, it is there no longer; only a luminous aureole remains to return you to the memory of stillness, as the wall turns transparent, from white to light. (Bhabha, 1998:12)

In the process of writing this essay I happened to visit an exhibition of the sculptor Anish Kapoor's work at the Hayward Gallery in London. The first installation looked from a distance like a large rectangular painting of the deepest blue imaginable. Close up, it invited the viewer to locate its surface on a two-dimensional plane which seemed to retreat into the distance the more one tried to fix it. The security guard had her work cut out to prevent people from leaning over the ropes to touch the blue surface, to feel with their hands what their eyes refused to tell them. In another room, the installation described above by Homi Bhabha had a similar effect although this time it was white and the perceptual disturbance was produced by the surface protruding into the room rather than disappearing into the wall. It was a curiously exhilarating experience trying to fathom what had happened to the bulge as you looked straight at it, seeing only a dense white flat surface. Only when you moved to the side could you see the profile re-emerge, and make sense of the title of this piece. I encountered a similar sensation with Kapoor's "White Dark" series as I stared into his hollow three-dimensional shapes without being able to see corners, sides, edges, and depths. The white space inside was uncannily vacant, but also powerfully empty. It was hardly surprising that many complained of dizziness once they left the building.

This experience of peering into the dark light, or the light dark, reminded me of the problems inherent in trying to speak about whiteness as a central feature of raciology – by which I mean the various discourses that bring and keep the idea of "race" alive. Richard Dyer, whose work on the representational power of whiteness has famously illustrated its all-or-nothing quality, was one of the first to draw attention to the way that whiteness can become invisible to those who are caught up in its glare (1988, 1997). From one angle whiteness appears as normality; in a white supremacist society those people and those ways of thinking, behaving, and talking that are deemed white, are the norm by which all else is measured. From another angle, to those who are placed outside this category, whether through birth or behavior, the parameters of whiteness are visible to a greater or lesser degree. Depending on experience and understanding, whiteness can be seen in many guises: as pure terror, as property, as "a desperate choice" (Roediger, 1998:23).

The 1990s has seen an extraordinary amount of work devoted to the examination of whiteness in different disciplines. Most of this recent work has emanated from the United States and is specifically addressed to US society and culture. It marks a potentially important shift in the way that the politics of "race" are understood, since it is premised on the belief that whiteness is a socially constructed category that exists in relation to ideas about blackness. Postcolonial theory in Europe has taken up this perspective, but here the struggle to recognize that "race" is a central structuring feature is always more difficult. Analyzing the ideological components of whiteness is a timely and urgently necessary project in the face of the continuing activity of far-right groups that take an overtly white supremacist stand. However, in circles that play down or deny the persistence of racial injustice, whiteness is often so far from being recognized as a racialized category, intimately and automatically connected to blackness, that it has become invisible to those who are able to claim privileged membership of the commonality it forms. To look "white" is to be "normal" as long as that is who you think you are. A perspective that challenges this apparent normativity is then ready to attend to the many ways in which ideas about whiteness are produced and reproduced through economics, politics, and culture.

Focusing on whiteness in this way also has the effect of energizing fresh theoretical and pragmatic debates about raciology, and the effects of race-thinking, which do not inevitably depend on investigations or comments on what it means to be black. This new ground has proved particularly fruitful to many designated "white" writers who are committed to a politics of accountability toward those who fall outside this illustrious category, a politics based not on guilt or patronage, but instead on the recognition that white supremacy has ways of diminishing the lives of everyone involved in its systemic power. Once the different constructions of racialized identity are perceived as interconnected and relational, though definitely not symmetrical, there ought to be greater opportunities for dialogue and alliance between those who find common aims against inequality and oppression. The conditional tense has to be underlined because there are, of course, no guarantees that these new ways of talking or thinking about "race" will necessarily lead to concerted political action, within or outside the academic world.

Just as it is difficult to describe the kind of sensory disorientation produced by the sculptures of Anish Kapoor, so it is hard at this point to delineate this new phenomenon of "whiteness studies" or "white critique," as some call it, which continues to expand at an exponential rate. What was recently perceived to be a radical and potentially subversive turn towards new perspectives on raciology and its effects can be described as something of a bandwagon to be jumped on by a host of writers anxious to explore their particular disciplinary take on the idea of whiteness. Given the proliferation of this work and the increasing difficulty of tracking its every direction, I intend to take issue with the field as a whole, without claiming to do justice to the key players. Having said this, there are dangers in trying to generalize about the work separately from the disciplinary contexts that the individual authors address. In other words, although it is appropriate to name David R. Roediger's *The Wages of Whiteness* (1991) as an original, pathbreaking book that is the first to chart the development of the white working class in the USA, it is clear from reading the introduction, "On autobiography and theory," that Roediger had been following a trajectory that made sense of his own political instincts informed by the work of other social historians and cultural theorists such as Alexander Saxton, Stuart Hall, and, above all, W. E. B. Du Bois (Roediger, 1991:10–11).

Similarly, one can point to the publication of Toni Morrison's important essays *Playing in the Dark* (1992) as an inspiration for concerted rereadings of US literary texts. But as Shelley Fisher Fishkin argues in an extraordinary review article on the "remapping of American culture" (1995), much of the groundwork for this new development in literary studies was laid in the previous decade by writers such as Eric Sundquist, Robert Stepto, and Aldon Lynn Nielson, and she claims that her own work was inspired by encouragement and support provided by Ralph Ellison, whose observations on "the true interrelatedness of blackness and whiteness" had intrigued her throughout her career. Similar arguments about genealogy may be made in other academic disciplines without playing down the relative explosion in books of all kinds that has sought to address the subject of whiteness in the 1990s.

Looking beyond the realm of scholarly activity, however, it is also important to connect this latest work to more accessible traditions of examining and challenging white racial attitudes and behavior that have accompanied black struggles for emancipation and justice. How new, radical, or subversive does this interrogation of whiteness look next to the hugely important work of earlier writers like Lillian Smith or John Howard Griffin who based their powerful deconstructions of Southern racism on their own experience as white Southerners; or the attempts of subsequent men and women who turned their attention to the history and psychology of white racism during the 1960s and 1970s – writers such as Joel Kovel, Winthrop Jordan, Dorothy Sterling, and David Wellman? And of course this list does not even try to encompass the work of African Americans and others whose experiences of slavery and the histories of European colonialism obliged them to develop an expertise about the ways of white folk. So, far from being new, the documentation and interpretation of whiteness that comes from the perspective of those who are not categorized as white has only just begun to be recognized as a valid contribution to the way those white folks see themselves. Who can claim to know about whiteness? David Roediger's most recent book *Black on White* (1998) reminds us of the view from the auction block, demonstrating how intimate knowledges of whiteness have been integral to what it means to be outside this category.

Ruth Frankenberg, author of one of the first feminist investigations into the way that "race" shaped white women's lives (1993:1), has provided a useful overview of recent work on whiteness in her introduction to a collection of essays entitled *Displacing Whiteness* (1997:1–33). Her summary is particularly useful because it does not limit the horizon of this work to the USA, unlike almost all other reviewers published there. She identifies four main areas. The first, historical studies, she notes, is arguably the fullest and best developed of these:

> This scholarship helps make it evident that the formation of specifically white subject positions has in fact been key, at times as cause and at times as effect, to the sociopolitical processes inherent in taking land and making nations. (Frankenberg, 1997:2)

The second and related area is cultural studies, where scholars and practitioners have been interested "both in the making of subjects and in the formation of structures and institutions." Third, and connected to this, is the whole question of whiteness as performance, "whether in daily life, in film, in literature, or in the academic corpus" (Frankenberg, 1997:3):

> At times what is at stake in such research is the "revealing" of the unnamed – the exposure of whiteness masquerading as universal. But at other times the stake is rather in examining how white dominance is rationalized, legitimized, and made ostensibly normal and natural. (Frankenberg, 1997:3)

Finally, Frankenberg suggests that there is an important body of work that examines racism in movements for social change. She draws attention here to the contribution of feminist critics of whiteness as well as "work on 'the other side of the coin' that monitors and analyzes the making of white supremacist identity and political movement ideology and practice" (p. 3).

The collection of essays that follows this introduction is interdisciplinary and the authors move between these four areas in their brief to show how "whiteness operates in particular locales and webs of social relations" (1997:3). Above all, whiteness is understood as a process that can be contested as well as deconstructed. Culture marked by whiteness is seen "as practice rather than object, in relation to racial formation and historical process rather than isolable or static."

In contrast with this type of politically engaged analysis of the new subject area, the mainstream media in the USA has observed its emergence into the public sphere with skepticism: Margaret Talbot, a senior editor of the *New Republic*, writing in the *New York Times Magazine*, questions the whole idea of analyzing the social construction of whiteness, asking whether it is "a symptom of the kind of agonized muddle that well-meaning Americans tend to find themselves in when it comes to racial politics. Wouldn't it be easier to retreat into transfixed contemplation of one's own racial identity than to try to breathe life onto the project of integration?" (Talbot, 1997:119) This interpretation of the new field of study happens to be grossly unfair in that it collapses together the projects of different authors mentioned in her article who are widely and openly at variance with one other. The idea that a new angle of reflexivity on the structures and processes of white supremacy automatically amounts to a bout of ineffectual navel gazing is absurd, but Talbot's caricature (published under the heading "Getting credit for being white") is made all the more convincing by her focus on an increasingly popular genre of writing that does indeed explore the concept of whiteness as "racial" identity from an autobiographical perspective. This, in my opinion, is an area fraught with contradictions, not least of which is that it tends to re-establish the first person firmly at the center of attention to whiteness, and also because it is in danger of reifying the whole notion of "race" as a system of human classification that can be understood outside the histories of its invention and brutal enforcement. This of course needs to be qualified because there are examples of insightful autobiography that illuminate this process just as there are narcissistic versions that obscure it. However, the difficult question of defining what whiteness is or is not is just one of the awkward theoretical issues that has been identified not only by those working outside the critical study of "race" but also firmly located within it. I want to move now to a more directed consideration of the problems and possibilities of this focus on whiteness.

Nothing Personal

The discovery of personal whiteness among the world's people is a very modern thing – a nineteenth and twentieth century matter indeed. (Du Bois, [1920] 1990:29)

Is White a race? The answer is *yes* it is ... The benefit in addressing race as an aspect of identity is beyond calculation. (Carter, 1997:206–7)

It is time we used our imaginations to invent alternative forms of white racial identity which, without having known victimization at the hands of other whites, nevertheless understand the disasters which constitute all forms of racial domination. (Wray and Newitz, 1997:6)

The key to solving the social problems of our age is to abolish the white race. Until that task is completed, even partial reform will prove elusive, because white influence permeates every issue in U.S. society, whether domestic or foreign. (Ignatiev and Garvey, 1996:10)

I use these four extracts to highlight the wide range of approaches to the analysis of whiteness. All four quotes are taken outrageously out of context. The first, by an African-American historian and sociologist, represents a black view of the historical development of white supremacy referred to earlier, and the phrase "personal whiteness" always makes me smile with its associations of bodily hygiene. It is tempting to update Du Bois's observation by saying that "The rediscovery of personal whiteness by some of the world's people is a very postmodern thing, a very late twentieth century matter indeed." The second quote, taken from an essay by the psychologist Robert Carter, enrages me since it illustrates the tendency mentioned above to give substance to the notion of "race" as a static and unchangeable fact of identity that marks groups of people for life regardless of their behavior and beliefs; in my view this undermines the whole project of demonstrating that whiteness is an exclusive social category produced through history. I feel more sympathy with the third extract, written by antiracist cultural theorists, but it still has me shouting "No, no that's where you're wrong!" From where I stand there is no need to perpetuate nineteenth and twentieth century notions of racial anything. As André Gorz says in *Farewell to the Working Class*, "The transformation of society ... requires a degree of consciousness, action and will. In other words it requires politics" (Gorz, 1982:12). If the twenty-first century is to transcend the color line inherited from earlier social, economic, political, and cultural formations, a progressive, forward-looking politics of social justice should embrace the will to abandon "race" as any kind of useful category, alternative or otherwise. There are other positions, of course, that share this possibly utopian but strictly necessary vision: the fourth extract is representative of a group called the new abolitionists, whose manifesto is the complete abolition of whiteness. Their motto – "Treason to Whiteness is Loyalty to Humanity" – has a rhetorical flourish that conveys the will to transform the state of things even if the theoretical or methodological details are not immediately clear.

These four perspectives do not begin to encompass the entire range of difficult questions I referred to earlier but they may suggest the divergent agendas of many writers who identify whiteness as a central factor in the study of "race." In particular, these quotes demonstrate the different ways that whiteness might be conceived as an aspect of cultural identity: the writers here suggest that white identity can be discovered, embraced, retained, or reimagined, or, given that whiteness is "nothing but an expression of race privilege" (Ignatiev and Garvey 1996:288), completely abolished. The point about these fundamental disagreements is not that they are surprising or unexpected, although it is distressing that the conservatism that argues that whiteness is still an integral aspect of a "nonracist" identity is in danger of diluting the radicalism that painstakingly provides evidence of the *making* of whiteness as a social category and the possibility of its unmaking. The scholars and activists who now address whiteness as a means to understand and analyze inequality, exploitation, and injustice are not automatically in dialogue with each other and are not guaranteed to speak the same language.

What is at issue here is the very meaning of "race" and its status in contemporary culture, whether local, national, or global. It is hard to reconcile Carter's suggestion that the way forward is to "develop a positive nonracist White racial identity ego status" (Carter 1997:207) with the perspective of historian Roediger, who quotes James Baldwin as saying: "As long as you think you're white, there's no hope for you" (Roediger, 1998:22). The scholarly tradition exemplified by Roediger, Alexander Saxton, Theodore W. Allen, and, more recently Hale (1998), whose book is entitled simply *Making Whiteness: The Culture of Segregation in the South 1890–1940*, can also be contrasted with the autobiographical, confessional tone of books like Jane Lazarre's *Beyond the Whiteness of Whiteness: Memoir of a White Mother of Black Sons* (1996). Both genres can be read as avowedly antiracist, but is one more effective than another in attacking mechanisms of exclusionary power or do they complement each other in theorizing the pervasive and insidious dynamics of racism in conjunction with localized social ecologies, gender relations, and sexualities?

This discrepancy in perception and understanding is familiar to anyone who has been involved in trying to develop effective and challenging ways of thinking about raciology. It would be dishonest to deny that many writers and activists try to muddle through in one way or another, possibly without realizing the dangers of falling between the cracks in their conceptual frameworks. In other words, many writers want to have their racial cake and eat it too. While it may be relatively easy to conclude that "race" refers to an outdated system of classification based on imagined notions of biological difference, the salience of skin color in everyday life still has to be reckoned with – in some places more than others. What does it mean to propose the abolition of whiteness in a world in which, as George Lipsitz (1995) puts it, structures of power offer all racialized minorities, not simply black and white, a "possessive investment in whiteness"? Or, to put it another way, how do we separate the simple, descriptive term "white" from the ideologically charged "White"? Perhaps those who argue for an alternative nonracist version of white identity are the pragmatists after all, while those who believe that it is possible to distance oneself from the trappings of light-skin privilege are in cloud-cuckoo-land. My point is that these opposing positions form a useful dialectic that can illuminate (as well as complicate) contemporary thinking about "race" as a feature of postmodern life.

My own work on whiteness – which I did not realize at the time was part of a new wave – stemmed from my involvement 20 years ago in both feminist and antifascist politics. Working for a journal that monitored the far right in Britain and its links with international white supremacist groups, my tasks entailed photographing their meetings and demonstrations, reading their propaganda, and constantly trying to anticipate and undermine their next moves. The ideology of these organizations was basically an updated German Nazi belief system: virulent antisemitism, hatred of communism, extreme antiblack (or anti-immigrant) racism, in a monochrome world in which people's skin color represented their history, their nature, their claim to belonging to race, to nation, to humanity. I was continually struck by their depiction of "Whites," especially women, as innocent victims, an endangered species battling to survive the onslaught from all sides (Ware, 1992). Long after I moved on to other employment I was highly suspicious of the word "white" as a description of racial type since it rarely allowed a distinction between the neo-Nazi fantasy and the vocabulary of common sense that did not "see" any political charge in this term. I mention this here because, however sinister and dangerous, the existence of overt white supremacist organizations can also demonstrate the effort required to create whiteness and to make it visible. At this level, the racial ideology of whiteness always depends on brute force to implement its strategies for domination, and carries with it associations with terror and death. In my opinion the presence and activity of these groups can be used to remind people of the mythic content of whiteness. They can also serve as a warning to those of us concerned to investigate the discursive power of whiteness in its less visible, less clean-cut, forms.

It is vital that the impulse to identify, mark, and analyze whiteness does not lead into a trap of reifying the very concept of "race" that it is intended to question. The growing interest in theoretical whiteness risks producing an indifferent cultural pluralism which does little to engage with the changing formations of local and global racisms. Mike Hill faces this area of contradiction that lies at the heart of the study of whiteness in another useful overview of recent work. He identifies the scholarship that emerged in the early 1990s as a "first wave of white critique," stating that it established whiteness as a distinct and relatively recent historical fiction (Hill, 1997:2). He views it as ironic that this work was quickly problematized, or rather, compromised, by this "newfound attention to the quintessentially unremarkable." Putting his finger directly on the erratic pulse of "white writing," he continues:

> ...the presence of whiteness alas within our critical reach creates a certain inevitable awkwardness of distance. Whiteness becomes something we both claim (single out for critique) and avoid (in claiming whiteness for critique, what else can we be, if we happen to be identifiably white?) (Hill, 1997:3)

Hill suggests that this conflict, characterized by "the epistemological stickiness and ontological wiggling immanent in whiteness" (Hill 1997:3) might be called a second wave of white critique. By this satisfyingly graphic formulation I think he is trying to represent the problem that many designated "white" writers confess to in their own work: their motivation stems partly from a recognition that their "whiteness" ties them historically into a system of race privilege from which it is hard to escape; but by providing a critique of whiteness they begin to situate themselves outside that system. Does this mean that they are in two places at once? This is the conflict that opens up questions of knowing and being which cannot be answered definitively. In a reference to Audrey Lorde's exhortation to her readers to "reach down into that place of knowledge...and touch that terror and loathing of any difference that lives there," Hill writes that the limits of this conflict over whiteness is "to articulate critically the power and banality of race privilege and to discover deep down (and of course on the surface) a 'face of terror' not unlike what one sees all around." He suggests that it is fruitful to return to feminist

111

writing from the 1970s and 1980s in order to understand how to theorize this fraught relationship between identity and politics, knowledge and consciousness. He specifically cites feminism as the place where activists, writers, and thinkers came to terms with the discovery that "distinctions of oppression are both portable and prolific" (Hill, 1997:5). Citing African American feminists like bell hooks and Lorde, he writes that "White feminists heard the charge that there were margins other than (and marginal to) those on which white women were located. That is, marginality is relational (but not relative or arbitrary)."

Hill is particularly interested in the way that some feminists responded to these charges. Marilyn Frye, for example, faced what she saw as a double bind inherent in white critique – a kind of "damned if you do, damned if you don't" situation. Her solution, as he reads it, is to call for disaffiliation from the structures of white privilege without losing sight of the way that gender and class compound identity and complicate the idea that individuals can simply choose to opt out of a category that they consider problematic: "It might indeed be said as a feminist lesson that 'disaffiliation' from the white race, its categorical disintegration, is perhaps a form of gendered interrogation already in progress" (Hill, 1997:7). This is a difficult argument to compress, but an important point to grasp because the "epistemological stickiness" and "ontological wiggling" are so frequently cited as a reason to doubt the efficacy of the whole project of white critique, throwing the baby out with the bathwater so to speak – or at least caricaturing it as narcissism in the manner of Margaret Talbot in the *New York Times*. Hill's optimism that many writers are becoming bold enough to face the "trouble spots" of identity politics by moving into a space that is "neither white nor its opposite" is welcome, but what does it suggest about the need for an explicit politics of location in order to carry it out? To put this bluntly – how do we – whether in the USA, in Europe, Australia, or South Africa – study the discursive production of whiteness in all its locally and socially differentiated forms, and how much does it matter not who we are when we do this, but where we are, theoretically when we do it? Where and how should critics and enemies of whiteness locate or reposition ourselves and what are the most effective strategies for forcing a separation between an imposed identity – still based primarily on skin color – on the one hand and the less visible signs of identification and political solidarity on the other? Adrienne Rich's insightful arguments in "Notes Towards the Politics of Location" (1986:210–31) have helped feminists to formulate similar questions in relation to gender, and I have also found it useful to adapt what Charles Taylor (1990) has called "a language of perspicuous contrast" in relation to the scrutiny of whiteness.

Although he is writing strictly about the relationship between social scientists and their anthropological subjects, Taylor's attempts to formulate an "interpretive view" of the structure of interaction between agent and subject is rather helpful in theorizing the position of the ethnographer of whiteness. Take this passage, for instance, which is worth quoting at length to illustrate his method of steering a course between two unwelcome opposites:

> The interpretive view, I want to argue, avoids the two equal and opposite mistakes: on one hand, of ignoring self-descriptions [of white identity, white culture, white experience] altogether, and attempting to operate in some neutral "scientific" language; on the other hand, of taking these descriptions with ultimate seriousness, so that they become incorrigible. Social theory in general, and political theory especially, is very much in the business

of correcting common sense understanding. It is of very little use unless it goes beyond, unless it frequently challenges and negates what we think we are doing, saying, feeling, aiming at. But its criterion of success is that it makes us as agents more comprehensible, that it makes sense of what we feel, do, aim at. And this it cannot do without getting clear on what we think about our action and feeling. That is, after all, what offers the puzzle which theory tries to resolve...For otherwise, we may have an interesting, speculative rational reconstruction...but no way of showing that it actually *explains* anything. (Taylor, 1990:124–5)

Although it might actually be quite appropriate to take the view of the modern ethnographer investigating the primitive tribalism of whiteness, I make no apologies for borrowing Taylor's insights on ethnographic work made in another context, nor am I suggesting that the whole of his argument fits here. My point is simply that the study of whiteness offers to every individual caught up in racial discourse against their will potentially new opportunities to make sense of self and other, and to recognize a degree of agency in challenging (and therefore changing) the many ways in which the beneficiaries of racial hierarchy are complicit with injustice.

Early on I used Homi Bhabha's elegant description of Anish Kapoor's installation to suggest the importance of looking at the structures and tentacles of white supremacy from different angles. The analogy ends here, however, for though it may be intriguing to wander to and fro in front of "When I am Pregnant," enjoying the sensation produced by the white bump disappearing before one's eyes, the student of whiteness requires a map of possibilities and a steady compass to make sense of the field. In societies structured so deeply by racial hierarchies that operate through and simultaneously with systems of gender, sexuality, and class, a politics for social justice must entail wilfully stepping beyond safe limits, without losing a sense of direction in exposing and destroying the technologies of white power.

References

Bhabha, Homi (1998) "Anish Kapoor: Making emptiness," in *Anish Kapoor*. Berkeley: University of California Press, pp.11–41.

Carter, Robert T. (1997) "Is white a race? Expressions of white racial identity," in Michelle Fine, Lois Weis, Linda C. Powell, and L. Mun Wong (eds.), *Off White: Readings on Race, Power and Society*. New York: Routledge, pp.198–209.

Delgado, Richard, and Stefancic, Jean (eds.) (1997) *Critical White Studies: Looking Behind the Mirror*. Philadelphia: Temple University Press.

Du Bois, W.E.B. ([1920] 1990) *Darkwater: Voices from Within the Veil*. Millwood, NY: Kraus-Thomson.

Dyer, Richard (1988) "White". *Screen* 29,4:44–65.

Dyer, Richard (1997) *White*. London: Routledge.

Ellison, Ralph (1964) *Shadow and Act*. New York: Random House.

Fisher Fishkin, Shelley (1995) "Interrogating 'whiteness,' complicating 'blackness': Remapping American culture." *American Quarterly* 47,3:428–66.

Frankenberg, Ruth (1993) *White Women, Race Matters: The Social Construction of Whiteness*. New York: Routledge.

Frankenberg, Ruth (ed.) (1997) *Displacing Whiteness: Essays in Social and Cultural Criticism*. Durham, NC: Duke University Press.

113

Gorz, André (1982) *Farewell to the Working Class*. London: Pluto Press.

Hale, Grace Elizabeth (1998) *Making Whiteness: The Culture of Segregation in the South 1890–1940*. New York: Pantheon Books.

Hill, Mike (ed.) (1997) *Whiteness: A Critical Reader*. New York: New York University Press.

Ignatiev, Noel and Garvey, John (eds.) (1996) *Race Traitor*. New York: Routledge.

Lazarre, Jane (1996) *Beyond the Whiteness of Whiteness: Memoir of a White Mother of Black Sons*. Durham, NC: Duke University Press.

Lipsitz, George (1995) "The possessive investment in whiteness: Racialized social democracy and the 'white' problem in American studies." *American Quarterly* 47,3:369–87.

Morrison, Toni (1992) *Playing in the Dark: Whiteness and the Literary Imagination*. Cambridge, MA: Harvard University Press.

Rich, Adrienne (1986) *Blood, Bread and Poetry*. London: Virago.

Roediger, David R. (1991) *The Wages of Whiteness: Race and the Making of the American Working Class*. London: Verso.

Roediger, David R. (1994) *Towards the Abolition of Whiteness*. London: Verso.

Roediger, David R. (1998) *Black on White: Black Writers on What it Means to be White*. New York: Schocken.

Talbot, Margaret (1997) "Getting credit for being white." *New York Times Magazine* 30 November, 1997:116–19.

Taylor, Charles (1990) *Philosophy in the Human Sciences*. Cambridge, UK: Cambridge University Press.

Twine, France Winddance (1998) "The white mother: Blackness, whiteness, and interracial families," *Transition* 73:144–54.

Ware, Vron (1992) *Beyond the Pale: White Women, Racism and History*. London: Verso.

Ware, Vron (1997a) "Purity and danger: Race, gender and tales of sex tourism," in Angela McRobbie (ed.) *Back to Reality?* Manchester, UK: Manchester University Press, pp.133–51.

Ware, Vron (1997b) "Island racism: Gender, place and white power," in Ruth Frankenberg (ed.) *Displacing Whiteness*. Durham, NC: Duke University Press, pp.283–310.

Ware, Vron and Back, Les (2001) *Out of Whiteness: Color, Politics, and Culture*. Chicago: University of Chicago Press.

Wray, Matt and Newitz, Annalee (1997) *White Trash*. New York: Routledge.

Chapter 10

Citizenship

Marco Martiniello

Introduction

The last decade has witnessed a return of the citizen and of citizenship both in academic and in political discourse (Kymlicka and Norman, 1994). The number of research projects, books, journals, conferences, and articles dealing with citizenship issues has also increased dramatically. The words "citizenship" and "citizen" are used in a growing number of different areas and social contexts. Whereas these words were traditionally linked exclusively to human beings, there are now discussions about the citizenship of plants, of animals, and of corporations. In many ways, the concept of citizenship has certainly become a political slogan.

But despite a renewed extensive academic interest in citizenship issues, a comprehensive theory of citizenship largely accepted by the academic community is still missing (Barbalet, 1988). Some scholars stress the formal dimension of citizenship, namely the juridical link between the individual and the state. Others reduce it to a set of rights enjoyed by the individual by virtue of her or his belonging to a national community. Others find it more useful to study the participatory dimensions of citizenship in order to understand new forms of political mobilization and social movements in contemporary societies. Dialogue and exchange between these scholars, who often seem to be actually interested in quite different phenomena and processes, is far from being easy. Dialogue between academics and policy makers and/or politicians is often even more problematic.

At least three features characterize current debates on citizenship issues. First, these discussions are very often linked to other topical academic and political discussions such as the debates on international migration, the debates on the management and the impact of cultural diversity, and the debate on the place of the nation-state in the post-Cold War era. Secondly, liberal approaches to all these issues seem to predominate in academia whereas among the general public and within the political field illiberal stands on ethnicity, nationalism, citizenship, and multiculturalism increasingly find a channel of expression in extreme right-wing and conservative politics. This gap between academic liberalism and a growing illiberalism of the general public and the political field is an important contextual data to be taken into account in our attempts. Thirdly, are misunderstandings and the confusion is often increased by the fact that they may be very difficult to distinguish in the literature between normative concerns, on the one hand, and explanatory concerns, on the other hand: sometimes considerations fundamentally aimed at answering the question "what ought to be?" are presented as mere analyses of the situation, and vice versa.

The aim of this chapter is to make sense of contemporary debates on citizenship. The first section defines modern citizenship. The second section locates citizenship in the social, economic, and political contexts in which it historically developed and which are associated with the nation-state. The third section examines the main challenges to citizenship which are a consequence of recent social, economic, and political changes and which call for a redefinition of citizenship. The fourth section deals with the issue of citizenship beyond the nation-state. On the one hand modern citizenship is deeply linked to the nation-state. On the other hand, the importance of the nation-state has recently been significantly reduced, with both the emergence of supranational forms of govern- ance and of subnational ones, as well as with the acceleration of the globalization of the economy. These developments undoubtedly raise the question of what citizenship beyond the nation-state means.

Defining Modern Citizenship

As pointed out above, there is no general agreement on the definition of citizenship, let alone on its meaning and scope. Conceptions of citizenship vary according to the academic discipline but also according to the school of thought within the various academic disciplines. Furthermore, language is often an obstacle to mutual understanding. For example, the English word citizenship can be translated in French by *citoyenneté* but also by *nationalité*. The distinction between *nationalité* and *citoyenneté* covers approximately the distinction between formal citizenship and substantive citizenship. The former refers to a formal link between an individual and a state, to the individual belonging to a nation-state which is juridically sanctioned by the possession of an identity card or passport of that state. The latter refers to the bundle of civil, political, social, and also cultural rights enjoyed by an individual, traditionally by virtue of her or his belonging to the national community. It also refers to the participation of the individual in the management of the public affairs of a given national and political community. These realities are clearly linked but they as clearly need to be distinguished.

Therefore, in order to avoid further misunderstandings, it is useful to adopt a starting definition of citizenship. Three main features characterize modern citizenship. First, citizenship is a juridical status granting civil, political, and social rights and duties to the individual members of a political collectivity, traditionally a state (Marshall, 1992). Secondly, citizenship refers to a set of specific social roles (voter, activist, etc.) performed by citizens and through which they express choices with regard to the management of public affairs and hence participation in government (Leca, 1991). Citizenship thus implies some sort of political competence. Citizens have the ability to use their status in order to defend their interests in the political game. Thirdly, citizenship also refers to a set of moral qualities thought to be crucial for the existence of the good citizen. These qualities are often referred to as the expression of civism. The recognition of the existence and the primacy of public interest transcending private ones are crucial aspects of civism.

Modern Citizenship in Context

A truly comprehensive account of citizenship would go back to antique Greece and Rome to find the first theories of citizenship (Heater, 1990). From there, on the trip back to the present century we would need to stop at the Italian Rinascita and at the French and American Revolutions which are generally seen as the cradles of modern citizenship (Falk, 1994). It developed simultaneously with the development and the propagation of the nation-state since the eighteenth century. For reasons of space, I will focus on the twentieth century and especially on the second part of it.

Contemporary citizenship has developed in a postwar context characterized by the predominance of the idea of nation-state, the reconstruction of democracy, a capitalist economy and a class-divided social system. Logically the concept of citizenship must be understood in relation with the concepts of nation-state, of democracy, of capitalism, and of social class.

Even though there was originally no conceptual link between citizenship and national identity or even nationality (Habermas, 1994), the boundaries between these categories have progressively been juridically blurred (Touraine, 1994): the individual enjoys the rights associated with citizenship (civil, political, social) because she or he belongs to a political community defined as a nation – the nation-state. In order to get full substantial citizenship rights, formal citizenship – that is, a juridically recognized belonging to the nation – is required. Modern citizenship is therefore largely national.

If the nation-state is the territorial boundary of citizenship, it is also the cultural boundary of citizenship. The nation-state supposes a perfect congruence between the political organization and the cultural organization. Citizens are assumed to share the same culture since they belong to the nation and to the state. Cultural homogeneity is considered to be a given, even in the work of T. H. Marshall. The notion of citizenship is also closely linked to democracy. The citizen ideally participates in the exercise of political power, at least through the voting process. Without the mandate temporarily given by the body of citizens the government has no legitimacy. The idea of citizenship supposes that elected governments and political leaders are accountable to the citizens (Falk, 1994). This principle of accountability is at the core of any democratic system.

Ideally, citizens are governed at the same time as they govern. In order to perform this double role, the citizen must enjoy some autonomy, some skills, and display loyalty toward the political community. There is nevertheless considerable disagreement between scholars about the degree and the nature of citizens' participation. It can be captured by the distinction between passive citizenship and active citizenship (Turner, 1990). Passive citizenship is developed from above by the state, which grants rights to the citizens. The latter are expected merely to exercise their rights. They are, for instance, supposed to cast their vote. On the contrary, active citizenship is developed from below through citizens' mobilization in various types of social and political movements. The citizens are not simply users of rights but active social and political agents who use their rights to claim new and/or better ones. The quality of democracy seems higher in the second case than in the first.

According to Marshall (1992) civil rights are a fundamental dimension of citizenship. The private property right, on which the whole capitalist economy is based, is one of those civil rights. Therefore, one could say that citizenship in its civil dimension has

117

made the development of capitalism possible and has contributed to reinforce social and economic inequalities in the capitalist mode of production (Barbalet, 1988).

After World War II economic growth and full employment made the creation of the welfare state possible in which citizenship (in its social dimension) served as a buffer between the impulses of the market and socioeconomic inequalities. Financed by income taxes collected by the state, social citizenship was in a way a method of redistribution of resources to the benefit of those citizens who were temporarily unable to fulfill their needs. It was a key element of a solidarity mechanism which relieved social and economic inequalities while simultaneously rendering them acceptable in principle. The current developments toward a global economy call for an adaptation of the capitalist welfare-state (Vogel and Moran, 1991). Citizenship will probably not be left untouched in this process.

In Marshall's view (1992), the concept of social class was central to make sense of divisions and differentiation in modern Britain. One of the main characteristics of British society was that it was a hierarchy of social classes between which the boundaries were hermetic. The development of modern citizenship would not have been possible without the struggle of the working class for its rights. But Barbalet (1988) may be correct when he states that it was the result of a convergence between the interests of the working class and those of the ruling class.

Citizenship is anyway paradoxical. On the one hand, it organizes the formal equality of all citizens in the face of the law. They all theoretically enjoy the same rights and duties. Citizenship is thus a form of social incorporation and a necessary condition for social integration. But on the other hand, persistent social and economic inequalities hinder the exercise of citizenship rights for those social classes located at the lower end of the class structure. This paradox can engender frustration and lead to social conflict when formally recognized rights cannot be satisfactorily exercised by all social groups (Turner, 1993).

The Main Challenges to Modern Citizenship

Political, social, economic, and cultural conditions which characterized the context in which modern citizenship developed have largely been altered in the last decades. The nation-state has lost the monopoly of economic and political regulation with the emergence of supranational and subnational regional powers. In many societies democracy is being challenged by extreme right-wing parties which had been totally discredited after World War II but which now find new fertile ground in poverty and social exclusion. With the collapse of most communist regimes, capitalism has no other enemy than itself. It has become increasingly global with the explosion of new technologies of information and communication. The class structure in the postindustrial capitalist era is also different than in the industrial era. The processes of inclusion and exclusion have taken new shapes. Furthermore, new groups organize and mobilize to claim rights, recognition, or special treatment (ethnocultural minorities, sexual minorities, etc.).

At least four main contemporary challenges to modern citizenship need to be explored: international migration, cultural diversity, gender relations, and social and economic exclusion. The issue of the impact of international migration on the evolution of citizenship is a difficult one. Migration flows always lead to the permanent settlement of migrants and their families on the soil of a state of which they are not formally members. Clearly, the presence of a migrant origin population questions the link between formal citizenship and substantial citizenship. Nowadays, is formal membership of a state (*nationalité*) still the main necessary condition for being granted integral substantial citizenship (*citoyenneté*) and should it be so (Bottomore, 1992)? In many immigration countries a denizenship regime conferring some citizenship rights (civil, social, and even political) to immigrant aliens has been established (Hammar, 1990) but nowhere is integral substantial citizenship granted to nonmembers of the nation. Some argue that it should not be the case and that newcomers should instead get a right to become full formal members of the state after a period of residence, in other words to naturalize (Carens, 1989). Others advocate a "new citizenship" (Bouamama, 1991; Withol de Wenden, 1987) in which residence in a country would replace formal membership as the main condition for gaining full substantial citizenship rights. Others claim for a postnational form of membership in which human rights would be the legitimizing principle of citizenship for nonnationals as well as for nationals (Soysal, 1994). It is anyway crucial to underscore that if the issue of the disconnection of formal membership and substantial citizenship is high on the academic agenda (Bauböck, 1996; Spinner, 1994; Jacobson, 1996) it is due to the globalization of migration. As in the past, migration has a crucial impact on the evolution of modern citizenship.

Cultural heterogeneity constitutes a real test of the strength of citizenship rights. Modern citizenship emerged in societies which saw themselves as profoundly mono-cultural. It rested on a universalist ideal according to which all citizens were granted the same rights and duties. Nowadays, most societies are *de facto* multicultural. Ethno-cultural and national minorities often make specific claims (recognition, autonomy, special treatment, etc.). Minority claims have for a long time been considered to be incompatible with modern citizenship precisely because they were considered to be particularistic as opposed to universalist and because they were asking for collective as opposed to individual rights. Attempts to reconcile universalism and particularism, individual rights and collective rights, in a renewed conception of citizenship have been developed by political theorists and sociologists who have introduced the notion of multicultural citizenship (Castles, 1994; Kymlicka, 1995).

Until recently citizenship studies did not pay much attention to gender and even less to sexual orientation. Citizenship was a gendered notion that did not take into account the various forms of discrimination and inequalities faced by women. According to feminist thinking, citizenship was in a way a tool of male domination. After World War II, the position of women improved in terms of civil rights, economic autonomy, and political power. But historically the unequal social position of women has been a challenge to the universalistic ideal of citizenship and any discussion on the evolution of citizenship now tends to avoid gender-biased views.

Finally, the rise of modern citizenship has not ended social and economic inequalities. On the contrary, the gap between the haves and the have-nots, the included and the excluded, seems to be growing even in overall wealthy countries. The growth of poverty coincides with the erosion of social rights. Increasingly, the poor and the excluded tend to be seen not as holders of rights but as objects of charity. Most of the poor and the excluded are formally members of the state but they are either denied some rights or unable to exercise them. This situation certainly challenges modern citizenship and its universalist and inclusive ideals.

The changes of context and the challenges to modern citizenship reveal what some authors see as a crisis of citizenship (Turner, 1993). It seems more to be a transition. What is at stake is not a return to a previous stage of citizenship but an enlargement of the social, political, temporal, and behavioral boundaries of citizenship (Vogel and Moran, 1991) by including new categories of individuals in the body of citizens and by including new citizenship rights in a renewed conception of citizenship rights (Barbalet, 1988).

Citizenship Beyond the Nation-state

The predominance of the nation-state in which citizenship historically developed has been seriously challenged over the past decades. Therefore, the exclusive location of citizenship within the cultural and geographical borders of the nation-state is increasingly problematic (Turner, 1993). In a global world in which political boundaries and cultural boundaries very rarely coincide, citizenship can be expected to develop beyond the nation-state. The idea is not new. Immanuel Kant, for example, imagined a global citizenship based on cosmopolitan institutions and laws. The question is: how is a citizenship beyond the nation-state going to develop? What are the various projects of postnational citizenship? Various projects have been presented, such as the postnational model of membership (Soysal, 1994), the global citizenship model (Falk, 1994), the multiple citizenship model (Heater 1990), and the ecological citizenship model (Van Steenbergen, 1994). For reasons of space, I will concentrate on the citizenship that is developing in the context of the European integration process: citizenship of the European Union.

Historically, the European integration process was from the outset the exclusive matter of small bureaucratic and political elites which were in charge both of the European decision-making process and of the production of knowledge about European integration. The citizens of the Member States did not show a deep interest in what was going on and, anyway, they were not often consulted by the European elites. According to several observers, the Maastricht Treaty which entered into force on 1 November, 1993 buried the old technocratic, economic, and elitist Europe and opened the way for a new political Europe in the making of which the citizens were going to play a central part. In other words, the Treaty on the European Union was supposed to mark a complete change of nature of the integration process. Whether this was the case or not is a very complex and and contested issue which is not going to be discussed here. But in terms of European Union citizenship, it is indisputable that the Maastricht Treaty, for the first time in the history of European integration, gave some juridical basis to that notion.

As a matter of fact, the Maastricht Treaty sets out citizenship of the Union. It concerns exclusively the nationals of one of the member states of the European Union. It consists of the following set of rights: the rights of freedom of movement and residence on the territory of the member states, the right to vote and to be elected in the local elections and in the elections of the European Parliament in the member state of residence, the right to diplomatic protection in a third country, the right to petition the European Parliament as well as the possibility to appeal to a European ombudsman. In legal terms, EU citizenship is undoubtedly only a minimal novelty in the sense that most of the rights it encompasses existed before either in some or in all the member states. But still it is clearly an attempt to conceive of citizenship beyond the nation-state.

Before and during the Intergovernmental Conference (IGC) which started in 1996 and led to the adoption of the Amsterdam Treaty in June 1997, several voices were raised calling for a revision and an extension of EU citizenship. In the end the IGC clarified the foundations of EU citizenship but it did not actually enlarge and expand the rights associated with it. The idea was to better define the rights and duties of both EU citizens and third-state citizens living in the EU as well as to enhance nondiscrimination and fundamental rights. Three changes introduced in the Amsterdam Treaty are worth mentioning: the changes in Article 8, the adoption of an antidiscrimination clause in the Amsterdam Treaty, and the adoption of Articles aimed at a better protection of human rights and fundamental liberties.

A sentence stating that EU citizenship completes national citizenship and does not replace it was added to Article 8.1. Clearly, this reinforces the approach of the Treaty of Maastricht, according to which EU citizenship is derived from national citizenship of one of the Member States. Consequently, this change closes the door for the time being to the granting of EU citizenship to third country nationals residing in the territory of the EU. The legal distinction between EU citizens and non-EU citizens is emphasized and this certainly harms the status of the latter. In that sense, this change can be interpreted as a setback since it emphasizes the link between EU citizenship and national citizenship, between citizenship and nationality, whereas EU citizenship was often presented as an attempt to break this link: more than ever the first condition to be recognized as a EU citizen is to be a national citizen of one of the member states.

Furthermore, a third paragraph is added to Article 8D. It states that EU citizens can write to any EU institution in the European language of their choice and get a reply in that same language. This is undoubtedly a step towards more transparency and non-discrimination but its scope remains quite limited.

For the rest, Article 8 of the Maastricht Treaty is left untouched in the new Amsterdam Treaty which has caused a huge disappointment among antidiscrimination and proimmigrant activists throughout Europe who had not abandoned their hopes earlier.

A more positive aspect is the introduction of an antidiscrimination clause in the Treaty of Amsterdam which could potentially strengthen EU citizenship. Article 6a of the Treaty states that the Council can adopt adequate measures to combat discrimination based on gender, race, ethnic origin, religion, age, sexual preference, and handicap. This new article is progress in the sense that for the first time the principle of nondiscrimination is given a legal basis on which political and legal action can be based. It seems to concern both EU and non-EU citizens. This would have been clearer if nationality had been included in the basis for discrimination list. For the time being discrimination based on nationality remains covered by the old Article 6. In practice, the implementation of Article 6a will depend on the emergence of the same political will at the EU level: a unanimous decision is required in order to implement any measure to combat discrimination as defined in Article 6a. This type of decision is never taken easily in the European context.

Finally, fundamental human rights are slightly reinforced through the introduction of paragraph 1 in Article F of the Treaty on European Union. It states that the European Union is grounded on the principles of democracy, freedom, the respect of human rights, and fundamental liberties. In other words, all member states are committed to respect these principles. In case of nonrespect by one of the member states, it may temporarily lose its voting right.

Clearly, despite some progress, the opportunity of the IGC to develop EU citizenship was more lost than taken. The Amsterdam Treaty confirms to a large extent the philosophy of the Maastricht Treaty as far as EU citizenship is concerned. For the time being EU citizenship as an attempt to develop citizenship beyond the nation-state is far from being an indisputable success.

Conclusion

It appears clearly that modern citizenship as it developed within the nation-state has become in part obsolete. But it also seems that we are still searching for a new multidimensional concept of citizenship which would be more adapted to the complexity of the global world. In the future, citizenship understood as a juridical status granting civil, political, and social rights and duties to the individual members of a political collectivity, as a set of specific social roles (voter, activist, etc.) performed by the citizen and as a set of moral qualities often referred to as the expression of civism, can be expected to be located not only at the nation-state level, but also locally at the regional level (for example, EU citizenship) and at the global level. Will it be possible to coordinate these various dimensions and locations of the multiple citizenship of the future? Only time will tell.

References

Barbalet, J. M. (1988) *Citizenship*. Milton Keynes, UK: Open University Press.

Bauböck, R. (ed.) (1994) *From Aliens to Citizens. Redefining the Legal Status of Immigrants in Europe*. Aldershot, UK: Avebury.

Bauböck, R. (1996) *Transnational Citizenship. Membership and Rights in International Migration*. Aldershot, UK: Edward Elgar.

Bottomore, T. (1992) "Citizenship and social class, forty years on," in T. H. Marshall and T. Bottomore *Citizenship and Social Class*. London: Pluto Press, pp.55–93.

Bouamama, S. (1991) *Vers une nouvelle citoyenneté. Crise de la pensée laïque [Towards a new citizenship. The crisis of secular thinking]*. Lille, France: La Boîte de Pandore.

Brubaker, W. R. (ed.) (1989) *Immigration and the Politics of Citizenship in Europe and North America*. New York: University Press of America.

Carens, J. H. (1989) "Membership and morality: Admission to citizenship in liberal democratic states," in W. R. Brubaker (ed.) *Immigration and the Politics of Citizenship in Europe and North America*. New York: University Press of America, pp.31–50.

Castles, S. (1994) "Democracy and multicultural citizenship: Australian debates and their relevance for Western Europe," in R. Bauböck (ed.) *From Aliens to Citizens. Redefining the Legal Status of Immigrants in Europe*. Aldershot, UK: Avebury, pp.3–27.

Falk, R. (1994) "The making of global citizenship," in B. Van Steenbergen (ed.) *The Condition of Citizenship*. London: Sage, pp.127–40.

Habermas, J. (1994) "Citizenship and national identity," in B. Van Steenbergen (ed.) *The Condition of Citizenship*. London: Sage, pp.20–35.

Hammar, T. (1990) *Democracy and the Nation State*. Aldershot, UK: Avebury.

Heater, D. (1990) *Citizenship. The Civic Ideal in World History, Politics and Education*. London: Longman.

Jacobson, D. (1996) *Rights Across Borders. Immigration and the Decline of Citizenship*. Baltimore, MD: The Johns Hopkins University Press.

Kymlicka, W. (1995) *Multicultural Citizenship*. Oxford: Oxford University Press.

Kymlicka, W. and Norman, W. (1994) "Return of the citizen: A survey of recent work on citizenship theory." *Ethics* 104:352–81.

Leca, J. (1991) "La citoyenneté en question [Questions of citizenship]," in P.-A. Taguieff (ed.), *Face au racisme 2. Analyses, hypothèses, perspectives [Confronting racism 2. Analyses, hypotheses, perspectives]*. Paris: La découverte, pp.311–36.

Marshall, T. H. (1992) "Citizenship and social class," in T. H. Marshall and T. Bottomore *Citizenship and Social Class*. London: Pluto Press, pp.3–51.

Marshall, T. H. and Bottomore, T. (1992) *Citizenship and Social Class*. London: Pluto Press.

Martiniello, M. (ed.) (1995) *Migration, Citizenship and Ethno-national Identities in the European Union*. Aldershot: Avebury.

Sorensen, J. M. (1996) *The Exclusive European Citizenship. The Case for Refugees and Immigrants in the European Union*. Aldershot, UK: Avebury.

Soysal, Y. (1994) *The Limits of Citizenship. Migrants and Postnational Membership in Europe*. Chicago: University of Chicago Press.

Spinner, J. (1994) *The Boundaries of Citizenship. Race, Ethnicity, and Nationality in the Liberal State*. Baltimore, MD: The Johns Hopkins University Press.

Touraine, A. (1994) *Qu'est-ce que la démocratie? [What is democracy?]*. Paris: Fayard.

Turner, B. S. (1990) "Outline of a theory of citizenship." *Sociology* 24,2:189–217.

Turner, B. S. (1993) *Citizenship and Social Theory*. London: Sage.

Van Steenbergen, B. (ed.) (1994) *The Condition of Citizenship*. London: Sage.

Vogel, U. and Moran, M. (eds.) (1991) *The Frontiers of Citizenship*. London: Macmillan.

Wiener, A. (1998) *"European" Citizenship Practice. Building Institutions of a Nation-state*. Boulder, CO: Westview Press.

Withol de Wenden, C. (1987) *Citoyenneté, nationalité et immigration. [Citizenship, Nationality and Immigration]*. Paris: Arcantère Editions.

Chapter 11

Multiculturalism

Stephen May

There is currently a growing awareness that the traditional organization of modern Western democratic nation-states is not as equitable, or as egalitarian, as many have assumed it to be. In particular, the notion of a singular, common culture has been brought into serious question by a wide range of minority groups who have argued that it no longer adequately represents, if it ever did, the multiethnic composition of modern nation-states. Concomitantly, minority groups have argued for greater public recognition and representation in the public or civic realm of their ethnic, cultural, linguistic and/or religious identities.[1] This ideology or movement, call it what you will, has come to be known as multiculturalism. Its cumulative effect over the last 30–40 years has recently led Nathan Glazer (1998), a long-time skeptic of multiculturalism, to concede that "we are all multiculturalists now." Multiculturalism, at least in his view, has finally "won" because the issue of greater public representation for minority groups is increasingly commonplace in discussions of democracy and representation in modern Western nation-states.

As a proponent of multiculturalism, I do not share Glazer's sense of wearied resignation. Nor, however, do I share his sense of inevitability, for it seems to me that while multiculturalism has accomplished much since its origins in the 1960s, it still has many obstacles yet to overcome. As Carlos Torres notes, for example:

> the multitude of tasks confronting multiculturalism is overwhelming. They include the attempt to develop a sensible, theoretically refined, and defensible new metatheoretical and theoretical territory that would create the foundations for multiculturalism as a paradigm; the attempt to establish its epistemological and logical premise around notions of experience, narrative, voice, agency and identity; the attempt to pursue empirical research linking culture/power/knowledge with equality/inequality/discrimination; and the need to defend multiculturalism from the conservative Right that has demonized multiculturalism as an unpatriotic movement. (Torres, 1998:446)

Taken in reverse order, the challenges Torres highlights can be usefully paraphrased as:

- the ongoing critique of multiculturalism from the right;
- the tendency of multiculturalism to concentrate on culture at the expense of structural concerns such as racism;

- the challenges that postmodernist understandings of identity present for multiculturalism;
- the urgent need to develop a multiculturalist paradigm that effectively addresses – and, where necessary, redresses – all of the above.

In what follows, I will chart the multiculturalist responses to these four broad challenges. I will conclude by arguing that "critical multiculturalism" offers us the best means by which multiculturalism as a paradigm might proceed in the twenty-first century.

"Preserving" the Nation-state

There are obvious advantages to the nation-state which help to explain its ongoing ascendancy. It liberates individuals from the tyranny of narrow communities, guarantees their personal autonomy, equality, and common citizenship, and provides the basis for a collectively shared way of life (Parekh, 1995). Or at least it does so in theory. As such, it is often viewed as the apogee of modernity and progress – representing in clear political terms the triumph of universalism over particularism, citizenship over identity, and individual rights over collective rights. This is certainly the view of the nation-state lionized by a wide range of conservative political commentators (e.g., Bloom, 1987; Bullivant, 1981; Glazer, 1975; Hirsch, 1987; Schlesinger, 1992). It is also, of course, the position most closely associated with the Rawlsian strain of orthodox liberal theory (see, in particular, Rawls, 1971).[2]

The critique of multiculturalism which inevitably ensues from this position can be usefully couched in terms of what Brian Bullivant (1981) has called "the pluralist dilemma." The pluralist dilemma, for Bullivant, is "the problem of reconciling the diverse political claims of constituent groups and individuals in a pluralist society with the claims of the nation-state as a whole" (1981:x); what he elsewhere describes as the competing aims of "civism" and "pluralism." Or, to put it another way, the pluralist dilemma requires a complex balancing act between two countervailing pressures – the need to maintain social cohesion on the one hand with, on the other, a responsibility to recognize and incorporate ethnic, linguistic, and cultural diversity within the nation-state.

Historically, two contrasting approaches have been adopted in response to the pluralist dilemma which Gordon (1978, 1981) has described as "liberal pluralism" and "corporate pluralism." Liberal pluralism is characterized by the absence, even prohibition, of any ethnic, religious, or linguistic minority group possessing separate standing before the law or government. Its central tenets can be traced back to the French Revolution and Rousseau's conception of the modern polity as comprising three inseparable features: freedom (nondomination), the absence of differentiated roles, and a very tight common purpose. On this view, the margin for recognizing difference within the modern nation-state is very small (Taylor, 1994). Corporate pluralism (aka multiculturalism) involves, in contrast, the recognition of minority groups as legally constituted entities, on the basis of which, and depending on their size and influence, economic, social, and political awards are allocated. Glazer (1975) and Walzer (1992, 1994) draw similar distinctions between an approach based on "nondiscrimination" – which involves, in Glazer's memorable phrase, the "salutary neglect" of the state towards ethnic minorities – and a "corporatist" (Walzer) or "group rights" (Glazer) model.

It is clear, however, that for conservative and orthodox liberal commentators only liberal pluralism will do. In the end, civism *must* be favored over pluralism while the corporatist intentions of multiculturalism must be specifically disavowed. This is because, in their view, only the current organization of nation-states – represented most clearly by the neutrality of the civic realm – can ensure personal autonomy, equality, and common citizenship (at least in theory). In contrast, multiculturalism is accused of replacing universalism with particularism and introducing ethnicity unnecessarily and unhelpfully into the civic realm – that is, "civil society" in Gramsci's (1971) sense of the term.[3] Where countenanced at all, alternative ethnic affiliations should be restricted solely to the private domain, since the formal recognition of collective (ethnic) identity is viewed as undermining personal and political autonomy, and fostering social and political fragmentation. As Will Kymlicka observes, "the near-universal response of [conservatives and] liberals has been one of active hostility to [multiculturalism]... schemes which single out minority cultures for special measures... appear irremediably unjust, a disguise for creating or maintaining... ethnic privilege" (Kymlicka, 1989:4). Any deviation from the strict principles of universal political citizenship and individual rights is seen as the first step down the road to apartheid.

How then can one respond effectively and convincingly to this broad conservative/liberal position; the first challenge facing multiculturalism?

The problem of individualism

First, the orthodox liberal construction of the person as *solely* a political being with rights and duties attached to their status as a *citizen* can be brought into question. Such a position does not countenance private identity, including a person's communal membership, as something warranting similar recognition. These latter dimensions are excluded from the public realm because their inevitable diversity would lead to the complicated business of the state mediating between different conceptions of "the good life" (Dworkin, 1978; Rawls, 1985). On this basis, personal *autonomy* – based on the political rights attributable to citizenship – always takes precedence over personal (and collective) *identity* and the widely differing ways of life which constitute the latter. In effect, personal and political participation in liberal democracies, as it has come to be constructed, ends up denying group difference and posits all persons as interchangeable from a moral and political point of view (Young, 1993).

However, this strict separation of citizenship and identity in the modern polity understates, and at times disavows, the significance of wider communal affiliations, including ethnicity, to the construction of individual identity. As Michael Sandel (1982) observes, in a communitarian critique of liberalism, there is no such thing as the "unencumbered self" – we are all, to some extent, *situated* within wider communities which shape and influence who we are.[4] Likewise, Charles Taylor argues that identity "is who we are, 'where we're coming from.' As such, it is the background against which our tastes and desires and opinions and aspirations make sense" (1994:33–4). These critics also highlight the obvious point that certain goods such as language, culture, and sovereignty cannot be experienced alone; they are, by definition, communally shared goods. A failure to account for these communal goods, however, has led to a view of rights within liberal democracy which is inherently individualistic and which cannot appreciate the pursuit of such goods other than derivatively (Taylor, 1994; Van Dyke, 1977). In short, individualistic conceptions of the good life may preclude shared community values that are central to one's identity (Kymlicka, 1989, 1995a). Conversely, as Habermas has put it, "a correctly understood theory of [citizenship] rights requires a politics of recognition that protects the individual in the life contexts in which his or her identity is formed" (1994:113).

The problem of neutrality

The dissociation of citizenship from individual identity, and the social and cultural context in which the latter is inevitably formed, highlights a related problem with conservative/liberal critiques of multiculturalism – a misplaced faith in the neutral state. Despite what conservative and liberal commentators would have us believe, ethnicity has never been absent from the civic realm. Rather, the civic realm represents the particular (although not necessarily exclusive) *communal* interests and values of the dominant ethnic group *as if* these values were held by all. In Charles Taylor's analysis, the "supposedly neutral set of difference-blind principles [that constitute the liberal] politics of equal dignity is in fact a reflection of one hegemonic culture.... [it is] a particularism masquerading as the universal" (1994:43–4). In a similar vein, Iris Marion Young argues that if particular groups "have greater economic, political or social power, their group related experiences, points of view, or cultural assumptions will tend to become the norm, biasing the standards or procedures of achievement and inclusion that govern social, political and economic institutions" (1993:133). The result, as Michael Billig observes, is a "banal nationalism" which is simply "overlooked, forgotten, even theoretically denied" (1995:17) by members of the majority (ethnic) group who tend to equate unconsciously their ethnic and national identities as being one and the same. This process of elision, of course, also helps to explain why dominant groups so seldom come to define themselves as "ethnic," regarding this as the preserve of "minority" groups.

The problem of the homogeneous nation-state

Taylor and Young's analyses point us to the third problem with conservative/liberal formulations: if there is no neutrality with respect to ethnicity, there is even less likelihood of any national homogeneity, and yet conservative and orthodox liberal commentators tend to accept such national homogeneity as a historical and political given, as simply the proper application of Reason (Goldberg, 1994). Conversely, these same commentators criticize multiculturalism's promotion of group-based identities (and the cultures associated with them) as both "ethnic cheerleading," and "nationalist myth making" (Schlesinger, 1992). However, this begs the obvious question, well-rehearsed by now in the literature on nationalism, of the artificial, sometimes arbitrary, construction of national identity itself (see, for example, Anderson, 1991; Gellner, 1983; Hobsbawm, 1990; May, 2001). In effect, national identity is no more immune to charges of contructionism and historical revisionism than the group-based cultures associated with multiculturalism that conservatives and orthodox liberals so decry.

127

Such recognition also makes problematic a related charge of conservative/liberal commentators that group-based affiliations are essentially preservationist rather than transformative in nature – that they constitute a mere "politics of nostalgia" at odds with the contemporary world and the inexorable forces of progress (see, for example, Glazer, 1975; Porter, 1975; Schlesinger, 1992; Waldron, 1995). There is some validity to this position, particularly with respect to the problematic concept of "authenticity," and I will explore its implications more fully in my ensuing discussion of postmodernist critiques of multiculturalism. However, for the purposes of this present discussion, it is enough to point out that when conservative/liberal commentators make this charge against the "preservation" of ethnic minority cultures, they are fatally undermined by their own attempts to invoke, in effect, a majoritarian version of the same process – a prior, pre-eminent, and apparently *static* "national" identity to which all should subscribe. Such a position not only considerably understates the possibilities of holding dual or multiple identities, except oppositionally, it also allows no room for a dynamic and multifarious conception of nationhood.

The end result is not too dissimilar to the preservationist and group-based conceptions that conservatives and liberals have purportedly set themselves against. As Sonia Nieto (1995) observes, the charge of ethnic cheerleading by conservatives may stem more from the fear that *their* ethnic cheerleading is being challenged than from any notion of wanting to retain a common national identity "for the good of all." When this is recognized, the associated notion of a "common culture" can be linked to hegemonic power relations, and successfully deconstructed. Common to whom, one might ask, and on whose terms? Who determines its central values and/or sets its parameters? Who is subsequently included and/or excluded from full participation in its "benefits" and, crucially, at what cost since the "price" minorities usually have to pay for full participation is the disavowal of their cultural, linguistic, and religious practices (cf. Howe, 1992)?

The problem of fragmentation

A fourth problem centers on the inevitable connections that are drawn by the broad conservative/liberal critique of multiculturalism between ethnic differentiation, conflict, and fragmentation. While conflict and fragmentation have undoubtedly occurred from ethnic, cultural and/or religious differentiation, they need not always do so. Likewise, the national integration envisaged by many conservatives and liberals has not always resulted in – indeed has seldom actually achieved – inclusion, consensus, and cohesion for all ethnic groups within nation-states. (Nor, one might venture, would some necessarily want it to.) Rather, as Iris Marion Young asserts, "when oppressed or disadvantaged social groups are different from the dominant groups, then an allegedly group-neutral assimilationist strategy of inclusion only tends to perpetuate inequality" (1993:133).

Young's assertion can be taken a step further here, since it is my contention that ethnic conflict and fragmentation arise most often *not* when compromises are made between ethnic groups or when formal ethnic, linguistic, and/or religious rights are accorded some degree of recognition – as conservatives would have us believe (see Frost, 1997; Schlesinger, 1992) – *but when these have been historically avoided, suppressed, or ignored* (see also Parekh, 2000). This is true, for example, of Canada, Belgium, and Sri Lanka – all cases, interestingly, that are employed by the conservative/liberal alliance as supposed exemplars of the fissiparous politics of multiculturalism.[5] If the contra-indicated position is actually the case, however, then far from ensuring national unity, the denial of ethnicity may well be a principal catalyst of *disunity*. In short, attempting to enforce ethnic, linguistic, and/or religious homogeneity is far more likely to foster disunity than to ameliorate it (see May, 2001).

A consistent failure to acknowledge the significance of hegemonic power relations, and the attendant inequalities of access and opportunity facing particular minority individuals and groups, is by no means limited to conservative and liberal commentators. Multiculturalism itself, particularly in its earlier formulations, tended to do much the same. Thus, the second challenge confronting multiculturalism is this: how can multiculturalism move beyond a well-meaning but ultimately vacuous approval of cultural difference to address adequately broader structural questions to do with inequality, racism, and discrimination, and the demand for greater formal recognition and representation of minority interests in the public realm?

Inequality, Racism, and Material Disadvantage

For much of its history, multiculturalism has been plagued by an idealistic, naive preoccupation with culture at the expense of broader material and structural concerns. If only cultural differences could be recognized, so the story went, the prospects of a harmonious multiethnic society could then (more easily) be achieved. This strain of multiculturalism is most evident in the rhetoric of early forms of multicultural education, developed throughout the 1970s and 1980s (see Modood and May, 2001). It is encapsulated, usefully, by Richard Hatcher's observation that while "culture is the central concept around which [this] multiculturalism is constructed, the concept is given only a taken-for-granted common sense meaning, impoverished both theoretically and in terms of concrete lived experience. It is a concept of culture innocent of class" (Hatcher, 1987:188).

Hatcher's acerbic assessment formed part of a sustained assault by "antiracist" theorists on what they perceived to be the endemic utopianism and naiveté associated with the multicultural education movement (and its municipal variants) of that era – a movement that has since come to be described as "benevolent multiculturalism" (see May, 1994; Troyna, 1993). Such critics, notably the late Barry Troyna (1987, 1993), argued that benevolent multiculturalism constituted an irredeemably "deracialized" discourse, an approach which reified culture and cultural difference, and which failed to address adequately, if at all, *material* issues of racism and disadvantage, and related forms of discrimination and inequality. While this broad antiracist position has been dominated by British commentators – a result of its origins there as a neo-Marxist critique of multiculturalism – it has also been articulated forcefully in the USA (see, for example, Alcoff, 1996; McCarthy and Crichlow, 1993; McLaren and Torres, 1999).

Proponents of multiculturalism have responded to this broad antiracist critique by acknowledging more directly the role of unequal power relations and the inequalities and differential effects that ensue from them (see Kanpol and McLaren, 1995; Kincheloe and Steinberg, 1997; May, 1999a; McLaren, 1995, 1997). This more critical response acknowledges that the logic of much previous multiculturalist rhetoric failed "to see the power-grounded relationships among identity construction, cultural representations and struggles over resources." Rather, it engaged "in its celebration of difference when the most important issues to those who fall outside the white, male and middle class norm often involve powerlessness, violence and poverty" (Kincheloe and Steinberg, 1997:17). In contrast, a more critical conception of multiculturalism:

> takes as its starting point a notion of culture as a terrain of conflict and struggle over representation – conflict for which resolution may not be immediate and struggle that may not cease until there is a change in the social conditions that provoke it. Rather than present culture as the site where different members . . . coexist peacefully, it has to develop strategies to explore and understand this conflict and to encourage creative resolutions and contingent alliances that move [away] from interpreting cultures to intervening in political processes. (Mohan, 1995:385)

However, in developing this broadly critical response, multiculturalists have also more recently come to face another, perhaps more intractable problem – a problem brought on to some extent by this very process of accommodation with antiracist theory. For example, the privileging of racism over other forms of discrimination in early conceptions of antiracism resulted in an increasing preoccupation with "color racism" and the black–white dichotomy. This, in turn, led to a "grand theory" approach which, in attributing racism as the primary modality in intercultural relations, came to be seen as both reductive and essentialist (see Donald and Rattansi 1992; MacDonald et al., 1989; Modood, 1992, 1998a, 1998b). Such an approach subsumes other factors such as class, religion, and gender, and fails to address adequately postmodernist accounts of identity as multiple, contingent, and subject to rapid change. These emphases in antiracist theory also considerably understate both the multiplicity of racisms and their complex interconnections with other forms of inequality (Gilroy, 1992; Modood, 1998a, 1998b; Rattansi, 1992, 1999). As McLaren and Torres observe of this: "[the] conflation of racialized relations into solely a black–white paradigm has prevented scholars from engaging more fully the specificities of particular groups and from exploring more deeply comparative ethnic histories of racism and how these are linked to changing class relations in late capitalism" (1999:45–6).

But this is not all, since antiracist theory, up until recently at least (see Gillborn, 1995), also consistently failed to conceptualize and address adequately the increasing articulation of new "cultural racisms," where "race" as a signifier is transmuted into the seemingly more acceptable discourse of "cultural differences" (cf. Rattansi, 1992, 1999; Short and Carrington, 1999). Thus, essentialist racialized discourses are "disguised" by describing group differences principally in cultural and/or historical terms – ethnic terms, in effect – without specifically mentioning "race" or overtly racial criteria (Barker, 1981; Small, 1994; Wetherell and Potter, 1992). New racisms, in this sense, can be described as a form of *ethnicism* which, as Avtar Brah describes it:

> defines the experience of racialized groups primarily in "culturalist" terms: that is, it posits "ethnic difference" as the primary modality around which social life is constituted and experienced. . . . This means that a group identified as culturally different is assumed to be internally homogeneous. . . . ethnicist discourses seek to impose stereotypic notions of common cultural need upon heterogeneous groups with diverse social aspirations and interests. (Brah, 1992:129)

And this brings us to the third key challenge facing multiculturalism, since the problems of cultural essentialism and the reification of group-based identities highlighted by Brah, and mobilized so effectively by new racist proponents, also continue ironically to haunt much multicultural theory and practice. This is particularly evident within multicultural education, for example, where the regular invocation of "cultural difference" often presents culture as *sui generis* (Hoffman, 1996). In the process, ethnicity is elided with culture and both come to be treated as "bounded cultural objects," to borrow a phrase from Richard Handler (1988), which are seen to attach unproblematically to particular individuals and/or groups. This naive, static, and undifferentiated conception of cultural identity, and the allied notion of the incommensurability of cultures, end up being not that dissimilar from the new racisms of the right. Both appear to abandon universalist notions of individual choice, rights, and responsibility in order to revalorize closed cultures, roots, and traditions (Lloyd, 1994; Werbner, 1997a).

It is perhaps not surprising then that criticism of multiculturalism with respect to this issue comes predominantly from what one might term the "postmodernist/left" (see Phillips, 1997) – although, of course, even a cursory glance at conservative/liberal critiques of multiculturalism will reveal a similar degree of skepticism on this issue (albeit for different reasons; see below). The challenge posed by postmodernist/left critics is this: how can multiculturalism, based as it is on a notion of group-based rights, avoid lapsing into reification and essentialism? In effect, how can it codify without solidifying corporate identities, thus accounting for postmodernist understandings of voice, agency, and the malleable and multiple aspects of identity formation? Not easily, is the short answer.

Groupness, Essentialism and the Politics of Identity

The principal problem for multiculturalism here is that any notion of group-based rights stands in direct contrast to much postmodernist theorizing on identities which – with its related concepts of hybridity, syncretism, creolization, and new ethnicities – highlights the "undecidability" and fluidity of much identity formation. Indeed, it is now almost *de rigueur* in this postmodernist age to dismiss *any* articulation of group-based identity as essentialist[6] – a totalizing discourse that excludes and silences as much as it includes and empowers (see, for example, Anthias and Yuval-Davis, 1992; Bhabha, 1994; Gilroy, 1993, 2000; Hall, 1992; Yuval-Davis, 1997a). Viewed in this way, multiculturalism's advocacy of group-based identities appears irredeemably passé.

Left/postmodernist critics are particularly exercised by, and skeptical of, any claims to the validity of distinct (ethnic) group identities, especially if such identities link cultural difference and identity ineluctably to a historical past of (supposed) cultural authenticity. Such critics argue that this form of "left-essentialist multiculturalism" (Kincheloe and Steinberg, 1997; McLaren, 1995), of which Afrocentrism is often seen as an exemplar (see Howe, 1998), may well be motivated by a principal concern to acknowledge positively cultural difference, to address historical and current patterns of disadvantage, racism, and marginalization, and, from that, to effect the greater pluralization of the nation-state, particularly in its public sphere. However, it does so at the cost of overstating the importance of ethnicity and culture, and understating the fluid and dialogic nature of inter- and intragroup relations. In effect, communitarian conceptions of multiculturalism are charged with operating a model of group membership which is at odds with the complexities of identity in the modern world (Burtonwood, 1996). As Edward Said argues, "no one today is purely one thing. Labels like Indian, or woman, or Muslim, or American are no more than starting points" (1994:407).

This broad critique of "left-essentialist multiculturalism" is illustrated by two allied, although theoretically quite distinct conceptions – cultural hybridity and the cosmopolitan alternative. Both celebrate the notion of cultural mixture and, concomitantly, disavow the validity of so-called "rooted" identities like ethnicity.

Cultural hybridity: the postmodern critique

The articulation of cultural hybridity – and related concepts such as *mestizaje* and creolization – is a prominent feature of the work of British theorists Stuart Hall, Homi Bhabha, and Paul Gilroy, among others. Hall's (1992) discussion of "new ethnicities," Bhabha's (1994) celebration of creolization and subaltern voices from the margin, and Gilroy's (1993, 2000) discussions of a Black Atlantic – a hybridized, diasporic black counterculture – all foreground the transgressive potential of cultural hybridity. Hybridity is viewed as being able to subvert categorical oppositions and essentialist ideological movements – particularly, ethnicity and nationalism – and to provide, in so doing, a basis for cultural reflexivity and change (Werbner, 1997a).

Within the discourses of hybridity, and of postmodernism more broadly, the new social agents are plural – multiple agents forged and engaged in a variety of struggles and social movements (Giroux, 1997). Conversely, hybridity theory is entirely opposed to universalism, traditionalism, and any idea of ethnic or cultural rootedness. In line with postmodernism's rejection of totalizing metanarratives, exponents of hybridity emphasize the contingent, the complex, and the contested aspects of identity formation. Multiple, shifting, and, at times, nonsynchronous identities are the norm for individuals. This position highlights the social and historical constructedness of culture and its associated fluidity and malleability. It also posits contingent, local narratives – what Lyotard (1984) has described as *petits récits* – in opposition to the totalizing narratives of ethnicity and nationalism. The rejection of totality and foundationalism in hybridity theory, and its replacement by a plethora of local identities, thus lends itself at one level to a politics of difference which is commensurable with multiculturalism. Like multiculturalism, the end result is the deconstruction and ultimate rejection of the idea of a "universal" neutral civic realm. Accordingly, hybridity theorists, like multiculturalists, are fundamentally opposed to the conservative and orthodox liberal defense of the nation-state discussed above and argue, instead, for a *differentiated* politics of representation.

However, where hybridity theorists differ from multiculturalism is in sharing with conservative/liberal commentators a view of ethnicity and nationalism as misconceived "rooted" identities. Similarly, these identities are ascribed with the negative characteristics of essentialism, closure, and conflict. Postmodernists, like multiculturalists, may thus argue for the pluralization of the nation-state via a differentiated local politics, but they do so via a *rejection*, not a defense of singular ethnic and cultural identities. Rather, as Homi Bhabha (1994) argues, it is the "inter" and "in-between," the liminal "third space" of translation, which carries the burden of the meaning(s) of culture in this postmodern, postcolonial world. Others have described this process as one of "border crossing" (see Anzaldúa, 1987; di Leonardo, 1994; Giroux, 1992; Rosaldo, 1989).

132

Hybridity theory, as part of the wider postmodern critique, appears to offer us, among other things, a more contingent, situational account of identity and culture – a process which involves "decentering" the subject (Rattansi, 1999) and contesting essentialism wherever it is found. But there are also limits to hybridity. First, in arguing for the inter- and in-between, hybridity is still predicated on the notion of (previous) cultures as complex wholes (Friedman, 1997; Wicker, 1997). In juxtaposing the merits of the heterogeneous hybrid against the homogeneous ethnicist or nationalist, hybridity as-sumes that the liminal "third space" is replacing the bounded, closed ones that preceded it. Border crossing, in effect, assumes that (closed) borders were there to begin with. However, as Jonathan Friedman (1997) points out, this simply perpetuates an essentialist conception of culture rather than subverting it since, as Lévi-Strauss (1994) has argued, all cultures are heterogeneous, arising out of cultural mixture. The juxtaposition of purity/hybridity, authenticity/mixture – so central to hybridity theory – is thus funda-mentally misconceived. In the end, hybridity is meaningless as a description of "culture" because it museumizes culture as "a thing" (Werbner, 1997a; see also Caglar, 1997; Modood, 1998a).

Second, an advocacy of hybridity carries with it the imputation that all group-based identities are essentialist. This is most clearly demonstrated in the conflation of ethnicity and nationalism with racism which, as so-called "rooted" identities, are all treated with equal disparagement (see Anthias and Yuval-Davis, 1992; Chambers, 1994; Gilroy, 1987). This is simply wrong. There are many examples of ethnic and national categoriza-tion which do involve the imputation of essentialized notions of racial and/or cultural difference, leading in turn to social and/or political closure, hierarchization, exclusion, and/or violence. The cultural racism of the New Right is an obvious example here, as indeed are some conservative conceptions of the nation-state (see, for example, Schlesinger, 1992). But while ethnic and national categories may be essentialized in the same way as "race" categories have been historically, they need not always be. Nor are ethnic relations necessarily hierarchical, exploitative, and conflictual in the same way that "race relations" invariably are (Jenkins 1994, 1997; Rex, 1973). Indeed, it has often been the case that the global impact of racism has overridden previously nonhierarchized ethnic categories (Balibar, 1991; Fenton, 1999). In similar vein, Werbner (1997b) has argued that the politics of ethnicity, which objectifies communities situationally and pragmatically with regard to questions of redistributive justice in the public sphere, can be clearly distinguished from the violent essentializing of racism.

The failure to make these crucial distinctions points to a third weakness of hybrid-ity theory – the considerable disparity between the intellectual celebration of hybridity and the reality of the postmodern world. This world *is* increasingly one of fractured, and fracturing identities. But these identities are generally *not* hybrid; just the opposite, in fact. Nation-states, as conservatives and liberals will be the first to tell you, are facing a plethora of ethnic, regional, and other social and cultural minority demands, many of which are couched in singular, collectivist terms. The tendency to rootedness and to boundary maintenance thus militates against ecumenism, and these tendencies are generated and reinforced by the real fragmentation occurring within and between nation-states in a global era (Friedman, 1997). Given this, as Friedman argues, the valorization of hybridization is largely self-referential and self-congratulatory:

hybrids, and hybridization theorists, are products of a group that self-identifies and/or identifies the world in such terms, not as a result of ethnographic understanding, but as an act of self-definition – indeed, of self-essentializing – which becomes definition for others via the forces of socialization inherent in the structures of power that such groups occupy: intellectuals close to the media; the media intelligentsia itself; in a sense, all those [and, one might add, *only* those] who can afford a cosmopolitan identity. (Friedman, 1997:81)

Ahmad (1995), in a similarly scathing critique, argues that articulations of hybridity fail to address adequately the social and political continuities and transformations that underpin individual and collective action in the real world. In that world, he argues, political agency is "constituted not in flux or displacement but in given historical locations." Moreover, it is sustained by a coherent "sense of place, of belonging, of some stable commitment to one's class or gender or nation" (Ahmad, 1995:16, 14).

The cosmopolitan alternative

These arguments and counterarguments with regard to hybridity theory are strongly echoed in debates within liberal political theory around the closely allied notion of the "cosmopolitan alternative" (Waldron, 1993, 1995; see also Hannerz, 1992). Jeremy Waldron, in a trenchant critique of group-based rights, objects to the idea that our choices and self-identity are defined by our ethnicity and asserts, instead, the need for a "cosmopolitan alternative." As he dismissively observes:

> though we may drape ourselves in the distinctive costumes of our ethnic heritage and immure ourselves in an environment designed to minimize our sense of relation with the outside world, no honest account of our being will be complete without an account of our dependence on larger social and political structures that goes far beyond the particular community with which we pretend to identify. (Waldron, 1995:104)

On this view, people can pick and choose "cultural fragments" from various ethnocultural sources, without feeling an allegiance to any one in particular. Thus, Waldron argues, an Irish American who eats Chinese food, reads Grimm's fairy tales to their child, and listens to Italian opera actually lives in a "a kaleidoscope of cultures." While Waldron concedes that we need cultural meanings of some kind, he argues that we do not need *specific* cultural frameworks: "we need to understand our choices in the contexts in which they make sense, but we do not need any single context to structure our choices. To put it crudely, we need culture, but we do not need cultural integrity" (1995:108).

As with hybridity theory, Waldron proceeds on this basis to argue that any advocacy of group-based identities, and specific rights which may be seen to attach to these, necessarily assumes a homogeneous conception of ethnic groups (see Waldron, 1995:103–5). Likewise, he is particularly critical of notions of cultural "purity" and "authenticity" which, he asserts, are regularly employed by ethnic minority groups in support of differential treatment in the public sphere. These attempts at cultural delineation are manifestly artificial in his view and can only result in cultural stasis and isolationism.

However, as Will Kymlicka (1995a) has countered, also from within liberal theory, the assertion of minority recognition and difference, and particular rights associated with this, is most often *not* based on some simplistic desire for cultural "purity." Advocates of multiculturalism are rarely seeking to preserve their "authentic" culture if that means returning to cultural practices long past. If it was, it would soon meet widespread opposition from individual members. Rather, it is the right "to maintain one's membership in a distinct culture, and to continue developing that culture in the same (impure) way that the members of majority cultures are able to develop theirs" (Kymlicka 1995a:105). Cultural change, adaptation, and interaction are entirely consistent with such a position. As Kymlicka argues elsewhere (1995b:8–9), minority cultures wish to be both cosmopolitan and to embrace the cultural interchange that Waldron emphasizes. However, this does not necessarily entail Waldron's own "cosmopolitan alternative" which denies that people have any deep bond to their own historical cultural and linguistic communities.

In a similar vein, Kymlicka asserts that minority rights "help to ensure that the members of minority cultures have access to a secure cultural structure *from which to make choices for themselves*, and thereby promote liberal equality" (1989:192; my emphasis). On this view, minorities continue to exercise their individual (citizenship) rights within their particular cultural (and linguistic) milieux and, of course, contextually, in relation to other cultural groups within a given nation-state. The crucial element, however, is that members of the minority are themselves able to retain a significant degree of control over the process – something which until now has largely been the preserve of majority group members. The key issue thus becomes one of cultural _autonomy_ rather than one of retrenchment, isolationism, or stasis.

In a related critique of Waldron's position, Margalit and Raz (1995) argue that people today may well adopt (and adapt) a varied range of cultural and social practices but that this does not necessarily diminish their allegiance to an "encompassing group" with which they most closely identify (see also Taylor, 1994). Moreover, if members of dominant ethnic groups typically value their own cultural membership, it is clearly unfair to prevent minority groups from continuing to value theirs. As Kymlicka again observes, "leaving one's culture, while possible, is best seen as renouncing something to which one is reasonably entitled" (1995a:90). Relatedly, he argues:

> The freedom which liberals demand for individuals is not primarily the freedom to go beyond one's language and history, but rather the freedom to move within one's societal culture, to distance oneself from particular cultural roles, to choose which features of the culture are most worth developing, and which are without value. (Kymlicka 1995a:90–1)

Developing a (Critical) Multicultural Paradigm

Which brings us to the fourth and final challenge currently facing multiculturalism: what components are essential for multiculturalism to develop into a sensible, theoretically refined, and defensible paradigm? In light of the above discussion, I want to suggest the following.

Theorizing ethnicity

What all the critiques of multiculturalism discussed in this paper uniformly fail to accomplish is an adequate *understanding* and *theorization* of the ongoing collective purchase of ethnicity, and the social and cultural practices which may be associated with it, in the modern world. We may well demonstrate, as individuals, a considerable degree of latitude in our attachment to, and choice of, particular social and political identities. As such, ethnic choices and identifications may vary in their salience – both in themselves, and in relation to other social identities – at any given time and place. Yet, at the same time, we need to acknowledge, and explain why "at the collective as opposed to the individual level, ethnicity remains a powerful, explosive and durable force" (Smith, 1995:34).

One way this can be achieved is via Pierre Bourdieu's notion of habitus (see Bourdieu, 1984, 1990a, 1990b; Bourdieu and Passeron, 1990; Bourdieu and Wacquant, 1992). The application of habitus to ethnicity and ethnic identity formation has been discussed at length elsewhere (see Bentley, 1987; May, 1999b, 2001; Smaje, 1997; Wicker, 1997). However, for the purposes of this discussion, it is enough to say that the four key dimensions of habitus highlighted in Bourdieu's work – embodiment, agency, the interplay between past and present, and the interrelationship between collective and individual trajectories – provide us with a useful means by which the continuing purchase *and* malleability of ethnicity, in its particular contexts, can be critically examined.

Another basis for theoretical analysis might be via a more Foucauldian approach to representation, discourse, and identity of which hybridity theory is an obviously prominent component. If the limits to such an approach are acknowledged (see above), ethnicity can be usefully examined here in relation to other discursive constructions of identity – both in terms of their complex interconnections and, crucially, their ongoing distinctions. The intersection of knowledge and power – that is, discourse as both a technique of power, and the terrain on which identity and meaning are contested – is also usefully highlighted by such analysis (see, for example, Fiske, 1996; Giroux, 1997; Hall, 1997; Shohat and Stam, 1994).

These examples are, of course, not meant to be taken as comprehensive, but they do point to the urgent need to theorize ethnicity, and its consequences, more adequately than we have hitherto. In so doing, both the durability and malleability of ethnicity, its varied forms of cultural expression, and its complex interconnections with other forms of identity, can be critically examined.

Acknowledging (unequal) power relations

In addition, a sensible and defensible theory of multiculturalism requires a central recognition of unequal power relations. Such recognition would allow one to avoid the mistake made by many hybridity theorists (as well as liberal advocates of the cosmopolitan alternative) of "flattening out" differences, making them appear equal (Alcoff, 1996). This is both inadequate as theory, and unreflective of practice, since it is clear that when it comes to ethnicity – or any other identity for that matter – some have more choices than others. In this respect, individual and collective choices are circumscribed by the ethnic categories available at any given time and place. These categories are, in turn, socially and politically defined and have varying degrees of advantage or stigma attached to them (Nagel, 1994). Moreover, the range of choices available to particular individuals and groups varies widely. A white American may have a wide range of ethnic options from which to choose, both hyphenated and/or hybrid. An African-American, in contrast, is confronted with essentially one ethnic choice – black; irrespective of any preferred ethnic (or other) alternatives they might wish to employ.

The preceding example highlights the different ethnic choices available to majority and minority group members; the result, in turn, of their differing access to the civic realm of the nation-state. In short, identities are not – indeed, *cannot* – be freely chosen and to suggest otherwise is to adopt an ahistorical approach which reduces life to the level of "a market, or cafeteria" (Worsley, 1984:246). Rather, identity choices are structured by class, ethnic, and gender stratification, objective constraints, and historical determinations (Hicks, 1991; McLaren, 1997). Both hybridity theory and the cosmopolitan alternative – as well as conservative/liberal critiques of multiculturalism – fail to recognize this.

Critiquing the "neutrality" of the civic realm

The recognition of unequal power relations highlights, in turn, the fiction of the supposedly neutral, formally egalitarian, and de-ethnicized civic realm. Thus a defensible multicultural paradigm must be able to deconstruct the apparent neutrality of civism – that is, the supposedly universal, neutral set of cultural values and practices that underpin the public sphere of the nation-state. Civism, as constructed within the so-called "pluralist dilemma," is *not* neutral, and never has been. Rather, the public sphere of the nation-state represents and is reflective of the *particular* cultural and linguistic practices of the dominant (ethnic) group. The principal consequence for many minorities – at both the individual and collective level – has been the enforced loss of their own ethnic, cultural, and linguistic practices as the necessary price of entry to the civic realm.

In short, culture has to be understood as part of the discourse of power and inequality. In particular, attention needs to be paid here to the processes by which alternative cultural knowledges come to be *subjugated*, principally through the hegemonies and misrepresentations – what Bourdieu (1991) has termed, for instance, "*méconnaissance*" or "misrecognition" – which invariably accompany such comparisons (see Corson, 1993, 1998; Kincheloe and Steinberg, 1997; May, 1999b, 2001). When this is grasped, alternatives become possible. For example, previously subjugated cultural knowledges can be revalued and simultaneously employed as counterhegemonic critiques of dominant forms of knowledge, along with the wider social, cultural, and material processes of domination to which the latter contribute (Kincheloe and Steinberg, 1997).

But even this may not be enough, since the recognition and incorporation of ethnic and cultural differences, even when allied to a critique of wider power relations, and the civic realm, does not necessarily resolve or redress the problem of essentialism. Indeed, the problem may be compounded, since an emphasis on distinctive ethnic and/or cultural boundaries may lead in turn to a further (unhelpful) implication of ethnic and/or cultural *boundedness*.

Maintaining critical reflexivity

Thus, the final, and perhaps key, tenet of a credible multicultural paradigm is the need to maintain at all times a reflexive critique of specific ethnic and cultural practices – one that avoids the vacuity of cultural relativism, and allows for criticism (both internal and external to the group), transformation, and change (see Phillips, 1997). This reflexive

137

position on culture and ethnicity is encapsulated by a distinction drawn by Homi Bhabha (1994) between cultural *diversity* and cultural *difference*. The former, he argues, treats culture as an *object* of empirical knowledge – as static, totalized, and historically bounded, as something to be valued but not necessarily *lived*. The latter is the process of the *enunciation* of culture as "knowledgeable," as adequate to the construction of systems of cultural identification. This involves a dynamic conception of culture – one that recognizes and incorporates the ongoing fluidity and constant change that attends its articulation in the modern world. Likewise, Stuart Hall has argued that a positive conception of ethnicity must begin with "a recognition that all speak from a particular place, out of a particular history, out of a particular experience, a particular culture, *without being contained by that position*" (1992:258; my emphasis). In other words, the recognition of our cultural and historical situatedness should not set the limits of ethnicity and culture, nor act to undermine the legitimacy of other equally valid forms of identity.

In the end then, this kind of critical, reflexive multiculturalism must foster, above all, people who can engage critically with all ethnic and cultural backgrounds, including (and especially) their own. Such an approach would allow all participants in the multicultural debate, however they may be situated, to recognize and explore the complex interconnections, gaps, and dissonances that occur between their own and other ethnic and cultural identities, as well as other forms of social identity.[7] At the same time, how ethnic and cultural identities differ in salience among individuals and across given historical and social contexts, and how these identities are situated in the wider framework of power relations, can also be highlighted, particularly with respect to the widely differing options available to majority and minority group members.

Conclusion

These four components, in combination, constitute what has come to be known as "critical multiculturalism." Critical multiculturalism combines both structural and culturalist concerns – linking culture to power, and multiculturalism to antiracism – in its deconstruction and critique of the organization of modern nation-states. Critical multiculturalism also engages actively with postmodernist conceptions and analyses of identity, while holding onto the possibility of an emancipatory, group-based politics. And, perhaps most importantly, critical multiculturalism provides a defensible, credible, and critical multiculturalist paradigm which can act as a template for a more plural, inclusive, and *democratic* approach to nation-state organization in this new century. Glazer, as much as he might not have wished it, may actually be proved right after all – it looks like multiculturalism, and its social and political consequences, are here to stay.

Notes

1 A particular problem that one soon encounters in any discussion of multiculturalism, and the various minority groups who lay claim to it, is the sheer diversity of so-called "multiculturalist" claims. Thus, while ethnicity and culture are most often, and perhaps most prominently, associated with multiculturalist demands, they are by no means exclusively so. Religious, gender, and other special representation rights also often come under the rubric, loosely

defined, of multiculturalism. It is not possible to pursue this issue further here, except to say that in what follows I will concentrate primarily on ethnicity and culture, since these remain the principal locus of multiculturalism. For a useful analysis of the various demands that are associated with multiculturalism, their legitimacy, and their limits, see Kymlicka (1995a) and Parekh (2000).

2 For the sake of simplicity, I will discuss both conservative and orthodox liberal commentators in broadly equivalent terms in what follows. In so doing, I acknowledge that this considerably oversimplifies the differences (both theoretical and political) between a wide range of commentators who could be said to fall within this broad "neoconservative" position. Be that as it may, my principal point is this: the conservative/liberal alliance reflects the complexities of a debate which often transcends and/or subverts traditional left/right political oppositions. Similarly, in the discussion of the postmodernist critique of multiculturalism which follows, we will encounter an equally complex alliance between postmodernist and (other) left-liberal commentators.

3 As Gramsci argues, in order to understand any nation-state as a whole, one must always distinguish between its "State" or political and administrative structure, and its "civil society." The latter comprises, for example, its principal nonpolitical organizations, its religious and other beliefs, and its specific "customs" or way of life. In making these distinctions, there are inevitably features which do not fit easily under either category. However, as Nairn (1981:131) summarizes it: "that is relatively unimportant. What matters is that they are distinguishable, and that the singular identity of a modern society depends upon the relationship between them."

4 Communitarians believe that we discover our ends embedded in a social context, rather than choosing them *ex nihilo*. Their principal objection to orthodox liberalism is thus to the idea of a self divorced from, or stripped of, the social features of identity.

5 In each of these nation-states, conflict between ethnic groups has centered around the historical denial of cultural and linguistic rights to significant minority communities – Flemish speakers in Belgium, French speakers in Quebec, and Tamil speakers in Sri Lanka (see Nelde, 1997; May, 2001).

6 Essentialism is taken to mean here the process by which particular groups come to be described in terms of fundamental, immutable characteristics. In so doing, the relational and fluid aspects of identity formation are ignored and the group itself comes to be valorized as subject, as autonomous and separate, impervious to context and to processes of internal as well as external differentiation (Werbner, 1997b).

7 In a parallel argument drawn from feminist discourse, Nira Yuval-Davis describes this process as one of "transversal politics" in which "perceived unity and homogeneity are replaced by dialogues that give recognition to the specific positionings of those who participate in them, as well as to the 'unfinished knowledge'...that each such situated positioning can offer" (1997b:204).

References

Ahmad, A. (1995) "The politics of literary postcoloniality." *Race and Class* 36,3:1–20.
Alcoff, L. (1996) "Philosophy and racial identity." *Radical Philosophy* 75:5–14.
Anderson, B. (1991) *Imagined Communities: Reflections on the Origin and Spread of Nationalism*, revised edn. London: Verso.
Anthias, F. and Yuval-Davis, N. (1992) *Racialized Boundaries: Race, Nation, Gender, Colour and Class and the Anti-racist Struggle*. London: Routledge.
Anzaldúa, G. (1987) *Borderlands/La Frontera: The New Mestiza*. San Francisco: Aunt Lute Books.
Balibar, E. (1991) "The nation form: History and ideology," in E. Balibar and I. Wallerstein (eds.) *Race, Nation, Class: Ambiguous Identities*. London: Verso, pp.86–106.

Barker, M. (1981) *The New Racism: Conservatives and the Ideology of the Tribe*. London: Junction.

Bentley, G. (1987) "Ethnicity and practice." *Comparative Studies in Society and History* 29:24–55.

Bhabha, H. (1994) *The Location of Culture*. London: Routledge.

Billig, M. (1995) *Banal Nationalism*. London: Sage.

Bloom, A. (1987) *The Closing of the American Mind: How Higher Education has Failed Democracy and Impoverished the Souls of Today's Students*. New York: Simon and Schuster.

Bourdieu, P. (1984) *Distinction: A Social Critique of the Judgement of Taste*. Cambridge, MA: Harvard University Press.

Bourdieu, P. (1990a) *In Other Words: Essays Towards a Reflexive Sociology*. Cambridge, UK: Polity Press.

Bourdieu, P. (1990b) *The Logic of Practice*. Cambridge, UK: Polity Press.

Bourdieu, P. (1991) *Language and Symbolic Power*. Cambridge, UK: Polity Press.

Bourdieu, P. and Passeron, J. (1990) *Reproduction in Education, Society and Culture*, 2nd edn. London: Sage Publications.

Bourdieu, P. and Wacquant, L. (1992) *An Invitation to Reflexive Sociology*. Chicago: Chicago University Press.

Brah, A. (1992) "Difference, diversity and differentiation," in J. Donald and A. Rattansi (eds.) *"Race", Culture and Difference*. London: Sage, pp.126–45.

Brandt, G. (1986) *The Realisation of Anti-racist Teaching*. Lewes, UK: Falmer Press.

Bullivant, B. (1981) *The Pluralist Dilemma in Education: Six Case Studies*. Sydney: Allen and Unwin.

Burtonwood, N. (1996) "Culture, identity and the curriculum." *Educational Review* 48:227–35.

Caglar, A. (1997) "Hyphenated identities and the limits of 'culture,'" in T. Modood and P. Werbner (eds.) *The Politics of Multiculturalism in the New Europe: Racism, Identity and Community*. London: Zed Books, pp.169–85.

Chambers, I. (1994) *Migrancy, Culture and Identity*. London: Routledge.

Corson, D. (1993) *Language, Minority Education and Gender: Linking Social Justice and Power*. Clevedon, UK: Multilingual Matters.

Corson, D. (1998) *Changing Education for Diversity*. Buckingham, UK: Open University Press.

Di Leonardo, M. (1994) "White ethnicities, identity politics, and baby bear's chair." *Social Text* 41:5–33.

Donald, J. and Rattansi, A. (eds.) (1992) *"Race", Culture and Difference*. London: Sage.

Dworkin, R. (1978) "Liberalism," in S. Hampshire (ed.) *Public and Private Morality*. Cambridge, UK: Cambridge University Press, pp.113–43.

Fenton, S. (1999) *Ethnicity: Racism, Class and Culture*. London: Macmillan.

Fiske, J. (1996) *Media Matters: Race and Gender in US Politics*. Minneapolis: University of Minnesota Press.

Friedman, J. (1997) "Global crises, the struggle for identity and intellectual porkbarrelling: Cosmopolitans versus locals, ethnics and nationals in an era of de-hegemonization," in P. Werbner and T. Modood (eds.) *Debating Cultural Hybridity: Multicultural Identities and the Politics of Antiracism*. London: Zed Books, pp.70–89.

Frost, G. (1997) *Loyalty Misplaced: Misdirected Virtue and Social Disintegration*. London: Social Affairs Unit.

Gellner, E. (1983) *Nations and Nationalism: New Perspectives on the Past*. Oxford: Blackwell.

Gillborn, D. (1995) *Racism and Antiracism in Real Schools*. Buckingham, UK: Open University Press.

Gilroy, P. (1987) *There Ain't No Black in the Union Jack*. London: Hutchinson.

Gilroy, P. (1992) "The end of antiracism," in J. Donald and A. Rattansi (eds.) *"Race", Culture, and Difference*. London: Sage, pp.49–61.

Gilroy, P. (1993) *Small Acts: Thoughts on the Politics of Black Cultures*. London: Serpent's Tail.

Gilroy, P. (2000) *Between Camps: Nations, Cultures and the Allure of Race*. London: Allen Lane/ Penguin Press.

Giroux, H. (1992) *Border Crossings*. London: Routledge.

Giroux, H. (1997) *Pedagogy and the Politics of Hope: Theory, Culture and Schooling*. Boulder, CO: Westview Press.

Glazer, N. (1975) *Affirmative Discrimination: Ethnic Inequality and Public Policy*. New York: Basic Books.

Glazer, N. (1998) *We Are All Multiculturalists Now*. Cambridge, MA: Harvard University Press.

Goldberg, D. (1994) "Introduction: Multicultural conditions," in D. Goldberg (ed.) *Multiculturalism: A Critical Reader*. Oxford: Blackwell, pp.1–41.

Gordon, M. (1978) *Human Nature, Class and Ethnicity*. New York: Oxford University Press.

Gordon, M. (1981) "Models of pluralism: The new American dilemma." *Annals of the American Academy of Political and Social Science* 454:178–88.

Gramsci, A. (1971) *Selections from the Prison Notebooks*, Q. Hoare and G. Nowell-Smith (eds.). London: Lawrence and Wishart.

Habermas, J. (1994) "Struggles for recognition in the democratic constitutional state," in A. Gutmann (ed.) *Multiculturalism: Examining the Politics of Recognition*. Princeton, NJ: Princeton University Press, pp.107–48.

Hall, S. (1992) "New ethnicities," in J. Donald and A. Rattansi (eds.) *"Race", Culture and Difference*. London: Sage, pp.252–9.

Hall, S. (ed.) (1997) *Representation: Cultural Representations and Signifying Practices*. London: Sage.

Handler, R. (1988) *Nationalism and the Politics of Culture in Quebec*. Madison: Wisconsin University Press.

Hannerz, U. (1992) *Cultural Complexity: Studies in the Organization of Meaning*. New York: Columbia University Press.

Hatcher, R. (1987) "Race and education: Two perspectives for change," in B. Troyna (ed.) *Racial Inequality in Education*. London: Tavistock, pp.184–200.

Hicks, E. (1991) *Border Writing*. Minneapolis: University of Minnesota Press.

Hirsch, E. (1987) *Cultural Literacy: What Every American Needs to Know*. Boston: Houghton Mifflin.

Hobsbawm, E. (1990) *Nations and Nationalism since 1780*. Cambridge, UK: Cambridge University Press.

Hoffman, D. (1996) "Culture and self in multicultural education: Reflections on discourse, text, and practice." *American Educational Research Journal* 33:545–69.

Howe, K. (1992) "Liberal democracy, equal opportunity, and the challenge of multiculturalism." *American Educational Research Journal* 29:455–70.

Howe, S. (1998) *Afrocentrism: Mythical Pasts and Imagined Homes*. London: Verso.

Jenkins, R. (1994) "Rethinking ethnicity: Identity, categorization and power." *Ethnic and Racial Studies* 17:197–223.

Jenkins, R. (1997) *Rethinking Ethnicity*. London: Sage.

Kanpol, B. and McLaren, P. (1995) *Critical Multiculturalism: Uncommon Voices in a Common Struggle*. Westport, CT: Bergin and Garvey.

Kincheloe, J. and Steinberg, S. (1997) *Changing Multiculturalism*. Buckingham, UK: Open University Press.

Kymlicka, W. (1989) *Liberalism, Community and Culture*. Oxford: Clarendon Press.

Kymlicka, W. (1995a) *Multicultural Citizenship: A Liberal Theory of Minority Rights*. Oxford: Clarendon Press.

Kymlicka, W. (1995b) "Introduction," in W. Kymlicka (ed.) *The Rights of Minority Cultures*. Oxford: Oxford University Press, pp.1–27.

Lévi-Strauss, C. (1994) "Anthropology, race, and politics: A conversation with Didier Eribon," in R. Borofsky (ed.) *Assessing Cultural Anthropology*. New York: McGraw Hill, pp.420–9.

141

Lloyd, C. (1994) "Universalism and difference: The crisis of antiracism in France and the UK," in A. Rattansi and S. Westwood (eds.) *Racism, Modernity, and Identity*. Cambridge, UK: Polity Press, pp.222–44.

Lyotard, J. (1984) *The Postmodern Condition: A Report on Knowledge*, trans. G Bennington and B. Massumi. Manchester, UK: Manchester University Press.

MacDonald, I., Bhavnani, R., Khan, L., and John, G. (1989) *Murder in the Playground*. London: Longsight Press.

Margalit, A., and Raz, J. (1995) "National self- determination," in W. Kymlicka (ed.) *The Rights of Minority Cultures*. Oxford: Oxford University Press, pp.79–92.

May, S. (1994) *Making Multicultural Education Work*. Clevedon, UK: Multilingual Matters.

May, S. (ed.) (1999a) *Critical Multiculturalism: Rethinking Multicultural and Antiracist Education*. London: RoutledgeFalmer.

May, S. (1999b) "Critical multiculturalism and cultural difference: Avoiding essentialism," in S. May (ed.) *Critical Multiculturalism: Rethinking Multicultural and Antiracist Education*. London: RoutledgeFalmer. pp.11–41.

May, S. (2001) *Language and Minority Rights: Ethnicity, Nationalism and the Politics of Language*. London: Longman.

McCarthy, C. and Crichlow, W. (eds.) (1993) *"Race", Identity and Representation in Education*. New York: Routledge.

McLaren, P. (1995) *Critical Pedagogy and Predatory Culture*. New York: Routledge.

McLaren, P. (1997) *Revolutionary Multiculturalism: Pedagogies of Dissent for the new Millennium*. Boulder, CO: Westview Press.

McLaren, P. and Torres, R. (1999) "Racism and multicultural education: Rethinking 'race' and 'whiteness' in late capitalism," in S. May (ed.) *Critical Multiculturalism: Rethinking Multicultural and Antiracist Education*. London: Routledge Falmer, pp.42–76.

Modood, T. (1992) *Not Easy Being British: Colour, Culture and Citizenship*. Stoke-on-Trent, UK: Runnymede Trust and Trentham Books.

Modood, T. (1998a) "Anti-essentialism, multiculturalism and the 'recognition' of religious groups." *Journal of Political Philosophy* 6, 4:378–99.

Modood, T. (1998b) "Multiculturalism, secularism and the state." *Critical Review of International Social and Political Philosophy* 1,3:79–97.

Modood, T. and May, S. (2001) "Multiculturalism and education in Britain: An internally contested debate." *International Journal of Educational Research* (in press).

Mohan, R. (1995) "Multiculturalism in the nineties: Pitfalls and possibilities," in C. Newfield and R. Strickland (eds.) *After Political Correctness: The Humanities and Society in the 1990s*. Boulder, CO: Westview Press, pp.372–88.

Nagel, J. (1994) "Constructing ethnicity: Creating and recreating ethnic identity and culture." *Social Problems* 41:152–76.

Nairn, T. (1981) *The Break-up of Britain: Crisis and Neo-nationalism*, revised edn. London: Verso.

Nelde, P. (1997) "Language conflict," in F. Coulmas (ed.) *The Handbook of Sociolinguistics*. Oxford: Blackwell, pp.285–300.

Nieto, S. (1995) "From brown heroes and holidays to assimilationist agendas: Reconsidering the critiques of multicultural education," in C. Sleeter and P. McLaren (eds.) *Multicultural Education, Critical Pedagogy, and the Politics of Difference*. Albany, NY: SUNY Press, pp.191–220.

Parekh, B. (1995) "Introduction." *New Community* 21:147–51.

Parekh, B. (2000) *Rethinking Multiculturalism: Cultural Diversity and Political Theory*. London: Macmillan and Cambridge, MA: Harvard University Press.

Phillips, A. (1997) "Why worry about multiculturalism?" *Dissent* 44:57–63.

Porter, J. (1975) "Ethnic pluralism in Canadian perspective," in N. Glazer and D. Moynihan (eds.) *Ethnicity: Theory and Experience*. Cambridge, MA: Harvard University Press, pp.267–304.

Rattansi, A. (1992) "Changing the subject? Racism, culture, and education," in J. Donald and A. Rattansi (eds.) *"Race", Culture, and Difference*. London: Sage, pp.11–48.

Rattansi, A. (1999) "Racism, 'postmodernism', and reflexive multiculturalism," in S. May (ed.) *Critical Multiculturalism: Rethinking Multicultural and Antiracist Education*. London: Routledge Falmer, pp.77–112.

Rawls, J. (1971) *A Theory of Justice*. Oxford: Oxford University Press.

Rawls, J. (1985) "Justice as fairness: Political not metaphysical." *Philosophy and Public Affairs* 14:223–51.

Rex, J. (1973) *Race, Colonialism and the City*. Oxford: Oxford University Press.

Rosaldo, R. (1989) *Culture and Truth*. London: Routledge.

Said, E. (1994) *Culture and Imperialism*. London: Vintage.

Sandel, M. (1982) *Liberalism and the Limits of Justice*. Cambridge, UK: Cambridge University Press.

Schlesinger, A. (1992) *The Disuniting of America: Reflections on a Multicultural Society*. New York: W.W. Norton.

Shohat, E., and Stam, R. (1994) *Unthinking Eurocentrism: Multiculturalism and the Media*. London: Routledge.

Short, G. and Carrington, B. (1999) "Children's constructions of their national identity: Implications for critical multiculturalism," In S. May (ed.) *Critical Multiculturalism: Rethinking Multicultural and Antiracist Education*. London: Routledge Falmer, pp.172–90.

Smaje, C. (1997) "Not just a social construct: Theorising race and ethnicity." *Sociology* 31:307–27.

Small, S. (1994) *Racialised Barriers: The Black Experience in the United States and England in the 1980s*. London: Routledge.

Smith, A. (1995) *Nations and Nationalism in a Global Era*. Cambridge, UK: Polity Press.

Taylor, C. (1994) "The politics of recognition," in A. Gutmann (ed.) *Multiculturalism: Examining the Politics of Recognition*. Princeton, NJ: Princeton University Press, pp.25–73.

Torres, C. (1998) "Democracy, education, and multiculturalism: Dilemmas of citizenship in a global world." *Comparative Education Review* 42:421–47.

Troyna, B. (ed.). (1987) *Racial Inequality in Education*. London: Tavistock.

Troyna, B. (1993) *Racism and Education*. Buckingham, UK: Open University Press.

Van Dyke, V. (1977) "The individual, the state, and ethnic communities in political theory." *World Politics* 29:343–69.

Waldron, J. (1993) *Liberal Rights*. Cambridge, UK: Cambridge University Press.

Waldron, J. (1995) "Minority cultures and the cosmopolitan alternative," in W. Kymlicka (ed.) *The Rights of Minority Cultures*. Oxford: Oxford University Press, pp.93–119.

Walzer, M. (1992) *What it Means to be an American*. New York: Marsilio.

Walzer, M. (1994) "Comment," in A. Gutmann (ed.) *Multiculturalism: Examining the Politics of Recognition*. Princeton, NJ.: Princeton University Press, pp.99–103.

Werbner, P. (1997a) "Introduction: The dialectics of cultural hybridity," in P. Werbner and T. Modood (eds.) *Debating Cultural Hybridity: Multicultural Identities and the Politics of Antiracism*. London: Zed Books, pp.1–26.

Werbner, P. (1997b) "Essentialising essentialism, essentialising silence: Ambivalence and multiplicity in the constructions of racism and ethnicity," in P. Werbner and T. Modood (eds.) *Debating Cultural Hybridity: Multicultural Identities and the Politics of Antiracism*. London: Zed Books, pp.226–54.

Wetherell, M. and Potter, J. (1992) *Mapping the Language of Racism: Discourse and the Legitimation of Exploitation*. London: Harvester Wheatsheaf.

Wicker, H-R. (1997) "From complex culture to cultural complexity," in P. Werbner and T. Modood (eds.) *Debating Cultural Hybridity: Multicultural Identities and the Politics of Antiracism*. London: Zed Books, pp.29–45.

Worsley, P. (1984) *The Three Worlds: Culture and World Development*. London: Weidenfeld and Nicholson.

Young, I. (1993) "Together in difference: Transforming the logic of group political conflict," in J. Squires (ed.) *Principled Positions: Postmodernism and the Rediscovery of Value*. London: Lawrence and Wishart, pp.121–50.

Yuval-Davis, N. (1997a) *Gender and Nation*. London: Sage.

Yuval-Davis, N. (1997b) "Ethnicity, gender relations and multiculturalism," in P. Werbner and T. Modood (eds.) *Debating Cultural Hybridity: Multicultural Identities and the Politics of Anti-racism*. London: Zed Books, pp.193–208.

Chapter 12

Discourse and Racism

Teun A. van Dijk

Introduction

For most people, and probably also for many readers of this chapter, the notion of racism is not primarily associated with that of discourse. More obvious associations would be discrimination, prejudice, slavery, or apartheid, among many other concepts related to ethnic or "racial" domination and inequality dealt with elsewhere in this book.

And yet, although discourse may seem just "words" (and therefore cannot break your bones, as do sticks and stones), text and talk play a vital role in the reproduction of contemporary racism.

This is especially true for the most damaging forms of contemporary racism, namely, those of the elites. Political, bureaucratic, corporate, media, educational, and scholarly elites control the most crucial dimensions and decisions of the everyday lives of immigrants and minorities: entry, residence, work, housing, education, welfare, health care, knowledge, information, and culture. They do so largely by speaking or writing, for instance, in cabinet meetings and parliamentary debates, in job interviews, news reports, advertising, lessons, textbooks, scholarly articles, movies or talk shows, among many other forms of elite discourse.

That is, as is true also for other social practices directed against minorities, discourse may first of all be a form of verbal discrimination. Elite discourse may thus constitute an important elite form of racism. Similarly, the (re)production of ethnic prejudices that underlie such verbal and other social practices largely takes place through text, talk, and communication.

In sum, especially in contemporary information societies, discourse lies at the heart of racism. This chapter explains how and why this is so.

Racism

To understand in some detail how discourse may contribute to racism, we first need to summarize our theory of racism. Whereas racism is often reduced to racist ideology, it is here understood as a complex societal system of ethnically or "racially" based domination and its resulting inequality (for detail, see van Dijk, 1993).

The system of racism consists of a social and a cognitive subsystem. The social subsystem is constituted by social practices of discrimination at the local (micro) level, and relationships of power abuse by dominant groups, organizations, and institutions at a global (macro) level of analysis (most classical analyses of racism focus on this level of analysis; see, e.g., Dovidio and Gaertner, 1986; Essed, 1991; Katz and Taylor, 1988; Wellman, 1993; Omi and Winant, 1994).

As suggested above, discourse may be an influential type of discriminatory practice. And the symbolic elites, that is, those elites who literally have everything "to say" in society, as well as their institutions and organizations, are an example of groups involved in power abuse or domination.

The second subsystem of racism is cognitive. Whereas the discriminatory practices of members of dominant groups and institutions form the visible and tangible manifestations of everyday racism, such practices also have a mental basis consisting of biased models of ethnic events and interactions, which in turn are rooted in racist prejudices and ideologies (van Dijk, 1984, 1987, 1998). This does not mean that discriminatory practices are always intentional, but only that they presuppose socially shared and negatively oriented mental representations of Us about Them. Most psychological studies of "prejudice" deal with this aspect of racism, though seldom in those terms, that is, in terms of their role in the *social* system of racism. Prejudice is mostly studied as a characteristic of inviduals (Brown, 1995; Dovidio and Gaertner, 1986; Sniderman et al, 1993; Zanna and Olson, 1994).

Discourse also plays a fundamental role for this cognitive dimension of racism. Ethnic prejudices and ideologies are not innate, and do not develop spontaneously in ethnic interaction. They are acquired and learned, and this usually happens through communication, that is, through text and talk. And vice versa, such racist mental representations are typically expressed, formulated, defended, and legitimated in discourse and may thus be reproduced and shared within the dominant group. It is essentially in this way that racism is "learned" in society.

Discourse

Definition

Without knowledge of racism, we do not know how discourse is involved in its daily reproduction. The same is true for our knowledge about discourse. This notion has become so popular, that it has lost much of its specificity. "Discourse" is here understood to mean only a specific communicative event, in general, and a written or oral form of verbal interaction or language use, in particular. Sometimes "discourse" is used in a more generic sense to denote a type of discourse, a collection of discourses, or a class of discourse genres, for instance, when we speak of "medical discourse," "political discourse," or indeed of "racist discourse." (For an introduction to contemporary discourse analysis, see the chapters in van Dijk, 1997.)

Although it is often used in that way, we do *not* understand by discourse a philosophy, ideology, social movement, or social system, as in phrases such as "the discourse of liberalism" or "the discourse of modernity," unless we actually refer to collections of talk or text.

146

In the broader, "semiotic" sense, discourses may also feature nonverbal expressions such as drawings, pictures, gestures, face-work, and so on. However, for brevity's sake, these will be ignored here, although it should be obvious that racist messages may also be conveyed by photos, movies, derogatory gestures, or other nonverbal acts.

Structural analysis

Discourses have many different structures, which also may be analyzed in many different ways depending on general approaches (linguistic, pragmatic, semiotic, rhetorical, inter-actional, etc.) or the kind of genres analyzed, such as conversation, news reports, poetry, or advertisements. It will be assumed here that both written/printed text and oral talk may thus be analyzed at various levels or along several dimensions. Each of these may be involved directly or indirectly in discriminatory interaction against minority group members or biased discourse about them, for instance, as follows:

- Nonverbal structures: A racist picture; a derogatory gesture; a headline size or page layout that emphasizes negative meanings about "Them."
- Sounds: An insolent intonation; speaking (too) loudly.
- Syntax: (De-)emphasizing responsibility for action, for instance by active vs. passive sentences.
- Lexicon: Selection of words that may be more or less negative about Them, or positive about Us (e.g., "terrorist" vs. "freedom fighter").
- Local (sentence) meaning: for instance, being vague or indirect about Our racism, and detailed and precise about Their crimes or misbehavior.
- Global discourse meaning (topics): selecting or emphasizing positive topics (like aid and tolerance) for Us, and negative ones (such as crime, deviance, or violence) for Them.
- Schemata (conventional forms of global discourse organization): presence or absence of standard schematic categories – such as a resolution in a narrative schema, or a conclusion in an argument schema – in order to emphasize Our Good things and Their Bad things.
- Rhetorical devices: metaphor, metonymy, hyperbole, euphemism, irony, etc. – again to focus attention on positive/negative information about Us/Them.
- Speech acts: e.g., accusations to derogate Them, or defenses to legitimate Our discrimination.
- Interaction: interrupting turns of Others, closing meetings before Others can speak, disagreeing with Others, or nonresponding to questions, among many other forms of direct interactional discrimination.

Although not yet very detailed, nor very sophisticated, this brief list of levels and some structures of discourse gives a first impression of how discourse and its various structures may link up with some aspects of racism. Note also that the examples given show the kind of group polarization we also know from underlying prejudices, namely, the overall tendency of ingroup favoritism or positive self-presentation, on the one hand, and outgroup derogation or negative Other-presentation, on the other.

In other words, with the many subtle structures of meanings, form, and action, racist discourse generally emphasizes Our good things and Their bad things, and

147

de-emphasizes (mitigates, hides) Our bad things and Their good things. This general "ideological" square not only applies to racist domination but in general to ingroup–outgroup polarization in social practices, discourse, and thought.

The cognitive interface

An adequate theory of racism is nonreductive in the sense that it does not limit racism to just ideology or just "visible" forms of discriminatory practices. The same is true for the way discourse is involved in racism. This is especially the case for "meanings" of discourse, and hence also for beliefs, that is, for cognition. Discourses are not only forms of interaction or social practices, but also express and convey meanings, and may thus influence our beliefs about immigrants or minorities.

The point of the analysis of discourse structures above, thus, is not only to examine the detailed features of one type of discriminatory social practice, but especially also to gain deeper insight in the way discourses express and manage our minds. It is especially this discourse–cognition interface that explains how ethnic prejudices and ideologies are expressed, conveyed, shared, and reproduced in society. For instance, a passive sentence may obscure responsible agency in the mental models we form about a racist event, a special type of metaphor (such as in "an invasion of refugees") may enhance the negative opinion we have about Others, and a euphemism such as "popular resentment" may mitigate the negative self-image an expression such as "racism" might suggest. In this and many other ways, thus, the discourse structures mentioned above may influence the specific mental models we have about ethnic events, or the more general social representations (attitudes, ideologies) we have about ourselves and Others. And once such mental representations have been influenced in the way intended by racist discourse, they may also be used to engage in other racist practices. It is in this way that the circle of racism and its reproduction is closed.

The social context: the elites

Research suggests that the discursive reproduction of racism in society is not evenly distributed over all members of the dominant majority. Apart from analyzing their structures and cognitive underpinnings, it is therefore essential to examine some properties of the social context of discourse, such as who its speakers and writers are. We repeatedly suggest in this chapter that the elites play a special role in this reproduction process (for details, see van Dijk, 1993). This is not because the elites are generally more racist than the nonelites, but especially because of their special access to, and control over, the most influential forms of public discourse, namely, that of the mass media, politics, education, research, and the bureaucracies. Our definition of these elites is thus not in terms of material resources that are the basis of power, such as wealth, nor merely in terms of their societal positions of leadership, but rather in terms of the symbolic resources that define symbolic "capital," and in particular their preferential access to public discourse. The elites, defined in this way, are literally the group(s) in society who have "most to say," and thus also have preferential "access to the minds" of the public at large. As the ideological leaders of society, they establish common values, aims, and concerns; they formulate common sense as well as the consensus, both as individuals and as leaders of the dominant institutions of society.

This is also true for the exercise of "ethnic" power – in which the dominant majority needs guidance in its relationships to minorities or immigrants. Given our analysis of the role of the "symbolic" elites in contemporary society, we conclude that they also have a special role in the reproduction of the system of racism that maintains the dominant white group in power. This means that an analysis of elite discourse offers a particularly relevant perspective on the way racism is reproduced in society.

At the same time, however, further sociological and political analysis is necessary to examine in more detail how the symbolic elites relate to the population at large, including incorporating and translating popular confusion or resentment into the forms of dominant racist discourse they deem to be most relevant to maintain their own power and status. For instance, critique of unemployment and urban decay against the (political) elites may thus be deflected by blaming them on the immigrants. More extremist forms of popular racism, whether or not organized in political parties, may then be publicly denounced so as to protect one's own nonracist face and to propagate more "moderate" forms of racism in mainstream parties. It is not surprising therefore that racist parties are "useful idiots" and, with reference to democratic values, seldom prohibited. The various social and political processes may easily be detected in an analysis of elite discourses in contemporary societies.

Of course, this special perspective on the role of the elites in the reproduction of racism, based on the simple argument that they control public discourse, also explains the role of small groups of elites in the nondominant forms of *antiracism*. If it is generally true that the leaders are responsible and need to give a good example, this conclusion also implies that antiracist policies and change should not so much focus on the population at large, but on those who claim to need it less: the elites. If the most influential forms of racism are at the top, it is also there where change has to begin.

The role of context

Current discourse analysis emphasizes the fundamental role of context for the understanding of the role of text and talk in society. As will also appear several times below, dominant discourses do not merely exercise their influence out of context. When defining discourse as communicative events, we also need to take into account, for example, the overall social domains in which they are used (politics, media, education); the global social actions being accomplished by them (legislation, education); the local actions they enact; the current setting of time, place, and circumstances; the participants involved, as well as their many social and communicative roles and (e.g., ethnic) group membership; and not least the beliefs and goals of these participants. These and other properties of the social situation of the communicative event will influence virtually all properties of text and talk, especially those properties that can vary, such as their style: *how* things are said. That is, similar prejudices may be formulated in very different ways depending on these and other context structures – for example, in government discourse or parliamentary debates, quality broadsheet or tabloid, on the left or on the right, and so on. In other words, the large variety of racist discourses in society not only reflect variable underlying social representations, but especially also adapt to different contexts of production: who says what, where, when, and with what goals. A theory of context also explains in part why, despite the dominant ethnic consensus, not all talk on minorities will be the same.

149

Conversation

After the more theoretical introduction about the way discourse is involved in racism and its reproduction, we now proceed to some examples of the various genres whose role in racism has been studied.

A genre is a *type* of discursive social practice, usually defined by specific discourse structures and context structures as spelled out above. For instance, a parliamentary debate is a discourse genre defined by a specific style, specific forms of verbal interaction (talk) under special contextual constraints of time and controlled speaker change, in the domain of politics, in the institution of parliament, as part of the overall act of legislation, engaged in by speakers who are MPs, representative of their constituencies as well as members of political parties, with the aim (for instance) to defend or oppose bills, with formal styles of address and argumentative structures supporting a political point of view ... And this is merely a short summary of such a definition of a genre, which usually needs both textual and contextual specification.

Thus, in the same way, everyday conversation is a genre, probably the most elementary and widespread genre of human interaction and discourse, typically defined by lacking the various institutional constraints mentioned above for parliamentary debates. Indeed, we virtually all have access to conversations, whereas only MPs have access to parliamentary debates. Much of what we learn about the world is derived from such everyday conversations with family members, friends, and colleagues. The same is true for ethnic prejudices and ideologies.

Study of conversations of white people in the Netherlands and California about immigrants (van Dijk, 1984, 1987) shows a number of interesting characteristics. Casually asked about their neighborhood, many speakers spontaneously begin to speak about "those foreigners," often negatively (see also the following studies of racist conversations: Jäger, 1992; Wetherell and Potter, 1992; Wodak et al., 1990).

Whereas everyday conversations are often about other people, and anything may come up in such talk, *topics* about minorities or immigrants are often limited to a few topic types, namely, the increasingly negative topic classes of difference, deviance, and threat. Thus, ethnic outgroups are first of all talked about in terms of how they look and act different from us – different habits, language, religion, or values. Such talk may still be neutral in the sense that such differences need not be negatively evaluated; indeed, differences may even be discussed in a "positive" way as being interesting, exotic, and culturally enriching. More often than not, however, different characteristics will be negatively framed when compared to those of the ingroup. Next, Others may be talked about even more negatively in terms of deviance, that is, of breaking our norms and values, in Europe typically so in negative remarks about Islam, or the way Arab men treat women. Finally, immigrants or minorities may be talked about even more negatively, in terms of a threat, for instance, in stories about aggression or crime or presented as taking away our jobs, housing, or space, or (especially in elite discourse) when seen as threatening "our" dominant culture.

Whereas topics are meanings that characterize whole conversations or large parts of them, a more local semantic analysis of everyday talk about minorities or immigrants reveals other interesting features. One of the best known are *disclaimers*, that is, semantic moves with a positive part about Us, and a negative part about Them, such as:

- Apparent Denial: We have nothing against blacks, but...
- Apparent Concession: Some of them are smart, but in general...
- Apparent Empathy: Of course refugees have had problems, but...
- Apparent Ignorance: I don't know, but...
- Apparent Excuses: Sorry, but...
- Reversal (blaming the victim): Not they, but we are the real victims...
- Transfer: I don't mind, but my clients...

We see that these local moves instantiate within one sentence the overall (global) strategies of positive self-presentation (ingroup favoritism) and negative other-presentation (outgroup derogation). Note that some disclaimers are called "apparent" here, because the first, positive part primarily seems to function as a form of face-keeping and impression management: the rest of the text or fragment will focus on the negative characteristics of the Others, thus contradicting the first "positive" part.

In the same way, we may examine several other dimensions of everyday talk about minorities. Thus it was found that in *narrative structures* of everyday negative stories about immigrants, often the resolution category was lacking. This may be interpreted as a structural device that enhances precisely the negative aspects of the complication category of a story: stories that have (positive) resolutions of problems or conflicts are less efficient as complaint stories about Others.

Similarly, stories also often have the role of premises that present the undeniable "facts" of personal experience in *argumentations* that lead to negative conclusions about minorities. It need hardly be stressed that such argumentations are replete with fallacies. Thus negative statements about the Others will typically be supported by the authority move that says that people "saw it on TV." In the same way as prejudices are stereotypical negative social representations, arguments themselves may be stereotypical and conventional. Thus, refugees will typically be described as a "financial burden" for Our society, who would be taken better care of "in their own region," dissuaded from coming because they may "suffer from popular resentment" here, or recommended to stay in their own country in order to "help build it up."

Finally, even at the surface levels of actual talk management, for instance, in turn-taking, fluency, and so forth, we may witness that white speakers appear to show insecurity or uneasiness, for example, by the extra use of hesitations, pauses, and repairs when they have to name or identify minorities.

As we have stressed before, these and other properties of discourse about Others have interactional-social conditions, functions, and consequences, as well as cognitive ones. Thus, outgroup derogation is itself a social, discriminatory practice, but at the same time its discursive manifestations express underlying prejudices, which may in turn contribute to the formation or confirmation of such prejudices with the recipients.

News Reports

Everyday conversations are the natural locus of everyday popular racism. Because they do not have active control over public elite discourse, ordinary people often have no more "to say" or "to do" against the Others than talking negatively to Them, and about Them.

Of course, ethnic stereotypes and prejudices, just like rumors, may spread fast in such a way.

As suggested, however, much everyday talk about minorities is inspired by the mass media. Speakers routinely refer to television or the newspaper as their source (and authority) of knowledge or opinions about ethnic minorities. This is especially the case for those topics that cannot be observed directly in everyday interaction, even in ethnically mixed countries or cities. Immigration is a prominent example, in which most citizens depend on the mass media, which in turn depend on politicians, bureaucrats, the police, or state agencies. Of course, in cities, regions, or countries with few minorities, virtually all beliefs about the Others come from mass media discourse, literature, textbooks, studies, or other forms of elite discourse. In other words, not only for ordinary citizens but also for the elites themselves, the mass media are today the primary source of "ethnic" knowledge and opinion in society.

It is not surprising therefore that the representation of minorities in the media such as television, newspapers, and movies has been extensively investigated (Dates and Barlow, 1990; Jäger and Link, 1993; Hartmann and Husband, 1974; van Dijk, 1991). Much earlier work is content-analytical, that is, quantitative research into observable features of text or talk, such as how often members of a specific ethnic group are portrayed in the news or advertising and in what roles. These studies offer some general insight, but do not tell us in detail *how* exactly the media portray minorities or ethnic relations. Sophisticated discourse analysis is able to provide such a study, and also is able actually to explain why media discourses have the structures they have, and how these affect the minds of the recipients. It is only in such a way that we get insight into the fundamental role of the media in the reproduction of racism.

If we focus more specifically on the media genre that is at the basis of most beliefs about minorities, namely the news, we may proceed in a way that is similar to that presented above for conversations. That is, we examine each of the levels identified above, and search for structures or strategies that seem typical for media portrayals of the Others.

News reports in the press, for instance, have a conventional schematic structure consisting of such categories as summary (headline + lead), main events, background (previous events, context, history), comments, and evaluation. Thus, we may focus on *headlines* and see whether these typical summaries of news reports are different for minorities than when they are about dominant group members. Following the general ideological square introduced above, we may for instance assume that headlines in the news tend to emphasize the negative characteristics of minorities. Much research has shown that this is indeed the case. In a Dutch study, for instance, we found that of 1500 headlines on ethnic issues, not a single one was positive when it involved minorities as active, responsible agents, whereas such is much more normal when one of Us is the semantic agent in a headline. Also the syntax of headlines may thus be biased in favor of the ingroup, for instance, when passive constructions diminish their responsibility for negative actions.

Headlines summarize the most important information of a news report, and hence also express its main topic. Further analysis of these overall meanings of discourse confirms what we already found in everyday conversations, which apparently seem to follow the media in that respect (and vice versa, the media in a sense also reflect commonsense beliefs), namely, that *topics* can be classified as being about difference, deviance, and threat. If we list the most important topics in "ethnic" news in different Western countries, or countries where Europeans are dominant, we always come up with a standard list of preferred topics, such as

- Immigration and reception of newcomers;
- Socioeconomic issues, (un)employment;
- Cultural differences;
- Crime, violence, drugs, and deviance;
- Ethnic relations, discrimination.

In other words, of the many possible topics, we again find a short, stereotypical list, in which the categories are usually defined in a negative way. Thus, immigration is always defined as a fundamental problem, and never as a challenge, let alone as a boon to the country, often associated with a financial burden. The same is true for the other main topics. Crime or crime-related topics such as drugs are virtually always among the top five of minority portrayals – even focusing on what is seen as "typical" ethnic crime, such as drug trafficking and sales, but also what is defined as political "terrorism" (for instance about Arabs). Cultural differences tend to be overemphasized, and cultural similarities ignored. Even discrimination and racism, which may provide a more balanced view of the "negative" aspects of society, are seldom news about the prevalence of discrimination and racism in society, but at most about popular resentment (very seldom or never about elite racism), about individual cases of discrimination, for example, on the job, or about extremist racist parties. In other words, discrimination and racism, when discussed at all in elite discourse, are always *elsewhere*.

Whereas topics are undoubtedly the most important, while also the most memorable aspect of news, they merely tell us *what* the media report about ethnic issues, not *how* they do so. Although we have less detailed insight into the local aspects of meaning, style, and rhetoric of news reporting on "race," there are a few findings that appear to be fairly reliable.

We already have observed for headlines that responsible agency may be enhanced or backgrounded by active or passive sentences. In the same way, backgrounding agency may occur in nominalizations, or word order of sentences. Again, the (largely unintentional) strategy that governs such local structures is the combined polarized tendency of positive self-presentation and negative other-presentation. Thus, we may find references to "resentment" or "discrimination" in the country, but it is not always spelled out *who* resents or discriminates against *whom*, as if discrimination or racism were phenomena of nature instead of practices of dominant group members.

Besides such aspects of discursive surface forms (syntax), it is especially the rich system of *meaning* that incorporates the many underlying beliefs that represent mental models of ethnic events, or more general, shared social representations of ethnic groups or ethnic relations. Following the now familiar ideological square, we thus may expect, and indeed do find, that in general information that is positive about Us or negative about Them will get highlighted, and vice versa. Semantically this means that such information will tend to be explicit rather than implicit, precise rather than vague, specific rather than general, asserted rather than presupposed, detailed instead of dealt with in abstractions. Thus, our intolerance, everyday racism, or discrimination will seldom be reported in much concrete detail, but their crimes, violence, and deviance will.

153

Taking into account the cognitive interface discussed above, we suppose that such meaning structures are a function of underlying mental representations which simply portray ethnic events and ethnic groups in that way. These may be *ad hoc*, personal mental models with personal opinions, but also widely shared stereotypes, prejudices, and ideologies. And the less these are conscious (as is often the case for more subtle forms of racism), the more the consensus is intertwined with dominant ethnic ideologies. Indeed, detailed news analysis about ethnic events provides a rich source for a study of contemporary social cognition.

Note though that what people say and mean in discourse is not only a direct function of their ethnic beliefs, but also a function of *context*, such as the setting, genre, speakers/ writers, the audience, and so on. Thus news on ethnic affairs in serious broadsheets and in tabloids is very different for those contextual reasons, even if the journalists' underlying mental models about the ethnic events would be roughly the same. These contextual differences especially manifest themselves in the variable surface structures of style (layout, syntax, lexicalization, rhetorical devices).

News reports also have an important intertextual dimension. Newsmaking is largely based on the processing of a large number of source texts, such as other news reports, press conferences, interviews, scholarly studies, and so on. Such intertextuality in news reports shows in various forms of citation and other references to other discourses. Thus, it comes as no surprise that newspapers will generally take (white) elite source texts (e.g., of government, scholars, or the police) as being more credible and newsworthy than source texts of minority group members. Indeed, minority groups have little direct access to the media. If they are cited, they are always accompanied by declarations of credible majority group members. Statements about discrimination and racism will often be downgraded to the dubious status of allegations.

Whereas these and many other aspects of news reporting about race clearly express and reproduce dominant ethnic attitudes and ideologies, and hence crucially influence racism, it should finally be emphasized that problematization and marginalization do not only apply to minorities in the news, but also in the newsroom. Especially in Western Europe, leading reporters are virtually always white Europeans. No wonder that these will follow a beat, search for sources, and believe opinions that are consistent with their own and other members of their group, and much less those of minority groups. So far, thus, minority journalists have had less access to the media, especially in leading positions. As we have seen, the elites, especially in Europe, are virtually always white, and they also control the contents, forms, style, and goals of news and newsmaking. And it comes as no surprise therefore that the mass media, and especially the right-wing tabloid press, is rather part of the problem of racism than part of its solution.

Textbooks

Arguably, after the mass media, educational discourse is most influential in society, especially when it comes to the communication of beliefs that are not usually conveyed in everyday conversation or the media. All children, adolescents, and young adults, are daily confronted for many hours with lessons and textbooks – the only books that are obligatory reading in our culture. That is, there is no comparable institution and discourse that is as massively inculcated as that of school.

The bad news is that this is also true for lessons about Them – immigrants, refugees, minorities, and peoples in the Third World – and that such discourses are often very stereotypical and sometimes plainly prejudiced. The good news is that there is no domain or institution in society where alternative discourses have more possibilities to develop than in education.

Many studies have been carried out on the portrayal of minorities and Third World people in textbooks. Even simple content analyses have repeatedly shown that such portrayal, at least until recently, tends to be biased, stereotypical, and Eurocentric, and in early textbooks even explicitly racist (Blondin, 1990; Klein, 1985; Preiswerk, 1980; van Dijk, 1993).

As suggested, much has changed in contemporary textbooks. Whereas minorities were earlier virtually ignored or marginalized in textbooks, at least until the late 1980s, and despite their prominent presence in the country and even in the classroom, current textbooks in the social sciences as well as other fields seem finally to have discovered that there are also minorities to write about. And whereas information about Us that could be negative (such as colonialism) used to be ignored or mitigated, there is now a tendency to want to teach children also about the less glorious aspects of "our" history or society.

And yet, this is a tendency but still far from the rule. Many contemporary textbooks in many Western countries remain basically Eurocentric: not only our economy or technology, but also our views, values, societies, and politics are invariably superior. They keep repeating stereotypes about minorities and other non-European people. Third World countries tend to be treated in a homogeneous way, despite the huge differences. As is the case in the press, the Others are invariably associated with Problems, for which however We tend to offer a solution. All this is equally true for minorities *in* the country, which largely are dealt with in terms of cultural differences and deviance, and seldom in terms of their everyday life, work, and contributions to both culture and the economy. Finally, textbook assignments too often ignore the presence of minority children in the classroom, and if not, these may be spoken about as Them, and not always addressed as part of Us.

These and many other properties of textbooks obviously are hardly an ideal preparation for the acquisition of ethnic beliefs that prepare children adequately for contemporary, increasingly multicultural, and diverse societies in Western Europe, North America, and elsewhere where Europeans are dominant over non-Europeans. As is the case for the media and the adult population, textbooks and lessons based on them form the discursive crucible for the everyday reproduction of biased ethnic beliefs and the often discriminatory practices based on them. We have argued that racism is learned and not natural or innate. This learning process already begins at school.

Political Discourse: Parliamentary Debates

Finally, among the influential symbolic elites of society, that is, those who have special access to and control over public discourse, we should mention the politicians. Indeed, sometimes even before the mass media, leading politicians have already preformulated a definition of the ethnic situation. State institutions such as the immigration service and the police, as well as their sustaining bureaucracies, are often the first to actually "talk to" new immigrants, as well as talk about them. Such discourse will rapidly become official, both as to meaning/content and style, and routinely adopted by the media which cover these agencies and institutions, thus spreading dominant definitions of the ethnic situation among the population at large. Also depending on political parties and contexts, such discourses may again be stereotypical, biased, or even racist, or indeed take a dissident, antiracist position based on human rights, multiculturalism, and diversity (see, e.g., Hargreaves and Leaman, 1995; Hurwitz and Peffley, 1998; Solomos, 1993).

Historically, political discourse on the Others, whether minorities within the country or non-Europeans in Third World countries or colonies, has been among the most blatantly racist forms of elite discourse (Lauren, 1988). Until at least World War II, leading politicians would openly derogate people of Asian or African origin, and claim their white, Western superiority. But due to the Holocaust and World War II, and as a result of the discrediting of racist beliefs because of their use by the Nazis, postwar political discourse has become increasingly less blatant on the right, and more antiracist on the left. This development, however, should not be seen as a steady form of progress, because in the 1990s problematizing and stigmatizing discourse on refugees and immigrants has reappeared more openly, even in mainstream parties.

Analysis of parliamentary debates on minorities, immigration, refugees, and ethnic issues more generally shows many features that are consistent with those of other elite discourses we have examined above (van Dijk, 1993). Specific for this discourse genre are of course especially its contextual characteristics: the political domain, the institution of parliament, the overall sociopolitical act of legislation, the participants in many different roles (politicians, party members, MPs, representatives, opposition members, etc.), and the local acts involved, such as defending or opposing a bill, giving a speech, criticizing the government, attacking opponents, and so on.

Large parts of parliamentary debates on immigration and ethnic issues are organized as a function of these context dimensions. Thus, populist strategies of talk, in which the will of the people is invoked, for instance, to restrict immigration, is of course a function of the position of MPs needing votes to stay in office or to toe the party line. Positions on ethnic policies taken and defended in parliament, thus, are not primarily personal opinions, but expressions of shared political party attitudes. And topics selected are those that are a function of the actual business of legislation at hand, such as dealing with an immigration bill or the arrival of refugees from Bosnia or Kosovo.

Political context similarly defines the nationalism that transpires in debates on immigration and minorities. In the same way as we find disclaimers in everyday talk, parliamentary speeches may begin with long sections of positive self-presentation in the form of nationalist glorification of "long traditions of tolerance" or "hospitality for the oppressed." But of course, "we can not let them all in," "we have no money," and so forth. That is, the rest of such debates will often be quite negative when it comes to the characterization of the others or the legitimation of further restrictions on immigration. That at least is the dominant voice – because occasionally we also find more tolerant, antiracist, dissident voices which make appeal to human rights and universal principles.

Structurally speaking, parliamentary debates are organized sequences of speeches, by government and opposition speakers respectively. Given the respective political positions and roles, thus, each speaker will speak "to" a specific issue, such as a recent ethnic event or a bill, and argue for or against a number of standpoints, for instance, aspects of ethnic or immigration policy. This means that such debates and their speeches will be largely argumentative and rhetorical.

Apart from the well-known rhetoric of nationalism, populism, or human rights mentioned above, what is perhaps most fascinating in parliamentary debates on immigration are the *argumentative moves*, for instance, those that are used to legitimate immigration restrictions. Many of these moves have become standard arguments or *topoi*, such as the reference to our ("white man's") financial burden, the regrettable reference to "resentment" in the country, the suggestion of receiving refugees in their own country, the need to listen to the will of the people, and so on. Similarly, such argumentations are replete with *fallacies* of various kinds. Credibility rather than truth is managed by referring to authoritative sources or opinion makers, such as scholars or the Church. Selected but emotionally effective examples are used either of immigration fraud or of torture by foreign regimes in order to argue against or for liberal immigration laws for refugees, in both cases giving in to the fallacy of generalization from single cases. Again, the overall strategy in the selection of argumentative moves is positive self-presentation and negative other-presentation. The Others in such a case may be not only the immigrants, but also those members of (opposed) political parties who defend their rights, or vice versa, those who are seen to infringe upon such rights.

Parliamentary debates are public, for the record, and official. This means that both content and style are strictly controlled, especially in written speeches. There is less formality in spontaneous debate, with large variation according to countries: in France such debates may be heated, with many interruptions, heckling, and many rhetorical styles, unlike the Netherlands and Spain, where parliamentary debates are formal and polite. This also applies to meanings and style of debates on minorities and immigration.

Self-control and public exposure prohibits, for instance, explicit forms of derogation or lexical selection that is obviously biased. This means that such official discourse will seldom appear very racist. On the contrary, tolerance and understanding may be extensively topicalized. But we have seen that this may also be a move, a disclaimer that introduces more negative topics. And in order to legitimate immigration restrictions, thus, speakers need to spell out why immigrants or immigration are bad for Us, and such an overall statement can only be conveyed by the general strategy, implemented at all levels of discourse, of negative other-presentation. Thus, in parliament, there will be references to fraud, drugs, or crime of immigrants, as well as to cultural differences and conflicts, and to the disastrous impact on the job market.

Concluding Remark

In sum, we see that influential public discourses, namely, that of the elites and elite institutions, show a large number of related characteristics. These not only reflect similar underlying mental models and social representations shared by the elites, but also similar ways of social interaction, communication, persuasion, and public opinion formation. Differences are mostly contextual, that is, depend on the aims, functions, or participants involved in them. But given similar aims, namely, the management of public opinion, legitimation, and decision making, we may assume that very similar structures and strategies will be at work in such discourse types. We will encounter stereotypical topics, conventional topoi, disclaimers that save face and hence manage impression formation; they engage in similar argumentative fallacies, make similar lexical selections when talking about Them, or use the same metaphors to emphasize some of their (bad) characteristics. All these different structures at different levels, and of different elite genres, contribute to the overall strategy of positive self-presentation and negative other-presentation. We have seen that precisely such structures may derive from and be geared towards the construction of similar mental structures, that is, negative attitudes and ideologies on minorities and immigration. And since among the elites as well as among the population at large such dominant group cognitions will again inspire similarly negative discourses and social practices, we may begin to understand how discourse, and especially public elite discourses, is crucially involved in the reproduction of racism.

References

Blondin, D. (1990) *L'apprentissage du racisme dans les manuels scolaires* [Racism Apprenticeship in Textbooks]. Montréal, Québec: Editions Agence d'Arc.

Brown, R. (1995) *Prejudice: Its Social Psychology*. Oxford: Blackwell.

Dates, J. L. and Barlow, W. (eds.) (1990) *Split Image: African Americans in the Mass Media*. Washington, DC: Howard University Press.

Dovidio, J. F. and Gaertner, S. L. (eds.) (1986) *Prejudice, Discrimination, and Racism*. Orlando, FL: Academic Press.

Essed, P. (1991) *Understanding Everyday Racism: An Interdisciplinary Theory*. Newbury Park, CA: Sage Publications.

Hargreaves, A. G. and Leaman, J. (eds.) (1995) *Racism, Ethnicity, and Politics in Contemporary Europe*. Aldershot, UK: Elgar.

Hartmann, P. and Husband, C. (1974) *Racism and the Mass Media*. London: Davis-Poynter.

Hurwitz, J. and Peffley, M. (eds.) (1998) *Perception and Prejudice: Race and Politics in the United States*. New Haven, CT: Yale University Press.

Jäger, S. (1992) *Brandsätze. Rassismus im Alltag* [*Inflammatory Sentences/ Firebombs. Racism in Everyday Life*]. Duisburg, Germany: DISS.

Jäger, S. and Link, J. (1993) *Die vierte Gewalt. Rassismus und die Medien* [*The Fourth Power. Racism and the Media*]. Duisburg, Germany: DISS.

Katz, P. A. and Taylor, D. A. (eds.) (1988) *Eliminating Racism: Profiles in Controversy*. New York: Plenum Press.

Klein, G. (1985) *Reading into Racism: Bias in Children's Literature and Learning Materials*. London: Routledge & Kegan Paul.

Lauren, P. G. (1988) *Power and Prejudice. The Politics and Diplomacy of Racial Discrimination*. Boulder, CO: Westview Press.

Omi, M. and Winant, H. (1994) *Racial Formation in the United States. From the 1960s to the 1990s*. London: Routledge.

Preiswerk, R. (1980) *The Slant of the Pen: Racism in Children's Books*. Geneva: Programme to Combat Racism, World Council of Churches.

Sniderman, P. M., Tetlock, P. E., and Carmines, E. G. (eds.) (1993) *Prejudice, Politics, and the American Dilemma*. Stanford, CA: Stanford University Press.

Solomos, J. (1993) *Race and Racism in Britain*. New York: St. Martin's Press.

Van Dijk, T. A. (1984) *Prejudice in Discourse: An Analysis of Ethnic Prejudice in Cognition and Conversation*. Amsterdam: J. Benjamins Co.

Van Dijk, T. A. (1987) *Communicating Racism: Ethnic Prejudice in Thought and Talk*. Newbury Park, CA: Sage Publications.

Van Dijk, T. A. (1991) *Racism and the Press*. London: Routledge.

Van Dijk, T. A. (1993) *Elite Discourse and Racism*. Newbury Park, CA: Sage Publications.

Van Dijk, T. A. (ed.) (1997) *Discourse Studies: A Multidisciplinary Introduction*. London: Sage.

Van Dijk, T. A. (1998) *Ideology. A Multidisciplinary Study*. London: Sage.

Wellman, D. T. (1993) *Portraits of White Racism*. Cambridge, UK: Cambridge University Press.

Wetherell, M. and Potter, J. (1992) *Mapping the Language of Racism: Discourse and the Legitimation of Exploitation*. New York: Columbia University Press.

Wodak, R., Nowak, P., Pelikan, J., Gruber, H., de Cillia, R., and Mitten, R. (1990) *"Wir sind alle unschuldige Täter." Diskurshistorische Studien zum Nachkriegsantisemitismus* [*"We are all innocent perpetrators." Discourse Historic Studies in Postwar Antisemitism*]. Frankfurt/Main: Suhrkamp.

Zanna, M. P. and Olson, J. M. (eds.) (1994) *The Psychology of Prejudice*. The Ontario Symposium, vol. 7. Hillsdale, NJ: Lawrence Erlbaum.

Chapter 13

Critical Race Feminism: Legal Reform for the Twenty-first Century

Adrien Katherine Wing

In this chapter, I hope to identify the intellectual threads that have contributed to this loosely woven tapestry I am labeling Critical Race Feminism (CRF). The notion expands upon the issues addressed in my first anthology *Critical Race Feminism: A Reader* (Wing, 1997a). That book was the first collection predominantly focusing on the legal status of women of color living in the United States, that is, African Americans, Latinas, Asians, and Native Americans. In the words of CRF foremother Professor Mari Matsuda, these women can experience "multiple consciousness," an awareness of oppression they face based simultaneously upon their race/ethnicity and gender (Matsuda, 1992). The volume emphasizes not only discrimination faced, but also resilience, resistance, and formation of solutions. It covers such diverse areas as antiessentialism, education, mothering, employment, welfare reform, criminality, domestic violence, and sexual harassment. A second volume is devoted to global legal issues affecting women of color, known as Global Critical Race Feminism (GCRF) (Wing, 2000).

In my travels I am frequently asked the meaning of this odd term "Critical Race Feminism." Some people have wondered if CRF adherents are "male-hating, bra burning feminazis in blackface." Some men of color have asked if we are race traitors who prioritize gender over racial solidarity. Professor Richard Delgado of the University of Colorado Law School coined the term CRF in the first edition of his anthology *Critical Race Theory: The Cutting Edge* (Delgado, 1995). The beauty of the strange expression is that each word represents one of the primary legal traditions from which it derives – those being Critical Legal Studies (CLS), Critical Race Theory (CRT), and feminist jurisprudence.

When I explain the derivation of CRF in some circles, I am sometimes met by a stony silence or a condescendingly polite response, "oh, that's very nice," as the conversation returns back to "real law." Implicit in the exchange or lack of exchange may be skepticism on several levels. Aren't the concerns of this subcategory of people covered adequately by "real law," that is, race and gender-neutral law? If not, doesn't the US race and gender discrimination law that has evolved primarily from the 1960s civil rights movements adequately protect women of color? Doesn't the post-World War II international legal regime that has developed principally since "First World" decolonization of most of the "Third World" encompass the legal problems of "Third World" women?

Critical Race Feminism is evolving as a richly textured genre interwoven with many areas of jurisprudence because the answer to all of the above questions is a resounding "No!" Existing legal paradigms under US, foreign, and international law have permitted women of color to fall between the cracks – becoming literally and figuratively voiceless and invisible. CRF attempts not only to identify and theorize about those cracks in the legal regime, but to formulate relevant solutions as well. We are consciously attempting to translate between cultures – the cultures of privilege of those who have the luxury of time and capacity to read a book like this, and those who will never have the opportunity to enjoy such intellectual largesse. As translators, we therefore are assisting in demarginalizing the lives and legal concerns of women of color.

Genesis

CRF originates from a collection of interrelated intellectual trends that emerged at the end of the twentieth century. It is my fervent hope that these colorful threads will continue to evolve into an increasingly interwoven tapestry that will have a place in global academic discourse in the twenty-first century. It is not that CRF is a simple hybrid, but that the trends are "elements in the conditions of its possibility" (Crenshaw et al., 1995:xix). The three strands I will now briefly discuss are CLS, CRT, and feminism.

The Conference on Critical Legal Studies was organized in the late 1970s by progressive white male academics who had been formed by the 1960s movements for social change. Like these men, Critical Race feminists endorse a left perspective on the role of law in American society. We critique both conservative orthodoxies and legal liberalism. We challenge the notion of law as neutral, objective, and determinate. We may also use the methodology of deconstruction of European postmodernists such as Jacques Derrida to expose how law has served to perpetuate unjust class, race, and gender hierarchies.

As part of CRT, CRF extends beyond the intellectual borders of CLS. CRT constitutes a race intervention in leftist discourse and a leftist intervention in race discourse. In illuminating the racist nature of the American legal system, CRT adherents are particularly interested in legal manifestations of white supremacy and the perpetuation of the subordination of people of color. While critical race theorists are concerned with class issues, since the majority of people of color are impoverished, we realize that poor communities of color have never been treated identically to the white underclass. Although CRT endorses the CLS notion that legal rights are indeterminate, we vehemently disagree that rights are therefore not important (Williams, 1987). Indeed the struggle to attain human rights remains critical for American minorities who have never had the luxury of taking such rights for granted.

In addition to challenging leftist discourse, critical race theorists also simultaneously engage in a leftist critique of liberal civil rights paradigms as well. We believe that racism has been an integral part of the American legal system since its founding, rather than an aberrational spot on the pristine white body politic. Racial progress is not necessarily inevitable, but may be cyclical. Gains often occur only if they are within white power elite self-interest (Bell, 1980). We thus reject the notion that the legal system has ever been color-blind, and specifically embrace color-consciousness and identity politics as the way to rectify today's racist legal legacies (Gotanda, 1991). Some of the CRT adherents may even agree with CRT founder, Professor Derrick Bell of New York University Law School, that racism is a permanent condition that can never be truly eradicated (Bell, 1992).

As Critical Race theorists, CRF adherents sometimes utilize the controversial story-telling technique as methodology (Bell, 1987). Opponents have attacked this approach as nonlegal, lacking intellectual rigor, overly emotional, and subjective (Farber and Sherry, 1997). This methodology, however, has significant value. Many of us prize our heritages in which the oral tradition has had historical importance – where vital notions of justice and the law are communicated generation to generation through the telling of stories. Also, using stories enables us to connect to those who do not understand hypertechnical legal language, but may nonetheless seek understanding of our distinctive voices (Delgado, 1990). We also believe in using critical historical methodology to demarginalize the roles people of color have played, usually outside the scope of the traditional historian's interests (Dudziak, 1994; Smith, 1994).

Additionally, we endorse a multidisciplinary approach to scholarship in which the law may be a necessary, but not sufficient, basis to formulate solutions to racial dilemmas. Thus there may be significant citation to disciplines such as history, sociology, political science, economics, anthropology, as well as African American studies, and Women's Studies.

Although CRF proponents endorse Critical Race *Theory*, we wholeheartedly embrace critical race *praxis* as well (Wing, 1990–91). Since many of us come from disenfranchised communities of color, we feel compelled to "look to the bottom," to involve ourselves in the development of solutions to our people's problems. We cannot afford to adopt the classic detached ivory tower model of scholarship, when so many are suffering, sometimes in our own extended families. We do not believe in praxis instead of theory, but that both are essential to our peoples' literal and figurative future.

There are many forms that praxis can take. In addition to working with various public interest and nongovernmental organizations, Critical Race feminists have engaged in law reform in the United States and internationally. Coalition building, political activism, board memberships, speeches, and even writing can all be forms of praxis. My own attempts at praxis have included working with actor and former star football player Jim Brown's Amer-I-Can Program Inc., a rehabilitative and preventive self-esteem curriculum ideally suited for youth at risk, ex-offenders, gang members and others. This praxis enabled me to enrich my own efforts at theorizing about gang life. Internationally, I have advised the African National Congress Constitutional Committee on options for a democratic South Africa, as well as the Palestinian Legislative Council as it drafted the first constitution. Once again, these efforts enriched my subsequent scholarship and teaching on these topics.

CRT now also includes related areas such as Critical White Studies (Delgado, 1990), Latino Critical Theory, Asian Crits (Chang, 1993), and Queer Theory (Valdes, 1995).

Another jurisprudential tradition that CRF draws from is feminism. CRF constitutes a race intervention in feminist discourse, in that it necessarily embraces feminism's emphasis on gender oppression within a system of patriarchy. But most CRF proponents have not joined the mainstream feminist movement. While reasons vary, in some cases the refusal to become associated is due to that movement's essentialization of all women, which subsumes the variable experiences of women of color within the experience of white middle-class women (Crenshaw, 1989). Mainstream feminism has paid insufficient attention to the central role of white supremacy's subordination of women of color, effectuated by both white men and women.

In addition to rejecting essentialism within feminism, Critical Race feminists reject CRT's essentialization of all minorities. As the experiences of males may differ significantly from females, we are thus a feminist intervention within CRT. Our antiessentialist premise is that identity is *not* additive. In other words, black women are not white women plus color, or black men plus gender.

CRF goes beyond the domestic focus on the United States that is typical of most scholarship on CLS, CRT, and feminism, and embraces global or transnational perspectives. Our analysis may embrace strands from international and comparative law, global feminism, and postcolonial theory as well. We are extending the narrow US notion of race to examine the legal treatment of women of color, whether they are living in developing or industrialized societies. We want to inspire scholars to engage in looking at multiple levels of discrimination and privileging that women may simultaneously face globally, not only on the basis of their race and gender, but also due to their nationality, ethnicity, color, class, sexual orientation, age, disability, religion, primary language, minority status, pregnancy status, and marital status.

Global Multiplicative Identities

As previously stated, Mari Matsuda coined the term "multiple consciousness" to describe the intersectional identities of women of color. In earlier scholarship, I have chosen to use the word "multiplicative" to configure identity (Wing, 1990–91). As a simplistic example, I am black × female. If you multiply my identities together, you have one indivisible being. You cannot subtract out any part of my identity, and ask me to pretend I am only a woman today or only a black. Currently, I am in the beginning stages of developing a global perspective on identity that I would like to share here (Wing, 1999). My initial premise is that everyone has multiple identities, not just women of color in the United States. Anglo-Saxon American males have multiple identities, and within a global context, most of their identities may privilege them. Women of color, on the other hand, may primarily possess a cluster of identities that lead them to face multiple forms of discrimination. But the analysis must become more complex. Even women of color, who are disproportionally impoverished, may have some identities that relatively privilege them. To assist women of color, we need to delineate their multiple identities, examine how those identities intersect to privilege or lead them to face discrimination, and then design multidimensional programs that would enhance their life situations.

I will now detail a number of identities that everyone has, and for simplicity's sake, discuss them separately. In reality, the impact of the intersection of the identities should be elaborated simultaneously.

For instance, one of the major identities we have is our nationality. While in our home country, that status might not be central to us on a daily basis. On the other hand, when traveling abroad, my American identity may privilege me or lead me to face discrimination. For example, every summer, I teach in South Africa. When I go shopping in the stores, the white shopkeepers often frown at my brown face. As soon as I speak in my American accent, their faces beam and they are most helpful. I represent the almighty dollar. That same status has caused me to fear being robbed or ripped off, since I might be regarded as a "rich American." It took me a number of trips before I realized that indeed I am a rich American, at least as juxtaposed to the majority of Africans.

Even within the United States, my US nationality may matter in many situations. I know that I can theoretically receive many benefits not open to "illegal aliens," legal tourists, foreign students, or even permanent residents.

Another central identity is race, which CRT and CRF naturally highlight. One tenet of CRT is that race is socially constructed, rather than biologically determined (Lopez, 1997). As a matter of fact, scientists have shown that there are often more genetic similarities across different so-called racial groups than within them. To illustrate how race is socially constructed globally, in the USA I am considered a member of the black race. Both my parents and both sets of grandparents are African Americans. In South Africa, based upon my light skin tone, shape of nose, and wavy hair texture, I am regarded as a Colored or mixed race person. I am far too light to be considered black. When I walk down the street there with my partner, who is a dark-skinned black American, we are considered an interracial couple. In Brazil, I discovered I am considered white! Only the darkest people of relatively unmixed African descent are considered black.

This example also illustrates the importance of an identity based on skin color. My skin tone has caused me to be called Latina, Indian, Arab, mulatto, biracial, and so forth. Within the Black American group, my coloring has historically led to a privileged position, because I am something known as "high yellow." The lighter skinned blacks have received benefits dating back to slavery, often because they were the master's illegitimate progeny. They may have become "house niggers" instead of field hands. Apparently, the only slaves former President Thomas Jefferson freed upon his death were the children of his long-time slave mistress, Sallie Hemmings. Several of these children immediately passed over into the white world, and the whereabouts of their descendants are unknown.

Today, lighter skinned African Americans remain overrepresented in the numbers of blacks who have attended college, attained professional status, and so forth (Russell et al., 1992). In my own maternal family's case, I am a third generation college graduate in part because of the actions taken by my maternal great-great-grandfather, Confederate General Pierre Gustave Toutant Beauregard, who apparently set his quadroon daughter Susan on the path of higher education. Internationally, I believe my skin tone has contributed to my warm acceptance in many countries. "You look just like my sister, mother, or aunt," I am often told.

Ethnicity is an interesting aspect of identity, but one that may be too often conflated with race, even in CRT-oriented scholarship. Although my skin color indicates many possible ethnicities, I am black American or African-American. Blacks living in the United States who are from the Caribbean or Africa may not consider themselves part of the same group as me. Imagine a white South African, who moves to the USA and becomes a citizen. Isn't she an African American? I have cousins who are Jamaican Americans and Liberian Americans. Some consider themselves Black Americans and some do not.

Another identity can be one's status as a member of a minority group. While a Nigerian American is a minority in the USA and may be subjected to some discrimination or relative privileging, in Nigeria this person is obviously not a minority. Instead it may be their ethnic status as Yoruba or Hausa that helps or hinders them.

Religious affiliation is an important aspect of identity for many people. In the US context, I am a secular mainstream-denomination Protestant, and I do not often think about this status. When I travel to the Middle East, my identity as a Christian is juxtaposed with those around me who are mainly Muslim or Jewish. During the Palestinian uprising from 1987 to 1993, I visited the Gaza Strip several times. At one point, Islamic fundamentalists were stoning or throwing things at women who were not wearing a *hijab*, or headscarf. Even though I was a Christian and thus technically not subject to the admonition against bare heads, I put on the *hijab* (Wing, 1994). Since my coloring and facial features indicate that I could be mistaken for a Palestinian, I was not willing to take a chance of trying to reason with a stone thrower.

With respect to gender, I will not belabor the point here since this identity is a central focus of CRF. On a personal note, I recall the numerous incidents where people have visited my office, looked at me behind my desk, and asked, "Where is Professor Wing, where is he?" The assumption of many men and women is still that only men can be professors.

Interestingly, when traveling globally, I am usually considered an "honorary male" and invited to dinners where no other women may be present. I have been served meals by women, who then retreat to a back room to eat with other women and children, as their men and I discuss politics, business, or international relations. My efforts to bridge the chasms of class, ethnicity, and culture that divide us are often defeated by our inability to speak the same language. Many wives have not had the same educational opportunities as their husbands to learn an international language like English. When I can communicate directly or through translation, I find that my identity as a mother is very valuable. As a mother of many sons, I am often considered multiply blessed and conversation may focus on the accomplishments of my fine young men.

My monolingual identity is a major inhibitor to my communication internationally, and to that of most Americans. The hodgepodge of French, Portuguese, Swahili, Spanish, and Arabic that I can utter does not substitute for the multilingual fluency needed for nuanced discourse. For example, if I must use male translators to ask uneducated Palestinian women how they feel about their lives, how am I to judge the filtered responses? What editing has occurred? What facial and tonal nuances have I missed because of my primary English-speaking identity? What fears do they have that I will get them in trouble with their menfolk in satisfying my outsider curiosity?

Sexual orientation is an identity that heterosexuals rarely think about, since they are privileged on this basis. I did not realize how much my heterosexuality was part of my identity until lesbian friends pointed out the privileges that I had every day, feeling free to talk about my partner, hold hands in public, place his picture in my office, slow dance at a club, and so forth. Thus even though I have felt discrimination as a black heterosexual woman, my situation is not the same as a black lesbian. It is the work of such lesbians, like the late Audre Lorde, that helped me understand the holistic nature of identity (Lorde, 1984).

Marx, Engels, Lenin, and their followers developed socialist theory and left the world the legacy of class analysis. In the legal academy, CLS has developed a literature that addresses this aspect. Much of CRT focuses implicitly or explicitly on class, but sometimes conflates lower or working class with minority racial/ethnic status.

Age is another aspect of identity, one that obviously changes over time. In some careers, such as athletics, modeling, or acting for women, youth is a privileging identity. In other fields, such as law, senior people may be accorded a respect and stature that eludes the young. I keep thinking that one day when I go totally gray, I will be treated with respect. My senior female colleagues assure me that this is definitely not the case for them as women. I also suspect that my relatively youthful appearance has exacerbated the voluminous amount of what is now termed "sexual harassment" in the United States, but is even more likely still to be viewed as good-natured, harmless fun abroad. My nationality and ethnicity intersect here to apparently lead some foreign men blatantly to ask me if I would go to bed with them. They think they know that American women are very promiscuous, and they have heard that black American women are the sexiest. In my youth, I deeply resented the insinuation of American promiscuity. It took me a number of trips to realize that these leering men were at least partially correct. At the risk of "essentializing," American women as a class are more likely to engage in premarital sexual activity than can be the case for women in many developing countries, where virginity and chastity are highly valued and tightly controlled. Maybe my new status as a "bifocal granny" will confer more respect, and the harassment may decrease.

There are a number of other identities that may have important consequences at different stages of one's life. The disabled is one group that anyone may become a part of at short notice. The stigma that still surrounds being mentally or physically disabled is often so profound as to cause those affected to hide or deny the status if they are able.

Marital status is a variable identity that has particular consequences for women. In the USA, a woman's marital status may be instantly known if she uses Mrs. or Miss. I am sometimes asked if I married a Chinese man, because my surname is Wing. This name is my father's name and thus my "maiden" name, which I have never changed, despite being married. The divorced, widowed, single, or never married status can imply certain stereotypes about the desirability of the woman.

By delineating all these identities, I am not calling for balkanization ad infinitum. Strategic essentialism can be theoretically useful and practically necessary, particularly when the goal is to enhance our ability to design solutions for those subordinated in society. For example, current US welfare reform efforts focus on class and gender – poor women. Often implicit in the analysis is race, that is, concern for the black "welfare queen." Yet there are many different types of welfare recipients. The needs of a minimum-wage black lesbian single parent may be very different than a single white male who is mentally disabled and homeless. A Latina migrant worker, speaking very little English, married to an illegal alien who is battering her, would have different requirements as well. These last examples have just highlighted several identities we have not mentioned previously, including immigration status.

Through this discussion of global multiplicative identity, I have provided a small example of what CRF can bring to the global study of race and ethnicity.

CRF in its global dimensions (GCRF) also enhances the development of international and comparative law, which includes the subfields of public international law, human rights, international business transactions, and the comparative law of different countries. These are fields that developed primarily based upon principles first enunciated by American and European white male scholars. Men of color from the developing world did not become involved until their respective nations gained independence or sufficient clout in entities like the United Nations. Their voices are still muted, but often rise in discussions of cultural relativism and human rights. European and American women have only recently become involved in attempting to reconceptualize international law from feminist perspectives. Global feminists have noted that international law has failed to address what takes place in the private sphere of the family, where most women spend a significant part of their time.

One final thread contributing to the GCRF tapestry is postcolonial theory.

> It is marked by a dialectic between Marxism, on the one hand, and poststructuralism/ postmodernism, on the other…manifesting itself in an ongoing debate between the competing claims of nationalism and internationalism, strategic essentialism and hybridity, solidarity and dispersal, the politics of structure/totality and the politics of the fragment. (Gandhi, 1998:viii).

According to Leela Gandhi, postcolonialism's constituency is the "Western academy and it enables nonwestern critics located in the West to present their cultural inheritance as knowledge" (Gandhi, 1998:ix).

CRF contributes to the development of international law, global feminism, and postcolonial theory by demarginalizing women of color in a theoretical and practical sense. Women of color may be simultaneously dominated within the context of imperialism, neocolonialism, or occupation as well as local patriarchy, culture, and customs. They have often had to choose between the nationalist struggle for independence or self-determination and the women's struggle against patriarchy. The nationalist struggle usually has prevailed, and it was often back to "women's work" of taking care of the house and the children. Open acceptance of feminism can be seen as an unpatriotic embrace of Western values that may be regarded as inimical to local culture. One of the dilemmas for those who do choose to be known as feminists is how to embrace the universality of women's international human rights within their own cultural context.

In conclusion, Critical Race Feminism emerged in the legal academy at the end of the twentieth century as a new level of sophistication and nuance in the study of race and ethnicity issues. In the new millennium, it is my hope that more disciplines will incorporate CRF analysis into their studies of the lives of women of color around the world.

References

Bell, Derrick (1980) "Brown v. Board of Education and the interest convergence dilemma." *Harvard Law Review* 93:518–33.

Bell, Derrick (1987) *And We are not Saved: The Elusive Quest for Racial Justice*. New York: Basic Books.

Bell, Derrick (1992) *Faces at the Bottom of the Well: The Permanence of Racism*. New York: Basic Books.

Chang, Robert (1993) "Toward an Asian American legal scholarship: Critical Race Theory, poststructuralism, and narrative space." *California Law Review* 81:1243–1323.

Cleaver Kathleen (1997) "Racism, civil rights and feminism," in Adrien Katherine Wing (ed.) *Critical Race Feminism: A Reader*. New York: New York University Press, pp.35–43.

Crenshaw, Kimberle (1989) "Demarginalizing the intersection of race and sex: A black feminist critique of antidiscrimination doctrine, feminist theory, and antiracist politics." *University of Chicago Legal Forum* 1989:139–67.

Crenshaw, Kimberle, Thomas, Kendall, Gotanda, Neil, and Peller, Gary (eds.) (1995) "Introduction," in *Critical Race Theory: The Key Writings that Formed the Movement*. New York: New Press, pp.xiii–xxxii.

167

Delgado, Richard (1990) "When a story is just a story: Does voice really matter." *Virginia Law Review* 76:95–111.

Delgado, Richard (ed.) (1995) *Critical Race Theory: The Cutting Edge*. Philadelphia, PA: Temple University Press.

Delgado, Richard (ed.) (1997) *Critical White Studies: Looking Behind the Mirror*. Philadelphia: Temple University Press.

Dudziak, Mary (1994) "Josephine Baker, racial protest and the cold war." *Journal of American History* 81:543–70.

Farber, Daniel and Sherry, Suzanna (1997) *Beyond All Reason: The Radical Assault on Truth in American Law*. New York: Oxford University Press.

Gandhi, Leela (1998) *Postcolonial Theory: A Critical Introduction*. New York: Columbia University Press.

Gotanda, Neil (1991) "A critique of our constitution is color-blind." *Stanford Law Review* 44:1–68.

Guinier, Lani (1990–1) "Of gentlemen and role models." *Berkeley Women's Law Journal* 6:93–106.

Gunning, Isabelle (1991–2) "Arrogant perception, world traveling and multicultural feminism: The case of female genital surgeries." *Columbia Human Rights Journal* 23:189–248.

Harris, Angela P. (1990) "Race and essentialism in feminist legal theory." *Stanford Law Review* 42:581–616.

Hernandez Truyol, Berta Esperanza and Kimberly Johns (1998) "Global rights, local wrongs, and legal fixes: An international human rights critique of immigration and welfare 'reform.'" *Southern California Law Review* 71:547–615.

Hill, Anita (1992) "Sexual harassment: The nature of the beast." *Southern California Law Review* 65:1445–9.

Ho, Laura, Powell, Catherine, and Volpp, Leti (1996) "(Dis)assembling rights of women workers along the global assembly line: Human rights and the garment industry." *Harvard Civil Rights-Civil Liberties Law Review* 31:383–414.

Lewis, Hope (1997) "Lionheart gals facing the dragon: The human rights of inter/national Black women in the United States." *Oregon Law Review* 76:567–632.

Lopez, Ian Haney (1997) *White by Law*. New York: New York University Press.

Lorde, Audre (1984) *Sister Outsider: Essays and Speeches*. New York: Crossing Press.

Matsuda, Mari (1992) "When the first quail calls: Multiple consciousness as jurisprudential method." *Women's Rights Law Reporter* 14:297–303.

Roberts, Dorothy (1991) "Punishing drug addicts who have babies: Women of color, equality, and the right of privacy." *Harvard Law Review* 104:1419–82.

Russell, Kathy, Wilson, Midge, and Hall, Ronald (eds.) (1992) *The Color Complex: The Politics of Skin Color among African Americans*. New York: Harcourt Brace Jovanovich.

Scales-Trent, Judy (1989) "Black women and the constitution: Finding our place, asserting our rights." *Harvard Civil Rights-Civil Liberties Review* 24:9–44.

Smith, J. Clay Jr. (1994) "United States foreign policy and Goler Teal Butcher." *Howard Law Journal* 37:139–215.

Valdes, Francisco (1995) "Queers, sissies, dykes, and tomboys: Deconstructing the conflation of sex, gender, and sexual orientation." *California Law Review* 83:1–377.

Williams, Patricia (1987) "Alchemical notes: Reconstructing ideals from deconstructed rights." *Harvard Civil Rights-Civil Liberties Review* 22:401–33.

Wing, Adrien Katherine (1990–91) "Brief reflections toward a multiplicative theory and praxis of being." *Berkeley Women's Law Journal* 6:181–201.

Wing, Adrien Katherine (1994) "Custom, religion, and rights: The future legal status of Palestinian women." *Harvard International Law Journal* 35:149–200.

Wing, Adrien Katherine (ed.) (1997a). *Critical Race Feminism: A Reader*. New York: New York University Press.

Wing, Adrien Katherine (1997b) "A Critical Race Feminist conceptualization of violence." *Albany Law Review* 60:943–76.

Wing, Adrien Katherine (1999) "Violence and state accountability: Critical Race Feminism." *Georgetown Journal Gender, Sexuality and Law*, 1:1.

Wing, Adrien Katherine (ed.) (2000) *Global Critical Race Feminism: An International Reader*. New York: New York University Press.

Chapter 14

Psychoanalysis and Racism: Reading the Other Scene

Phil Cohen

Introduction

One of the most important features of the Macpherson Report into the murder of Stephen Lawrence (a black teenager who was killed in an unprovoked racist attack in 1993), and one not much remarked upon, was the insistence upon the distinction between unconscious racism, operating covertly or unwittingly, behind the scenes, or perhaps behind the backs of well-intentioned governance, and the malevolent, consciously directed forms of racial hatred so clearly manifested by Stephen's killers. But in all the controversy surrounding the failure to bring Stephen's killers to justice, and the mixture of inaction, incompetence, silence, and cover-up that for once brought the police and the white working-class community of South London into the same side of the dock, there was one piece of evidence which both broke that complicity and put into question the distinctions upon which the report's recommendations were made.

As part of their attempt to "nail" the five young white men who are widely regarded as having committed the murder, the police set up a concealed camera to film the suspects at home. In the footage that has been released we see the group prancing about the living room, brandishing knives, and chanting racist obscenities. It is a pantomime of racial violence, and many observers have been struck by the histrionic quality of the whole episode. These are young men getting off on the racial fantasies that bond them together as a gang and acting "as if" they were performing for each other's benefit a script written to be staged for quite another audience – only to discover retrospectively, of course, that this mimicry was in reality being observed and that having apparently got away with their public misdeed because no witnesses would come forward, they had "unwittingly," as a result of a "private indulgence" made themselves into the object of the whole world's fascinated, and officially horrified, gaze. The video was not admitted as legal evidence in the case but it leaves us with a series of unresolved questions: just what can be reliably inferred from such material about racist states of mind? What does it tell us about the role of fantasy in the committal of racial violence, and about the complicity of certain kinds of prurient and moralistic stances in the construction of the anti/racist spectacle?

As soon as the question is posed in this way we have to begin to consider how the *mise en scène* of racial violence and hatred works simultaneously at the level of private fantasy and public mythography, in terms of what is consciously avowed and unconsciously disavowed, to create a series of impasses at the level of engagement with the real. In other words we have entered, whether we like it or know it, or not, into the domain of psychoanalysis (see Dalal, 1998; Rustin, 1996).

As we will see, there are many different schools of thought within psychoanalysis, each with its own preferred strategy for defining and reading the symptomatic signs of racism, each claiming to be the royal road to a proper interpretation of the phenomenon. Nevertheless there are some common denominators, and these may provide us with a starting point.

The first is the concept of the Unconscious itself. For psychoanalysis, this does not simply denote a lack of consciousness or reflexive awareness, a kind of "absentminded-ness," nor is it "that which is not consciously intended"; rather, the Unconscious is defined positively as constituting an autonomous domain of psychic reality and its representation. Unconscious fantasy may not be directly accessible, but through the coded forms of dreams, bodily symptoms, and slips of the tongue, through certain characteristic frames of mind and forms of symbolization, it does speak. What it speaks about are elemental feelings of rage, persecution, anger, and jealousy consequent on primordial fears of separation, abandonment, loss, or death; and the no less strong impulses to possess and bond with people or things that are felt to offer safety and protection against these destructive drives. It is with these Other scenes – scenes initially dominated by extreme ambivalence towards the (m)other and with the defenses that are mobilized by the child in order to deal with it – that psychoanalysis is primarily concerned, both as a general theory of human development and as a specific practice of therapeutic intervention (Richards, 1995; Frosh, 1998).

From a psychoanalytic standpoint, "unconscious racism" is therefore first and fore-most a description of what happens to certain elementary structures of feeling and fantasy when they become racialized. Or to put it another way round, we are looking at how processes of racialization (which may be variously political, cultural and/or economic, institutional or informal, depending on context and conjuncture) engage with and affect the "other scenes" of self-identification. The staging of these transform-ations, in both public and private settings, is the story of how the Unconscious (qua "discourse of the Other") animates racist practices (qua strategy for excluding or eliminating the Other from the body politic).

The payoff for adding a properly psychoanalytic dimension to the account is that instead of simply demonstrating the illogicality of racist beliefs – a relatively easy task whose accomplishment may make us feel useful as intellectuals but does little to tackle the underlying problem – we look at how these beliefs are underpinned by certain indicative structures of feeling or emotional investment that have their own rationale in the psychic economy of desire. It may then become possible to pinpoint hitherto unrecognized sources of undercover resistance to antiracist policies and to devise more effective ways of engaging with them. In this way psychoanalytically informed antiracist work may be able to tackle some of the more intractable forms of popular and insti-tutional racism in a way that left antiracism, with its overwhelming attachment to rationalist and prescriptive modes of address, has so far failed to do (Cohen, forthcom-ing).

In principle then psychoanalysis should have a lot to contribute. In practice it has been a different story. Key psychoanalytic assumptions about the nature of mental and emotional life and its interaction with social, cultural, and political orders have been used to generate arguments about the causes, effects, and meaning of racism which are often absurdly reductive, demonstrably false, and even highly racist in their implication. In so far as these difficulties have not been addressed or overcome they continue to be seized on by those who have their own reasons to discredit the psychoanalytic enterprise.

In the next section I shall summarize the main criticisms that have been leveled at psychoanalytic readings of racism. The chapter then goes on to look at the work of Adorno and Fanon in some detail as exemplars of the attempt to overcome some of these difficulties. The final section reviews recent developments and debates in which post-structuralist theories of discourse and desire, largely informed by the work of Jacques Lacan, have attempted to engage with contemporary forms of racism. The chapter concludes by returning to the Stephen Lawrence case to argue that the psychoanalytic frame, applied within the limits and conditions that are proper to it, adds a valuable dimension to understanding and engaging with the deeper reaches of the popular racist imagination.

The Hermeneutics of Suspicion

It has recently been suggested that in many respects race is the Unconscious of psycho-analysis, the constitutive but disavowed foundation of its project, yet its fatal blind spot. Certainly the special relationship between race and psychoanalysis must be understood in both historical and structural terms (Rustin, 1996).

Freud's work was born out of two of the critical experiences of the twentieth century: migration and racism. Fin de siècle Vienna, as Carl Schorske (1988) shows so brilliantly in his book, was nothing if not a multicultural city, inhabited by large numbers of refugees from Russia, Poland, and Eastern Europe. The founding members of Freud's circle were predominantly from Jewish backgrounds, and, as such, were multilingual in a triple sense. They spoke and read German (amongst other European languages), as well as Hebrew; many used Yiddish to converse amongst themselves on everyday, nonscientific topics; even more importantly they were teaching each other a quite new foreign language, one which had never been spoken in this way before, the language of the Unconscious.

But if they imagined that by mastering *this* discourse of the Other, they would somehow be accepted into the non-Jewish establishment which ruled the medical and other scientific faculties of the European university, they had another think coming. Psychoanalysis was from the outset attacked as "the Jewish science," its concern with questions of infant sexuality, memory, desire, and identity were regarded as symptomatic expressions of the unhealthy and febrile temperament of the Jewish race, or an expression of the neurotic self-hate engendered by their hopeless attempt to assimilate into modern European culture and society.

There is a large literature now on the ambivalent relationship between early psycho-analysis, Judaism, and Jewish culture, and how this was played out both in Freud's own work and in the politics of affinity and enmity within the Viennese circle (Bakan, 1990). We know about the virulent antisemitism of Groddeck, "the wild analyst," who fulmin-ated against the evils of miscegenation and the threat to the Aryan master race (Grod-deck, 1997); we have learnt to detect the more subtle prejudices of Ernest Jones (1953–7), Freud's official biographer, who developed a hygienicist model of the body politic to argue that total assimilation was the only solution to the Jewish question. Freud, worried about the effect of antisemitism on the fledgling discipline, hoped that Carl Jung's presence would give psychoanalysis a more acceptable Christian face. Jung's own theory of "racial memory" and his deployment of his model of individuation to characterize the African psyche as primitive did not however save psychoanalysis for long from its "Jewish" tag.

How far did early psychoanalysis give a gloss to commonsense Victorian thinking about race, biology, and human evolution? Many commentators have noted the tension between, on the one hand, the tactical appropriation of bioenergetic models and discourses drawn from positivistic science (including at this time racial science and anthropology), in order to situate psychoanalysis within the Western Enlightenment tradition, and on the other, the persistence of themes and idioms deriving from Jewish mysticism and German romanticism, which gave psychoanalysis its currency in bohemian, intellectual, and artistic circles (Gilman, 1996; Nandy, 1989; Gay, 1978). The tension can be found, of course, in Freud's own work; it is there for example in the dissonance between his libido theory and his method of dream interpretation; and in the non sequiturs of his early theory of recapitulation (ontogeny repeating phylogeny as stone age baby transits to civilized man) considered in the light of his later reflections on the culture of modernity and the return of its repressed to be found in *Civilisation and its Discontents* (Freud, 1962).

Issues of race and ethnicity were thus current, if largely disavowed within the psychoanalytic circle itself. Long before *Kristallnacht* and the book burnings, long before the trains began carrying Jews back from their asylum in the West to torture and death in the East, race was the largely unacknowledged touchstone of the early psychoanalytic debates. Yet with the fall of Vienna to the Nazis and the dispersal of the founding psychoanalysts to other countries, mainly of course to Britain and the USA (but also in some cases further afield to Latin America and South Africa), race paradoxically disappeared from the agenda. In so far as psychoanalytic concepts were applied to the analysis of racism it was largely by others, by sociologists, anthropologists, or historians, themselves often Jews and exiles from Nazism (viz. the Frankfurt School/New School for Social Research) who were sympathetic to Freud's ideas.

From the 1940s onwards the professional culture of psychoanalysis took on an increasingly dual character. The diasporic communities of analysts made a concerted attempt to assimilate to the scientific conventions of the host society, to give their discipline a distinctively local, or rather national, character, reflecting its most cherished values. The other, more negative sides to the English or American dream (including of course racism and colonialism) were therefore ignored. These "other scenes" became part of the repressed in the collective memory of psychoanalysis. At the same time great efforts were made to preserve the integrity of clinical theory and practice through the operation of training institutes. Their goal was to create an enduring base from which to assert the distinctiveness of the psychoanalytic tradition, even and especially by those who were most concerned to revise it. Inevitably this meant that any "foreign influences" that might compromise or contaminate the corpus – and the body politic – of Freudianism were regarded with deep suspicion (Turkle, 1992).

It is against this background that we have to understand the ambition of psychoanalysis as a critical hermeneutics – and its failure of nerve. For we have here the paradox of a discipline that prides itself on unflinchingly confronting the ambition, greed, power hunger, perversity, and murderous rage of the individual patient yet unquestioningly accepts a sanitized version of its own history from which all these nasty elements (including racism) have been magically purged!

Two moves make this possible. First by instituting intensive forms of professional self-scrutiny directed at the mastery and evaluation of its own internal clinical practice, psychoanalysis seeks to place itself "above suspicion" of cultural bias, and to lay claim to objectivity as a natural science of the Unconscious. Yet this scrutiny has proved to be highly selective; it has not, for example, extended to the fact that very few analysts or patients are recruited from black, Asian, or other nonwhite ethnic minorities, nor does it consider the structured neglect of questions of race and ethnicity in the conduct of training and the talking cure. Instead suspicion is directed outwards; the motivations of all those who raise the issue of "institutional racism," whether from their position on the couch, or the academic podium, are interpreted "psychodynamically" in such a way as to invalidate the arguments being made (Dalal, 1998).

There are many instances in the literature of this abuse of clinical insight. Thus for example, in the USA there was a notorious case in which a female patient's involvement in black power groups was interpreted as a flight from rage with the analyst; another patient who suffered from an "irrepressible urge to take part in race riots" and had failed to make progress at work (due to race discrimination!) was made to see "through the analytic work" that her protestations warded off self-loathing and, as such, were a defence against recognizing her internal rage. Both these patients, be it noted, had black therapists! Similarly a white patient who showed a strong sense of identification with black causes became actively involved in antiracist struggles, and eventually got assaulted by a racist policeman in a demonstration, was told by his analyst that he was acting out a regressive masochistic fantasy of being beaten by his father.

Of course there are bad analysts, and bad interpretations; the normalization of bias under the guise of "objective" clinical judgment is what has given psychoanalysis – like psychiatry – such a bad name. Ironically what makes such reactionary positions tenable is the very radicalness of psychoanalytic skepticism *vis à vis* ideology. In *Civilisation and its Discontents* Freud suggests that the way to psychic hell may well be paved with good intentions. In what may today be read as a pioneering study of the culture of complaint, he suggests that behind charitable deeds and fine – or politically correct – words we may frequently discern far less creditable motivations at work. Political activism always has its "other scene." He does not, however, say that this is always or automatically the case, or even where it is, that the effect is to invalidate the "do gooding." Black militants who make knee-jerk denunciations of racism when something goes wrong in their own private lives may be using political rhetoric as means to evade their existential responsibility, or they may be giving an entirely accurate and dispassionate account of some process of discrimination they have personally suffered. And conceivably they may be doing both! There is no law of automatic inversion whereby what is consciously affirmed is inevitably unconsciously denied. It is always a matter of investigation, not *a priori* judgment, and the answer – the unconscious meaning of the situation – will vary from case to case.

In principle, then, psychoanalysis gives no support to abusive generalizations along the lines "all whites are unconsciously racist," or "all black militants secretly envy, and hence want to destroy, the achievements of European civilization." In practice, however, whole metapsychologies of racism have been constructed on the basis of selective clinical evidence and inflated overinterpretation. Richard Sterba (1947), in a famous study based on his white patients who had taken part in the 1943 antiblack riots in Detroit, argues that negrophobic violence derives from repressed sibling rivalry. Kovel (1988), drawing on a mixture of clinical and documentary material for his "psycho-history" of white racism in the American Deep South, suggests that the motivation is more directly oedipal. But in both cases sweeping generalizations are being made, by extrapolating evidence about individual psychopathology to collective and institutional processes.

The unresolved question which recent critics of psychoanalysis have raised is how come that in a discipline that prides itself on such rigorous self-scrutiny, whose metapsychology boasts of its radical skepsis, and whose therapeutic endeavors are directed towards releasing the patient from the toils of compulsive repetition and the "false self," such strategies of misrecognition persist, especially in the areas of race and ethnicity? Is there perhaps something intrinsic to the psychoanalytic method as such, something built into the structure of its hermeneutics, that not only makes such interpretations possible, but also actively generates and endorses them?

The Analytic Epoche – A reductio ad absurdum?

The French psychoanalyst Jacques Lacan is famous, amongst other things, for his aphorism that the efficacy of analysis as a talking cure lies in the fact that within its special setting and frame "nothing real happens." He was referring to the fact that everything that is brought into play in the analysis from outside – events in everyday life, social or political situations in which the patient is caught up – all this is interpreted in relation to the patient's feelings towards the analyst, which in turn are held to be a repetition of earlier patterns of relatedness towards parents, dominated by infantile fantasies and defense mechanisms. In other words, the analyst suspends judgment as to the wider significance or facticity of the external event in order to concentrate on its unconscious meaning for the patient through the chain of associations and memories it evokes.

This procedure has been called the analytic epoche; the interpretive frame wrapped around the patient's utterances systematically brackets out everything to do with the "real referent" and instead considers them as communications between different, split-off, parts of the inner self or (m)other, as mediated by the analyst's presence and hence overdetermined by the dynamics of transference (Spence, 1994).

From this vantage point, external social reality only enters into consideration in so far as it functions as a form of camouflage for processes of internal sabotage or psychic disavowal (denial by means of the real), or alternatively serves to focus strategies of evasion or acting out that take no account of self-preservation (denial of the real). These can be two sides of the same coin. For example a white boy is set upon and attacked by a group of Asian boys on his way home from school. The boy's mother uses the incident as a rationale for her agoraphobia, and her racism – just look what happens when you go out, you get set upon by blacks – and attempts to implicate her son in both (denial by means of the real); meanwhile the son, in order to protect himself against becoming drawn into a *folie à deux* denies that such a thing has ever happened, and ignores warnings that the gang is still out to get him (denial of the real).

The analytic epoche is an essential device of clinical treatment, but it can also lead to abusive interpretations. A frequent example is the way transference resistance on the part of black patients towards white analysts (which frequently focuses on differences of color or culture) is regarded by the analyst as arising from purely internal instinctual sources, rather than as a carryover, maybe inappropriate, from valid external social experience. Clearly such an approach may do great damage and jeopardize the therapeutic outcome; but the epoche has even more dire consequences when it is extrapolated from the consulting room and applied as an epistemological principle for explaining racism in the society outside. Yet this is just what Freudian metapsychology attempts to do.

Different tendencies within psychoanalysis operate with different models of the interaction between psychic and social structure, but they all tend to assume as given the following set of distinctions:

A	B
Fantasy	Rationality
Internal	External
Biological	Cultural
Individual	Group
Latent	Manifest

Whichever instance is taken as axiomatic (and this varies), the items in column B are invariably treated as secondary, symptomatic, or even epiphenomenal, while the items in column A are regarded as primary in terms of causation and/or meaning. The aim of the analytic work is to uncover the workings of Set A in and through Set B, and then to map B back onto A in order to recover from the social items their true (i.e., psychological) significance or explanation. This procedure is therefore intrinsically reductive, and the reduction takes two main forms: Set B is explained as the effect and Set A as the cause (libido theory and ego psychology); Set B is interpreted as a site of symbolic displacement and Set A as a locus of symbolic condensation (Kleinian object relations theory and Lacanian discourse theory).

Although the two approaches yield radically different accounts of mental life they both operate a general reduction of the structural properties of social institutions and groups, to the psychological characteristics of the individual human subjects who inhabit them. From the point of view of constructing a theory of racism, one of the key effects of psychoanalytic reductionism is that positions of powerlessness, inequality, or exclusion are devalorized as instances of the real; instead they are treated as the site of unconscious projections or compensations drawing on fantasies of omnipotence, castration, or abandonment. We have already seen how this might work as a racially invalidating device in the clinical setting, but as the basis of a metapsychology of racism it produces even more dire results. For example in some accounts racism is reduced to a form of xenophobia which in turn is linked to infantile stranger anxiety. A more general tendency is to subsume racism under the general rubric of prejudice and scapegoating – i.e., the splitting off and projection of bad, internally persecutory aspects of the self into Others. Racist attitudes and behavior are then explained as the expression or acting out of internal psychological dynamics located within the individual, dynamics which in turn are mapped into the sphere of intergroup relations where the world is split into a Good Us and Bad Them.

In such theories, the real objects of racial hatred (blacks, Jews, etc.) are present only as the containers, screens, or vectors of more or less paranoid projections. This might in itself be useful in indicating the phantasmagoric nature of racist constructions. But this derealization is capped by another, far more dangerous process of *deracialization*. For the real object of racial fantasy is not, in this view, the Jew or the black at all. These are merely displacements – substitute figures standing in for the subjects' own father and mother, the phallus (castration anxiety) or the womb (separation anxiety).

The key authorization for this move is to be found in Freud's 1922 paper "Some neurotic mechanisms in jealousy, paranoia and homosexuality." In this essay, centered on a clinical study of the Daniel Schreber case, Freud argues that in paranoid states of mind socially taboo impulses are transferred from the subject to the object where they can become the focus of aggression. In the case of men, the forbidden subject is the boy's submissive homosexual desire for the father, which covers over the underlying parricidal impulse; in the case of the paranoiac this repressed hatred is displaced into a generalized hatred and urge to destruction randomly expressed against socially undesirable objects.

This paper has been the single most important influence on subsequent psychoanalytic interpretations of racism. In Sterba's analysis, blacks are interpreted as playing the role of an imaginary young sibling – they are unwelcome intruders and as such provide a defense against or displacement of the patient's oedipal anxieties. Sterba argues that the repressed fear/hatred of the father associated with the boy's passive homosexual desire for him is projected onto blacks. Why? Because in the culture of the Deep South at this time blacks were legitimate scapegoats; therefore they could be the substitute object of both homosexual desire and its aggressive disavowal, thus allowing a benign paternal imago of the (white) father to be sustained.

For Kovel, too, race fantasies are applied only at second hand to "races"; the full range of meanings in race fantasies cannot be understood, he says, unless their infantile root is taken into account; racism is a kind of acting out, a system which facilitates the expression of infantile desire without conscious knowledge. For him racism is a special kind of negative Oedipus; the black man represents both the father and the son in their destructive aspects – the father with the omnipotent phallus, the son who lusts after the mother's body. In attacking and dominating blacks the white man is both a father castrating the son and the son castrating the (black) father; that is why the more black men are humiliated, the more they are invested with prodigious sexual capacities and are the object of sexual envy, that is, they are envied for possessing the libidinal power (the phallus) that has been renounced or lost by the whites.

Recently this idea has been taken up and reworked by historian David Roediger (1991, 1994) in his account of the transformation of European immigrants (including Jews and Irish) into the standard bearers of a "new white race in the USA." Roediger argues that Native Americans and African Americans came to unconsciously represent the sexual and social freedoms of the preindustrial world which the white populations of the American frontier towns were being forced to surrender in making the transition into the work disciplines of capitalism and modern times. The racial ambivalence of the Irish in particular stemmed from the fact they belonged in both worlds; their love/hate relation to blacks was part of a historical "return of the repressed" (Roediger, 1991).

Kovel explores the other, positive, side of the oedipal triangle in discussing the role which "black mammies" play in the upbringing of many white children from well-to-do families in the plantation society of the Deep South. The contrast between the strong "libidinal" bond established with wet nurse or nanny, and the emotional distance created by the mother, sets the template for the sexual/racial double standard: black women being regarded as warm and sexually available (objects of lust and disregard), and white women as unapproachable "southern belles" (objects of idealization and longing).

Almost all the analyses that proceed in this vein focus on the racialization of quasi-oedipal relations between white men and black women. In other words they follow Freud in privileging the masculine standpoint. One refreshing exception to this is the work of Joan Riviere. Trained by Melanie Klein, Riviere was concerned to explore feminine positioning as a relatively autonomous dynamic within the oedipal triangle. In her famous theory of masquerade she elaborated a model of the feminine psychic defenses that were mobilized against the destructive, castratory effects of patriarchal authority. To illustrate her ideas she discusses the case of a patient who had fantasies of being attacked by a "Negro" whom she would first seduce and then hand over to the police. Riviere notes that this fantasy had been very common in her patient's childhood and youth, which she had spent in the southern states of America; in fantasy then, her patient asserts the power of female desire in the face of male violence, by exploiting her position of racial superiority to attack black potency. Riviere argues that the symbolic father that figures in this scenario is not represented by the attacking Negro who (in other scenes) takes his place as an object of desire, but by the law asserted in the father's name by the white male authorities who punish the black for daring to cross the race line. In this way this white woman is "free" to substitute the black male body (= the black phallus) for the (white) father's penis that she already has inside her. Riviere calls this series of displacements, through which the place of the sexual and racial other is assumed only to be disavowed, a process of masquerade, and she links it to the arts of seduction which women learn as the only way of asserting their own desire within the field of male sexual dominance (Hughes, 1991).

It is not that such analyses do not shed some interesting light on structures of feeling and fantasy that may be evoked by popular iconographies of race, or that the dispositions they describe may not feature in the biographies of some individual racists. The problem arises in the conflation of different levels of analysis and/or their reduction to a single all-determining principle of psychological causation. For, to take Kovel's example, the double standard cannot simply be read off from child-rearing patterns, even in their most normative aspect. Why? Because the actual affective relations with mother or nurse, however mediated by race, will vary drastically depending on the inner world of the child, the workings of a given family fantasy system, and what Freud calls "the vicissitudes of the instincts." And Riviere's suggestion that her white female patient's fantasies of seduction/betrayal/revenge over a black man are part of a common culture of racism in the Deep South leaves unresolved the question as to whether this is a normative instance of the racialization of female desire, or of the feminization of racist desire. Are we dealing here with the translation into primary process thinking of narrative themes integral to the popular culture of this time and place; or is it a case of secondary elaboration of a perverse sadomasochistic fantasy, couched in the idioms of racist myth and folk tale?

In principle it would be possible to tackle such questions by applying the model of overdetermination that governs psychoanalytic interpretation (Laplanche and Leclaire). It is a clinical commonplace that the same dream image (e.g., a train running into a wall) can have many different meanings, the exact one only being established through a process of free association that explores the network of signifiers in which it is embedded. The same principle applies to understanding racism's "other scenes." Take the example of a white schoolboy who writes "Pakis go home" all over the playground wall in a school with a strong antiracist policy. This *may* involve acting out a whole range of nonracial fantasies (e.g., to do with the desire to be caught and punished by expulsion, or hatred of the school, or the desire to be sent home); such feelings *may* have become racialized by a process of cultural habituation or repetition setting up a fixed association between the symbolic position which Asian children or teachers occupy in this boy's inner world and their situation in external social reality. *Perhaps* this may be linked *in some cases* to envy for the warm protective family environment and success at school which Asians are felt to enjoy and/or to anxiety about the loss of such patterns of kinship and community amongst whites. *In so far as* those connections are made, writing the slogan *might* allow this boy to unconsciously identify with Asians, by getting himself excluded and sent home, so putting himself symbolically and materially in their place in a way that allows him to consciously "get his own back" while disavowing his racial envy and anxiety.

Such conjectures will readily come to the mind of anyone who is at all familiar with how to apply the procedures of psychoanalytic thinking to the study of popular racism. But the point is that they are just hunches, not explanations, and treating one as if it were the other is precisely the kind of *a priorism* that we have to guard against. In fact we could only arrive at a fully fledged interpretation if these initial conjectures were tested through a lengthy process of working through the boy's fears and fantasies about school and home, as well as what he thinks about blacks. The same graffiti written by another boy might turn out to have quite a different unconscious resonance.

Overdetermination works the other way as well, of course, so that many different signifying acts can get cathected to the same object. So, for example, if we shift the focus to consider the public meaning of racist graffiti it becomes clear that the performative power of the message "Pakis go home" (i.e., to actuate the reality it refers to, by "persuading" Asians to move from the area) depends for this "graphic" effect on its material functioning within a whole network of other signifying practices mobilized in strategies of racial harassment (i.e., spitting, obscene gestures, insults, verbal threats, threatening letters and phone calls, vandalism, feces put through letter boxes, etc.). In other words a whole lot of disparate practices, each with their own "logic of signification" may nevertheless by habitual association come to have a shared symbolic meaning bound up with their application to a common object, and this indeed is the work of "racialization."

The notion of overdetermination thus allows us to address the complex, multifaceted nature of racism. It indicates that there is no automatic principle of one-to-one corres-pondence between culture and personality, biography and social structure, culture and identity, such that the institutional forms of racism automatically mirror and/or under-write the psychic structure of the individual racist. Even in the most racialized, hom-ogenized, and totalitarian kinds of society, where mechanical solidarities rule OK (one thinks of Nazi Germany, or certain settler colonialisms, or South Africa under apart-heid), such a tight fit does not obtain.

There have been some attempts to complicate the picture by building intervening variables into the analysis, but these do not apply the notion of overdetermination to the task. Kovel, for instance, distinguishes between dominative racism (based on oedipal desire and the equation black = phallus = paternal signifier), and aversive racism which is anal sadistic in orientation, and centered on fantasies about dirt and bodily functions repudiated in the search for some purified notion of a "higher" culture or civilization. Young-Bruehl (1996) similarly distinguishes between different types of racism in terms of their characteristic psychopathologies. Antisemitism is an obsessional prejudice displayed by people with overrigid superegos, whilst negrophobia exemplifies hysterical prejudice in which a group is chosen to act out forbidden sexually aggressive drives that the racist has repressed. This is contrasted with ethnocentrism and xenophobia which are based on a narcissistic refusal to value difference for its own sake.

All these examples show, however, is that in making these correlations Freudianism has not so much overcome its reductionism as diversified its effects. So how does it come about that a theory which so radically "deconstructs" the myth of the unitary subject in the clinical setting should operate with such an integrationist model of self and society when it comes to generalize its findings? To understand this turnabout we have to look at the intellectual division of labor between the various branches of the human sciences, and in particular the special relationship that psychoanalysis has come to entertain with sociology (Craib, 1998).

How (Not) to Construct a Psychoanalytic Theory of Racism Without Really Trying

If you want to go about constructing a psychoanalytic theory of racism the lazy way, you take a number of short steps. First you concentrate on what are widely assumed to be the clinical strengths – the analysis of transference and resistance; the operation of the major defense mechanisms (projection, introjection, splitting, denial, foreclosure); the theory of narcissism, and borderline personality; the psychodynamics of envy, guilt, and anxiety. These are the bedrocks of clinical judgment and treatment concerning individual psychopathology.

Secondly you look at the more explicit or ideal typical forms of racist behavior and belief and you try to find there evidence for the operation of the structures which you have already identified in clinical practice as examples of individual psychopathology. And lo and behold you do indeed find that individuals with pronounced or extreme racist views, or who carry out violent racial attacks, exhibit a common pattern of psychopathology. Some of them suffer from contagion phobias, others get anxiety attacks if they are in a lift with a black person; quite a few white men exhibit deeply ambivalent or envious feelings about what they see as the superior sexual potency or license enjoyed by black men; others entertain sexual fantasies of a sadistic kind towards black women; a lot of them of them project the bad part of themselves into their preferred racial hate object, and they indulge in a magical or primary process thinking in scapegoating ethnic minorities and blaming them for all manner of social ills.

So far so simple. It seems that we have located certain invariant (or at least frequently recurrent) psychological traits, which can be found strongly associated (if not statistically correlated) with certain invariant (or at least frequently recurrent) features of racist thought and practice. So, it can be safely concluded there must be a causal relation between the two. Starting from this fatal equation psychoanalysis goes one step further and claims that it can explain the causal link in terms of its own theory of individual or group psychodynamics. This gives us some of the most richly absurd theories of racism in the whole canon. For example, the equation of black people with feces or Jews with "dirty money" is explained in terms of anal sadistic fantasies on the part of people who have been too rigidly potty trained. The rape and castration fantasies about black men which are found amongst members of the Klu Klux Klan or the participants in urban race riots in the USA are explained as a displacement of their sibling rivalry or oedipal ambivalence towards their own fathers who are perceived to be cruel, powerful, and engaging in extramarital sex with black women. Alternatively white American males project onto black American men their own sexual repressions, making the latter in their fantasies the object of their own homosexual desire.

But then a sociologist joins the party and points out that many of the young people who were members of the Hitler *Jugend* were not authoritarian personality types but fun-loving and sexually liberated *wandervogel*; someone else brings up evidence to show that rape and castration fantasies about black men are not confined to the Klu Klux Klan, but are quite widely distributed, being entertained by large numbers of people, including other black men, who in no way can be described as white supremacists; so already things are beginning to look a little bit more complicated. Finally our sociologist tactfully suggests that these so-called common psychopathological traits of the racist can be found occurring in nonracists, and even antiracists, and are not specific to racism itself. They are present in political witchhunts and purges conducted by totalitarian regimes, in religious sectarianisms, and ethnic nationalisms of every kind, in the fanatical loyalties generated by football teams, or socialist groupuscules; in almost any social ideology you care to name similar mechanisms of projection/splitting/denial and so on can be seen at work. At this level the psychodynamics of a lynch mob and a chauvinistic gang of football supporters have more in common with each other than they do with other forms of racism or nationalism, but that hardly helps us to understand the differences between the culture of the American Deep South and Southern Suburban England!

So, our social scientist concludes, what does it really help to explain about racisms, or even racists, to point out their formal similarities with all these other instances? At best it reduces racism to a subset of a generic prejudice, a particularly acute form of xenophobia or ethnocentrism. At worst it regards racism as the symptomatic expression of a particular, pathological personality type: rigid, anally fixated, authoritarian, narcissistic, sexually repressed, paranoid and so on. Worse still, by insisting that racism is an irrational residue of primitive thinking, and racists are infantile, perverse people who for one reason or another have failed to grow up into mature, fulfilled, and democratic individuals, psychoanalysis reintroduces by the back door its own version of the great moral dividing line between civilized and primitive, between the educated who speak with the voice of reason, and the rest who do not. And that distinction, we hardly need reminding, has been a characteristic device of European racism since the eighteenth century Enlightenment first introduced it (Cohen, 1992).

At this point psychoanalysis may become rather defensive in its claims to explain racism. What is then modestly proposed is a rather crude division of intellectual labor. Psychoanalysis will explain the psychological mechanisms at work in creating the subjective conditions of affiliation to particular kinds of social ideology, and historians, anthropologists, or sociologists will explain why in one context the social ideology has a fascist or a socialist content, or here takes a religious and there a political form, or why in this time and place Jews or Asians are the object of fear or attack.

So for example the Kleinians will say: look, we have a perfectly serviceable theory of envy as a fantasy system. But it is socially opportunistic – the fantasy will attach itself to whatever object or group is socially sanctioned in a particular culture or group as being habitually enviable. So you historians or sociologists go away and work out whether this or that group is more or less likely to be envied because of their race, for reasons x, y, and z, and we will explain to you what kind of people are most likely to be drawn into the psychodynamics of racial envy.

It seems like a perfectly reasonable deal, until you realize that psychoanalysis has done little or no work. It has simply sat back and said: we have the theory of psychic reality which does not require us to have a theory of racism. So let the social scientists produce a theory of racism, which does not have a theory of the unconscious. Then we add our model of psychic structuration to their theory of social structuration and hey presto, we have a fully fledged theory of racism.

But actually we have nothing of the kind. The psychoanalysts think they have solved the interaction of the psychic to the social when all they have done is brought them into a purely mechanical and mutually reductive relation. And en route, they have given the social scientists an alibi for thinking they do not need to explain the deeper, more unconscious reaches of the racist imagination, in order to understand its versatility and power of resistance to rational argument or structural reform.

This mutual inertia governing the relationship between the two disciplines continued throughout most of the twentieth century. It was not shaken by the rise and fall of Nazism, the decline of Empire, and the postcolonial crisis of Western culture. Yet throughout this period, there were also some notable attempts to "square the circle" and establish a more integrated approach to understanding the psychosocial conditions of racism, with or without its "other scene."

Prejudice theory

In the late 1940s and early 1950s, as a new postfascist and postimperial world order began to dawn in the West along with the Cold War against communism, a new discipline developed in the USA aiming to provide a rational scientific basis upon which the forces of unreason in society could be combated, and the world made safe for democracy. The foundations for a social psychology of prejudice were laid by Gordon Allport's *The Nature of Prejudice* (1954), a project designed from the outset to eliminate the need for a special theory of the unconscious *and* a specific theory of racism.

On the side of psychology Allport's theory was heavily cognitivist, drawing on and further elaborating the notion of stereotypification advanced by gestalt psychologists and phenomenologists in the 1920s and 1930s. Stereotypes are here considered as a form of profile construction applied to information processing under conditions where there is either too much or too little data to work on. Stereotyping is regarded as both functional, in reducing cognitive dissonance between expectation and perception, and dysfunctional in reducing the flow of new information generated by social interactions. Stereotypes might be benign – and sustain positive images – or they might be negative, underwriting all manner of social discrimination, depending upon the circumstances in which they operated. As for the sociological side to the argument, Allport's theory was influenced in equal measure by Moreno's sociometry and, in its later development, by Mead's symbolic interactionism. Studies of the pressures of social conformity at work in group relations should be able to pinpoint the role of negative stereotypes of the outgroup in rendering normative the key mechanisms of scapegoating and deviancy amplification to be found in cultures of popular prejudice (see Young-Bruehl 1996; Allport, 1954).

Prejudice theory served to eliminate the structural dimensions of both the psychic and the social by reducing both to their lowest common denominator in interpersonal process. Methodologically the theory attempted to operationalize its constructs by introducing attitudinal scales and behavioral indices as measures of personality and group traits that predisposed to prejudice. Within this perspective then, racism or xenophobia (and the two were again conflated) was simply one amongst many examples of unreasonable behavior governed by personal attitudes based on hostility and/or ignorance. By implication, the practice of Western democracy was associated with the education of the private citizen into norms of individual rationality that happily coincided with the values and aspirations of the American Way of Life (AWOL); this in turn would inoculate them against totalitarian ideologies (whether fascism or communism) associated with mass capitulation to collective forms of irrational race and class hatred.

The social psychology of prejudice was one of the great academic success stories of the second half of the twentieth century and it continues to inform the dominant enlightenment model of how to combat popular racism through public education programs. But in its rush to arrive at a normative solution prejudice theory destroyed the delicate dialectic between the structure of fantasy, the object which it invests with unconscious significance, and the pattern of habitual association encoded in particular kinds of social discourse. Within its truncated conversation between the social and the psychic, the principles of overdetermination at work in racial formations of power and identity became literally unthinkable.

Nevertheless there were alternative attempts to develop a theory of social ideology and combine it with a theory of unconscious psychic process in order to make a more radical critique of the roots of racism in Western culture. And it is to these we must now turn.

The Odd Coupling: Marx and Freud with Adorno and Fanon

Adorno

Theodor Adorno et al.'s (1950) *The Authoritarian Personality* and Frantz Fanon's *Black Skin, White Masks* (1986) are not often bracketed together as belonging within the same intellectual or political conjuncture. Adorno's book was published in 1950, in that brief interlude between the defeat of fascism and the onset of the Cold War; Fanon's first appeared in English in the 1960s at the height of the anticolonial struggle in North Africa. There are, self-evidently, differences in approach and focus. *The Authoritarian Personality* is a study of the psychosocial roots of antisemitism and fascism which, despite its commitment to critical theory, makes use of attitudinal scales and all the other objectifying apparatus of American social science; *Black Skins, White Masks* is an impassioned study of the impact of French settler colonialism and negrophobia on the black African psyche, based on clinical case studies.

Yet despite these differences the middle European Jewish philosopher, exiled in New York, and the Algerian psychiatrist, active in the national liberation struggle and in Parisian left-wing intellectual circles, have written texts whose problematics have much in common. Both books are attempting to couple key elements of Marxist and Freudian thinking in such a way as to push them beyond their encapsulation in the Enlightenment tradition; both writers seek to adumbrate a more self-critical standpoint capable of recognizing the implication of the human sciences (including historical materialism and psychoanalysis) in the prosecution of Western racism. And both authors, because of their own intellectual formation and social situation, remain deeply ambivalent about the direction in which their respective lines of thought are leading them, an ambivalence that surfaces in certain key contradictions in their arguments.

Adorno's book begins where his earlier *Dialectics of the Enlightenment* left off, namely with the dominative attitude of Western reason. For Adorno both bourgeois democracy and the Enlightenment were linked to the notion of capitalist modernity and the ethics of possessive individualism; that set of articulations had their psychic underpinning in a common personality structure centered on a rational calculating ego. Within this ideological frame, and specifically under the influence of antisemitism, Jews were made to represent all the modes of life that Western people have had to learn to repress in the transition to modernity; as Europe's internal others they are made to figure the forces of nature and the id, relics of the past, practicing a mimetic impulse that cannot be completely destroyed, and so forth. In so far as Jews enter into the world of modernity (e.g., as business people and entrepreneurs) they are made to represent its "bad" or savage side – the unacceptable face of capitalism.

In this way Adorno neatly turns the tables on prejudice theory. Prejudice theory sees racial prejudice as an archaic residue, operating in the substructure of the personality, and which under certain conditions might be mobilized by political ideologies such as fascism to overwhelm rational thought. Adorno suggests that it is the very form of Western rationality that constructs the Jew as the bearer of atavistic impulses and gives rise to racism as its necessary false consciousness.

Adorno then turns to psychoanalysis to provide an explanation as to why some individuals, and not others, formed within the same historical conditions, become active antisemites and supporters of racist or fascist causes. For this purpose he draws extensively on familiar sources – Sterba's (1947) study and Freud's theory of male homosexuality and paranoia. For Adorno then the boy's ambivalent submission to strong paternal authority is the key to understanding the male authoritarian personality. In this view he is very close to Wilhelm Reich, another German exile living in New York. Reich's *Mass Psychology of Fascism* had already pointed the finger at what he called "the puritanical sex economy of the patriarchal bourgeois family" as the nursery of fascism.[1] In Reich's view the popularity of regimes of homosocial racial bonding promoted by the Hitler *Jugend* lay in the fact that they provided a legitimate outlet for the expression of passive homosexuality via worship of the Führer father figure, while at the same time making "weak effeminate" Jews the target of displaced male aggressivity.

While Reich focused on fascist youth culture as providing the antilibidinal defenses or character armoring needed to deal with the adolescent body's unruly desires, Adorno preferred to focus on the social conditions which might facilitate the development of authoritarian personalities: chronic economic insecurity, mass unemployment, rapid social change, and cultural anomie; under these conditions trust in conventional authority structures begins to break down, and releases all kinds of fears, anxieties, and negative feelings. People whose character formation is based on a rigid and punitive superego would lack the psychic defenses needed to deal creatively with the ambivalent positionalities created by uncertain times (see Bauman, 1989). Instead they would need to identify with strong authority figures, especially if these were lacking in their own families, leaders who could embody "strong" solutions and publicly sanction attacks upon scapegoats while relieving the perpetrators of any personal feelings of guilt.

As Adorno's study proceeds, however, the analysis moves ever further away from its initial Marxist starting point and the Reichian focus on collective psychopathology, and ever closer toward a reductionist account of the social conditions of individual psychopathology. In my view this shift has less to do with the invocation of Freud's theory of paranoia than with the choice of research methodology. With the help of Elsie Frenkel-Brunswick, a social psychologist, Adorno devised the famous "F" scale, combining measures of ethnocentrism, political and cultural conservatism, and racial intolerance into a single attitudinal profile. Whether or not he wanted to give his study a veneer of academic respectability and get its arguments taken seriously by the intellectual establishment of the day, and whether or not this strategy was overdetermined unconsciously by a desire to assimilate into the AWOL, there is no doubt that this attempt to operationalize a complex theory in narrow empiricist terms served radically to decontextualize much of the argument, and allow it to be read from a purely psychologistic point of view.

As a statement of its time, Adorno's concept of the authoritarian personality had the advantage of rendering fascism and communism into equivalent instances in a way that simply effaced the ideological differences (not to mention the world war that had just been waged) between them. This certainly suited the emergent Cold War mentality of the USA.[2]

The fact is that in Adorno's model the concrete forms of racism and nationalism are only contingently related to the ideal typology of authoritarianism which, in turn, is simply conflated with fascism. The claim that the study had discovered a new "anthropological species" – in the figure of the omniprejudiced fascist – now reads like a rather desperate attempt to provide some empirical foundation for the Hegelian teleology that underlay the Frankfurt school's doom-laden prognostications about the future of Western democracy. It is perhaps no coincidence that the personality traits associated with the "omniprejudiced fascist" could just as easily be found in the heroes of rugged American individualism – a connection that Martin Scorsese was to make brilliantly explicit in *Taxi Driver*, where a screwed-up, sexually bigoted ex-marine cabbie goes on the rampage, committing serial murders against New York low life only to wake up the next morning to find himself headlined in the press as an Alger Hiss type all-American hero.

Fanon

This is just the kind of link that Fanon would have made, as it were from the other side. Writing in the context of anticolonial struggle, he distinguished between three kinds of violence – the systemic racism through which colonialism attempts to reduce its subjects to subhuman status; the individualized black on black violence which arises from identification with the aggressor and the inversion of political hatred into neurotic self-hatred; and finally the revolutionary violence which liberates blacks from the structures of oppression that have imposed a false white self upon them (Fanon, 1986; Macey, 2000).

Fanon's project is complementary to Adorno's in a number of ways. Both were outsiders writing from a standpoint that was highly critical of the liberal enlightenment tradition. Just as Adorno is concerned to disentangle Marxism from its implication in dominative reason, by means of psychoanalysis, so Fanon seeks to rescue psychoanalysis from its Eurocentric bias, which he sees as legitimating its abusive clinical applications within the domain of colonial psychiatry, by introducing a Marxian perspective.

He begins the task with his famous critique of Octave Mannoni's theory of a "colonial dependency complex." In his book *Prospero and Caliban* Mannoni (1964) had argued that the coming of the colonizers was unconsciously expected and even desired by the future subject peoples. On the basis of clinical evidence Mannoni suggested that the germ of this complex is latent in the adult Malagasy from childhood – that is, it is a genetic and real inferiority. This quasi-infantile dependency gives rise to insatiable and unrealistic demands for adult autonomy, associated with struggles for political independence. Mannoni's model, which incidentally he subsequently repudiated, is derived from Adler's notion of the inferiority complex. Paradoxically Adler, as a socialist, was unique in the Freudian circle for his concern to link and even derive frames of the unconscious mind from social conditions. Fanon, in fact, adopts a more properly Adlerian perspective when he writes "if there is an inferiority complex it is the outcome of a double process: primarily economic and subsequently the internalisation – or better the epidermalisation – of this inferiority" (Fanon, 1986). If the black African patient is suffering from an inferiority complex, and desires to be white, this desire has to be derived from the social structure and the fact that he (sic) lives in a society which makes his inferiority complex possible by proclaiming the superiority of one race over another.

For Fanon, the aim of critical psychotherapy was to demystify both the external social and the internal psychic reality by demonstrating their dialectical interdependence. Intervention, he argued, must be at the level of both the individual and the group – to make the patient conscious of his unconscious desire and abandon attempts at hallucinatory whitening, but also to act in the direction of changing the social structure – and hence to transcend individualism, and become involved in the group, in the collective struggle for liberation.

The focus of Fanon's work is thus the interplay between the material and social as this is mediated through the psychic envelope that racism wraps around the body. He brings to his analysis two dimensions of understanding which are utterly lacking in previous work on racism. The first derives from his experience as an Algerian psychiatrist, treating African patients within the framework of French colonial psychiatry; the second comes from his formation as a French intellectual heavily influenced by the work of Sartre and Lacan. Combining these two perspectives enabled him to look at racism and colonialism from the point of view of their impact on the black psyche. Blacks are no longer present in Fanon's psychoanalysis merely as shadows thrown onto the wall by white projective identification; they appear in their own right, as historical agents fully engaged in the process of their own psychic formation. He looks clinically, and also with passion, at how racism entraps its subjects, and imposes alienating identifications upon them. For this purpose he draws heavily on Sartre's theory of objectification (the famous "*en soi*" adumbrated in *Being and Nothingness*) and Lacan's seminal essay on *The mirror stage of ego development*.

From Lacan he gets the central idea that the structure of language splits the subject (i.e., between a speaking and a spoken subject) in a way that also constitutes the other as the repressed, unspoken "third" party which makes the discourse possible. When Lacan says that the Unconscious is the discourse of the Other, this is what he means. But what happens when the subject is interpellated in racist discourse? In that case the splitting of the subject in and by language becomes itself racialized; the effect is to insinuate a split between a real but bad black self (i.e., fully embodied but denied full access as a speaking subject to the symbolic order) and a good but false white self (i.e., a disembodied subject who can however speak volubly, but only in its master's voice). Fanon insists that this alienation effect is not only produced by language – it becomes active existentially in the physical interface between colonizer and colonized through the medium of the racist gaze.

Fanon is concerned here with how rituals of racist misrecognition are introjected – his word is "epidermalized" – so as to induce a form of a narcissistic trauma. Following on from Sartre's model of the "petrification" of the subject's desire in the look of the Other, Fanon suggests that when blacks discover themselves objectified in the negrophobic, or even merely clinical, gaze of the white colonialist, in so far as they recognize themselves in that structure of misrecognition, they can only become Other to themselves.

Fanon's emphasis on the *epidermalization* of racist discourse, on the way it "gets under the skin" and undermines the integrity of the black bodily ego, plus his advocacy of revolutionary violence as a means of disalienation, has led many cultural commentators, especially in the USA, to see him as a pioneer and champion of black identity politics. Fanon undoubtedly saw himself as a cultural nationalist, albeit in a largely tactical sense – it was, he believed, a necessary stage along the road to pan-African socialism. He canvassed the return to cultural roots in order to create a sphere of psychoaffective equilibrium in which the damage wreaked by colonialism could be worked through and undone. He certainly tended to argue that black pathology was a function of contact with white society, and that left to their own devices black societies were incapable of producing neuroses. He was also highly critical of the cosmopolitan mind set of the black middle class. Underlying both stances was a normative view of the black psyche based on an organicist model of culture and cultural oppression. In terms with which Margaret Thatcher might well agree, Fanon argued that disjuncture between family and nation leads to social anomie; his vision of the healthy, liberated black civil society follows W. E. Du Bois in seeing the family as its essential cornerstone. Or to put it another way, Fanon's analysis, having boldly advanced psychoanalysis beyond the consulting room and the white middle-class reference group into the thick of the battle against Western colonialism, suddenly retreats back into the "familialism" of classical Freudianism, in proposing a corporatist vision of the "good society." At this point he uncritically reoccupies the ground that Adorno and, to a lesser extent, Reich had cleared in their critique of the emotional foundations of fascism.

Many of these attitudes come out in Fanon's famous case studies of two of his patients – whom he calls Capecia and Veneuse. Capecia is a mulatto. She has only one possibility and one concern, Fanon writes: to turn white. She is barred from herself, and he adds, may she add no more to the mass of imbecilities. Veneuse is a neurotic intellectual, and for him his color is only an attempt to explain his psychic structure. If this objective difference did not exist he would have manufactured it out of nothing. Everything about him can be explained by his devaluation of self (self-hatred) consequent on his fear of maternal abandonment. The "crime" of both patients for Fanon is thus that they have both epidermalized colonial ideology and found neurotic rather than political solutions to their internal conflicts.

As can be imagined, Fanon's harsh and unforgiving portrayal of these two patients has become the subject of heated controversy. There has been no shortage of feminists who have argued that Fanon's unsympathetic view of Capecia is typically misogynistic, and no shortage of psychoanalysts who have suggested that if Fanon dissociates himself so strongly from Veneuse, it is precisely because he has so much in common with him. Afrocentrics and black roots radicals then enter the fray to suggest that these attacks on Fanon are motivated by racial spite and become part of a wider attempt by the white intellectual establishment to discredit a revolutionary black thinker.

Fanon's take-up has been uneven, to the point of lopsided. His work was initially embraced enthusiastically by the student and countercultural left in the 1960s as part of their general anticolonialism. Once African independence came and brought civil wars and a whole lot of other complications in its aftermath, many of this generation turned towards more home-grown interests and pursuits: green politics, feminism, and finally, of course, postmodernism. The antipsychiatry movement, strong in both France and Italy, and linked to the libertarian left, claimed Fanon as one of its chief inspirations in the struggle to de-institutionalize mental health care, close the asylums, and end compulsory medication and ECT treatments. But the romantic view of madness – and more especially schizophrenia – as a metaphor for capitalist alienation, the attempt to portray the schizophrenic as a poet or revolutionary manqué, which came to be associated with antipsychiatry through the work of R. D. Laing (e.g., 1959) and David Cooper, (e.g., 1971), would have horrified Fanon who not only accepted the classical Freudian distinction between neurosis and psychosis, but as we've seen equated both with political false consciousness.

He might not have been much more sympathetic towards recent attempts to focus on patterns of racial discrimination within the mental health system, and to create a transcultural psychiatry more responsive to the nuances of lifestyle that shape the patient's attitude and behavior (Littlewood and Lipsedge, 1989; Littlewood 1998; Macey, 2000). Fanon the social revolutionary would have roundly condemned, as abjectly reformist, any attempt to ameliorate the black patients' lot that did not transform their social and material conditions at the same time. Indeed one of the least recognized influences on his work was the transcultural school of French psychiatry that took just this line and whose complicity with colonialism Fanon was much concerned to expose.

Within the world of black or Afro-American cultural studies, the story has been very different. Fanon's star has risen steadily to its current point of ascendancy where there are whole journals, conferences, and academic careers devoted to the pursuit of "Fanon Studies." His corpus is fought over by essentialists and post-structuralists, by those who claim him as the forefather of Afrocentrism, and those who see him as a practitioner of postcolonial studies *avant le lettre* (Macey, 2000) Yet by definition such scholarly debates are about situating or celebrating Fanon, not about going beyond the limits necessarily set by his life and times. But nor is any such critical engagement forthcoming from those arguably best placed to do so, namely his fellow psychiatrists.

Within the psychoanalytic profession Fanon's work was almost completely ignored during his lifetime, and continues to be scarcely referred to – let alone deferred to – in the literature (Macey, 2000). There are a number of reasons for this. He was not, it is true, a profound clinician; his case histories, compared to those written by Ernst Binswanger, Manfred Bleuler, Françoise Dolto, or Marion Milner, are perfunctory and one-dimensional. Nor did he produce any new models or reformulations of intraspychic process, like Bion, Lacan, Kohut, or Balint. He did not manage to combine theoretical originality with therapeutic innovation like Freud himself, or D. W. Winnicott, Melanie Klein, or Octave Mannoni (Mannoni, 1964).

But the suspicion remains that these shortcomings, if that is what they are, are not the main reason for his neglect. His "original fault" in the eyes of the analytic establishment was that he broke the analytic rule distinguishing the patient's internal world (which is the domain proper of psychoanalysis) from external social reality (which is supposedly none of its business); he abandoned the analytic epoche for cultural interventionism, and in so far as he did so, he betrayed his true vocation as a "doctor of souls."

How should this charge be answered? It may be the case that in some instances Fanon's ideological enthusiasm clouded his clinical judgment. And it may be that for all his political revolutionism, Fanon was, in strictly professional terms, a conservative thinker. But then this is hardly unique. In fact in the history of psychoanalysis it is the norm. Those whose ideas or practice have challenged or transformed the internal culture of the profession have tended to be conservative on wider social and political questions. This is certainly the case with Klein, Winnicott, Bion, and Balint. But equally the political radicals – Reich and Adler – have exercised an altogether retrograde influence vis à vis the sophistication of analytic ideas. Only in the case of Ferenczi do we find someone whose work is capable of pushing at both the external boundaries and internal limits of Freudianism at one and the same time.

Fanon in fact does not fit into the either/or category; he deployed ideas at the cutting edge of philosophical and analytic thinking in his time to explore the psychic violence committed by racist and colonialist regimes in the name of a "superior" Western reason. En route he turned Adorno's negative dialectics off its Hegelian head and onto its materialist feet by demonstrating how racist discourse is embodied in and through the desire of the other. As such his work constitutes a fresh starting point for a consideration of unconscious racism and how it might be critically, and politically, engaged.

New Directions

In the last decade of the twentieth century, as virulent movements of nationalism and racism emerged in the "old countries" of Europe, especially in the wake of collapsing communist regimes, psychoanalytic ideas became increasingly central to attempts at making sense of these "postcolonial" or "postmodern" forms (Rattansi, 1998). The notion that racism (or nationalism) could be understood as simply a displaced – and hence "false" – type of class consciousness no longer stood up once it became clear that class – at least in its Marxian sense – was no longer a sufficient concept to explain either the persistence or the transformation of structural inequalities in these societies (Goldberg, 1993).

The impact of feminism not only switched the focus from class to gender, but served to highlight those aspects of racism which psychoanalysis had always made central to its account – namely the sexual dynamics of racial desire and hatred (Mitchell, 1974). For some this made it possible to revisit libido theory, if only to overturn its patriarchal bias through a radical re-reading of the "desiring machine" (Deleuze and Guattari, 1983). At the same time the Lacanian "revolution" made possible a cultural turn unhampered by any reference to the instincts. It was cultural theorists who increasingly turned to Freudian texts in search of clues to the power which signifiers of race and nation continued to exert over the social imaginary, especially in the realm of popular culture (McClintock, 1995). Some profited from a deconstructive reading of Freud, to challenge the "universalism" of his formulation of the Oedipus and complete the decolonization of psychoanalysis itself; others engaged with ethnic identity politics by interrogating pre-Oedipal positions linked to Freud's notion of a "narcissism of minor differences." Finally, and perhaps most radically, there were attempts to link the body politic of racism with Freudian notions of the death instinct, the uncanny, and the compulsion to repeat. We will deal with each of these developments briefly in turn.

Is the Oedipus universal?

One of the earliest debates between psychoanalysis and the other human sciences concerned the applicability of Freud's reading of the Oedipal myth to non-Western cultures. Just how invariant was the Oedipal triangle as a foundation stone of the "law of sexual difference"? There has been no shortage of critics to argue that the attempt to create a general theory of the human condition out of an ancient Greek myth and on the basis of clinical data obtained from neurotic white middle-class Viennese is a case of blatant ethnocentrism. Freud's defenders, whilst conceding that some of his attitudes and opinions are undoubtedly those of a "man of his culture and time," nevertheless argue that his fundamental discoveries transcend these limitations and, with suitable modification, can be applied to other cultures and other times. Not surprisingly this debate has run and run and has been given new impetus by the cultural relativism preached by some forms of postmodern epistemology.

Anthropologists took an early interest in Freudian concepts (Devereux, 1980). Although most remained sceptical of Freud's own anthropological speculations, especially his theory of the parricidal "primal horde," many found his formulation of the Oedipus complex of great pertinence to their ethnographic work. Malinowski, in his field study of Trobriand Islanders, had argued the case for a matrilineal variant in which the maternal uncle rather than the father plays the key role in the Oedipal triangle. In this culture the young man must become a mother's brother to his sister's children when he grows up and hence must renounce identification with his father at an early stage of the game. In other words different patterns of authority, power, and kinship generate different structures of emotional attachment and conflict (Malinowski, 1954).

A. K. Ramanujan, in his more recent study of the Indian Oedipus, has argued along rather similar lines; the deep structure of the myth is the same but the narrative viewpoint which governs the unfolding of the plot is that of the mother/son. In so far as a father figure is involved at all the conflict is enacted through surrogates. The usual pattern here is for the son to submit to the father's authority and then to be allowed access to the mother's desire. In other words we are dealing with a reversed or negative Oedipal structure where mother/son form a mutually seductive couple and the father is jealous of the son's erotic attachment to Mum. The daughter equivalently has a strong identification with her father and takes her mother's place in the field of paternal desire. This structure of feeling and fantasy therefore underwrites the rules of the Indian caste system which both demands the absolute submission of the son to the father and uses the bond with the mother to tie him into loyalty to the family. Here once again we have a version that does not conform to the European norm.

The recent republication of Wulf Sachs's *Black Hamlet* (1996), the classic psychoanalytic biography of a black South African healer written by his Jewish South African analyst, first published in 1937, has served to highlight many of the issues of cultural relativism focused by the original Oedipus debate. In her introduction to the new edition, Jacqueline Rose, writing from a literary Lacanian perspective, makes no bones about the historical implication of psychoanalytic theory and practice in ethnocentric constructions of the Other; but she also argues that pushed to its limit the notion of projective identification opens up a symbolic space in which it is possible to interrogate just these assumptions. Ironically it may have been Sachs's own political identification with the cause of Black Liberation, his desire to free his patient from his neurotic entanglements so he could fully participate in the struggle to emancipate his own people, that led him to both assimilate the distinctive features of African Oedipus, as described by Ortigues, to a Eurocentric model and to foreclose that space of uncertainty and unknowing where a proper working through of cultural differences might proceed in the conduct of the talking cure.

As these examples show, there are "family resemblances" between different Oedipal forms but also crucial differences. It is not the case that the positive Greek Oedipus is the universal norm and all the others variants, or that where the "normal" features do not exist there are no Oedipal relations at all. Rather, within the erotically desirable circle of kin (including servants and other members of the household), a particular culture selects certain relations for Oedipalization, that is, as the source of its myths and the focus of psychic conflict, because these relations are structurally significant for its reproduction. It also follows that some relations which are erotically charged may not in fact be "Oedipalized" at all. This raises the intriguing possibility that in Western cultures where "race relations" have become increasingly sexualized, this may be the result of a process of de-Oedipalization, or rather a cultural regression to pre-Oedipal formations of self and other.

Piggybacking on the Oedipus debate, there is an increasingly powerful current of work, primarily by psychoanalysts from non-Western cultures questioning the universality of Freud's first topological model. The picture Freud draws of the "skin-encapsulated ego," caught between the blind instinctual drives of the "id" and the moralizing collective voice of the superego, could be read as an accurate enough transcription of the psychodynamics of Western individualism; but in societies where the "we self" predominates over the "I self" as the matrix of identification, where consequently conventional ego boundaries are blurred and symbiotic relations the norm, the notion of what is a "transitional object" clearly has to undergo revision. As psychoanalysis develops further outside Europe many of its key concepts can expect to come under further pressure, leading no doubt to an enrichment of both theoretical vocabulary and clinical practice.

Male fantasies or the authoritarian personality revisited

Almost all the work inspired by Adorno and by Freud's 1922 paper on paranoia, focuses on the Oedipal structuration of racist desire. As a result the forms of pre-Oedipal identification and aggressivity which the work of Melanie Klein and her followers put on the psychoanalytic map, have, until very recently, been virtually ignored. The publication of Klaus Theweleit's *Male Fantasies* (1987) changed all that.

Theweleit's book is a study of letters written home by young men serving in the German *Freikorps* after World War I. The *Freikorps* was an elite military unit, many of whose members subsequently became leading supporters of the Nazi party. Theweleit is concerned to show, through a close "Freudian" reading of these texts, how the emotional roots of racism and fascism can be traced to the way male psychology is organized by and into a military machine. He takes a leaf out of Reich's *Mass Psychology of Fascism* to argue that rituals of militarism wrap the body up in a physical and emotional straightjacket and provide an institutionalized defense against disturbing sexual desires, by giving them a perverse sadistic organization.

That would, however, be true of any military machine in the world (with the possible exception of the Cuban army, that supposed last bastion of Stalinism in the Western hemisphere, which has its own inimitable style of marching, halfway between a shimmy and a samba!). Unless you take the view that all armies are intrinsically fascistic, the argument does not get us very far, and certainly represents little advance on Reich's own reductive applications of libido theory. However, at this point Theweleit introduces a new twist into the argument; he suggests that the unique contribution of fascist and racist discourses with their essentialized binaries of (good) Self and (bad) Other is to provide a second line of defense against regression to more fluid and polymorphously perverse forms of identification set in motion by the infantilizing effects of authoritarian regimes. He argues that the life-destroying reality principles that are mobilized in fascism cannot be analyzed using classical Freudian formulations of the Oedipal complex but instead require us to look at what is in play in pre-Oedipal structures.

For these purposes Theweleit draws extensively on Deleuze and Guattari's famous notion of *machine désirante* – a sucking pumping machine linking mother's breast and baby's mouth in a symbiotic matrix of libidinal energy "without subjects." In their book *Anti-Oedipus* Deleuze and Guattari (1983) argue that this "psyborg" entity constitutes the very aliveness of the real, characterized as it is by teeming polysemy, and an endless flux of desire; this productive power, which, they argue, is that of the Unconscious itself, is by definition associated with the fertility of women's bodies. Theweleit now takes over to argue that it is precisely this feminine force of production that is so threatening to the patriarchal order – and hence has to be crushed, stamped out, or otherwise neutralized before being reinvented in a monolithic order invested with a sterile dynamism dominated by the death drive. That, in his view, is the psychodynamic work which fascist ideology does on behalf of the soldier males of the *Freikorps* and whose effects can be read between the lines of the letters they send home to their mothers.

The recent emergence of racist skinhead youth movements in Germany, Austria, Scandinavia, the UK, and the USA, often with affiliations to far right nationalist or neo-Nazi groups, would seem to argue for the prescience of much of Theweleit's analysis (Kaplan and Bjorgo, 1998). These "home boys" with their sentimental odes to "mother-love" tattooed on one arm and death or glory swastikas emblazoned on the other certainly seem to have found in fascist symbolism and racist acts a means of asserting a "strong" form of masculinity that is otherwise disintegrating all around them. The collapse of the culture of manual laborism along with its patriarchal codes of apprenticeship and inheritance, coupled with the deterritorialization of related communities of aspiration, would certainly point to a radical "de-oedipalization" of subject positions (Cohen, 1999). However this may just as easily mobilize white projective identifications with the macho stance of black rap and street culture, setting in motion a very different dynamic based on racial envy. Once again it is dangerous to "read off" the object choice – however racialized – from some presumed common psychological disposition of the group.

The main difficulty with this argument, however, is its practical corollary – namely that the only viable antiracist strategy is somehow to persuade these boys to embrace their repressed feminine side and explore the polymorphously perverse possibilities opened up by the postmodern world. Not only is this to set up a normative libertarian ideal which is highly contradictory in its own terms, but it obviously invites a further defensive "hardening" of the racist body armor on the part of these young men. But are there other ways of looking at the problem?

A narcissism of minor differences? Racist desire and its disavowal

Once pre-Oedipal relations became the center of attention, the way was open to shift the focus from the more overt rationalizations of racism to a consideration of its secondary gains – the more covert pleasures afforded by racist desire.

In this perspective there has been renewed interest in Freud's notion of a "narcissism of minor differences." In a famous passage in his paper Freud commented:

> every time two families become connected by marriage each of them thinks itself superior to the other. Of two neighbouring towns each is the other's most jealous rival. Closely related races keep each other at arm's length. The south German cannot endure the north German, the Englishman casts every kind of aspersion on the Scot, the Spaniard despises the Portuguese. And elsewhere we are no longer astonished that greater differences should lead to an almost insuperable repugnance such as the Gallic people feel for the German, the Aryan for the Semite and the white races for the coloured. (Freud, 1921:121)

Underlying this argument is Freud's view of the role of aggression in narcissism. As he puts it:

> In the undisguised antipathies and aversions which people feel towards strangers with whom they have to do, we may recognise the expression of narcissism, that works for the self preservation of the individuals as though the occurrence of any divergence from their own particular lines of development involved a criticism of them and a demand for their alteration. (Freud, 1921:122)

Freud's theory of narcissism seemingly sanctions the conflation between "fear of the stranger," xenophobia, national chauvinism, and racism. But is that actually consistent with his formulation? He starts by stating what amounts to a law: the greater the proximity/similarity of the Other the greater its perceived threat to the Ideal Self, hence the greater the fear evoked and the stronger the urge to invent difference and assert distance. So far so good. This is a great advance on all the liberal and humanist platitudinizing that suggest that the more alike we are the easier it should be for us to get on, and that after all there is only one race – the human race. Where Marx saw merely a dumb generality, without purchase on the real world, Freud detects a cover story which seeks to deny the narcissistic dynamics at work in these identifications.

But then Freud adds a rider: in moving from "minor differences" to major ones – let us say in moving from ethnocentrism to racism – we are, according to this argument, simply seeing the same principle "writ large." This is the fatal leap in the argument which many Freudians have been only too keen to take (Kovel, 1988). Major differences, that is, differences that are based on structures of power and domination, are not simply interpersonal or intergroup differences aggregated. That is the prime fallacy of methodological individualism.[3] An explanation that might plausibly apply to relations of sibling rivalry, or the territorial rivalry between two neighboring gangs, and which might also apply to rivalries between socialist or Christian sects, or between different groups of black immigrants, does not translate into a model for understanding imperial rivalries, genocidal attacks, or systematic racial discrimination. These structures simply operate at another level of determination. This is first because where the other sex, race, nation, or class is concerned, difference is primary or constitutive, and similarity is, at best, something constructed after the event. Secondly, in terms of Freud's formula we might expect heterophobic patterns only in cases where there is some demonstrable similarity – something sufficiently alike to make potentially invidious comparison almost inevitable, and hence requiring some move to foreclose the possibility. But when Freud is talking about the "greater differences" between whites and blacks he is clearly talking about the *absence* of demonstrable similarities. Now according to the logic of his argument this should play on an unconscious fear that blacks are really the same as whites under the skin, and this in turn will call forth, through the circuit of its disavowal, a strategy of *dedifferentiation* applied to the object, namely: "blacks all look the same – you can't tell one from the other (unlike us whites)." And this is indeed the case.

Xenophobia, or its more general term heterophobia, thus turns out to imply a quite different structure of feeling to that of racial hatred. This is not to say that rivalries between close similars (qua narcissism of minor differences) cannot become racialized – as the horrible example of ethnic cleansing in ex-Yugoslavia clearly demonstrates – but this entails a qualitative transformation not a mere quantitative increase in the amount of libidinal energy invested in the construction (Ignatieff, 1995).

Much of the most interesting recent work has therefore concentrated on spelling out just what this transformation consists of. What happens when narcissism, and pre-Oedipal object relations generally, become racialized, what changes and what stays the same about the structure of the fantasy and its object?

Sibony and the Lacanians

Perhaps the most radical attempt to outline a theory of racist desire from within a Lacanian perspective comes from the work of Daniel Sibony (1978, 1998). Sibony asks "what do racists want from racism?" and he answers "to eliminate the desire of the other." It is the enjoyment of being black, the pleasure Jews take in their Jewishness, that is hated because it represents a joy in being alive *and* in being different. Racist desire then is a form of what Ernest Jones called aphanasis. The aim of racist discourse, especially in its institutionalized forms, is not to impose the State's own desires on the Other (as in assimilationist strategies), but to expel the Other from the realm of desire, and hence from life itself. In this sense, Sibony says, all racism has a genocidal impulse. In terms of the structure of this desire, Sibony notes that it takes as its preferred object the body that leaves nothing to be desired, a body that is immaculately conceived, pure, phallic, immortal – and dead. The stiff and the statue are the model bodies of the "master race" and as such are juxtaposed to the body of the subject race, a body which is fecund, secretive, excretive, mortal, blemished, impure – and indubitably alive. Following Theweleit, Sibony creates a dual image of the racialized body politic, on one side formed by the figure of Thanatos, on the other by Eros, and he too attributes the split representation to a perverse dialectic of narcissistic identification. But rather than seeing this as a simple polarity, he suggests that one of the more unconscious functions of racist discourse is to reanimate the dead phantom body, to invest it magically with a biological life force – which is precisely its "race"; it is this which secures the perpetual regeneration of the master body and ensures that the transmission of its powers of social propagation from generation to generation do not have to pass through the defiles of sexual difference, or historical individuality.

This is a very fruitful formulation and one which I have developed further in my own work on the racialization of the body within "home boy" cultures and "homely racism" (Cohen, 1993). Janine Chasseguet-Smirgel (1985) has also taken this line of thought for an interesting walk; focusing on the maternal body as a fantasy object within racist and national discourse, she insists that its idealization is inscribed in territorial claims of every kind, from the assertion of autocthony to "we were here first" nativism; this sense of belonging always contains within it the germs (sic) of a more or less violent repudiation of the Other and indeed of the symbolic order as a whole.

Homely racism also has as its necessary correlate a fascination, and abhorrence, of the unhomely – what Freud called the *unheimlich* or uncanny. Sibony suggests this is because three dimensional human beings (i.e., "real" blacks or Jews) continue to bear an uncanny resemblance to the stick figures created by the racist imagination; as such they evoke ambivalent feelings associated with "the other scene" populated as it is with aliens, zombies, ghosts, "psyborgs," and all the other hybrid beings whom we imagine to have taken our rightful place as denizens of the "first home" that is the mother's body (Cohen, 1998). The visible presence of these flesh and blood shadows in everyday social encounter serves to unblock racial fantasy from its compulsive repetition by reanimating it in the register of the real – it is always a story about a real incident that literally authorizes the fantasy. The function of the scapegoat in this perspective is to unfold a narrative that justifies our own "right of return" to the primordial home in order to expel "unwanted intruders" and make the world safe for our own kind.

The uncanny is also a key feature in Julia Kristeva's (1994) analysis of racism and nationalism. However, for her what evokes the characteristic figures of the *unheimlich* is not so much the Other (class, race, nation, sex) in the external world but the Other Within – in the words of the title to her book "the stranger we are to ourselves." This sense of the foreign in the midst of the familiar she relates to the death drive (Bion, 1991). The diffuse narcissistic anxiety experienced in the face of what cannot be symbolically represented in and by the self is linked by Kristeva to a state of abjection. By this she means the sense of self-abandonment habitually associated with what is repudiated about bodily needs and their satisfaction, and which comes to be socially anchored to habits or habitats of those living on the margins of society, on the other side of the race, class, or sex tracks.

Yet Kristeva also sees this position of liminality from its other side, as offering the immigrant and the exile a freedom from the burdens of historical representation carried by those who feel they have to defend the physical integrity of the nation or the race. It is just this transcendance of an imposed inheritance, and the license it gives to invent new forms of identity and belonging, that becomes the focus of envy on the part of "the indigenous": a Lacanian version, then, of the classic Freudian theme of the return of the repressed.

Sibony and Kristeva tend to follow Sartre in deriving an epistemology of racism from an ontology of "the racist." The work of Slavoj Žižek (1989, 1991) proceeds in the opposite direction and derives structures of racist feeling and fantasy from the epistemophobic structures of the body politic. Žižek too homes in on the notion of the *unheimlich* as an indivisible remainder/reminder of otherness that resists symbolization in language. For him the foundation myths of race and nation are premised on a primordial act of disavowal: they assert that nothing can be lacking in the reality guaranteed by their written or unwritten constitutions of the sovereign subject. It is precisely this foreclosure that in Žižek's view underwrites a constitutive split between the universal categories of citizenship and the particularism of identitarian politics based on race or ethnicity. At the same time it founds a powerful principle of racist or ethnicist reiteration – the compulsion to repeat (or somatize, or act out) what is unrepresentable about desire. For what is repeated, across all the banal insults and slurs, slogans, graffiti, and jokes that make up the everyday rhetorics and pragmatics of racism, is a degree zero of representation – an "x marks the spot that is not y." It is this inscription which draws a fatal line under the feet of those whom the body politic will assign to the side of life or death and which also triggers performatively the passage to acts of gratuitous racial violence, through its equivalence with the real (Butler, 1990, 1993).

In the last 10 years many of these Lacanian ideas have been taken up and developed further by writers operating within the paradigms of feminism and postcolonial studies (McClintock et al., 1997). In some cases, for example in the work of Homi Bhabha (1994), and Gayatri Spivak (1988), Lacanian terms are deployed to underwrite a post-structuralist model of "decentered subjectivity" which is then made into a cultural paradigm of a certain version of postmodern identity. Bhabha's notion of "mimicry," for example, derives largely from Fanon's appropriation of Lacan's model of the mirror stage. Mimicry here is a device through which the colonial subject subverts its master's voice and gestures of authority in the very act of echoing their cadences. Then by a shift in problematic that is never properly conceptualized, Bhabha begins to write in almost identical terms about mimicry in postcolonial settings as if all that was involved in the decolonization process was a reconfiguration/reversal of the "play of signifiers." The implicit idealism of the Lacanian theory of desire, with its emphasis on lack in relation to the real (based ultimately on Hegel's master/slave dialectic), comes out strongly here. Spivak's notion of a subaltern subject who "does not speak" but for whom the ideal speech situation is to throttle the loquaciousness of the master, in a reverse form of aphanisis, is another example of how psychoanalytic ideas can be wrenched out of context and twisted to lend support for normative political projects with which they have little affinity (Spivak, 1988).

One of the main criticisms that can be leveled at this body of work is that it is highly normative. It posits an ideal typical racial, colonial, or postcolonial encounter with the Other, which is illustrated only indirectly, usually through the citation of literary texts or films, but in a way which bears only the flimsiest relation to the empirical complexities of real positions and practices within cultures of racism. Kristeva's figures of The Exile or The Orphan are metaphorical constructions, not recognizable social beings.

This process of abstraction is also related to the style of presentation, especially the penchant for writing dense prose sprinkled with obscure but poetic or scientific images after the laconic manner of the master (sic). Sibony, for example, has not been translated into English for the very good reason that he is virtually untranslatable. Even more than Lacan, his style is full of allusive word play that hints at plumbing Unconscious depths but does little to clarify the argument and in fact seems primarily designed to impress the reader with the author's verbal dexterity and encyclopedic knowledge. Žižek's work is often difficult, relies on puns and double entendres which only make sense to someone steeped in the entire oeuvre of Western philosophy, linguistics, and the human sciences as well having an intimate grasp of the finer points of Lacanian theory. A familiarity with contemporary film, popular culture, and political debate also helps! Bhabha and Spivak are equally at home doing headstands on the high wire of postcolonial theory or deconstructing popular movies but it must be said that little of their stream of theoretical consciousness comes down to earth for long enough to dwell usefully on the specifics of conjunctural analysis at the level of policy or practice. Julia Kristeva stands out as someone who writes clearly and elegantly, and is concerned to take the reader along with her as she worries at a problem.

Despite this caveat, this is an enduringly important body of work, albeit one that has yet to be taken up by the psychoanalytic profession itself. The reasons are not difficult to find. Almost without exception these Lacanians are academics whose primary formation and interests have been in the arts, humanities, or social sciences, and who have engaged with psychoanalytic ideas *en passant*. The "difficulty" of the texts and their seeming irrelevance to the clinical setting have given analysts a good alibi for ignoring them. In general the profession remains closeted in discussions of clinical technique and interpretation and leaves questions of metapsychology to others "better equipped." At one level, this is somewhat surprising given that the scope of analytic treatment is increasingly being extended outwards from the private consulting room, clinic and mental hospital, to the fields of social work, education, and institutional management. It is in just these contexts that issues of racial discrimination have come to the fore. Yet at another level, for the reasons I discussed at the outset, the professional culture and conventions of psychoanalytic practice militate against any such wider engagement and "race" remains its special blind spot.

Conclusion: After Lawrence

So what finally is the payoff for adding a psychoanalytic perspective to the understanding of unconscious racism? First of all let us be clear that it has nothing to do with providing psychotherapy for racists! It might have something, or indeed a lot, to do with making the psychoanalytic profession more aware of ethnocentric assumptions in its own clinical theory and practice, and in persuading it to tackle the forms of institutional racism operating in its procedures for recruiting both analysts and analysands.

More generally, however, a case must be made that psychoanalytic insights provide a powerful resource for getting to grips with some of the trickier aspects of both popular and institutional racism, provided they are applied in a nonreductive manner, and in a way that supplements rather than replaces other readings.

With this in mind let us return to the scene of the racist crime with which we began or rather to its "other scene." What can we add to our understanding of this bizarre episode? The suspects are, of course, unaware that they are being filmed; if they knew that the police had bugged their houses we might expect them to have been more circumspect in their behavior. However, the fact is that even in areas known for their high levels of antagonism towards ethnic minorities, as in this part of South London, the successful commission of a racial murder requires that there be no witnesses. So between the performativity of the racist insult and the performance of the murderous act there opens up an all too fatal gap, a gap that can only be widened by further acts of intimidation. For what is a performance without an audience?

Yet in this case the gap is filled, not so much by the pantomime of racial violence these boys stage for their own benefit, as by its alteration through police surveillance into a medium of voyeurism for the rest of the world. But as we watch these boys cavorting about, entering through the eye of the hidden lens into their "secret world" of racial fantasy, what – or rather whose – game are we really playing?

We could say that it is a game that centers on the fantasy of seeing, hearing, and hence knowing everything about the Other, without oneself being seen, heard, or recognized as Other. It is about eavesdropping and peeking through invisible keyholes into worlds from which one is normally excluded. The ideal is to participate secretly, without being observed to be doing so, and to observe without in any way disturbing what is going on. What is to be seen and heard in this way is usually some excitingly illicit, dangerous, or forbidden, but pleasurable scene. In other words, it is about what Freud called the primal scene, the scene staged in the imagination even and especially if it is witnessed "for real," in which the child observes its parents making love, and which may be interpreted as an act of violence, but at the very least is experienced as something which may be observed *but not told*, on pain of castration or death.

So as watchers of this video we have unwittingly been made to occupy the vantage point of an ideal audience for a racist murder to be publicly staged, as witnesses who do not have to be silenced "after the event" because it is always and already after the event and we have nothing to say that may be usefully taken down and used in evidence against these boys; we may be fascinated or repulsed by the spectacle of the crime, but we are powerless to intervene. We can of course press the button and stop the video, but we cannot interrupt this unfolding scenario of racist hatred, we can only replay it, and indeed we may well find ourselves caught up in the compulsion to repeat. This drive for "action replay" is not only because we are not in fact material witnesses to the original scene of the crime, but because what is being reiterated is the fact that there can be no denouement, no possibility that the intricacies of plot might be finally unraveled and the mysteries of racism revealed. We always and already know "who dunnit " but that knowledge, like the video itself, does not constitute proof. Since the case and its narrative cannot be closed by these means, the only thing left for us to do is to play it again, and again, and again.

What we have to face therefore is the fact of structural complicity between the spectacle of racist violence and the standpoint of official antiracist horror. I am not talking here of a certain "mirroring" between the rhetorical styles of racist/fascist/far right organizations and some antiracist/antifascist/far left groups, although this certainly exists. I mean that we have to begin our analysis, and our activism, from a recognition that in racism's Other scene there are no hard and fast lines to be drawn between "two legs bad" and "four legs good." In this context it will not help to remember Hegel's dictum that in the night all cows are black. For under the aegis of that legacy we find, when dawn comes, that the Old Mole of History is still burrowing away in the belief that it was ever thus. Psychoanalysis both indicates the role that racism plays in the construction of that nightmare and helps us wake up to what it is we need to do to unearth a less split principle of hope.

Notes

1   Reich (1975). It is worth noting that for Adorno, in contrast to Reich, it is the weak or missing father, rather than the overbearing patriarch, who creates the emotional conditions for fascism,

an idea that was subsequently to be followed up by Mittserlich in his famous study of *Society Without the Father*. In either case, however, from a strictly psychodynamic viewpoint, the effect is the same and results in weak, fragmented narcissistic personality types who need to identify with strong leaders and lose themselves in a sense of oceanic oneness with the racial mass in order to maintain a precarious sense of identity and self-worth.

2 Of course it could be argued that these differences were more apparent than real. The proclaimed internationalism of Soviet style communism was given the lie by the virulent antisemitism and covert nationalism practiced under its regimes.

3 This is commonly regarded as a form of methodological individualism, and it is, except that in the case of psychoanalysis the individual is disaggregated into a series of discrete and conflicting molecular functions: id, ego, superego in Freud's first libido theory; real, imaginary symbolic, in Lacanian theory. In this way way psychoanalysis actually puts in question some of the basic tenets of Western individualism, including the autonomy of the skin-encapsulated ego and the primacy of the rational calculating self. Even ego psychology, which comes closest to endorsing the John Wayne/Frank Sinatra view of the world, has to wrestle with the recalcitrance of the Unconscious when it comes to rationalizing the American Dream.

References

Adorno, Theodor W., Frenkel-Brunswick, E., Levinson, D. J., and Sanford, R. N. (1950) *The Authoritarian Personality*. New York: Harper.

Allport, Gordon W. (1954) *The Nature of Prejudice*. Garden City, NY: Doubleday.

Bakan, David (1990) *Sigmund Freud and the Jewish Mystical Tradition*. London: Free Association Books.

Bauman, Zygmunt (1989) *Modernity and the Holocaust*. Cambridge, UK: Polity.

Bhabha, Homi (1994) *The Location of Culture*. New York: Routledge.

Bion, Wilfred R. (1991) *Experiences in Groups and Other Papers*. London: Tavistock.

Butler, Judith (1990) *Gender Trouble: Feminism and the Subversion of Identity*. New York: Routledge.

Butler, Judith (1993) *Bodies that Matter: On the Discursive Limits of "Sex."* New York: Routledge.

Chasseguet-Smirgel, Janine (1985) *The Ego Ideal: A Psychoanalytic Essay on the Malady of the Ideal*. New York: Norton.

Cohen, Phil (1992) " 'It's racism what dunnit': Hiddden narratives in theories of racism," in Ali Rattansi and James Donald (eds.) *"Race," Culture, and Difference*. London: Sage.

Cohen, Phil (1993) *Home Rules: Reflections on Racism and Nationalism in Everyday Life*. London: University of East London New Ethnicities Unit.

Cohen, Phil (1998) *Strange Encounters: Adolescent Geographies of Risk and The Urban Uncanny*. London: Centre for New Ethnicities Research, Finding the Way Home Working Paper 3.

Cohen, Phil (ed.) (1999) *New Ethnicities, Old Racisms*. London: Zed Books.

Cohen, Phil (forthcoming) *Race and the Other Scene*. London: Routledge.

Cooper, David (1971) *The Death of the Family*. Harmondsworth, UK: Penguin.

Craib, Ian (1998) *Experiencing Identity*. London: Sage.

Dalal, Farhad (1998) *Taking the Group Seriously: Towards a Post-Foulkesian Group Analytic Theory*. London: Taylor and Francis.

Deleuze, Gilles and Guattari, Felix (1983) *Anti-Oedipus: Capitalism and Schizophrenia*. Minneapolis: University of Minnesota Press.

Devereux, George (1980) *Basic Problems of Ethnopsychiatry*. Chicago: University of Chicago Press.

Fanon, Frantz (1986) *Black Skin, White Masks*. London: Pluto.

Freud, Sigmund (1921) "Further problems and lines of work," in *The Complete Psychological Works of Sigmund Freud*, vol. XVIII. London: The Hogarth Press.

Freud, Sigmund ([1922] 1955) "Some neurotic mechanisms in jealousy, paranoia and homosexuality," in *The Complete Psychological Works of Sigmund Freud*. London: Hogarth Press, pp.221–34.

Freud, Sigmund (1962) *Civilisation and its Discontents*. New York: W. W. Norton.

Frosh, Stephen (1998) *The Politics of Psychoanalysis: An Introduction to Freudian and Post-Freudian Analysis*. New York: New York University Press.

Gay, Peter (1978) *Freud, Jews and Other Germans: Masters and Victims in Modernist Culture*. Oxford: Oxford University Press.

Gilman, Sander (1996) *Freud, Race and Gender*. Princeton, NJ: Princeton University Press.

Goldberg, David Theo (1993) *Racist Culture: Philosophy and the Politics of Meaning*. Oxford: Blackwell.

Groddeck, Georg (1997) *The Meaning of Illness: Selected Psychoanalystic Writings*. New York: International University Presses.

Hughes, Athol (ed.) (1991) *The Inner World of Joan Riviere*. London: Karnac Books.

Ignatieff, Michael (1995) *Blood and Belonging: Journeys into the New Nationalism*. London: Noonday Press.

Jones, Ernest (1953–7) *The Life and Times of Sigmund Freud*, 3 vols. London: Hogarth Press.

Kaplan, Jeffrey and Bjorgo, Tore (eds.) (1998) *Nation and Race: The Developing Euro-American Racist Subculture*. Boston: Northeastern University Press.

Kovel, Joel (1988) *White Racism: A Psychohistory*. London: Free Association Books.

Kristeva, Julia (1994) *Strangers to Ourselves*. New York: Columbia University Press.

Laing, R. D. (1959) *The Divided Self*. London: Tavistock.

Littlewood, Roland (1998) *The Butterfly and the Serpent: Essays in Psychiatry, Race and Religion*. London: Free Association Books.

Littlewood, Roland and Lipsedge, Maurice (1989) *Aliens and Alienists: Ethnic Minorities and Psychiatry*, 2nd edn. London: Unwin Hyman.

Macey, David (2000) *Frantz Fanon: A Life*. London: Granta.

Macpherson, Sir William of Cluny (1999) *The Stephen Lawrence Inquiry: Report of an Inquiry by Sir William Macpherson of Cluny*. London: The Stationery Office.

Malinowski, Bronislaw (1954) *Magic, Science, and Religion and Other Essays*. New York: Doubleday.

Mannoni, Octave (1964) *Prospero and Caliban: The Psychology of Colonization*. New York: Frederick A. Praeger.

McClintock, Ann (1995) *Imperial Leather: Race, Gender and Sexuality in the Colonial Context*. New York: Routledge.

McClintock, Ann, Mufti, Aamir, and Shohat, Ella (eds.) (1997) *Dangerous Liaisons: Gender, Nation, and Postcolonial Perspectives*. Minneapolis: University of Minnesota Press.

Mitchell, Juliet (1974) *Psychoanalysis and Feminism*. New York: Pantheon.

Nandy, Ashis (1989) *The Intimate Enemy*. New Delhi: Oxford University Press India.

Rattansi, Ali (1998) "Just framing: Ethnicities and racisms in a 'postmodern' framework," in L. Nicholson and S. Seidman (eds.) *Social Postmodernism: Beyond Identity Politics*. Cambridge, UK: Cambridge University Press.

Reich, Wilhelm (1975) *The Mass Psychology of Fascism*. Harmondsworth, UK: Penguin.

Richards, Barry (1995) *Disciplines of Delight: The Psychoanalysis of Popular Culture*. London: Free Association Books.

Roediger, David (1991) *The Wages of Whiteness*. London: Verso.

Roediger, David (1994) *Towards the Abolition of Whiteness*. London: Verso.

Rustin, Mike (1996) *Towards the Good Society and the Inner World: Psychoanalysis, Politics and Culture*. London: Verso.

Sachs, Wulf (1996) *Black Hamlet*, introduction by Saul Dubow and Jacqueline Rose. Baltimore, MD: Johns Hopkins University Press.

Sartre, Jean-Paul (1990) *Being and Nothingness*. London: Routledge.

Schorske, Carl (1988) *Fin de Siècle Vienna*. New York: Vintage Books.

Sibony, Daniel (1978) "L'affet ratial," in *La Haine et la Désir*. Paris: Grasset.

Sibony, Daniel (1998) *Ecrits sur le "racism", ou, La haine identitaire*. Paris: C. Bourgois.

Spence, Donald (1994) *The Rhetorical Voice of Psychoanalysis: Displacement of Evidence by Theory*. Cambridge, MA: Harvard University Press.

Spivak, Gayatri (1988) *In Other Worlds: Essays in Cultural Politics*. New York: Routledge.

Sterba, Richard (1947) "Some psychological factors in negro race hatred and in anti-negro riots," in Geza Roheim (ed.) *Psychoanalysis and the Social Sciences*, vol. 1. New York: International University Press.

Theweleit, Klaus (1987) *Male Fantasies*. Minneapolis: University of Minnesota Press.

Turkle, Sherry (1992) *Psychoanalytic Politics*. London: Free Association Books.

Young-Bruehl, Elisabeth (1996) *The Anatomy of Prejudices*. Cambridge, MA: Harvard University Press.

Žižek, Slavoj (1989) *The Sublime Object of Ideology*. London: Verso.

Žižek, Slavoj (1991) *For They Know What They Do*. London: Verso.

Chapter 15

Everyday Racism

Philomena Essed

Everyday racism is racism, but not all racism is everyday racism. From everyday racism there is no relief.

Introduction

Until recently the day-to-day realities of racism did not have a place in political and sociological histories. Barry Adam, one of the first authors to analyze strategies employed to cope with everyday inferiorization, puts his finger on the spot when he states that "Behavior which is mundane, routine, and taken for granted tends to escape the notice of the more dramatic macro histories" (Adam, 1978:1–2). This does not mean that everyday experiences of racial discrimination have been absent from discourse and collective memory. Written materials on everyday racism could be found in poems, literary narratives, and autobiographies. Many readers are familiar with Ralph Ellison's extraordinary story of a "race" invisible, which opened ignorant eyes to the emotionally consuming impact of daily injustices (Ellison, 1952). Likewise, personal accounts of day-to-day life, whether under segregation in the USA (Maya Angelou, 1970; Audre Lorde, 1982) or under South African apartheid (Ellen Kuzwayo, 1985) have been documents of learning. From the fiction of Richard Wright, James Baldwin, Alice Walker, and Toni Morrison to the real life account of Angela Davis, across the world people of color recognize their own stories. They share these painful experiences with family and friends, often to lighten the burden (Feagin and Sikes, 1994). In her book, *The Black Notebooks* (1997), Toi Dericotte analyzes brilliantly not only the immediate situation and its aftermath, the repetitiveness of racism, but also how racism has a vicarious and cumulative impact:

> I was looking through the eyes of my mother, cousins, and aunts . . . I began to see how our most intimate relationships, our abilities to love, express ourselves, and indeed to live, are deeply and permanently affected by racism. (Dericotte, 1997:20, 188)

In many instances autobiographical materials and personal accounts or life stories prove to be insightful testimonies. Stories are one of the best rhetorical tools because they connect the storyteller and the message with the audience. Stories help to show the listener how to identify with a topic because of the detailed manner in which the stories are contextualized. Accounts are useful in revealing the emotional toll of constant exposure to discrimination (Williams et al., 1997). Personal accounts of the lived experience prove most illuminating in telling what everyday racism is about: injustices recurring so often that they are almost taken for granted, nagging, annoying, debilitating, seemingly small, injustices one comes to expect. The concept of everyday racism relates day-to-day experiences of racial discrimination to the macrostructural context of group inequalities represented within and between nations as racial and ethnic hierarchies of competence, culture, and human progress. In this article I examine the various ways in which everyday racism is expressed and contested in ordinary situations. I will share, for purposes of illustration, selected stories about everyday racism, stories reflecting my personal experiences, and stories that were recently related to me informally by friends and family in the course of my own everyday life.

The Denial of Racism

Each and every government in the world is aware that the Universal Declaration of Human Rights includes agreement on the elimination of racial discrimination (Lauren, 1988, 1998). Parliaments are prone to engaging in positive self-presentation, and when it comes to racism often claim their country as more equal, humane, tolerant, and fair than anywhere else (van Dijk, 1993). This does not mean that racism is a problem long gone, that there are only a few die-hards left out there who can be pointed at as "the racists" when they openly propagate white supremacy.

Criticized but still firmly embedded in our societies are the universal claims of Western knowledge, the domination of Western norms for progress, and the globalization of Western standards for cultural and human development (Amin, 1989). Racism – or, historically speaking more accurate, racisms (Goldberg, 1990, 1993) – covers ideological and social processes which discriminate against others on the basis of their being associated with different racial or ethnic group membership. In the course of the twentieth century a shift of discourses has occurred, replacing the focus on quasi-scientific myths of biological inferiority by a concern with cultural (under)development (Solomos, 1989). In the course of the twentieth century we have also witnessed processes of decolonization, the Civil Rights Movement in the USA, and the formal ending of apartheid in South Africa, developments indicative of more tolerant attitudes, explicit rejection of racist positions and skillful positive self-presentations on race issues. Intertwined with the emerging culture of international human rights (Lauren, 1998), the denial of racism has come to be part of dominant commonsense discourses, effects of which taint the everyday lives of groups who continue to struggle against racial injustices (Razack, 1998). Inherent in the denial of everyday racism is the discrediting of voices of discontent:

> I was on guard. So many times if a black person admits discomfort, the white person then says that the black person must be "sensitive-paranoid" – responding not to the present environment, which is safe and friendly, but to something of the past. They want to hear that the white people in this environment (themselves) are fine. It's the black person who is crazy. (Dericotte, 1997:146)

Ellis Cose comments in his book on black middle-class anger against the persistence of racism that they are probably "less afraid of being called Uncle Toms than of being penalized for speaking out against racism" (Cose, 1993:12). In Europe, the tendency to associate racism with World War II, to see racism primarily as a moral problem, as the ultimate "sin," has created a taboo against confronting individuals with the racism of their behavior. In the USA, according to some authors, to deny racism and to blame the black victims of racism have become intellectually fashionable (Feagin and Sikes, 1994).

Despite the Universal Declaration that there should be no place for racism in our lives, there is insufficient inter/national commitment to educate children, inform adults, and provide citizens with relevant information about how to identify racism, how it is communicated, how it is experienced, and how it can be countered. The notion of everyday racism can be a helpful tool for understanding that racism is a process involving the continuous, often unconscious, exercise of power predicated in taking for granted the privileging of whiteness (Frankenberg, 1993), the universality of Western criteria of human progress, and the primacy of European (derived) cultures.

Why distinguish between racism and everyday racism? Everyday racism is not about extreme incidents. The crucial characteristic of everyday racism is that it concerns mundane practices. This does not make everyday racism a racism of a more humane kind. Although everyday racism has such an informal ring that it may sound as if it concerns relatively unharmful and unproblematic events, it has been shown that the psychological distress due to racism on a day-to-day basis can have chronic adverse effects on mental and physical health (Fulani, 1988; Jackson et al., 1996). According to Thomas La Veist (1996) several studies have demonstrated a link between exposure to racism and high blood pressure. Everyday racism, though felt persistently, is often difficult to pinpoint. As a result these microinjustices become normal, fused into familiar practices, practices taken for granted, attitudes and behaviors sustaining racial injustice. Continuous disrespect and hostilities nurture alienation from society, or even from self (McGary, 1999). This is not meant to say that targets of racism are only victims, powerless or passive against the forces of exclusion. In their study on the black middle-class experience of racism Joe Feagin and Melvin Sikes point out that there has been a significant increase in the number of African Americans with the professional and financial recourse to fight discrimination (Feagin and Sikes, 1994).

Conceptual Issues: Nature and Characteristics of Everyday Racism

The concept of everyday racism has two constituent parts: one part says that it is about racism and the other part that it is about the everyday. For a long time traditional bias in the social sciences favored "grand" developments, while excluding everyday life from what was considered a relevant area of research. Changes in the late 1960s and 1970s came about with the emergence of microsociology, most notably the leverage of phenomenology (Luckmann, 1978). Advocates of the study of meaningful social phenomena on their own grounds claimed that "we must begin all sociological understanding of human existence with an understanding of everyday life" (Douglas, 1974:x). Pathbreaking in their analytical eye for the details of everyday situations, many phenomenological and ethnomethodological interpretations of everyday events fall short where they fail to take into account the social and political framework of intergroup relations. Significant for the development of a theory of everyday racism has been a small number of theoretical attempts to link micro events to macro structures, in order to show "how practice is structured by organizational context and the distribution of power" (Alexander and Giesen, 1987:36).

The notion of "everyday" is often used to refer to a familiar world, a world of practical interest, a world of practices with which we are socialized in order to manage in the system. In everyday life, sociological distinctions between "institutional" and "interactional," between ideology and discourse, and between "private" and "public" spheres of life merge and form a complex of social relations and situations. The concept of everyday racism, originally developed in two comparative studies between the Netherlands and the USA (Essed, 1984, 1990a, 1991), has been adopted and successfully applied to the study of racism in other countries, including South Africa (Louw-Potgieter, 1989; Essed 1990b), Switzerland (Shaha, 1998), Canada (das Gupta, 1996), the UK (Twine, 1998), and in specific areas such as public health (Jackson et al. 1996), private business organizations (Human and van Schalkwyk, 1998) and neighborhood shopping (Lee, 2000). The focus on everyday manifestations of systemic inequality extends outside the field of race relations as well, which has contributed to granting "the everyday" generic meaning: everyday inequalities (O'Brien and Howard, 1998); everyday sexism (Ronai et al., 1997). Does this mean that these phenomena are the same? Ideologies of racial and gender domination, though (in)directly rooted in social constructions of biological differences, are both increasingly cultural in their discursive expressions (Hecht, 1998; Benokraitis, 1997). Gender and race are social constructions comprising a combination of ingroup favoritism and outgroup exclusions. Everyday manifestations of racial and gender discrimination have many similarities, such as being patronizing, talking down, assuming lack of confidence, hiring token blacks or women, or favoring white men (Human and van Schalkwyk, 1998). But there are also many differences. A prevalent form of everyday racism is contact avoidance, whereas everyday discrimination against women can take the reverse form: uninvited touching. A serious problem with analogizing is that women of color are made invisible in comparing "blacks" and "women." Furthermore, analogies do not do justice to the fact that racisms and genderisms are rooted in specific histories designating separate as well as mutually interwoven formations of race and gender. I have called intersections of genderism and racism "gendered racism" (Essed, 1991) a notion which has been adopted and worked out in more detail in a number of studies (Bento, 1997; St. Jean and Feagin, 1998).

The concept of everyday racism defies the view that racism is either an individual problem or an institutional problem. When we reduce racism to personal prejudices we get easily misled into believing that the psychology of the prejudiced person is the main problem. The development of alternative conceptualizations of racism, that is, a shift from intent (the motive behind discrimination) to outcome (the effect of discrimination to the lives of discriminated groups) has greatly benefited from critical US publications. The Kerner Report (Kerner Commission, 1968) a study of the conditions of black riots, benchmarked a structural approach, later captured in the notion of "institutional racism" (Carmichael and Hamilton, 1967). The institutional dimension refers to cooperative systems forming part of the ruling apparatus. Institutions embody cultural values organized around a distinctive function – education, health care, law, housing, media, and the like (Smith, 1987). Racism is ideologically mediated through actual practices in all these institutions. This means that the taken-for-granted feeling that one's own group comes first, the idea that people of a different racial and ethnic background are less competent, less civilized, a cultural threat, or less intelligent operates (latently) when "individuals in carrying out the routine practices of their employment or institution produce outcomes which in their effect discriminate against members of ethnic minority populations" (Husband, 1991:53). Discrimination occurs whether or not actors are aware of their attitudes and motives.

Racism is not confined to institutional settings, because our everyday lives are not confined to institutional settings either. Furthermore, racism is not only a set of outcomes, but intrinsically a process which sustains unequal relations of power. As a process, everyday racism is interwoven in ongoing negotiations over resources, whereby the one party "can gain and maintain the capacity to impose its will repeatedly upon another, despite any opposition, by its potential to contribute or withhold critical resources from the central task, as well as by offering or withholding rewards, or by threatening or invoking punishment" (Lipman-Blumen, 1994:110). The following story, related to me by the project coordinator, illustrates the point of negotiation:

> City of den Haag, the Netherlands. A management consultancy firm offers internship positions to three candidates of color, the first "nonwhites" to work for that particular firm. The internship trajectory is part of a government project where the Ministry of Social Affairs agrees to finance one year of training and internship, on the condition that if completed successfully the trainees get offered a contract as junior advisers. The project coordinator, a white woman, is an expert in leadership coaching. The three trainees who are placed with the management consultancy report to the project coordinator that they feel underestimated constantly. Typos in their writing are immediately misconstrued as language deficiency, there is lack of encouragement, and the consultancy firm director, a white man, expresses openly his view that ethnic minorities are generally incompetent. The situation calls for intervention. The project coordinator has a meeting with the director, who explains that he had this gut feeling all along that the candidates would not succeed in the consultancy world. The project coordinator is not very impressed by the director's appeal to his gut feeling. She wants to see the evaluation reports identifying the specific tasks the candidates were asked to perform, their learning progress, their successes and failures, the mentoring input from the side of the firm and their results. The director responds that he does not work like that, explaining: "it is common knowledge that ethnic minorities have language problems and educational deficiency." The project coordinator discusses the situation at length, the attitude of the director, his prejudices, questioning whether he is competent at all to supervise ethnic minority candidates. This creates further trouble. The director feels devastated and demoralized. How dare she question his attitude? After the meeting he calls her again, and spends hours on the phone complaining that she has upset him, and that he is not a racist. The project coordinator pursues the case, which results in improvement of work conditions. Ultimately two of the candidates stay – they are in the process of completing their internship and are likely to get offered a contract.

It can be disquieting for people to be told that "independently of their own sense of personal agency they are perpetuating a form of racist practice" (Husband, 1991:53). In the case discussed, the accusation of racism shifts the focus of attention away from the initial problem. The director demands time and energy from the project coordinator in order to deal with his hurt feelings, in the course of which he tries to redefine the situation as a question concerning whether he is a racist or not. The problem is the organizational culture, which seems hostile to the career aspirations of the trainees. This example also shows that when sensitive to recognizing racism in everyday life, white people – the project coordinator for one – can make successful interventions to counter discrimination.

Everyday racism is never a singular act in itself, but a multidimensional experience (McNeilly et al., 1996). One event triggers memories of other, similar incidents, of the beliefs surrounding the event, of behavioral coping and cognitive responses. Joe Feagin and Melvin Sikes, who studied at length black Americans' accounts of racism, agree that the "recurring experiences … with whites who discriminate are at the heart of the racial problem" (1994:15). In other words, each instantiation of everyday racism has meaning only in relation to the whole complex of relations and practices. Iris Young speaks in this respect of systemic constraints:

> … the vast and deep injustices some groups suffer as a consequence of often unconscious assumptions and reactions of well-meaning people in ordinary interactions, media and cultural stereotypes, and structural features of bureaucratic behavior and market mechanisms – in short, the normal processes of everyday life. (Young, 1990:41)

In my study, *Understanding Everyday Racism* (Essed, 1991), I found that expressions of racism in one particular situation are related to all other racist practices and can be reduced to three strands of everyday racism, interlocking as a triangle of mutually dependent processes: the *marginalization* of those identified as racially or ethnically different; the *problematization* of other cultures and identities; and symbolic or physical *repression* of (potential) resistance through humiliation or violence. Across and between everyday situations, from workplace to restaurant, from classroom to shopping, from house hunting to public transportation, and from watching television to staying in a hotel, racism operates through the characteristics of the specific situation and through the situational resources by means of which power can be expressed. The power of the teacher includes, among other things, power to give or to withhold rewards. Marginalization in the classroom comprises a range of practices promoting the image of the model student as white, where ethnic minority students are tolerated but not accepted as equally important to the intellectual body of the nation. Students of color in mostly white colleges face discrimination from epithets to professional indifference and social isolation (Feagin, 1992; Romero, 1997). The teacher is supposed to grade with fairness, but some teachers do not succeed in acknowledging achievements of black students when acknowledgment is there for white students (Essed, 1991). Everyday racism can mean that the teacher withholds information about applications for scholarships. Research has pointed at the problem of chronic inflexibility when black students ask for help or additional explanation. There is negligence in classroom discussions, or symbolic marginalization where instruction materials are exclusively based on white experiences (Essed, 1990a, 1991).

As a process, the *marginalization* of ethnic minority students is anchored ideologically through explanations associating them one-sidedly with *problems*: less intelligent, language deficiency, lack of cultural sophistication, insufficient work ethic or social skills. Some ethnic groups, notably Asians, are accused of an exaggerated work ethic compared to the white norm. The status quo of marginality is maintained through the *repression* of resistance. A major form of everyday repression concerns the privileging of the definition of reality through the denial of racism. Accusations of oversensitivity about discrimination, continuous ethnic jokes, ridicule in front of others, patronizing, rudeness, and

207

other attempts to humiliate and to intimidate can all have the effect of discouraging action against discrimination.

The main characteristics of everyday racism can be summarized as follows: Everyday racism is a *process* in which (1) socialized racist notions are integrated in meanings that make practices immediately definable and manageable, (2) practices with racist implications become in themselves familiar and repetitive, and (3) underlying racial and ethnic relations are actualized and reinforced through these routine or familiar practices in everyday situations. Everyday racism is experienced *directly* and *vicariously*. Because it permeates everyday life, it has a more damaging effect on health than incidental major confrontations with racism. Everyday racism involves cumulative practices, often covert and hard to pinpoint. Specific incidents acquire meaning in terms of the three major processes through which racism operates in everyday life: the marginalization of racial and ethnic groups, the problematization of (attributed) group characteristics and culture, and the repression of (potential) counter action.

Comparative Analysis: Everyday Racism across Locations and Nations

Everyday racism is rooted in the history of particular societies and adapts to the structure and nature of that society. In societies where segregation is institutionalized, systematically recurring forms of racism are likely to include obstruction of attempts to integrate. One of my experiences with everyday racism in South Africa is a case in point. The account that follows is extended, as I will use it later on as a basis for illustrating a method for analyzing accounts of covert racism.

> Cape Town, South Africa. We have booked a room for two at the President Hotel in Sea Point, an upscale, previously white-only area. Upon arrival the receptionist, a young white man, first registers my (white) partner – fair enough, the reservation got made in his name. Upon our request to include my name, the receptionist replies that one name will do. We insist that he add my own name to the room number. The receptionist gapes at me, no doubt categorizing me as "Cape Colored," and blurts out: "Do I take it that you share the same room?" "Of course we share the same room" is our reply, somewhat surprised at this weird question. Since the receptionist does not look as though he is going to make a move to process my name in the computer, I ask for the reservation form, add my name, commenting "now you have the correct spelling to put into your computer." I am expecting a call at 7 p.m. that evening from a colleague at the University of Cape Town concerning the exact arrangements for a talk I have agreed to give. The expected call does not come through. Upon return from the restaurant, later that evening, we check at the reception whether there has been a call at all, unwilling to believe that my colleague has forgotten about me. Our skepticism appears to have ground: the receptionist who had registered us had bluntly refused to file my name into the computer. The evening receptionist, a man of color, apologizes and corrects the exclusion immediately. Another receptionist, a white man who stands next to the "colored" receptionist, throws a hostile stare, disappears for a moment and returns with the message that he has checked with the operator: there has been absolutely no call that evening from anyone asking for a supposedly unlisted name anyway. Upon our profuse objections that there must have been a call, another white man sticks his head from behind a door in the back only to retreat immediately, but long enough for us to notice that the door he shuts behind him is that of the manager's office. Displeased by the situation, we call the manager from our room. He identifies himself as the deputy evening manager. His tone is hostile to begin with and,

upon our asking whether the refusal to register me has to do with my being black, he becomes plainly rude, loses it, adding volume to his voice over the phone: "we do not have any racism in this hotel, how dare you make such a suggestion." The next morning my colleague calls. Relieved to find me at last, she confirms that she did indeed call at the time we had agreed on and had insisted that someone under my name must be staying in the hotel. Suspecting misconduct on the part of the hotel, she had refused to take no for an answer, recognizing what she referred to as the "same old white chauvinism"; and probably realizing also that the operator had picked upon her Indian background identifiable from her voice. She had wisely asked for the name of the operator, a woman who likewise grew impolite and dismissive. "This is outrageous," I commented, "but at the same time too good to be true – now we have evidence of deceit, we have nailed them right here." We call for the general manager, asking for her to come up to our room in order to provide an explanation of how this can happen in a hotel that Nelson Mandela himself had opened a couple of years before. She handles the situation professionally. No denials, no excuses in defense of her staff – she simply listens, shakes her head with disgust and agrees that this should never have happened, wondering how she can make up for the damage done. We comment that we are not interested in any personal compensation, but would rather see that she provide her staff with proper diversity training. She firmly states that she will do something about her staff. A huge basket with fruit and exclusive wine gets sent up with a note: "our very sincere apologies." Throughout the remaining part of the stay, the staff goes out of their way to behave overcorrectly. How sincere the apologies are can be judged by other mixed couples or people of color who choose in the future to stay at the same hotel.

This event exemplifies everyday racism in a country in transition from formal segregation where race mixing was against the law to the new situation where racial discrimination is in violation of the law. Nevertheless racism in everyday life in what many see as the new South Africa is alive and kicking. The story also shows that racism is not only targeted against those perceived as racially or ethnically different, but it also implicates whites who transgress racial boundaries.

Everyday racism adapts to the culture, norms, and values of a society as it operates through the prevalent structures of power in society. The more status or authority involved, the greater the damage resulting from commonsense prejudiced statements and discriminatory behavior. When members of parliament make discriminatory statements or sanction discriminatory policies in the course of their normal everyday duty, as politicians, the safety and civil rights of ethnic minorities and refugees are at stake. When teachers underestimate, discourage, or ignore ethnic minority children, the futures of ethnic minority generations are at stake. When employers discriminate against people of color, jobs, incomes, or career mobility are at stake as in the following example which my sister mentioned when we talked over the phone preceding my visit to South Africa. It concerns her son Nelson. Since then, he has read my draft version of his story, made comments, and added a follow-up:

Nijmegen, the Netherlands. Nelson, a Dutch student of economics who has completed his freshman year with terrific grades, seeks a summer job in order to finance his vacation. He registers at Tempo Team, one of the largest agencies for temporary jobs. The official, a white woman, having processed his data on a system card, suggests that he return within a few days, which he does, but she has nothing for him. The third time another white woman official in charge fetches Nelson's card from the files, glosses through the job offers, and approaches the counter while reading his card. It appears that something has been written on the back of the card. Nelson reads: "nice young man, but he does not look too bright." Nelson does not say anything, wants to reject the two job offers because they seem boring and simple, but accepts one because time is running out and he really wants a job. He feels awkward about the text on his card, realizing that the quick judgment about his intelligence when he has hardly communicated with the woman with whom he registered must have been triggered by his brown face. Fortunately, the accusation that he is not smart does not really affect him – he has always been at the top of his class. Furthermore, his uncle happens to work for the local antidiscrimination office. They discuss the case – it matches a pattern of exclusion with which the office is familiar. There have been complaints before about agencies discriminating against ethnic minority candidates. Yet, Nelson feels too intimidated by the idea that he is dependent on a job to file an official complaint. His anger about it does not leave him, however. A few days before the completion of his job he returns to the Tempo Team office to voice his discontent about the derogatory remarks on his card – a brave thing to do about which he feels pretty nervous. The woman at fault is not in, colleagues insist there must have been some kind of mistake, but "unfortunately" – so they claim – someone must have displaced his card, so they cannot verify his complaint.

Personal stories, such as Nelson's experience, give body and voice to cold statistics of unemployment for ethnic minorities in the Netherlands: 20 percent compared to only 5 percent for the population at large. Unemployment figures are not just there in the abstract, they are the outcome of negotiations between individuals who all have personal stories, a number of which are likely to include experiences of racial discrimination in the labor market.

Methodological Questions: Identifying Racial Meaning in Everyday Experiences

Insufficient insight into the systemic nature of racism fuels denial and the generic accusation that black people are oversensitive and resort too quickly to charging racism. The presupposition that those exposed to discrimination are not competent to make sound judgment about the situation is a powerful tool of everyday racism. Racial privilege is perpetuated when those who claim superior judgment are insensitive to recognizing everyday racial injustices, while claiming exclusive power to define reality as void of racism. Privileging dominant views, the knowledge and insights accumulated on the basis of repetitive exposure to and experience of racism are discharged as useless. In two sequential studies, I have worked out a methodology to recover those knowledges and to show that accounts of racism are not *ad hoc* stories. Accounts are reflective interpretations of realities based on heuristics of inference from general knowledge, and on heuristics of rational comparisons – with nonracist situations (for inconsistency) and with other forms of discrimination (consistency). The pain, anger, or disempowerment which discrimination often causes targets to feel are strong incentives for careful examination of an event before judging it discriminatory and taking action, the latter often at the risk of retaliation. Nelson's story is indicative of hesitation and strategic timing of his response for fear of victimization. It has been shown repeatedly in research that careful observation is a norm rather than an exception when suspicion of discrimination is involved (Dummett, 1973; Essed, 1990a, 1991; Feagin and Sikes, 1994; St. Jean and Feagin, 1998). This is not meant to deny that there are occasions where one can make a wrong judgment while spotting discrimination where it is not present. We will see later that general knowledge of what is to be expected under "normal" circumstances – that is, "nonracialized" circumstances – is a prerequisite for recognizing when something goes wrong. At the same time, knowledge about when things "go wrong" irrespective of race is relevant in order to see that an "unjust" situation might not be racist. Finally, it is also feasible that people play strategically on white sensitivity about being charged with racism by doing just that against better knowledge.

Eliciting accounts of racism provides a wealth of information otherwise invisible to scholarly eyes. In a project about everyday racism at a so-called integrated South African university, then still during the period of apartheid, we tested the method of careful listening and inquiring about observations of racism in order to expose hidden racism at the very university that claimed to have nondiscrimination policies. A racially diverse group of students, black, "colored," Asian, and white, were instructed to interview black fellow students about their experiences in college. In preparation for the interviews the students studied reading materials about racism – the teacher wanted them to have sufficient general knowledge about racism before they were allowed to engage in fieldwork. The students were instructed to elicit extended information about experiences of racism, not by attacking the interviewees with quick accusations of oversensitivity but by non-directive probing for overt and hidden signs of racism, inviting the interviewee to "tell about it as much as possible in detail" (Louw-Potgieter, 1989:311). The account was to be the interviewee's own reconstruction of the event that she or he felt had been an expression of racism. I had introduced this method earlier in two projects about everyday racism in the USA and in the Netherlands, but it had not been tested in another context, and with diverse interviewers (Essed, 1984, 1990a, 1991). Each account was analyzed twice, first by the interviewer, then by the project supervisor.

The findings were revealing. First, the project confirmed the hypothesis that everyday racism can be considered a generic concept. Second, on the face of it, the method of interviewing – creating maximum space for interviewees to contextualize and explain their experiences in their own words and according to their own judgment – reduced the impact of the race of the interviewer on the interview situation. All of the interviewers across color and gender elicited similar stories. They found that the interviewees, black students, "tended to test all other possibilities and hypotheses before judging an actor's behavior racist" (Louw-Potgieter, 1989:313). The author concludes that this evidence is in sharp contrast to the stereotype that blacks are so obsessed with racism that they will construe well-intentioned behavior as racist. The methodological value of accounts concerns competency at the level of meaning through the careful reading of observations of discrimination on a day-to-day basis. Careful listening and probing, which was the disposition of the President Hotel manager, underscores the relevance of emotional intelligence (Goleman, 1995, 1998) in dealing with everyday racism. Unlike the deputy manager, her professionalism kept her from jumping to the hasty conclusion that whatever had happened could be everything but racism.

Experience is a central concept in the study of everyday racism. Accounts of racism locate the narrators as well as their experiences in the social context of their everyday lives, giving specificity and detail to events and inviting the narrator carefully to qualify subtle experiences of racism. Experiences of racism are a relevant source of information because racism is often expressed in covert ways and because racism is denied and mitigated by the dominant group. Elsewhere I have discussed in detail a method for systematically analyzing accounts of racism in the Netherlands and in the USA (Essed,

1988, 1991). Accounts, verbal reconstructions of experiences with racism, are likely to include (some of) the following information: *context* (where did it happen, when, who were involved?); *complication* (what went wrong?); *evaluation* (was it racism?); *argumentation* (why do you think it was racism?); and *reaction* (what did you do about it?). Let us apply this to the hotel event in South Africa.

Context

This category gives information about the participating actors, the time, place and social circumstances in which racism events are situated: A mixed couple registers at the President Hotel. A white male receptionist handles the registration.

Complication

This part of the account says something about "what went wrong," what was unacceptable. In the particular event the receptionist refused to register the woman of color, and showed disbelief about a white man and a woman of color sharing a room. In order to know why this was unacceptable you need to have knowledge of how it should have been: the receptionist is supposed to file both names in the computer upon demand, and is not supposed to question, let alone disapprove of, a couple. Later complication upon complication adds to the racism already active: lies about the phone call, rudeness against my colleague when she calls for me in vain, a badly-behaving night manager, who grows aggressive when we criticize the hotel for racial discrimination.

Evaluation

The story suggests that this was a case of racism, even when no reference was made to color.

Argumentation

Arguments are relevant to explain why the complications are seen as forms of everyday racism. In the context of covert racism, this is the most interesting category because it deals with the question: "Why did you think what happened was discrimination?" This category makes plausible, defensible, or acceptable the hypothetical evaluation that particular actions are manifestations of racism, even when at face value they might appear nonracial.

A relevant argument can be that the complications we have identified are *consistent* over time – postapartheid is still oversensitive to mixed couples. There is consistency over situations – under apartheid any hotel could have openly refused to allow a woman of color in an upscale (white) hotel, today refusal is off limits, but personnel may still attempt to make one's stay an unpleasant one. There can be consistency in the behavior of the same actor – in this case we have no knowledge about behavior of this particular receptionist with other visitors of color. It is not unlikely that gender has played a role too, that the first receptionist took me for an occasional girlfriend and hence refused to treat me as a regular hotel guest. According to this consideration the evaluation of the situation can be seen as

212

gendered racism. Consistency can also be found in the behavior of other personnel with the same profile – white men, in this case – another white male receptionist lies in order to cover up for their negligence; yet another white male, the night manager, is rude. Transcending gender, one finds also rudeness from the side of the phone operator, a woman whose racial background is unknown to us.

Comparison for *inconsistency* with other (nonracist) situations is also a useful tool. This heuristic poses the question: how should service have been in a nonracialized situation? Or, do you know of similar situations (staying in a hotel) where racism had not been a problem, what happened in that case? Preceding our visit to the President Hotel, we stayed at the one of the Mövenpick hotels. The staff ranking followed traditional color lines: management white, reception and services black, Colored, Asian, kitchen black. But the service was impeccable. From waitress to manager, customer friendliness was the code. When we questioned some pictures on the wall reflecting affiliation to the former regime of President Botha, the manager we spoke to appeared sensitive to our critique. He explained that Botha had his residence around the corner of the hotel, was a frequent visitor to their restaurant, and indeed had opened the hotel in the mid 1980s while still president. Removal of all the pictures at once was considered too confrontational and awkward. According to the manager they had taken down a lot already, the rest would go with the major reconstruction coming soon. At the writing of this article, two months later, I received word through a colleague who had just stayed at the same hotel that only one Botha picture is left. As the above shows, despite the obvious remains of the apartheid system in staffing hierarchy and hotel decoration, the personnel seemed competent to avoid racial discrimination in day-to-day interactions with the hotel guests.

Another relevant comparison, for *consistency*, concerns similar discrimination (marginalizing the party of color, while centralizing the white party), but in a different situation, for instance, a restaurant rather than a hotel, within walking distance from the President Hotel. The evening of the missed phone call we had to admonish a young white waitress at the Avanti restaurant for invariably only addressing and first serving my partner, and me only through him. This breach of gender rules expressed disrespect, to say the least. Finally, the fact that the colleague who called me in vain recognized immediately that "same old white chauvinism" points to the fact that her experience with the President Hotel is consistent with other experiences.

Reaction

Individuals are actors in a power structure. Power can be used to reproduce racism, but it can also be used to combat racism. Immediate emotional reactions can include anger, frustration, powerlessness. Targets of racism have been found to employ a range of behavioral responses: speak up, remain silent, ignore racism, work harder to prove them wrong, pray, get violent, repress the memory (McNeilly et al., 1996). In the South African example, we speak up, and challenge the hotel management to provide sustainable improvements.

The categories of accounts have not only qualitative value. They have also been used as a basis for quantitative data collection (McNeilly et al., 1996; Williams et al., 1997). The first category, the *context*, provides information about the range of situations where discrimination occurs. The second category, the *complication*, holds information about the patterns of discrimination. The final category, the *reaction*, if quantified, gives information about the frequency of protest, who is involved in action against racism, and which actions have been successful and why.

Conclusions

Once it is recognized that racial oppression is inherent in the nature of the social order, it becomes clear that the real racial drama is not simply racism, but the fact that racism is an everyday problem. When, as we have seen, racism is transmitted in routine practices that seem "normal," this can only mean that racism is often not recognized, not acknowledged, let alone problematized. In order to expose racism in the system it does not make sense to fight people, to wonder whether he or she is a racist. It is relevant to focus on when, where, and how racism operates through everyday life, how and when ordinary situations become racist situations. What I am claiming is that there is no structural racism without everyday racism. On all levels of society, within and outside of institutions, we must analyze ambiguous racial meanings, expose hidden currents, and generally question what seems normal or acceptable.

By the same token, everyday racism is always structurally contextualized. Speaking up against racism when it invades our everyday lives, though seemingly an individual act, is conducive to critical change because countering everyday racism is contesting the racial inequalities at large. It has been shown that people of all racial backgrounds can learn to recognize and to contest racism in everyday life. Careful listening to the stories of those exposed to racism on a daily basis is a crucial tool in updating our collective knowledge about racism, which can be useful to counter its manifestations in everyday life.

Acknowledgment

I am grateful to David Theo Goldberg for his very useful comments on an earlier draft of this paper.

References

Adam, B. D. (1978) *The Survival of Domination. Inferiorization in Everyday Life*. New York: Elsevier.

Alexander, J. and Giesen, B. (1987) "From reduction to linkage: The long view of the micro – macro debate," in J. Alexander, B. Giesen, R. Münch, and N. Smelser (eds.) *The Micro – Macro Link*. Berkeley: University of California Press, pp.1–42.

Amin, S. (1989) *Eurocentrism*. London: Zed Books.

Angelou, M. (1970) *I Know Why the Caged Bird Sings*. New York: Bantam Books.

Benokraitis, N. V. (ed.) (1997) *Subtle Sexism. Current Practice and Prospects for Change*. Thousand Oaks, CA: Sage.

Bento, R. F. (1997) "When good intentions are not enough," in N. V. Benokraitis (ed.) *Subtle Sexism. Current Practice and Prospects for Change*. Thousand Oaks, CA: Sage, pp.95–116.

Carmichael, S. and Hamilton, C. (1967) *Black Power*. New York: Vintage.

Cose, E. (1993) *The Rage of a Privileged Class*. New York: Harper Collins.

das Gupta, T. (1996) *Racism and Paid Work*. Toronto: Garamond Press.

Dericotte, T. (1997) *The Black Notebooks. An Interior Journey*. New York: Norton.

Douglas, J. D. (ed.) (1974) *Understanding Everyday Life*. London: Routledge & Kegan Paul.

Dummett, A. (1973) *A Portrait of English Racism*. Harmondsworth, UK: Penguin.

Ellison, R. ([1952] 1972) *The Invisible Man*. New York: Vintage Books.

Essed, P. (1984) *Alledaags Racisme* [*Everyday Racism*]. Amsterdam: Sara (2nd edn. 1988, Baarn/ den Haag: Ambo/Novib.)

Essed, P. (1988) "Understanding verbal accounts of racism". *TEXT* 8,1:5–40.

Essed, P. (1990a) *Everyday Racism: Reports from Women in Two Cultures*. Claremont, CA: Hunter House.

Essed, P. (1990b) "Against all odds: Teaching against racism at a university in South Africa." *European Journal of Intercultural Studies*. 1,1:41–56.

Essed, P. (1991) *Understanding Everyday Racism: An Interdisciplinary Theory*. Newbury Park, CA: Sage.

Feagin, J. (1992) "The continuing significance of racism: Discrimination against black students in white colleges." *Journal of Black Studies*. 22,4:546–78.

Feagin, J. R. and Sikes, M. P. (1994) *Living with Racism. The Black Middle Class Experience*. Boston: Beacon Press.

Frankenberg, R. (1993) *White Women, Race Matters. The Social Construction of Whiteness*. London: Routledge.

Fulani, L. (ed.) (1988) *The Psychopathology of Everyday Racism and Sexism*. New York: Harrington Park Press.

Goldberg, D. T. (ed.) (1990) *Anatomy of Racism*. Minneapolis: University of Minnesota Press.

Goldberg, D. T. (1993) *Racist Culture. Philosophy and the Politics of Meaning*. Oxford: Blackwell.

Goleman, D. (1995) *Emotional Intelligence*. New York: Bantam Books.

Goleman, D. (1998) *Working With Emotional Intelligence*. New York: Bantam Books.

Hecht, M. (ed.) (1998) *Communicating Prejudice*. Thousand Oaks, CA: Sage.

Human, L. and van Schalkwyk, C. (1998) "Communicating racism and sexism: An exploratory study in two South African organisations." *Bestuursdinamika* 7,1:53–75.

Husband, C. (1991) "Race, conflictual politics, and anti-racist social work: Lessons from the past for action in the 90s". *C.D. Project Steering Group. Setting the Context for Change*. London: CCETSW, pp.46–73.

Jackson, J., Brown, T. N., Wiliams, D. R., Torres, M., Sellers, L. and Brown, K. (1996) "Racism and the psychical and mental health status of African Americans: A thirteen year national panel study." *Ethnicity and Disease*, 6, Winter/Spring: 132–53.

Kerner Commission ([1968] 1988) *Report of the National Advisory Commission on Civil Disorders*. New York: Pantheon Books.

Kuzwayo, E. (1985) *Call Me Woman*. London: The Women's Press.

Lauren, P. G. (1988) *Power and Prejudice. The Policy and Diplomacy of Racial Discrimination*. Boulder, CO: Westview Press.

Lauren, P. G. (1998) *The Evolution of International Human Rights*. Philadelphia: University of Pennsylvania Press.

La Veist, T. A. (1996) "Why we should continue to study race ... but to do a better job: An essay on race, racism, and health." *Ethnicity & Disease* 6, Winter/Spring: 21–9.

Lee, J. (2000) "The salience of race in everyday life: Black customers' shopping experiences in black and white neighborhoods." *Work and Occupations*, 27,3:353–76.

Lipman-Blumen, J. (1994) "The existential bases of power relationships: The gender role case," in H. L. Radke and H. J. Stam (eds.) *Power/Gender. Social Relations in Theory and Practice*. London: Sage, pp.108–35.

Lorde, A. (1982) *Zami. A New Spelling of My Name*. Trumansburg, NY: The Crossing Press.

Louw-Potgieter, J. (1989) "Covert racism: An application of Essed's analysis in a South African context." *Journal of Language and Social Psychology* 8:307–19.

Luckmann, T. (1978) (ed). *Phenomenology and Sociology*. Harmondsworth, UK: Penguin.

McGary, H. (1999) *Race and Social Justice*. Oxford: Blackwell.

McNeilly, M. D., Anderson, N. B., Armstead, C. A., Clark, R., Corbett, M., Robinson, E. L., Pieper, C. F. and Lepisto, E. M. (1996) "The perceived racism scale: A multidimensional assessment of the experience of white racism among African Americans." *Ethnicity & Disease*, 6, Winter/Spring: 155–67.

O'Brien, J. and Howard, J. (eds.) (1998) *Everyday Inequalities*. Oxford: Blackwell.

Razack, S. (1998) *Looking White People in the Eye. Gender, Race, and Culture in Courtrooms and Classrooms*. Toronto: University of Toronto Press.

Romero, M. (1997) "Class-based, gendered and racialized institutions in higher education: Everyday life of academia from the view of Chicana faculty." *Race, Gender & Class* 4,2:151–73.

Ronai, C. R., Zsembik, B. A. and Feagin, J. R. (eds.) (1997) *Everyday Sexism in the Third Millennium*. New York: Routledge.

Shaha, M. (1998) "Racism and its implications in ethical-moral reasoning in nursing practice: A tentative approach to a largely unexplored topic." *Nursing Ethics* 5,2:139–46.

Smith, D. E. (1987) *The Everyday World as Problematic*. Toronto: Toronto University Press.

Solomos, J. (1989) *Race and Racism in Contemporary Britain*. London: Macmillan.

St. Jean, Y. and Feagin, J. R. (1998) *Double Burden. Black Women and Everyday Racism*. Armonk, NY: M. E. Sharpe.

Twine, F. (1998) "Managing everyday racisms: The anti-racist practices of white mothers of African-descent children in Britain," in J. O'Brien and J. Howard (eds.) *Everyday Inequalities*. Oxford: Blackwell, pp.237–51.

van Dijk, T. A. (1993) "Denying racism: Elite discourse and racism," in J. Wrench and J. Solomos (eds.) *Race and Migration in Western Europe*. Oxford: Berg, pp.179–93.

Williams, D. R., Yu, Y. and Jackson, J. S. (1997) "Racial differences in physical and mental health. Socioeconomic status, stress and discrimination." *Journal of Health Psychology* 2,3:335–51.

Young, I. M. (1990) *Justice and the Politics of Difference*. Princeton, NJ: Princeton University Press.

Chapter 16

Science, Race, Culture, Empire

Sandra Harding

Is Science Racist?

Three practices with racially discriminatory consequences initially seemed to justify an affirmative response to this question. From the beginning of the nineteenth century until well after World War II, sciences sought to divide and rank human groups, persistently "discovering" the natural inferiority of non-Europeans, as well as Jews, women, and other groups. Craniology was just one such now discredited comparative science: skin color, hair texture, and virtually every other body feature were carefully compared by the sciences. A second critical focus has been on racist misuses and abuses of the sciences, their applications and technologies, such as Nazi eugenics, the Tuskegee syphilis experiments, discriminatory testing and uses of reproductive technologies, and the environmental racism that disproportionately locates toxic industries and dumps in nonwhite neighborhoods and Third World societies. Finally, people of non-European descent have been disfavored in the social structure of European and US science through exclusion, marginalization, and restriction to lower-level jobs.

Those who reject such criticisms, whom I shall refer to as the defenders of autonomous or neutral science, often acknowledge that such projects have been unjust and ill-founded. Nevertheless, they reply, the racism of such projects, where it does exist, does not challenge the fundamental cultural neutrality of the sciences. Modern science cannot legitimately be charged with racism on the basis of these kinds of criticisms. In the first case of attempts to discover the natural distinctions between the races, they argue that the vast majority of such projects – such as craniology, or other problematic comparative studies of intelligence or of body parts – are simply examples of bad science, not of real science. However, we cannot yet discount the possibility that there are real differences between the races. Such findings would be beneficial to the patients of medical and health institutions. The second and third criticisms point only to bad social practices, they argue; not to racism within the sciences themselves. How the information produced by neutral sciences is used, and who gets to do science, are both social matters decided in civic life, not scientific matters controlled by the rigorous methods that can create culturally neutral sciences. Furthermore, these defenders of autonomous science conceptualize the racism claimed to be apparent in these practices, where it exists, to be the consequence of false beliefs and bad attitudes of unenlightened individuals. The production of accurate scientific information is the best way to eliminate the appeal of such prejudices and biases, they argue.

Yet the antiracist critics do not find compelling these defenses of the autonomy of science from society, this way of conceptualizing racism, or this remedy for racist practices. For one thing, they point out that we now have many decades of more accurate scientific information about racial differences and similarities between the races, and of the inadequacies of the very concept of racial types to explain human variation. Race is not natural in the ways assumed by the studies of racial types. Moreover, many scientists who are not overtly prejudiced – in the sense that they do not hold false beliefs nor have "bad attitudes" toward nonwhites continue to engage in all three kinds of scientific projects that have racially discriminatory consequences. Why has the widespread availability of more accurate information about racial difference had so little positive effect on scientific practices?

From the very beginning of the early criticisms there could be heard hints of deeper links between scientific, racial, and Eurocentric projects than prejudice analyses of the causes of these three criticisms could capture. Is racism limited to the intentional acts of individuals, as the prejudice analyses assume? What about discriminatory principles, projects, practices, and cultures of institutions such as the law, the economy, or modern science and its philosophies? What about racist and Eurocentric assumptions made by whole societies, not just by individuals, and assumptions held over even larger historical eras and cultures, such as "modern life," "the developed world," or five centuries of European expansion? Are individuals' biases and prejudices the causes or effects of such larger social projects and eras?

Slowly but surely a horrible truth has come to light: the smartest and best-intentioned individuals can find themselves contributing to what other cultures and later eras identify as racist and ethnocentric projects. Thus some of the most powerful recent analyses have sought to identify racist and ethnocentric assumptions of first world institutions, societies, and civilizations (or philosophic standards), ones that are to be found beyond or outside the intentions of individuals.

The following account first identifies current issues in thinking about the natural and/or cultural elements of racial types; racist misuses and abuses of the sciences, their applications, and technologies; and racism in the social structures of sciences. Then it turns to new directions in research on other cultures' science and technology traditions, and on the connections between European expansion, the growth of modern sciences in Europe, and the decline of other cultures' science traditions. It concludes by identifying challenges to standard philosophies of science and epistemologies – those deepest and most pervasive forms of racism and Eurocentrism – that have emerged from such research on race, culture, empire, and sciences.

Natural Racial Types?

Three lines of thinking have developed in response to the question of whether there are natural race differences and, if so, what they are. The first assumes that the fundamental "truth of race" is part of the natural order, can be discovered by biology, and has valuable social implications and consequences. The second argues that race is entirely a socially constructed category, that it is not a useful scientific concept, and that these facts destroy the foundation for racist prejudice and discrimination. The third challenges both of these views, arguing that the second insufficiently questions the nature/culture dichotomy that provides the foundation for scientific race difference debates. Since bodies are physiological entities that are shaped by social practices, race is always both biological and social. What we need to learn is just how social practices produce socially and biologically raced bodies.

The "natural races" view has a long and by now well-documented scientific history, emerging at the end of the eighteenth century and flourishing by the mid-nineteenth century (Gould, 1981; Proctor, 1988; Stepan 1982). (Of course European racism has a far longer history.) It employed different methods at different times, favoring morphology and classification in the eighteenth century, but comparative histology, functional analyses, and the analysis of internal organization in the nineteenth century. Measuring racial differences in intelligence is just one of the projects in this history; scientists have sought racial classification of human differences also in shapes of skulls, lips, noses, foreheads, pelvises, or sexual organs, in sensitivity to pain, in genetic or hormonal makeup, in skin color, hair texture, and yet other traits. It is disturbing to discover that such projects have been pursued by some of the most distinguished scientists using state-of-the-art methods for their day. Nor were these scientists disproportionately racist; many were among the most politically progressive figures of their day on race and gender issues. As historians have pointed out, Nazi eugenics programs were only following the lead of mainstream scientific research in the USA and elsewhere in Europe (Proctor, 1988). While the emergence of population genetics in the 1930s and 1940s marginalized the older focus on racial typologies, traces of the older search for biological determinants of racial differences have lingered on in such fields as the IQ debates and controversies over sociobiology (Gould, 1981; Jensen, 1980; Lewontin et al., 1984; Wilson, 1975). Indeed, assumptions of "natural races" are by no means archaic, since racial classification systems remain useful in physical anthropology, forensic pathology, physiology, and some areas of public health (Hammonds, forthcoming).

Nevertheless, the second approach has rejected the "natural race" view in favor of the argument that racial categories are always socially constructed (Harding, 1993). Reflection on the World War II atrocities committed in the name of maintaining "racial purity" decreased the attractiveness of continuing to search for biological determinants of racial differences. Moreover, the "social race" defenders pointed out the immense cultural variation in systems of racial classification. The US had had a complex system of classifying people of African descent as quadroons, octoroons, and those legally counted as black because their ancestry gave them 1/32 "black blood." In parts of the Caribbean class has shaped racial classification so that the richer one is, the whiter one is perceived to be. South Africa, Japan, and other cultures have their own systems of racial classification. Furthermore, the emergence of population genetics, as indicated, made it compelling to treat alike variation in human populations and in animal and plant populations. Purported "racial difference" is best understood on the model of classifying butterflies or petunias. By the 1960s this social race approach was well-established in biology and the social sciences. According to this view, racial prejudice, now deprived of its scientific grounds, should soon wither away.

A third approach argues that the social race position is also flawed (Hammonds, forthcoming). For one thing, it can't account for why the "natural race" assumption is still scientifically useful in such fields as physical anthropology, forensic pathology, physiology, and some areas of medical and health sciences – areas where well-intentioned scientists are well aware of the criticisms of the biological determinist accounts. Further-more, the social race view simply substitutes reification of the social determinants of race for the natural determinants favored in the older view. Thus it reinstates the problematic Western assumption underlying both positions that nature and culture are discrete categories. This third approach argues that cultures introduce changes in those biological entities that are bodies. For example, culturally established "mating" ideals shape genetic distributions, such as those that occur through limiting or expanding the numbers of mixed-race children in a community. (Consider that Spanish colonial policies sometimes encouraged and at other times forbade marriage between the Con-quistadores and indigenous women. The British had similarly shifting policies in India and Africa.) Nutrition, access to health care, exposure to toxins, and other socially shaped processes have different impacts on different social groups from conception on. Bodies are always both natural and cultural, both biologically and socially raced. More-over, given the diversity of culturally produced racial classifications and the consequent lack of a common definition of race difference, any search for racial differences will always be able to find them. (One can always find at least some similarities or differences between any two objects.) Thus the apparent reality of various scientific criteria for racial difference is a product of searches for difference rather than a pre-existing aspect of natural or social orders. What we need to seek is not the "truth of race difference" in nature or in social relations, but how social practices do change bodies in ways that conform to racial projects (Hammonds, forthcoming).

These three approaches reveal in different ways how thinking about race difference has always been permeated by a focus on sex difference also. The critics of "natural race" have approached this topic through, for example, analyses of scientific uses of race/sex analogies, of the manipulation of reproductive practices to preserve racial and culturally valued sexual differences, and of primate studies that have been used to generate scientific arguments for the service of racial and sexual sterotypes to racist, colonial, and androcentric projects (Hammonds, forthcoming; Haraway, 1989; Stepan, 1986).

The Racist Misuse and Abuse of Sciences, Their Applications and Technologies

A second focus of criticism has been on the uses of scientific information and technologies for racist projects. Sterilizing African American welfare recipients; medical experimen-tation on Jews, gypsies, African Americans and Puerto Ricans; patterns of environmental toxicity and environmental destruction due to military and industrial practices, and the racially discriminatory uses of reproductive technologies are some of the best-known examples of such projects (Braidotti et al., 1994; Headrick, 1981; Jones, 1981; Proctor, 1988; Sachs, 1992; Shiva, 1989). These criticisms, like the other two, support the more general argument that the benefits of modern sciences and technologies disproportionately have been distributed to the already most economically and politically advantaged groups and the costs to the already least advantaged groups (Harding, 1993). Moreover, critics point out that mainstream philosophies of science obscure such patterns by an accounting system that disclaims any responsibility the sciences might have for discriminatory or destructive uses or consequences of the sciences, foreseen or unforeseen, yet claims credit for any and all good uses and consequences of sciences, foreseen or not. Because individual scientists often do not intend such consequences, the argument goes, it is simply wrong to attribute any responsibility for such bad uses and consequences to the sciences. On this view, sciences are not fundamentally social institutions intricately imbedded in larger social formations. Instead, they are only value-free methods, pieces of information disconnected from any social aspects of their production, use, or consequences, and the purely technical (and thus value-free) intentions of basic science researchers.

Of course it would be absurd to blame the sciences alone for the problematic applications and technologies identified by the critics, let alone to blame individual scientists. That is not the point of these criticisms of the neutral science position. Rather, it is to understand the functions of scientific projects in their historic contexts, and how racist and ethnocentric consequences follow from apparently innocent assumptions about human variation, causes of social change, human progress, the functions of value-neutrality, and what constitute good methods. Science-and-society are one social formation, each aspect of which is deeply rooted in assumptions of the other.

Racist Social Structures in the Sciences

A third concern has been racist patterns of discrimination in the social structure of the sciences. Gaining access to scientific training and jobs has often required heroic struggles and tolerance of insulting and demeaning treatment by education and science institutions and by racially privileged teachers, employers, and peers. Even when trained as scientists, few people of color have been promoted to the most distinguished teaching positions, directorships of the most prestigious laboratories, or the most powerful science policy positions (Manning, 1983; Pearson, 1985; *Science*, 1992).

Many explanations have been offered for these patterns. Until the 1960s US racial minorities had only restricted access to higher education (in some states, even to high school) and to professional-track preparation for a scientific career. Moreover, it has been difficult for youngsters in these groups to see themselves as scientists, mathematicians, or engineers, given the absence of relevant role models. Nor have they had access to mentors – white or not – as have their white peers. Furthermore, a community service ethic has tended to direct career choices for racial and ethnic minorities. Given the sciences' other racist and Eurocentric practices, these fields have not ranked high as enabling service to minority communities. (One can wonder if a kind of mirror-image "community service ethic" covertly attracts many whites to scientific careers since advances in science are routinely rhetorically associated with progress for "civilization," where "civilization" is defined in terms of distance from the lives of "primitive peoples.")

There have been notable exceptions to such generalizations. In the early part of the twentieth century, biologist George Washington Carver experimented with peanuts in order to create products useful for African Americans and that they could produce. In the 1920s and 1930s African American Ernest Everett Just made important contributions to developmental biology. African American Charles Drew discovered blood platelets. And in the last few decades many more US scientists of color have risen to the top of scientific institutions (Manning, 1983; *Science*, 1992; Van Sertima, 1986). Moreover people of color have seized opportunities for careers in science and medicine when they have appeared. For example, Darlene Clark Hine (1985) has documented the struggles and achievements of 115 African-American women who received M.D.s in the quarter century following the end of US slavery. Furthermore, some of the achievements attributed to scientists and engineers of European descent have been misattributed; they were produced by their slaves, servants, or other employees (as well as their sisters and wives) – a pattern found in the history of science in Europe as well.

In recent years there have been intensified efforts to increase the numbers of minorities in the sciences, mathematics, and engineering through improving elementary and high school science education and introducing outreach programs in universities and industries (*Science*, 1992). We are used to seeing pictures of at least token African Americans, Hispanics, and Asians in photographs of laboratories, university science classes, and ads for science, medical, and engineering products and jobs. Scientific honors now occasionally go to scientists of non-European descent in the USA. Yet there is a long way to go before racial discrimination disappears from the social structure of the sciences.

Today a walk through any lab – university or industrial – will reveal large numbers of scientists of non-European descent. The vast majority are foreign-born. Becoming an engineer or scientist is an attractive way for people in many Third World societies to join an international elite, as well as to enjoy the other benefits that come from a career in these fields. Indeed, the "brain drain" in the sciences is one way in which human resources from around the world continue to be appropriated into Northern projects half a century after the beginning of the end of formal European and American colonial rule. Yet even this is an advance of sorts against earlier forms of racism which strictly limited access to scientific educations and careers to people of European descent. As historian Michael Adas (1989) points out, an extreme form of this policy was visible in the refusal of the British rulers of India to let Indian science and math students learn even of the contributions to international mathematics that had been made by distinguished Indian mathematicians.

Three more recent approaches to "race" and science issues provide broader horizons within which to think about the issues raised by these first three analyses. The first argues against conventional ways of contrasting modern sciences and "ethnosciences." The second argues for setting the history of science and technology within larger social projects, especially European expansion. The third argues against the purported immunity of epistemologies and philosophies of science from racial, cultural, and imperial projects.

Real Science vs. Ethnosciences?

Recent research in comparative ethnosciences has challenged the conventional contrast between real, modern, transcultural, European sciences and the mere ethnosciences of other cultures. This shift was already prefigured in Thomas Kuhn's *The Structure of Scientific Revolutions*. Kuhn pointed to the importance for philosophy and history of science of the new social histories of European science that were learning "to display the historical integrity of that science in its own time" (Kuhn 1962:1). Crucial to the advance of European sciences, argued Kuhn and the generation of historians, sociologists, and ethnographers that have pursued this lead, has been (and remains) their immersion in cultural and political projects of their day.

Meanwhile, comparative ethnoscience researchers have been describing other cultures' achievements in pharmacology, medicine and health care, agriculture, mathematics, engineering, navigation, and every other kind of knowledge about mathematics and the natural order needed for a culture to survive. Partially independently, they have developed two lines of argument that conjoin with the Kuhnian project. One is to show the high achievements of non-Western science and technology traditions, made possible by their immersion in local cultural projects (Goonatilake, 1984; Hess, 1995; Joseph, 1991; Lach, 1977; Needham, 1954; Sabra, 1976; Van Sertima, 1986; Watson-Verran and Turnbull, 1995; Weatherford 1988). This argument counters the devaluation of these traditions in the West, and their exclusion from the category of "real science" because of their cultural imbeddedness. The other line of argument delineates the distinctive Europeanness of European sciences: it creates a "Europology" of modern sciences by showing their imbeddedness in specifically European cultural assumptions and projects (Harding, 1998; Hess, 1995; Nandy, 1990; Needham, 1969; Petitjean et al., 1992). This research counters claims about the purported cultural neutrality of modern sciences. Thus in their opportune use of historical and cultural resources, all knowledge systems are distinctively "local" ones – an issue to which we return. Localness does not insure good quality on this account. Individuals and their cultures can easily disappear because of faulty local assumptions; indeed, the extinction of our species perhaps may be the already inevitable consequence of faulty modern assumptions about environments. Modern European-American sciences differ from other cultures' knowledge systems in important ways, but the specification of how and why this is the case must be sought elsewhere than in the contrast between the purported cultural neutrality of the former and the "ethno" character of the latter.

The comparative ethnoscience projects are one important stream in what has come to be referred to as "postcolonial science and technology studies" (a designation originating with South Asian science and technology scholars, but somewhat problematically used more generally). A second focuses on the mutually supportive relations between the development of modern sciences and successes of European expansion.

Science and Empires

Is it entirely the irrelevant coincidence suggested by conventional European histories that the "voyages of discovery" and the "birth of modern science" started in Europe during the same period? To the contrary, each required the success of the other for its own successes, according to the science and technology scholars writing the new postcolonial global histories. And this symbiotic relation between European expansion and the advance of modern sciences continues today, according to critics of Third World development policies.

These accounts chart how the voyages of discovery produced exactly the information about nature's order needed for Europeans successfully to establish global trade routes and settlements in the Americas and, eventually, Australia, New Zealand, Africa, and elsewhere around the globe. The success of such expansionist projects required advances in navigation, cartography, oceanography, climatology, botany, agricultural sciences, geology, medicine, pharmacology, weaponry, and other scientific fields that could provide information enabling Europeans to travel far beyond the boundaries of Europe, and to survive encounters with heretofore unfamiliar lands, climates, flora, fauna, and peoples. In turn, the production of such information required European expansion. Expansion enabled Europeans to forage in other cultures' knowledge systems, absorbing into European science useful information about the natural world Europeans encountered, new research methods, and new conceptual frameworks. Expansion permitted Europeans to appropriate access to nature around the globe, so as to compare, contrast, and combine together new observations of nature's regularities. Moreover, through expansion, potentially sophisticated competitors to European science were vanquished (intentionally or accidentally, e.g., through the effects of European-introduced infectious diseases), along with the flourishing and, sometimes, the very existence of the cultures that had developed those other knowledge systems. Thus the voyages of discovery and subsequent European expansionist projects greatly contributed to the way modern sciences flourished specifically in Europe, rather than also or instead in other cultures of the day (Brockway, 1979; Crosby, 1987; Goonatilake, 1984; Headrick, 1981; McClellan, 1992; Nandy, 1990; Petitjean et al., 1992; Reingold and Rothenberg, 1987).

The argument here is not that all European sciences equally benefited from European expansion; for example, modern physics was developed during a somewhat similar process of increased travel, warfare, and social movement that occurred within Europe. Nor is it that Europeans, including scientists, were vicious, evil-minded creatures who always intended the destructive consequences of their expansionist projects. Indeed, European expansion was justified through appeals to improving the quality of life for Europeans and bringing "civilization" to the savages, doing God's work in the world, and in other "noble" ways not so very different from how Third World development policies have been justified since their inception in the 1950s. The development decades have produced humanitarian appeals to bring the so-called undeveloped societies up to the standard of living of the developed Western societies through the transfer to the undeveloped societies of Western scientific and technological expertise, rationality, and the democratic political forms that these purportedly encourage. Yet the policies responding to such appeals have, intentionally or not, largely continued to direct the flow of natural, human, and economic resources from the South to the North. Maldevelopment and dedevelopment for the majority of the world's peoples have tended to characterize the introduction of scientifically rational agriculture, manufacturing, health care, and so forth into the already economically and politically disadvantaged societies of the Third World (Bass, 1990; Braidotti et al., 1994; Sachs, 1992; Shiva, 1989). The appearance of so many Third World scientists and students in US labs, and the skepticism about whether a career in the sciences will permit one to serve communities of color, mentioned earlier, are just two of the issues raised in the early criticisms of the racism of science that are illuminated by viewing US and European sciences in the context of the new global histories produced by postcolonial science and technology studies.

Conclusion: Eurocentric Philosophies of Science and Epistemologies

The preceding themes and issues in recent studies of race, culture, empire, and science have challenged fundamental assumptions of conventional philosophies of science and theories of knowledge. Such civilizational or philosophic assumptions provide general and abstract standards that have racist and ethnocentric consequences. Four such challenges are particularly noteworthy.

First, the histories of science upon which philosophies of science and theories of knowledge depend have been doubly Eurocentric. In reporting the history of science, they have reported only the history of European sciences, and only as that history is understood by "the natives," that is, those groups of Europeans who have most benefited from the development of modern sciences in Europe. Such histories have encouraged philosophies of science to avoid the disinterested, objective, criticism of this particular range of their own assumptions that these philosophies otherwise recommend for advancing the growth of knowledge, scientific and philosophic. Thus the purportedly universally valid standards for what counts as science, as good method, as objective and value-free research, as human progress, have themselves been permitted to be permeated by ethnocentric assumptions.

Second, all knowledge systems are local knowledge systems in important and valuable ways. Culture is not only a "prisonhouse" for knowledge, as the conventional view correctly holds; it is also a "toolbox," providing valuable resources through which a culture's members can come to understand and interact effectively with their environments. We can see how this is so by reflecting on how different cultures have four kinds of different resources on which to draw in their knowledge-seeking projects. They have different locations in heterogeneous nature (in deserts, in rain forests, on the borders of oceans, in mountains), and different interests in the parts of nature in which they find themselves. Thus they are led to ask different questions about nature's order – ones useful for enabling from Genoa to the Caribbean, or from Cape Canaveral to the Moon. Moreover, cultures bring different discursive metaphors, models, and narratives to the ways they think about their environments and about their interests. For example, European cultures have thought of the earth as a living organism, a creation of God's mind, an endless cornucopia of resources for human use, a mechanism, and as a spaceship or lifeboat, to mention just a few models from the last five centuries. These discursive resources direct scientific attention to different regularities of nature, and to different kinds of explanation of these regularities. Furthermore, cultures organize the production of scientific knowledge in ways that tend to be characteristic of how they organize work more generally. Thus the voyages of discovery are one way to organize the production of such knowledge, no less than are the laboratories of field-trips that have been the focus of conventional philosophic attention. Economic and political relations shape the distribution of these local resources, giving greater access to knowledge about more of nature's order to those groups already well-positioned to make use of such knowledge. From the perspective of this kind of account, the insistence on the purported universality of Western scientific claims and philosophic standards obscures the valuable ways that such claims and standards are always local, generated and subsequently maintained because of their usefulness for historically local projects – their integrity with their historic eras, as Kuhn would have put the point. In important respects, the universality ideal is scientifically, philosophically, and politically dysfunctional. Some claims and standards travel far and long, as they are found useful in different cultures and over extended eras. But long trips are not the same as eternal ones (Harding, 1998).

Third, these accounts challenge the very ways science is defined in the conventional accounts. They challenge the value of contrasting real, modern, European sciences with ethnoscience traditions, of regarding science and technology as mutually exclusive categories, and of excluding scientific institutions, their cultures and practices from what we count as real science. These accounts show how sciences and their societies co-constitute each other in important ways: scientific projects are always part of larger social projects; "the social" permeates how sciences think about "the natural" (and vice versa). The argument here is a strategic one: let us see what we can learn by refusing these conventional contrasts.

Finally, a theory of knowledge that directs researchers to start off their thought from the lives of those marginalized or exploited by the dominant conceptual frameworks can more effectively maximize the objectivity of research claims than research processes that restrict their issues to those legitimated within the dominant forms of thought. These standpoint epistemologies have in effect guided the production of the antiracist and anti-Eurocentric analyses of scientific and technological traditions around the world (Harding, 1998).

Is science racist? Pursuing this question has led critics of the neutral science ideal to far more accurate, comprehensive, objective, and rational ways to understand human variation, natural and cultural, and humans' interactions with their environments. It has led them to visions of sciences that could indeed be *for* comprehensively human welfare.

Acknowledgment

I thank Judith Branzberg, Evelynn Hammonds, and Gilda Zwerman for helpful comments on this paper.

References

Adas, Michael (1989) *Machines as the Measure of Man*. Ithaca, NY: Cornell University Press.

Bass, Thomas A. (1990) *Camping with the Prince and Other Tales of Science in Africa*. Boston: Houghton Mifflin.

Blaut, J. M. (1993) *The Colonizer's Model of the World: Geographical Diffusionism and Eurocentric History*. New York: Guilford Press.

Braidotti, Rosi, Charkiewicz, E., Hausler, S. and Wieringa S. (1994) *Women, The Environment, and Sustainable Development*. London: Zed.

Brockway, Lucille H. (1979) *Science and Colonial Expansion: The Role of the British Royal Botanical Gardens*. New York: Academic Press.

Crosby, Alfred (1987) *Ecological Imperialism: The Biological Expansion of Europe*. Cambridge, UK: Cambridge University Press.

Goonatilake, Susantha (1984) *Aborted Discovery: Science and Creativity in the Third World*. London: Zed.

Goonatilake, Susantha (1998) *Mining Civilizational Knowledge*. Bloomington: Indiana University Press.

Gould, Stephen Jay (1981) *The Mismeasure of Man*. New York: Norton.

Hammonds, Evelynn (forthcoming) *The Logic of Difference: A History of Race in Science and Medicine in the U.S.* Chapel Hill: University of North Carolina Press.

Haraway, Donna (1989) *Primate Visions: Gender, Race, and Nature in the World of Modern Science*. New York: Routledge.

Harding, Sandra (ed.) (1993) *The "Racial" Economy of Science: Toward a Democratic Future*. Bloomington: Indiana University Press.

Harding, Sandra (1998) *Is Science Multicultural? Postcolonialisms, Feminisms, and Epistemologies.* Bloomington: Indiana University Press.

Headrick, Daniel R. (ed.) (1981) *The Tools of Empire: Technology and European Imperialism in the Nineteenth Century.* New York: Oxford University Press.

Hess, David J. (1995) *Science and Technology in a Multicultural World: The Cultural Politics of Facts and Artifacts.* New York: Columbia University Press.

Hine, Darlene Clark (1985) "Co-laborers in the work of the Lord: Nineteenth century black women physicians," in Ruth J. Abram (ed.) *"Send Us a Lady Physician": Women Doctors in America 1835–1920.* New York: W. W. Norton, pp.107–20.

Jensen, A. R. (1980) *Bias in Mental Testing.* New York: Free Press.

Jones James H. (1981) *Bad Blood: The Tuskegee Syphilis Experiment.* New York: The Free Press.

Joseph, George Gheverghese (1991) *The Crest of the Peacock: Non-European Roots of Mathematics.* New York: I. B. Tauris.

Kuhn, Thomas S. (1962) *The Structure of Scientific Revolutions.* Chicago: University of Chicago Press.

Lach, Donald F. (1977) *Asia in the Making of Europe*, vol. 2. Chicago: University of Chicago Press.

Lewontin, R. C., Rose, Steven and Kamin, Leon J. (1984) *Not In Our Genes.* New York: Pantheon.

Manning, Kenneth R. (1983) *Black Apollo of Science: The Life of Ernest Everett Just.* Oxford: Oxford University Press.

McClellan, James E. (1992) *Colonialism and Science: Saint Domingue in the Old Regime.* Baltimore, MD: Johns Hopkins University Press.

Nandy, Ashis (ed.) (1990) *Science, Hegemony, and Violence: A Requiem for Modernity.* Delhi: Oxford University Press.

Needham, Joseph (1954) *Science and Civilization in China*, 7 vols. Cambridge, UK: Cambridge University Press.

Needham, Joseph (1969) *The Grand Titration – Science and Society in East and West.* Toronto: University of Toronto Press.

Pearson, Willie Jr. (1985) *Black Scientists, White Society, and Colorless Science: A Study of Universalism in American Science.* Milwood, NY: Associated Faculty Press.

Petitjean, Patrick, Jami, Catherine, and Moulin, Anne Marie (eds.) (1992) *Science and Empires: Historical Studies About Scientific Development and European Expansion.* Dordrecht: Kluwer.

Proctor, Robert (1988) *Racial Hygiene: Medicine Under the Nazis.* Cambridge, MA: Harvard University Press.

Reingold, Nathan and Rothenberg, Marc (eds.) (1987) *Scientific Colonialism Cross-Cultural Comparisons.* Washington, DC: Smithsonian Institution Press.

Sabra, I. A. (1976) "The scientific enterprise," in B. Lewis (ed.) *Islam and the Arab World: Faith, People, and Culture.* New York: Alfred Knopf, pp.181–200.

Sachs, Wolfgang (ed.) (1992) *The Development Dictionary: A Guide to Knowledge as Power.* Atlantic Highlands, NJ: Zed.

Science (1992) Special issue on "Minorities in Science: The Pipeline Problem." 258:1175–1237.

Shiva, Vandana (1989) *Staying Alive: Women, Ecology, and Development.* London: Zed.

Stepan, Nancy Leys (1982) *The Idea of Race in Science: Great Britain 1800–1960.* London: Macmillan.

Stepan, Nancy Leys (1986) "Race and gender: The role of analogy in science." *Isis* 77:261–77.

Stepan, Nancy Leys and Gilman, Sander (1991) "Appropriating the idioms of science: The rejection of scientific racism," in Dominick LaCapra (ed.) *The Bounds of Race.* Ithaca, NY: Cornell University Press, pp.72–103.

Traweek, Sharon (1988) *Beamtimes and Lifetimes.* Cambridge, MA: MIT Press.

Turnbull, David (forthcoming.) *Masons, Tricksters, and Cartographers: Makers of Knowledge and Space.* New York: Guilford.

Van Sertima, Ivan (1986) *Blacks in Science: Ancient and Modern*. New Brunswick, NJ: Transaction Books.

Watson-Verran, Helen and Turnbull, David (1995) "Science and other indigenous knowledge systems," in Jasanoff, S., Markle, G., Pinch, T. and Petersen, J. (eds.) *Handbook of Science and Technology Studies*. Thousand Oaks, CA: Sage, pp.115–39.

Weatherford, Jack McIver (1988) *Indian Givers: What the Native Americans Gave to the World*. New York: Crown.

Wellman, David (1977) "Prejudiced people are not the only racists in America," in *Portraits of White Racism*. New York: Cambridge University Press.

Wilson, Edward O. (1975) *Sociobiology: The New Synthesis*. Cambridge, MA: Harvard University Press.

Political Economy

Introduction to Part III

David Theo Goldberg and John Solomos

There has been considerable focus on the political economy of race and ethnicity in the past few decades. Partly influenced by the emergence of Marxist and neo-Marxist approaches in this field during the 1960s and 1970s, there was a notable flowering of studies concerning the relationship between race and racism and wider sets of political and economic relations. It is to this dimension that we turn in this part of the *Companion*.

The first paper, by David Theo Goldberg, focuses on a dimension that has in many ways remained largely ignored in much of the contemporary discussion, namely, the role of the state in the reproduction of complex forms of racism and racial exclusion. Goldberg's account points to the relative silence on this topic in the most prominent currents in scholarly debate. He suggests that there is an urgent need for more careful analysis if we are to come to terms with the role of state institutions and agencies in shaping contemporary forms of racial subjugation and inequality. Taking his starting point as the historically formed interrelationship between the modern nation-state and patterns of racial ordering, he then goes on to suggest ways in which the role of the state could be brought back into theorizing about racism.

In a more particular vein, Stephen Small's paper focuses on the history of racial structures in the United States. He asks in what sense racism might be a useful analytic concept for analyzing contemporary social relations in a state such as the USA, or whether we need new conceptual frameworks to make sense of the changing forms of racial politics and exclusion at present. Small's analysis is framed around the continued relevance of racialized patterns of social, economic, and political exclusion. Drawing on a range of examples from a wide variety of arenas, including museum-plantation sites in the South, he seeks out both the continuities and the discontinuities between the past and the present.

The account provided by Small of the new morphology of racialized social relations in the United States is complemented and extended by Jennifer Hochschild's vibrant account of the war of position about the politics of affirmative action in the United States. This contribution provides an insight into the cross-currents of public debate about this issue over the past two decades, focusing particularly on what current controversies tell us about the racial culture of American society. In many ways, argues Hochschild, recent controversies about affirmative action are symbolic of a crisis of confidence about the meaning, as well as the validity, of the "American dream" in the current environment. They tell us more about the levels of anxiety about the core ideologies of American society than about how affirmative action works in practice.

One of the most important arenas of recent scholarship on race and ethnicity has focused on patterns of political mobilization and their impact on the position of minorities. This is the core concern of the paper by John Solomos and Liza Schuster, which engages critically with the emergence and development of the main analytical models in this field. Highlighting the relatively recent development of the rigorous study of the politics of race and racism, Solomos and Schuster provide an account that is focused on the key theoretical frameworks in this field as well as on examples of the changing role of political mobilization in shaping the position of racial and ethnic minorities. Drawing on research in a variety of political settings, they suggest the need to move beyond generalizations about the nature of political mobilization towards a more nuanced and situated account of the changing boundaries of political involvement and exclusion.

Chapter 17

Racial States

David Theo Goldberg

The Race from State Theory

One of the most telling evasions in these past two decades of thinking about race has concerned the almost complete theoretical silence concerning the state. Not just the way the state is implicated in reproducing more or less local conditions of racist exclusion, but how the *modern* state has always conceived of itself as racially configured. The modern state, in short, is nothing less than a racial state. It is a state or set of conditions that assumes varied racially conceived characters in different sociospecific milieus. So, in one sense, there is no singular totalized phenomenon we can name *the* racial state; more precisely, there are racial states and racist states. Yet it is possible at the same time to insist that there are generalizable conditions in virtue of which the modern state is to be conceived as racial, and as racially exclusionary or racist. The history of the modern state and racial definition are intimately related. So it is surprising perhaps that the theoretical literature on state formation is virtually silent about the racial dimensions of the modern state. And the theoretical literature on race and racism, given the culturalist turn of the past two decades, has largely avoided in any comprehensive fashion the implication of the state in racial formation and racist exclusion.

This is not to say that there haven't been microstudies focused more empirically on the racial experiences of particular states such as South Africa (Greenberg, 1987; Wolpe, 1988; Magubane, 1990, 1996; Posel, 1991); or on state implication in policies regarding race, for instance, in the United States or in Britain or in South Africa (Marx, 1998); or considerable work on the use of state apparatuses like law to advance racially configured projects (e.g., critical race theory, critical feminist theory, LatCrit theory). In contrast to the strong body of recent feminist theorizing about the state (Pateman, 1988; MacKinnon, 1989; Brown, 1995; Ferguson, 1984) those thinking about the state in racial terms have tended to delimit their conceptions to the obvious, extreme and so seemingly exceptional cases like Nazi Germany or South Africa or the segregationist South in the USA (cf. Burleigh and Wippermann, 1991). Eric Voegelin's provocatively prescient intervention, *Race and State*, first published in 1933 and recently released in translation, offers the hints of an analytic vocabulary. Yet he reduces the relational scope between race and the state – between "the race idea," "race theory," and the state – not unsurprisingly, to the case of Nazi Germany and the Third Reich (Voegelin [1933] 1997, [1933]/1998).

There has been little recent theoretical work nevertheless – especially since Stuart Hall's timely intervention in the late 1970s (Hall, 1980/Hall et al., 1978) or Arendt's and Cassirer's insightful interventions in the immediate aftermath of World War II (Arendt, 1951; Cassirer, 1946) – focused explicitly on how the modern state came to be racially conceived, on the historical codefinition of race and the state in their modern manifestations, and on state articulation of racially configured and racist commitments (cf. Joseph and Nugent, 1994). It is all the more remarkable then that Stuart Hall, of all analysts, writes a genealogy of the modern state around this time that makes no mention whatsoever of the role of race in its conception or institutional emergence (Hall, 1984).

One notable exception to the prevailing contemporary oversight may be Omi and Winant's book on racial formation in the United States which includes a chapter explicitly entitled "The Racial State" (Omi and Winant 1986:70–86, revised in 1994). In light of the wide citation of that book in both its editions it is notable therefore that there is virtually no reference to their chapter on the state.[1] Omi and Winant at least raise the question sociologically and outline a theory regarding the racial forming of states. Their chapter is helpful in posing the problem, in drawing attention to the central implication of the state in racial definition and management, and in *outlining* a theory about how the state assumes racially conceived and racially expressive projects. The structure of their proposed theory nevertheless presumes a conceptual discreteness about the state and race that I am concerned here to challenge.

Race is integral to the emergence, development, and transformations (conceptually, philosophically, materially) of the modern nation-state. Race marks and orders the modern nation-state, and so state projects, more or less from its point of conceptual and institutional emergence. The apparatuses and technologies employed by modern states have served variously to fashion, modify, and reify the terms of racial expression, as well as racist exclusions and subjugation.

Thus racial definition is entwined with modern state elaboration from what Dussel calls the "first modernity" in the orbit of Spanish expansion and onward. Racial definition of modern states is elaborated with the "voyages of discovery" (the very concept bears racial significance) and the debate in the 1550s between Las Casas and Sepulveda over Indian enslavement, through the second "planetary modernity" (Dussel, 1998:11ff.) from the seventeenth century and Enlightenment debates over the constitutions of colonial and liberal states, "national character" and citizenship criteria, to the postapartheid moment. It accordingly marks contemporary population shifts via extensive migration, policy debates, and legal decisions revolving around color blindness, the emergence of "fortress Europe" and the American "prison industrial complex." Indeed, racial configuration fashions the terms of the founding myth, the fabrication of historical memory, necessary (as Charles Tilly insists) to both the discursive production and ideological rationalization of modern state power (Tilly, 1994b). But it is also the case, especially since the racial project and racist exclusions became obvious in the eighteenth century, that the figure of the racial state – and of particular racist states – was fashioned in part by the resistant response of those it most directly and viscerally affected, namely, the racially characterized, marginalized, exploited, and excluded.

Classical liberalism (which includes in its range much of the commitments of contemporary conservativism in the form of neoliberalism) thus was a key element historically in promoting racial reasoning and its racist implications as central to modernity's common moral, sociopolitical, and jurisprudential sense. And it is not far-fetched to suggest that racially conceived compromises regarding racist exclusions – ranging from constitutional endorsements of slavery to formalized segregation, colonial rule and its aftermath, affirmative action, immigration and crime policy – have been variously instrumental in sustaining a consensual dominance of liberalism in modern state formation over the past century and a half.

In general, modern states are intimately involved in the reproduction of national identity, the national population, labor, and security in and through the articulation of race, gender, and class. The view of the state I am suggesting here, and relatedly of the complex, nuanced, and subtle entanglement (Tilly, 1994a) of identity processes, cultural and commodity flows, and state institutions, apparatuses, and functions is clearly more complex than dominant critical accounts of the state. The latter have tended to reduce the state and its apparatuses in one of two prevailing ways. The state is conceived on one set of views as a purely autonomous political realm. Here it is taken as analytically distinguishable from civil society or the public sphere, as well as from the economic processes of the society. On another set of views, the state is considered an epiphenomenon, a reflection and so effect of deeper underlying determinations (like the mode of production, class relations, or the economy).

Catharine MacKinnon (1989) rightly dismisses this epiphenomenalism of the state and of liberal theory's view that the law is society's text, its rational mind. The law and the state are not simply rationalizations of dominant social relations. MacKinnon argues that this epiphenomenalism hides the state's gendered/sexual definition from view. But in critiquing these forms of Marxist and liberal epiphenomenalisms of the state, MacKinnon explicitly reinstates an epiphenomenalism of her own, by making the state reflective of – reducible to – sex/gender interests. The state in her view simply rationalizes male power (MacKinnon, 1989, esp. p. 161). This again views the state and law as nothing else than instrumental to interests set elsewhere, a set of institutions and texts whose nature is imposed upon it from outside itself, from a defining condition external, prior in ontological logic, to the state. Thus MacKinnon, like almost all Marxist and liberal theorists, fails really to theorize the nature and definition of state constitution in itself. She continues to share with these views the image of the state as an unmarked medium, a set of institutions themselves abstractly neutral, autonomously fashioned, that get taken over, invaded, and invested with content or interests by groups vying for and expressing power. Autonomy theory and epiphenomenalism collapse, necessarily seeking each other out. Like others, MacKinnon imputes specificity to a state whose constitution is taken to be autonomously defined only by indirection, only by theorizing what it is the state reflects, what it is supposedly an epiphenomenon of.

In states that are racially conceived, ordered, administered, and regulated, the racial state could be said to be everywhere – and simultaneously seen nowhere. It (more or less invisibly) defines almost every relation, shapes all but every interaction, contours virtually all intercourse. It fashions not just the said and the sayable, the done and doable, possibilities and impermissibilities, but penetrates equally the scope and quality, content and character, of social silences and presumptions. The state in its racial reach and expression is thus at once supervisible in form and force and thoroughly invisible in its osmotic infusion into the everyday (Essed, 1990), its penetration into common sense, its pervasion (not to mention perversion) of the warp and weave of the social fabric.

States of Racial Rule, States of Racial Being

The racial state accordingly is as much a state or condition of being as it is a state of governance. Actually, it is more accurate to speak of racial states, for the forms and manifest expressions are multiple and multiplicitous, diverse and diffuse. Racial states are places among others where states of being and states of governance meet. For instance, race has long enabled citizens both to deny the state's implication in violence and, where acknowledged, to deny any personal implication or to abrogate responsibility. Citizens of racial states thus are able to trade on the ambiguity between condition of being and form of governance, at once benefiting from (the historical and contemporary effects of) reproducing racisms and distancing themselves from any implication in them.

It is important to recognize here that the racial state trades on gendered determinations, reproducing its racial configurations in gendered terms and its gendered forms racially. Bodies are governed, colonially and postcolonially, through their constitutive positioning as racially engendered and in the gendering of their racial configuration. White men enacted the "dirty" governance of colonialism; white women, excluded from the formalities of colonial governance almost altogether, in very large part were excluded also from the colonies, or from those colonial spaces least like Europe. Largely ripped from traditional forms of labor, "non-European" men were put to work manually, where they were employed at all, under grueling, debilitating, ultimately crippling conditions. Under historicist regimes, namely, those colonial forms of governance predicated on seeing the local inhabitants not as inherently inferior but historically immature and so in principle capable of development, the more educated indigenous middle and educated classes of men would be employed at lower levels of local colonial administration, their sons ultimately becoming the nationalist leaders of the decolonizing movements a half century or more later. Black women, black women of mixed origin, and Asian women likewise were racially devalued and driven to lesser or deskilled work in domestic or manufacturing or agricultural arrangements. And they were under constant threat of sexual invasion and exploitation by white men (and often by men generally), as too were young boys not classed as white, though to a lesser extent than girls and women (Haym, 1991).

So racial violence perpetrated in the name of and by the state invariably assumes gender-specific expression, and state-shaped racially figured labor policies and practices are almost always contoured to reproduce a state of gendered effects. The promotion of migrant labor flows by the colonial state in South Africa in the late nineteenth century, through the imposition of hut and poll cash taxes, drove black men from the land to seek work in mining, secondary industry, and urban domestic settings. Rural women were left to tend for children, agriculture, and the rural homestead, with devastating effects on family units. Urban black women were driven mainly into domestic labor, menial manufacturing jobs, managing shebeens (illegal home bars), or prostitution, reduced almost invariably to servicing whites and men. The statutory restriction of mixed marriages throughout the southern United States until 1968 principally affected black women, effectively restricting them from claiming paternity support for the children fathered by white men as a result of rape and coercion.[2]

Defining States, Refining States

There is a deep tension here between the state as a set of institutions representative of specific political interests, or a site around which the struggle for such political representation takes place, and the political as more diffuse, as infusing all social relations and subject formation. Theoretically, this tension emerged explicitly in the wake of the 1960s. It manifests most clearly in the swirl of views around Althusser and his followers regarding repressive and ideological state apparatuses as well as the interpellation of subjects, renewed deployment of Gramsci's analysis of hegemony as social reproduction through popular consent, and Foucault's critical interventions concerning subjection, normalization, and governmentality (Gramsci, 1971; Althusser, 1971; Buci-Glucksmann, 1980; Hall, [1986] 1996).

The modern state was never simply an epiphenomenon or conduit of capital. This is especially so when one considers the state in its colonial – colonizing or colonized – form, or more broadly in its racial shape and ordering. Racial states most broadly construed, as modern states generally, often have served capital's interests, more or less self-consciously, and certainly always have expressed its gendered interests. They have done so not least by regulating the (racially ordered and deeply gender-differentiated) labor supply and by policing the gates and terrain of bourgeois access and style, substance, and aesthetics, the shapes and roles of families. Thus they have ensured economic well-being for some and social law and order diffusely. Capitalist states have drawn heavily on these racial possibilities. They have concerned themselves virtually throughout their formation accordingly with three conditions that have deep racial definition: first, with regulating migration and immigration, not least with the labor supply and labor costs in mind; second, with shaping social, and particularly sexual, interaction with the view to sculpting the face of demographic definition; and third, with controlling crime, predicated primarily in relation to property rights.

Capitalist states – or more carefully, states that operate in the terrain of capitalist economic formation and a more or less expansive capitalist world system – nevertheless are not simply reflective of capital's interests. Indeed, one could make the matter more complex still by insisting that capital's interests are never singular, and often not unitary, either intra- or internationally.[3] Capitalist states are capitalist, as Poulantzas points out, not for their class composition – not simply for representing the interests of the capitalist class. They are capitalist rather for occupying a particular "objective" structural position in virtue of reproducing an historically specific and internally contradictory mode of production, locally and globally (Poulantzas, 1969:73; Holloway and Picciotto, 1977:4–6).

There are times when states have insisted on representing or mobilizing interests antithetical to those of capital. Particular states, for instance, have insisted upon working protections and improved living conditions for the working classes over bourgeois objections. Many states regulate im/migration even in the face of labor shortages that would drive wage rates and so labor costs up. And many support greater leisure as a mode of social control in the face of pressures to extend the working day, while recently some economically developed states have moved at least nominally to equalize wage rates across race and gender.

A state can be called capitalist, then, primarily in the structural sense of enabling the reproduction of capital overall, of mediating in some general and contingent sense the

237

contradictions that capital and its fractious factions almost inevitably generate. So states are not in any narrow sense functional for capital's reproduction, or for the extension and expansion of accumulation. Rather, capitalist states constitute at most the terrain of struggle over the range of selected strategies (what Jessop calls "strategic selectivity") for capital's reproduction and accumulability locally and globally, short and long term. They offer the field for fashioning the sort of underlying hegemony, the (re)production of consent, that would sustain overall such reproduction and accumulation across classes (Jessop, 1990:9–10).

Thus, as Comaroff concludes, "the history of governance is irreducible to the history of political economy or vice versa" (Comaroff 1998:338), though they do, and interactively, set horizons and so define the range of possibilities available for each other (cf. Williams 1981:83–9). States of governance and political economy offer for and in relation to each other the limits of conceivability and possibility rather than the specificities of their discretely or mutually produced outcomes. State institutions seek to control capital's resources to their own political ends, just as the representatives of capital undertake to bend the state to its instrumental concerns. They do so not least by attempting to massage the contradictions within and between capitals and their fractions so that these tensions remain productive rather than implosive.

Where Marxists like Poulantzas theorize the state as "relatively autonomous" from infrastructural material production, then, they still maintain the primacy of the mode of production in setting the limits of social conception and comprehension. State derivation theorists, for instance, insist that the political and its expressions are derivable from the forms that capital and the economic assume at any historical moment (Holloway and Picciotto, 1977). This is preferable perhaps to liberal political theorists such as Habermas, Offe, Rawls, or Kymlicka who claim to theorize the political in almost complete absence of discussion regarding capital formation and accumulation. Yet in shaking social theory loose of these moorings, in undoing the hold of the base–superstructure metaphor on thinking the social, "relative autonomy" should not give way to thinking of material production, politics, and economics as totally autonomous or independent of each other. Rather, the shift makes the causal connections multidirectional and historically specific. Thus it no longer is necessary to maintain determination of the state by the interests of capital "in the last instance." There are historical moments when the forces and resources of capital have been deployed by design to reproduce the conditions of sustaining the racial state – the racial conditions of the state – either generally or in a historically specific form like apartheid even to the detriment, short- or long-term, of capital's interests.

The *relative* autonomy of state and capital, accordingly, concerns their autonomous logics. These in turn prompt the possibilities of state and capital defining themselves in and through each other, their strategic deployment in relation to each other, their strategic selection of elements from each other necessary for their existence and survival or to craft outcomes each defines in its best interests. But relative autonomy here concerns also the relative "need" to define themselves through – and so by means of the terms of – each other (cf. Jessop, 1990:83–4). Neither economic nor political spheres are inherently privileged, though both at least are necessary, and mutually so. To these historically specific and so contingent purposes, the state and capital (and to these one could add law and culture) look to mediating terms to effect a language of mutual comprehension and deployability, and of common practice. They are, in short, terms of reasoning – logics – that make it look like they are at one, of a piece, engaged in common projects that are seemingly the product of common sense. People after all don't live out their economic, political, social, legal, and cultural lives discretely but inter-actively, in interconstitutive and mutually determining terms.

It must be insisted relatedly that the racial state is racial not *merely* or reductively because of the racial composition of its personnel or the racial implications of its policies – though clearly both play a part. States are racial more deeply because of the structural position they occupy in producing and reproducing, constituting and effecting racially shaped spaces and places, groups and events, life worlds and possibilities, accesses and restrictions, inclusions and exclusions, conceptions and modes of representation. They are *racial*, in short, in virtue of their modes of population definition, determination, and structuration. And they are *racist* to the extent such definition, determination, and structuration operate to exclude or privilege in or on racial terms, and in so far as they circulate in and reproduce a world whose meanings and effects are racist. This is a world we might provocatively identify as a *racist world order*. But more about this in conclusion.

Racial Subjects, Racial Selves

Racial rule is caught always in the struggle between subjection and citizenship, as Comaroff (1998:329) characterizes the contradiction of colonialism (Cooper and Stoler, 1997). In the case of racial governance, this (set of) tension(s) is "resolved" pragmatically though always contingently in different directions for racial rule naturalistically predi-cated than for the historicist. Under naturalist regimes – those defining their marginal-ized subjects as inherently inferior – this dilemma between social belonging and its conditions of enactment tends to be fashioned in terms of the terror of abject subjection, of physically threatened and imposed violence. This is a belonging conceived only as property relation, whether enslavement, debt peonage, coercive contractual work, or nominally waged labor.

For historicist racial regimes, by contrast – those conceiving their racially identified subjects as historically differentiated in maturity and development – the tension is played out formatively in favor not principally of physical terror but rather the (never to be?) fulfilled promise of citizenship. Here social belonging does not privilege some form of property relation but the deferred longing for a common humanity ideologically fash-ioned. If for racial naturalism the inherently inferior could never qualify for citizenship, for racial historicism racial subjection was effected through the holy grail of legal citizenship and its attendant rights (Comaroff, 1998:339). Citizenship was a status and standing not only never quite (to be) reached for the racially immature but for whom the menu of rights was never quite (as) complete. Even *within* naturalist and historicist scope, the multiplicity of the dimensions as well as the variability in styles of rule imply that the modes of racial rule and regulation are never fixed, given, or singular, but multiple, shifting, site-specific, temporally and discursively defined.

So subjection is internalized and to that extent seemingly self-designed and fashioned. The racial state, thus, could be said to strive for a racial subjection which, though usually perceived as externally imposed upon subjects, actually is self-fashioned and self-pro-moted. "Racial subjection" seeks as such to turn imposition into self-assumption, assertive charge into autonomous, self-imposed choice, harness into hegemony. Thus, there is no clear-cut contrast between state and individual, between asserted institutional power and capillary governmentality. Foucault shows, in short, that the distinctions between the state as institutional power and power vested in and through the state of being, between "what is within the competence of the state and what is not, the public versus the private" are fictions of modern sociodiscursive formation (Foucault, 1991:103).

All modern states – not least the colonial, as Comaroff comments, but one could extend the point to cover the racial state more extensively also – exercise themselves in good part by way of the capillary, by local instrumental and institutional forms of coercion, physical and symbolic forms of violence. They trade on various more or less implicit modes of discipline and surveillance, and on hegemony as the fashioned and diffuse production of consent (Comaroff, 1998:338). This represents a project of governance that, even where relatively effective from the point of view of racial rule, was never quite complete. One might say it never could be complete, for subjection in both (and related) senses of the term promotes its resistance; imposition from the outside – the external – calls forth at least redefinition internally, in terms of the already (pre-) existing sum of defining conditions of the self, and at most outright, explicit rejection, denial, dismissal. The self accordingly is always caught – split – between the past and the present, the self itself (so to speak, as already socially defined and conditioned) and the social, between self-assumption and imposition, in short, between "my"-self and its other. This is especially so in the context of race: race as socially (and state) imposed and as taken on "freely," assumed as a project, as a self-making.

One little-emphasized implication of Foucault's focus on governmentality, on the logics of (self-)governance, and on the interiorization of state power and subjection, I want to suggest then, has been to collapse the artificial distinction between ambiguous meanings of the public: as civil society and as state power, of individuals acting "in public" and of the "*res publica*," of economy and society, and state formations as discrete entities somehow acting upon each other rather than as mutually and depthlessly defined. In the sense I am suggesting, economy and society, private and public spheres, are coconstitutive of the possibilities even of their distinction. Kim Crenshaw shows that segregation in the United States, historically and contemporarily, is sustained by the legally maintained and managed distinctions between formal and informal racial distinctions, and between public and private discriminations (Crenshaw, 1998:286). In a deep sense, then, the "publics" of public spheres, public goods, public sectors, and public culture are not as distinct or as discrete as the obtuse literatures constituting them often would have it. Race, I am insisting, makes it less easy to sustain (as discrete and distinguishable) the seams between civil society, public sphere or sector or goods or culture, and governmentality. Race is codefined by such domains in the particularity of its local expression and significance. What makes this more complex, though, is that race simultaneously serves to cohere these domains, to imprint upon them their seeming specificity, the mark of their common state(d) definition.

It follows that race is more than simply threaded through the fabric of modern and modernizing racial states. States are drawn into racial frames of reference, into the rings of racial globalities, in entering into the circles of modernity, in becoming modern states. Race then is not a premodern condition but a quintessentially modern one masquerading in the guise of the given and the ancient, bloodlines and genetic pools. States have acquired their modernity more or less and partially through racial assumption, through being drawn into the terms and forms, shapes and spaces, temporalities and rhythms of racial world ordering and world racial definition.

The historical trajectory of the colonial state developed in relation to European discovery, pacification, commerce, and rational administration of non-European peoples (Comaroff, 1998:323ff), of those deemed without history and culture. By contrast, the genealogy of the racial state is more complex. Obviously it includes, precisely because implicated in, the colonial trajectories identified so insightfully by Comaroff. But the racial state cannot be delimited to its obvious colonial form. There are two conceptual reasons for this beyond the clearly political one that to do so would be to bury responsibility for the racial state in and with a colonial past that even where transformed leaves its traces, more or less firmly imprinted, upon the present.

First, as I have insisted, the racial state trades in its emergence on the shaded space between the state as lived condition and the more formal mode of governance, between subjection in the sense of existential constitution and subjection as a mode of governmental imposition and political constitution. Gramsci captures this connection between the political sphere, civil society and coercion in his classic formulation of the state: "State = political society + civil society, in other words hegemony protected by the armour of coercion" (Gramsci, 1971:263). The racial state accordingly is the embodiment, the exemplar *par excellence*, of the shift in theorizing the political from institutional forms to governmentality, from politics as domain and discipline to politics as disciplinary practices embedded in the everyday. Thus it must be presumed to outlive its colonial expression not least because in penetrating the everyday the racial state was destined to "survive" its institutional forms.

Second, and this by way of periodization, the racial state at least in its emerging form as a set of assumptions about the nature of being and living, was deeply implicated not only in fashioning and effecting the outcome of the colonial imperative but in making it conceivable. In short, the presumption of the racial state opened up the possibility of thinking the colonial project at all. As sets of institutions, and as ways of thinking and institutionalizing the governance of societies racial in both their metropolitan and their colonial expression, racial states emerged materially out of, as they were elaborated in response to, the "challenges" of colonial rule. And so conceptually they gave rise to conceiving the possibility of the colonial, while they emerged institutionally in elaborating rule in the colonies and – though less visibly but at least as presumptively – to marking the nature and scope of metropolitan societies in Europe too. Racial states accordingly have shaped the possible and marked out the impossible in the latter also. The charged atypicality of the Irish or Jews in the European context, for instance, is comprehended and sustained only by identifying each respectively with and in terms of the conjunction of blackness, (European) femininity, and the lumpenproletariat, as I have revealed elsewhere in Carlyle's case (Goldberg, 2000).

The (racial) state, in its institutional sense, must be seen thus not as a static thing but as a *political force* fashioning and fashioned by *economic, legal*, and *cultural forces* (forces of production, of sociolegality, and of cultural representation). It is a player not just in productive, distributive, circulating, and consumptive patterns and tensions, and in their reproduction. It has been central to political contestations over control of the materialities of society but also (and especially) of its own instrumentalities, its means and modes of rule and representation, of social supervision and control, over the style and substance of social governmentality. In short, the state is a contestant in the markets of representation, of who speaks for whom and in and on what terms.

241

Racial Governmentalities

In their particularities, then, racial states oversee a range of institutional, definitive, and disciplinary practices. They are engaged in definition, regulation, governance, management, and mediation of racial matters they at once help to fashion and facilitate. For one, racial states *define* populations into racially identified groups, and they do so more or less formally through census taking, law, and policy, in and through bureaucratic forms, and administrative practices.

Second, racial states *regulate* social, political, economic, legal, and cultural relations between those racially defined, invariably between white citizens and those identified as neither white nor citizen, and most usually *as* black (or more or less *with* blacks[4]). These are relations more often than not tense and internally fraught, exacerbated by their racially imposed character. The racial complexity may be intensified by the fact that their shape is determined in part by the externalization of tensions, ethnically or nationally or in some other sense politically defined, within and among those competing for the benefits, privileges, and profits of whiteness. Historical examples of these intrawhite tensions abound: between northerners and southerners in the USA, between Afrikaner and those of British background in South Africa, or between Flemish and Walloon, Dutch and French-speaking in Belgium.[5]

Relatedly, racial states *govern* populations identified in explicitly racial terms. The identification legally and administratively of groups as inherently inferior or historically immature, as native or indigenous to colonized spaces, is taken invariably to entail – *to require* – their management and oversight. Such regulation commands not just what the racially regulated can do but where they can and cannot go, what educational institutions they can access, with whom they can fraternize, and where they can reside. But it commands also under what conditions the racially marginalized are profiled and criminalized – which is to say, subjected to surveillance and suspicion, punished, imprisoned, placed on probation, and paroled.

Fourth, racial states *manage economically*. They oversee economic life, shape the contours of racially conceived labor relations, structure the opportunities or possibilities of economic access and closure. To these ends, racial states will intervene to secure the conditions for the reproduction of capital, not least by ordering resources and attempting to ameliorate tensions threatening the conditions for capital's expansion externally and internally. Thus states will open or stem the flow of the racially figured labor supply in response to the needs of capital, but delimited also by political demands and worries. Racial governance accordingly assumes different forms under naturalist and historicist presumption, for states insisting on the claim to inherent inferiority, in the first instance, and reproducing historical immaturity, in the second: most notably, slavery, segregation, and forced labor in the former mode; assimilationism, indirect rule and developmentalism in the latter. In the naturalistic extreme, racially identified groups are treated much like the natural resources found in the environment, no different than the objects of the landscape available for the extraction of surplus value, convenient value added to raw materiel. Thus the racial state participates in, as it promotes, racial rule – whether locally or at a colonial distance. It rules not just through labor regulation but by insisting on managing most if not all forms of exchange, commerce, intercourse, raw materials, production, trade, markets, labor circulation, distribution, and redistribution. At the extreme, then, the racial state is a peculiar sort of totalitarianism, seeking (only more or less successfully) to pervade all social forms, institutions, and expressions.

These considerations again reveal the irreducibility of the political to the economic. States may enact policies, rules, and instrumental modes of operation conducive not to the maximizing of surplus value, short or long term, but in the name of some politically driven logic like maintaining security, or white supremacy, or "principled" racial segregation irrespective of the duplicate costs it entails. In fact, it is specious to think that the cost–benefit calculation can be divided so discretely between the economic and the political. The fine line between the two likely collapses in the face of the calculation, just as it is manufactured by and in the interests of those whose power is identified artificially on one or other side of the dividing line.

Finally, racial states not only regulate but also claim to *mediate* relations between those (self-)identified as "white" or "European" and those declared "nonwhite" or "Native." Such mediation manages disputes and conflicts over land, labor, and mixed racial intercourse, socially and sexually. As adjudicator, the state claims a nominal neutrality. Yet its actions historically have been largely partial. In reproducing a racial system, a mode of being and governance, the actions of racial states are representative mostly of those belonging to the ruling racial class, whose racial status as privileged – indeed, as ruling – the state in its racial configuration has helped to define, refine, and promote.

These considerations raise the obvious question whether the racial state is *necessarily* representative of the interests of the ruling racial class – defined as whites, Europeans, or those of European descent – and thus inherently implicated in racial subjugation and exclusion. In short, is the racial state inherently a racist state?

Racial States and Racist States

Racial states employ physical force, violence, coercion, manipulation, deceit, cajoling, incentives, law(s), taxes, penalties, surveillance, military force, repressive apparatuses, ideological mechanisms and media – in short, all the means at a state's disposal – ultimately to the ends of racial rule (Comaroff, 1998:324–6), which is to say, to the ends of reproducing the racial order and so representing for the most part the interests of the racial ruling class. This entails in the history of fabricated racial configuration that racial rule by definition serves the interests of those conceived as white. "Whiteness" then is not some natural condition, phenotypically indicative of blood or genetic or intellectual superiority but the manufactured outcome of cultural and legal definition and political and economic identification with rulership and privilege. If we go by history – and in this instance what else is there to go by? – then in class terms whiteness definitionally signifies social superiority, politically equates with control, economically equals property and privilege.

This equation of racial states with privilege and power requires qualification. Clearly, the racial powers and privileges of whites are magnified or tempered by class position, gender, even the standing of and within a nation-state. Thus those otherwise considered as white in the scheme of common sense and who occupy social positions of disprivilege or disempowerment become referenced precisely as less or other than white. They are characterized with the likes of "white niggers" or "half-niggers," as "temporary Negroes" (Dollard, [1937] 1988), "hunky" (Hungarian), "dago" (Italian and Spanish), "polak" (Poles), "spicks" (Spanish) and "kikes" (Jews). The characterization in an 1898 debate over the disenfrachisement of Italians in the USA exemplifies the power and (dis)privilege at work in racial identification: "... according to the spirit of our meaning when we speak of 'white man's government,' [the Italians] are as black as the blackest negro in existence" (quoted in Cunningham, 1965:34; Barrett and Roediger, 1997, esp. p. 9).

It follows that the racial state is at once implicated in the possibility of producing and reproducing racist ends and outcomes. Race has been invoked normatively in institutional terms and state contexts almost always to hierarchical purposes. This fact deeply delimits the taking up of race as an organizing theme to antiracist ends. It is not simply the invocation of race *per se* that is fraught with this danger, for as historically contingent on social determinations race conceptually is open to the ends of antiracist mobilization. Rather, it is the deep historical implication of race in state structure, its relative penetration of state definition, organization, and determination that delimits its resistant potential even as it renders strategic racial invocation essential. It means that race can be mobilized to antiracist purposes at best only as a short-term and contingent strategy. We have witnessed the limits of affirmative action recently in just these ways, for instance. The effects of antiracist race mobilization have tended to be ambivalent and ambiguous. In invoking the very terms of subjugation, in "standing inside them" to transformative purposes, racial invocation likely re-inscribes elements of the very presumptions promoting racist exclusions it is committed to ending. Hence Sartre's struggling over what in *Antisemite and Jew* he nominates "antiracist racism," the conceptual contradiction hinting at the pragmatic tension.

We might usefully bear in mind here the distinction Etienne Balibar insists upon between "*(official) State racism*" and "*racism within the State*," between what Balibar characterizes as the "exceptional state" and "exceptional moments" of the normal state (Balibar and Wallerstein, 1991:39; Balibar's emphasis). A state may license racist expression within its jurisdiction simply by turning a blind eye, by doing nothing or little to prevent or contest it, by having no restricting rules or codes or failing to enforce those on the books. By contrast, a state like Nazi Germany, apartheid South Africa, or Jim Crow Louisiana may assume racism as a state project, definitive of state formation, articulation, in a word, (national) state identity. Between the two instances lies a myriad of racially articulated expressions both licensed and practiced by state mandate. One set of examples concerns the racial characterization of the criminal classification system (i.e., activities or profiles associated with a devalued racially identified population treated more harshly than otherwise comparable activities or profiles of those not so devalued). Another covers civil service job classifications (e.g., white prison guards of predominantly black prisons in states with a long history of racist structures most notably in the criminal justice system; white truck drivers and black manual workers; white male bosses and black female clerical staff).

In these many microexpressions, as well as more explicitly at the macro level, the racially conceived and reproducing state is characteristic of, not exceptional to, modernity. Modernity is defined by racial conditions even as it characterizes those conditions as abnormal or exceptional. So while *racist* states may seem exceptional, their very possibility is underpinned by the normalcy of the *racial* state. But there does remain a difference, captured by Balibar's distinction, in degree if not kind between states in and through which race is sewn into the social fabric by way of racial routinization and those where racist exclusion is explicitly defined as *the* principal (and "principled") state project.

Racial invocation by the state and definition of the state by race, it follows, almost invariably restricts the range of critical intervention and transformative potential to a dualistic and mutually exclusionary choice. On one hand, it elevates the narrowing naturalization of the assimilationist or integrationist; on the other, it begrudgingly spawns the separatist (in the Black Nationalist contrast to the segregationist). Ranging between the promisingly reactive and a reactionary politics, race-based antiracism may be pragmatically necessary in some historical moments, but it clearly reifies under the weight of its own logic into racial essentializing once those historical openings close down. It is for just this reason that both Angela Davis and Philomena Essed strongly urge political mobilization around common *political* interests rather than pre-existing or prefashioned common identities. Here, the common identity is to emerge out of the mobilization rather than essentialistically (and so exclusionistically) giving rise to it (Davis, 1998:319–20; Essed, 1996:109–10).

Racial Penetration, Racial Routinization

In Foucauldian terms, the state not only invades the body of subjects. It goes a long way in making bodies what they are, and by extension who they are. It is thus instrumental in subject formation. The more the racial state is implicated in fashioning the form and content of subject formation, the more it penetrates into everyday social life, and the greater the hold of race over the social horizons of the conceivable. Consider how the racial state defines, manages, and regulates family formation: who can form a family racially, who can belong to a family, who can marry, how the offspring will be defined and designated racially and so what the life opportunities are for them. Women thus are implicated in reproducing the nation-state's population, its citizenry (though even this might become contested technologically before too long). Again, examples are numerous: the 1950 Mixed Marriages Act in South Africa prohibited not just interracial marriage but any interracial sexual activity. The Serbian men who impregnated while raping Bosnian and more recently Kosovan women of Muslim background were self-consciously pursuing a policy of diluting the "national stock," at once mockingly reducing Muslim men to a sense of impotence. Antimiscegenation laws abounded throughout the colonial and then state legal codes of the American South until they were called into question in a 1948 California case, *Perez v. Sharp*, and then ultimately rendered completely unconstitutional in 1968 in the appropriately named *Loving v. Virginia* (see Furumoto and Goldberg, 2001).

The racial state sets limits on social possibilities, or enacts them, not just formally through law but through *routinization* (Comaroff 1998:331 ff.; Omi and Winant, 1994:85; Hesse, 1999:99–100). Rendering these practices normal by their routine repetition hints at their presumed naturalization; they are taken as given and therefore (in the collapse of social imperative into the natural) coterminously unalterable. Besides sexual routines, permissibilities and prohibitions, the examples are more or less pervasive. Consider birthing practices licensed and prohibited. Similarly, birth certificates define what and how one is named and thus recognized legally and administratively, how such recognition or its failure furnishes social standing.

245

Nevertheless, racial routinization in states that are more or less racially predicated runs deeper still by invading all aspects of sociomaterial life. It colors child-rearing (members of "races" regarded as "alien" or of "lesser value" in Nazi Germany were forced into abortion, castration, and sterilization), schooling, recreational activities like sports and recognizable religious practice. It manifests through marriage licensing and annulment, technical training and higher education; through spatial design and control, especially urban planning, apportioning residential and labor spaces, and relatedly property ownership; as well as through laboring conditions. In the extreme instance, again, the Law for the Reduction of Unemployment introduced by Hitler in 1933 extended marriage loans to citizens, the conditions for repayment of which they could satisfy by producing children. As Burleigh and Wippermann (1991:46) note, this law was designed to effect three principal outcomes: to multiply a "pure" German population, to reduce unemployment of men, and most notably, by forcing women to return to their traditional maternal roles. As examples such as these reveal, racial routinization is reproduced in temporal templates, marking life by a racial brush from early childhood, for example, through health practices such as inoculation injections; driving, drinking, and conscription ages; as well as voter registration and voting rolls. And racial routinization is licensed materially in the card of identity registration that serves as the codification and so condition of these social acts and duties, responsibilities and rights, all of which are more or less racially thick.

The routinization of race silently in social life is reproduced also through criminalization, taxation, retirement, death, burial, and inheritance formalities, all factors the state regulates or oversees, manages and mediates. In short, the modern state has come to enact racial configuration in virtually all, or at least all significant, social practices and conditions, markers and indices from birth to death and burial, from the personal to the institutional. The more penetrating racial categories are in a state's lexicon and bureaucratic practice, the more such practices routinize racial reference and social shaping.

Thus all these domains and practices, conditions and regularities, codes and orders come at various moments in modern states to be racially conceived and enacted, ordered and structured, produced and reproduced, color and culture coded. They constitute regulative and regulated regimes in good part through state administrative apparatuses like the census, tax forms, passports, lending and banking practices. In short, the exercise of racial states in the merging of their institutional forms with – their penetration into – daily life renders the trace of the state's racial dimensions relatively invisible. Racial regulation is reproduced through routinized governance of/over family, civil society, labor and markets, private and public morality, ownership, public monuments and parades, open and closed ceremonies, common and commonly restrictive and restricted social practices in living and in death (Comaroff 1998:337–8). In racial states, as Benjamin Disraeli commented over a century ago, all comes to be race. And in the twist of their most extreme manifestations, in the penetrating institutionalization of race, race comes to be all.

One should be careful here, however, as Foucault and those he has influenced have emphasized, not to reduce all subject formation and subjection to the political, directly or indirectly to the state institutionally conceived. This is a position one might call politicism or statism in the face of economism. Subjection in both senses is at least multiply determined and most likely overdetermined, often (though *pace* Foucault also not completely) internalized. So social subjection (mostly) becomes self-regulating and self-directing. The institutional state assumes as its necessary condition the state or condition of being, of lived culture and cultural life, the imposed becoming the self-chosen, the fabricated the given, the historically fashioned the state of things, the social the natural. If there is anything approaching a "national character" perhaps this is all it amounts to, the (informal) codification of the cultural characteristics and values of a dominant or majority group whose definition is state-related or directed. Again, imposition may be more or less violent, more or less coercive, more or less subtle. Coercion is more the former in the case of naturalist racial regimes, sustained principally by repressive apparatuses, while more the latter in historicist ones, reproduced largely by ideological and discursive apparatuses though underpinned always by the threat of repressive violence.

Racial Assertion and the Nation-state

Race and nation

These remarks raise the distinction between race and nation. Race may be thought of as the social or cultural significance assigned to or assumed in physical or biological markers of human beings, including the presumed physical or physiognomic markers of cultural attributes, habits, or behavior. Nation, by contrast, is the significance of cultural markers as assumed or assigned (imagined) indicators of common originary belonging, where race (or ethnicity, as cultural socialization) might be one of those (imagined) markers assigned significance or dominance in picking out members. Where this is so, race and nation overlap, more or less isomorphically.

It is worth observing that race (or ethnoracial identification) has a thickish history of being legislated – directly, baldly, and in its own (mostly unmediated) terms. Nation has not been so legislated, at least not directly and unmediated. Thus the restrictions of immigration law historically have been predicated in terms either of ethnoracial identification or state origin. Here the reference in some laws to "national origin" is actually to where people were born, or the citizenship they hold. This difference between race and nation has to do with the very basis of their conception. So it is thought possible to legislate race directly, in its own terms, in ways in which nationhood is deemed not so amenable to legislation (in contrast to nationality, which really is the legislation of state belonging and potential access to state rights, privileges, and resources). This difference in legislative amenability may have to do with the privileging of a presupposed physical optics thought to make racial identification accessible in ways the cultural references of nation are not (or less so). The former is imagined to have a "substance" available to the latter only through some more readily questionable idealist metaphysics. German law, for instance, establishes German national belonging only in virtue of marking nationhood in racial terms. German origin is defined as the claim to German blood. Belonging to the nation is a matter not just of being born in Germany but of being born to parents whose blood or genes awkwardly are considered "to run German," who in that sense are "racially" German.

Racial assertion

The German citizenship codes make clear that it is the business of the state to state, of authorities to author the law, to assert themselves (Comaroff, 1998:340, 342). Historically, it has been the business of racial states to assert themselves – to state their conditions – racially. It has been their business to generate the possibilities of their boundaries in no more or less than racial terms. The institutionalization of race by the state, its routinized assumption in the structure of state institutions, has made it possible for contemporary states to assert themselves racially without explicit invocation of racial terms (Goldberg, 2001: ch. 8). The racial state, then, is never complete, always (as Comaroff says of the colonial state, 1998:341) on the make, a work in progress, a Sartrean project. This is necessarily so in the case of racial states not simply because race is, as the cliche says, socially constructed. It follows multiply and interactively from the very interface of the state and race.

The state is a condition of assertion. As a prevailing form of power it is, and necessarily, the effect of constant reassertion. This reiteration is required in so far as the state provides the principal modern institutional sites through which social status is claimed, and the gains of status quickly dissipate if not guarded, in the absence of their reassertion. The state then can never not speak itself, for as soon as it stops stating itself, so to speak, it ceases to be a state. Likewise, in so far as race in its status claims is dialogical and ideological, discursive and illocutionary, it presupposes for its enactment its assertibility, its required capacity at every moment of being stated. Thus, in the face of its own social silence race ceases to reproduce itself; it cannot reproduce and replicate *sans* the state, in the absence of its more or less invisible institutionalization. But once institutionalized in and through the state, the state now racially conceived cannot speak, cannot state itself, other than in the terms of race. So modernity's race to the state became at once the stating of race, its institutional assertion. Race stated, in short, is the state raced.

To say this, however, and once again paradoxically, is to give the racial state perhaps too much coherence. For as suggested above, the state may be thought of as the phantom of governance and authority, a territorial placeholder for sets of often competing and more or less local institutional interests and powers. In this sense, the state provides media and a measure of scope for the assertion and authorization, legislation and legitimation of institutional power(s). The latter two institutional practices offer to the former two a semblance of coherence, a singularity of style and voice, a common language and mode, the shadow of an institutional sphere in the face of prolific heterogeneous messiness. They offer, that is, the artifice of national, cultural, and expressive unity – community – in the face of fractured disunity and anarchy, the artifice of homogeneity in the face of proliferating heterogeneities.

Comaroff (1998:329) distinguishes between colonizing states in Europe that concerned themselves in their metropolitan conditions with "manufacturing homogeneity" and colonized states devoting themselves to "managing difference," regulating the threat of heterogeneity, of anarchy (statelessness). Fabricating homogeneity in the metropoles, at home, it might be said, was predicated upon displacing heterogeneity to the outside. Colonized states thus were initially shaped to represent racial otherness as exteriority. Conceived as embodiments of material states, they were considered in naturalist terms to lie outside the civil(ized) societies of metropolitan order. As the colonies became increasingly sewn into a world capitalist system (offering raw materials, consumptive agricultural products, mineral wealth, and markets) and as colonial governmentality took shape over time (offering employment, opportunity, adventure, excitement, and the exercise of power), managing heterogeneity shifted from the semiavoidance of exteriority to the regulative and ordered intimacy of "containerization" (Tilly, 1994a). The shift transformed unknown objects of adventurous discovery and examination into elaboration of a logic of colonial rule, first through imposing direct rule and later mediated via indirect management of more peripheral units in a growing global order. The colonial state accordingly turned "savages" dialogically and governmentally first into "colonial subjects," by subjecting them to colonial rule and regulation, and then again into "units of labor." And in doing this, the colonial state transformed "savages" ironically into legal persons (cf. Baker, 1998).[6] The ambivalence of colonial subjectivity is revealed here, for "legal persons" were extended little more than formal personhood. These are persons for or really "before" the law, regulable units or administrative entities rather than fully human beings.

The modern state may be conceived accordingly as a container. It has enabled the internal dynamics of modernity to be played out by offering not just a backdrop for pressing modern tensions but structural constraints on their explosiveness, and so on the scope of their effects. These are the tensions between futurism and nihilism, revolutionary zeal and conservative denial; between technological imperative and antitechnological commitment; between a retrospective *ancien régime* and a prospective avant-grade; between repression of the new and its celebration; between fixity and the given in tension with flux and change, speed and motion. The modern state is tied then to a fixed mode of managed accumulation with the logic of production largely dictating the limits of circulation, exchange, and consumption.

In their racial framing, thus, the freedom of the modern state (and perhaps this is the state condition generally) is necessarily illusory. It is predicated always and necessarily on an unfreedom both for those ruled and for those ruling. Racially ordered and manifested freedom – the freedom of whites, historically speaking – accordingly is no freedom at all. Power, generally, and racially predicated and ordered power particularly, requires always its own reproduction, its reiterated assertion, freedom's necessity a logic of determination that at once discounts the freedom such necessity dictates (cf. Butler, 1997).

Relatedly, as states have increased their scope and range, their growth in institutional determination and (formal) authority over the lives of their inhabitants – both citizens and noncitizens, those in and out of the state alike – *de facto* control, efficiency, and effect have diminished (Comaroff calls this "the Minogue Paradox," 1998:336). There is, one could say, a point of diminishing returns, a marginal effectivity of rule. The more repressive, the more likely resistant. And the more cemented, the more internally cracked. This is especially so regarding racial repression and rule. States, as Weber famously insisted, are those institutions effecting a monopoly over the legitimate means of physical force. Thus the greater state insistence on effecting and exercising such monopoly, the more visible. The greater the violence states promote in everyday life, the more they have to resort to threatened or explicit violence as the mode of rule. And the more violence becomes a norm, the readier those within and without the state are loosened, if not licensed, to resort to forms of personalized and anonymous violence. This is especially exacerbated by racial terms, for race, while making institutionally visible the perpetrators, picks out the objects of violence in emphatically identifiable ways.

In becoming systemic and institutionalized, racial violence effectively renders its perpetrators individually irresponsible, in both senses of the term. If racial violence is normalized as a given of daily life, individual responsibility is abrogated either to invisible social forces (ancient histories of antagonism, poverty of culture, etc.) or to errant individuals. The perpetration of racial violence in the state's name is clouded over,

249

mediated, rationalized away by those reserving (relative) humanity or progress to themselves while cast(e)ing off or out as inhuman or less human the objects of the violation and as exceptional the particular perpetrators. Racelesssness, or color blindness as a particular expression, is the project to re-institute the relative invisibility, the anonymity, of racial rule in the wake of its postcolonial and globalizing excavation (Goldberg, 2001: ch. 8).

Laying Down Racial Law

Racial states attempt accordingly to assert themselves, to regulate through the rule of race, to impose race upon a population so as to manage and control, divide and rule. In these attempted assertions, though, racial states paradoxically divide by rule and so destabilize the very order they supposedly are designed to produce. In subjecting to (and through) race, states race subjection and so too cohere the response, reaction, and resistance by the terms through which they seek to repress. In insisting on the universalizing rationality of raced regulation, racial states delimit rationality to that of race, thus racially inscribing rationality and circumscribing reasonableness. In insisting on racial order, they impose racial violence upon the very violence they claim to be staving off, thus rattling the order they are seeking to reproduce. In the final solution, to rule racial brutes that are brutish by state assumption – brutes, as Hobbes at the dawn of the modern state insisted, are those the modern state must necessarily exclude from its domain – the brutes must all be exterminated, materially or symbolically: and this in the name of – executed by – the written law of the state.

Modern states – and here racial states once more are the norm of modern statehood, not the exception – speak through the law, in legal codes and terms. The institutionalization of race in and through the state is a form of legal reasoning (Goldberg 2001: ch. 6). It consists in the claim to displace brutish custom, to substitute for the idiosyncrasy and variability of everyday practice the systematicity and normativity of written codicils, and the assertion of atemporal order. Yet the extermination of all the brutes in the name of the law, and the project to institute racial arrangements through law, can only be effected brutally. In seeking to exterminate brutishness – the self-professed racial project *par excellence* – the state necessarily reveals at once its racial conception and becomes nothing short of brutal.

The racial state, then, is a genus of forms and processes, an analytic generality the specificities of which differ case by case. Colonies of Britain, Belgium, France, Netherlands, or Germany differed in their particularities, as indeed in racial specificity they differed from each other as well as from those of Portugal or Spain. It is because of these overdeterminations – in number and nature, in variation, and in the variety of their interaction – that one could begin to differentiate not only between particular expressions or institutions of racial rule but also their forms. In their spatio-temporal specificities regarding racial rule, the USA differs not just from Canada but also from those societies with which it has been most compared, namely, South Africa and Brazil (contra Marx, 1998). Colonized states and metropolitan ones differed almost as much between as from each other, as too have the postcolonial from their colonial manifestations. So "the racial state" as a category offers no more than a template for rule, the contours rather than the content.

States of Racial Violence

In its visible assertibility racial rule developed into a form of crisis management. It is in moments of perceived crisis that the routinized obscuring of racial rule evaporates to leave evident behind it the force upon which it is necessarily predicated. It renders evident, in addition, the (threat of) violent physical enforcement that racial rule is driven to invoke so as to reinstate the threatened order. The Congo (and perhaps this is generally the case for naturalistically driven racial regimes) was perceived by the Belgians in its otherness as inherently threatening, as state crisis constantly under construction. The virtually ceaseless states of emergency under mature apartheid exemplify this notion of rule through racially fashioned crisis also. With historicist racial regimes the overriding pursuit has been to rule through routinization, to normalize racial governance through the order of law, resorting to naked force only when the threads of racial order have torn at the seams of the social fabric as the administrative routines failed to contain(erize) the racially dominated "in their place."[7]

If crisis is the dominant medium of the visibility of racial rule, power is its mode, its defining condition. Power may be considered a potency, the capacity to act (Habermas, 1986:75–6). In social terms (as Arendt says), power is the capacity to act in concert (Arendt, 1986:64). The social power to act, however, is not to be defined simply in terms of capacity; it is more fully the potency to affect the standing of other people. Social power accordingly is not merely a capacity but a relation of relative capability, at basis a political relation. It is the active shaping of people's social standing, or the social positioning and possibility so to shape. The state effects social accessibility and status by way of its institutionalized apparatuses. It does so not only in class terms but interactively also in racial and gendered ones. Race in particular delimits acknowledgment of the grounds of such social (in)accessibilities, attributing them to the force of individual or group (in)capacities (Sartre [1960] 1976:720).

It follows that the state is (an institutionalization of) the exercise of power. It is, by both design and effect, the institutionalized elevation of the interests – political, economic, legal, social, cultural – of some to the exclusion or devaluation of others. State power thus is exercised and embodied in the name of, and through the institutionalized apparatuses of, the state on behalf of some (always more or less contested) interests to the exclusion of others. These interests may be narrowly those of the group directly holding and exercising political power, or more broadly of those whose class interests are represented by administrators of the state apparatus (or some combination). They may be exercised in concert with the logic of systemic imperatives mandating the terms of its own reproduction. In modern terms, such institutional commitments, interests, and imperatives have been advanced through the order of law, underpinned by the threat of force.

Race is an especially convenient form of conceptual social cement here. For just as the state is an expression of power, so it is possible to reconceptualize race in terms of power. Race covers over the "magical" nature of the modern state, making its fetishistic characteristics appear all too readily as naturally given, as sacred and so unchallengeable (Taussig, 1997). Thus even the historicist conceptions of race appear naturalized. Race is conceived as a container or receptacle of power, a medium through and in the name of which power is expressed. All too often race is projected as a rationalization for, an epiphenomenon of, power's expression, the determinants of which are otherwise established (for instance, economically). While this is not always inaccurate, I have been arguing by contrast that race is itself the expression of relations of power. It is the embodiment and institutionalization of these relations.

Jewsiewicki and Mudimbe (1995) argue that it is not some naturally pre-existing nation in the name of which state creation is mobilized. Rather, states instrumentally invent nations as a form of generalized socialization. By the same token, I am claiming, states are instrumental in inventing races both as a form of socialization and as technologies of order and control. States fabricate races, imputing to them a semblance of coherence. They do not create races artificially from whole cloth, however, but pick up the threads for designing the racial fabric from various sources, scientific and social, legal and cultural. States then are fundamental to weaving race into the social fabric, and indeed the fabric of the modern state is fashioned with racially woven threads. States thus are endowed or endow themselves with "races"; they adjust and adopt races to governmental purposes. While states are instrumental in the institutional conceptualization of races, racial conceptions define and refine state formation.

That race is a marker, an expression, indeed, constitutive of modern relations of power makes it especially amenable to the expression of state power, one might say, to the central defining condition of modern statehood *per se*. Through race there is displaced from the modern state, covered over, the raw expression of state power. Such power, nothing more than created, is projected through racial terms as the given order of things, seemingly intractable and so established by natural or teleological law. The consensual rationalization of modern statehood acquires the anchor of racial naturalization; and the givenness of race, its teleology, becomes legitimated – rein*forced* – through the veneer of consensual agreement of citizens to the state and state fabrication. Those rendered racially inferior or different are locked in and away. The almost conceptual vacuity of race (Stoler, 1997) enables configuration of transnational extrastate identities – for example, "the white race" or diasporic Pan-Africanism – as well as the reification and magnification of local, intrastate racial exclusions (cf. Balibar, 1990). These two movements do not simply pull away from each other. Rather, the elasticity of race pulls them back as they stretch apart into a taut, mutually reinforcing racial order.

Now violence is conceived usually as the invocation and use of instruments (in the case of the state, state apparatuses) to implement the effects of power's exercise at the expense of those upon whom it is exercised (Arendt, 1986). But we might think of violence more extensively also as the dispersal throughout the social of arrangements that systematically close off institutional access on the part of individuals in virtue of group membership, and indeed that render relatively hidden the very instrumentalities that reproduce that inaccessibility. This is violence not just in virtue of wrenching life's possibilities from some in order to elevate those of others, though it is clearly that. It is violent the more so in refusing to acknowledge the sources of the inaccessibility, attributing them through the forces of racial subjection to the individualized or group capacities, or their relative absence, of those who lack access. It follows that racial conditions of life as we have come to experience them throughout modernity – the racial state in that broader sense of the term identified above – are inherently violent. So racial states in both their institutional and existential senses are not simply the exercise of power but equally states of violence. And the more violent the racist imposition, the more likely will it be that effective resistance will have to respond violently to some degree also. Here the violence of resistance is generically that of breaking the conceptual and social strangleholds, the yoke, of "given" and naturalized relations and conditions that have been enacted and reified historically in the name of race.

Thus, on this conception, not only were colonial conditions in the Congo Free State and later the Belgian Congo violent, or colonial administration in Bechuanaland or India, but also those colonizing regimes licensing the instrumentalities of exclusion and refusing to do anything about them. The same point extends to the racial regimes in the United States, southern *and* northern, but also to the federal government that not only failed to curtail lynching but through constitutional law enabled the implementation of the "one drop rule," the institutionalization of the "separate but equal" principle, and segregated social space.

A Racist World Order

Finally, racial states are elaborated, reproduced, extended, and sustained – in short, they exist over time – in virtue of their relative positioning in the establishment of a complex global arrangement. Race was discursively fashioned as its elaborating definition helped to imagine and create a world known even by its protagonists as colonization (Merivale, [1841] 1928). Bodies were racially produced, constituted as bearers of political and economic, legal and cultural, power and meanings. They were constituted as perpetrators and objects of racial violence in relation to their insertion into a world process of racial states, conditions, and arrangements. Belgian military and missionary men flocked to Central Africa. Indigenous people were dehumanized and delimbed as they or their relatives were Christianized. European women traveling in the colonies at the end of the nineteenth century could see their patriarchal homelands as free by comparison despite the fact that they still lacked the vote (Grewal and Caplan, forthcoming).

We find in these examples and countless others like them the representation of a worldly web of racial arrangement, relationally produced over time, positioning not only people(s) but nation-states in terms of the fashioned hierarchies. As Balibar notes, Wilhelm Reich characterized this as "nationalist internationalism."[8] These meanings and the institutional arrangements upon which they depend and which they recreate have shaped the outlines of possibility for their inhabitants.

As much as power was cemented racially in state formations within a global ordering, resistance to any part of the racial ordering of states, affairs, and people ultimately has had to assume proportionate global reach. Not only was the abolitionist movement transnational in organization, so too the debate in America concerning postslavery prospects for freed slaves conjured global movements. Thus the American Colonization Society, founded in 1817 by the likes of Jefferson, insisted on African repatriation (as did Lincoln famously later) because the racial differences between whites and blacks were deemed so naturalistically deep as to prevent "the races" living peaceably together. The Society was infamously instrumental in founding and funding the free state of Liberia. On the other side of the divide, the African Civilization Society, led by the likes of early "black nationalists" Alexander Crummell and later Edward Blyden, likewise looked to Africa as postabolition salvation for freed slaves. Crummell in particular argued that emigrating American blacks had the resposibility to "civilize" Africa into the virtues of Christianity and commerce (Crummell, [1861] 1996; Blyden, [1862] 1996).

253

Anticolonial and antiracist campaigning, most notably in the wake of massive migrant mobilization, have recognized the global scope of racial conditions. Racial states anywhere are shored up in larger or smaller ways, more or less directly, by their connectedness to racial states everywhere. Resistance movements have understood the need to respond to racist conditions in appropriately global terms. The campaign led by Morel against Leopold's regime in Central Africa grew from London but certainly looked for support to the USA and Europe. Colonial subjects, upon studying at the likes of Oxford and Paris, Amsterdam and Heidelberg, Moscow and Louvain, returned to their homelands to lead nationalist decolonizing movements in the name of Pan-Africanism and Negritude. Both sought and secured international connections, reflected not only in the Conference on Race in 1911 but also in the international sites of the various Pan-African Conventions (New York, London, Paris, Manchester). Among the earliest mobilizations at the fledgling United Nations was the Convention Against Genocide in 1946 and the first of many Declarations on Race followed just two years later.

There is a negative implication to this globalizing of racial conditions, however, well worth closing by noting. At the turn of the nineteenth century, the emergence of Afrikaner nationalism enabled the British to think themselves free of discriminatory spirit. We see here how the interconnectedness of what I have tentatively identified as a loosely ordered racial world systemic process has served not merely to mobilize racist structures, nor simply to sustain racial resistance movements. Relations between the Civil Rights Movement and the antiapartheid struggle, between Black Power and Black Consciousness, jump to mind. This racial world system equally shores up racially exclusionary conditions globally and locally. It has enabled denial of their own implication in racial state formation and conditions of those claiming greater racial tolerance, displacing their implication behind the veil of those more extreme expressions. The international antiapartheid campaign reproduced this logic: conservatives and liberals alike in Europe and the United States could declare themselves against apartheid and for color blindness, against racism and at least ambivalent about affirmative action, at once blind to the relation. The implications of these questions of law, violence, and globalization for more or less contemporary manifestations of racial states call for sustained analysis, but I must leave this to another occasion (see Goldberg, 2001: ch. 6).

Notes

1 Etienne Balibar, most notably in his focus on issues of nationalism and nation formation, offers useful distinctions concerning race and the state, but he too provides no sustained analysis of the racial forming of the modern state (Balibar, 1991; Balibar and Wallerstein, 1991). There have appeared recently a couple of books on the state, race, and culture (Lloyd and Thomas 1998; Bennett, 1998). Helpful on the intersection of these phenomena, it is notable that their focus is culturally fashioned and driven. Thus while they theorize aspects of racially conceived states, they fail to address comprehensive accounts of the founding, framing, and forming of modern state making *per se*.

2 I do not mean to make too much of this, in light of Stephen Small's careful empirical research revealing that the white men fathering mixed black offspring were usually poor and hardly in any position to extend advantages to their children, other than their nominal whiteness, even where unusually they might have wanted to (Small, this volume)

3 " ... the state ... does not have this unity, this individuality, this rigorous functionality ... " (Foucault, 1991:103).

4 For instance, the legislature of the State of California in 1850 prohibited the conviction of a white defendant in criminal proceedings on the strength of testimony offered by a black, mulatto, or American Indian witness. In *People v. Hall* (1954), the murder conviction of a white man was overturned on appeal on the argument that, as a member of "the Mongoloid race," the principal witness, a Chinese man, was identifiable with blacks and so his testimony was ruled inadmissible because unreliable (see Goldberg, 1997:39).

5 Anthony Marx (1998) has argued recently that political elites resorted to racist exclusion, most notably in the form of *de jure* segregation, to consolidate whites in the face of intrawhite conflict (Civil War in the USA, the Boer War in South Africa), national instability, and potential demise in power. So *de jure* segregation apparently was fashioned to unite whites in these societies. By contrast, Brazil suffered no internalized conflict among whites, and so there was no need to resort to segregation of blacks as a way of uniting a divided nation identified with whiteness. In Brazil, discrimination accordingly assumed less overt forms. Marx takes racial formation in these societies to be imposed more or less top down by elites seeking to ensure solidity in their nation building in the late nineteenth and twentieth centuries. He adds in a nod to nuance that formal exclusion prompted resistant racial identities among people of color which were necessary in turn for protesting such exclusion and mobilizing for inclusion and resource sharing. Here again Brazil is differentiated from the other two instances, for in the former lack of formalized racism is deemed to result in the relative lack of resistant race-based identity formation.

Marx conceives the state minimally and traditionally in a Hobbesian vein, as using race instrumentally to the ends of stability and security (Marx 1998:4, 13). He accordingly offers no account of race and race making beyond what elites and resisters are taken superficially and obviously to do in relation and response to each other. So he fails to show how race is used, what it stands for materially and symbolically, what work and conditions in different contexts it is able to effect beyond the bald unification of whites in the face of their own potential conflict. Accordingly, he suggests a totally reductionistic sense of race as functional to social definition, determined by a mix of economics and politics, the effect of which is to force an artificial similitude between the USA and South Africa in order to save the thesis. Superficially both the Civil and Boer Wars were conflicts for control over territories and wealth. By contrast, however, the Civil War was not an *ethnic* conflict among whites that necessitated state imposition of segregation to resolve. Nor in a more subtle reading of their respective histories are either simply reducible to black–white bifurcation, even as that racially created division has dominated both. Indeed, as I have argued above, the state was implicated in modern race creation from the outset, as race was mobilized to mold modern state definition in different ways at different times. And if ethnic tensions among whites in the making of modern states supposedly are resolved through a broader black–white bifurcation, how is it that Belgium fails to fit that model?

6 Charles Mills (1998:187–9) calls this "subpersonhood." He insists, again, that the creation and elaboration of the category of subpersonhood is a product only of what I have identified above as the naturalist tradition. As he says, " .. *for these beings [subpersons], a different set of normative rules applies; natural law speaks differently*" (Mills 1998:188; his emphasis). A little later Mills insists that Kant, "preeminent Enlightenment theorist of personhood and the founder of the modern concept of race," places Native Americans at the bottom of his hierarchy of races, a rung beneath blacks. But nothing Kant says bears this ordering out. Quite the contrary, Kant's characterization of "Negroes" – as "stupid" with "no feeling rising above the trifling" – is in clear contrast to his sometime, if begrudging, praise for "the savages of North America" whom he insists are not one of "the four original races" but derivative from the "Hunnic (Mongolian or Kalmuck) race" of northern Asia (Kant, [1775] 1950:17–18). Thus he says of the latter that "Among all the savages there is no nation that displays so sublime a mental character" for "they

255

have a strong feeling for honor" and are "truthful and honest" and above all driven by "valor" (Kant [1764] 1960:110–12).

7   While devoting relatively few pages to the use of military force and only late in his large book, Lugard nevertheless recommends that a soldier shoot quickly to kill a single or few insurrectionists as a show of power. He promotes the willingness to use force rather than sparing immediate life at risk of revealing weakness and facing the need for a much larger response later (Lugard [1922] 1965:580). For an elaboration of "principles of imperial policing," see Gwynn (1934). Since its establishment over 50 years ago, the state of Israel has had in effect a legal state of emergency designed for the most part to deal with its internal "Arab question," legislation that enables "the Israeli cabinet to supersede the legislative process" (*New York Times*, April 7, 2000: A10).

8   Balibar understands this to begin with Nazism (Balibar, 1990:287). I am suggesting that it was initiated at least with colonial formations in the nineteenth century.

References

Althusser, Louis (1971) *Lenin and Philosophy and Other Essays*. London: New Left Books.

Arendt, Hannah (1951) *The Origins of Totalitarianism*. London: André Deutsch.

Arendt, Hannah (1986) "Communicative power," in S. Lukes (ed.) *Power*. New York: New York University Press, pp.59–74.

Baker, Lee (1998) *From Savage to Negro: Anthropology and the Construction of Race, 1896–1954*. Berkeley: University of California Press.

Balibar, Etienne (1990) "Paradoxes of universality," in D.T. Goldberg (ed.) *Anatomy of Racism*. Minneapolis: University of Minnesota Press, pp.283–94.

Balibar, Etienne (1991) "*Es gibt keinen Staat in Europea*: Racism and politics in Europe today." *New Left Review* 187 (May–June): 5–19.

Balibar, Etienne and Wallerstein, Immanuel (1991) *Race, Nation, Class: Ambiguous Identities*. London: Verso.

Barrett, James and Roediger, David (1997) "In between peoples: Race, nationality and the 'new immigrant' working class," *Journal of American Ethnic History* Spring: 3–44.

Bennet, David (ed.) (1998) *Multicultural States: Rethinking Difference and Identity*. New York: Routledge.

Blyden, Edward Wilmot ([1862] 1966) "The call of providence to the descendants of Africa in America," in Wilson Moses (ed.) *Classical Black Nationalism: From the American Revolution to Marcus Garvey*. New York: New York University Press, pp.188–208.

Brown, Wendy (1995) *States of Injury: Power and Freedom in Late Modernity*. Princeton, NJ: Princeton University Press.

Buci-Glucksmann, Christine (1980) *Gramsci and the State*. London: Lawrence and Wishart.

Burleigh, Michael and Wippermann, Wolfgang (1991) *The Racial State: Germany 1933–1945*. Cambridge, UK: Cambridge University Press.

Butler, Judith (1997) *Excitable Speech: A Politics of the Performative*. New York: Routledge.

Cassirer, Ernst (1946) *The Myth of the State*. New Haven, CT: Yale University Press.

Comaroff, John (1998) "Reflections on the colonial state, in South Africa and elsewhere: Factions, fragments, facts and fictions." *Social Identities* 4,3:321–62.

Cooper, Frederick and Stoler, Ann Laura (eds.) (1997) *Tensions of Empire: Colonial Cultures in a Bourgeois World*. Berkeley: University of California Press.

Crenshaw, Kimberle (1998) "Color blindness, history and the law," in Wahneema Lubiano (ed.) *The House that Race Built*. New York: Vintage, pp.280–8.

Crummell, Alexander ([1861] 1966) "The progress of civilization along the West African Coast," in Wilson Moses (ed.) *Classical Black Nationalism: From the American Revolution to Marcus Garvey.* New York: New York University Press, pp.169–87.

Cunningham, George (1965) "The Italian: A hindrance to white solidarity in Louisiana, 1890–1898." *Journal of Negro History* 50 (January).

Davis, Angela (1998) "Reflection on race, class, and gender in the USA: Interview with Lisa Lowe," in Joy James (ed.) *The Angela Y. Davis Reader.* Oxford: Blackwell, pp.297–328.

Dollard, John ([1937] 1988) *Caste and Class in a Southern Town.* Madison: University of Wisconsin Press.

Dussel, Enrique (1998) "Beyond Eurocentrism: The world-system and the limits of modernity," in Frederic Jameson and Masao Miyoshi (eds.) *The Cultures of Globalization.* Durham, NC: Duke University Press, pp.3–31.

Essed, Philomena (1990) *Everyday Racism.* Claremont, CA: Hunter House.

Essed, Philomena (1996) *Diversity: Gender, Color, and Culture.* Amherst: University of Massachusetts Press.

Ferguson, Kathy (1984) *The Feminist Case Against Bureaucracy.* Philadelphia, PA: Temple University Press.

Foucault, Michel (1991) "Governmentality," in G. Burchell, C. Gordon and P. Miller (eds.) *The Foucault Effect: Studies in Governmentality.* Chicago: University of Chicago Press, pp.87–104.

Furumoto, Kim Benita and Goldberg, David Theo (2001) "Boundaries of the racial state: Two faces of racist exclusion in U.S. law." *Harvard Blackletter Law Journal* 17.

Goldberg, David Theo (1997) *Racial Subjects: Writing on Race in America.* New York: Routledge.

Goldberg, David Theo (2000) "Liberalism's limits: Carlyle and Mill on 'The Negro question'." *Nineteenth Century Contexts* 22,2:203–16.

Goldberg, David Theo (2001) *The Racial State.* Oxford: Blackwell.

Gramsci, Antonio (1971) *Selections from the Prison Notebooks*, ed. Quentin Hoare. London: Lawrence and Wishart.

Greenberg, Stanley (1987) *Legitimating the Illegitimate: State, Markets, and Resistance in South Africa.* Berkeley: University of California Press.

Grewal, Inderpal and Caplan, Karen (forthcoming) "Postcolonial feminist scholarship: Theorizing gender in a transnational way," in Philomena Essed, Audrey Kobayashi, and David Theo Goldberg (eds.) *Companion to Gender Studies.* Oxford: Blackwell.

Gwynn, Sir Charles (1934) *Imperial Policing.* London: Macmillan.

Habermas, Jürgen (1986) "Hannah Arendt's communications concept of power", in S. Lukes (ed) *Power.* New York: New York University Press, pp.75–93.

Hall, Stuart (1980) "Race, articulation and societies structured in dominance," in UNESCO *Sociological Theories: Race and Colonialism.* Paris: UNESCO.

Hall, Stuart (1984) "The state in question," in Gregor McLennan, David Held, and Stuart Hall (eds.) *The Idea of the State.* Buckingham, UK: Open University Press, pp.1–28.

Hall, Stuart [1986] 1996 "Gramsci's relevance for the study of race and ethnicity," in D. Morley and K-H. Chen (eds.) *Stuart Hall.* London: Routledge, pp.411–40.

Hall, Stuart, Critcher, C., Jefferson, T., Clark, J., and Roberts, B. (1978) *Policing the Crisis: "Mugging," the State, and Law and Order.* London: Macmillan.

Haym, Ronald (1991) *Empire and Sexuality: The British Experience.* Manchester, UK: Manchester University Press.

Hesse, Barnor (1999) " 'Reviewing the Western spectacle: Reflexive globalization through the black diaspora,' " in Avtar Brah, Mary J. Hickman, Mairtin Mac an Ghaill (eds.) *Global Futures: Migration, Environment and Globalization.* London: Palgrave, pp.122–43.

Hesse, Barnor (ed.) (2000) *Un/Settled Multiculturalisms: Diasporas, Entanglements, Transruptions.* London: Zed Press.

Holloway, John and Picciotto, Sol (eds.) (1977) *State and Capital: A Marxist Debate*. Austin: University of Texas Press.

Jessop, Bob (1990) *State Theory*. Oxford: Polity.

Jewsiewicki, Bogumil and Mudimbe, V. Y. (1995) "Meeting the challenge of legitimacy: Post-independence black African and post-Soviet European states." *Daedaelus: Journal of the American Academy of Arts and Sciences* 124, 3 (Summer): 191–208.

Joseph, G. M. and Nugent, Daniel (eds.) (1994) *Everyday Forms of State Formation: Revolution and the Negotiation of Rule in Modern Mexico*. Berkeley: University of California Press.

Kant, Immanuel ([1775] 1950) "On the different races of man," in Earl Count (ed.) *This is Race: An Anthology Selected from the International Literature on the Races of Man*. New York: Henry Schuman, pp.16–24.

Kant, Immanuel ([1764] 1960) *Observations on the Feeling of the Beautiful and Sublime*, trans. John Goldthwait. Berkeley: University of California Press.

Lloyd, David and Thomas, Paul (1998) *Culture and the State*. New York: Routledge.

Lugard, Lord Frederick ([1922] 1965) *The Dual Mandate in British Tropical Africa*. Hamden, CT: Archon Books.

MacKinnon, Catharine (1989) *Toward a Feminist Theory of the State*. Cambridge, UK: Cambridge University Press.

Magubane, Bernard (1990) *The Political Economy of Race and Class in South Africa*. New York: Monthly Review Press.

Magubane, Bernard (1996) *The Making of a Racist State: British Imperialism and the Union of South Africa 1875–1910*. Trenton, NJ: Africa World Press.

Marx, Anthony (1998) *Making Race and Nation: A Comparison of South Africa, the United States, and Brazil*. New York: Cambridge University Press.

Merivale, Herman ([1841] 1928) *Lectures on Colonization and Colonies*. Oxford: Oxford University Press.

Mills, Charles (1998) *Blackness Visible: Essays on Philosophy and Race*. Ithaca, NY: Cornell University Press.

Omi, Michael and Winant, Howard (1986) *Racial Formation in the United States: From the 1960s to the 1990s*. New York: Routledge.

Omi, Michael and Winant, Howard (1994) *Racial Formation in the United States: From the 1960s to the 1990s*, revised edn. New York: Routledge.

Pateman, Carole (1988) *The Sexual Contract*. Princeton, NJ: Princeton University Press.

Posel, Deborah (1991) *The Making of Apartheid, 1948–1961: Conflict and Compromise*. Oxford: Clarendon Press.

Poulantzas, Nicos (1969) *Political Power and Social Classes*. London: New Left Books.

Sartre, J.-P. ([1948] 1965) *Antisemite and Jew*. New York: Schocken Books.

Sartre, Jean-Paul ([1960] 1976) *Critique of Dialectical Reason*. London: New Left Books.

Stoler, Ann Laura (1997) "Racial histories and their regimes of truth," in D. Davis (ed.) *Political Power and Social Theory*, vol. II. Ann Arbor: JAI Press, pp.183–206.

Taussig, Michael (1997) *The Magic of the State*. New York: Routledge.

Tilly, Charles (1994a) "Entanglements of European cities and states," in Charles Tilly and Wim Blockmans (eds.) *Cities and the Rise of States in Europe: A.D. 1000–1500*. Boulder, CO: Westview, pp.1–27.

Tilly, Charles (1994b) "The time of states." *Social Research* 61:269–95.

Voegelin, Eric ([1933] 1997) *Race and State*, Collected Works, vol. 2, trans. Ruth Hein. Baton Rouge: Louisiana University Press.

Voegelin, Eric ([1993a]/1998) *The History of the Race Idea*, Collected Works, vol. 3, trans. Ruth Hein. Baton Rouge: Louisiana University Press.

Williams, Raymond (1981) *Marxism and Literature*. New York: Oxford University Press.

Wolpe, Harold (1988) *Race, Class, and the Apartheid State*. London: J. Currey.

Chapter 18

Racisms and Racialized Hostility at the Start of the New Millennium

Stephen Small

Introduction

When analyzing earlier periods of US history, it is easy to identify who was a racist and who was the victim of racism. The Europeans who ordered the murder of Native Americans, who stole their land, and forced them on the "Trail of Tears" and into community blight on reservations were racist. The owners of plantations (what I call "master-enslavers"[1]) who bought and sold, raped and exploited, Africans and African-Americans, were racists, as were the poor whites who served as overseers and "slave-catchers." The so-called scientists who classified blacks at the bottom of the "chain of being," suggesting they had smaller brains, the men had bigger genitals, the women were more able to handle childbirth[2] – these were the racists. So were the supporters of the idea of the Manifest Destiny of whites to rule the world "from sea to shining sea," the Social Darwinists who saw whites as the "fittest of the fit" and envisaged that the unfit "races" would become extinct; and the eugenicists who advocated the sterilization of the unfit races (Hawkins, 1997; Larson, 1995). The Ku Klux Klan, who bombed and burnt, and raped and castrated, were racists; in California, the politicians and corporations that first encouraged as cheap labor, and then attacked and abused, Chinese and Japanese immigrants, paid them less for the work they did, denied them access to land ownership and forced them into dilapidated areas that became the first "Chinatowns" were racists. Throughout the twentieth century, the immigration laws that prevented Chinese migrants from entering the USA, that deported Mexicans and Mexican-Americans *en masse* when no longer needed for labor, the restrictive covenants that prevented people of color from living in certain neighborhoods, the laws that prevented them from attending certain schools, or from working in certain police forces and fire departments, or paid them less for doing the same work as whites – all of these were racist (Almaguer, 1994).

The various politicians who framed the Constitution, and the 3/5 Clause; who wrote the Chinese Exclusion Act of 1882, and the National Quotas Act, who annexed one third of Mexico and turned it into the United States; who outlawed interracial marriage and classified the children of such marriages as biologically degenerate, psychologically unstable and social misfits – these were the racists (Takaki, 1982; Spickard, 1989). The politicians who interned thousands and thousands of Japanese Americans in concentration camp conditions were racists. The Governors of Arkansas and Alabama, who said segregation today and forever, these were racist. In times gone by, the racists were far from

259

hesitant to say who was superior and who was inferior (invariably whites at the top, blacks at the bottom, Native Americans, Asians, and Latinos in between); and they were far less hesitant to implement laws to support this, and to organize the distribution of jobs, pay, housing, and education to ensure that this remained the case (Wilson, 1978). Here it is possible to see racism as the content of an ideology, or as prejudice, or as discriminatory actions; racism here is both individual and group intentions, and institutional and systematic outcomes; and racism was perpetrated by politicians and judges, the police, managers of companies, and individual citizens with malicious intent and for personal gain. These kinds of racisms were outright, explicit and clear. Racism was a ubiquitous set of beliefs and practices that systematically devalued the lives of people of color, and ensured that they were treated worst.

But times have changed, and it's not so easy to identify the racists any more. Nor are they so enthusiastic about announcing it themselves. Scientists almost unanimously agree that there are no biological races, and that populations called races are more likely to be defined in political, cultural, and economic terms. The laws are no longer explicitly racist, in fact, many of them are shaped by explicit opposition to racism. Funds have been invested to offset the effects of past racism and discrimination, and to prevent current discrimination; to support businesses and organizations for people of color, and to help the settlement and adjustment of immigrants and their families, or the assimilation of Native Americans. Organizations have been established to promote equal opportunity and cultural diversity. Politicians are far more likely to publicly decry racism, to highlight the need for diversity, and to advocate what they call a "color-blind" approach. President Clinton's race initiative is a prominent example.

Where racism still exists, it is represented as the work of extremist individuals and organizations, psychologically unstable, monstrous individuals, who castrate and drag black bodies for miles; as the work of a tiny minority, the rotten apples in the police force; or as the unintended consequences of organizational features and policies. These are the remnants of earlier eras and the source of outrage and condemnation by all Americans when they happen today. Even more, they have been joined by other racists, so called "reverse racists." According to this interpretation, the main racists of today are blacks, or other people of color, and the victims are whites, or other people of color. Counter claims see white people who call for "color-blind" approaches, as racist; those who call for an end to preferential policies of affirmative action, who argue that blacks and other people of color are "reverse racists" – they are called racist. In this climate, all Americans are urged to embrace a "color-blind" philosophy, so that society might get rid of extremists of both types, an approach to which they appeal for authority to the wisdom of Martin Luther King, in which people will be judged "on the content of their character rather than the color of their skin." If it were only that simple.

Has racism really disappeared or has the current climate seen it transformed into new forms of hostility and discrimination? Some analysts talk of a "new racism," the "re-articulation of racism," focus on the ways in which past discrimination shapes the contemporary situation, and they point out that many of the old types of racist atrocities – murders, violence, abuse, discrimination – have far from disappeared (see Goldberg, 1990b). These analysts have turned the analytical microscope away from people of color, and back on to whites and whiteness – looking at the ways in which whiteness – ethnicity, identity, racism – operates to perpetuate power, even while it is not explicit, hostile, or individually intentional (Morrison, 1992). Collectively they call for a new language and conceptual framework of analysis, a new understanding of different types of racism and racialized hostility, and a new appreciation of the complex connection between the past and present, and between racialized hostility and class and gender inequalities and hostilities; between the local and national, the national and international contexts. They insist that racialized hostility, and racisms, remain central in the lives of blacks in particular, people of color in general (Miles, 1989; Goldberg, 1990b; Small, 1994b).

In this chapter I explore the changing manifestations of racialized hostility in the United States in the 1990s, in order to interrogate the concept of racism and assess its continued usefulness. I suggest we can understand the continuing role of racialized hostility in the lives of people of color in general, and blacks in particular, in the United States.[3] I examine racisms of various kinds – in terms of content, intent, and outcomes on people's lives. I suggest that the US society is thoroughly racialized – in the distribution of resources, both material and symbolic, and in the organization of group, especially ethnic, identities. Ideas about race remain a primary operating principle in the organization of social life and interactions. This can only be understood by looking at the links with the past; and by focusing on structures, ideologies, and images that are racialized. The best way of doing this is by discarding the antiquated language of the nineteenth century, and developing new concepts for interpreting and explaining the complexities at the start of the twenty-first century. This can be done via the racialization problematic, a framework within which we should reject the old concept of racism, and employ the more sophisticated formulation of racisms. And I provide evidence from one area of US life – museum-plantation sites in the South – that has not been the focus of substantial research, but which offers insights into some of these intricate linkages.

The Racialized Social Formation of the United States Today

When police officers in Los Angeles attempted to subdue Mr. Rodney King, or police officers in New York arrested a Haitian immigrant, they were not interacting as individuals. When the senior managers of a large oil corporation mimic the actions of African Americans; or banks lend money to whites but not to blacks; when citizens of Mexico are targeted for specific consideration by the Naturalizaton and Immigration Service, or Asian students are regarded as a model minority, this is not because they are individuals. When some white students fail to gain entry to the University of California at Berkeley, and they notice that some African–American students do gain entry, they are not noticing them as individuals. When American-owned companies relocate to Mexico it's not because the workers there are individuals. When an African–American woman walks into a Korean store in New York or Los Angeles, neither she nor the store owners interact simply as individuals. When African–American men say they only date white women, or white men say they only date Asian women these are not actions unique to them as individuals.

When Tiger Woods wins a flurry of golf tournaments it becomes national and international news not because he is an individual but because we live in a world in which the vast majority of golf players are white men. When Venus and Serena Williams attain high rankings in tennis they attract dramatic attention in a world in which most successful professional tennis players are white. When Spike Lee produces a film called *White Men Can't Jump*, its meaning is understood in a society in which the vast majority of NBA players are black men. Without a shadow of a doubt, the same meaningfulness would prevail should an Asian become a prominent basketball player or 100 meter runner, should a white man win the world heavyweight boxing championship, or should a black woman win chess or swimming championships. Similar successes in the world of work (Asians CEOs), or education (blacks overrepresented in UC, Berkeley's freshman class); or crime (whites overrepresented in prisons), or politics (a Native American president!) would evoke similar discordant emotions.

In all these instances the individuals do not act as individuals alone, nor are their actions interpreted as those of individuals alone – they are not the specific expressions of individual selves, but rather are shaped by definite forms of social relationships, ideologies and images. The interactions and actions occur in concrete contexts between clearly identified groups, usually marked by ideas of race and ethnicity. And the meaning attributed varies with these groups. These concrete contexts are characterized by disparities in resources – jobs, housing, education, health, social status – between groups that are called races, groups that reveal physical and cultural differences. These contexts are characterized by a particular history of interactions which are usually familiar to the individuals from these different groups, who bring to their interactions the meanings, stereotypes, and notions that they hold about one another. These groups are social categories that are racialized, rather than randomly formed groups of individual people. This is what it means to say that society is racialized – that it is systematically organized around beliefs about race; that the distribution of power, resources, and images, corresponds closely with membership of racialized groups; and that members of these groups are conscious of such organization (see Goldberg, 1993; Small, 1999). Racialization includes macro and micro level aspects, collective and individual aspects, and institutional and ideological aspects. Some of these result directly from past arrangements, as in the growth of reservations, ghettoes, barrios, and Chinatowns. But some are primarily the result of recent or current arrangements and actions. However varied, uneven, and contradictory they seem, they are routine, recurrent and institutionalized aspects of the social order. I propose that we think of the racialization of society in terms of structures, ideologies, and images.

The idea of racialized structures has two key components. In the first instance, it refers to the distribution of people and their access to valuable resources such as political power, employment, education, housing, and health. Primarily this aspect involves who owns what, works and lives where, and has good health. When we examine the evidence on people of color and whites in the USA we see tremendous disparities across the racialized groups. Blacks and Asians are less likely to hold political office than their numbers in the population suggest. Blacks are far more likely than other groups to be urban and inner-city, segregated and in poor housing; whites are more likely to be suburban, in affluent housing, and to attend private schools (O'Hare et al., 1991; Massey and Denton, 1993). Latinos are overwhelmingly resident in south-western states, are largely segregated, and attend inferior schools. Asians live overwhelmingly in the West (Darder et al., 1997; Hamamoto and Torres, 1997). Data from the 1990 Census indicated that six states account for around 75 percent of all foreign-born immigrants and their families. Poor blacks live in segregated communities with inferior resources and heavy policing; middle-class blacks live in "gilded ghettoes," wealthy but segregated from whites; middle-class whites live in suburban communities, which are gated and often have private security to prevent apparent intruders (read people of color); and middle-class blacks and Asians work in a context of surveillance and "glass ceilings." Blacks who are in poverty are poorer than whites and are there longer.

Asians have higher levels of education than other groups, are higher earners, and far more of them, especially national groups, are self-employed (Hamamoto and Torres, 1997). Blacks and Latinos get less earnings and less retirement income – just over half of what whites get. Blacks inherit less than whites, and their businesses have less capital (Oliver and Shapiro, 1995). Most of the workers in California who plant and pick the food that we eat, who cook and serve it to us in restaurants or supermarkets, and who clean up after we eat it are people of color, many are recent immigrants, some undocumented. Blacks are now 42 percent of the Army, 32 percent of the Navy and 25 percent of the Air Force. Black women represent about 33 percent of all the women in the services. The main universities in the South are more than 80 percent white. It's easy to see black faces on any major university campus, but these are in clerical, support, or maintenance positions, rather than students (Platt, 1997). In 1993 the average life expectancy of blacks was 7.1 years less than whites. The health treatment they receive is generally worse – "fewer mammograms, immunizations and ambulatory care visits than for white people, but greater mortality and admissions to hospital." (Bhopal, 1998:1971).

The second component of racialized structures refers to the normal, recurrent, and routine procedures of institutions that shape and constrain our daily lives, from politics (voting and political representatives), economics (businesses, employment), education (universities, schools), health (hospitals) and other spheres of social life (family, media, music, sport). The practices of key institutions shape and determine who succeeds and who fails, who is rewarded and who is punished. Hospitals offer fewer tests to blacks, especially where they involve expensive technology. Police forces deploy their officers in the streets of communities of color; the Immigration and Naturalization Service targets Mexican immigrants; employers deny jobs to people of color; welfare agencies target women of color (Marable, 1995; Feagin and Vera, 1995; Collins, 1994; Hamamoto and Torres, 1997). The abolition of affirmative action in California has significantly decreased the number of African Americans attending UC, Berkeley, and UCLA. Media institutions stereotype and caricature the lives of people of color (Guerrero, 1993; Rodriguez, 1997; Hamamoto, 1994). The outcomes of these actions are reflected in the low numbers of people of color in universities and positions of political power; and in the high numbers in prisons (Duster, 1995). When we look at the distribution of blacks and Latinos across different institutional realms – employment and education, health and housing, sport and the media – we see common sets of distributions and concrete examples.

Ideologies are systematic statements about the way in which society is organized, or ought to be organized, if it is to function well – they include systematic statements about democracy, individual freedom, the rule of law and order, and equality. There are different types of racialized ideologies, including those with explicit racialized content, and those with coded racialized content (that is, reference to racialized groups is implied). But all ideologies are racialized, even where there is no explicit or obvious mention of race, because all ideologies have differential consequences for populations labeled "black," "Asian," "Latino," and "white." Statements of policy, statements made by institutions or groups, and statements made by individuals, can be clearly and explicitly racist in their content. When white supremacist groups say blacks are inferior, degenerate, or polluted; when individual politicians argue that Native Americans are lazy

263

or slovenly; when white students claim that Asian-American students work too hard, or raise grade levels; when police officers claim that blacks are more prone to violence; when sports managers claim blacks are better boxers or runners, these views are based on the idea of different racialized abilities. When senior company managers claim African Americans don't have the ability to manage, or senior sports administrators claim they only have the ability to excel in the performance of sport, but not its management; when public officials claim black women have too many babies, or individuals claim Mexican women are good housekeepers, these are based on the same notions. In these instances only closer inspection will make it clear whether such views are based on presumed biological differences, or on issues of culture or economic competition. In either case, these are racist ideologies.

Other ideologies lack explicit racialized reference, relying instead on coded racialized reference. Here, words are heavily saturated with meanings and interests as the result of a specific history in which a particular social group is attributed with a particular fixed nature and/or whose presence is associated with a set of (usually undesirable) social consequences (Omi and Winant, 1994). When politicians refer to "muggers" and crime in the "inner city," the burden on the Welfare State, to children outside wedlock, or to "reverse racism," and when they claim that multiculturalism devalues Western civilization, these all have a "racialized" reference. They are understood to be promoting policies believed to benefit "whites" while penalizing blacks and other people of color. Another type are ideologies in which the policies of the government are blamed for exacerbating racialized conflict, for example, where they fund black businesses. Here it is suggested, or stated, that such policies favor black people who are thereby privileged illegitimately.

All ideologies are racialized because of the differential, often adverse, impact that they have on racialized populations. In some ideologies (including those without any racialized reference) it is often possible to identify the hostile intentions of those advocating them, or the likely adverse consequences of the ideology for people of color. Many supporters of Proposition 187 in California, while claiming they were interested in justice and equality for all legal residents of the USA, made it clear that they held stereotypical and despicable attitudes towards Mexicans. Many policies around policing exemplify this type of ideology. For example, the practice of police officers stopping African American car drivers, colloquially called "driving while black," is defended by weakly veiled arguments about the need to act directly to deal with street crime. In others, the effect of the policy itself, even where no explicit mention is made, and where no clear hostile intentions can be established, can still be disadvantageous. For example, it is the law in the United States to deprive a convicted felon of the right to vote. That means that a significant number of black men will be unable to vote for the rest of their lives.

And "color-blind" policies are also racialized. To understand this it is indispensable to understand today's context in light of history, because US society has always been racialized. As Toni Morrison argues:

> In what public discourse does the reference to black people not exist? It exists in every one of this nation's mightiest struggles. The presence of black people is not only a major referent in the framing of the Constitution, it is also in the battle over enfranchising unpropertied citizens, women, the illiterate. It is there in the construction of a free and public school system; the balancing of representation in legislative bodies; jurisprudence and legal defin-

itions of justice. It is there in theological discourse; the memoranda of banking houses; the concept of manifest destiny and the preeminent narrative that accompanies (if it does not precede) the initiation of every immigrant into the community of American citizens. The presence of black people is inherent, along with gender and family ties, in the earliest lesson every child is taught regarding his or her distinctiveness. Africanism is inextricable from the definition of Americanness – from its origins on through its integrated or disintegrating twentieth-century self. (Morrison, 1992:65)

To pretend race has not been central is a fallacy; and to organize society as if it is irrelevant will only exacerbate racialized inequalities. One cannot abolish the effects of past racism simply by pretending they do not exist today. We cannot just reverse these entrenched experiences simply by declaring society "color-blind." White Americans have tried to deny the significance of race, but "insisting on the meaninglessness of race to the American identity, are themselves full of meaning. The world does not become raceless or will not become unracialized by assertion" (Morrison 1992:46). Or, in other words, "in a wholly racialized society, there is no escape from racially inflected language" (Morrison 1992:12–13). Even something as ostensibly simple as "American identity" is racialized. Because

Deep within the word "American" is its association with race. To identify someone as a South African is to say very little; we need the adjective "white" or "black" or "colored" to make our meaning clear. In this country it is quite the reverse. American means white, and Africanist people struggle to make the term applicable to themselves with ethnicity and hyphen after hyphen after hyphen. (Morrison, 1992:47)

The existence of different types of racialized ideologies means that we cannot focus only on ideologies that have explicit racialized content – it is more complex than that.

Racialization is also pervasive in the images of different groups, for example, in the media, film, and advertising (Guerrero, 1993; Hamamoto, 1994; Rodriguez, 1997). Despite the fact that blacks now occupy a wide variety of locations, reflecting a range of lifestyles, in the movies blacks remain tragic mulattos, amazons, mammies and maids, pimps and whores, gangsters, faithful servants and lovable sidekicks. Now, too, we have black drag queens as in the film *To Wong Foo*. Blacks continue to be sports figures – *The Fan*, *Jerry Maguire*. Men are emasculated fathers and oversexed ineffectual lovers. Women are "betraying butch bitches," "hot pussies," sluts and slags, or strippers and prostitutes, as in *Set it Off*, *Boomerang*, *Harlem Nights*, *A Thin Line Between Love and Hate*, *Independence Day*, *Gridlocked*. If a woman is dark she is a villain, if light-skinned, sexy, and desirable she is dumb, as with Vanessa Williams in *Eraser*. Nor is interracial sex allowed, especially if it involves men of color and white women – *Pelican Brief*, *The Long Kiss Goodbye*. Alternatives do exist, but they don't prevail – *Once Upon a Time When we Were Colored*, *Philadelphia*, *The President's Wife*, dysfunctional families as in *Soul Food*, biracial buddy movies – *48 Hours*, *Lethal Weapon*, *Shawshank Redemption* – preserve the image that color is irrelevant.

Latinos remain stereotyped as illegal immigrants who don't (and won't) speak English, as gangsters and drug dealers; and Latinas are represented as hypersexual and sensuous (Berg, 1997; Cortes, 1997). Asian men remain effeminate and timid, drug dealers or gamblers, or otherwise employed in small businesses, especially restaurants (Hamamoto, 1994). They have also been identified in recent years as particularly corrupt, especially in politics. The film *Rush Hour* provides a good example of blacks and Chinese making fools of one another, and of themselves at the same time.

But it's not all bad, it seems. Another aspect of racialized images are those that reflect the rhetoric of equality and diversity: the prevalence of multiracial sports teams, dance groups, and the like on television; the presentation of news reports and weather by, especially, women of color. This is common in music videos of the most diverse kinds, in magazines, and in advertising for clothes, music, cars, and all manner of products, as well as among the catalogs and promotional literature of major universities. This has become particularly common in California after the passage of Proposition 209. These are designed to promote the philosophy of diversity and multiculturalism. And there are films and literature in which one can find counternarratives and images that reflect the variety and vitality of the lives of people of color (Rodriguez, 1997).

These are what we might call external, institutional, organizational aspects of racialization. But racialization is also constituted of sets of attitudes, and beliefs. The ways different racialized groups look at the their world, and understand and explain it, is different. Whites overestimate the proportion of blacks in poverty, and are more likely to explain it in terms of individual failings; whites estimate levels of black/white disparity consistently lower than blacks estimate it (Gandy and Baron, 1998). Whites are more likely to dismiss the effects of past racism and discrimination as irrelevant to the way society works – about two thirds of whites opposed offering an apology to African Americans for slavery; at the same time, African Americans see a direct relationship between past racism and current inequality and discrimination, and almost exactly the same number of them are in favor of an apology. Whites also underestimate the nature and extent of contemporary discrimination; blacks are more likely to estimate it correctly. We might say that not only do blacks and whites live and work in a different world, but their mindsets are in a different world as well.

The structures, institutional practices, ideologies, and images of racialization interact in ways that shape one another. For example, discrimination causes poverty and material hardship and media institutions routinely employ images of people of color in poverty and on welfare dependency. Businesses move to locations to maximize profits, locations difficult for people of color to access. Similarly, communities of color continue to be the subject of degradation and vilification in images disseminated by politicians, press, and television, and through literature and popular culture so that "white" people fear and despise them and some people of color are suspicious, distrustful, resentful, or fearful of one another. The psychological consequences are immense. At the same time, ideologies of "color blindness" create the appearance of equality and fairness, while hiding practices of discrimination, and hostile intentions.

What this means is that any understanding of racism must be based on a recognition of the racialized nature of society, and the processes that maintain both stability and social change. This requires explicit consideration of the aspects of racialization related to state policies and actions; the relationship between racialization and class and gender inequality; and, especially today, its relationship with international politics and trade, that is, patterns of globalization. Ideologies, images, and attitudes, alongside actions, both individual and institutional, that might be called racist, spread their effects throughout all areas of society. Thinking about racism in this way requires us to develop a new language and a new conceptual framework. No simple notion of racism will work. We must first discard much of the commonsense language that we use (Miles, 1982; Small, 1994a). This language leads to an oversimplified focus on race by positing the existence of a distinct category of social relations (i.e., relations between supposedly distinct "races") while ignoring the relevance of economic and political processes and the consequences of the routine operation of key institutions in contemporary life. Yet "race relations" makes no sense, because there are no "races" and so there cannot be any social relations between them (Miles, 1982).

But if "race relations" are not the relationship between biologically different "races," why are certain types of social relation defined as "race relations"? An answer to this question requires us to adopt a framework that turns our attention to economic and political processes and to the ways in which structures, images, and ideologies operate to sustain inequality. Additionally, we need to consider the impact of the ideological dimension of resistance to such inequality. A framework of this kind does not presume that "race" is a variable in and for itself. Rather, it is argued that ideas and beliefs about "race" have shaped these relationships, alongside the impact of, for example, ideas about class and gender. This approach is usually described as the *racialization problematic* (or framework) (Miles, 1989). This framework is a set of assumptions and concepts which explore the multiple factors that shape what has previously been described as "race relations." Some of these factors entail explicit reference to "race," for example, beliefs about the existence of "races," and discrimination based on such beliefs. But other factors – such as competition for economic and political resources (education, jobs, housing, elected office) – may seem to have no "racial" reference. The racialization problematic enables us to draw out the relationship between these seemingly unrelated variables, and to assess the significance of each of them. What this conceptual approach requires, rather than presumes, is that there is a need to question and explain the social and cultural boundaries and identities by which groups called "races" have been, and continue to be, defined. The best way to do this is via an historical and comparative approach.

The key concept within the racialization problematic is the process of *racialization* (and hence the notion of racialized social relations) which has been defined in a number of ways (see Small, 1994b for an overview). I use it to refer to a historically specific ideological process, and to the accompanying structures, that result in certain social collectivities being thought of as constituting naturally (often biologically) distinct groups, each possessing certain ineradicable features. The groups so racialized vary, but racialization speaks to the nature of the relationship between these different groups. The example most relevant to this is the racialization of diverse ethnic groups from Africa and Asia in order to constitute a "black race" and an "Asian race," both of which stand in opposition to (even in conflict with) the "white race." This particular instance of racialization is founded in part on colonization, slavery, and the growth of the United States. Racialization also refers to the institutional arrangements usually associated with these historical patterns: the legal system (in slavery, Jim Crow and later, including legislation on immigration and Civil Rights), the economic system (the plantation economy, separate and unequal work and pay), as well as housing (including ghettoes, barrios, and Chinatowns).

Old and New Racisms Rearticulated

But where does the concept of racism fit into all of this? In the past racism was seen as an ideology that classified human populations as if they were permanently distinctive racial groups (Banton, 1977). Or racism was the explicit hostile intentions of people with power – politicians, employers, police captains. Or it was individual acts of extremist groups like the Ku Klux Klan; or of extremist individuals with psychological problems (Carmichael and Hamilton, 1967). There were biological racists, institutional racists, psychological racists, and so forth. But the complexities of today make such examples seem out of date. There is no consensus today on how to define racism. Any approach must recognize the continuities with the past. To think about racism today, we have to think about some of the ways racism was defined in the past, and how its usage has been modified. There is a vast literature on the history, expression, and variations in racism and racisms (see Goldberg, 1993; Small, 1994b for overviews). A chapter of this length cannot cover all of these analyses. Many aspects of them, particularly as they apply to other historical periods and other nations, are addressed in other chapters in this volume. I focus on some of the most central sociological analyses of racism. If the USA is racialized, is it also racist? Not necessarily. It's better to think of racism as one aspect of racialization.

The first statements of racism were those made by scientists working in anatomy who claimed the world was naturally divided into distinct human categories (called species or races) and that they were hierarchically arranged by levels of physique, intelligence, and culture. Most books on this topic were published in the 1840s and 1850s, but Michael Banton (1977) describes Robert Knox as one of the first racists, having lectured and published his books several decades earlier. In these analyses the role of science in producing racist ideologies is highlighted and racism is seen as an effort by scientists to explain human physical, mental, and cultural variations. As scientific methods and knowledge changed, there developed what might be called different types of racisms, including "biological racism," "Social Darwinism," "manifest destiny," and "eugenics" as different types of racism (Gossett, 1965; Larson, 1995; Hawkins, 1997). While these ideologies reveal many striking differences, what they all share is the view that Africans, Europeans, Asians, and Native Americans can be seen as more or less naturally distinctive human populations, with different characteristics and attributes. Nor were such views marginal: they were all systematically developed ideologies, advanced by formally trained scientists, many holding positions at top universities, advocated using the claims of scientific research and evidence, and embraced by the foremost academics, politicians, and others of their periods. This approach has tended to see the growth of racism as a scientific error. There were also analyses that focused on the psychological effects and gains (Kovel, 1971).

A different approach highlights the role that economics and politics played in European conquest and colonization, in which claims about biology were inextricably related to the economic motives of those advancing them. The belief that Africans were naturally capable of working on plantations in the full heat of the sun, were physically stronger than Europeans and intellectually inferior (it was suggested they did not mature beyond the age of a teenage white person), arose primarily because it suited the economic needs of plantation slavery. Whites were seen as intellectually and culturally superior, especially with regard to Christianity, and civilization required that whites be relieved of any burdensome work in order that they might concentrate on cultural matters of a higher order, such as government, education, art, and music. Where working-class whites expressed racist beliefs this was seen as a consequence of manipulation and encouragement by powerful whites – they were told that their white skin was the badge of superiority. Thus, says Eric Williams: "Slavery was not born of racism; rather, racism was the consequence of slavery" (1944:7).

In many of these theories the link between racism and other ideologies, such as sexism, nationalism, and religion are highlighted. "Whites viewed white women as chaste and pure, charged with the task of ensuring that white men remained 'civilized,' while whites saw black women as natural whores who enticed white men into sexual relationships" (Amott and Matthaei, 1991:x). In this way, it becomes clear that racism as an ideology is closely, perhaps inextricably, linked to other ideologies of difference. This is evident today.

A statement issued by UNESCO in the 1950s, after the racism of Nazi Germany, was meant to offer a decisive scientific view of "race": "Racism falsely claims that there is a scientific basis for arranging groups hierarchically in terms of psychological and cultural characteristics that are immutable and innate."[4] UNESCO argued that the groups usually designated as races in political and social or even religious terms were better understood as social groupings. At the biological level, if the word "race" was used at all, it meant populations that shared common pools of genes (a definition which follows from Darwin – see Goldberg, 1993:66). This was very different from what people in the street understood by race. Apparently, people in the street did not pay much attention to the scientists, because ideologies, attitudes, and actions that were clearly racist, continued throughout the world, no less so than in the United States. The 1960s saw some more explicit formulations of racism. Carmichael and Hamilton argued:

> Racism is both overt and covert. It takes two, closely related forms: individual whites acting against individual blacks, and acts by the total white community against the black community. We call these individual racism and institutionalized racism. The first consists of overt acts by individuals, which cause death, injury or the violent destruction of property.... The second type originates in the operation of established and respected forces in the society, and thus receives far less public condemnation than the first type (Carmichael and Hamilton, 1967:4)

This approach was concerned with the atrocious acts of violence committed on a day-to-day basis. Here, racism was highlighted as something done by whites against blacks, especially in the context of slavery, Jim Crow, and their legacies. Carmichael and Hamilton emphasized the difference between individual and institutional racism to indicate that it was not just a matter of individual prejudices, whether of extremists or most whites, that might be changed with education or by the law; rather that the routine operation of the institutions of US society served to ensure that blacks (and other groups of color for that matter) remained at a disadvantage. This approach distinguished intention and outcome – a society could still be racist if the outcomes were systematically detrimental to blacks, even where there was no clear expression of intent.

The changing conditions of the 1950s and 1960s in the United States – the end to formal legal segregation, the introduction of Civil Rights legislation to guarantee access to resources and rights for all blacks, and other people of color, the introduction of affirmative action, and the increasing opposition to racism voiced by successive presidents (right up to the race initiative of President Clinton in the late 1990s) – has led others to say racism is a thing of the past. William Julius Wilson, one of the foremost sociologists of recent decades, has argued that racism is a thing of the past. Wilson argued

269

that a "racist society" is one "in which the major institutions are regulated by racist ideology" and that in such a society "the life chances of the members of individual minorities are essentially more a function of race than of class" (1978:ix–x). However, "race relations in America have undergone fundamental changes in recent years, so much so that now the life chances of individual blacks have more to do with their economic class position than with their day-to-day encounters with whites" (1978:1). This is the premise underlying the abolition of affirmative action in California, and is certainly the view of most whites in the United States today. Wilson drew a distinction between past discrimination and present discrimination, arguing that much racial inequality today was the result of past discrimination, but that the effects of past discrimination would disappear over time. He highlighted the successes of young, university educated, professional blacks as example (Wilson, 1987). Others have highlighted the dramatic changes in the organization of US society, the changing nature of employment and education, the increasing internationalization of work, and dramatic changes in immigration, particularly of people from Asia, South America, and the Caribbean.

Even accepting that much of what Wilson says is true, there still seems to be an awful lot of racism around:

> Black churches are still being burned to the ground by white supremacists in the South . . . and white men in Texas still think it's a sport to hunt down and kill African Americans . . . and the police still think nothing of beefing up the arrest of urban Chicanos and Mexican migrants with a good beating; and a natural restaurant chain like Denny's would still be enforcing racial quotas for their customers if they had not been sued by black Secret Service agents; . . . Most people of color in the United States, on a daily basis, think twice about how they can best survive the day without experiencing paternalism, pity, humiliation, insults, rudeness, or much, much worse. (Platt, 1997:8)

In this context analysts have talked of different kinds of "racisms," have insisted on the need for an appreciation of the varying ideological, cultural, political, and economic motivations for such "racisms," as well as the far more varied forms such hostility takes, particularly as it has become far more symbolic and far more covert. These scholars emphasize the "new racism," or the rearticulation of racism (Omi and Winant, 1994; Ansell, 1997; Gabriel, 1998). The concept of a *new racism*, formulated in England initially by Barker (1981) and the *rearticulation of racism*, formulated in the United States by Omi and Winant (1994), has been especially influential. These approaches are grounded in the view that biological or scientific racism has declined in significance, and new forms of racialized hostility have grown to take its place. It is argued that this "old racism" has been superseded by a new racism or by the rearticulation of racism which is characterized by an assertion of the naturalness of both a desire to live amongst "one's own people" (Us) and hostility towards a culturally or racially distinct immigrant presence (the Other) that threatens the existence of "our way of life."

Omi and Winant describe the rearticulation of racism as: "A practice of discursive reorganization or reinterpretation of ideological themes and interests already present in the subjects' consciousness, such that these elements obtain new meanings or coherence" (1994:173). Elsewhere, Omi has defined rearticulation as "the strategic use of race to deflect the issue of race" (Omi and Takagi, 1996:157). Focusing on the 1980s they highlighted "codewords," that is, the ways in which the demands for a "color-blind" society were manipulated to preserve white privilege, and to make claims of "reverse racism" by blacks against whites. In the 1990s manipulations of this kind have also been common, and whites in general, right-wing politicians in particular, have engaged in subterfuge by manipulating Asian Americans to suggest that affirmative action harms Asian Americans and therefore is not a black/white issue. In fact, argue Omi and Takagi, the assault on affirmative action is designed to preserve white privilege (Omi and Takagi, 1996). After all, when the focus on meritocracy resulted in more Asian Americans being admitted to the University of California, they faced discrimination.

So today we have two clearly identifiable sociological approaches to racism. In the first instance are those analysts who draw largely on earlier definitions and focus on an ideology that the world is divided into a number of separate "races" (for example, Europeans, Africans, and Asians) who are endowed with different physical and mental attributes, that "race" determines culture, and that Europeans are superior both mentally and culturally. Public expressions of such views are very infrequent because they run counter to the dominant government ideologies and public discourses. In the second instance are those who have a larger, revised definition. They claim that the original concept refers to only one specific form of racism, and that today there is more than one racism, constituted of different facets, and motivated by different factors. This second notion itself has two approaches. First, there are those who emphasize racism as a specific form of ideology and who argue that there are a variety of historically specific racisms which refract the particular context in which they are formed and expressed. Second, there are those who see racism in such a way as to include both beliefs and practices which lead to the subordination of specific racialized groups. For many in this latter approach, evidence of the existence of racism is found in the patterns of racialized inequality described at the start of this chapter. Both of these approaches imply a difference between "individually oriented" notions, and those that are based on a "structural approach" (Goldberg, 1993: 92).

Racialization and Racisms

While recognizing that society is racialized, I do not think that it is useful to think of it as all racist; and I don't think it is useful to approach ideologies by asking whether they are racist or not. Some appear to be clearly and explicitly racist. Others, which make no explicit mention of race, can still be motivated by racisms of various kinds. But explicit racist hostility, especially that based on a belief in an ideology of the natural inequality of races, is not always the primary motivation. I believe it is more useful to acknowledge the diverse array of ideologies that speak to issues of race, ethnicity, national or religious identity, and to examine them for their racialized intentions, content, and consequences. Another way of putting this is to think of all ideologies in terms of the intentions of those promoting them, the content of the ideologies themselves, and the outcomes that they have or are likely to have for different racialized groups. This requires us to focus our attention on specific ideologies and to undertake research to assess them. In analyzing the content of ideologies we should assess those with explicit racialized reference, those with coded reference, and those without any clear racialized referent but in which we can identify hostile intentions and/or adverse consequences for blacks, or other people of color. This creates a considerable challenge, but it means that we are no longer

271

subordinate to the binary idea of racist/nonracist, it highlights the need for empirical scrutiny, and it means that with such clear definition and evidence, we are likely to have a more compelling case.

Racist motivation may occur for a variety of reasons: "psychosexual fear, economic or social disparities; for cultural exclusions; or for political entitlement" (Goldberg, 1990a:297). When we examine many intentions it is often clear that there is present expressed hostility towards a racialized group that is based on a belief in the existence of races, and a belief that society should be organized in accord with this belief. This may happen even where no mention of race is made. Many of these people mask their real intentions behind rhetoric and codewords, as with many of those who supported the abolition of affirmative action. This is also the case when police forces claim to treat all citizens in the same way, but in practice target communities of color, as well as targeting blacks who drive cars. Or where white students claim university courses are too difficult (and imply that it is Asian Americans who drive up the grades). We can clearly infer racist aggression when black churches are bombed and burnt.

Ideologies are racist in terms of their content, and so too can specific statements be racist in this way. When the Ku Klux Klan says "keep America white"; when individual politicians say that Mexicans are inferior, or that Asians are a "model minority," these views are based on the idea of different racialized abilities, as also when senior company managers claim African Americans don't have the ability to manage, or senior sports administrators claim they only have the ability to excel in the performance of sport, but not its management. In these instances only closer inspection will make it clear whether such views are on presumed biological differences, or on issues of culture or economic competition. In either case, these are racist ideologies. Institutional racism occurs when the outcomes of specific policies, organizational arrangements, or the actions of the powerful result in adverse consequences for people of color. When real estate agents direct people of color to purchase homes in a limited number of neighborhoods, when police target certain areas for crime, when employers do not recruit from black colleges, when prosecutors exclude black jurors, when hospitals do not offer expensive techno-logical examinations, all of these have an adverse effect on communities of color.

As can be seen, there are complex links between intention, content, and outcomes. These things are not mutually exclusive. Sometimes it's possible to identify clear relationships; at other times it is not. But in each instance it is necessary to empirically investigate the matter. And even where we do not conclude that these ideologies are racist (say in intent, or content), where they have adverse effects for people of color I think we can still conceptualize them as expressing racialized hostility. For example, Omi and Takagi see racism as hostility:

> We tend to think of racism as hostility directed against those of a different skin color believed to be "inferior" – in terms of class and status, in intellectual ability, or in cultural orientation. This hostility is coupled with structural forms of discrimination – in the job market, in politics, in residential patterns – and negative cultural representations. (Omi and Takagi, 1996:159)

I have suggested elsewhere that while one primary concern should be an analysis of racism, it is equally important to identify what might be done (Small, 1994b). I have introduced the concepts of racialized integration, harmony, and parity as reflecting the goals usually described as equal opportunities or diversity. Racialized integration is usually meant to indicate physical and social integration of different racialized groups in housing, employment, and education. Racialized harmony usually means where social relations are nonantagonistic, and is often suggested by events like carnivals and festivals, or where there are high levels of dating and marriage across racialized groups. Racialized parity refers to equal access to, and enjoyment of, valued resources such as wealth and health, earnings and education, and access to power and privilege. I have also suggested that the primary goal of blacks in particular is parity; while whites emphasize harmony or, less frequently, integration. I doubt that satisfactory levels of harmony or integration will be reached without sustained attack on the disparities in resources. This must be a primary concern.

Racialization Over Here: Museum-plantation Sites[5]

There are several thousand museum-plantation sites across the US South which comprise a major tourist infrastructure in the economies of Southern States. These sites include state, county, and private museums and exhibitions, actual and reconstructed plantation complexes, working plantations, "slave quarters" and related buildings. The vast majority of these sites are physical structures, but some are organized around tours, both vehicular and walking. Some of them are staffed by African Americans. Hundreds of "Welcome Centers," county, city, and town tourist offices provide institutional support to these sites. The sites are advertised across the South, the nation, and the world in travel and tourist books, in newspapers and magazines, in videos that are distributed or sold, and via the World Wide Web. Hundreds of thousands of visitors, both American and from numerous other nations, visit these sites each year. Here I offer some examples from Louisiana and Georgia. The social organization of these museum-sites, the cultural practices, ideological underpinnings, and the images physically presented in them, reveals important dimensions of racialization, and enables us to examine indicators of racialized intention, content, and outcomes which don't lend themselves so easily to accusations of racism, but which clearly constitute racialized hostility.

The institutional infrastructure of museum-plantation sites comprises thousands of sites across all the southern states, private and public ones, supported by a massive range of tourist agencies. The sites appeal for legitimacy to the historical legacy of "great men" – Thomas Jefferson in Virginia, Jimmy Carter in Georgia, James Oglethorpe in Georgia (the founder of Savannah), and of "great events," foremost of which is the Civil War, reflected in the "Little White House of the Confederacy" in Montgomery, Alabama, Sherman's March to the Sea, and the home of Alexander H. Stephens (Vice-president of the Confederacy) in Crawfordville, Georgia. These sites do not stand alone, but are linked to many other historical men and events, from earlier or later periods (such as Elvis Presley), all under the rubric of the noble and culturally rich South. This institutional infrastructure displays an uneven though frequently explicit attention to African-American history, once again, via "great men" (Martin Luther King, Arna Bontemps), "great events" (Montgomery bus boycott), "great structures" (Ebenezer Baptist Church, Atlanta, Georgia). Vast resources are invested in these sites in an attempt to attract visitors; for example, around the Olympics in 1996, when Georgia made sustained efforts to entice visitors to the Atlanta Olympics to stay in the state and visit its many delightful sites, including the "Plantation Trace" and "Colonial Coast." A delightfully colorful guidebook, *Georgia on my Mind*, was produced to invite visitors to the state's "rich Indian and Civil War heritage" and the "more than 60 state parks and historical sites" (*Georgia on my Mind*, p. 8). In the sites themselves, the vast majority of docents are elderly white Southern women, selected, no doubt, for their authenticity, rather than for any particular impartiality they might exemplify. And the vast majority of visitors seem to be whites.[6]

The grand narrative of the museum sites – the key images and language used, the (moral) assumptions made, and the framework of thinking which is encouraged – is one preoccupied with the grandeur of the architecture, the splendor and luxuriousness of the décor and furniture, the opulence and affluence of the white residents, and the gentility of the lifestyles that they led. The context is a contrast with the royalty and aristocracy of Europe, and comparisons are often explicitly made. It is expressed in the enormous scale and cost of the homes and architecture; the origins of the house contents – silver from England, pianos from Italy, furnishings from France, stone from Germany; in the lavishness of the owners, who spared no expense for the parties organized for their wives and children, or in honor of the nation. No more striking exemplification of this is to be found than in the fact that when docents heard my clearly English accent, they almost invariably offered what amounted to an apology, more or less saying, "We know you must have seen far better than this in England and we're sorry that our homes don't match up to what you have in Europe."

A prime example is Nottoway Castle, advertised as the biggest plantation house in the South, and which, in its video "Nottoway Memories," invites visitors to "experience and savor the aristocratic splendor that was the old South. Nottoway is the ultimate in Southern Grandeur; Southern hospitality at its finest." To me it seems more like an imitation castle than a plantation. It is a massive white structure with six major columns, and huge extension sections on either side of the main structure. The house boasts an unequalled 365 "openings" – 200 windows and 165 doors – one for every day of the year. It has Louis XIV furniture, Rosewood beds, a piano from London, numerous mirrors, marble fireplaces, chandeliers, exuberant dining tables with extensive layouts of china plates, crystal wear, candelabras, and silver. The tour takes you through the two floors, and numerous rooms. If you have not had enough during the tour you can stay overnight – Nottoway has 10 rooms and three suites serving bed and breakfast, at a paltry figure of $200.00. The commercial planners of this plantation complex left nothing to chance, and visitors are required to pass through the gift shop as they enter the premises in order to get to the house, a gift shop abundantly stocked with all sorts of plantation memorabilia – dolls, books, pictures, and a sundry array of souvenirs.

Extremely comprehensive details of the house and the former owners are provided – details of the cost of building and furnishing it, down to each door and window, along with the names of family members, dates of birthdays and important events, family and individual idiosyncrasies, right up to the current owner, who, we are told, currently lives here, is 89 years old, and "is a delight." If we want to see her she will be in the doll room in a short while, we are told. The owners were described by the tour guide with awe and admiration for their accomplishments. But the (meticulous) attention apportioned to the former owners was spared for blacks. We are told that the family that built it had "300 slaves" and "57 household servants," but we are told no more about them. It was also spared for the two large statues of black servants, with dark black faces and gold paint, as if from Ancient Greece, that were in the hall. They were about 8ft tall, with candelabras on their heads, adding another 18 inches or so. There was no mention, no description, they were simply ignored, as if they were not there.

Central to this narrative is the link with the movie *Gone with the Wind* and its mansion, "Tara," to which each site compares itself favorably, or just compares itself in some way to the narrative presented in that movie: a narrative of love and romance, affluence and success, majesty and pride, dashed away in the crass industrial might of the white north. Some plantations claim to be bigger; others to be almost as big. Some have the same number of columns, or more, or less; others have the same stairway, or the same style, or a different style. Others have similar chairs, or doors, or carpets. Others have something that is vaguely similar to Tara. In Nottoway Castle the tour guide casually remarks, "If you saw *Gone with the Wind* then you'll remember the drapes – Scarlett used them to make a dress." Of course, Georgia has the indisputable claim to authenticity – after all it was there that the events of the film took place – and at Stone Mountain, there is a "Tara" museum, along with the most meticulously researched and laid-out memorabilia. All in all, one could come away with the impression that the fiction which is the film has a reality larger than the facts – it certainly plays a bigger role in shaping the social organization of museum-plantation organization and culture in the South. Even in the attempt at counternarrative, one which highlights the role of poor and working-class white men as frontiersmen, white women as the backbone of Southern society, the contrast is still there. In "Old Alabama Town" in Montgomery, Alabama a composite of buildings of impeccable working-class credentials, we are told that while many states had massive mansions, and affluent exuberant lifestyles, the workers of Alabama (meaning white workers) lived, hard and hearty, rough and rugged, and eked a humble existence out of a hard land, an existence which was the basis for this great nation. In this narrative it is the wealth produced by the working-class whites of the South that led to the economic success of the nation.

The key images presented are of homes and furniture and splendor. When guides mention humans, whites are described in (extensive) details; blacks are passed over in a perfunctory manner, except perhaps in the case of "faithful old servants" about whom cursory details are provided, and the enslaved person is deployed to highlight the generosity and magnanimity of the master-enslaver. Thus, we are told, Alexander Stephen's bondspersons said that "if they had to be slaves they wouldn't want to be anywhere else than with Mr. Stephens." Or, where enslaved persons were allowed to stay on a plantation after the Civil War, they were welcomed with open-handed, open-hearted warmth. It is the impressive Southern hospitality which accompanies the impressive structures.

The primary intent of such institutions is not to be racist, not to denigrate African Americans, not to deny the exploitation, the suffering, the resilience, the contributions. I doubt that the organizers of these sites, or those that fund them, would deny that these things occurred. It's just that these issues are simply not part of this story. You may be part of the universe of this history, but our telescope is focused elsewhere. As I exited Nottoway Castle, I noticed a brown barn-type building at the rear of the house. I asked two Clack women on a path, discussing the linen and cooking in the house, who informed me that it was "Just an old building, an old slave building." My inspection revealed that it was piled from floor to ceiling with junk. A fitting tribute. The intention of these sites is to tell one aspect of that history, to recapture the splendor and glory of the past, in a way similar to British castles and stately homes, and to offer something for (white) people to be proud or. But the content of the narrative is marginalization of the African American presence in Southern history in general, slavery in particular. This is accomplished not by outright bigotry, or by simple lies; rather it is achieved via distoritions and exaggerations, silences and erasures. What the outcome of such museum-plantation sites might be on the understanding and psyches of the visitors is not clear from the data collected so far. A complete understanding would require us to undertake interviews with such visitors. In lieu of more complete information I want to suggest that it is far more likely to provide reassurance for whites – things were not so bad, whites suffered also – and vexation for blacks – our struggles, suffering, misery, resilience has been denied, abused. This is implied by the fact that the organizers of black tours say that you will not get the pretty distortions of white tours, for example, in South Carolina. Given that such an overwhelming proportion of white visitors are at the extremes of the age profiles – elderly, presumably retired, whites, accompanied by young children (probably their grandchildren) – I suspect that it reminds the former of times gone by, and inculcates into the latter the impression that the past was not so bad, and the USA is a nation to be proud of.

This dominant narrative is contested. A small but significant number of sites are organized and staffed by African Americans. These include, for example, the Harriet Tubman Museum in Macon, Georgia, the Gullah Tour in St Helena, South Carolina, and the Arna Bontemps House in Alexandria, Louisiana. They offer a stark contrast to the narratives of the mainstream sites, and visits to them offer a glaring illustration of the partiality of these sites. They start their stories in Africa, rather than in slavery; they are more explicit on the suffering and exploitation, they are more likely to highlight African American resistance, especially through narratives of famous blacks (Martin Luther King, etc.); they are more likely to offer personal details of individual African Americans; and to highlight the contributions made by African Americans (who built the house, polished the furniture, grew the food, cooked and served the meals in these "great houses") including the inimitable artwork or weaving and music. Theirs is not a story of admiration for the buildings that were built by the enslaved, nor sorrow for the days gone by, but of critique for an inherently abusive institution and praise for the spirit of resilience in the face of oppression. Such sites offer a necessary corrective to the partiality and distortion of the larger congeries of museum-plantation sites; but obviously they operate under far more severe finanancial and institutional constraints. They tend to be smaller in size, have more limited funds, and fewer visitors.

Collectively, these sites reveal many aspects of the racialization of which they are constituted. All of these sites demonstrate the inextricable links between the past and present. Many of the sites are housed in the very structures in which blacks labored in the fields, and went into labor in the homes, and died; and in which wealthy whites dined and danced. And at the ideological level they reflect the connective tissue of the collective memory of the white South for the nostalgic days gone by, a memory that is partial, distorted, and biased. These sites attract a significant number of international visitors; they create jobs for local people, and help pay for them with funds from international sources. The Atlanta-based Olympics exemplifies this, but it is a regular occurrence at other times.

There are several contradictions one experiences during these visits. First, there is an almost palpable disjuncture between the social construction of the sites – beautifully laid-out, well-organized, preserved buildings, exquisite gardens, immaculately kept buildings – and the historical reality of the atrocities which were the basis of their coming into being. The overall construction today makes visitors feel physically comfortable, while the tours make them psychologically comfortable. Secondly, the majesty of the scenery at some sites is severely compromised by the juxtaposition of the house alongside contemporary structures – gigantic advertising boards, huge electricity pylons or (in the case of Nottoway) massive oil refineries – that punctuate the landscape immediately surrounding them. In this respect the sites appear that much more anachronistic. Finally, the sites themselves are irreducibly anachronistic, as in the way that extensive time periods of history are collapsed into one another, from room to room, to create coherence and good impressions. Collectively, the loquacity of such lack of fit speaks volumes to the many other silences that prevail.

Is it racism? Not in the old-fashioned sense. There is no formal expression of a belief in white superiority and black inferiority, no explicit hatred directed towards African Americans, no mention of the word "Nigger," no explicit praising of the Ku Klux Klan. Nor is there obvious derogation of Native Americans. But I believe it constitutes racialized hostility. Overall there is a level of symbolic hostility and a clear manifestation of superiority and distortion. These sites pretend to offer an accurate, even comprehensive, account of Southern history. The institution of slavery in all its atrocities, the suffering and exploitation of African Americans, the impressive resilience and resistance that they offerered, is depersonalized, marginalized, deflected, rendered secondary to the splendor and opulence of stately homes, the exuberant lifestyles of affluent whites, which is emphasized and articulated. In sum this is a society "gone with the wind." In this narrative it is the white South which is the victim, and the white North which is victimizer, as when the whites working to make uniforms for the Confederacy are imprisoned and dragged off to the North; or when the owners of impressive houses find them ransacked and burnt. Overall it is an affront to African Americans, one which at the same time pacifies and reassures White southerners. Earlier generations would call it institutional racism in its outcomes. I prefer to think of these museum-plantations as the sites of a racialized ideology.

If these sites are not motivated by racism, then by what? I believe it is an array of material, political, and psychological factors. These institutions seek to make a profit in an age in which national and global tourism is expanding exponentially. They seek to present the United States as a nation with an impressive architectural and cultural history, and the South as the backbone of that history (especially in comparison with Europe, in whose historical shadows the USA cowers). And they seek to assuage White southerners in particular, perhaps all whites in general, that slavery was not so bad for those who lived it, that the real victims were White southerners, and that the past houses many memories that one should be proud of.

An examination of these sites is important because it makes a contribution to the analysis of collective memory and the continuing racialization of US society. These sites are a concrete example of the connective links of the past and present, and of the local and the international, and they manifest all the aspects of racialization described in this chapter. They are a prime example of how ideologies are racialized even where race is not explicitly mentioned, and even where conscious, explicit racialized hostility is not intended. Such racialized ideologies cannot be reduced primarily to the motivations of political actors, or the actions of the state; they demonstrate that racialized ideologies

277

today continue to be shaped by a remarkable combination of factors, including economic profit, political gain, nostalgia, the evasion of guilt, as well as hostility to black people. It is particularly concerned with the symbolic dimensions of ideologies. Collectively they are a clear example of racialized hostility.

Conclusion

The institutional arrangements of contemporary American society are far more complex than in the past. Patterns of distribution of resources, power, and privilege are no longer allocated on the basis of laws, or explicit government and corporate institutional policies and actions, that privilege whites over people of color. Nor are the attitudes and actions of individuals towards people of color as explicitly stated as they used to be. Moreover, with the crude infrastructure of racism gone, and with the ubiquitous evidence of success by significant sections of communities of color, the prevailing discourse of equality and inequality has a "persuasiveness" that is resilient (Goldberg, 1990a:309). In this context a simple concept of racism no longer works. Earlier analyses of racism that suggested a monolithic "white racism" which was economically motivated, or predicated on beliefs of biological and cultural superiority, have given rise to an acknowledgment of varied types of racialized ideologies and discourses, shaped by increasingly complex sets of factors. The continuing disparities in resources that are evident across racialized groups, and the patterns of discrimination that sustain such disparities, cannot be explained primarily as the result of the conscious racist intentions of whites. Rather a combination of factors shapes them, including economic factors, political factors, sexism, and psychological needs. Better to look at all ideologies and explore the content, intent, and outcomes. This gives us a better handle on racialized hostility.

In this context I have argued that all social formations are thoroughly racialized, but not all are racist. We can draw a distinction between racialized and racist – this distinction being an empirical matter which must be investigated. Instead of thinking of racism, it is better to think of racisms and racialized hostility; and we should resist a definition of racism that is preoccupied with the content of an ideology alone. We must also think about addressing expressed intentionality, and thinking about the outcomes of intended and unintended institutional behavior. Collectively these can be seen as constituting the terrain of racialized hostility, of which racisms of various kinds (as sets of ideologies) are but a limited feature. Or, as Goldberg has argued elsewhere, "a very wide set of conditions, often quite different from one another, make up the range of racisms," and that means we should not expect racist expression to be clear and unequivocal; rather we must constantly explore exclusions, definitions, explanations, and rationalizations (Goldberg, 1993:103). It's clear, too, that we should have clear goals of the alternative institutional arrangements and discourses that might counter the consequences of past and present racism (Goldberg, 1990a:312; Small, 1994b).

This approach sees many links between the past and present, between local, national, and international contexts, and between race and other lines of stratification, including gender and class; these interact. I suggest that we focus on structures, institutions, ideologies, and consideration of content, intent, and outcome, with a concern for distinguishing harmony, integration, parity. All require empirical focus and research, which focuses on local contexts, but sees them as constituted by national and international forces.

Notes

1 I find that the label "slave master" invests a finality and legitimation to a relationship that was always challenged. This term offers a more accurate reflection of the contestation that was inevitably present under slavery. I am developing this approach in a manuscript currently being prepared on enslaved blacks and blacks of mixed origins (usually termed "mixed-race") in the Caribbean and the United States in the nineteenth century. As I shall argue in this chapter, it is necessary to be skeptical of much of the language that we use in our analyses.

2 I'm hesitant to call them scientists uncritically because none of them had the kind of scientific skills, technology, or resources that we associate with scientists today; many of them were competent in one broad area of science, say biology, but not in its application to human population variance; and because many of them simply falsified their findings (see Gossett, 1965).

3 Limitations of space require me to focus primarily on African Americans, though I believe that this analytical framework also applies to other racialized groups, with necessary attention to the historical, demographic, and cultural specificities of each group.

4. Montagu, 1972:158. For a brief history of these ideologies see Small, 1994c.

5 A "museum-plantation site" is a museum that is organized to exhibit artifacts and offer accounts of the history of slavery, and/or Southern society. It most frequently comprises the actual buildings used during the period of slavery. Museum-plantation sites can be public or private. There are several thousand of them throughout the 13 states which comprised the first colonies of what became the United States. The data reported here are from a larger collaborative program of research on sites across the entire South, but with a particular focus on Virginia, Louisiana, and Georgia, which is being carried out with Professor Jennifer Eichstedt of California State University, Humboldt.

6 I make this observation on the basis of observations at visits to over 100 sites, in eight states between 1996 and 1999. Similar observations have been made by my colleague, Jennifer Eichstedt, at the site visits she has undertaken.

References

Almaguer, Tomas (1994) *Racial Faultlines. The Historical Origins of White Supremacy in California.* Berkeley: University of California Press.

Amott, Teresa L. and Matthaei, Julie A. (1991) *Race, Gender and Work. A Multicultural Economic History of Women in the United States.* Boston, MA: Southend.

Ansell, Amy (1997) *New Right, New Racism. Race and Reaction in the United States and Britain.* New York: New York University Press.

Banton, Michael P. (1977) *The Idea of Race.* London: Tavistock.

Barker, Martin (1981) *The New Racism.* London: Junction Books.

Berg, Charles Ramirez (1997) "Stereotyping in films in general and of the Hispanic in particular," in Clara E. Rodriguez (ed.) *Latin Looks. Images of Latinas and Latinos in the U.S. Media.* Boulder, CO: Westview Press, pp.104–20.

Bhopal, Raj (1998) "Spectre of racism in health and health care: Lesson from history and the United States." *British Medical Journal* 316,7149:1970–3.

Carmichael, Stokeley and Hamilton, Charles V. (1967) *Black Power. The Politics of Liberation in America.* New York: Vintage Books.

Collins, Patricia Hill (1994) "Shifting the center: Race, class, and feminist theorizing about motherhood," in Evelyn Nakano Glenn, Grace Change, and Linda Rennie Forcey (eds.) *Mothering. Ideology, Experience, and Agency.* New York: Routledge, pp.45–65.

Cortes, Carlos E. (1997) "Chicanas in film: History of an image," in Clara E. Rodriguez (ed.) *Latin Looks. Images of Latinas and Latinos in the U.S. Media*. Boulder, CO: Westview Press, pp.121–41.

Darder, Antonia, Torres, Rodolfo D., and Gutierrez, Henry (1997) *Latinos and Education. A Critical Reader*. New York: Routledge.

Duster, Troy (1995) "The new crisis of legitimacy in controls, prisons and legal structures." *The American Sociologist* 26,1:20–9.

Feagin, Joe R. and Vera, Hernan (1995) *White Racism. The Basics*. New York: Routledge.

Gabriel, John (1998) *Whitewash. Racialized Politics and the Media*. London: Routledge.

Gandy, Oscar H. and Baron, Jonathan (1998) "Inequality: It's all the way you look at it." *Communication Research* 25,5:505–27.

Goldberg, David Theo (1990a) "The social formation of racist discourse," in David Theo Goldberg (ed.), *Anatomy of Racism*. Minneapolis: University of Minnesota Press, pp.295–318.

Goldberg, David Theo (ed.) (1990b) *Anatomy of Racism*. University of Minnesota Press, Minneapolis.

Goldberg, David Theo (1993) *Racist Culture. Philosophy and the Politics of Meaning*. Oxford: Blackwell.

Gossett, Thomas (1965) *Race. The History of an Idea in America*. New York: Schocken.

Guerrero, Ed (1993) *Framing Blackness. The African American Image in Film*. Philadelphia, PA: Temple University Press.

Hamamoto, Darrell Y. (1994) *Monitored Peril. Asian Americans and the Politics of TV Representation*. Minneapolis: University of Minnesota Press.

Hamamoto, Darrell and Torres, Rodolfo (eds.) (1997) *New American Destinies: A Reader in Contemporary Asian and Latino Immigration*. New York: Routledge.

Hawkins, Mike (1997) *Social Darwinism in European and American Thought, 1860–1945*. Cambridge, UK: Cambridge University Press.

Kovel, Joel (1971) *White Racism: A Psychohistory*. New York: Vintage Books.

Larson, Edward J. (1995) *Sex, Race and Science. Eugenics in the Deep South*. Baltimore, MD: The Johns Hopkins University Press.

Marable, Manning (1995) *Beyond Black and White*. London: Verso.

Massey, Douglas S. and Denton, Nancy A. (1993) *American Apartheid. Segregation and the Making of the Underclass*. Cambridge, MA: Harvard University Press.

Miles Robert (1982) *Racism and Migrant Labour*. London: Routledge & Kegan Paul.

Miles, Robert (1989) *Racism*. London: Routledge.

Montagu, Ashley (1972) *Statement on Race*. London: Oxford University Press.

Morrison, Toni (1992) *Playing in the Dark. Whiteness and the Literary Imagination*. New Haven, CT: Harvard University Press.

O'Hare, William P., Pollard, Kelvin M., Mann, Taynia L., and Kent, Mary M. (1991) *African Americans in the 1990s*. Washington, DC: Population Reference Bureau, 46, 1.

Oliver, Melvin L. and Shapiro, Thomas M. (1995) *Black Wealth, White Wealth. A New Perspective on Racial Inequality*. New York: Routledge.

Omi, Michael and Winant, Howard (1994) *Racial Formation in the United States. From the 1960s to the 1980s*. 2nd edn. London: Routledge.

Omi, Michael and Takagi, Dana (1996) "Situating Asian Americans in the political discourse on affirmative action." *Representations* 55:155–62.

Platt, Anthony M. (1997) "The land that never has been yet: U.S. race relations at the Crossroad." *Social Justice* 24,1:7–23.

Rodriguez, Clara E. (1997) *Latin Looks. Images of Latinas and Latinos in the U.S. Media*. Boulder, CO: Westview Press.

Small, Stephen (1994a) "Concepts and terminology in representations of the Atlantic slave trade." *Museum Ethnographers Journal* December: 1–14.

Small, Stephen. (1994b) *Racialised Barriers: The Black Experience in the United States and England*. New York: Routledge.

Small, Stephen (1994c) "Racist ideologies," in Anthony Tibbles (ed.) *Transatlantic Slavery. Against Human Dignity*. London: HMSO, pp.111–15.

Small, Stephen (1999) "The contours of racialization: Structures, representations and resistance in the United States," in Rodolfo D. Torres, Louis F. Miron, and Jonathan Xavier Inda (eds.) *Race, Identity, and Citizenship. A Reader*. Maldon, MA: Blackwell, pp.47–64.

Spickard, Paul (1989) *Mixed Blood: Intermarriage and Ethnic Identity in Twentieth-Century America*. Madison: University of Wisconsin Press.

Takaki, Ronald T. (1982) *Iron Cages. Race and Culture in 19th Century America*. Seattle: University of Washington Press.

Torres, Rodolfo D, Miron, Louis F. and Inda, Jonathan Xavier (1999) *Race, Identity, and Citizenship. A Reader*. Maldon, MA: Blackwell.

Williams, Eric (1944) *Capitalism and Slavery*. London: Andre Deutsch.

Wilson, William Julius (1978) *The Declining Significance of Race: Blacks and Changing American Institutions*. Chicago: University of Chicago Press.

Wilson, William Julius (1987) *The Truly Disadvantaged*. Chicago: University of Chicago Press.

Chapter 19

Affirmative Action as Culture War

Jennifer Hochschild

If one examines any collection of books or syllabi on the subject of affirmative action over the past 25 years, one observes two phenomena – a huge outpouring of legal and philosophical analyses of its merits and a paucity of empirical examinations of its mechanisms and effects.[1] The legal and philosophical analyses range from passionate assertions that quotas are essential in order to mitigate American racism, to equally fervent arguments that any racial or gender-based preference violates core American values of equality of personhood and opportunity. One can even find a few carefully nuanced intermediate positions that subtly distinguish among recipients, procedures, triggering circumstances, and the like (e.g., Appiah and Gutmann, 1996). Without denigrating the energy and creativity of many of these efforts, I believe it is fair to say that the core legal and philosophical positions were laid out in the first few years of this debate. With the exception of the recent claim about the intrinsic benefits of diversity for an organization, the succeeding volumes have mostly developed or elaborated upon these original claims.[2]

What We Don't Know About Affirmative Action

There are, in contrast, huge holes in the corpus of what we know about how affirmative action actually works in practice.[3] For example, we know very little about just how people are hired or admitted to most universities. When is race or gender a tie-breaker; when does minority status still count against the applicant; when are less-qualified African Americans or women hired/admitted over more qualified whites, Asians, or men; when does the reverse occur? Do certain kinds of professional schools or firms consistently treat affirmative action in ways different from that of other kinds of professional schools or firms? I know of virtually no research within and across nonelite university admissions offices, corporate personnel offices, professional schools' admissions offices, or police or fire departments that carefully traces these processes and analyzes them comparatively or theoretically.[4]

This is a revision of an article by the same name in *The Cultural Territories of Race:White and Black Boundaries*, ed. Michèle Lamont (Russell Sage Foundation Press and University of Chicago Press, 1999).

What happens after a person is hired or admitted in circumstances where affirmative action is presumed to have played a role? Do blacks or white women feel stigmatized, inferior, insecure? If so, do they overcompensate by rigidity or racial paranoia or timidity? Do they feel any more insecure than, for example, alumni children admitted to universities as legacies, or white working-class athletes admitted to bolster Big Ten football teams, or the boss's nephew put in charge of the front office? Alternatively, if they do feel insecure or are stigmatized, are they able to overcome their initial obstacles and succeed at about the same rate as other workers or students? What are the processes by which people who are initially labeled as "affirmative action hires" move toward success or failure; do they have more to do with internal fortitude, organizational culture, structural opportunities, or what? Do some contexts facilitate success or reify stigma more than others? Again, there are very few careful and systematic studies of co-workers' interactions and corporate or university practices in which affirmative action is a central part of the organizational context.

Another set of questions: how many whites or men are told by admissions officers or personnel directors that they would have been hired/admitted if it were not for affirmative action pressures? After all, that is an easy and mutually gratifying response from a gatekeeper to an angry or disappointed candidate – and to many such candidates in a row, so long as each is addressed in the absence of the others. An example: one man reported on an e-mail list his stellar undergraduate record and his admission to several excellent law schools, but with little funding. "At least three admissions counselors stated outright, and others implied, that had I been anything but white male and had those numbers [GPA, LSAT scores etc.], I would've been immediately full-ride plus living expenses" (Finley, 1996). If his experience occurs frequently, that would explain why so many more whites than is arithmetically possible believe that they or someone they know about was denied a job or promotion because of affirmative action. (See my discussion of survey results below.) But to my knowledge, no one has conducted research on how affirmative action is presented to nonminorities denied jobs or admission or promotion.

We know very little about how minority set-asides for contracts work. Conventional wisdom holds that the process is corrupt, with the most common allegation being that an African American (or woman of any race) is used as a "front" for predominantly white (or white male) owners of a firm (for example, see Oreskes, 1984). How often does that occur? Why cannot those who grant contracts find out about it? Do they try? Conversely, how often do minority set-asides function as they were presumably intended to – giving a start to a firm headed by a woman and/or person of color who would not otherwise be able to find clients or win contracts due to racial or gender stereotypes? How and when does that more positive dynamic work, and what distinguishes successful from unsuccessful firms once set-asides are in place? Some analysts have begun to answer these questions, but the disproportion between assertion and knowledge is enormous (House Government Operations Committee, 1994; Bates and Williams, 1996; Enchautegui et al., 1996; Myers and Chan, 1996).

Broader political research would also be useful. Why did affirmative action surface as an especially "hot" political issue in 1995, given that white men (and to a lesser degree, white women) have always disliked strong versions of it (Bennett et al., 1995: tables 2, 3)? Conversely, why haven't corporations, universities, most political candidates, and city governments jumped on the antiaffirmative action bandwagon? Do they see benefits in affirmative action policies that they would not be able to attain absent an apparently coercive governmental mandate? (An analogy here might be school superintendents who welcomed judicial decisions mandating desegregation because the mandate allowed them to make changes in the school system that were otherwise politically too difficult.)[5] Why has there been an antiaffirmative action referendum only in two states (California and Washington) and one city (Houston) so far?[6] How should we understand the conflicting views of affirmative action held by white women and Asians?[7]

Broader historical research would similarly be illuminating. In the 1960s, as Stephen Carter (1991) reminds us, many on the left saw affirmative action as an individualistic sell-out. In their view, affirmative action encouraged personal mobility of the most energetic, articulate, and effective actors within a racial or gender group at the expense of structural transformation that would benefit the whole group. Regardless of whether it was right or wrong, what happened to that view? Why did support for affirmative action move from being a relatively right-wing position (President Nixon established the Philadelphia plan partly to give more blacks a stake in the extant economic system, and endorsed set-asides in order to encourage black capitalism) to being a relatively left-wing position over the past 30 years? Conversely, why hasn't the political right embraced affirmative action as a classic case of sponsored mobility, a process of carefully and selectively admitting a few outsiders into the elite and defusing the claims of the rest?

Who is eligible for affirmative action in various locations and venues, and why? In Richmond, Virginia, for example, the city's set-aside program covered Hispanics, "Orientals," American Indians, Eskimos, and Aleuts as well as blacks; as Justice O'Connor pointed out in *Croson*, "there is absolutely no evidence of past discrimination against" members of most of these groups; "it may well be that Richmond has never had an Aleut or Eskimo citizen."[8] When are women treated as a distinct class, and why? Do they receive different (better? worse?) treatment under employers' affirmative action guidelines than African Americans, or Hispanics, for example? Who decides about cases of mixed or ambiguous racial or ethnic identity, and to what effect?

I could list other arenas in which empirical research about the processes and effects of affirmative action are scarce or missing, but the point should be clear: Americans' elaborate and sophisticated legal and normative debate about the legitimacy, desirability, and impact of affirmative action has until very recently taken place in something close to a factual vacuum.

That might not be surprising in the political arena – after all, debates in Congress about abortion funding, illegal immigration, the effects of nuclear fallout, intervention in Kosovo, and other highly controversial issues, often ignore what evidence exists, or occur in the absence of much evidence at all. Such ignorance might not even be always inappropriate; elected officials and judges must sometimes make decisions regardless of whether they know enough about the choices confronting them. Similarly, the relative paucity of empirical knowledge might not be disconcerting to advocacy groups. Advocates of a particular policy position – whether support or opposition to affirmative action, nuclear disarmament, abortion rights, or something else – either are not primarily motivated by empirical considerations, or believe that they know enough facts or the right facts in order to espouse their position with confidence.

But the disproportion between legal and philosophical analysis on the one hand, and empirical analysis on the other, *is* inappropriate in the academy. Social scientists *do*, one normally assumes, believe that knowledge – about how processes work, what effects policy innovations have, how historical and institutional contexts affect behaviors and outcomes – matters. But except for a few crucial exceptions, mostly buried in scholarly journals or legal briefs, they have not expended much effort on empirical analyses of affirmative action.[9] Why not? And what does the relative paucity of research compared with argumentation tell us about the policy of affirmative action, the cultural context of American racial and gender politics, and – most broadly – the ideology of the American dream?[10]

My argument, in brief, is the following: in the current American racial culture, affirmative action is more important to participants in the policy debate as a weapon with which to attack enemies in order to win some other battle than as an issue in and for itself. To be useful as a weapon, affirmative action must remain at the level of moral claims and single-dimensional outrage; the messy and complex realities that are likely to surface in careful empirical analyses do not help much in political and cultural warfare.[11] This phenomenon is as true in the university as in the explicitly political realm, because most scholars do not pursue the traditional objective of scholarly neutrality in the arena of racial politics and policy choices. To put it most succinctly, the debate over affirmative action is predominantly a culture war over who is an American and what it means to be a good American, and only secondarily a dispute between political parties or policy analysts over how best to improve the status of African Americans or women.

I do not make this assertion only to deplore it, although I will do some of that below. Nor do I claim that the culture war over affirmative action is unique; on issues ranging from a national bank in the 1830s to communists in the State Department in the 1950s, Americans have always become passionately concerned about social "crises" that in fact matter little to their daily lives.[12] Instead, I want to explore the culture war over affirmative action for a more analytic reason: comparing what we believe about affirmative action with what we know and what we have chosen not to find out tells us a great deal about Americans' hopes, fears, and self-images.

What Do We Know About Affirmative Action?

There has been, of course, some excellent empirical research on the subject of affirmative action (almost all of which has appeared only in esoteric professional journals or in unpublished legal briefs).[13] A review of what it tells us will begin to substantiate my claim about the symbolic functions of the debate over affirmative action.[14]

To begin with, a few solid historical analyses of the development and implementation of affirmative action policy have been published (Burstein, 1985; Graham, 1999; Skrentny, 1996). With one clear exception (Skrentny), these analyses seldom address the issue of "why affirmative action?" and "why at a given historical moment?" Instead, their main burden has been to demonstrate that federal policy was in fact effective. That is, once federal officials, especially several presidents in a row beginning with Lyndon Johnson, decided to endorse affirmative action and develop an institutional structure to implement and enforce the policy, it happened. Graham (but not the other historians of affirmative action) even argues, roughly, that the federal government was *too* effective in the sense that affirmative action policy created an elaborate system of social regulation by bureaucrats and courts that is now unresponsive to public wishes, excessively interventionist, and counterproductive.

Thus affirmative action was encouraged, or at least not halted, by both conservative Republican presidents (Nixon, Reagan, Bush) and liberal Democratic ones (Johnson, Carter, Clinton). Federal laws and executive orders to foster or mandate affirmative action could have been reversed, but were not, when both houses of Congress were controlled by Republicans (or by Democrats); they could have been declared unconstitutional, but were not, when the Supreme Court was dominated by either liberal or conservative activists. The historical record is one of growth and persistence, with considerable trimming (especially of business set-asides) and usually more lip service than effort – but without rejection of its core mission – at the federal level (Rice and Mongkuo, 1998; Leadership Conference on Civil Rights, 1997:2; Anderson, 1996). Thus with a few exceptions, conservative opponents have not fought hard to eliminate affirmative action when they might have succeeded; that is the first suggestion of a gap between rhetoric and practice among policy actors and advocates purportedly on the same side of the issue.

A little research provides evidence about the economic effects of affirmative action policies on African Americans (and/or white women) and on the corporations that hire them (Leonard, 1984a, 1984b, 1986, 1990; Heckman and Wolpin, 1976; Heckman and Payner, 1989; Badgett and Hartmann, 1995; Holzer and Neumark, 1999; Holzer, 1998; Rodgers and Spriggs, 1996). Aggregate analyses of employment suggest that affirmative action did target blacks during the 1970s, and that it contributed to the creation of a substantial black middle class that has persisted over the succeeding three decades.[15] Thus federal regulations not only institutionalized the initial policy but also produced the desired outcomes, at least to some degree.[16] Affirmative action did not, moreover, target only those already well-educated or in the middle-income brackets; its initial effects were greatest for people in unskilled and semiskilled job categories (Leonard, 1984b).[17] There is no evidence that affirmative action policies have harmed productivity of participating firms (Leonard, 1984c).[18]

The same story appears to hold for university admissions. During the 1980s, the most selective four-year colleges were most likely to admit African American and Hispanic students preferentially. In nonelite schools, which 80 percent of college students attend, students of different races with similar characteristics were admitted at essentially the same rate (Kane, 1998). Elite colleges were not harmed by their energetic affirmative action practices; by the end of the decade, their tuition had risen disproportionately compared with other universities', as had the number of students applying for admission.[19]

For universities as for firms, individual participants as well as the institution appear to gain from being associated with affirmative action. Attending a high-quality school yields higher earnings in adulthood, even after controlling for family background and school achievement; studies even show higher payoffs to blacks than to whites of attending an elite school (Brewer et al., 1999; Kane, 1998; Daniel et al., 1995; Bowen and Bok, 1998). Thus affirmative action beneficiaries at elite universities did indeed benefit, to no apparent detriment to their fellow white students.[20]

Affirmative action was not, however, the most important factor in decreasing the racial wage gap between the 1960s and 1980s. Enforcement of laws against employment discrimination, as well as increasing educational attainment and achievement among blacks, did more (Heckman and Verkerke, 1990; Leonard, 1990; Smith and Welch, 1984, 1989). During the 1980s, when enforcement of federal affirmative action regulations was all but halted and there was no demonstrable aggregate impact of affirmative action policy, the wage gap between fully employed blacks and whites fluctuated, but did not fundamentally change (Farley, 1996:249; see also Leonard, 1986).

Thus analyses of firms and universities, while thin, suggest several results: when implemented with at least a little pressure for compliance, affirmative action has had slight positive effects on beneficiary groups and no discernible negative effects on employers or colleges. When all pressure for compliance disappears, affirmative action mostly disappears. Even at its strongest, affirmative action has had less impact on racial wage inequality than have the much less controversial policies of improving educational attainment and achievement and enforcing the law against employment discrimination.

Another small arena of empirical research encompasses psychological experiments (Clayton and Crosby, 1992; Crocker et al., 1991; Steele, 1999; Nacoste, 1985, 1994; Blanchard and Crosby, 1989; *Basic and Applied Social Psychology*, 1994). Results from these experiments are important, but so far do not move much beyond a demonstration of common sense. If people are told that affirmative action has influenced their attainment of a position, they devalue the position or their performance – more so if they disapprove of affirmative action to begin with or if it was described as playing a central role, and less so if they see the apparent authority as racially biased. White women feel more demeaned by "unwarranted help" than do African Americans, who are more likely to see affirmative action as an entitlement. Co-workers may change their initial judgment that a new black manager is incompetent if he demonstrates that he is not or if they want to help him succeed. African Americans perform less well than they are capable of if they believe that they are underqualified compared with white students, but must nevertheless uphold the honor of their race. In short, affirmative action may or may not have harmful psychological and interpersonal effects, depending on who is involved, how the policy is deployed, and the context within which it is deployed – extremely useful knowledge, but hardly grounds for passion in either defense or opposition.

Another arena of scattered but important research findings treats the organizational effects of affirmative action (Kelly and Dobbin, 1998; Dobbin et al., 1993; Edelman, 1990, 1992; Sutton et al., 1994; Konrad and Linnehan, 1995). Since the laws and executive orders creating affirmative action did not detail concrete compliance mechanisms, managers have constructed a wide variety of practices and structures. "Personnel professionals, in particular, saw opportunities in these new areas of law and promoted responses that would expand their power and numbers" (Dobbin, 1996). The elaborate array of rules, offices, grievance procedures, plans, tests, and other mechanisms has come to have a life of its own; "over time, these structures, more than any particular substantive result, tend to be equated with compliance" (Edelman, 1996). Forms of affirmative action that comport with the economic goals of a corporation – such as "diversity" for certain firms or in certain markets – become part of the corporate culture and are thereby domesticated. They neither disrupt conventional practices of hiring and promotion very much, nor do they generate much opposition. If anything, many executives and managers strongly support affirmative action *as they understand it* for several reasons: they believe that they are doing something socially productive, they believe that if properly handled "diversity" can increase their profits, and they are not paying high costs for endorsing affirmative action (Thomas and Ely, 1996; Cox and Blake, 1991; Badgett, 1995). Again, there are few grounds for intense defense or opposition here.

The very small amount of aggregate data available shows no evidence that affirmative action creates a sense of stigma or inferiority in its recipients. African Americans in firms that have affirmative action programs are at least as happy in their jobs as African Americans in firms that do not. The former demonstrate greater occupational ambition and are more likely to believe that people are helpful than the latter (Taylor, 1994; Blanchard and Crosby, 1989). Blacks who believe that affirmative action played a part in their hiring or promotion have no less confidence in their ability to do their job than do other workers (Hochschild, 1995:98–102, 290–2).

Surveys of public opinion offer the most fully developed research arena (Kinder and Sanders, 1996; Pettigrew and Martin, 1987; Bobo and Kluegel, 1993; Bobo and Smith, 1994; Gamson and Modigliani, 1987; Sniderman and Piazza, 1993; Kluegel and Smith, 1983; Schuman et al., 1997; Bobo, 1998). Surveys provide several results crucial to my claim that the debate over affirmative action is more symbolic than substantive. About a third of white Americans cannot make any association with the phrase "affirmative action" (Steeh and Krysan, 1996:129).[21] Those who do have an opinion on the topic (most of whom presumably have some idea of what it means), produce more consensus than one would imagine possible if one listened solely to the political activists and news media.

Although about three-fourths of white Americans consistently agree that blacks should "work their way up ... without any special favors," so do about half of black Americans. Although 85 percent or more of whites endorse "ability" rather than "preferential treatment" to determine who gets jobs and college slots, so do about three-fifths of blacks. Conversely, fully seven in ten whites (compared with over eight in ten African Americans) favor affirmative action programs "provided there are no rigid quotas." Solid majorities in both races endorse special job training and educational assistance for women and people of color, extra efforts to identify and recruit qualified minorities, redrawing of voting districts to ensure minority representation, and other "soft" forms of affirmative action (Steeh and Krysan, 1996; see also Gallup Organization, 1995). One quarter of those who voted for California's referendum banning affirmative action in 1996 would have preferred a "mend it, don't end it" option (Lempinen, 1996).

If one can trust survey data, then, it seems possible to develop a workable political consensus around some "soft" affirmative action policies. African Americans and Latinos will always support these policies more strongly than will whites, and women will support them somewhat more strongly than will men. But that is no different from the pattern of support for any policy measure that benefits some citizens more than or at the expense of others. The likelihood of different levels of enthusiasm does not stop politicians and policy planners from initiating new laws and regulations, so long as they can forge a set of rules that some people strongly endorse and most can tolerate. There might be such a set of rules to be found within the wide range of possibilities for affirmative action policy, if the troops would declare a truce in the culture war long enough to move warily toward a no-man's-land in the center.

Other survey data, however, suggest caution; this no-man's-land will be safely occupied only if perceptions of affirmative action are brought more closely into line with its practice. Relatively few whites (under 10 percent) claim to have been harmed by the workings of affirmative action policy. Nevertheless, more (up to 20 percent) claim to know someone who has been so harmed, and still more (30 to 40 percent) claim to have heard about someone who was so harmed. Up to 80 percent of whites believe it likely that a white will lose a job or promotion to a less-qualified black due to affirmative action. One third of whites think affirmative action programs frequently "deprive someone . . . of their rights," and half of white youth (compared with one-fifth of black youth) think that more whites lose out to blacks due to "special preference" than blacks lose to whites due to prejudice (Hochschild, 1995:144, 308; Steeh and Krysan, 1996:139–40).

Unless they define affirmative action as any situation in which an African American bests a white, regardless of why, these survey respondents are wrong. In 1994, only 2 percent of 641 government contractors polled complained of quotas or reverse discrimination. Of the more than 3,000 discrimination cases to reach courts between 1990 and 1994, fewer than 100 charged reverse discrimination; most of those, like most claims about any kind of discrimination, were dismissed due to lack of merit (Stephanopoulos and Edley, 1995: Sec. 6.3; Blumrosen, 1995). Possibly political correctness inhibits firms from complaining about quotas, and perhaps white men suffer under the same constraint when they consider bringing charges of reverse discrimination. But surely a strong legal case would sweep aside those hypothesized constraints at least sometimes. Thus it seems safe to conclude that many more people are exercised by fears of the policy of affirmative action than are harmed by its implementation. *If* views about affirmative action are subject to rational consideration (a large "if," and one which I dispute over the next few pages), then wide dissemination of information about who actually benefits from or is harmed by affirmative action would be an essential component of finding a workable middle position.

I have saved until last any discussion of the central exception to my complaint about the paucity of empirical studies of affirmative action. Bowen and Bok's *The Shape of the River* is a very important work, both for its arguments themselves and because it is so unusual in this field. It confirms some of the critics' fears; many African-American students who attend elite colleges and universities do indeed enter with lower test scores and exit nearer the bottom than the top of their class. But it does more to confirm the supporters' hopes: the more selective the school they attend, the better black students do in the short and long runs; white as well as black students value and benefit from racial diversity; black students are not paralyzed by insecurity, and black alumnae contribute importantly to their communities. The authors themselves, of course, are not neutral observers of the policy but they have striven – mostly successfully – to engage in serious social science research rather than in polemics. Responses have also been politically influenced, but they too have enhanced the discussion by reporting countervailing data of their own. Overall, *The Shape of the River* reinforces my basic points – that the consequences of affirmative action are mixed, like those of most complex policies, that it is possible to do solid research on the subject, and that there are a huge number of unexamined questions remaining.

Affirmative Action as Cultural Warfare

Unfortunately, many people's views about affirmative action are not subject to rational consideration, any more than people could be persuaded to think coolly about the "monster bank" or communism. If people did think about affirmative action by weighing its costs against its benefits, passions would not run so high. After all, the research record gives complete warrant to neither the hopes of supporters nor the fears of opponents.

The policy has certainly aided specific individuals applying to elite colleges (Bowen and Bok, 1998) and professional schools or to middle-level public service jobs (Collins, 1983, 1997). It has arguably harmed those who would have been admitted or hired absent affirmative action (Lynch 1989; Taylor 1991). It may even have simultaneously helped *and* harmed a few people (Carter, 1991; Steele, 1999; Clayton and Crosby, 1992). It has had great impact on police and fire departments, on a few law and medical schools, and on the Army. But compared to legislation and litigation against employment discrimination or barriers to voting and office-holding, or desegregation of schools, affirmative action has had relatively little aggregate impact. And it has, perhaps, benefited professional personnel officers and attorneys more than any other single group of people.

We face therefore two puzzles. Why are a lot of people so exercised over this particular policy, which distributes outcomes about as most other policies do and which has done less to change American racial hierarchies than have a variety of other less controversial policies? And why is the empirical base for understanding the practice and effects of affirmative action so thin and in most cases publicly invisible compared with the rich philosophical and legal arguments that the issue has evoked?

These two puzzles are both resolved by one answer: political actors find affirmative action an immensely valuable issue over which to debate, and therefore have little desire to figure out just how it operates. That is, affirmative action is too precious as a political weapon in a broader cultural war about what America stands for to be blunted by attention to real-life complexities.

Many opponents of affirmative action are less concerned with the policy *per se* than with a wider assertion that racial (or gender) discrimination no longer exists, and that African Americans' continued claims of its persistence are merely whining or self-seeking. At their crudest, opponents are racially hostile. Less crudely, they are unable or unwilling to see structural barriers or institutional advantages that are independent of individual intentions or awareness. The most sophisticated opponents are more concerned about class or individual, rather than racial or gender, barriers (Lind, 1995; Woodson, 1996), or they judge the costs of a continued focus on racial differences to be too great now that the black middle class is fairly well-established (Sleeper, 1997) Gitlin, 1995), or they judge that laws and regulations against employment discrimination are strong enough to take care of the remaining racial bias in jobs (James Heckman, personal communication with the author, 1997). Alternatively, they espouse a principle of individual meritocracy which supersedes caveats or shadings (Glazer, 1975; Eastland, 1996; Thernstrom and Thernstrom, 1997).

Many proponents of affirmative action demonstrate an equal but opposite dynamic. They are less concerned with the policy *per se* than with a wider assertion that racial (or gender) discrimination is just as virulent as it has always been, and that whites' opposition is merely covert racism or inexcusable naivete (Preston and Lai, 1998; Motley, 1998). At their crudest, proponents are paranoid or self-seeking. Less crudely they believe, as one of my students put it, that blacks have just as much right to a class structure as whites do and just as much right to use all means legally available to reach the top of it. The most sophisticated proponents see affirmative action as a means for individual blacks to overcome persistent racism and attain resources that will help the African American community and the nation as a whole to overcome its shameful past – DuBois's talented tenth (Rosenfeld, 1991). Alternatively, they see employment discrimination (or biases in universities' admissions policies) as sufficiently subtle as well as widespread that standard laws and litigation are insufficient. In this view, people of color and/or white women must be inserted into the core of the hiring/promotion/admissions processes in order to identify and bring to justice persistent hidden biases that work on behalf of white men (Bergmann, 1996; Edley, 1996; Reskin, 1998).

Political elites within these groups do not talk to one another and have no electoral, social, or organizational incentive to do so. Legally, they each have a rich set of court cases, laws, and regulations to bolster their claims. Normatively, each group has available to it more philosophical justifications for its position than anyone can possibly read or use. Historically, each group can point to its preferred victories and defeats. Politically, each group has a core constituency and a wider set of citizens to whom it can turn for occasional support. Organizationally, each group has well-established but complex and constantly renegotiated (thus energy-draining) internal ties of communication, bargaining, and resource extraction to maintain. Socially, members of the two groups seldom encounter one another outside of formal, scripted disputes. Neither group has, in short, much reason or incentive to question its own position or give serious consideration to the other's.[22]

Academic research does not fit very clearly anywhere in this picture, which may explain why there has been so little of it compared with argumentation that is not empirically based. That is unfortunate for at least two reasons. First, some fascinating research questions are so far left untouched. Second, in my view only reasonably dispassionate analyses could provide the possibility of intellectual space for people to separate their broad beliefs about the role of race in America from their particular judgments about the efficacy of affirmative action compared with other possible routes to racial equality. Only if there is a cohort of people who can persuasively say, "it works in this regard but not in that one ..." or "it works better than X but not as well as Y to achieve goal Z ..." have we as a nation any chance to get past the shouting.[23]

Why have advocates on all sides of the debate over American racial policy seized on affirmative action rather than, for example, wage discrimination or the quality of schooling in inner cities as the battleground for deciding what race means in the United States today? After all, affirmative action neither affects many whites nor comes close to solving the deepest problems of African Americans. So why is it "the highest pole in the storm"?[24] Partly because opposition to affirmative action is one of the few remaining respectable vehicles for seeking to maintain white domination. No public figure can any longer argue, as one could 50 years ago, in favor of lesser schooling for black children or different wages for the same work based on one's gender and race.[25] In that sense, "ascriptive Americanism" lost the public debate to liberalism in the last third of the twentieth century (Smith, 1997). But even if part of one's motivation is to resist black competitive success, one *can* oppose affirmative action in the name of values that all Americans publicly claim to share (see Hochschild, 1995: chapter 7, on white opposition to black competitive success).

Opposition to affirmative action remains respectable because both sides to this dispute call on Americans' deepest and most cherished values (often the same value, in fact). The set of values most closely associated with passion about affirmative action can be characterized as the American dream. The ideology of the American dream is the promise that all Americans, regardless of their race, sex, or background, can reasonably anticipate the attainment of some success, if they use means under their own control such as talent, ambition, and hard work. The pursuit of success is associated with virtue, and so can legitimately be seen as noble and elevating, rather than merely materialistic or selfish (Hochschild, 1995). The ideology implies a balanced contract between the public sector and private individuals. The government is expected to provide equality of opportunity – thus no discrimination by race, gender, class, or religion – and a structure that makes anticipation of success reasonable – thus a strong system of public education, a flourishing economy with plenty of jobs, physical security from enemies without and crime within the nation. Citizens, in turn, are expected to act within that framework to take care of themselves – to attain skills, support themselves and their families, refrain from discrimination or false claims of victimization, and follow a moral code.

Most Americans believe in each component of the American dream and most share an implicit conviction that the balance between governmental and personal responsibility is about right (Hochschild, 1995: chapter 1). Hence the United States lacks strong libertarian and Marxist political parties, as well as widespread white racist or black nationalist social movements. But, partly because their shared convictions are so strong, Americans contend fiercely over just how to translate those convictions into concrete practice.

To some, the American dream is necessarily individualist. The ideology is intended to create a structure within which each person can rise or fall according to his or her merit alone. Some individualists reluctantly support affirmative action on the grounds that it is a necessary way station on the path from racial domination to race-blind individualism. But most see affirmative action as a denial of the deepest tenets of the American dream, since in their eyes it gives special privileges to some at the expense of others. The government formerly discriminated in favor of whites, and now it discriminates in favor of blacks – those are equal violations of the ideology of the American dream and they should be equally prohibited.

To others, the American dream is not necessarily individualist. The ideology can be just as well interpreted to mean that *groups* have the right to pursue success collectively. Until a group succeeds according to its members' own shared vision, the individuals within it cannot attain their dreams (alternatively, the pursuit of group success shapes and directs individuals' dreams). In the eyes of those committed to group identity as a defining characteristic of social engagement, prior (or current) discrimination in favor of whites is not symmetrical with current proactive efforts to benefit blacks. Until the two races are equal in political power, economic means, social status, and cultural autonomy, equality of opportunity does not exist in the United States and calls for symmetry are a mere pretence for continued domination.

Just as principled opposition to affirmative action may reinforce or be a cover for a desire to retain white racial domination, principled support for affirmative action may similarly reinforce a desire to use public policies to benefit oneself or one's group. After all, Americans (like most other humans, probably) have historically shown themselves adept at making normative arguments that coincide with their self-interest. There is no reason to suppose that middle-class African Americans are any different from anyone else in this regard.

Thus some Americans see strong forms of affirmative action as violating the values of individualism, equal opportunity, and meritocracy that instantiate the American dream. Some of them may have less respectable grounds for opposition that merge with those values. Others see strong forms of affirmative action as the only lever available to pry open the hypocritical claim of purported equality but actual racial domination that characterizes "Amerikkka."[26] Some of them too may have other, less publicly compelling, reasons for support that merge with their understanding of the American dream.

Where self-interest and ideology coincide so powerfully and in two such directly opposed camps, nuanced views do not flourish.

The clash between contending sets of interests and values is exacerbated by a growing perceptual gap between the races. On the one hand, the best-off African Americans – those best poised to take advantage of the opportunities that affirmative action offers – increasingly distrust white Americans' racial values and practices. In the 1960s, poorly educated blacks were more likely than well-educated blacks to agree that "whites want to keep blacks down"; by the 1980s, the positions of the two groups were reversed (Hochschild, 1995:74). In 1990 and again in 1996, well-educated blacks agreed more than did poorly educated blacks that "the Government deliberately makes sure that drugs are easily available in poor black neighborhoods in order to harm black people" (Hochschild, 1995:74 and analyses of *New York Times*/CBS News survey of October 13, 1996, in possession of author).[27] Given a perception of intransigent and even growing white racism in the United States, affirmative action becomes a crucial weapon in well-off African Americans' arsenal (Hochschild, 1995: chapters 4–7; Bositis, 1997; Gallup Organization, 1997).

On the other hand, whites are increasingly convinced that racial discrimination is declining, and that blacks no longer suffer much from the effects of previous discrimination. In 1995, 55 percent of whites (compared with 29 percent of blacks) mistakenly agreed that "the average African American" is as well off as or better off than "the average white person" in terms of jobs and education. Over 40 percent of whites (and about 20 percent of blacks) held the same mistaken view with regard to housing and income (*Washington Post* et al., 1995). By the 1990s a majority of whites typically agreed that blacks have equal or greater opportunities than do whites to get ahead generally, to attain an education, to be admitted to college, and to get a job (Hochschild, 1995:60–64, Appendix B). They see the existence of the new black middle class as evidence to support that perception. And given that 15 percent of whites agree with the very strong statement that "almost all of the gains made by blacks in recent years have come at the expense of whites," it is especially striking that the "average American" estimates up to one-third of Americans to be black and one-fifth to be Latino (the real figures are 12 percent and 9 percent) (Hochschild, 1995:143; Gallup and Newport, 1990; Nadeau et al., 1993; *Washington Post* et al., 1995: table 1.1).

Thus for some whites as well as for some middle-class blacks, perceptions unite with interests and values to create passionate convictions about affirmative action, regardless of whether it "works" or not. No wonder there is a culture war over an issue that directly affects only a small fraction of the American population.

Is There an Escape from the Impasse?

I noted earlier a broad band of rough consensus in the survey data – quotas or preferences are bad (the Supreme Court agrees) but extra efforts to identify and train people who have been disadvantaged by race or gender is good (the Supreme Court agrees here also). That is a workable starting point for designing a policy that could achieve many of the purposes of affirmative action without generating so much hostility – if people are susceptible to compromise on this issue.[28]

Even those who voted for California's Proposition 209 in the November 1996 election were not all strongly opposed to affirmative action, and even those who voted against it were not all strongly supportive. A Field Poll conducted several days after the vote found that fewer than half of opponents agreed that "affirmative action policies should not be changed." A third of the opponents further agreed that "affirmative action policies should be relaxed somewhat." Conversely, about a quarter of the proposition's supporters agreed that affirmative action policies should not be changed, or should be relaxed but not eliminated (Lempinen, 1996). Some of these voters may simply have been confused about what they were voting for. But many apparently would have preferred a middle ground to the two stark alternatives they were offered. Similarly, 65 percent of respondents to a national survey the day of the 1996 presidential election hoped that President Clinton would "put more emphasis on affirmative action to improve educational and job opportunities for women and minorities" in a second term ("Clinton's Second Term" 1996:1). In Houston, Texas, 55 percent of the voters in November 1997 rejected a proposition that would have banned "affirmative action" in city contracting and hiring (Verhovek, 1997b).[29] In all of these cases, we see the glimmering of a political context in which citizens' opinions on affirmative action could come to stand for something other than racism or denial of meritocracy.

Similarly, many public officials and corporate officers seem wiser than either the activists or the academics. They focus more on the actual workings of affirmative action than the latter, and they find affirmative action more manipulable and less revolutionary (for better or for worse) than the former (Wolfe, 1996; Hochschild, 1998). Local public officials find that appointing a few well-connected black advocates has symbolic as well as substantive pay-offs in the next election. Corporate managers find that affirmative action has shifted from a pesky problem to a core management tool. A decade ago, problems of "equal employment opportunity" came in almost last (just above sexual harassment) on a list of executives' "human-resource management issues"; by 1992, "cultural diversity" led corporate executives' list of "workforce concerns." Almost two-thirds of companies surveyed by the Conference Board in 1991 offered diversity training to their employees, and most of the rest planned to do so soon (Schein, 1986; Towers Perrin, 1992:3; Wheeler, 1994:9; Glater and Hamilton, 1995). The Conference Board now promotes conferences and publishes reports on "Managing Diversity for Sustaining Competitiveness" (Conference Board, 1997).

We have, then, an electorate and many public and private officials who apparently seek a middle ground of "extra help" but not "reverse discrimination," faced with a paired set of fiercely vocal activists who portray their opposites as either racist or un-American. For the former group, affirmative action is a policy with virtues and defects, appropriate interpretations and outrageous distortions – much like any other policy. Its members have little use for academic analyses of the policy, but for the same reason that they have little use for academic analyses of virtually all policies; scholars are too slow, too methodologically driven, or too attuned to deep structures rather than useable facts. For the latter group, affirmative action is a symbol of deep racial claims and anxieties. Its members too have no use for empirical evidence, not because they find scholars irrelevant (often they are themselves scholars), but because the most careful analyses show that affirmative action seldom has dramatic impact, whether positive or negative, and that it frequently has unintended and ironic consequences.

At the most general level, affirmative action serves as a litmus test for anxieties about the meaning and validity of the American dream. Many African Americans fear, perhaps rightly, that the American dream was never meant to include them and can never be wrenched from its historical role of enabling some white men to legitimately dominate all other residents of the United States. In their eyes affirmative action instantiates a new and more sympathetic interpretation of the nation's core ideology. It is also one of the only levers available to pry apart the tightly linked chains of meritocratic beliefs, personalistic practices, and structural biases in favor of the well-off. Many whites (especially but not only men) fear, perhaps rightly, that the American dream is losing its hold on Americans' moral imagination. They see affirmative action as the tempter leading people to believe that what they *do* does not matter as much as who they *are*. For both groups, the devil is at the gate, and affirmative action is implicated in the defense of the city. Under these circumstances, we should not be surprised that evidence on how it actually works is irrelevant to all except those who have to put the policy into practice and live with the results.

Acknowledgment

My thanks for comments on an earlier version of this article to Marianne Engelman Lado, Amy Gutmann, Luke Harris, Ira Katznelson, Michèle Lamont, Dale Miller, John Skrentny, Alan Wolfe, and the participants in various seminars at Princeton University.

Notes

1   For example, Edley (1996) devotes 12 of the 280 text pages of his book to "facts" about America's racial situation (and of them, only three pages address the effectiveness of affirmative action policies). A special issue on affirmative action of the National Council for Research on Women (1996) devotes one of its 12 substantive pages to "the evidence." The main counter-evidence to my claim is, of course, *The Shape of the River* by William Bowen and Derek Bok. I will discuss it below; for now, it is important to note only that it was published fairly recently (1998), that it was *not* written by research scholars as that term is usually understood, and that it stands out as a dramatic and unique exception to the circumstances I describe in the text.

2   The past decade and a half has seen important judicial decisions on the extent of and reasons for legally acceptable affirmative action. These include *City of Richmond v. J. A. Croson Co.* (1989), *Adarand Constructors, Inc. v. Peña* (1995), and *Hopwood v. University of Texas (1996)*. These decisions, however, did more to specify (mostly to narrow) the conditions under which affirmative action may be used and to define more precisely what the term itself may legitimately mean than to change the nature of the underlying debate over the need for affirmative action.

3   Note the obvious but important point that there is no single entity or process called "affirmative action"; the term is used to mean everything from efforts to ensure a broad applicant pool to strict quotas. Both proponents and opponents play verbal games with the term.

4   Another caveat: individual institutions and agencies sometimes analyze their own practices, and occasionally compare their own with similar institutions' practices. But these analyses are seldom made public, and by definition are not conducted by neutral evaluators. Policy analysts have known for decades that it is virtually impossible for an organization to evaluate its own practices in ways that are uncontaminated by internal politics or by the goals of the evaluators, no matter how hard they try. So even if these analyses exist, they do not count much against the claim in the text.

5   Many journalists have made some variant of this claim, but researchers have not investigated it carefully (Broder and Barnes, 1995; Langfitt, 1995; DelVecchio, 1996; Pulley, 1996; Kahlenberg, 1996).

6   See Hochschild (1998) for one effort to answer some of these questions.

7   Half of women (compared with 57 percent of men) and 45 percent of Asian Americans (compared with 60 percent of whites, 26 percent of blacks, and 30 percent of Latinos) voted for Proposition 209 (the California Civil Rights Initiative) in November 1996 (Ness, 1996). White men and women supported the antiaffirmative action proposition more strongly than did men or women of color. In Washington, 65 percent of men, and 50 percent of women supported Initiative 200, which was modeled after Proposition 209. Almost 60 percent of whites, and 46 percent of nonwhites (almost all of whom are Hispanic or Asian American) similarly supported the initiative (Ladd, 1998:129). Onishi (1996) provides a good analysis of the Asian-American college students' ambivalent views about affirmative action.

8   Richmond is not alone. In San Francisco, those eligible for preference in bidding on city contracts include descendents from all nations in Asia, the Pacific islands, Africa, and Latin America, as well as Asian Indians, Arab Americans, Native Americans, women of all races, and locally owned business. In 1999, the city government considered adding Iranian Americans to the list.

9   To give only one example of the many observations similar to my own: "affirmative action's detractors have generally sidestepped time-consuming, substantive research to verify their suppositions about who actually participates in or benefits from such programs. Even scholarly opponents of affirmative action have resorted to emotionally-charged rhetoric without offering clear evidence of their claims of reverse discrimination" (Washington State Commission on African American Affairs, 1995a:10). I would simply add that advocates have done little more.

10 The argument in this paper extends and develops my analysis in Hochschild (1995). That book eschewed discussion of specific policy or political issues, since it focused on variations within and across broad ideologies, especially the ideology of the American dream. Disputes over the meaning of the American dream, however, are often played out in the political and policy arena; I argue below that affirmative action is one of the most important sites for such a dispute.

11 Holzer and Neumark (1999) observe that "despite the intensity of the viewpoints held, the evidence to date on this issue [specifically, the underqualification of affirmative action beneficiaries] remains quite thin." I agree with them on the intensity and the thinness; in my view, however, the evidence is thin *because of* rather than *despite* the intensity of the viewpoints.

12 On the Bank War, see Meyers (1957); on McCarthyism, see Fried (1997) and Schrecker (1986). On the social construction of crises more generally, see Larana et al. (1994), and Gamson (1990).

13 Two comprehensive recent surveys of empirical research on affirmative action in employment are Reskin (1998) and Holzer and Neumark (2000); the latter points to many "shortfalls between what we do know and what we would like to know," but also points to a "growing literature that . . . begins to ask and answer some of the right questions. They are speaking explicitly, however, only from the perspective of economists (Holzer and Neumark, 2000:484). Readers of an earlier version of this chapter pointed out that "much of the debate over affirmative action has taken place in the legal arena . . . [Therefore] the lawyers and their experts build a record to support or oppose an affirmative action policy . . . Moreover, . . . many public agencies and other organizations that receive federal assistance have conducted searching reviews of their affirmative action policies and extensive fact-finding" (personal communication from Marianne Engelman Lado and Luke Harris). They are, of course, correct, and this huge subterranean literature would be a gold mine for researchers seeking to make comparisons and draw generalizations about how and why affirmative action functions. But part of my point is the fact that researchers have seldom dug into this gold mine. And in any case each analysis in this literature is by definition biased in favor of or against affirmative action.

14 From here on, I will focus mostly on race-based rather than gender-based affirmative action, simply because I know more about the former than the latter. As I understand it, the evidence is roughly similar with regard to outcomes for white women as it is for black women and men. The symbolic politics of affirmative action, however, probably differ significantly between race and gender, and it would be illuminating to develop their differences in more detail.

15 For example, "between 1970 and 1990, the number of black electricians more than tripled (from 14,145 to 43,276) and the number of black police officers increased almost as rapidly (from 23,796 to 63,855)" (Karabel, 1993:159).

16 However, in Washington State "*whites* [including men as well as women] are the primary beneficiaries of the state's affirmative action program affecting hiring, . . . of special admissions programs at public institutions of higher learning, . . . [and] of programs designed to assist minority- and women-owned firms seeking to do business with the state" (Washington State Commission on African American Affairs, 1995a:1; see also 1995b and 1995c). We do not know how extensively or when these counterintuitive results hold.

17 However, Holzer (1998:225) finds "a strong *positive* correlation between education levels of hires and Affirmative Action." See also Holzer and Neumark (1999).

18 Echoing my complaint above, Holzer (1998:43) points out that "we have little strong evidence to date on the efficiency effects of these programs, or on whether they generate any net new employment for less-educated workers." Firms subject to affirmative action regulations experience an increase of about 5 percent in labor costs compared with firms not so subject, according to the only set of scholars who have studied the issue (Griffin et al., 1996).

19 Average undergraduate tuition charges in private four-year colleges rose from under $4,000 in 1980 to almost $13,000 in 1996–7. Tuition charges in public four-year colleges rose during the same period from about $1,000 to $3,000 ("Tuition Trends," 1997). For more detail, see Clotfelter, 1996.

20 Would-be students who are not admitted to elite universities have stronger grounds than almost anyone else for opposing affirmative action. But their claim of harm or injustice is weak for two reasons. First, the overwhelming majority of applicants would not be admitted to Harvard or Princeton even if every beneficiary of affirmative action were denied a slot in the freshman class. (About 12 percent of applicants to Princeton or Harvard are admitted.) Second, no one has a right to admission to an elite private (or public) university or to a given job; one may be deeply disappointed by rejection, but one cannot claim unjust treatment.

21 Over four in ten Americans (41 percent of whites and Asians, 62 percent of blacks, and 57 percent of Latinos) perceive that "white men are generally covered under federal affirmative action" (Morin, 1995). Legally they are correct. But I think it fair to assume that in the context of public opinion surveys, this result indicates ignorance of how affirmative action normally operates rather than subtle knowledge of the law.

22 Skerry (1997) gives a somewhat similar analysis.

23 As President Clinton put it rather plaintively in his conversation with a group of racial conservatives, "I'd like to . . . hear from you . . . on the question of, 'Do you believe that race . . . is still a problem in some ways?' And if so, instead of our getting into a big fight about affirmative action . . . " His plea was largely ignored; most responses to his and Vice-president Gore's questions came back to a statement of opposition to preferences ("Excerpts from Round Table", 1997).

24 Comment by Christopher Edley, in Holmes (1997). Edley goes on to observe, "You can look at those figures [on how many are affected by federal contracts and elite college admissions] and ask, why are black folks making such a big deal out of affirmative action? That's the wrong question. The real question is why are white folks making such a big deal out of it?"

25 In 1942, only 32 percent of Americans agreed that white and black students should attend the same schools, and only 46 percent opposed "separate sections for Negroes in streetcars and

buses." As late as 1963, fewer than half of Americans agreed that they would vote for a black presidential candidate of their political party even if he were qualified. Most importantly for this paper, in 1944 and again in 1946, fewer than half of white Americans agreed that "Negroes should have as good a chance as white people to get any kind of job." (The alternative response was "white people should have the first chance at any kind of job" (Schuman et al., 1997:104 [all responses are percentages of those giving a substantive answer]).

26 This is the spelling of "America" sometimes used by strong critics from the left, and intended to evoke an association of the United States with the Ku Klux Klan.

27 The 1990 survey was of residents of New York City; the 1996 survey was a national random sample.

28 If I were made race czar, I would work to strengthen at least the "soft" forms of affirmative action. In the long run, however, it would be more valuable for the state of California, for example, to engage in structural reforms of inner-city schools rather than merely allowing U.C. Berkeley to pick out the few black or Latino students who have somehow triumphed over the wasteland that has demoralized all of their fellow students. The university has taken tentative steps in that direction, in response to the brutal abolition of affirmative action through Proposition 209 (Tien, 1999; Ponessa, 1997).

29 Polls prior to the election showed that two-thirds of Houston's voters would have supported a proposition to "not discriminate against or grant preferential treatment to" any person on group based on race, sex, or ethnicity (Verhovek, 1997a). The two propositions would have had identical effects; all the difference lay in the wording or, in my terms, in which variant of the American dream is invoked by the fluid concept of affirmative action.

References

Anderson, Bernard (1996) "The ebb and flow of enforcing Executive Order 11246." *American Economic Review* 86:298–301.

Appiah, K. Anthony and Gutmann, Amy (1996) *Color Conscious*. Princeton, NJ: Princeton University Press.

Badgett, M. V. Lee (1995) "Affirmative action in a changing legal and economic environment." *Industrial Relations* 34:489–506.

Badgett, M. V. Lee and Hartmann, Heidi (1995) *The Effectiveness of Equal Employment Opportunity Policies*. Washington DC: Joint Center for Political and Economic Research.

Basic and Applied Social Psychology (1994) Special issue on affirmative action. 15 (1 and 2).

Bates, Timothy and Williams, Darrell (1996) "Do preferential procurement programs benefit minority businesses?" *American Economic Association Papers and Proceedings* 86:294–7.

Bennett, Stephen Earl, Tuchfarber, Alfred, Smith, Andrew, and Rademacher, Erick W. (1995) "Americans' opinions of affirmative action." Unpublished paper, Institute for Policy Research, University of Cincinnati.

Bergmann, Barbara (1996) *In Defense Of Affirmative Action*. New York: Basic Books.

Blanchard, P. A. and Crosby, Faye J. (eds.) (1989) *Affirmative Action in Perspective*. New York: Springer-Verlag.

Blumrosen, Alfred W. (1995) "Draft report on reverse discrimination commissioned by Labor Department: How courts are handling reverse discrimination cases," *Daily Labor Report*, March 23. Washington, DC: Bureau of National Affairs.

Bobo, Lawrence (1998) "Race, interests, and beliefs about affirmative action," *American Behavioral Scientist*. 41,7:985–1003.

Bobo, Lawrence and Kluegel, James R. (1993) "Opposition to race targeting." *American Sociological Review* 58,4:443–64.

Bobo, Lawrence and Smith, Ryan A. (1994) "Antipoverty policy, affirmative action, and racial attitudes," in Sheldon Danziger, Gary Sandefur, and Daniel Weinberg (eds.) *Confronting Poverty: Prescriptions for Change*. New York: Russell Sage Foundation and Harvard University Press, pp.365–95.

Bositis, David (1997) *1997 National Opinion Poll: Race Relations*. Washington DC: Joint Center for Political and Economic Studies.

Bowen, William and Bok, Derek (1998) *The Shape of the River: Long-Term Consequences of Considering Race in College and University Admissions*. Princeton, NJ: Princeton University Press.

Brewer, Dominic, Eide, Eric, and Ehrenberg, Ronald (1999) "Does it pay to attend an elite private college?" *Journal of Human Resources* 34 (1): 104–23.

Broder, David and Barnes, Robert (1995) "Few governors join attack on racial policies." *Washington Post*, August 2: A01ff.

Burstein, Paul (1985) *Discrimination, Jobs, and Politics*. Chicago: University of Chicago Press.

Carter, Stephen (1991) *Reflections of an Affirmative Action Baby*. New York: Basic Books.

Clayton, Susan D. and Crosby, Faye J. (1992) *Justice, Gender, and Affirmative Action*. Ann Arbor: University of Michigan Press.

"Clinton's Second Term" (1996) *The Polling Report* 12, November 18:1, 6.

Clotfelter, Charles (1996) *Buying the Best: Cost Escalation in Elite Higher Education*. Princeton, NJ: Princeton University Press.

Collins, Sharon M. (1983) "The making of the black middle class." *Social Problems* 30:369–82.

Collins, Sharon M. (1997) *Black Corporate Executives: The Making and Breaking of a Black Middle Class*. Philadelphia, PA: Temple University Press.

Conference Board (1997) "Managing Diversity for Sustaining Competitiveness." New York:Conference Board.

Cox, Taylor H. and Blake, Stacy (1991) "Managing cultural diversity:Implications for organizational competitiveness." *Academy of Management Executive* 5:45–56.

Crocker, Jennifer, Voellel, Kristin, Testa, Maria, and Major, Brenda (1991) "Social stigma:The affective consequences of attributional ambiguity." *Journal of Personality and Social Psychology* 60,2:218–28.

Daniel, Kermit, Black, Dan, and Smith, Jeffrey (1995) "College quality and the wages of young men." Unpublished paper, University of Pennsylvania, Wharton School.

DelVecchio, Rick (1996) "Cities trying to detour past Prop. 209." *San Francisco Chronicle*. November 25:A1ff.

Dobbin, Frank (1996) "Organizational response to affirmative action and equal employment law." Memo to Conference on Social Science Perspectives on Affirmative Action, American Sociological Association, Washington DC.

Dobbin, Frank, Sutton, John, Meyer, John, and Scott, W. R. (1993) "Equal opportunity law and the construction of internal labor markets." *American Journal of Sociology* 99,2:396–427.

Eastland, Terry (1996) *Ending Affirmative Action:The Case for Colorblind Justice*. New York: Basic Books.

Edelman, Lauren (1990) "Legal environments and organizational governance:The expansion of due process in the workplace." *American Journal of Sociology* 95,6:401–40.

Edelman, Lauren (1992) "Legal ambiguity and symbolic structures: Organizational mediation of civil rights law." *American Journal of Sociology* 97,6:1531–76.

Edelman, Lauren (1996) "Affirmative action in employment." Memo to Conference on Social Science Perspectives on Affirmative Action, American Sociological Association, Washington DC.

Edley, Christopher Jr. (1996) *Not All Black and White:Affirmative Action and American Values*. New York: Hill and Wang.

Enchautegui, Maria, Fix, Michael, Loprest, Pamela, van der Lippe, Sarah, and Wissoker, Douglas (1996) "Do minority-owned businesses get a fair share of government contracts?" *Policy and Research Report* (of the Urban Institute) Summer/Fall:4–7.

"Excerpts from round table with opponents of racial preferences" 1997 *New York Times* December 22:A24.

Farley, Reynolds (1996) *The New American Reality*. New York: Russell Sage Foundation.

Finley, Steve (1996) "Re: Being a privileged white male." on Listserv Athena-discuss@info. harpercollins.com. June 5.

Fried, Albert (1997) *McCarthyism: The Great American Red Scare*. New York: Oxford University Press.

Gallup, George Jr. and Newport, Frank (1990) "Americans ignorant of basic census facts." *Gallup Poll Monthly* 294:2–5.

Gallup Organization (1995) *Affirmative Action: A Gallup Poll Special Report*. Princeton, NJ: Gallup Organization.

Gallup Organization (1997) *The Gallup Poll Social Audit on Black/White Relations in the United States*. Princeton, NJ: Gallup Organization.

Gamson, William (1990) *The Strategy of Social Protest*, 2nd edn. Belmont, CA: Wadsworth Publishers.

Gamson, William and Modigliani, Andre (1987) "The changing culture of affirmative action." *Research in Political Sociology* 3:137–77.

Gitlin, Todd (1995) *The Twilight of Common Dreams*. New York: Metropolitan Books.

Glater, Jonathan and Hamilton, Martha (1995) "Affirmative action's corporate converts." *Washington Post* March 19:H1, H6.

Glazer, Nathan (1975) *Affirmative Discrimination: Ethnic Inequality and Public Policy*. New York: Basic Books.

Graham, Hugh Davis (1999) "The paradox of American civil rights regulation, 1964–1994," in Morton Keller and R. Shep Melnick (eds.) *Taking Stock: American Government in the Twentieth Century*. New York: Cambridge University Press, pp.187–218.

Griffin, Peter, Getis, Arthus and Griffin, Ernst (1996) "Regional patterns of affirmative action compliance costs." *Annals of Regional Science* 30:321–40.

Heckman, James and Payner, Brook (1989) "Determining the impact of federal antidiscrimination policy on the economic status of blacks: A study of South Carolina." *American Economic Review* 79:138–77.

Heckman, James and Verkerke, J. Hoult (1990) "Racial disparity and economic discrimination law: An economic perspective." *Yale Law and Policy Review* 8,2:276–98.

Heckman, James and Wolpin, Kenneth (1976) "Does the contract compliance program work? An analysis of Chicago data." *Industrial and Labor Relations Review* 29:544–64.

Hochschild, Jennifer (1995) *Facing Up to the American Dream: Race. Class, and the Soul of the Nation*. Princeton, NJ: Princeton University Press.

Hochschild, Jennifer (1998) "The strange career of affirmative action." *Ohio State Law Journal* 59,3:997–1037.

Holmes, Steven (1997) "Thinking about race with a one-track mind." *New York Times*, Section 4. December 21:1.

Holzer, Harry (1998) "Employer hiring decisions and antidiscrimination policy," in Richard Freeman and Peter Gottschalk (eds.) *Generating Jobs: How to Increase Demand for Less Skilled Workers*. New York: Russell Sage Foundation, pp.223–57.

Holzer, Harry and Neumark, David (1999) "Are affirmative action hires less qualified? Evidence from employer–employee data on new hires." *Journal of Labor Economics* 17,3:534–69.

Holzer, Harry and Neumark, David (2000) "Assessing affirmative action." *Journal of Economic Literature* 38:483–568.

House Government Operations Committee, U.S. Congress (1994) *Problems Facing Minority and Women-Owned Small Business Including SBA Section 8(a) Firms in Procuring U.S. Government Contracts: An Interim Report*. HRPT. NO. 103–870. Washington, DC: US Government Printing Office.

Kahlenberg, Richard (1996) "Bob Dole's colorblind injustice." *Washington Post* June 2:C1, C4.

Kane, Thomas (1998) "Racial and ethnic preferences in college admissions," in Christopher Jencks and Meredith Phillips (eds.) *The Black–White Test Score Gap*. Washington, DC: Brookings Institution, pp.431–56.

Karabel, Jerome (1993) "Berkeley and beyond." *American Prospect* 12:156–60.

Kelly, Erin and Dobbin, Frank (1998) "How affirmative action became diversity management." *American Behavioral Scientist* 41,7:960–84.

Kinder, Donald and Sanders, Lynn (1996) *Divided by Color*. Chicago: University of Chicago Press.

Kluegel, James and Smith, Eliot (1983) "Affirmative action attitudes:Effects of self-interest, racial affect, and stratification beliefs on whites' views." *Social Forces* 61:797–825.

Konrad, Alison and Linnehan, Frank (1995) "Formalized HRM structures: Coordinating equal employment opportunity or concealing organizational practices?" *Academy of Management Journal* 38:787–820.

Ladd, Everett (ed.) (1998) *America at the Polls 1998*. Storrs, CT:University of Connecticut, Roper Center.

Langfitt, Frank (1995) "GOP abandons effort on minority set- asides." *Baltimore Sun* May 23:1B.

Larana, Enrique, Johnston, Hank, and Gusfield, Joseph (eds.) (1994) *New Social Movements:From Ideology To Identity*. Philadelphia, PA:Temple University Press.

Leadership Conference on Civil Rights (1997) *Affirmative Action for Women and Minorities:It Works Well, it is Necessary, and it Benefits America*. Washington DC: Leadership Conference on Civil Rights.

Lempinen, Edward (1996) "Affirmative action foes span spectrum." *San Francisco Chronicle* November 22:B1ff.

Leonard, Jonathan (1984a) "The impact of affirmative action on employment." *Journal of Labor Economics* 2:439–63.

Leonard, Jonathan (1984b) "Employment and occupational advance under affirmative action." *Review of Economics and Statistics* 66:377–85.

Leonard, Jonathan (1984c) "Anti-discrimination or reverse discrimination:The impact of changing demographics, Title VII, and affirmative action on productivity." *Journal of Human Resources* 19,2:145–74.

Leonard, Jonathan (1986) "What was affirmative action?" *American Economic Review* 76:359–63.

Leonard, Jonathan (1990) "The impact of affirmative action regulation and equal employment law on black employment." *Journal of Economic Perspectives* 4:47–63.

Leonard, Jonathan (1996) "Wage disparities and affirmative action in the 1980s." American Economic Association *Papers and Proceedings* 86:285–9.

Lind, Michael (1995) *The Next American Nation:The New Nationalism and the Fourth American Revolution*. New York: Free Press.

Lynch, Frederick R. (1989) *Invisible Victims:White Males and the Crisis of Affirmative Action*. New York: Greenwood.

Meyers, Marvin (1957) *The Jacksonian Persuasion: Politics and Belief*. Stanford, CA: Stanford University Press.

Morin, Richard (1995) "Affirmative action for white guys?" *Washington Post* October 22:C5.

Motley, Constance Baker (1998) *Equal Justice Under Law*. New York: Farrar, Straus, and Giroux.

Myers, Samuel and Chan, Tsze (1996) "Who benefits from minority business set-asides? The case of New Jersey." *Journal of Policy Analysis and Management* 15,2:202–26.

Nacoste, Rupert (1985) "Selection procedure and responses to affirmative action." *Law and Human Behavior* 9,3:225–42.

Nacoste, Rupert (1994) "If empowerment is the goal . . .:Affirmative action and social interaction." *Basic and Applied Social Psychology* 15:87–112.

Nadeau, Richard, Niemi, Richard, and Levine, Jeffrey (1993) "Innumeracy about minority populations." *Public Opinion Quarterly* 57,3:332–47.

National Council for Research on Women (1996) "Affirming diversity: Building a national community that works." *Issues Quarterly* 1:1–28.

Ness, Carol (1996) "Prop. 209 wins, heads for courts." *San Francisco Examiner* November 6:A1ff.

Onishi, Norimitsu (1996) "Affirmative action: Choosing sides." *New York Times*, Section on "Education Life" March 31:26–35.

Oreskes, Michael (1984) "The set-aside scam." *New Republic* December 24:17–20.

Pettigrew, Thomas and Martin, Joanne (1987) "Shaping the organizational context for black American inclusion." *Journal of Social Issues* 43,1:41–78.

Ponessa, Jeanne (1997) "Higher ed. Outreach plan targets at-risk Calif. youths." *Education Week* June 4:5.

Preston, Michael and Lai, James (1998) "The symbolic politics of affirmative action," in Michael Preston, Bruce Cain, and Sandra Bass (eds.) *Racial and Ethnic Politics in California*, vol. 2. Berkeley, CA: University of California, Institute of Governmental Studies Press, pp.161–98.

Pulley, Brett (1996) "Affirmative action: Can Whitman stand firm?" *New York Times*, New Jersey section November 24:2.

Reskin, Barbara (1998) *The Realities of Affirmative Action in Employment*. Washington DC: American Sociological Association.

Rice, Mitchell and Mongkuo, Maurice (1998) "Did *Adarand* kill minority set-asides?" *Public Administration Review* 58:82–6.

Rodgers, William III and Spriggs, William (1996) "The effect of federal contractor status on racial differences in establishment-level employment shares: 1979–1992." *American Economic Review* 86:290–93.

Rosenfeld, Michael (1991) *Affirmative Action and Justice: A Philosophical and Constitutional Inquiry*. New Haven, CT: Yale University Press.

Schein, Lawrence (1986) "Current issues in human-resource management." *Research Bulletin* (of The Conference Board), 190.

Schrecker, Ellen (1986) *No Ivory Tower: McCarthyism and the Universities*. New York: Oxford University Press.

Schuman, Howard, Steeh, Charlotte, Bobo, Larry, and Krysan, Maria (1997) *Racial Attitudes in America*, revised edn. Cambridge, MA: Harvard University Press.

Skerry, Peter (1997) "The strange politics of affirmative action." *Wilson Quarterly* 21, Winter:39–46.

Skrentny, John (1996) *The Ironies of Affirmative Action*. Chicago: University of Chicago Press.

Sleeper, Jim (1997) *Liberal Racism*. New York: Viking Press.

Smith, James and Welch, Finis (1984) "Affirmative action and labor markets." *Journal of Labor Economics* 2:269–301.

Smith, James and Welch, Finis (1989) "Black Economic Progress after Myrdal." *Journal of Economic Literature*. 27:519–64.

Smith, Rogers (1997) *Civic Ideals: Conflicting Visions of Citizenship in U.S. History*. New Haven, CT: Yale University Press.

Sniderman, Paul and Piazza, Thomas (1993) *The Scar of Race*. Cambridge, MA: Harvard University Press.

Steeh, Charlotte and Krysan, Maria (1996) "The polls–trends. Affirmative action and the public, 1970–1995." *Public Opinion Quarterly* 60,1:128–58.

Steele, Claude (1999) "A threat in the air: How stereotypes shape intellectual identity and performance," in Eugene Lowe (ed.) *Promise and Dilemma: Perspectives on Racial Diversity and Higher Education*. Princeton, NJ: Princeton University Press, pp.92–128.

Stephanopoulos, George and Edley, Christopher Jr. (1995) "Affirmative action review. Report to the President." Washington, DC: Unpublished report to the President.

Sutton, John, Dobbin, Frank, Meyer, John, and Scott, W. Richard (1994) "The legalization of the workplace." *American Journal of Sociology* 99,4:944–71.

Taylor, Bron (1991) *Affirmative Action at Work*. Pittsburgh, PA: University of Pittsburgh Press.

Taylor, Marylee C. (1994) "Impact of affirmative action on beneficiary groups: Evidence from the 1990 General Social Survey." *Basic and Applied Social Psychology* 15:143–78.

Thernstrom, Stephan and Thernstrom, Abigail (1997) *America in Black and White: One Nation, Indivisible*. New York: Simon and Schuster.

Thomas, David and Ely, Robin (1996) "Making differences matter: A new paradigm for managing diversity." *Harvard Business Review* 74,5:79–90.

Tien, Chang-Lin (1999) "What a university can learn and teach about conflict and difference," in Eugene Lowe (ed.) *Promise and Dilemma:Perspectives on Racial Diversity and Higher Education*. Princeton, NJ: Princeton University Press, pp.193–8.

Towers Perrin (1992) *Workforce 2000 Today:A Bottom-Line Concern*. New York:Towers Perrin.

"Tuition Trends" (1997) *Chronicle of Higher Education* May 30:A11.

Verhovek, Sam (1997a) "Houston to vote on repeal of affirmative action." *New York Times*. November 2:28.

Verhovek, Sam (1997b) "Referendum in Houston shows complexity of preferences issue." *New York Times* November 6:A1, A26.

Washington Post, Kaiser Family Foundation, and Harvard University (1995) *The Four Americas:-Government and Social Policy Through the Eyes of America's Multi-racial and Multi-ethnic Society*. Washington DC: *Washington Post*.

Washington State Commission on African American Affairs (1995a) *Affirmative Action:Who's Really Benefiting? Part 1: State Employment*. Olympia, WA:Washington State Commission on African American Affairs.

Washington State Commission on African American Affairs (1995b) *Affirmative Action:Who's Really Benefiting? Part 2: Public Higher Education*. Olympia, WA:Washington State Commission on African American Affairs.

Washington State Commission on African American Affairs (1995c) *Affirmative Action:Who's Really Benefiting? Part 3: Contracting in State Government*. Olympia, WA:Washington State Commission on African American Affairs.

Wheeler, Michael (1994) *Diversity Training*. New York: Conference Board.

Wolfe, Alan (1996) "Affirmative action, inc." *New Yorker* November 25:106–15.

Woodson, Robert (1996) "Affirmative action is no civil right." *Harvard Journal of Law and Public Policy* 19:773–8.

Chapter 20

Racism, Politics, and Mobilization

John Solomos and Liza Schuster

Introduction

During the past two decades one of the most contested and thorny problems in scholarship about race and ethnic relations has been the question of how political processes and identities are shaped and constructed through the meanings attributed to racial and ethnic identities. This is partly the result of the growing politicization of questions about race and ethnicity in various parts of the globe, a trend that has been particularly noticeable in Europe, North America, and parts of Africa. It is also linked to an increasing awareness by researchers working in a variety of disciplines that the role of political institutions is central to any rounded analysis of forms of racial and ethnic conflict (Alex-Assensoh and Hanks, 2000).

As a result of these trends we have seen a noticeable growth of research and writing on various aspects of the racialization of political life in a wide range of advanced industrial societies and on forms of political mobilization and action (Bulmer and Solomos, 1999). This trend has been evident in political science and, perhaps more significantly, within sociology and urban studies. This growth of interest is partly because political events in a variety of countries across Europe and other parts of the globe have emphasized the fact that the question of how to conceptualize the interplay between questions about race and politics is not purely an academic matter. It is also very much connected with wider political questions and cultures in any given historical conjuncture, and in a very real sense therefore the study of the politics of race involves an engagement with everyday political debates and dilemmas (Gilroy, 2000; Parekh, 2000). But another reason why this dimension of the study of race and ethnicity has become heavily contested can be found in the growth of forms of political mobilization that are framed around questions of race and ethnicity. The experience of a wide range of European societies during the 1980s and 1990s, along with the continuing salience of race in American political culture, are perhaps the most notable examples of a wider global pattern. At the same time we have seen important changes in forms of political mobilization among racialized minority communities in Europe, North America, and other parts of the globe (Hanchard, 1999).

It is not surprising, given this background, that we have seen a growing body of work on the interrelationship between race, politics, and society in recent years. In this paper we want to explore key dimensions of the study of race and political mobilization by focusing on the history of research and scholarship in this field and the evolution of contemporary research agendas. In doing so we hope to provide an overview of the key questions that have shaped existing research agendas, and pinpoint some of the directions of research and public debate.

Conceptualizing Race, Ethnicity, and Politics

Most of the early studies of race and ethnic relations were based within sociology or anthropology. Few political scientists became involved in research concerned with race or ethnicity in the early stages of scholarly research in this area. This did not mean that there were no studies that explored aspects of racialized politics or forms of social mobilization in ethnically divided societies, but the study of race, politics, and power became an important aspect of studies of race and ethnicity relatively late (Solomos, 1993; Saggar, 2000). There are some classic studies that date back to the 1960s, many of which were focused on community politics or changing forms of racial ideology in the USA during the period of the Civil Rights Movement and Black Power. Such studies, however, remained relatively marginal to the field as a whole until the 1980s and 1990s.

This growth of interest in the study of the politics of race has helped to clarify some questions, but others remain open and contested. Take, for example, the following two seemingly simple questions: what explains the role of race in political mobilizations and conflicts in contemporary advanced industrial societies? How does political agency connect with social structure in shaping what is popularly called the politics of race? These questions are also at the heart of the main theoretical debates about the changing politics of race and ethnicity that have developed in recent years. Such debates have focused particularly on how we can understand the relationship between race, politics, and social change in the present environment.

Despite some progress in clarifying issues raised by these questions we still lack a clear analytic framework for analyzing the interrelationship between race, politics, and social change, and know relatively little about key features of contemporary racialized politics.

Race, Racism, and Politics

In the midst of this growth of interest in the politics of race it is also clear that crucial theoretical and conceptual issues have remained untheorized and, perhaps most importantly, underresearched. This situation is partly the result of (1) the abstract and generalized nature of much of the theoretical debates that have developed in recent years, and (2) the lack of theoretically informed research on the dynamics of racialized politics in the contemporary period.

Both of these points may seem surprising, on first sight, particularly when we take into account the highly politicized nature of research on race and ethnic issues in recent years. But it is not surprising when we take into account the fact that much of the research on the politics of race in contemporary societies has been concerned with either local case studies or very specific studies of policy formation and the impact of policies on racial issues.

Perhaps no other country exemplifies the growth of research on race and politics than the United States of America. In the aftermath of the transformation of public debates

305

about race in American society during the 1950s and 1960s there was a growing range of studies of issues such as urban politics and race, the role of minority politicians, race and public policy, and the dynamics of racialized politics. Although some of the issues and processes addressed in this body of work are in some sense specific to the political institutions and culture of American society, and could not be seen as directly relevant to the situation in Britain or other European societies, it remains an important point of reference for scholars working in a variety of national environments.

The earlier development of American research in this field can partly be explained by the impact of black, Hispanic, and other minority politicians on political institutions in the United States since the mid-1960s (Marable, 1985; Omi and Winant, 1994). During the past three decades there has been a rapid growth in the number of elected black officials at all levels of American political life, leading to what some commentators have called a "new black politics." Additionally, during the 1980s and 1990s politicians such as Jesse Jackson sought to use this growth of minority representation as one of the means of building a "rainbow coalition" of various excluded groups in order to challenge the established political order (Alex-Assensoh and Hanks, 2000; Sears et al., 2000).

It is in the context of this growth of a vibrant minority political culture that we have seen the development of an extensive body of research on black and minority political mobilization in the United States. Much of this research has been concerned with two key issues. First, the growth of black political empowerment in the aftermath of the Civil Rights Movement and the urban uprisings of the 1960s. Second, the emergence of new forms of black and minority political mobilization in the United States, particularly during the 1980s and 1990s. Both of these trends have led to wide-ranging research on the dynamics of black and minority political mobilizations, the role of alliances in changing the relative powerlessness of minority communities, and the growth and role of black political elites.

An influential American study that derives from this period is a study by Browning et al. (1984) entitled *Protest is Not Enough*, which examined the politics of Hispanic and black mobilization in 10 northern Californian cities. Their aim was to develop a "conception of minority political action and position that linked mobilization to policy, that demonstrates the connection between the passions, interests and actions of mobilization and the government response – if any." Browning et al. (1984:2) suggest a simple sequence of political activity: mobilization – incorporation – responsiveness. They identify two kinds of mobilization, demand protest and electoral. Their model is concerned with the outcome and response to political mobilization. Their conclusion is provocative:

> The key to higher levels of responsiveness was not representation but coalition: minority inclusion in a coalition that was able to dominate a city council produced a much more positive government response than the election of minority council members who were not part of the dominant coalition. (Browning et al., 1986:576)

They also point out that white support for minority incorporation was not a matter of benign altruism because the existence of these coalitions depended on the support of black and Hispanic politicians. The attraction of this model is that it focuses on the political system as a whole, rather than narrowly focusing on the activities of minority politicians. The responsibility for change is placed squarely within the political system itself. It also captures the dynamic nature of the political process where any advance may be subject to what they refer to as "roll backs" (Browning et al., 1984:262–3).

There are of course problems in applying the American experience to other societies. If we take the examples of Britain and France, perhaps the most important of these problems is the ideological character of party politics and their preoccupation with discouraging caucusing along sectional interests. This was evident in the response of the Labour Party in the 1980s and 1990s to pressures to increase minority representation in its institutions, and more generally in its responses to other forms of minority mobilization. France has traditionally been hostile to identity politics, which are seen as dangerous to the unity of the Republic. In this sense the pluralist model which is found within the American situation cannot be simply applied. Nevertheless, there are elements of the account given by Browning et al. for American cities that link up with the transformations which we have seen over the past two decades in both national and local politics in Britain and other European societies.

Urban Politics and Racial Conflict

One of the earliest attempts to situate the role of political mobilization in the construction of racial identities can be found in studies of the role of race and ethnicity in urban politics. John Rex and Robert Moore's classic account of "race, community and conflict" in Birmingham in the West Midlands of England during the 1960s remains an important account of this phenomenon. Rex and Moore's (1967) study represents an early attempt to develop a conceptual framework for the analysis of the politics of race in contemporary societies. The starting point of this study was that the position of ethnic minority communities must be understood primarily in terms of their status as migrants. Rex combined a Weberian notion of class analysis with elements of the urban sociology developed by the Chicago School, and what he has termed in his later work a "loose marxism" (Rex, 1989). Rex subsequently attempted to provide a sociologically based explanation for racial discrimination and conflict by identifying inequalities in "market situations" which fuel conflicts between indigenous workers and newcomer populations (Rex, 1973:32).

In this study Rex refers to the political work that took place in organizations within immigrant "colonies" and the development of organizations which acted for the specific class interests of migrant workers (Rex, 1973:4). He argues that it is through such forms of political mobilization that minority communities attempted in the period after their arrival in Britain to establish their social and economic position, as well as ensure a degree of access to political institutions.

In the study conducted by Rex and Tomlinson in Handsworth, an inner-city area of Birmingham, during the mid-1970s this type of analysis was further developed to take account of the changing social and political situation (Rex and Tomlinson, 1979). The basic research problem of this study was structured by the objective of researching the extent to which immigrant populations shared the class position of their white neighbors and white workers in general. The substance of the analysis outlined a class structure in which white workers had been granted certain rights which had been won through the working class movement and the Labour Party. The result was, argued Rex and Tomlinson, that by the 1970s a situation of "class truce" developed between white

307

workers and the dominant social groups. Basing their analysis on Marshall's account of citizenship and the welfare state, in which the salience of a shared citizenship outweighed the political importance of class as a source of political action, they argued that the development of welfare state institutions provided an important mechanism for shaping political mobilization within the working class.

For Rex and Tomlinson the position of migrant workers and their communities was one where they were located outside this process of negotiation that had taken place between white workers and capital. They experienced discrimination in all the areas where the white workers had made significant gains, namely, employment, education, housing. It followed from this that the position of migrant workers placed them outside the working class, in the position of an *underclass*:

> The concept of underclass was intended to suggest . . . that the minorities were systematic-
> ally at a disadvantage compared with their white peers and that, instead of identifying with
> working class culture, community and politics, they formed their own organisations and
> became effectively a separate underprivileged class. (Rex and Tomlinson, 1979:275)

From this point Rex and Tomlinson developed a model of political action and even a political agenda for black populations as they become a "class for themselves." This highlighted the ways in which minorities are forced into a series of reactive or defensive political strategies in order to deal with their exclusion from full citizenship in all the key economic and social arenas.

Drawing on their research in Handsworth, Rex and Tomlinson argued that this process of political mobilization was likely to take on different forms within Asian and West Indian communities. Within Asian communities it resulted in a concentration on capital accumulation and social mobility. In the West Indian community it took the form of withdrawal from competition altogether with an emphasis on the construction of a black identity. This all led to what Rex refers to elsewhere as the "politics of defensive confrontation" (Rex, 1979).

Rex and Tomlinson identified a number of tiers in the political process in which minority politics operated. First, there were government-sponsored paternalistic agencies, such as the Community Relations Councils. In many ways this tier of political involvement acted as a buffer which kept the issue of race outside of the mainstream political arenas. Second, there existed community-led projects based in specific localities. These organizations explicitly aimed at promoting "racial harmony." Third, there existed numerous self-help organizations which developed within the minority communities themselves. Amongst West Indians this took the form of independent black political action, black cultural development, and identity groups. Within Asian communities there existed the various Indian Workers Associations, kinship-based organizations, and elite negotiations with the host society (Rex and Tomlinson, 1979:240–74).

It was on the basis of this model that Rex and Tomlinson claimed in their study of Handsworth in the mid-1970s that West Indian political action was not in the main channeled through the Labour Party, although their normative class position as workers led them to give electoral support to the Labour Party and membership of trade unions. They also claimed that the community politics which was in operation within self-help groups was not articulated within mainstream left politics. Labour's relationship to Asian communities was characterized in a very different way. Here the labor movement as a whole, and kinship, played a more important role in meeting the needs of Asians in all areas of community life. This resulted in a situation where Asian community organizations were engaged in constant negotiation with the host society, with Labour politics and left politics in general (Rex and Tomlinson, 1979:250).

The notion that ethnic minority communities form distinct classes which exhibit distinct political interests has informed all of Rex's later theoretical work (Rex 1986a, 1986b). This is perhaps his most interesting contribution, for in this idea of separate class interests there exists a model of political action which reflects the class structure of metropolitan urban systems. Rex uses the Weberian notion of ideal types to describe forms of minority political structure and action (Rex, 1970). He defends this method-ology as a way of "defining concepts, of refining them in the course of historical studies, of arguing about them, and then applying them again as yardsticks against which reality can be measured" (Rex 1979:306).

One of the key problems of his work, however, which a number of critics have highlighted, is that in the process of constructing a series of ideal types Rex runs dangerously close to reiterating stereotypical statements about the culture and history and organization of migrant groups. One of the great weaknesses of Rex's sociology of race relations is that he refers to minority communities as if they possessed unitary cultures which have some kind of informing spirit that is sociologically and even politically meaningful. In this sense Rex reproduces an essentially idealist view of culture which is at worst stereotypical and at best a part truth. His paradigm in no way addresses the material and historical specificity of the cultural production of racialized political identities (Gilroy, 1987). Culture for him becomes an explanatory concept in itself, and not in relation to political and economic conditions. There exists a tension in Rex's work between this kind of culturalism and his utilization of a Weberian conceptual framework which locates relationships between ethnic groups and social structures in sets of class and market situations.

What is perhaps more surprising is that with regard to minority politics Rex's work includes little in the way of detailed analysis of specific political activity and involvement of minority politicians and communities. Rather what we find is a series of sociological frameworks where specific movements and incidents are either dealt with briefly or remain unexplored. While many of Rex's formulations can be criticized as being both narrow and somewhat stereotypical, there are a number of useful insights in his analysis of minority politics and culture. Perhaps the most useful ideal type that comes from his sociology is the hypothesis that migrant workers and their children occupy a distinct class position within British society that will ultimately lead to distinct forms of political engagement. This framework at least allows for the possibility of new and autonomous forms of minority political mobilization.

The main weakness of Rex's analysis, however, is that it tells us little about the development of new forms of political engagement since the mid-1970s. Rather he seems to think that his analysis of the situation in Handsworth in the early 1970s is an adequate model for the present situation. As we shall attempt to show, however, it is important to retain some analytical flexibility in order to comprehend the rapidly changing political cultures within political institutions and minority commu-nities.

Political Mobilization and Racial Politics

From the 1980s onwards more attention began to be directed at the role of political processes and institutions in the construction of racial and ethnic questions. Research at both the national and local political level has highlighted the changing political strategies and ideologies that have helped to shape policies on issues such as housing, employment, education, policing, and equal opportunity. This research has shown clearly that over the years political and ideological processes have played a very important role in the construction of popular images of minorities and in shaping the development of particular types of policy intervention.

What has also become clear in recent years, however, is that minority groups are themselves playing an active role within national and local political institutions. This phenomenon has certainly become important at the level of local politics, with the election of a sizeable number of black local councilors over the past decade. But it is also becoming increasingly important within the context of national party politics and within parliamentary institutions (Solomos and Back, 1995).

What is surprising at first sight, however, is that there have been few attempts to produce detailed accounts of the processes that may help to explain these changes, especially in Europe (Favell, 1998). In Britain, Solomos and Back's study of race and political mobilization in Birmingham during the early 1990s highlighted the need for detailed case studies of the changing terms of the relation between race, politics, and social change (Solomos and Back, 1995). One of the starting points of this research was the hypothesis that race is first and foremost a political construct. From this starting point Solomos and Back argue that the racialization of political mobilization has to be contextualized within processes of social change and identity formation, within specific political cultures and discourses and within wider processes of social and economic change.

Studies such as this have provided suggestive accounts of the complex ways in which ideas about race and ethnicity manifest themselves in plural and complex forms within political institutions. In this context unitary or simplistic notions about race and political action become hard to sustain.

Yet it is clear that within the main strands of literature in this field little attempt has been made to develop a theoretical discussion of the processes through which ideas about race gain political salience and have an impact on patterns of political mobilization. Most studies have been largely descriptive and undertheorized, particularly as they have not sought in any meaningful sense to provide a theoretical framework for the analysis of race and political action.

This has resulted in a number of useful descriptive accounts of the role of race in electoral politics, the impact of racialized agendas on public policy, and case studies of specific events or cities. But within this body of work the political processes involved in the making of racial politics have received little or no attention, either from a theoretical or empirical perspective. Indeed, it is surprising to see how little research has explored in any detail the contemporary dynamics of racial politics. This has resulted in serious lacunae in the analysis of racial politics in contemporary societies. More significantly little attention has been given either to forms of political and social mobilization among minorities or to the responses of political institutions to minority struggles for empowerment.

Race Politics or Class Politics?

An underlying theme in much of the contemporary discussion of the politics of race is the question of the interrelationship between race, ethnicity, and class in shaping forms of political mobilization. The class basis of racial and ethnic minority political action has been a key concern in political writings that can be referred to as falling broadly within neo-Marxist and post-Marxist thinking. Though there are clear differences of approach about what is meant by "class analysis" the relationship between class formation and racial formation has been an important concern of both scholars such as Rex and Marxist writers working on these issues. A case in point is the work of Robert Miles, which represents perhaps the most consistent attempt to develop a class analysis of racialized politics. Miles has consistently opposed the notion that *race* is a useful analytical category, preferring what he sees as a Marxist analytic framework in which racism is viewed as integral to the process of capital accumulation (Miles, 1989). For Miles the idea of race refers to a human construct, an ideology with regulatory power within society: "The influence of racism and exclusionary practices is always a component of a wider structure of class disadvantage and exclusion" (Miles, 1989:9).

Within the framework race constitutes an idea that should be seen as having no analytical value as such. It is here where Miles diverges from Rex's approach. While Rex is concerned with models of social action (i.e., for Rex it is enough that race is utilized in everyday discourse as a basis for social action), Miles is concerned with the analytical and objective status of race as a basis of action. While Miles would agree that the struggle against racism is a vital political issue confronting contemporary societies, he argues that race in itself is not a scientifically valid medium for political action. Race is an ideological effect, a mask which hides "real" socioeconomic relationships. Thus the forms of class consciousness which are legitimate for Miles must ultimately be seen in terms of class relations, which are hidden within the regulatory process of racialization. A good example of the way this framework is applied to empirical situations is the study by Miles and Annie Phizacklea (1980) of "working class racism," where they argue that black and white workers share significant political commonalities within specific class locations. Within this framework the political usages of race as a mechanism for political mobilization only make sense within an analysis of the class and ideological relations that shape the meaning of notions of race in specific societies. To signify this process of the social construction of the category of race within specific social relations Miles uses the concept of racialization.

For Miles processes of racialization are intertwined with the material conditions of migrant workers and other racialized groups. Its effects are the result of the contradiction between "on the one hand the need of the capitalist world economy for the mobility of human beings, and on the other, the drawing of territorial boundaries and the construction of citizenship as a legal category which sets boundaries for human mobility" (Miles, 1988:438). Within the British setting this ideological work is conducted primarily by the state and acts as a means of crisis management (Hall et al., 1978; CCCS, 1982; Miles and Phizacklea, 1984). From this perspective Miles argues that the construction of political identities which utilize "racial" consciousness plays no part in development of a "progressive politics." In this sense he views black political movements as ultimately operating on false premises and he disputes the analytic value of talking about the politics of race.

311

Interestingly enough, there exists a paradox in Miles's thinking with regard to the kinds of political mobilization that black and migrant workers have participated in. On the one hand he applauds the participation of black workers in the labor movement, while at the same time he is cynical of the political fruits of the labor movement, that is, the Labour Party and the trade unions. This is particularly apparent in his appraisal of the election of black and ethnic minority Labour MPs to the House of Commons (Miles, 1988:456). It seems that all current forms of political participation are viewed as reformist, regressive, and ultimately untenable. For Miles it appears that any form of political incorporation results in a form of cooption that merely legitimates the British social formation and capitalist democracy. There is a sense in which Miles seems to be striving for a theoretically defensible form of political action. However, it could be argued that his concentration on the illusory and repressive nature of racial ideology ultimately leads to a situation where all forms of action are dissolved into class-based terms of reference (Gilroy, 1987:25).

Miles's work has been a major influence in contemporary debates about race and racism, and the limits of political strategies based on race. But it says surprisingly little about the issue of political action and mobilization within migrant communities which is based on ideas about racial and ethnic identity. A key argument that could be derived from his analysis is that black and minority politics are really distillations of class conflict. If this is true any movement away from class-based political action (i.e., movements towards black community politics) is doomed to failure (Miles, 1989). If one takes this argument further, class-based political action is ultimately in opposition to any sort of sustained political organization around notions of race and ethnicity. This is largely because for Miles the politics of race is narrowly confined to the struggle against racism. This is neatly captured in the way he reformulates Stuart Hall's famous statement on the relationship between class and race. Reversing Hall's argument somewhat, Miles concludes that it is not race but "racism (which) can be the modality in which class is 'lived' and 'fought through'" (Miles, 1988:447).

In contemporary Europe, for example, the emphasis of most research has been on racism and the mobilization of racist movements rather than on constructions of race or the political mobilization of minority groups (Hainsworth, 2000; Koopmans and Statham, 2000). In France, one of the best known theorists of race is Michel Wieviorka, and his work emphasizes the social, economic, and political contexts that give rise to racism and the shift that has manifested itself from what he calls a racism of inequality to one of difference. Wieviorka considers a number of different political factors such as the breakdown of social movements, the crisis of the left, including the decline of the French Communist Party, and the perception of a "communitarian" threat to the Republic. He argues that social movements, such as the labor movement in Western societies, structure and confer meaning on a wide range of behaviors that extend beyond their strict field of action, and that when such movements decline they leave the actors for whom that movement was a central reference point orphaned and weakened. This weakness has a substantial impact on racism, both in the working- and middle-class milieu. The labor movement, according to Wieviorka, offered a "project of collective action in which all workers were united without distinction of race" (Wieviorka, 1995:97).

He suggests that when this began to break up, the project of social integration gave way to racial and social segregation. This process also affected the middle class, which had previously been polarized, forced to take up positions against either the labor movement or the employers. This class was then demobilized by the crisis of industrial society and the labor movement and space for attitudes and behavior that tend towards racism opened up. The space has to an extent been filled by the *Front National*.

Wieviorka (1994) has described the simultaneous rise of the far right and the decline of the Communist Party in the municipal councils of some of the districts around Paris during the 1980s, a shift that also occurred elsewhere in France. He uses the rhetoric of various political actors during this process to illustrate the links between conceptions of the republic, nation, and religion that inform racist discourse by reference to a "we" and that defines the "other" as non-Judeo-Christian, as decadent and as anti-French.

Antiracism in France has been closely connected with antifascism, but Wieviorka and others have noted the attempts by the far right to make antiracism synonymous with being anti-French, while rejecting the label of racist themselves. According to Wieviorka (1994), a differentialist racism has grown up, one which argues that every culture has value, and that one has a right to protect one's own – French – culture. Similar types of cultural racism have become part of the political scene in a number of European societies in recent years, particularly in the context of political debates about the impact of immigration on social and cultural institutions.

The Politics of Racial Formation

Another major influence in recent debates about the politics of race can be traced to the work of authors who have at one time or other been associated with the Birmingham Centre for Contemporary Cultural Studies (CCCS). This research was stimulated in many ways by the publication of Hall's (1980) programmatic essay on "Race, articulation and societies structured in dominance." Hall's most important argument was that while racism cannot be reduced to other social relations, it cannot be explained autonomously from them. Thus racism commands a relative autonomy from economic, political, and other social relations. Taking as their theoretical starting point Hall's rather abstract and programmatic argument, a number of attempts were made by writers associated at one time or another with the CCCS to retheorize the significance of the nature of racism within the British society (CCCS, 1982; Gilroy, 1987, 2000; Solomos, 1993). The works of these writers explored the changing political dynamics of race in the environment of the 1980s and 1990s, by focusing on the emergence and impact of new discourses and political agendas about race.

While Hall essentially initiated a reconceptualization of race within Marxist theory at CCCS, this position achieved a more developed expression in the work of the Race and Politics Group, resulting in the publication of *The Empire Strikes Back* (CCCS, 1982). This volume initiated a fierce controversy when it was first published and it still occupies a controversial position in the history of studies of race in British society. It sought to use Hall's theoretical insights to analyze race and politics in British society, but it can be seen as differing from his work in two significant ways. First, it placed a greater emphasis on the role of authoritarian state racism, especially in managing a British social formation that was undergoing a period of crisis. Second, the degree of autonomy given to race from class social relations was reworked (Gilroy, 1987; Solomos, 1993). It is this second development which is most significant with regard to the study of political action and social change. It is also the key area where the approach of these writers can be seen as

313

differing from the analytic framework about the relationship between race and class proposed by Miles among others.

A key theme of *The Empire Strikes Back* is that the working class in Britain does not constitute a continuous historical subject; and that black communities can constitute themselves as a politically conscious, "racially demarcated class fraction." It is in this sense that class cannot always be assumed to be the primary political force in any specific conjuncture. Thus black communities can act as autonomous political forces in any specific situations where their interests are threatened or attacked.

In recent years this kind of approach to the analysis of the role of racial politics has become more influential. Significant analytical frameworks which have foregrounded a political analysis of race are to be found in the work of British writers such as Paul Gilroy and Michael Keith and American writers such as Michael Omi, Howard Winant, and David Theo Goldberg. Although all of these writers can be seen as starting out from within a neo-Marxist or post-Marxist analytic framework, their works also engage with other theoretical and conceptual approaches. Without wanting to ignore the obvious differences between these writers it can fairly be said that their work reflects (1) an uneasiness with the limits of the Marxist model represented by Miles and other researchers and (2) a concern to investigate the mechanisms through which race and ethnicity are constructed through social, cultural, and ideological processes.

Gilroy has developed this line of analysis further in *There Ain't No Black in the Union Jack*, where he moves more clearly towards a perspective which he calls *race formation* (Gilroy, 1987). Rejecting the various analytical arguments associated with a neo-Marxist analysis of race and class, Gilroy emphasizes the need to conceive of race as the key aspect of the black experience in British society. In developing this argument he rejects any argument that prioritizes class over race in the analysis of political change. He argues forcefully:

> The proletariat of yesterday, classically conceived or otherwise, now has rather more to lose than its chains. The real gains which it has made have been achieved at the cost of a deep-seated accommodation with capital and the political institutions of corporatism. (Gilroy, 1987:246)

Here there exists, perhaps surprisingly, a great deal of similarity between Gilroy's notion of the relationship between class and race and Rex's theoretical conclusions (Rex and Tomlinson, 1979). Both authors are arguing that the continuous historical project of working-class struggle has been fractured, leaving a number of classes or class/race fractions involved in specific struggles. Equally, Gilroy and Rex both emphasize that their formulations are models of social action. It is essential to both positions that the significance of race is located within the salience that this term of reference has developed in the world of political actors.

It is here that Gilroy utilizes the concept of race formation, a notion he shares with the analysis of Omi and Winant (1994) in the United States. The notion of race formation emphasizes above all that race is not simply a concept that can be dispensed with. Gilroy, for example, accepts that the meaning of race as a social construction is contested and fought over. In this sense he is suggesting something close to a Gramscian position on ideology whereby race is viewed as an open political construction where the political meaning of terms like "black" are struggled over. He makes the case for the existence of an inclusive black community in which political identities are formulated that address numerous but linked everyday struggles against racism (Gilroy, 1987:38). It is this political possession of race by actors that leads to a social movement located around notions of racial identity: "Collective identities spoken through 'race,' community and locality are for all their spontaneity, powerful means to coordinate action and create solidarity" (Gilroy 1987:247). Gilroy, like a number of other authors working in this field, utilizes the literature on social movements to provide theoretical support for an interpretation of "nonclass-motivated" political action. Gilroy argues that it is in this context that both black community politics in general and the black sections movement within the Labour Party take on a political meaning of their own outside of specific class locations (Gilroy, 1987).

Along with Gilroy a number of other researchers have sought to develop an analytical model to simultaneously incorporate a number of political engagements without necessarily having to attempt to qualify these sites of struggle in terms of a class reductionism. Within this model of political action a multiplicity of political identities can be held. For example, an inclusive notion of black identity can prevail and at the same time allow heterogeneity of national and cultural origins within this constituency. Omi and Winant's analysis of the United States provides a good example of this kind of approach to the question of political mobilization. Taking as their starting point the changing politics of race in the period since the 1960s they argue for the need to see processes of racial formation as the outcome of the unique social, cultural, and political processes that have characterized the United States over the past three decades (Omi and Winant, 1994). In this sense their model of the United States experience ties up quite closely with a key strand in the theoretical literature on the politics of racialized mobilization in Britain and other European societies.

While these accounts of racial formation are at one level perceptive and contain important theoretical insights on the politics of race there are some serious omissions. The most important of these is (1) that there is no substantive analysis of the impact of black and minority participation in the political system, and (2) there is little analysis of the transformation of political discourses about race. Such conceptual and theoretical discussions have provided an important contribution to the debate on political agency and race, but they have shed little light on processes of minority mobilization within political institutions. Gilroy, for example, is ambivalent about the possibility of applying the notion of race formation to the electoral arena and party politics. On the question of establishing alliances within the Labour Party and promoting greater black representation he points out:

> The campaign to secure parliamentary places for black MPs and for the development of "black sections" inside the Labour Party has been one of the very few voices holding the idea of Afro-Asian unity although in their case, the political basis for this alliance remains vague. (Gilroy, 1987:40)

Two questions which come to mind are: why is the political basis for alliances of this nature vague? Would it be impossible to conceive of electoral politics connecting with the kinds of politics of race and community that is identified by Gilroy and other writers? Both these questions cannot be adequately dealt with on the basis of abstracted assumptions. Given the important changes in forms of black and ethnic minority political

315

involvement over the past decade it is of some importance to address these questions on the basis of research in the context of everyday political situations.

As yet we have seen little of this kind of research, and this has meant that we know surprisingly little about the new forms of black and ethnic minority political mobilization. Additionally it is important to note that little research has been done on the everyday processes of political change and conflict within political institutions. Key questions about the role of party politics, claims to representation, pressures on the policy agenda, and the role of black and minority politicians remain largely unexplored. Whatever the merits of attempts to question the limits of class-based models of the politics of race, it has to be said that as yet they have not provided a rounded analysis of the complex ways in which racialized political identities have been constructed and reconstructed in recent years. It is also interesting to note that all the approaches we have discussed say very little about the whole issue of democratic politics and the role of minorities in party politics. Indeed it is clear that writers as diverse as Rex, Hall, Miles, and Gilroy hold little hope that an oppositional politics can be developed within the arena of representative democracy, and they therefore say very little about what is perhaps the key aspect of new forms of black political involvement in British society over the past decade.

Gilroy, for example, views pressure group strategies which have evolved out of community struggles that utilize a specifically black political vernacular as the way forward. Along with Miles he has reservations about the possibility of political participation within the institutions of the labor movement. In particular he questions the degree to which the Labour Party can effect a defensible strategy on racial equality. He has also developed important critiques of the antiracist initiatives that were implemented during the 1980s within local government agencies (Gilroy, 1993). But arguments such as this leave a number of questions unanswered. For example: how have racialized political identities been shaped by political ideologies and party politics? What explains the emergence of minority politicians within mainstream party politics? What impact have mobilizations such as the black sections movement had on the political agenda? To what extent can political institutions in societies such as Britain be described as multicultural?

Trends in Racial Politics

The discussion in this paper has focused on key aspects of the complex sets of issues that need to be thought through in developing a conceptual framework for the analysis of the changing forms of racialized political mobilization in contemporary societies. Its main theme has been that the frameworks developed to analyze race and political action have important limitations. We are suggesting that the theoretical engagements of these frameworks cannot adequately conceptualize the political transformations and debates about race and politics which have taken place in recent years and which are likely to proceed apace during the early part of the twenty-first century. The political struggles that underscored the debates of the 1980s and 1990s have moved on. In many ways the turn towards the conceptualization of culturally defined racisms and the politics of identity has been led by political events which have shaped the political environment since the late 1980s (Gilroy, 2000; Saggar, 2000; Alibhai-Brown, 2000). This is perhaps best exemplified by the continuing debates over the changing boundaries of political mobilization in the contemporary period, which suggests that a range of sites for social antagonism and resistance exist within contemporary societies that cannot be conceptualized within a conventional class analysis. Equally, in the context of the complex forms of identity politics that have arisen in the past few decades, race and ethnicity are likely to remain important sites of political mobilization.

It is essential for any analysis of the contemporary politics of race and ethnicity to come to terms with the everyday processes and practices which help to give some meaning to ideas that articulate a politics of race. This necessitates an analysis that can help us to understand the complex and changing forms of political mobilization around questions of race and ethnicity that have emerged in contemporary societies. It also requires a fuller analysis of the similarities and differences between the experiences of different nation-states.

References

Alex-Assensoh, Y. M. and Hanks, L. J. (eds.) (2000) *Black and Multiracial Politics in America*. New York: New York University Press.

Alibhai-Brown, Y. (2000) *Who Do We Think We Are? Imagining the New Britain*. London: Allen Lane.

Browning, R. P., Marshall, D. R., and Tabb, D. H. (1984) *Protest Is Not Enough: The Struggle of Black and Hispanics for Equality in Urban Politics*. Berkeley: University of California Press.

Browning, R. P., Marshall, D. R., and Tabb, D. H. (1986) "Protest is not enough: A theory of political incorporation." *PS* 14,3:576–81.

Bulmer, M. and Solomos, J. (eds.) (1999) *Ethnic and Racial Studies Today*. London: Routledge.

Centre for Contemporary Cultural Studies (CCCS) (1982) *The Empire Strikes Back*. London: Hutchinson.

Favell, A. (1998) *Philosophies of Integration: Immigration and the Idea of Citizenship in France and Britain*. Basingstoke, UK: Macmillan.

Gilroy, P. (1987) *There Ain't No Black in the Union Jack*. London: Hutchinson.

Gilroy, P. (1993) *Small Acts: Thoughts on the Politics of Black Cultures*. London: Serpent's Tail.

Gilroy, P. (2000) *Between Camps: Nations, Cultures and the Allure of Race*. London: Allen Lane.

Hainsworth, P. (ed.) (2000) *The Politics of the Extreme Right*. London: Pinter.

Hall, S. (1980) "Race, articulation and societies structured in dominance," in UNESCO *Sociological Theories: Race and Colonialism*. Paris: UNESCO, pp.305–45.

Hall, S., Critcher, C., Jefferson, T., Clarke, J., and Roberts, B. (1978) *Policing the Crisis: Mugging, the State, and Law and Order*. London: Macmillan.

Hanchard, M. (ed.) (1999) *Racial Politics in Contemporary Brazil*. Durham, NC: Duke University Press.

Koopmans, R. and Statham, P. (eds.) (2000) *Challenging Immigration and Ethnic Relations Politics: Comparative European Perspectives*. Oxford: Oxford University Press.

Marable, M. (1985) *Black American Politics*. London: Verso.

Miles, R. (1988) "Racism, Marxism and British politics." *Economy and Society* 17,3:428–60.

Miles, R. (1989) *Racism*. London: Routledge.

Miles, R. (1993) *Racism after "race relations."* London: Routledge.

Miles, R. and Phizacklea, A. (1980) *Labour and Racism*. London: Routledge.

Miles, R. and Phizacklea, A. (1984) *White Man's Country: Racism in British Politics*. London: Pluto Press.

Omi, M. and Winant, H. (1994) *Racial Formation in the United States: From the 1960s to the 1990s*, 2nd edn. New York: Routledge.

Parekh, B. (2000) *The Future of Multi-Ethnic Britain: Report of the Commission on the Future of Multi-Ethnic Britain*. London: Profile Books.

Rex, J. (1970) *Race Relations in Sociological Theory*. London: Weidenfeld and Nicholson.

Rex, J. (1973) *Race, Colonialism and the City*. London: Routledge and Kegan Paul.

Rex, J. (1979) "Black militancy and class conflict," in R. Miles and A. Phizacklea (eds.) *Racism and Political Action in Britain*. London: Routledge and Kegan Paul, pp.72–92.

Rex, J. (1986a) *Race and Ethnicity*. Buckingham, UK: Open University Press.

Rex, J. (1986b) "The role of class analysis in the study of race relations – A Weberian perspective," in J. Rex and D. Mason (eds.) *Theories of Race and Ethnic Relations*. Cambridge, UK: Cambridge University Press, pp.64–83.

Rex, J. (1989) "Some notes on the development of the theory of race and ethnic relations in Britain," unpublished discussion document, Centre for Research in Ethnic Relations, University of Warwick.

Rex, J. and Moore, R. (1967) *Race, Community and Conflict*. London: Oxford University Press.

Rex, J. and Tomlinson, S. (1979) *Colonial Immigrants in a British City*. London: Routledge and Kegan Paul.

Saggar, S. (2000) *Race and Representation: Electoral Politics and Ethnic Pluralism in Britain*. Manchester, UK: Manchester University Press.

Sears, D. O., Sidanius, J., and Bobo, L. (eds.) (2000) *Racialized Politics: The Debate About Racism in America*. Chicago: University of Chicago Press.

Solomos, J. (1993) *Race and Racism in Britain*, 2nd edn. Basingstoke, UK: Macmillan.

Solomos, J. and Back, L. (1995) *Race, Politics and Social Change*. London: Routledge.

Solomos, J. and Back, L. (1996) *Racism and Society*. Basingstoke, UK: Macmillan.

Wieviorka, M. (ed.) (1994) *Racisme et Xénophobie en Europe: une comparaison internationale*. Paris: Editions la Découverte.

Wieviorka, M. (1995) *The Arena of Racism*. London: Sage.

PART IV

Space

Introduction to Part IV

David Theo Goldberg and John Solomos

Issues of location, space, and territory have played key roles in the history and development of racial and ethnic formations in various parts of the globe. The location of race and ethnicity within spatial boundaries, whether it be the colonial state or the metropolitan city, the urban "ghetto" or the suburban sprawl, has been a recurrent theme in theoretical debates and in empirical studies of urban life. From the very earliest stages of the genesis of the academic study of race and ethnicity, metaphors of race and territory have abounded, inherent features of the field of study. Indeed, in many ways racially marked images of "the city" and urban spaces have played a key role in the configuration of urban politics and social change.

Michael Keith provides a powerful reminder of both the breadth and the power of images of "the city" in different historical and geographical settings. Drawing on a diverse range of sources and situated examples, Keith provides a sharp reminder that many of the social scientific ways of conceiving the city that developed during the twentieth century were deeply inflected with racially composed or saturated imagery and with the boundaries of whiteness. He also provides a critical overview of the ways in which governmental intervention in urban contexts across Europe and North America have been rationalized by reference to the place of race and ethnicity within the iconography of "the city." Keith's paper concludes by suggesting avenues of research that could be pursued if we are to achieve a more nuanced understanding of increasingly multicultural but deeply racialized cities.

While Keith's account is wide-ranging in coverage, the following two papers in Part IV offer overviews of two of the key conceptual frames shaping much of the scholarship about urban racial and ethnic conditions. Robert Bernasconi's paper provides an account of both the historical and contemporary usages of the term "ghetto." He begins by tracing its lineage to the way it was used to describe the areas of cities in which Jews were confined during the sixteenth century. He then explores the evolution and development of the notion of "the ghetto" during the twentieth century, noting that it is used much more broadly today while it is still linked to the core practice of segregation. In doing so he provides a suggestive insight into the impact of new forms of ghettoization and exclusion on the social fabric of cities, drawing particularly on the experience of white flight and gated communities as symbols of urban life in the USA.

The next paper, by Douglas S. Massey, has important links to Bernasconi's account of the ghetto, focusing as it does on residential segregation. Pointing to the ways in which interest in questions of residential segregation was at the heart of the work of the Chicago School of Sociology in the early twentieth century, Massey provides a sharply focused account of the evidence about segregation that has emerged in more recent research in US metropolitan areas. In particular, he highlights the increasingly complex forms of segregation that are current in the present environment and the need to develop new conceptual and empirical tools in order to analyze them.

In a creative reading of various bodies of literature, Claudia Milian Arias analyzes the ways in which borders – physical and geographical, metaphysical and metaphorical, philosophical and linguistic – fashion interlocking identities. She reveals how these bordered identities create selves that are inscribed racially, sexually, culturally, and linguistically. These selves, she suggests, dialogue with what become "other" border-lands, other identities marked by distinct boundaries. She is particularly interested to show how borders are thus the conditions of possibility for interstitial identities such as mixed race formations.

Les Back's paper on race and the Internet neatly supplements Milian Arias's. Back explores the increasing role of new technologies of communication within racist subcultures. He examines the changing boundaries of race and ethnic identities prompted from within urban settings but projected cybernetically well beyond the sociospatial confines of the urban. His account focuses specifically on the role of the Internet and related technologies as mechanisms to configure what he calls "translocal whiteness" among activists involved in neofascist and extreme right-wing subcultures. He investigates, in particular, the possibilities to be found through the Internet to construct forms of imagined identities across networks of racist activists living in different localities or nation-states, as well as the implications of such activism in terms of everyday political mobilization and intervention.

Part IV thus stretches ethnoracial experience from the materialities of its urban underpinnings in the past century to its more recent global extension through the virtualities of the new cybertechnologies.

Chapter 21

The Mirage at the Heart of the Myth? Thinking about the White City

Michael Keith

In the early 1990s Birmingham, the second largest city in the United Kingdom, reinvented itself. Formerly the metal–bashing heart of manufacturing Britain and re-nowned for both its civic culture and brutal postwar redevelopment around a shopping market and traffic roundabouts, the city was traumatized by each of the postwar depressions. Like many another postindustrial metropolis across the globe it attempted to foster the creation of a new site of mass consumption for the present and future, rationalized by a narrative of renaissance that was based on the tapestry of historical tales of the past. Mass consumption focused on new shopping malls, a theater district, an international conference center and associated hotels and new sports developments to host international events.[1] The story line that stitched this tapestry together was in some ways more interesting.

The Council "reimagineered" the marketing of the city by relocating it. A council promotion exercise, captured by the accidentally ironic strap line "More than meets the eye"[2] drew on images of gondolas to boast that the city had more miles of canal than Venice; of Stratford on Avon and Coventry Cathedral to highlight the city's cultural heritage; empty shopping malls and (white) nuclear families walking through villages of Warwickshire to highlight lifestyle opportunities. Given that a 1988 quality of life report had placed Birmingham 38th out of 38 cities in the UK and that in 1988 the French newspaper *Le Point* had ranked the city 49th out of the 50 largest cities in Europe it is perhaps not surprising that "image" and reputation were central to the project to regenerate the city. But whilst the politics of the city clearly reflected the fact that over 25 percent of the city's population were drawn from black and ethnic minority back-grounds (Solomos and Back, 1995) the regeneration reconstructed a sense of the city that was profoundly white in its refusal to acknowledge the needs, presence, or aspirations of such communities as Patrick Loftman has described in great detail (Loftman, 1990).

In stark contrast, on becoming mayor of London in the year 2000, Ken Livingstone took dinner with the members of the City Corporation. Whilst flouting the dress code by refusing to wear the normal dinner jacket (tuxedo) he told the assembled audience representing the greatest concentration of wealth in Europe that:

> If London is to remain the financial centre of Europe, and to attract the inward investment and skilled labour for this, it cannot do so without internalizing and adopting the same international cultural norms and approach. Those who believe that London can survive as

Europe's leading financial centre while adopting, explicitly or implicitly, a narrow racist or intolerant culture do not understand the challenges of globalisation.[3]

Across the city[4] the rhetoric of globalization has created for the twenty-first century a celebration of cultural diversity. The "regeneration" of cultural quarters and "ethnic enclaves" has become part of the mainstream rhetoric of projects promoting urban transformation. At first glance this may appear a welcome change from the whitening waves of gentrification in the 1970s and 1980s property booms on both sides of the Atlantic. But it was not for nothing that black civil rights groups in 1960s America proclaimed that "urban renewal equals nigger removal" and so it is perhaps important to greet the meeting of global capitalism with niche-marketed multiculturalism with a degree of caution as this particular postcolonial encounter begins to reshape the cities of the twenty-first century.

Such stories are open both to easy derision and proper critique. On the one hand, in any particular city location it is imperative to subject the representations of a new urbanism to a realistic analysis of the political economy and the political possibilities of the juxtaposition of the all too grim litany of socioeconomic indicators of poverty and inequality that are both generated by and sit alongside increasing concentrations of affluence (Feagin, 1998; Harvey, 1990; Katznelson, 1992, Lash and Urry, 1994). But on the other hand it is also essential to question the hidden dreams and desires that shape the future visions of the city that are at the heart of major changes in urban living that are characteristic of most of the cities of contemporary capitalism. And in descriptions of such city transformations the analytical salience of issues of race and racism is far too often either peripheral or silent. In part this chapter suggests that such silence is not necessarily racially unmarked, that normality itself can be implicitly epidermal.

At the heart of this chapter is an assertion that it is not possible to disassociate the deep cultural roots of such narratives from the lived experiences of people in modern cities that are divided by imaginary but very powerful vectors of race thinking and racial categorization. The simultaneously real and imaginary nature of the social life of cities demands that we think carefully about the manner in which the cultural traces of thinking about the cosmopolitan present owes much to techniques of governing, mapping, and categorizing populations that draw on ostensibly objective value-loaded lexicons of race and urbanism. If we take seriously the deep cultural roots of these structures of sensibility we might think seriously about their impact, not so much to validate the polarities of opposition on which they hinge but more to acknowledge the deeply implicated binary thinking that they invoke. For an understanding of the interplay between race thinking and contemporary urbanism cannot escape the seemingly contradictory observation that the abstract basis of both of these sociologically powerful terms is tendentious at best; race a perennially powerful mirage and the city a normative myth as much as an empirical locus of analysis. For these reasons an understanding of the interplay of race and the city is in part an articulation of the myth within the mirage.

The Powerful Mirage of Race Thinking

Race – with its uncertain relationship to "ethnicity" – appears to be a term that captures one of the key fractures within both contemporary industrialized societies of affluent capitalism and also – after the end of history – increasingly structures thinking and writing about Second and Third World societies after the collapse of state socialism (Goldberg, 1993; Solomos and Back, 1996). In their particular realizations, race and ethnicity are historically and geographically produced forms of identification that acquire a self-referential analytical power. It is a prosaic paradox that the more that people *understand* their political systems and allocation mechanisms of power and resources in terms of race and ethnicity, the more the terms themselves acquire analytical *significance* in making sense of particular social moments. Across many of the metropolises of capitalism in every continent, a child's educational future may be determined by where they live, a settlement pattern structured by a racialized allocation of housing resources that reflects a historically determined ethnic migration of labor that still bears an imprint on the niched divisions of labor markets and racialized labor processes in a particular city. The conflicts that result from these histories in particular sites in the city may determine struggles for community rights, the party or movements that individuals are likely to campaign or vote for, and the processes of recognition and resource allocation that potentially reproduce social divisions of race and ethnicity as meaningful ways of understanding the social world.

Across the globe narratives of empire, of slavery, of varying degrees of forced and unforced labor migration all articulate cultural differences in very real terms as differences in life chances that people from one racialized group may experience in relation to others. But also as these differences in power, in rights and in wealth become entrenched through time in particular locations, the universality of humanity is potentially compromised by the legacies of history and geography (Butler et al., 2000). Drawing attention to this academically may at times appear to cut against both a liberal tradition of thinking about relations between individuals and a communitarian sense that such patterns of racialization create in some sense spurious forms of collective identity. Analytically, scholars of race and ethnicity are consequently caught between emphasizing the often hidden significance of the imprint of racialization (Goldberg, 1993; Omi and Winant, 1987; Winant, 1994) and invoking another world beyond "raciology" (Gilroy, 2000). Put crudely, whilst the fundamental building blocks of race thinking are themselves ethically compromised it does not make the edifice of racialized social divisions any less powerful a mirage.

The Returning Myth of the City

The city likewise is often offered up as an analytical centerpiece of social analysis. At the highpoint of urban social theory in the Anglophone academy, the tension between cities as ever more powerful *empirical descriptions* of places where the vast majority of humanity lived and cities as *objects that might succumb to theoretical understanding* foundered on the problem of the analytical unity of the urban. Effectively, by the early 1980s scholars from diffuse ideological perspectives implicitly or explicitly agreed that the city could no longer be considered a basic building block of analysis or a coherent theoretical unit (Saunders, 1981, 1986; Savage and Warde, 1993: chapters 5 and 6). A chaotically conceptualized *object* of analysis ill served the task of an aspirant sociological rendering of contemporary life. And yet the *subject* of the city refused to disappear from the way in which academics, politicians, and artists organized their ways of thinking about social and economic life. It has been argued elsewhere that it is consequently more productive to think about the manner in which the city comes to serve as an organizing concept in writing and thinking about social and economic life than it is to attempt to "theorize" the urban (Keith, 2000). A focus on the relationship between observation of the city and the cities that are being observed problematizes both subject and object, disrupts any simplistic invocations of theorizing the city, and concentrates on the manner in which an urban sensibility structures our narratives of the real. In this sense, the city has stubbornly refused to disappear as a category of social analysis. Livable cities, networked cities, sustainable cities, global cities, dual cities, are all central to ways of thinking about the present and organizing our ways of thinking about the possible and probable futures (Osborne and Rose, 1999).

Race and city: both terms share an anchor at the heart of commonsense discussions about the way in which we live our lives. Both terms are the invisible center of subdisciplinary studies in both social sciences and humanities. Both terms mean something and yet when scrutinized more carefully they appear to expand to include everything or else melt into air as conceptually flawed caricatures of reality. More significantly still there is a straightforward proposition from which this chapter flows. It is suggested here that the binary relationships that inform "race thinking" and the uncertain values that are invoked through vocabularies of urbanism are mutually implicated in the history of descriptions that make the social life of cities comprehensible across a wide range of related sources, ranging through the imaginary world of novelists, the ideologically loaded paradigms of the academy, the seemingly mundane texts of governmental reform, and the hyperreal excesses of Sim City and the virtual experience of the computer game. In this context we need to think carefully about the technologies through which representational practices create their own subjects and draw simultaneously upon "race thinking" and "city talk" if we are to understand the complex and recursively defined way in which people from different cultures live in cities of today's globe (Der Derian, 1998; Robins and Webster, 1999).

In an exemplary work in 1973 Raymond Williams used the couplet country and city as key organizing themes in structuring the manner in which people thought – and wrote – about their lives. Drawing on the literary traditions from the seventeenth century onwards, but citing a tradition in which a "contrast between country and city, as fundamental ways of life, reaches back into classical times" (Williams, 1973:1), he outlined the metaphoric and metonymic associations which allowed landscapes in general, and the city/country binary couplet in particular to stand for a much wider structure of sensibility, to invoke sets of social relations and power relations that were crystallized in specific buildings, aesthetics, characters, and moralities. Williams suggests that the insinuation of the country and the city into a way of thinking about everyday life is always about something more than just a descriptive vocabulary, that "whenever I consider the relations between country and city... I find this history active and continuous: the relations are not only of ideas and experiences, but of rent and interest, of situation and power; *a wider system*" (Williams, 1973:7; my emphasis).

Through a volume which focused on the English literary tradition but also touches on the work of Dostoievsky, Engels, Balzac, and Baudelaire, Williams describes the manner in which urban life connoted a series of positive and negative values, the corollaries of which were logically identified with the rural way of life. He highlights notions of learning, of communication and of light as the positively signified aspects of city life in contrast to the peace, innocence, and simple values of the country. Yet the stigmas of noise, worldliness and ambition that are associated with the city (and often the court as a metonym for the urban) are also juxtaposed against the backwardness, ignorance, and limitations of the rural way of life (see table 21.1).

If we take seriously the deep cultural roots of these structures of sensibility then we might also think seriously about their import, not so much to verify or falsify the polarities and oppositions but more to acknowledge the deeply implicated binarisms that are at the heart of ways of thinking about cities and the techniques of modernizing, rebuilding, beautifying, regulating, regenerating, and governing them.

If these values lie just beneath the ways in which cities are represented they also condition changing attitudes towards the contemporary metropolis; the characteristics of an urbanism that is not straightforwardly (after Simmel or Wirth) a specific cultural form or a way of life but can be understood as a tangle of ambivalent feelings, sentiments, and commonsense "knowledges" about the nature of city life. Moreover, if we take the spirit of Williams slightly further it is possible through simplification (and a degree of caricature) to identify a *diagnostic cartography* of this urbanism (see table 21.2). Crucially it is not just that there are particular positive and negative valorizations of city life but also that they resonate within the tensions between attraction and repulsion that echo in other structures of feeling. Space prevents a systematic reading of the canon of urban studies in this chapter through such a lens. But it is possible at least to suggest that a deconstructive reading of both the more dystopian and the more utopian analyses of contemporary city life across the social sciences draws at least occasionally from such implicit normative and profoundly cultural understandings of the potential of the urban; whether even in recent times we consider texts as diverse as Peter Hall's study of the links between cities and civilization (Hall, 1998), Castells' networks of global economic change (Castells, 1996, 1997, 1998), Sassen's treatises on the nature of globalization (Appiah and Sassen, 1999; Sassen, 1999), or the detective-like investigations of American capitalism scholars such as Mike Davis and Ed Soja (Davis, 1998, 2000; Soja, 1989, 1996, 1999).

The psychoanalytic is important in this context and some authors have taken further its relevance to urban studies (Pile, 1996; Donald, 1999). But in the world of symbolic values it is not necessary to resort to a full scale psychoanalytic reading of the urban to identify both the tensions between attraction and repulsion implicit in the various representations of city life and the manner in which a reading of the city can provide a "topos for the exploration of anxiety and paranoia" (Vidler, 1996:xiii). It is also the case

Table 21.1 The country and the city for Raymond Williams

The city	The country
Learning	Peace
Communication	Innocence
Light	Simple value
Noise	Backwardness
Worldliness	Ignorance
Ambition	Limitation

Table 21.2 Cultural cartographies and the urban imagination

The city	The country
Disgust	
Debauchery	Propriety
Instability	Security
Danger	Stability
Transgression	Order
Desire	
Lust	Repression
Culture	Nature
Avant-gardism	Tradition
Cosmopolitanism	Parochialism

that such a topos is both malleable and potentially pernicious in the manner in which the positive and negative valorizations of specific characteristics can become transcoded through particular processes that articulate representations of city spaces (Stallybrass and Whyte, 1986). In novels (Moretti, 1998), in cinema (Donald, 1999), in contemporary art (Collings, 1997), as much as in planning and in local economic development, the lexicon of the city provides both subjects that are analyzed and a set of values and meanings that are not reducible to mere bricks and mortar.

Again space prohibits exhaustive categorization here but it is possible to point to a genre of writing that might be exemplified by Paul Rabinow's work *French Modern*. Rabinow identified the links between French urbanism in the early twentieth century and its colonial antecedents in the late nineteenth. Rabinow's work is important because it details the ties between the heroic technocrats who dreamed the future of the cities, the image *de la ville* which provided the armature for the realization of these dreams (Rabinow, 1989:5) and the management of urban populations.[5] He demonstrates the realization of the colonial imperative to administer in the built form of colonial cities and the subsequent translation of such rationalities to the cities of the French mainland. Regimes of governmentality emerge through the histories of design: "Both in the garden cities and in the colonies, the symbolic central point of the city had been reserved for public administration. Administration was evolving from an organizing symbol to a technical consideration" (Rabinow 1989:358). Similarly – though initially without the Foucauldian framing – a related project lay at the heart of Christine Boyer's landmark early work *Dreaming The Rational City* (Boyer, 1986) in its consideration of the relationship between ideologies of the built form and the development of Los Angeles. In both cases the authors unpick the rationality that lies behind the organization of city form and the technologies of power through which such rationality is realized in the built environment; put simply to answer David Harvey's perennial question "in whose image is the city built"? In each case and in similar work (e.g., Wright, 1991; Sennett, 1994) the city emerges as a sociological subject through specific regimes of power, both echoing and drawing on Michel Foucault's understanding of a notion of the conduct of conduct that lies at the heart of specific forms of governmentality (Foucault, 1991). For the purposes of this chapter it is necessary to link the Foucauldian genre of writing about the city, which takes the city as subject at its heart, to other investigations of the historical and cultural roots of city thinking.

There are three pieces to this analytical jigsaw. It is possible to imagine an intellectual project that takes both the vocabulary of the spaces of the city – (*inter alia*) the plan, the neighborhood, the suburb, the inner city, the ghetto, the street, the tower block – and secondly the technologies of their representation – (*inter alia*) the map, the visual, the virtual, the textual, the oral, the perspectival – and subjects both to a genealogical examination. It is not that the vocabulary is contaminated in some way but it is instead important to identify and recognize the provenance of the representations that we deploy (De Certeau, 1984; Barth, 1996; Deutsche, 1996) if, for example, we are to dig beneath the quintessentially urban celebrations of the "neighborhood" promoted by Tony Blair's Social Exclusion Unit or the suspect past, present, and future rural spaces of the village of sociality espoused by Hillary Clinton (Social Exclusion Unit, 2000; Clinton, 1996).

Such genealogies relate to popular culture and to economic rationale, to the rule of law and the etymological city roots of the nature of civilization. It is precisely in this context that it is important to think about the manner in which the European Commission might suggest that "the past decades have seen a rediscovery of the value of urban living and a growing appreciation of quality of life in the cities of Europe" and that " 'Urban areas' are a statistical concept. Cities are *projects for a new style of life and work*." (European Commission, 1991:7, my emphasis) It is also precisely in this context that alongside the spaces of the city and the technologies of their representation it becomes important to interrogate the third piece of the jigsaw: the characters that explicitly and implicitly, historically and geographically, inhabit these new spaces.

In this sense it has been argued elsewhere that the characters of the modern city have a similarly complex provenance (Keith, 1995). In the imagined worlds of the government bureaucrat, as much as in the anticipated urbanisms of the city architect, a cast of citizens occupies the city stage. The nuclear family, the squatter, the single parent, the key worker, the cultural worker, the rioter, the anarchist, the class-mobile entrepreneur, are just a few of the iconic subject positions that become reified in social policy and catered for in city plans. They too come loaded with their own histories of respectability and transgression, they too might logically form the subject matter of independent genealogical volumes. The inspiration for such an analysis might again be the work of Walter Benjamin – whose "types" populated his work and served more than a merely analytical role (Buck-Morss, 1989; Bullock and Jennings, 1996; Gilloch, 1996; Missac, 1995, Szondi, 1995; Keith, 2000). Yet of central significance to this chapter is that while we can speak through a historically loaded vocabulary, it remains essential to understand that such spaces, such technologies, and such characters are rarely racially unmarked.

The similarity between the structures of such sensibility that fascinated Raymond Williams and the structures of racial thinking is far from coincidental.[6] The fundamental premise of racism identifies a distinction between self and various others that are associated with particular characteristics and a casual glance at the attributes of urbanism detailed in table 21.2 cannot fail to notice the resemblance with much "commonsense" discussion of racial caricature. The sometimes crude boundaries of bigotry echo the crude binary oppositions of town and countryside, just as the more nuanced valorizations of disgust and desire hide the more complex racisms of the contact zones between different cultures (Pratt, 1992) and the ambivalence of some writers about the possibilities of cultural fusion and hybridity (Bhabha, 1994; Gilroy, 2000).

The burgeoning literature on "whiteness" (Dyer, 1997; Frankenberg, 1997; Ware, 1992; Ware and Back, 2000) is significant here. Absence can be as powerful a racializing force as presence. Racism at times works by a process of substitution, a coding of phrases and terms which conveys racist meaning without specific reference to explicitly racist beliefs. The urban renaissance currently promoted in the United Kingdom needs to look at its constituent parts as closely as the glibly multicultural globe celebrated by the new Mayor of London. Periclean Athens promoted an enlightenment polis yet simultaneously subsumed slavery. An architecturally rooted urbanism can at times produce streets and neighborhoods purged of racial impurity (Lokko, 2000). Conversely, discussions of mugging, of faith, of sexuality can be racialized in a moment through the selective representation of the street, the mosque, and scene of domestic motherhood.

Such binarism has been subjected to a stringent criticism in much contemporary social theory (Bhabha, 1994). However, what is rarely contested is that at the heart of much thinking in the United Kingdom about a sociology of "race relations" and in the USA about the centrality of racial thinking is precisely such a phenomenology of self and other, transcoded through the epidermal, governmental, and the cultural into a model of normality and stranger, the latter potentially either "assimilated" or rejected by a dominant – commonly implicitly white – social world. And as always what is often most negatively stigmatized is at times most desired, a covetous tradition with scopophilic roots at the very heart of all social observation.

In the British historiography of writing about race, the barely postcolonial dark strangers that inhabited the writings of Richmond, Patterson, and Banton through the Weberian constructions of John Rex and on to the more politically engaged models that focused on the problems of raciology that emerge in the crucibles of racism, the building blocks remain firmly binary in nature. Even the work in more recent cultural theory that has focused on issues of hybridity, syncretism, and "new ethnicities" is potentially open to the critique of synthesizing alternative purities, or creating "an essentialist opposite to the now denigrated cultural purity" (Maharaj, cited in Mercer, 2000:238).

Likewise in the USA, for all the nuances of the Chicago school tradition (Abbott, 1999) and the occasional investigations of the construction process behind race thinking (Goldberg, Harris) the empirical horror of the racialized city leads unerringly back to a dominant trend of investigation that begins with the categoric indictments of William Julius Wilson's mapping of socioeconomic disadvantage, moves through Mike Davis's cartographic certainties of Hispanic city life (M. Davis, 2000) and on to Angela Davis's archaeology of the American Prison Industrial complex (A. Davis, 2000). The point is not to underestimate the political power or the academic value of such work but just to stop and think for a second about some of the categories on which it relies – the racial subjects that inhabit such narratives – and the relationship of these categories to particular strands of thinking about the city. The apparent statistical solidity implicit in the demographics of migrant minorities needs to be set alongside the contingent nature of the creation of sociological and political subjects and the mediating force of cultural racialization on which this contingency rests.

Even in a mainland European contemporary context that emerges from the phenomenon of migrant flows and the unspeakability of race thinking after the Holocaust, the categoric refusal of multiculture from writers as distinguished as Michel Wieviorka

(Wieviorka, 1998) is in part reliant upon a distinction between the normal and the alien that fits precisely within both the longstanding traditions of French secularism and the categoric oppositions of Fanon's "look a negro" (Fanon, 1986).

One possibility of moving beyond deconstructive critique of writing about cities is to reconsider the conventional relationship between empirical and rationalistic traditions of intellectual investigation. If the premise that racial categorization seeps into writing and thinking about cities has a degree of validity, it may be worth developing the outlines of a synthesis of empirical and theoretical analyses of the contemporary city. Such a stance might take as its starting point the possibility of combining the rigorous empirical exploration of the forms of racialized newness that come into the world through the continuously mutating urban landscape alongside a more rigorous skepticism about the plurality of representational practices that are used to capture such diversity in print and in film.

Towards Some Exemplary Thinking: Technology, Landscape, and Character

It is possible to argue that the strength of urban studies is the logical corollary of its weakness. A predilection for interdisciplinarity both transgresses disciplinary boundaries but also potentially neglects the logics on which conventional academic divisions of labor are based. To suggest that architecture, cultural studies, sociology, politics, history, and geography might all be talking about a different city when they invoke notions of the urban is perhaps unsurprising. More significantly in the contemporary academy, as disciplinary boundaries collapse it becomes more important to examine the sorts of leakage that occur across previously sealed silos of knowledge production.

Social policy debates may be simultaneously structured by architectural concerns in the search for "cities for a small planet" (Rogers, 1997), a postnationalist political theory that attempts to develop an Athenian invocation of the urban as a basic building bloc (Young, 1990, 1997), a social theory that attempts to relate trajectories of visual culture with regimes of urban design (Boyer, 1994), or a philosophy that celebrates the characters of the city as the bearers of the possibility of living with difference. The productive intellectual crossings of such debates does not render it any less significant to understand where different trajectories are emerging from.

In a similar fashion academic discourse draws upon particular representational technologies. The relationships between the plan and architecture, perspective and empirical observation, photography and anthropology, the map and geography, the archive and historical narrative, virtual space or spaces of governance and political theory, experience and ethnography all demonstrate particularly diverse technological processes through which city life comes to be represented.

In this context the racialized nature of the contemporary city is likewise dependent on the processes through which the analytical world is rendered comprehensible as an object of study. At a simple level it becomes important to ask why it is that in Sim City you can have a riot but never a revolution; to think about the status of the film evidence that made it plausible that the police officers attacking Rodney King were innocent (Butler, 1993). The case demonstrated that the field of vision is so starkly racialized. As Martin Jay has demonstrated, it is possible to link particular regimes of the visible to alternative ways of thinking about the city (Jay, 1992, 1994). It is also plausible – after Lefebvre (1991) – to think of the city acting both as a product of representational technologies (a representation of space) and also as a theater of representational practices (a space of representation).

Through specific regimes of representation the city emerges as a political subject in relation to particular and specific configurations of the countryside, race, and nationalism. Put crudely, studies of nationalism have long identified correspondent relations between the strength of nation-states and the genesis and the artifice of national cultures. In a sense the assimilatory uniformity of the nation–state and its correspondent relationship with genocide identified by Bauman is inversely significant in relation to the power of city-based identities. The weakening of the nation-state and the strengthening of cities in the networks of global capitalism in North America and a potentially federal Europe need to be placed in the context in which the weakening of national ties is not without benefits. This is not to invoke a utopian urbanism characteristic of some of Iris Marion Young's work or the cherished urbanism promoted by architect Richard Rogers in his work heading the British Urban Task Force.

The "old new" racism of national rights and belonging in 1980s Europe is superseded by a debate about the racism of global capitalism tied to the German decision in 2000 to restart the *Gastarbeiter* system directed at South Asian IT skilled labor, an investigation by the British government into the possibility of further selective large-scale "skilled" immigration, ongoing mass migration to the major American metropolises, an auction by the mainstream political parties in the UK to provide the most intolerant articulations of refugee asylum law, and the obscene deaths in June 2000 of 58 "illegal" Chinese migrants in the back of a refrigerated grocery van just down the road from the not so white cliffs of Dover.

Such weakenings of national ties are linked directly to the new flows of global migrant labor (Sassen, 1999) which both rely on cities as the reference points in which newly racialized populations coalesce, and amplify the city as a representational site of refugee presence personified through beggars in streets and claimants in the town hall. The three pieces of the jigsaw – landscape, technology, and iconic characters – can be manipulated precisely because of the cultural depths of race thinking and city talk on which they draw.

In a complementary fashion at times of national crisis the landscapes of nationalism can resonate through the countryside as much as the city.[7] The novelist Kazuo Ishiguro cleverly played with such a notion in tracing the seething growth of 1930s fascism to the bastion of Englishness in the country house at the center of *The Remains of the Day*.[8] Likewise it should be of no surprise at all that the British National Party in 2000 turns towards the countryside, with a Cambridge University-educated leadership based on a rural small landholding in Wales (Back, 2000) to identify discontented nationalist sentiment, with its launch of a new journal *The Countryman*.

At a different scale of analysis within the city theater itself we might consider the relationship between spaces of representation and the characters that such spaces are inhabited by (Jacobs, 1996). The nature of such an iconographic understanding of contemporary metropolitan life has been recently touched on by Bourdieu in his notion of "site effects" where

> These days referring to a "problem suburb" or ghetto almost automatically brings to mind, not "realities" – largely unknown in any case to the people who rush to talk about them – but phantasms, which feed on emotional experiences stimulated by more or less uncontrolled words and images. (Bourdieu, 1999:123)

By definition the structures of feeling that inform the languages through which we imagine the cities of the past, the present, and the future are culturally specific. Just as the work of Raymond Williams was itself always subject to critiques of Eurocentricity, the way in which the city has been imagined in different national traditions generates related but different cultures of urbanism. The long-standing antiurbanism of mainstream twentieth century America that generated the twin totemic symbols of the city automobile and the free suburb alongside the *fin de siècle* gentrifying reconquest of the city frontier documented in detail by Neil Smith (1996) is self-evidently different from a mainland European sensibility that is most readily identified with Simmel, Benjamin, and a cherished urbanism that lends itself so easily to the Parisian *grands projects* of the Mitterand era in 1980s France and the millennial London of Blair's Britain (Frisby, 1985: chapter 4). As James Donald has noted "juxtaposing the category of the city with the concept of modernity is to ask about an experience, a repertoire of ways of acting and feeling that is culturally and historically bounded" (Donald, 1999:xi). Differences and similarities in the histories of articulation of cities structure the specificities of thinking about the racialized urban even as they reinforce the analytical power of the categories themselves.

But the purpose of this chapter is not, in the spirit of comparative sociology, to typologize geographies of city thinking and their cognate ideologies of city planning. It is rather to suggest that beginning to understand the genealogy of vocabularies of the urban alongside the spatially concrete forms of race formation provides an alternative perspective on ways of thinking about race and the city. Put simply it is sometimes most productive to think about the invoked racial worlds of the urban social that are implicit when people talk of the ghetto and the community, the street and the projects, the problem estate and the regenerated neighborhood, the "burbs" and the "hood."

For most writing and thinking about cities shares at least some degree of cultural provenance which makes both imaginative similarities and the unique trajectories equally interesting. To take a case in point it is precisely the historical and geographical specificities of the *banlieu* in contrast to the American suburb and the British new town that can make particular cartographies of racism comprehensible and the grim toll of racist murders meaningful in the white light that illuminates the social life of Thamesmead, Woolwich, Eltham, and Welling in London and Howard Beach in New York.

Indeed such a call for the iteration between a continual questioning of the concepts and vocabulary that we use to investigate the social world and a sustained wonder at the possibilities of the empirical remains constant to the spirit of an investigative engagement with the nature of racialized city life across the globe. Through an acknowledgment that academic speech draws on language that is so deeply culturally embedded can begin an acceptance that just as people make their social worlds in circumstances not of their own choosing, investigations of the racialized urban demands both a rigorous empirical open-mindedness and simultaneously an acknowledgement of the genealogical cultural traces within which such investigation is generated. As a recent investigation of the American ghetto suggested:

> One must go against the flow of the dominant American tradition of research on the topic and break with the moralistic schemata and naturalistic reasoning inherited from the early Chicago school to posit that the ghetto does not suffer from "social disorganization" but

constitutes a dependent universe, finely differentiated and hierarchized, organized according to distinct principles generative of a *regular form of social entropy*. (Wacquant, 1998:12)

Conclusion: Under the Skin of the City?

So what does such an archaeology produce? It should in the very least make us consider carefully the historical problem of thinking about racialized city life. The gentrification of the ethnic enclave is causally related to the stigmatization of the city ghetto and only a detailed examination of the interface of culture, political economy, and social policy can explain to us how this comes to be the case. It is essential both to understand the progress that has been made in celebrations of cultural diversity that litter the policy arenas of today's mainland Europe and North America whilst simultaneously understanding that they do not necessarily present us with either an "end of racism" or even a significant improvement in the life chances of racialized minorities. And it is imperative to identify the manner in which racialized images inform city descriptions that may rationalize governmental intervention and then erase a racialized presence.

What is suggested here is not merely an iconography of the urban. Much productive work in recent cultural geography has pointed to both the possibilities and the limitations of taking forward the project of Walter Benjamin and Roland Barthes in reading the signs of the city (Barthes, 1973; Benjamin, 1999; Caygill, 1998; Raban, 1974; Wright, 1992).

To get under the skin of the city is partly a task that demands an unpacking of the forms of collective memory that structure our ways of thinking (Boyer, 1994) but is also about a constant iteration between the concepts and vocabularies that are being used in academic analysis and the hidden racialized genealogies of precisely these same concepts. To accept the significance of technologies of representation of the urban is to point to a reconsideration of the valorization of alternative forms of academic labor. The oral history and the graffiti tag generate an urbanism that is related to, but distinct from, the architectural plan and the urban futures envisioned by city hall. To investigate either is insufficient; the myth in the mirage of the racialized city comes into focus only when the two are triangulated through a sustained labor that does not return us to Chicago but does place gossip, interview, and memory alongside the more rarefied theoretical considerations of commodification and governance.

The creation of the risk society potentially opens up particular cartographies of the underground and invisible worlds of the city where interrelated complexities of race, class, and criminality are always rewriting new stories of symbolic spaces and places (Beck, 1992). In terms of mainstream debate in the USA and Europe in the twenty-first century it is essential to link a concern with notions of urban regeneration with a debate about pollution and displacement of the body politic, to link a celebration of the urban public sphere with the racial subject positions of those included and excluded from within it, to tie the street and the tower block to the images of the street robber and the racially marked victim, and to link the studies of "risk" to the architecture of the racialized imaginary in the urban uncanny.

Notes

1   It is certainly the case that the city has been transformed and for some commentators the success
    of the project was identifiable at an early stage:

    Birmingham is replicating Glasgow's success in initiating a strategic, long-term process of
    regeneration. This is due to the sheer number of initiatives, now reaching a threshold
    of synergistic activity; to the broad scope of initiatives addressing the complex equation of
    urban renewal; to a history of pragmatic partnerships between the private sector and local
    government; and to a long-term strategic perspective shared between alternating Labour
    and Conservative controlled governments. (Carley, 1991:100). See also Kearns and Philo,
    1993; Sorkin, 1992.

2   Birmingham City Council (1991). The strap line was drawn from the poet of Empire, Rudyard
    Kipling's verse:

    Our England is a garden that is full of stately views,
    Of borders, beds and shrubberies and lawns and avenues,
    With statues on the terraces and peacocks strutting by;
    But the Glory of the Garden lies in more than meets the eye

3   Taken from the speech of Ken Livingstone, Mayor of London, to the Lord Mayor's Dinner on
    "The Government of London" at the Mansion House in the City Corporation, May 22, 2000.
4   In Brixton, in Brent, in Lewisham, Greenwich and the East End of London a range of urban
    regeneration projects currently promote cultural diversity as one of the strengths of their
    locality.
5   For Rabinow, "social technicians were articulating a normative or middling modernism. In
    their discourses, society became its own referent, to be worked on by means of technical
    procedures which were becoming the authoritative arbiters of what counted as socially real"
    (Rabinow, 1989:13).
6   Again space prohibits an extensive examination here but the cultural construction of gender
    draws on related diagnostic cartographies of the urban that both render a gendered analysis of
    the sites of the city equally germane (cf. Pollock, 1988) and guarantee that the constructions of
    character examined later in this chapter are invariably simultaneously gendered and racialized
    (Heron, 1993; Wolff, 1985; Wilson, 1992).
7   The work of George Mosse (1975) provides an exemplary case of the intricate and contextual
    relationships between landscapes of nationalism and the configuration of the urban.
8   At one point in the novel the central protagonist, as ever with Ishiguro gradually awakening to
    the fragile construction of his lifeworld, comments:

    And yet tonight, in the quiet of this room, I find that what really remains with me from this
    first day's travel is not Salisbury Cathedral, nor any of the other charming sights of this city,
    but rather that marvellous view encountered this morning of the rolling English country-
    side. Now, I am quite prepared to believe that other countries can offer more obviously
    spectacular scenery. Indeed, I have seen in encyclopaedias and the *National Geographic
    Magazine* breathtaking photographs of sights from various corners of the globe; magnificent
    canyons and waterfalls, raggedly beautiful mountains. It has never, of course, been my
    privilege to have seen such things at first hand, but I will nevertheless hazard this with some
    confidence: the English landscape at its finest – such as I saw it this morning – possesses a
    quality that the landscapes of other nations, however more superficially dramatic, inevitably

335

fail to possess. It is, I believe, a quality that will mark out the English landscape to any objective observer as the most deeply satisfying in the world, and this quality is best summed up by the term "greatness". For it is true, when I stood on that high ledge this morning and viewed that land before me, I distinctly felt that rare, yet unmistakable feeling – the feeling that one is in the presence of "greatness". We call this land of ours *Great Britain*, and there may be those who believe this a somewhat immodest practice. Yet I would venture that the landscape of our country alone would justify the use of this lofty adjective. (Ishiguro, 1989:28)

References

Abbott, A. (1999) *Department and Discipline*. Chicago: Chicago University Press.

Appiah, K. A. and Sassen, S. (1999) *Globalization and its Discontents: Essays on the New Mobility of People and Money*. New York: New Press.

Back, L. (2000) "Guess who's coming to dinner: investigating in the grey zone." in V. Ware and L. Back, *Dark Thoughts on Whiteness*. Chicago: University of Chicago Press, pp.167–92.

Barth, L. (1996) "Immemorial visibilities: Seeing the city's difference." *Environment and Planning A* 28,3:471–93.

Barthes, R. (1973) *Mythologies*. London: Granada.

Beck, U. (1992) *The Risk Society: Towards a New Modernity*. London: Sage.

Benjamin, W. (1999) *The Arcades Project*. London: Verso.

Bhabha, H. (1994) *The Location of Culture*. London: Routledge.

Bourdieu, P. (1999) "Site effects," in P. Bourdieu et al. *The Weight of the World*. London: Polity Press, pp.123–30.

Boyer, C. (1986) *Dreaming The Rational City: The Myth of American City Planning*. Cambridge, MA: MIT Press.

Boyer, C. (1994) *The City of Collective Memory: Its Historical Imagery and Architectural Entertainments*. Cambridge, MA.: MIT Press.

Boyer, C. (1996) "Electronic disruptions and black holes of the city: The issues of gender and urbanism in the age of electronic communication," in C. Boyer *Cybercities*. New York: Princeton Architectural Press.

Buck-Morss, S. (1989) *The Dialectics of Seeing. Walter Benjamin and the Arcades Project*. London: MIT Press.

Bullock, M. and Jennings, M. (1996) *Walter Benjamin: Selected Writings. Volume 1:1913–1926*. Cambridge, MA: Harvard University Press.

Butler, J. (1993) "Endangered/endangering schematic racism and white paranoia," In R. Gooding-Williams (ed.) *Reading Rodney King, Reading Urban Uprising*. London: Routledge, pp.15–22.

Butler, J., Laclau, E., and Žižek, S. (2000) *Contingency, Hegemony, Universality: Contemporary Dialogues on the Left*. London: Verso.

Carley, M. (1991) "Business in urban regeneration partnerships: A case study in Birmingham." *Local Economy* 6:100–15.

Castells, M. (1996) *The Information Age: Economy, Society, Culture, vol 1, The Rise of the Network Society*. Oxford: Blackwell.

Castells, M. (1997) *The Information Age: Economy, Society, Culture, vol. 2, The Power of Identity*. Oxford: Blackwell.

Castells, M. (1998) *The Information Age: Economy, Society, Culture, vol. 3, End of Millennium*. Oxford: Blackwell.

Caygill, H. (1998) *Walter Benjamin: The Colour of Experience*. London: Routledge.

Clinton, H. (1996) *It Takes a Village: And Other Lessons Children Teach Us*. New York: Touchstone Books.

Collings, M. (1997) *Blimey! From Bohemia to Britpop: The London Artworld from Francis Bacon to Damien Hirst*. Cambridge, UK: 21.

Davis, A. Y. (2000) *The Prison Industrial Complex* (CD ROM). New York: AK Press.

Davis, M. (1998) *Ecology of Fear: Los Angeles and the Imagination of Disaster*. New York: Metropolitan Books.

Davis, M. (2000) *Magical Urbanism: Latinos Reinvent the US Big City*. London: Verso.

De Certeau, M. (1984) *The Practice of Everyday Life*. Berkeley: University of California Press.

Der Derian, J. (1998) *The Virilio Reader*. Oxford: Blackwell.

Deutsche, R. (1996) *Evictions*. Cambridge, MA: MIT Press.

Donald, J. (1999) *Imagining the Modern City*. London: Athlone Press.

Dyer, R. (1997) *White*. London: Routledge.

European Commission (1991) *Green Paper on the Urban Environment*. Brussels: European Commission.

Fanon, F. (1986) *Black Skin, White Masks*. London: Pluto Press.

Feagin, J. (1998) *The New Urban Paradigm: Critical Perspectives on the City*. Lanham, MD: Rowman and Littlefield.

Foucault, M. (1991) "Governmentality," in G. Burchell, C. Gordon, and P. Miller (eds.) *The Foucault Effect: Studies in Governmentality*. Hemel Hempstead, UK.: Harvester and Wheatsheaf, pp.87–104.

Frankenberg, R. (1997) *Displacing Whiteness: Essays in Social and Cultural Criticism*. Durham, NC: Duke University Press.

Frisby, D. (1985) *Fragments of Modernity*. Oxford: Polity.

Gilloch, G. (1996) *Myth and Metropolis: Walter Benjamin and The City*. Oxford: Polity.

Gilroy, P. (2000) *Between Camps: Race, Identity and Nationalism at the end of the Colour Line*. London: Allen and Lane.

Goldberg, D. (1993) *Racist Culture. Philosophy and the Politics of Meaning*. Oxford: Blackwell.

Hall, P. (1998) *Cities in Civilization*. London: Weidenfeld and Nicholson.

Harvey, D. (1990) *The Condition of Postmodernity*. Oxford: Blackwell.

Heron, L. (1993) *Women Writing the City: In Streets of Desire*. London: Virago.

Ishiguro, K. (1989) *The Remains of the Day*. London: Faber and Faber.

Jacobs, J. M. (1996) *Edge of Empire: Postcolonialism and the City*. London: Routledge.

Jay, M. (1992) "Scopic regimes of modernity," in S. Lash and J. Friedmann (eds.) *Modernity and Identity*. Oxford: Blackwell, pp.178–95.

Jay, M. (1994) *Downcast Eyes*. Berkeley: University of California Press.

Katznelson, I. (1992) *Marxism and the City*. Oxford: Clarendon Press.

Kearns, G. and Philo, C. (1993) *Selling Places: The City as Cultural Capital*. Oxford: Pergamon Press.

Keith, M. (1995) "Ethnic entrepreneurs and street rebels: Looking inside the inner city," in S. Pile, and N. Thrift (eds.) *Mapping the Subject: Geographies of Cultural Transformation*. London and New York: Routledge, pp.355–70.

Keith, M. (2000) "Walter Benjamin, urban studies and the narratives of city life," in G. Bridge and S. Watson (eds.) (1999) *Blackwell Companion to Urban Studies*. Oxford: Blackwell, pp.410–29.

Lash, S. and Urry, J. (1994) *Economies of Signs and Space*. London: Sage.

Lefebvre, H. (1991) *The Production of Space*. Oxford: Blackwell.

Loftman, P. (1990) *A Tale of Two Cities: Birmingham, the Convention Centre and the Unequal City*. Birmingham, UK: Birmingham Polytechnic.

Lokko, L. (2000) *White Papers, Black Marks: Architecture, Race, Culture*. Minneapolis: University of Minnesotsa Press.

Mercer, K. (2000) "A sociography of diaspora," in P. Gilroy, L. Grossberg, and A. McRobbie (eds.) *Without Guarantees: In Honour of Stuart Hall*. London: Verso, pp.233–45.

Missac, P. (1995) *Walter Benjamin's Passages*. Cambridge, MA: MIT Press.

Moretti, F. (1998) *Atlas of the European Novel*. London: Verso.

Mosse, G. (1975) *The Nationalization of the Masses: Political Symbolism and Mass Movements in Germany from the Napoleonic Wars through the Third Reich*. New York: New American Library.

Omi, M. and Winant, H. (1987) *Racial Formation in the United States: From the 1960s to the 1980s*. London: Routledge.

Osborne, T. and Rose, N. (1999) "Governing cities: Notes of the spatialisation of virtue." *Environment and Planning D: Society and Space* 17:737–60.

Pile, S. (1996) *The Body and the City. Psychoanalysis, Space and Subjectivity*. London: Routledge.

Pollock, G. (1988) *Vision and Difference: Feminism, Femininity and the Histories of Art*. London: Routledge.

Pratt, M. L. (1992) *Imperial Eyes: Travel Writing and Transculturation*. London: Routledge.

Raban, J. (1974) *Soft City*. London: Collins.

Rabinow, P. (1989) *French Modern. Norms and Forms of Social Environment*. Cambridge, MA: MIT Press.

Robins, K. and Webster, F. (1999) *Times of the Technoculture: From the Information Society to the Virtual Life*. London: Routledge.

Rogers, R. N. (1997) *Cities for a Small Planet*. London: Faber and Faber.

Sassen, S. (1999) *Guests and Aliens*. New York: New Press.

Saunders, P. (1981) *Social Theory and The Urban Question*. London: Hutchinson.

Saunders, P. (1986) *Social Theory and The Urban Question*, 2nd edn. London: Hutchinson.

Savage, M. and Warde, A. (1993) *Urban Sociology, Capitalism and Modernity*. Basingstoke, UK: Macmillan.

Sennett, R. (1977) *The Fall of Public Man*. New York: Alfred A. Knopf.

Sennett, R. (1994) *Flesh and Stone: The Body and the City in Western Civilization*. New York: W. W. Norton.

Smith, N. (1996) *The New Urban Frontier: Gentrification and the Revanchist City*. London: Routledge.

Social Exclusion Unit (2000) *National Strategy for Neighbourhood Renewal: A Framework for Consultation*. London: The Stationery Office.

Soja, E. (1989) *Postmodern Geographies*. London: Verso.

Soja, E. (1996) *Thirdspace: Journeys to Los Angeles and other Real and Imagined Places*. Oxford: Blackwell.

Soja, E. (1999) *Postmetropolis: Critical Studies of Cities and Regions*. Oxford: Blackwell.

Solomos, J. and Back, L. (1995) *Race, Politics and Social Change*. London: Routledge.

Solomos, J. and Back, L. (1996) *Racism and Society*. Basingstoke, UK: Macmillan.

Sorkin, M. (ed.) (1992) *Variations on a Theme Park: The New American City and The End of Public Space*. New York: Hill and Wang.

Stallybrass, P. and Whyte, A. (1986) *The Politics and Poetics of Transgression*. London: Methuen.

Szondi, P. ([1962] 1995) "Walter Benjamin's city portraits," in G. Smith (ed.) *On Walter Benjamin: Critical Essays and Recollections*. Cambridge, MA: MIT Press, pp.18–32.

Vidler, A. (1996) *The Architectural Uncanny*. Cambridge, MA: MIT Press.

Wacquant, L. (1998) "Inside the zone: The social art of the hustler in the black American ghetto." *Theory, Culture and Society* 15,2:1–36.

Ware, V. (1992) Beyond the Pale: White Women, Racism and History. London: Verso.

Ware, V. and Back, L. (2000) *Dark Thoughts on Whiteness*. Chicago: University of Chicago Press.

Wieviorka, M. (1998) "Is multiculturalism the solution?" *Ethnic and Racial Studies* 21,5:881–910.

Williams, R. (1973) *The Country and the City*. London: Chatto and Windus.

Wilson, E. (1992) "The invisible flaneur." *New Left Review* 191:90–110.

Winant, H. (1994) *Racial Conditions: Politics, Theory, Comparisons*. Minneapolis: University of Minnesota Press.

Wolff, J. (1985) "The invisible flaneuse: Women and the literature of modernity." *Theory, Culture and Society* 2,3:37–48.

Wright, G. (1991) *The Politics of Design in French Colonial Urbanism*. Chicago: University of Chicago Press.

Wright, P. (1992) *A Journey Through Ruins: The Last Days of London*. London: Radius.

Young, I. M. (1990) *Justice and the Politics of Difference*. Princeton, NJ: Princeton University Press.

Young, I. M. (1997) *Intersecting Voices: Dilemmas of Gender, Political Philosophy and Policy*. Princeton, NJ: Princeton University Press.

Chapter 22

The Ghetto and Race

Robert Bernasconi

The word *ghetto* was introduced in the sixteenth century to describe a controlled area of a town or city within which Jews were confined at night, at which time members of other groups were forbidden entry. During the twentieth century a much broader usage of the term has developed, although it continues to reflect the practice of segregation that was at the root of the original idea of a ghetto. Today a ghetto can be any area of a city or town in which the living quarters of an ethnic minority are concentrated, although the term is usually reserved for poor, densely populated, inner-city districts. Because the ghettos have been the site of so much suffering, the definition of the ghetto is not a scholastic matter, but a contested issue in which members of different ethnic groups are heavily invested. Some claim that the "true" ghetto is the ghetto imposed by law and that the extension of the word *ghetto* beyond the original strict sense that it acquired in sixteenth century Italy blurs historical reality. Others argue that if the place where almost all members of an ethnic group live is racially segregated, and if it is difficult for them to move to an area that is not racially segregated, what matters is less whether the segregation is *de jure* or *de facto* than the conditions inside and outside the ghetto. This article will consider both the narrow and the broad senses of the term, focusing particularly on the Jewish and African-American ghettos.

The Jewish Ghetto in Europe

There has been a long-standing tendency of Jews, like other foreign groups, to seek to live together, both for convenience and protection. Sometimes Jews sought the assistance of the secular authorities in securing for themselves an enclosed area of the city. At a time when cities were often divided into separate districts by gated areas, Jews wanted their own secured residential quarter to protect them against violence and threats of violence arising from the growth in antisemitism. The Church authorities also had an interest in separating the Jews from ordinary Christians. In 1179 the Third Lateran Council decreed that Christians who lived in proximity to Jews should be excommunicated from the Catholic Church. This reflected a growing fear within the Church hierarchy that the faith of ordinary Christians might be contaminated by close contact with Jews. Similar concerns were directed against Saracens. In some places legislation was enacted enforcing residential segregation. For example, in 1412 John I of Castile ordered that both Jews and Moors be consigned to walled enclosures and in 1462 one of the most important Jewish ghettos was established in Frankfurt. However, such legislation was not consistently enforced. The same was true of the legislation following the proposal of the Fourth Lateran Council of 1215 requiring Jews and Saracens to wear distinctive markings. Hostility against Jews led to massacres and, in the fifteenth century, to expulsions, including most famously, the expulsion from Spain of 1492. In this context, when there was a reassertion of the policy of segregating Jews in enclosed areas, it appeared to be a moderate course of action, somewhere between death or expulsion and acceptance.

The ghetto was from the outset a site of ambiguity: a means of housing the Jews while holding them at arm's length. Christian societies had need of the Jews, not least because they were not bound by the prohibitions against usury. Jewish loans assisted the poor, helped finance trade, and provided governments with an additional source of funds through taxation. The ghetto provided a way in which Christians could enjoy the commercial benefits that the Jews provided without having to live alongside them. It was a way of incorporating those who would nevertheless continue to be treated as outsiders.

The term "ghetto" derives from the Venetian word for iron foundry. In 1516 a decree of the Venetian Senate had ordered all Jews to move their residence to the area of the new foundry, the *ghetto nuovo*, to which they would be confined at night. The Venetians had already given the Germans a compound in which they had to reside but from which they could trade. In 1573 the Turks applied to the Venetian authorities for an area similar to the Jewish ghetto and in 1621 their request was finally granted. The Turks came under great suspicion, not only because they were linked to a rival military power, but also because their religion was considered more alien. Although the ghetto was in certain respects a privilege, it was severely overcrowded, making it necessary to expand the area twice in the 60 years after its foundation. The ghetto also made Jews an easy target. In his autobiography, *Life of Judah*, Rabbi Leon Modena described how in the first half of the seventeenth century, when one Jew was found guilty of a crime, all Jews suffered and the whole of the ghetto would be subjected to scrutiny (Cohen, 1988). Nor did the existence of the ghetto stop the Venetians from threatening the Jews with expulsion, which they did from time to time throughout the sixteenth century.

In addition to being both a refuge and a trap in which the Jews were caught, the Venetian ghetto was also an intellectual center for Jewish culture. It became a gathering point for Jews from different places and the dissemination point of the vigorous intellectual activity that took place there. Venice became, for example, a publishing center for Hebrew books. Jewish thought turned inward and came to focus predominantly on searching the biblical and talmudic traditions for clarification of the unique characteristics and destiny of the Jews. The practice of religion in the Venetian ghetto was also transformed in a way that mirrored the ghettoization process itself. Whereas religious activity previously had often taken place in private homes, now the synagogues and the activities that took place there came to be regarded as more sacred. The space surrounding the synagogue took on a correspondingly more profane character. Jacob Katz (1961) has argued that the social exclusiveness of life in the Jewish ghetto led to Jewish indifference to conditions outside the ghetto that was reflected in a decline in Jewish polemics against Christianity. But one should beware overstating the case. The stability of the ghetto also allowed for contact between Jewish and Christian cultures.

Jews had access to Christian learning as well as to developments in science. Rabbi Leon Modena can serve as an example of those Jews who was open to the world outside the ghetto. Modena adopted certain techniques from Christian sermonizing, introduced choral music, and, like many other Jews, studied at a distance the developments in Christian thought, beginning a process that would eventually make assimilation possible.

Although the word "ghetto" is Venetian, not all the ghettos that were instituted in its wake shared its redeeming features. In 1555 Pope Paul IV ordered that all Jews in Rome should live on a single street and that if that did not suffice they should be given a larger area on condition that it had only one gate. He also sought to impose a similar arrangement on Jews throughout the papal states. Soon Pope Sixtus V obliged the Jewish men of Rome to attend Christian sermons at least six times a year. Before long this *vicus Judaeorum* or *seraglio degli hebrei* was given the Venetian name *ghetto*, which was also the word used when an area was set aside for the Jews of Florence in 1571, in Siena in 1572, and in a number of other Italian towns that adopted similar arrangements over the next hundred years. Ghettos were also imposed on Jews throughout the Germanic lands, but elsewhere Jews tended to live alongside each other without being obliged to do so by law.

The strict compulsory ghettos of Italy and Austro-Germany were dismantled at the end of the eighteenth century and early in the nineteenth century. For example, in 1797 the gates of the Venetian ghetto were demolished. The Jews were able to participate more fully in society. Nevertheless, the word "ghetto" survived to designate the areas in which Jews tended to congregate, even when they had the opportunity to live elsewhere. Israel Zangwill described such ghettos in his *Children of the Ghetto* (first published 1892) when he characterized the London ghetto as of "voluntary formation" and yet nevertheless an imposition: "People who have been living in a Ghetto for a couple of centuries are not able to step outside merely because the gates are thrown down, nor to efface the brands on their souls by pulling off the yellow badges" (Zangwill, 1925:1–2).

Tragically, that was not to be the last chapter in the history of the Jewish ghettos of Europe. During World War II, the Nazis collected Jews in ghettos before rounding them up for transportation to the death camps. This ghettoization was more readily accomplished in Eastern than in Western Europe in part because the Eastern Jews were a more closely knit identifiable group than their Western counterparts. The Nazis established their ghettos on the site of the old Jewish quarters, thereby confirming a continuity with the old order. Indeed the Nazis themselves distinguished between 13 Polish "ghettos" that were completely sealed and a larger number of "Jewish quarters" that were closely guarded but were not fully enclosed. The German authorities announced the plan to set up ghettos in Poland for the Jews in 1939. The first ghetto to be established was at Lodz in February 1940. It remained in existence for over four years because of its importance as a manufacturing center. The largest Polish ghetto, the Warsaw ghetto, was created in October 1940 when 140,000 additional Jews were moved in after the evacuation of 80,000 non-Jews. Following an edict of October 15, 1941, any Jew found outside the ghetto was under a death sentence. A policy of extermination by starvation was pursued. The massacre of the Polish Jews began in 1942 and in the middle of that year forced deportations began from the Warsaw ghetto. Amidst heavy resistance the Warsaw ghetto and the remaining inhabitants were finally destroyed in April and May of 1943. The Nazi ghettos were not a way of accommodating the Jews, but a transit point to their extermination.

Ghettos in the USA

In the remainder of this article I will focus on the ghettos of the United States. There are, of course, numerous ghettos elsewhere, but it was in the United States that the term "ghetto" developed a new range of meaning. The word was used in the United States at the end of the nineteenth century, much as it was used in England at the same time, to refer to distinct Jewish districts within the major cities. Almost one million Jews entered the United States in the 25 years following 1881. Many of these congregated in New York, so that at the end of that period there were about 600,000 Jews there. There were some Jews in most of the better residential districts, but there were at least four identifiable ghettos where the residents were predominantly Jewish. The so-called Great Ghetto was on the lower east side of Manhattan and covered about 500 acres. One of its wards averaged more than 57 residents to a house. In spite of the overcrowding, the death rate was low, thereby giving some confirmation to reports that clean living conditions were maintained. The Jewish ghetto in Philadelphia was also densely populated, even though land was less scarce. As in New York, the Jewish population was mainly from Eastern Europe. They tended to congregate in the same area in which the German Jews had already settled. As their numbers increased through immigration, the area of the ghetto expanded, displacing the Italian population alongside it. This expansion of the Jewish district conformed to a pattern of social mobility whereby the arrival of each new immigrant group had an impact on the location in the social hierarchy of the other immigrant groups. The place of an ethnic group on the social ladder was reflected not only in housing, but also in forms of employment, for example, whether or not they worked in sweatshops. Mobility up the social ladder in this way led to assimilation, although it seems that the assimilation of European immigrant groups, like the Italians, the Poles, and the Irish, into the ethnic alliance of whiteness seems to have been dependent on assimilation to the specific forms of antagonism against nonwhite races found in the United States. In other words, Anglo-Americans could welcome other groups as white to the extent that they were ready to distance themselves from blacks, East Asians, and Hispanics, a price they were almost always ready to pay.

The use of the term *ghetto* to describe "colonies" of East European Jews in northeastern cities began to be extended to apply to other immigrant groups and also to African Americans at least as early as the second decade of the twentieth century. Chinese, Italian, and other immigrant groups, had already taken possession, as it were, of defined areas of the city. Streets that they had occupied overflowed to become districts. To outsiders these districts looked like racialized slums, but they were often unaware of the close ties binding together the members of these neighborhood communities that shared a culture and sometimes even a language that could not be found elsewhere in the city. External observers also tended to ignore the fact that there was more variation in education and income among the inhabitants of these ghettos than would have been the case if income had been the sole determinant of where one lived. Four of the preconditions of ghettoization are ethnic diversity, racism, poverty, and urbanization. The United States had the first three in abundance at the beginning of the twentieth century and was about to add the fourth. Because racism is a decisive factor in the formation of a ghetto, most of the ghettos in the United States are black.

343

Black migration from the rural districts to the cities in the early part of the twentieth century led whites to want to control the location of blacks within the city boundaries. In the South with its "Jim Crow" laws, the strategy adopted was to enforce residential segregation through laws. In 1910 the Baltimore city council established separate neighborhoods for blacks and for whites. Similar laws were passed in other cities, including Atlanta, Louisville, St. Louis, Oklahoma, and New Orleans. However, in 1917, the Supreme Court declared this procedure unconstitutional. Thereafter the residential segregation of African Americans into extensive ghettos developed more quickly in the North, with Chicago and Cleveland the first. In 1910 there were no areas of Chicago where blacks were more than 61 percent of the population. By 1930 almost two-thirds of Blacks lived in concentrations of more than 90 percent. At that time three-quarters of all residential property in Chicago was covered by restrictive covenants. Other Northern cities had ghettos in place by 1940. In the South, city blocks were segregated early, but the large well-defined ghettos of contemporary Southern cities are largely the product of the White flight that began in the 1950s.

The difference between ghettos and what were called "foreign districts" can be illustrated with reference to the situation in Chicago in the 1920s. There were in the city at that time some 27 ethnicities led by the Italians, the Poles, and the Irish. However, even though almost all of these groups had their own identifiable neighborhood, the areas they occupied were always ethnically mixed. Although one or two ethnicities might dominate an area visibly, the statistics told a different story. The Mexicans, who increased from 1200 to almost 20,000 during the 1920s, never became the dominant ethnic group in any part of the city; they were not subjected to segregation in spite of there being some hostility towards them. By contrast, at the end of the nineteenth century there was already a Jewish ghetto where some 14,000 of Chicago's 75,000 Jews were concentrated. Nevertheless, many Jews lived outside the ghetto and this tendency for the Jews to be dispersed throughout the city grew with further Jewish immigration. There were few African Americans living outside the ghettos and these were mainly live-in domestic servants. If the ghetto is defined as an area inhabited almost exclusively by an ethnic group, such that the vast majority of members of that group live in ghettos, then only African Americans have been confined to ghettos in the United States for any length of time.

The main factor in the creation of the Northern ghettos was the refusal of whites to live alongside blacks. The fact that the courts upheld restrictive covenants until 1948 gave whites legal support, just as the tendency of the police to ignore violence directed against blacks trying to escape the ghettos meant that they could do much as they liked to impose their will. The discrimination exercised by the financial institutions in the distribution of loans also contributed to the formation of the ghettos. Neither the eventual collapse of the system of restrictive covenants, nor the dissolution of legalized segregation in education and social activities, has abolished racial segregation as a *de facto* system. Indeed in some of the major metropolitan areas it is arguably getting worse, leading to what is called hypersegregation. Residential segregation has also thwarted integration of the schools. The uneven distribution of funds for education has left many blacks with a separate but unequal schooling long after *Brown v. Board of Education*. The migration of jobs from the cities has also denied economic opportunities to inner-city residents. Furthermore, white flight left the cities with a declining tax base to address the problems of poverty and a deteriorating superstructure. As the Kerner Report of 1968 explained, "What White Americans have never fully understood – but what the Negro can never forget – is that white society is deeply implicated in the ghetto. White institutions created it, white institutions maintain it, and white society condones it" (National Advisory Commission on Civil Disorders, 1968:2). This remains true today. The ghetto represents institutional racism, that is to say, a racism that is enshrined in the social fabric and that would continue to exist even if the antiblack racism of individuals would cease tomorrow.

In many towns and cities, especially in the Southern United States, African Americans are no longer in the minority. Large portions of a city are the almost exclusive preserve of ethnic minorities. In this context, the tendency is to identify the ghetto with the poorest sector, usually the inner city, where so-called urban renewal worked in conjunction with highway construction and misguided housing policies to destroy the integrity of the old black neighborhoods. Because many of the black middle class moved either to the suburbs or to the housing stock formerly occupied by whites before the latter left the city, there is no longer the same range of wealth in the historically black areas of the city as there had been in the past. Nevertheless, it remains true that even though the black middle class have left the inner-city ghetto there is still much less class separation among African Americans than among either whites or Hispanics. Furthermore, the black middle class, even in the suburbs, remain segregated to an extent that is not true of any other group.

The fact that the ghetto has been in place so long has led to the development of what is sometimes called "ghetto culture." Scholarly characterizations of ghetto culture have varied considerably. In the wake of the Moynihan Report on "The Negro Family," Kenneth B. Clark in *Dark Ghetto* (1965) characterized the ghetto in terms of a chronic, self-perpetuating, institutionalized pathology. Clark's study provoked numerous responses designed to show that ghetto behavior was functional, a creative attempt to adapt to a racist society. The debate entered a new stage with William Julius Wilson's (1987) *The Truly Disadvantaged*. Wilson attacked the cultural values of "the ghetto underclass," but argued for an economic solution to what he called the "concentration effects" of living in a neighborhood in which the mass of the population were overwhelmingly disadvantaged. This allowed him to characterize his contribution as a refocusing of the liberal perspective. Addressing social isolation rather than the culture of poverty, which he understood as an effect of social isolation, Wilson proposed programs to promote social mobility. But this is insufficient if mobility is defined by the ability to leave the ghetto, particularly if at the same time others are being pushed back into it. One cannot address ghettoization without addressing what is aptly called "redundancy of place," a phrase used to describe locations that have effectively fallen outside the economy and so remain cut off from any upsurge in the economy. Redundancy of place is reflected in the fact that there is less a housing shortage in many big cities than a neighborhood shortage, because the ghettos, and the immediate area surrounding them, are regarded by both the financial institutions and the housing market, not to mention the politicians, as blighted or off the map.

Conclusion

The Jewish ghettos of Europe, the black ghettos of the United States, and the immigrant ghettos wherever they are found, arise as the dominant group's solution to the problem of how to contain that which it wants to exclude but is unable to do without or eradicate. The Jews were a source of finance and blacks, like the various immigrant groups, are a source of cheap labor. The ghetto is the location handed over to "the others" so that they disappear into it. But the project of ghettoization failed because the ghetto preserves minorities as minorities and enables their cultures to flourish. Although the ghetto was for many immigrants the stepping-stone on which, or "decompression chamber" through which, they assimilated and passed into the larger society, for others it has provided a context in which they could maintain a sense of their old identity, traditions, and language. Furthermore, these ethnic minorities were not passive. They used the space of the ghetto to develop their own organizations and counterculture. "Ghetto" has come to signify a whole style of being black in the United States including a form of dress and dialect. White suburban youths have even sought to imitate this style, albeit while showing little understanding of the conditions which gave rise to it.

Exclusive focus on the ghetto can be misleading. There is also widespread poverty in rural districts. The ghetto, at least as presently understood, is strictly an urban phenomenon. This is because of the contemporary association of the ghetto with extreme poverty and poor housing that are not yet found in the suburbs. Nevertheless, if the suburbs are often an escape from the inner city, as the suburban housing stock of these suburbs declines the distinction is likely to seem more tenuous, just as today people's determination of which parts of a city are "ghettos" will tend to vary depending on their own ethnic identity. On some definitions, any predominantly black neighborhood is a ghetto. Sometimes the ghetto is identified only with what scholars occasionally call "the second ghetto" of public housing. In that case "the ghetto" is used as a relative term, reserved for the neighborhood of those who are regarded as being at or near the bottom of the social hierarchy within a system of racial segregation.

The all-white suburbs of contemporary America represent an abandonment of the cities. Whites fled the cities in part because ghettoization failed to keep the cities under white control. By an extraordinary reversal, numerous members of the white majority declare they do not "feel" safe in large sections of the city, including downtown. The gated communities of the rich are the mirror image of the ghettos. Their determination to live away from the city, in districts where their neighbors resemble them financially and ethnically, has the effect of maintaining residential segregation along racial, ethnic, and class lines. If racism and ethnocentrism created the ghetto, one effect of ghettoization is that it means that members of the dominant group remain ignorant of ethnic minorities, leading to a lack of appreciation of their culture and problems, as well as a persistence of stereotyping. The ghetto as an effect of racism contributes to the persistence of racism.

References

Baron, S. W. (1965) *A Social and Religious History of the Jews*, vol. 9. New York: Columbia University Press.

Bullard, R. D., Grigsby, J. E., and Lee, C. (1994) *Residential Apartheid: The American Legacy*. Los Angeles: CAAS Publications.

Clark, Kenneth B. (1965) *Dark Ghetto*. New York: Harper and Row.

Cohen, Mark R. (ed.) (1988) *The Autobiography of a Seventeenth-Century Venetian Rabbi. Leon Modena's "Life of Judah."* Princeton, NJ: Princeton University Press.

Drake, St. Clair, and Clayton, Horace (1993) *Black Metropolis*, revised and enlarged edn. Chicago: The University of Chicago Press.

Haverkamp, Alfred (1995) "The Jewish quarters in German towns during the late Middle Ages," in R. Po-Chia Hsia and Hartmut Lehmann (eds.) *In and Out of the Ghetto*. Cambridge, UK: Cambridge University Press, pp.13–28.

James, Edmund (ed.) (1907) *The Immigrant Jew in America*. New York: B. F. Buck.

Katz, Jacob (1961) *Exclusiveness and Tolerance*. Oxford: Oxford University Press.

Katz, Michael (ed.) (1993) *The "Underclass" Debate*. Princeton, NJ: Princeton University Press.

Massey, Douglas and Denton, Nancy (1993) *American Apartheid*. Cambridge, MA: Harvard University Press.

National Advisory Commission on Civil Disorders (1968) *Report of the National Advisory Commission on Civil Disorders*, The Kerner Report, ed. Tom Wicker. (1968). New York: E. P. Dutton.

Philpott, Thomas Lee (1978) *The Slum and the Ghetto. Neighborhood Deterioration and Middle-Class Reform, 1880–1930*. New York: Oxford University Press.

Poliakov, Leon (1954) *Harvest of Hate. The Nazi Program for the Destruction of the Jews of Europe*. Syracuse, NY: Syracuse University Press.

Ravid, Benjamin (1987) "The religious, economic and social background of the establishment of the ghetti of Venice," in Gaetano Cozzi (ed.) *Gli Ebrei e venezia secoli xiv–xviii*. Milan: Edizioni di Comunità, pp.211–59.

Ravid, Benjamin (1992) "From geographical realia to historiological symbol: The odyssey of the word *Ghetto*," in David B. Ruderman (ed.) *Essential Papers on Jewish Culture in Renaissance and Baroque Italy*. New York: New York University Press, pp.373–85.

Wilson, William Julius (1987) *The Truly Disadvantaged*. Chicago: The University of Chicago Press.

Zangwill, Israel (1925) *Children of the Ghetto*. London: Globe.

Chapter 23

Residential Segregation

Douglas S. Massey

Segregation is the differential location of two or more groups within distinct categories of a social structure. The positioning of group members in different structural locations may arise from voluntary choices, whereby members of one group freely choose to occupy locations that are different from those of other groups; or it may reflect involuntary forces, whereby systematic barriers are erected to restrict the mobility of one class of people and confine them to particular positions within the structure. Segregation may also reflect a combination of voluntary and involuntary forces. As a social fact, however, the term "segregation" implies no particular judgment about how the configuration came about; only that groups are separated from one another within a well-defined social structure.

Over the years social scientists have examined the separation of social groups across a variety of social and economic structures. They have studied the differential location of men and women in occupational categories to measure the degree of gender segregation in the workforce (Jacobs, 1989); they have examined the degree to which rich and poor children attend different schools to measure the class segregation within the educational system (Orfield, 1993); and they have studied the differential location of elderly and young within separate communities to examine age segregation in housing (Cowgill, 1986). Given two or more groups and a social structure composed of multiple categories, the measurement of segregation follows axiomatically from whatever operational definition is chosen.

By far the most studied kind of segregation involves the differential distribution of racial or ethnic groups across neighborhoods of a city, a topic that is generally considered under the rubric of *residential segregation*. This field has attracted strong interest over the years because sociologists have long recognized the close connection between where people live and the social and economic outcomes they experience (Park and Burgess, 1925). Interest in residential segregation has intensified in recent years as virtually all industrialized nations have become multiracial/multiethnic societies through mass immigration during the postwar era (Massey et al., 1998).

The identification of residential segregation as an important factor in social stratification can be traced to theorists of the Chicago School of Sociology in the early twentieth century. As Robert Park noted in 1926, "it is because social relations are so frequently and so inevitably correlated with spatial relations; because physical distances so frequently are . . . indexes of social distances, that statistics have any significance whatever for sociology" (Park, 1926:8). In virtually all societies, social and economic resources are unevenly distributed in space, so where one lives plays a significant role in determining one's prospects for education, health, employment, income, and prestige (Massey and Denton, 1985). If members of a particular racial or ethnic group are highly segregated, therefore, they probably do not have access to the full complement of public and private resources necessary for success in modern society.

Ernest Burgess (1928) was the first social scientist to measure patterns and levels of residential segregation using objective methods, but he was unable to establish a consensus about how best to do so. In subsequent years, social scientists became bogged down in a prolonged debate about the most appropriate way to measure racial and ethnic segregation. The issue was finally settled by Otis and Beverly Duncan (1955), who recommended using the index of dissimilarity in most situations. This straightforward measure varies between 0 (no segregation) and 100 (complete segregation) and represents the percentage of minority members who would have to exchange neighborhoods with majority members to achieve an even, or integrated, residential distribution.

For the next 20 years, social scientists working in the tradition of the Chicago School of Sociology employed this index to measure levels of residential segregation across a variety of different urban settings. Duncan and Duncan (1957) undertook their classic study of the causes, patterns, and levels of black segregation in Chicago. Lieberson (1963) followed with an analysis of segregation among European-origin groups living in US industrial cities. In their ambitious study, Taeuber and Taeuber (1965) documented patterns of segregation and neighborhood transition for Africans in cities throughout the United States. Finally, as the racial and ethnic composition of other nations was transformed by postwar immigration, social scientists applied the index of dissimilarity to study minority segregation outside the United States – in Britain, Germany, France, the Netherlands, Israel, Canada, and Australia (see Massey, 1985, for a review).

In 1976, Cortese and colleagues ignited a vigorous new debate about how segregation should be measured by questioning the universal applicability of the index of dissimilarity. In response to their critique, numerous alternatives were proposed, yielding a proliferation of indices and considerable confusion in the literature. Massey and Denton (1988) sought to bring some order to the field by demonstrating that residential segregation was actually multidimensional, characterized by five distinct axes of spatial variation – evenness, exposure, clustering, concentration, and centralization – which comprehensively characterized the spatial circumstances of any racial and ethnic group. They showed that the index of dissimilarity measured the evenness dimension quite well, thus confirming Duncan and Duncan's earlier work; and after clarifying the conceptual and empirical properties of the remaining dimensions, they went on to recommend a specific index for each one.

Massey and Denton (1989) built on the conceptualization of segregation as a multidimensional construct to demonstrate that Asian and European ethnic groups in US metropolitan areas *never* achieved a high level of segregation on more than one dimension at a time, whereas blacks in 20 metropolitan areas displayed high levels of segregation on at least four dimensions *simultaneously*, a residential pattern they termed "hypersegregation." According to their data, more than one third of all African Americans lived under conditions of hypersegregation in 1980, a pattern that persisted into the 1990s (Denton, 1994).

Despite widespread recognition that residential segregation is a multidimensional construct, the most commonly used measure continues to be the index of dissimilarity,

349

often employed in concert with the P* isolation index, which Massey and Denton (1988) recommended to measure the exposure dimension. The latter index states the percentage of minority members living in the neighborhood of the average minority person. An index of 80 for African Americans, for example, means that the average black person lives in a neighborhood that is 80 percent black. Unlike the index of dissimilarity, this index is strongly influenced by the minority proportion within an urban area. Other things equal, the isolation index tends to rise as the relative size of the minority increases.

Given this sensitivity, intergroup and intercity comparisons are best made using the index of dissimilarity. A convenient rule of thumb for interpreting the dissimilarity index is that values under 30 are "low"; those from 30 to 60 are "moderate"; and those above 60 are "high" (Kantrowitz, 1973). In general, voluntary processes of segregation yield index values in the low-to-moderate range. Two voluntary processes have received the most attention from social scientists: the self-selection of households into different neighborhoods based on income, and the self-selection of migrant households into different neighborhoods based on family and friendship connections.

Whenever a minority group is poor and a majority group affluent, members of each group display a propensity to sort themselves into different segments of the housing market based on their ability to bear housing costs. Since the time of Homer Hoyt (1939), social scientists have known that high- and low-cost dwellings tend to cluster together to form rich and poor neighborhoods, yielding a differential distribution of minority and majority members on the basis of income alone, regardless of racial or ethnic preferences. Socioeconomic differences thus translate directly into some degree of racial or ethnic segregation between groups, but typically these selective processes produce dissimilarity indices that are in the low to moderate range, rarely exceeding 40 and usually remaining below 35.

Another voluntary form of segregation stems from chain migration, whereby in-migrants to a city are attracted to specific neighborhoods by social connections to friends and relatives who already live there. Drawing upon the social capital embedded in personal networks, arriving migrants obtain jobs and housing in close proximity to their social contacts, leading to a concentration of certain ethnic or racial groups in specific neighborhoods, which is observed objectively as residential segregation.

Periods of rapid immigration are generally characterized by rising levels of segregation for the ethnic or racial minorities involved, especially if the new arrivals are also of low socioeconomic status. Such processes of self-selection typically yield dissimilarity indices in the moderate range, although during periods of exceptionally rapid immigration values may go somewhat higher. For example, from 1970 to 1990 the Hispanic population of Los Angeles, California, increased by 350 percent, mainly through the massive entry of poor Latin American immigrants. Over the same period, the Hispanic–white dissimilarity index rose from 47 to 61 (Massey, 2000).

In general, segregation levels rarely exceed a dissimilarity value of 60 in the absence of involuntary factors; and they are almost never sustained at such high levels for any length of time. As immigrant generations succeed one another and socioeconomic status rises, the high levels of residential segregation that are created through rapid immigration tend to dissipate. Even in Los Angeles, the Hispanic–white dissimilarity index dropped markedly as one moves from the foreign-born to the native-born generation, and from low to high income groups (Denton and Massey, 1988). In urban areas of most countries, therefore, dissimilarities for minorities range from 0 to about 60, depending on a group's average socioeconomic status, generational composition, and recency of arrival of its immigrants. This characterization appears to hold for immigrants and their descendants in the United States, Canada, Australia, Western Europe, and Israel (Massey, 1985).

Whenever residential dissimilarity persists at levels above 60 for any length of time, it usually involves involuntary forces of one sort or another. Studies done in the United States show that African Americans continue to experience remarkably high levels of discrimination in real estate markets, banking, and insurance, and that as potential neighbors they remain objects of considerable prejudice by whites, leading to a range of avoidance behaviors (Massey and Denton, 1993). As a result, black–white residential dissimilarities in US urban areas generally range upward from 60, and unlike those of other ethnic minorities, they do not fall as socioeconomic status rises (Denton and Massey, 1988). Moreover, black residential segregation has displayed little tendency to decline over time, except in places where the number of blacks is so small that complete desegregation yields little interracial mixing (Krivo and Kaufman, 1999).

Thus, among US metropolitan areas with the 30 largest black populations the average dissimilarity index in 1990 was 73, down only slightly from the rather extreme value of 81 two decades earlier. In contrast, the average dissimilarity index for the 30 largest Hispanic populations was only 50, up slightly from 47 in 1970 owing to the rapid influx of Hispanic immigrants. The largest urban concentrations of Asians, meanwhile, displayed an index of just 41 in 1990, a figure that was actually down four points from 1970 despite extensive Asian immigration during the intervening period. Other than African Americans in the United States, the only documented case where a racial or ethnic group experienced prolonged, high segregation was that of black Africans in the Union of South Africa under apartheid (Christopher, 1993). Neither blacks in Canada (Fong, 1996) nor Brazil (Telles, 1992) display the extreme segregation of their US counterparts.

New interest in the consequences of residential segregation was stimulated by William Julius Wilson, who argued in 1987 that the growing social isolation of minorities (particularly African Americans) within neighborhoods of intensely concentrated poverty systematically lowered their chances for success in employment, marriage, and education, controlling for their individual and family characteristics. Although Wilson attributed the growing isolation of minorities to structural shifts in the US economy and the changing geography of employment, Massey and Denton (1993) showed that rising income inequality caused by these changes *necessarily* produces high concentrations of poverty when they occur to a highly segregated group, such as African Americans. Given rising income inequality and a high degree of racial residential segregation, the concentration of black poverty is mathematically *inevitable*.

Thus, high levels of involuntary segregation undermine the socioeconomic well-being of minority groups by subjecting them to uniquely disadvantaged neighborhood environments brought about by the concentration of poverty and its correlates. Recent studies drawing on longitudinal data files reveal that growing up in a very poor neighborhood has negative socioeconomic consequences that are independent of personal characteristics or family circumstances. Specifically, coming of age in a poor neighborhood undermines cognitive development in early childhood, reduces academic achievement in later adolescence, and elevates the risk of antisocial behavior throughout the life course (Brooks-Gunn et al., 1997). Males experience a higher likelihood of withdrawing from the labor force and increased risks of criminal involvement, while women are less likely to marry and more likely to become single parents (Massey and Shibuya, 1995).

351

In sum, the combination of a rising rate of poverty and a high level of racial or ethnic segregation inevitably yields a geographic concentration of poverty that markedly lowers the odds of socioeconomic success for individual minority members. This finding implies that residential segregation is a key factor within broader processes of racial and ethnic stratification, and centrally implicated in the reproduction and maintenance of social inequality.

This link between segregation and stratification should prevail no matter what one assumes about the degree to which members of the same group are segregated by social class, but obviously when high levels of income or occupational segregation occur *in addition to* racial or ethnic segregation, the concentration of poverty will be exacerbated. Although the necessary data are not available in most countries, studies done in US cities reveal a marked rise in the degree of segregation by income from 1970 to 1990 (Massey, 1996), a trend that occurred within all regions and racial/ethnic groups (Jargowsky, 1996). In the United States, at least, the rich are increasingly living apart from the poor.

Although rising income inequality and growing class segregation clearly serve to undermine the socioeconomic welfare of all racial and ethnic groups in the United States, the consequences have been particularly severe for African Americans because they are so highly segregated by race. As a result of the hypersegregation of more than one third of all African Americans, and the very high segregation of most of the rest, poor blacks experience far higher concentrations of neighborhood poverty than the poor of any other group. Although few studies have explored the intersection of class, racial, and ethnic segregation in any detail, to the extent that rising income inequality, growing class segregation, and rising or persisting racial/ethnic segregation coincide in other nations, a similar ecology of inequality is expected to prevail.

As social science approaches the millennium, therefore, interest in residential segregation has broadened not only to include issues of measurement and causality, but increasingly to focus on the consequences of segregation by class as well as race and ethnicity. In order to disentangle the independent effects of metropolitan structure, neighborhood composition, and family circumstances on individual social and economic outcomes, researchers have turned increasingly to multilevel models and longitudinal data sets. Although the questions may be similar to those raised by the Chicago School theorists so long ago, the measures, methods, and data are now far more complex and sophisticated. Specifying the theoretical nature and empirical strength of connections between ecological structure, neighborhood conditions, and individual outcomes nonetheless remains a central preoccupation of social science.

References

Brooks-Gunn, J., Duncan, G., and Aber, L. (eds.) (1997) *Neighborhood Poverty, Volume I: Context and Consequences for Children.* New York: Russell Sage.

Burgess, E. W. (1928) "Residential segregation in American cities." *Annals of the American Academy of Political and Social Science* 140:105–15.

Christopher, A. J. (1993) "Segregation levels in the late-apartheid city 1985–1991." *Tijdschrift voor Economische en Sociale Geografie* 83:15–24.

Cortese, C. F., Falk, R. F., and Cohen, J. C. (1976) "Further considerations on the methodological analysis of segregation indices." *American Sociological Review* 41:630–37.

Cowgill, Donald O. (1986) *Aging Around the World*. Belmont, CA: Wadsworth.

Denton, N. A. (1994) "Are African Americans still hypersegregated?" in R. D. Bullard, J. E. Grigsby III, and C. Lee (eds.) *Residential Apartheid: The American Legacy*. Los Angeles: CAAS Publications, pp.49–81.

Denton, N. A. and Massey, D. S. (1988) "Residential segregation of blacks, Hispanics, and Asians by socioeconomic status and generation." *Social Science Quarterly* 69:797–817.

Duncan, O. D. and Duncan, B (1955) "A methodological analysis of segregation indices." *American Sociological Review* 20:210–17.

Duncan, O. D. and Duncan, B. (1957) *The Negro Population of Chicago: A Study of Residential Succession*. Chicago: University of Chicago Press.

Fong, E. (1996) "A comparative perspective on racial residential segregation: American and Canadian experiences." *The Sociological Quarterly* 37:199–226.

Hoyt, H. (1939) *The Structure and Growth of Residential Neighborhoods in American Cities*. Washington, D.C.: U.S. Government Printing Office.

Jacobs, J. A. (1989) *Revolving Doors: Sex Segregation and Women's Careers*. Stanford, CA: Stanford University Press.

Jargowsky, P. A. (1996) "Take the money and run: Economic segregation in U.S. metropolitan areas." *American Sociological Review* 61:984–98.

Kantrowitz, N. (1973) *Ethnic and Racial Segregation in the New York Metropolis*. New York: Praeger.

Krivo, L. J. and Kaufman, R. L. (1999) "How low can it go? Declining black–white segregation in a multiethnic context." *Demography* 36:93–110.

Lieberson, S. (1963) *Ethnic Patterns in American Cities*. New York: Free Press.

Massey, D. S. (1985) "Ethnic residential segregation: A theoretical synthesis and empirical review." *Sociology and Social Research* 69:315–50.

Massey, D. S. (1996) "The age of extremes: Concentrated affluence and poverty in the 21st century." *Demography* 33:395–412.

Massey, D. S. (2000) "The residential segregation of blacks, Hispanics, and Asians:1970 to 1990," in G. D. Jaynes (ed.) *Immigration and Race Relations. New Challenges For American Democracy*. New Haven, CT: Yale University Press, pp.44–73.

Massey, D. S., Arango, J., Hugo, G., Kouaouci, A., Pellegrino, A., and Taylor, J. E. (1998) *Worlds in Motion: Understanding International Migration at the Millennium*. Oxford: Oxford University Press.

Massey, D. S. and Denton, N. A. (1985) "Spatial assimilation as a socioeconomic process." *American Sociological Review* 50:94–105.

Massey, D. S. and Denton, N. A. (1988) "The dimensions of residential segregation." *Social Forces* 67:281–315.

Massey, D. S. and Denton, N. A. (1989) "Hypersegregation in U.S. metropolitan areas: Black and Hispanic segregation along five dimensions." *Demography* 26:373–93.

Massey, D. S. and Denton, N. A. (1993) *American Apartheid: Segregation and the Making of the Underclass*. Cambridge, MA: Harvard University Press.

Massey, D. S. and Shibuya, K. (1995) "Unravelling the tangle of pathology: The effect of spatially concentrated joblessness on the well-being of African Americans." *Social Science Research* 24:352–66.

Orfield, G. (1993) *The Growth of Segregation in American Schools: Changing Patterns of Separation and Poverty since 1968*. Alexandria, VA: National School Boards Association.

Park, R. E. (1926) "The urban community as a spatial pattern and a moral order," in E. W. Burgess and R. E. Park (eds.) *The Urban Community*. Chicago: University of Chicago Press, pp.3–18.

Park, R. E. and Burgess, E. W. (1925) *The City*. Chicago: University of Chicago Press.

Taeuber, K. E. and Taeuber, A. F. (1965) *Negroes in Cities: Residential Segregation and Neighborhood Change*. Chicago: Aldine.

Telles, E. E. (1992) "Residential segregation by skin color in Brazil." *American Sociological Review* 57:186–97.

Wilson, W. J. (1987) *The Truly Disadvantaged: The Inner City, the Underclass, and Public Policy*. Chicago: University of Chicago Press.

Chapter 24

New Languages, New Humanities: The "Mixed Race" Narrative and the Borderlands

Claudia M. Milian Arias

Once in a while through all of us there flashes some clairvoyance, some clear idea, of what America really is. We who are dark can see America in a way that white America cannot. And seeing our country thus, are we satisfied with its present goals and ideals? (W. E. B. Du Bois, 1995:509)

Artists and writers are currently involved in the redefinition of our continental topography. We see through the colonial map of North, Central, and South America, to a more complex system of overlapping, interlocking, and overlaid maps. Among others, we can see Amerindia, Afroamerica, Americamestiza-y-mulata, Hybridamerica, and Transamerica.

... We try to imagine more enlightened cartographies: a map of the Americas with no borders; a map turned upside down; or one in which the countries have borders that are organically drawn by geography, culture, and immigration, and not by the capricious hands of economic domination and political bravado. (Guillermo Gómez-Peña, 1996:6)

In Chicana and Chicano scholarship and cultural productions, the US–Mexico border zone is conceptualized not only as a point of multiple migrations, but also as a site informing and housing the various identity formations for this ethnoracial group. Because border theory principally relates to US and Mexican terrains, I focus on the ways that Chicana and Chicano configurations of border identities interlock and overlap with the redesignation of various investigations of self – racially, sexually, culturally, and linguistically – dialoguing with what become "other" borderlands. This exchange builds on the visionary qualities of Chicana and Chicano theoretical, cultural, literary, and political underpinnings, expanding the politics and pedagogy of liberation within the borderlands and pointing to border realities within communities of color in the United States. Undoubtedly, we must retain the specificities that Chicana, Chicano, and Mexican bodies encounter when they migrate and cross the US–Mexico border, but forging other border discourses concerning alienization, otherization, exploitation, and oppression would enrich Border Studies. At stake here is the construction of new meanings of border identities; the critical engagement of Chicana and Chicano in relation to "Latina," "Latino," and "black"; and the insertion and alteration of different interpretations of the borderlands that address associations between larger cultures. These connections between Chicanoness and blackness – or even how blackness is configured within Chicana and Chicano narratives – is highly underdeveloped and therefore merits close considerations.

This discussion of the borderlands and mixed race ties the ontological concerns of border cultures to blacks on the peripheries confronting issues of dispossession, exile, racialization, and marginalization. First, we examine responses to disparaging locations of ethnoracial subjects and how "problematic" peoples – through "mixed race" – counter the negation of their humanity by articulating a "different" language and by bearing the weight of the English alphabet in ways that mark, reverbalize, and theorize a "colored" experience. I start with James Weldon Johnson's (1995) *The Autobiography of an Ex-Colored Man* to punctuate a childhood consciousness demanding explanations to W. E. B. Du Bois's prognosis of being a problem. Next, I briefly shift to Zora Neale Hurston's (1998) passing reference to Janie's childhood as "Alphabet" in *Their Eyes Were Watching God*. Hurston illuminates a path where the *meanings* of living as a problem are deciphered in childhood through symbols impelling an ethnoracial and gendered subject to investigate questions such as "what am I?" and "where am I?" I explore these uncertainties through the construction of "the Elemenos" in Danzy Senna's novel, *Caucasia* (1998). The Elemenos are "a shifting people constantly changing their form, color, [and] pattern, in a quest for invisibility" (Senna, 1988:7). Indeed, "a quest for invisibility" and being assigned insignificance are two different realities.

I conclude by examining patterns of linguistic racialization by linking literary forms that investigate how "ambiguous," multiracial subjects speak their meanings in contemporary contexts that deracialize, if not "reproblematize" their existence by "unproblematizing" it. How does a subject that "can be anything," like journalistic graphs and sidebars cautioning that "Hispanics can be of any race," negotiate experiences of marginalization within the black and white binary? My objective is to study literary tropes that exercise a textual, yet highly symbolic, power by positioning people of color as floating signifiers of language. At present, we paradoxically witness not only a racialized turn, but also a deracialized linguistic turn within multicultural approaches that do not account for cultural workers' skillful agency in the construction of their text, or in the retelling of their particular story. I call attention to alternative perspectives that provide provocative linguistic connections to the instability of race, immigration, and a sense of place within the makings of the nation, while also focusing on the tensions and contradictions that construct ethnoracialized subjects as cultures of display.

The Text and the Body: Rereading Alphabetical Mixtures

In *The Autobiography of an Ex-Colored Man*, Johnson's multiracial protagonist, upon returning from school, desperately seeks a response from his closest relative. The anonymous narrator forcefully implores, "Mother, mother, tell me, am I a nigger?" (Weldon Johnson, 1995:8). Posing this question as a nine-year-old, the little boy realizes that blackness is "wrong." As the brown-skinned mother tearfully replies, "No, my darling, you are not a nigger," she recognizes her son's pain and attempts to disengage him from an injurious meaning of blackness. Calling him "my darling" – not "my baby," or "my child" – she underscores an endearment that does not infantilize her son. While expressing her affection, she simultaneously reveals an anguish that, despite her emotional attachment, confronts the color-line. Her evocation of "my darling" precedes the last word in her statement. Unlike Jack in Langston Hughes's short story, "Passing," (Hughes, 1990) who while making the transition into the white world, commends his mother for not publicly disclosing his blackness, the mother's grief in *The Autobiography of an Ex-Colored Man* illustrates the location of her son's humanity.

This mother points to a child's capacity to realize a humanity ("of color") that echoes Janie, Hurston's heroine in *Their Eyes Were Watching God*. Here, Janie declares that she did not know she was not white until she was about six years old, when a childhood photograph taken with her white schoolmates revealed her blackness. Janie narrates:

> So when we looked at de picture and everybody got pointed out there wasn't nobody left except a real dark little girl with long hair standing by Eleanor. Dat's where Ah wuz s'posed to be, but Ah couldn't recognize dat dark chile as me. So Ah ast, "where is me? Ah don't see me."
>
> Everybody laughed, even Mr. Washburn. Ms. Nellie, de Mama of de chillun who come back home after her husband dead, she pointed to the dark one and said, "Dat's you, Alphabet, don't you know yo' ownself?"
>
> Dey all useter call me Alphabet cause so many people done named me different names. Ah looked at de picture a long time and seen it was mah dress and mah hair so Ah said:
>
> "Aw, Aw! Ah'm colored!" (Hurston, 1998:9)

As Janie points to someone else's recognition of "her" blackness, Ms. Nellie's revealing question – "don't you know yo' ownself?" – directs Alphabet to a black self, outside of herself. Ms. Nellie assigns Janie's blackness to a level of consciousness that must come from within Janie, so that she knows "her place," and follows a systematic order like the letters of the alphabet. That Janie embodies the Alphabet suggests her anonymity while struggling with a language that Toni Morrison identifies as having the ability to "powerfully evoke and enforce hidden signs of racial superiority, cultural hegemony, and dismissive 'othering' of people" (Morrison, 1993:x). Alphabet details a particular kind of training in literacy and race relations, preparing Janie for the white social world as her "colored" consciousness attempts to answer and live with *what* she is. In this moment, *being* Alphabet means documenting her experiences, as she becomes a resistant agent to Ms. Nellie's version of blackness.

Janie's forming and informing patterns of language serve as a point of departure as they become a mechanism for survival within ethnoracial subjects who are mixed, or in the case of *Caucasia's* protagonist, slightly "off-white" (Senna, 1988:119). These subjects struggle to make meaning between "white" America as well as "black" and "brown" America. *Caucasia* – a provocative and absorbing exploration of racial tensions within the familial sphere and within the makings of "the nation" – is the poignant, coming-of-age narrative of Birdie, who "looks like a little Sicilian" (p. 23) and the search for her sister, Cole, "cinnamon-skinned, curly-haired, [and] serious" (p. 5). Raised in Boston's South End during the 1970s, when the city "still came in black and white [but] yellowing around the edges" (p. 1), Birdie and Cole Lee, the offspring of a white mother and a black father, are compelled to maneuver their own racial locations. When the parents divorce, they racialize and segregate the siblings by picking a daughter that approximates their skin tone, accentuating the particular racial formations and ideological underpinnings that have informed each parent's asymmetrical positionalities in US structures. The father takes Cole to Brazil in pursuit of racial equality, while the mother takes Birdie to the various locations of race in the United States, what Birdie identifies as "the underneath," Caucasia, "a world without names, without pasts, [and] without documents" (p. 115). Senna provides new meanings in the construction of border identities through *black* mixture and illustrates how blackness is linked to mestizaje by virtue of its myriad ethnoracial compositions, coupled with the legacies of violence of how these colors came to be racially marked. When mixed blackness is penned into the "black" novel, it does not only destabilize the meanings of what "pure" blackness entails, but also the meanings of Latina and Latino literary and cultural projects that overlook blackness because "Latina" and "Latino" is misread and misunderstood as "not black."

In Chicana and Chicano cultural productions, racial and cultural mixture emerge through the transformation of the US–Mexico border as a geographical and perceptual site, recognized by José David Saldívar as "a paradigm of crossings, intercultural exchanges, circulations, resistances, and negotiations as well as of militarized 'low-intensity' conflict" (Saldívar, 1997, ix). This line of investigation allows Chicanas and Chicanos to contest the violence of the border alongside the racist and discriminatory practices of US structures and among other things, to confront the implications of living with the legacy of not only being internally colonized, but of being "Americanized" as well. The aim of border crossings is not to provide a complete blueprint of what constitutes Chicananess and Chicanoness. Memory – lacunae, absences, recollections – plays a pivotal role in the re-evaluation and reinscription of Chicana and Chicano pluralities, fragmented histories, geographic terrains, and political borders.

The borderlands are where "America" is transformed as the here and the now, so to speak, as US normative culture invariably positions and reduces their reality as an alien and un-American (read: Chicano and Mexican) "there." Yet, while these lines of cross-cultural crossings and exchanges overlap with diasporic groups throughout the Americas, Chicanas and Chicanos often exclusively construct and understand the conditions of the 2,000-mile, US–Mexico border as a unique Chicana and Chicano situation. Chicanas and Chicanos insist that the assertion of their ethnoracial subjectivities requires investigation of their pluralities, but they tend to almost always be situated in dualistic terms of Chicano and normative culture. Such extremes bypass the overall racial compositions of the United States exceeding a brown and white binary. Like the borderlands, Senna's novel clearly illustrates that multiple border crossings become the experience through which subjectivity is continuously made, unmade, and transformed.[1] Birdie's notions of elsewhereness lead us to border consciousness, or awareness by racialized ethnicities struggling to make sense of identity formations that correspond to the US internal lines along race. Birdie – a transient subject consistently unmasking and clearly reconstructing the meanings of white normativity by inhabiting that forbidden ideological as well as material space – proclaims: "I disappeared into America, the easiest place to get lost. Dropped off, without a name, without a record. With only the body I traveled in. And a memory of something lost" (Senna, 1988:1).

In *Caucasia*, memory is constantly activated through a language that Birdie and Cole perfect, called Elemeno, in honor of their four favorite letters of the alphabet. Elemeno is a language, a method, and a space to identify the social and political problems of their time, while localizing them to the domestic sphere. Birdie acknowledges: "We could hear our parents fighting through the heating vent. Muted obscenities. We were trying to block them out with talk of Elemeno" (Senna, 1988:7). Richard Rodriguez, in dialogue with the complexities Senna evokes of a black and white world, reveals in *Days of Obligation*: "When I was growing up, I heard Americans describing their nation as simply bipartate: black and white. When black and white America argued, I felt I was overhearing some family quarrel that didn't include me" (Rodriguez, 1992:166). Arguments in the Lee household, in black and white, also exclude Birdie and Cole. Trying to decipher the racial tensions of the outside world, the girls' father invariably asks, "What's wrong with this picture?" (Senna, 1988:62), neglecting to examine the types of racial pictures in his own family. Elemeno, we are told, "is a complicated language, impossible for outsiders to pick up – no verb tenses, no pronouns, just words floating outside time and space without owner or direction. Attempting to decipher our chatter, my mother said, was like trying to eavesdrop on someone sleeptalking, when the words are still untranslated from their dream state – achingly familiar, but just beyond one's grasp" (pp. 5–6) The mother reduces the intensity of the girls' language to sleeptalking, relegating them to a state of nonbeing. Elemenos merit no explanations about the social world. In this way, Senna invokes Ralph Ellison's *Invisible Man*, whose protagonist became alive upon discovering his invisibility.

Efforts to decipher Elemeno, described as a "high-speed patois" (Senna, 1988:6), accentuate mystification with the unlocatable people who verbalize that dialect. In Birdie's case, the racialized uncertainties that consistently surface are: " 'Who's that?' 'She a Rican or something?' " (p. 36). By contrast, Cole has "a face of those accustomed to being watched" (p. 41). In a contemporary context, Birdie and Cole become Hurston's new "Alphabets," whose color – or being – is a mystery to the outside world, since they are continually misinterpreted. Yet, Janie, Birdie, and Cole share a new awareness that allows them to name things in their particular environment. Not surprisingly, the first chapter is titled "Face," and Birdie explains that Elemeno was developed in the attic bedroom of their home on Columbus Avenue (p. 5). Senna playfully inverts the discovery of the New World as the two sisters, "amid the dust and stuffed animals," make cities out of them (pp. 5–6). In reconstructing the United States, Senna documents what Du Bois described as the lives of those who find themselves "outside of the American world, looking in" (Du Bois, 1997:157).

Imaginatively, the siblings create a geographical and linguistic site we can call Elemeno City, or a "secret and fun and make-believe" place (Senna, 1988:5–6), where they also become queens of their make-believe nation (p. 53). In *Borderlands*, Gloria Anzaldúa explains that her " 'home' tongues" are languages she speaks and shares with her family and friends to create a sense of place (Anzaldúa, 1999:78). Likewise, Birdie aspires to live in her home space, where stuffed animals – generally given to children for cuddling and protection from the dark – shield the sisters from incriminating stares that intimate "something like exhaustion" (Senna, 1988:32–6). Their attic, then, is a discursive and material space that enables Birdie and Cole, in Anzaldúan terms, to "trust and believe in themselves as speaker[s]" and "as voice[s] for the images" they embody (Anzaldúa, 1999:95). Birdie and Cole fragment and displace normative discourses about the racialized meanings and subsequent positionings of whiteness, detailing how the subaltern subject is able to shape and shift in order to survive. In *White Reign*, Peter McLaren reminds us that whiteness is a material and discursive space serving as "an articulatory practice that can be located in the convergence of colonialism, capitalism, and subject formation. Whiteness displaces blackness and browness – specific forms of nonwhiteness – into signifiers of deviance and criminality within social, cultural, cognitive, and political contexts" (McLaren, 1998:67). Senna transgresses the siblings' nonwhite "signifiers," embodying an undetermined space of continuous transition.

Accounting For Self and Place

Cole reveals that Elemenos are a language as well as racialized and gendered subjects. They have the capacity to "turn not just from black to white, but from brown to yellow to purple to green, and back again" (Senna, 1988:7). Through Elemeno, this "unracialized" invisibility takes a "racialized" linguistic turn. Anzaldúa amplifies the function and necessity of a language like Elemeno, or what she calls in a Chicana and Chicano context, "border tongues" (Anzaldúa, 1999:77) Anzaldúa explains: "for a people who live in a country in which English is the reigning tongue but who are not Anglo . . . what recourse is left to them but to create their own language? A language which they can connect their identity to, one capable of communicating the realities and values true to them" (p. 77). For Birdie, the transient subject who answers to various deviations of her name – Patrice, Jesse, Birdie, Birdie Lee, Bird – "with a schizophrenic zeal" (Senna, 1988:17), Elemeno evokes a double self struggling to find what has place within the multiple mappings of America, where racial compositions are constructed in ways that "erase" ethnicity. Like Janie, or Alphabet, as well as the protagonist in *The Autobiography of an Ex-Colored Man*, their racial designations, and subsequent ideological attachments to *being* reduced to interchangeable "names," depends on who is doing the naming. Indeed, Birdie's mother reminds her that she has "a lot of choices, babe. You can be anything, Puerto Rican, Sicilian, Pakistani, Greek. I mean anything really. And of course, you could always be Jewish" (p. 110).

This index of deracializing identities creates a hierarchical and otherizing understanding of race. The myriad of ethnicities the mother posits implies that they are not as "bad" as being black. Birdie reveals that people of color see themselves in her face – and through that racial "anything," as her mother puts it – some individuals expect Birdie to respond to their specific racial *and* linguistic identifications. In one instance, a man who looks "Indian" attempts a conversation with Birdie, reminding her of Elemeno. The ways that this exchange echoes Elemeno resonates with Lorna Dee Cervantes's uses of language in her "Poem For The Young White Man Who Asked Me How I, An Intelligent, Well Read Person, Could Believe In The War Between Races" (1990). Cervantes leads us into a moment of instability, where the poet is unplaceable and "childlike." Cervantes acknowledges the infantilizing effects of racialization, colonization, and marginalization, and how language bears these marks in its syllables – or scars she must recite to survive. As the poem delineates itself dialectically, Cervantes' address includes her reader in an argument, or a discussion already in progress. She first invokes a collective voice rendering a self-contained topographical region into existence, through the lines, "In my land/people write poems about love." This land from which she speaks is fraught with a childlike instability evoked through the notion of illiteracy. It is a broken language, "full of nothing but contended childlike syllables."

Senna delineates Cervantes' rawness of language in Elemeno, where a childlike state evokes exhilaration with "the little world they create" (Senna, 1988:6). Cervantes' land is forced to rely on the fragments of words to reconstruct her identity against the dehumanizing elements that appear as threats in the first stanza, what she deems as "The barbed wire politics of oppression" (Cervantes, 1990:4). The "barbed wire politics of oppression" allude to notions of being denied access to certain spaces, borders, or in Mary Louise Pratt's term, "contact zones" like the US–Mexico border pointing to the expected, but deportable, presence of a racialized subject (see Pratt, 1992). Cervantes' fence imagery, published in her 1981 collection of poetry, *Emplumada*, lays the ground-work for a poetics contesting the militarization of the US–Mexico border. In *Borderlands*, first published in 1987, Anzaldúa recognizes the US–Mexico division as a site where the "Third World grates against the first and bleeds" (Anzaldúa, 1999:25). Anzaldúa and Cervantes reverse Latin American notions that position indigenous communities as being tainted by bad blood (or "*mala sangre*"). This type of bleeding references the physical violence by US Border Patrol agents and the economic and environmental exploitation along the border by US corporations.

At the airport, Birdie explains to the "Indian" man that she is "American," and that her parents are black and white. After her clarification, the man's expression, "changed slightly. I had disappointed him, deeply. He had been homesick and had seen his home in my face. Now he turned away, no longer interested" (Senna, 1988:323). Birdie's explanation seems parenthetical. This initial racial association indicates a search for a home pointing to multiple geographies that nonetheless lack a specificity or materiality behind that ethnoracial identifier. Looking alike, in other words, does not necessarily constitute a community. Tellingly, however, they both speak "English" in "America" to not only grasp the meanings of their ethnoracial specificities, but to also emphasize that the center remains linguistically unchanged. Birdie thus shows the twofold face of language and race and how people have different associations with "racial exchanges."

Like her phenotype, Birdie simultaneously intimates linguistic possibilities. Yet, present political movements indicate these linguistic possibilities need to be restrained, if not dismissed through policies advocating an end to bilingual education, like Califor-nia's Proposition 227 and efforts to nationally designate English as the "official" language. Despite these "English Only" proposals, English is countered, mimicked, and transformed by subjects who are discriminated against for presumably not speaking it. Anzaldúa, for example, reveals that she uses "anglicisms, words borrowed from English: *bola* from ball, *carpeta* from carpet ... *cookiar* for cook, *watchar* for watch, [and] *parkiar* for park" (Anzaldúa, 1999:79). In *Urban Exile*, Harry Gamboa, Jr. notes that a subject that is linguistically marked and ranked evokes a nationality other than "American." He recalls that his first art lesson in an East Los Angeles elementary school consisted of "cutting and pasting a dunce cap out of construction paper, onto which the teacher wrote the letters, 'S-P-A-N-I-S-H' " (Noriega, 1998:14), forcing him to embody a tongue that supposedly impedes his advancement in US society.

Anzaldúa also recalls the ramifications of being caught speaking Spanish, or the act of embodying the "other" nonwhite side: "I remember being caught speaking Spanish at recess – that was good for three licks on the knuckles with a sharp ruler. I remember being sent to the corner of the classroom for 'talking back' to the Anglo teacher when all I was trying to do was tell her how to pronounce my name" (Anzaldúa, 1999:75). Language becomes a type of bad behavior, if not mode of life that must be controlled. Whereas for Anzaldúa the mispronunciation of her name leads to her discipline and to an orderly classroom, for Rodriguez the pronouncement of his name as "*Rich-heard Road-ree-guess*" directs him to his education. In *Hunger of Memory*, Rodriguez outlines his "new" designation, Richheard – not Ricardo, as his mother calls him – in consecutive syllables that reposition, and become, a riddle bearing his name.[2] The screeching sound, particularly as we pause midway through his last name, *Road-ree-guess*, clarifies Rodriguez's role in US society, a chatter that intones "Richard heard a road to guess." This sound suggests that Rodriguez must navigate a road – or various color-lines – to become what he calls a "scholarship boy," or an "American story" (Rodriguez, 1983:5).

By contrast, Gamboa demonstrates the limits of the English language by employing the shadows of history through a linguistic collage that shapes his own as well as a collective identity formation. Resourcefully, Gamboa builds on his childhood incident to make the English language bear the weight of Chicana and Chicano conquest. Gamboa examines the incorporation of Chicanas and Chicanos to the United States through the Mexican–American War in 1848, brought by US doctrines of expansion, justified through ideologies of Manifest Destiny. In one of his pieces, "Jetter's Jinx," a character utters:

> Many festivals destroy tiny successes.
> Many fest, Dest, Tiny suck excess.
> Mani, Fest, Des, Tiny, Suck excess.
> Manifest Destiny Sucks.
> (Gamboa, 1998:233)

The fragmented structure of this excerpt suggests the ways that Manifest Destiny needs to be revisited, revised, and challenged. Tellingly, Gamboa employs periods throughout these semantically fragmented lines, providing a foundation for self-representation that questions and remaps the United States through continuous linguistic, geopolitical, and cultural border crossings. Through border culture, Chicanas and Chicanos struggle to transform oppressive social and cultural conditions in the theory and practice of their subjectivities. Because of the absence of a definition of culture, border theory precipitates a manifestation of consciousness, a way of life meaning and forming beings. Border culture allows Chicanas and Chicanos, racially and sexually marked by US structures and practices, to (1) trace their lineage to indigenous cultures; (2) mix deviations of languages, including English, Nahuatl, Spanish, and Spanglish; (3) claim Mexican and US ties as political rhetoric and policies represent them as a questionable, problematic population and legislation militarizes the border; (4) confront issues of labor exploitation alongside social and cultural inequalities; (5) occupy various unevenly deployed geographical spaces; and, among other things, (6) insert queer and feminist configurations in heterosexual- and masculine-centered constructions and assertions of Chicanoness. These avenues of thinking, points of interaction, and ways of generating new forms of interpretation and meaning demonstrate an engagement with sociocultural processes of being and becoming human in a popular mainstream in which Chicanas and Chicanos are "aliens." Gamboa and Senna thus open "space" for larger, social discourses about subjects who fluctuate as black, white, and with varying shades between these two categories.

Side by side, Gamboa and Senna indicate that while Latina, Latino, and "multiracial" may seem to be exclusive categories, they also speak to different levels of racial "sameness." Latina and Latino do not replace black, nor vice versa, but they can supplement it. Senna's and Gamboa's work illustrates that they do not linearly fit the imagined role of how a racialized subject lives. They show the specific realities of the supposedly nonspecific, easily recognizable "nonwhite." In so doing, they echo an African proverb: "It is not what you call me, it is what I answer to" (quoted in Sandoval-Sánchez, 1999:11).

Notes

1 While I single out the agency of subaltern subjects within contradictory locations, I do not mean to suggest that the formation of subjectivity is a self-selecting phenomenon. Subjects become who they are in relation to larger sociocultural politics, and they learn to maneuver within ever-increasing attempts to stifle their growth, progress, and creativity.
2 Rodriguez, 1983:11. In *Hunger of Memory*, Rodriguez amplifies: "I needed my teachers to keep my attention from straying in class by calling out *Rich-heard* – their English voices slowly prying loose my ties to my other name, its three notes, *Ri-car-do*" (Rodriguez, 1983:21; italics in original).

References

Anzaldúa, Gloria (1999) *Borderlands/ La Frontera: The New Mestiza*, 2nd edn. San Francisco: Aunt Lute Books.

Cervantes, Lorna Dee (1981) *Emplumada*. Pittsburgh, PA: University of Pittsburgh Press.

Cervantes, Lorna Dee (1990) "Poem for the young white man who asked me how I, an intelligent, well-read person, could believe in the war between the races," in Gloria Anzaldúa (ed.) *Making Face, Making Soul/ Haciendo Caras: Creative and Critical Perspectives by Feminists of Color*. San Francisco: Aunt Lute Books, pp.4–5.

Du Bois, W. E. B. (1995) "Criteria of negro art," in David Levering Lewis (ed.) *W. E. B. Du Bois: A Reader*. New York: Henry Holt, pp 509–15.

Du Bois, W. E. B. (1997) *The Autobiography of W. E. B. Du Bois: A Soliloquy on Viewing My Life from the Last Decade of its First Century*. New York: International Publishers.

Gamboa, Harry Jr. (1998) *Urban Exile: Collected Writings of Harry Gamboa, Jr.*, ed. Chon A. Noriega. Minneapolis: University of Minnesota Press.

Gómez-Peña, Guillermo (1996) *The New World Border: Prophecies, Poems, and Loqueras for the End of the Century*. San Francisco: City Lights Books.

Hughes, Langston (1990) "Passing," in *The Ways of White Folks: Stories by Langston Hughes*. New York: Vintage Classics, pp.50–7.

Hurston, Zora Neale (1998) *Their Eyes Were Watching God*. New York: HarperPerennial.

McLaren, Peter (1998) "Whiteness is . . . the struggle for postcolonial hybridity," in Joe L. Kincheloe, Shirley R. Steinberg, Nelson M. Rodriguez, and Ronald E. Chennault (eds.) *White Reign: Deploying Whiteness in America*. New York: St. Martin's Press, pp.63–75.

Morrison, Toni (1993) *Playing in the Dark: Whiteness and the Literary Imagination*. New York: Vintage Books.

Noriega, Chon A. (1998) "No introduction," in *Urban Exile: Collected Writings of Harry Gamboa, Jr.*, ed. Chon A. Noriega. Minneapolis: University of Minnesota Press, pp.1–22.

Pratt, Mary Louise (1992) *Imperial Eyes: Travel Writing and Transculturation*. (New York: Routledge.

Rodriguez, Richard (1983) *Hunger of Memory: The Education of Richard Rodriguez*. New York: Bantam Books.

Rodriguez, Richard (1992) *Days of Obligation: An Argument with My Mexican Father*. New York: Viking.

Saldívar, José David (1997) *Border Matters: Remapping American Cultural Studies*. Berkeley: University of California Press.

Sandoval-Sánchez, Alberto (1999) *José, Can You See?: Latinos On and Off Broadway*. Madison, University of Wisconsin Press.

Senna, Danzy (1988) *Caucasia*. New York: Riverhead Books.

Weldon Johnson, James (1995) *The Autobiography of an Ex-Colored Man*. New York: Dover Publications.

Chapter 25

The New Technologies of Racism

Les Back

The New York Police Department expressed concern yesterday at the number of Hairless Vagrant Youths hanging around underpasses, dark alleyways and latrines holding Personal Computers with the intent to Maim and Rob. One such unhirsute youth was questioned by reporters:
Our man in Brooklyn: So, Dave – can I call you Dave?
Dave: That's me name.
OMIB: So, Dave, you – hit people with this Personal Computer thing?
Dave: I do. Ram the screen down straight over their 'ead. IBM PC's work best, then the 'ole 'ead goes right down the cathode tube. Macintoshes only works on folks with small 'eads, like children and creationists.
OMIB: But . . . why don't you just . . . hit them. With your hands?
Dave: I'm a child of the Information Age.[1]

This joke conjures up the image of a brainless skinhead for whom the only use for a computer is in its ability to inflict physical harm. It is the quintessential stereotype of what a racist looks like – male, maniacal, the uncivilized "white-faced" minstrel of the antiracist imagination. But such lampoonery masks a deadly serious reality. The success of the white power music scene today is in large part the product of the information age. The key exponents and distributors of white power rock have utilized computer technologies to advertise, network, and market their products in unprecedented ways. In this sense the neo-Nazi moguls of the music scene are certainly the children of a digital era. Such current realities undermine any crude correspondence between ignorance or stupidity and racism or fascism. Technological advances such as the Internet have provided a means for contemporary fascists within Europe and the white diasporas of the New World to garner a digitally enhanced translocal culture in cyberspace and a truly international market. The Internet provides much more than just another publishing tool for propaganda, for it has offered an immediate and direct form of access to people with networked personal computers and a means to participate interactively in racist movements without face-to-face contact.

This chapter will explore the intersection between fascism and the technologies of a translocal whiteness. Critical discussion of cyberculture has in the main focused on its

This chapter is an edited excerpt from Vron Ware and Les Back (forthcoming) *Out of Whiteness: Color, Politics, and Culture*. Chicago: University of Chicago Press.

potential to realize new forms of human subjectivity. Cyberspace illustrates the contemporary resonance of poststructuralist philosophy which emphasises *becoming* over *being* (Deleuze and Guattari, 1986) and *performance* over *essence* (Butler, 1990). Sherry Turkle has commented on how computer simulation demonstrated the relevance of French social theory:

> ...more than twenty years after meeting the ideas of Lacan, Foucault, Deleuze, and Guattari, I am meeting them again in my new life on the screen. But this time, the Gallic abstractions are more concrete. In my computer mediated world, the self is multiple, fluid, and constituted in interaction with machine connections, it is made and transformed by language; sexual congress is an exchange of signifiers; and understanding follows from navigation and tinkering rather than analysis. And in my machine generated world...I meet characters who put me in a new relationship with my own identity. (Turkle, 1995:15)

It is here too that Sadie Plant and Donna Haraway have argued that within these virtual domains new utopian possibilities exist for women to inhabit a world beyond the constraints of gender (Plant, 1998; Haraway, 1991; see also Featherstone and Burrows, 1995). All this stands in stark contrast to the profoundly essentialist arborescent quality of Net-Nazi activism. But such a possibility, in which digital culture might enhance rather than undermine modern fascisms, was anticipated by some of these theoreticians and particularly in the work of Deleuze and Guattari.

In *A Thousand Plateaus*, Deleuze and Guattari argue that part of the nature of fascism is a "proliferation of molecular focuses in interaction, which skip from point to point, before beginning to resonate together..." (Deleuze and Guattari, 1986:214). This comment might well have been made about the lateral connectedness found in cyberspace. Rather than seeing fascism enshrined in a totalitarian bureaucracy, they argue that fascism was and is manifest in the microorganization of everyday life. The power of fascist culture here is in its "molecular and supple segmentarity, [with] flows capable of suffusing every cell...What makes fascism dangerous is its molecular or micropolitical power, for it is a mass movement: a cancerous body rather than a totalitarian organism" (pp. 214–15). There is, however, little discussion in the theoretical literature on cyberculture which looks at the ways in which the extreme right has utilized the medium. On the other hand, the work produced by antifascist monitoring organizations adds little to the qualitative understanding of how virtual fascism might relate to its previous media incarnations (see Capitanchik and Whine, 1996; Anti-Defamation League, 1995; Simon Wiesenthal Center, 1998). In this sense, there is a real gap between the politically engaged and empirically extensive forms of antifascist monitoring and the academic and theoretical work on virtual culture. This chapter situates itself somewhere between these ways of looking at the politics of cyberspace in an attempt to make critical theory speak to political realities and vice versa. In a technological age the morphology of whiteness is changing because, as Sherry Turkle (1995) points out, the modernist preoccupation with calculation is being superseded by simulation and invention at the interface between flesh and machines.

Media, Fascism, and New Technosocial Horizons

The contemporary cultures of the ultra-right pose real difficulties with regard to definition and classification. A wide range of terms are currently used to describe these groups, including neo-Nazi, Nazi, Ultras, white supremacist, fascist, and racist. These labels are used to describe a complex range of ideologies, movements, and groups. For the sake of conceptual clarity I shall be deploying the notion of cyber-Nazis to speak about a range of subcultural movements in Europe, North America, and beyond. While these movements are diverse they exhibit the following common features:

• a rhetoric of racial and/or national uniqueness and common destiny,
• ideas of racial supremacy, superiority, and separation,
• a repertoire of conceptions of racial Otherness,
• a utopian revolutionary worldview that aims to overthrow the existing order.

In line with Umberto Eco's (1995) insightful comments we would argue that these diverse movements possess a "family of resemblances" while recognizing that there is no necessary reason why specific groups should hold to all of the social features outlined above.

For some conventional scholars of the far right the current interest in the relationship between xenophobia, popular culture, and new technologies is little more than a fashionable intellectual chimera.[2] They caution that the "real issue" is what is happening in terms of the ballot box and the macroeconomic and political trends that underpin political mobilizations. Such a view misses the importance of vernacular culture – be it mediated by technology or other forms – in sustaining what Deleuze and Guattari call the "molecular nature" of authoritarian politics. Alternately, there is a tendency within cultural studies to politicize all aspects of youth culture, reading style as a prosaic statement of protest without establishing the connections between its symbolism, action, and political affiliation.[3] In order to understand fascism, either in its generic or contemporary forms, it is crucial to develop a sensitivity to the relationship between politics, culture, and the mass media. The relative absence of a clear analysis of these issues in contemporary scholarship is somewhat at odds with the focus of some classical studies of fascist ideas and values. Walter Benjamin, for example, in his essay on "Art in the Age of Mechanical Reproduction" commented that new technologies, like photography, enabled the mass character of Nazism to be captured in unprecedented ways:

> Mass movements are usually discerned more clearly by a camera than by the naked eye. A bird's eye view best captures gatherings of hundreds of thousands. And even though such a view may be accessible to the human eye as it is to the camera, the image received by the eye cannot be enlarged the way a negative is enlarged. (Benjamin, 1968:244)

From this perspective the medium *and* the message are important if we are to understand the dynamics of these movements. This is no less true today. In this sense, Benjamin's suggestive comments about the potential of technology to express aesthetic politics in a new dimension can usefully be applied to simulation, style, and digital culture. The simple point that follows from this is that it is both important and necessary to map the matrices of contemporary fascist politics through their specific forms of cultural expression.

It is for this reason that it is important to combine an analysis of the politics of racism and fascism with a focus on the ways in which racist ideas and values are expressed through particular cultural modalities (Back et al. 1996). The first of these is the

367

technosocial (Escobar, 1994). A particular technology – be it pop music or the Internet – has no inherent ideological orientation. Rather, the relationship between form and content is found at the interface between particular technologies and their utilization. In the context of Nazism the technosocial modalities of photography and film contributed to the mass choreography of moral indolence. They provided a way for state authority to be embodied and a means by which individual conscience could be dissolved in the volkish reverie of mass art (Solomos and Back, 1996). As Benjamin rightly argues, this is made possible by the form itself, along with the historical forces which put it to work. This approach stresses the realm of possibilities that are opened up by the deployment of a particular technology in the context of racist cultures. The key point to emphasize here is that the Internet and other related media allow new horizons for the expression of whiteness. In fact, as will be argued, the rhetoric of whiteness becomes the means to combine profoundly local grammars of racial exclusion within a translocal and international reach that is made viable through digital technology.

From this perspective, the Internet, subcultural style, or pop music each constitutes a particular kind of cultural modality which needs to be evaluated within its own technical apparatus and form. The second element identified here is the mechanisms of circulation and their spatial distribution. In particular this means identifying how these cultural forms of expression address particular audiences and their spatial patterns of reception. The last element focuses on the way symbolic and linguistic elements are combined within particular technical modes. For example, it seems possible within the white power music scene for staunchly nationalistic sensibilities to be maintained while common images and icons and musical forms are shared between subcultures throughout the world.

"Resistance Through Digital"

At its most basic, the Internet is an interconnected computer network that enables hyper forms of communication which compress the relationship between time and space. Its origins go back to 1969 when the Defense Advanced Research Project Agency (DARPA), a United States defense department, developed a method of exchanging military research information between researchers based at different sites. By the mid-1980s, these computer networks were expanded by another US government agency, the National Science Foundation (NSF). The NSF established supercomputer centers whose resources were required to be accessible to any educational facility who wanted them. The NSF network was gradually refined and evolved into what we know as the Internet. Evidence first appeared in the 1980s that electronic mail and Bulletin Board Systems (BBS) which lie outside of the Internet were being used by neofascists. It is really in the last three years that the level of right-wing Internet activity has increased dramatically.

Resource pages on the World Wide Web are closest to a broadcast model of propaganda. They enable white power groups to circulate articles, CD catalogs, images, and symbols. Rick Eaton, of the Simon Wiesenthal Center, sums up the pace of change: "At the time of the Oklahoma city bombing there was one white supremacy page on the web – that was Don Black's page, *Stormfront*. Now there are literally hundreds and there's new ones that come up all the time."[4] Estimates of exactly how many sites vary and the transient nature of these pages make it difficult to establish an exact figure. There are around 200 white supremacist web sites but some estimates put the number of hate sites as high as 600. These include Hammerskin[5] sites and music dedicated pages, most notably Resistance Records, originally based in Detroit. Eaton concludes: "The Internet was one factor in giving new life to that music scene. The skinhead movement in general was in decline three years ago. Now it is international and big business. Resistance Records brought it all together and through their web site established an international market."[6] The web has been particularly effective for advertising white power music on mail order. Previously, the music could only be bought at concerts or through advertising in skinzines but, through the web, CD catalogs potentially reach millions.

Resistance Records was founded in 1994 by George Burdi (a.k.a. Eric Hawthorne) and Mark Wilson, both of whom were in their early twenties. The label's 12 bands sold 50,000 CDs in their first 18 months of business. By 1996 the label made a profit for the first time from a total of $300,000 worth of sales. They also sold their own glossy magazine called *Resistance*, which had a circulation of 15,000. Their web page was highly sophisticated, including sound samples of each band that could be downloaded and heard online. Burdi, formerly of the Church of the Creator, is also the lead singer of RAHOWA (*RA*cial *HO*ly *WA*r), one of the leading American Nazi bands. His voice is evocative of Roger Waters from the English progressive rock band Pink Floyd, providing another example of how particular images of Englishness are utilized within white musical authenticity. Burdi's story is interesting precisely because he is an example of a middle-class and highly media-literate youth being drawn into the white power scene. He grew up in an upper-middle-class family in a suburb of Toronto, the son of an insurance broker who was not known for espousing racist views. A bright child, he received his first computer at the age of 10. Mark Potok, of Klanwatch, comments: "The music scene is important because – along with the Internet – it has helped The Movement reach people it has never reached before, specifically, middle-class and upper-middle-class teenagers. Kids who live in their parents' two and three and four hundred thousand dollar homes." Currently, in America, racist recruitment is more focused on the suburbs than the working-class trailer parks. Mark Potok concluded:

> There was a great deal of interest in the 1980s in recruiting thugs, your typical racist skinhead. There's a lot less interest in that now and a lot more in recruiting college-bound or college-educated upper-middle-class bright kids because they are looking for strategists not street soldiers. It is not about beating people up in bars but looking for the leaders of tomorrow.[7]

When Stuart Hall and Tony Jefferson published *Resistance Through Rituals* in 1976, the analysis of youth culture was connected with an antihegemonic politics of "the popular." It is not without some irony that over 20 years later the chief exponent of fascist music should have stolen the language of "Resistance" in the name of popular racism. White power rock is a form of ritualized resistance but in ways that the early cultural studies writers would not have anticipated. In the United States, Resistance Records have been successful in constructing a well-packaged and alluring form of media-generated racist rebellion. This music has garnered an international market and its appeal in different national contexts is varied and driven by contrasting social forces. In Britain, white power music may be an appeal to a racist notion of proletarian authenticity; in America it might be invoked by middle-class kids to shock their parents' pretensions to liberal multiculturalism; while in Sweden it may be used by rebellious young people to goad the nation's Liberal Democratic self-image.

Cyberspace offers a relatively safe space to participate in an interactive way in a largely autonomous, although not hermetic, racist Networld. Here, social networks and aspects of the everyday life of racists can be carried into cyberspace and sustained. The existence of the *United Skins Webring* is a good example of this kind of networking. The Webring enables skinhead sites to be entered as part of a connected circle of sites. However, not all skinheads are invited. "Baldies, commies, queers and trads [i.e. traditional skinheads] that can't admit they like Skrewdriver need not apply," they warn. Another highly sophisticated site is Micetrap's *White Pride Network*. This page also provides a library of 250 white power tracks that can be downloaded through a form of sound file compression called mp3s, which make it possible to record a whole song in a file that takes up only a few megabytes of memory. The web page also offers links to the home pages of bands like Berserkr and Intimidation One, music reviews, and sections dedicated to racist jokes and white power video retailing. When you open the NS88 page, messages flash beneath the logo: "Welcome to NS88 Websites/The best in white power video/ committed to the highest quality." As each message flashes on the screen the sound of a whip being cracked is heard on the speakers.

The combination of intimacy and distance found in cyberspace provide a new context for racist harassment through abuse or digital tools like "mail bombs." They also provide a context in which racism can be simulated. Elsewhere I have talked about the use of computer games that offer the "pleasure" of simulated racial violence (Back et al. 1996). These technologies make new types of racist behavior possible. They combine all of the fruits of the digital era to produce interactive visual forms that are alluring and attractive to a particularly youthful audience. Virtual forms of racial violence relate to chilling lived experiences while remaining in the "other world" of computer simulation. They are politically slippery because they blur the distinction between social reality and fantasy. This issue was brought sharply into focus in April 1996 when a photograph of a young black man, face down on the floor being beaten and kicked, was posted on the *Skinheads USA* website. The site is maintained by 28-year-old Dallas resident, Bart Alsbrook, known by his online name "Bootboy." Another photograph entitled "Mexican Getting Smashed" showed two men beating a bleeding victim. The incident was reported in the local newspaper (Copilevitz, 1996). The Dallas police examined the possibility of using the images as evidence, and since this incident the web site has been closed down. Mark Briskman, a director with the Anti-Defamation League, commented at the time: "It reminds me of Nazi Germany and the way they meticulously documented all their atrocities in stills and on film."[8] This incident is a dangerous example of the use of the Internet to celebrate real incidents of racist violence. The tension between national chauvinism and the increasingly transnational matrices of neofascist culture can be managed within cyberculture. It seems possible for staunchly nationalistic sensibilities to be maintained while common images and icons are shared.

The World Wide Web also allows the symbols and regalia of racist youth culture to be displayed and disseminated. The *Hammerskin Nation* page includes a rogue's gallery of racists displaying their tattoos as examples to assimilate and reproduce. But, more than this, these cyberstudios produce incarnate portraits of skin and bodies marked by whiteness. This highlights two further points, namely: that racialized bodies are an achievement rather than a given, they are acted upon in the creation of whiteness; and, secondly, that the processes of simulation and authenticity are being combined within these cultures. To have tattoos is the ultimate mark of white power authenticity, this is to indelibly mark and fix light skin in racialized terms. However, these images are being digitally disseminated producing fascist cyborgs that can be downloaded and admired narcissistically as artefacts of racial authenticity (see Levinas, 1990). Anne Miller's article on "Racist Tattoos," posted on the *Aryan Dating Page*, argues that ancient Celtic tattoos might be more appropriate for "main-stream racists":

> Why get a Celtic design instead of another kind? One reason is acceptance. There are other racialist symbols that are viewed as extremist by today's society. The symbols could affect your job security and middle-of-the-road friends might avoid you if your *tattoo* is too wild. But a Celtic tattoo would say to the World, "I'm proud to be white" without causing too much fuss with your boss or friends (and it looks neat too!).[9]

Examples are also provided on this page in digitally enhanced color. The Net fosters a kind of closet form of white supremacism that people can participate in from the privacy of their computer terminals.

News groups are an important interactive aspect of the medium. They operate within USENET and offer forms of exchange, debate, and chat concerning particular themes and special interests. Articles and responses are sent to news groups by electronic mail. Racist Net activists have established their own groups within the alternative or "alt." areas of USENET. The most important of these news groups are *alt.politics.nationalism.-white*, *alt.revolution.counter*, *alt.skinhead*, and *alt.revisionism*. The news groups become a context for racist sentiments to be countered by antifascist activists or nonracist skin-heads but they also allow for networking, exchanging information and correspondence between white power music fans. This can vary from posting lists of CDs for "tape trade," to advertising or simply posting information about new web sites or channels for Internet Relay Chat and online discussion groups. One recent posting to the *alt.skinheads* newsgroup offered a list of 340 Oi! and white power CDs and vinyl recordings for trade, along with an offer to make copies of a further 163 tape recordings.

In 1996 former Net-Nazi Milton J. Kleim made an application to establish a main-stream white power music newsgroup within the recreation or "rec" part of USENET. Although USENET has no formal governing body, there is a requirement that additions to the "big seven" newsgroups (i.e., *comp.*, *misc.*, *news.*, *rec.*, *sci.*, *soc.*, *talk.*) should be sanctioned by the wider Net community. So, in order for *rec.music.white-power* to be established it had to pass a vote open to all USENET users. The vote which took place between February 26 and March 18, 1996 gave an insight into the numbers of active Net-Nazis. The vote was organized by the USENET Volunteer Votetakers, a group founded in 1993. In total, 592 votes were cast in favor of the white power music group and a massive 33,033 votes against, with 6,200 invalid votes. Resistance Records' mailing list was made available to the campaign and George Burdi put his support behind it. Regardless, the campaign failed to muster more than 600 votes. Two years on, the number of white racists actively involved in the Internet globally is probably somewhere between 1,000 and 1,500 people.

Attempts have also been made to combine Net activism with "real world" association. The *RaceLink* web page offers a list of activists' contact details and locations. It aims to put racists in contact with each other. The page includes mostly American links but it also provides contact e-mail addresses and post office boxes in Canada, Germany, Portugal, South Africa, and the United Kingdom. Additionally, The *Aryan Dating Page* offers a contact service for white supremacists. Entries are listed for men and women, sometimes including pictures. While most of the profiles are American, there are also personal ads from a range of countries including Brazil, Canada, Holland, Norway, Portugal, UK, Slovakia, and Australia. In June 1998 the page included 140 advertisements from white men, of which 80 percent were from the United States and 15 percent from Canada. There were also 60 personal advertisements from white women. Again these were mostly American (68 percent) but the page also links to a considerable number of white South African women (17 percent of all ads) through a mailing list compiled by Zunata Kay.

One of the interesting things about scrolling through the personal ads is that the faces that appear are nothing like the archetypal image of "The Racist." There are very few skinheads with Nazi tattoos: these white supremacist "lonely hearts" – mostly in their twenties and thirties – look surprisingly prosaic. Take 36-year-old Cathy, who lives in Pennsylvania but who is "desperate to move to a WHITE area!" She appears in the photograph in a rhinestone outfit with glitzy earrings: "The picture of me is a little over done," she explains. "I had photos down with the girls at the office. I am really a blue jean natural gal, but I look like an Aryan Princess when I get dressed up. But I am really the girl next door type."[10] Or 19-year-old Debbie from New England, who writes: "I am [a] young white power woman who seeks someone seriously devoted to the white power movement. A person whose commitment is undaunting. I am a member of several WP organizations, and would like to speak with men who share the same values as I."[11] The male ads provide an equally unexpected set of portraits of white supremacy. Frank, a 48-year-old divorced single parent from Palo Alto, California, writes: "Today I'm a responsible parent and have my views but don't go out of my way to let it be known unless confronted, I have tattoos, and am down for the Aryan race, So hope to hear from you fine ladies in the near future. Ps know how to treat a lady and that's with love and respect."[12] Here Frank presents himself as a kind of white supremacist "new man." This is contrasted with the ad from John Botti, a 25-year-old from Los Altos who presents himself as a kind of preppy, "going places" nineties man. He writes "I am looking for someone who is as conservative and pretty as hell. Equally as important is someone with a quality education."[13] These are images of fascism in the information age that bear little resemblance to previous incarnations. This was brought home very powerfully by the image of Max, a 36-year-old Canadian, who described himself as a "long-time Movement activist." He listed his interests as anthropology, Monty Python's humor, the Titanic story, Celtic music, and Civil War re-enacting. Max chose to have his photograph taken at his computer keyboard, where he presents himself as the picture of technological proficiency. This struck me, the first time I saw it, as a very appropriate image of the face of late twentieth century fascism.

The *Aryan Dating Page* was pushed off the Internet server that carried it in 1998 and today it has been assimilated and reconstructed on Don Black's *Stormfront* web page, where it is renamed as "White Singles." Through these accounts, we glimpse the ways in which these people move between mainstream society and the world of the cyber-Nazi and white power movements. This is signalled by Cathy's mention of having photographs taken with the girls from the office, or the idea of Frank going down to pick up his seven-year-old daughter from school and who keeps his views to himself "unless confronted." In this sense, the different cultural modalities discussed in this chapter allow different types of whiteness to be inhabited at various times. In one moment, the mainstream whiteness of the school, or workplace – coded here as normality – is occupied, while at other times at the computer terminal the public privacy of the Internet digitally facilitates the communion with a whiteness that announces itself openly. The technological clothes of these identities provide an ontological milieu in which the interplay between symbol and self can be established in new time/space coordinates.

"White Pride World Wide"?

The circuit of this international system is made possible by a shared translocal notion of race. This is reflected and enshrined in Don Black's slogan "WHITE PRIDE WORLD WIDE" which has been used by Resistance Records as a title for their compilation albums of white power music. Racist rock fans belong to distinct national settings, yet they can all position themselves within a shared translocal racial lineage. These connections are rendered explicit; consider this passage from an a e-mail sent to *Stormfront*:

> I am a 20 year old white American with roots in North America dating back 300 years and then into Europe, Normandy, France. Well anyways, I am proud to here [sic] of an organization for the advancement of whites.[14]

The Internet provides a context to trace these genealogies fostering a transnational notion of whiteness that unites old world racial nationalisms (i.e., in Europe and Scandinavia) with the white diasporas of the New World (i.e., United States, Canada, South Africa, Australia and New Zealand, and parts of South America). New connections are being established between ultra right-wing sites in North America, Western Europe, and Scandinavia at a considerable pace. Yet, it is still the American web sites and news groups that are the most sophisticated. A survey of *Stormfront's* archived letters shows that 70 percent of all correspondence comes from the United States and Canada, with only 14 percent from Western Europe and Scandinavia.[15] Similarly, most of the activity on the Web, be it the Aryan *Dating Page* or *Hammerskins* sites, is predominantly American in focus.

The use of computer simulation and transnational information networks provides a key context in which the theoretical and political tensions between the ethnocentric and Eurocentric elements of contemporary racism can be worked through. In this sense it is necessary not only to explore the impact of technological change on racist cultures but also to reconceptualize how racism works within and beyond the boundaries of particular nation-states. Ethnocentric forms of racism seem to be targeted at particular minority groups depending on the specific national context and their histories of migration and racialization. Similar patterns of substitution and commensurability apply to the understanding of ethnocentric racism within the context of the networld. The nationalists in Germany focus on the Turks, whereas their compatriots in Britain will demonize Afro-Caribbeans and South Asians. The processes of racialization are commensurable even though the complexion of the racial Other varies.

The International Jew is an omnipresent figure of hate within the cultures described here. It seems that the pre-existing histories of antisemitism in North America and Europe are being given a new lease of life within cyberculture. Antisemitic ideas are

373

enhanced by the Internet's global framework precisely because these discourses have historically been articulated through a notion of an international conspiracy. This may go some way to explaining the high level of antisemitic sentiment found within the neofascist networld. The cover of a white power music compilation *Leaderless Resistance* represents the Jew as a serpent preying on a shackled white man. Taken from the *Resistance Records* web site, this extreme antisemitic image reinvigorates the historical legacy of the Jew represented as a predatory subhuman. Similarly, a cartoon that was posted on the *White Aryan Resistance* web site showed the Jew as a parasite to be exterminated, the caption reading:

> They sting like a bee
> Dart like a flea
> Strip you bare like a locust
> You, too, will make a ready meal
> If you remain unfocused
> Stand up! Take arms!
> Defend yourself...
> Like the heroes of the past
> When the Kikes come crawlin'
> Just send them sprawlin'
> With a dose of poison gas!

These are images which are not in themselves new, since they have been part of antisemitic ideas for some time and were articulated in a different form by the Nazis in their attempt to dehumanize Jews. Sophisticated digital technology is enabling these products of the racist imagination to be circulated in an unprecedented way.

It might be possible to talk here about an emergent elementary structure that can describe this translocal whiteness. Picking up the point made by Deleuze and Guattari at the beginning of this chapter, these networks possess a supple segmentarity that combines recombinant, molecular qualities with lateral connection. They operate both through the boundaries of nation-states and national particularity, while at the same time these supple white rhizomes possess a series of discursive strands. First, this notion of whiteness promotes a *racial lineage* that is plotted through, and sustained by, cyberspace. This transnational technology, which in many respects has come to personify the permeability of human cultures, is used here to foster and articulate an ethos of *racial separation*. The racist Networld itself becomes the embodiment of this ideal, individuals at their computers projecting themselves into a simulated "racial homeland" – this, despite the fact that it is almost impossible to maintain a hermetic digital world without the potential intrusion of "outsiders." At a deeper level many extreme-right users of the Internet are also concerned that their enemies have access to the very technology that they are using. In a posting to *alt.politics.* white-power leader Reuben Logsdon articulated a key concern when he argued: "The main problem with racial separation is that with all this damn communications technology, Jewish media can still be broadcast into the country to corrupt whites, and whites can still meet marriage partners over the net from outside Greater White Amerikkka."[16]

Such views reflect the very real ambivalence which extreme-right activists have in supporting the right to "free speech," but, within the present political climate, it is also clear that their strongest defense is to argue for unhindered access to the technology that they also see as a threat to their notions of racial and cultural purity. An essay posted on *Stormfront* in 1996 by L. R. Beam warns of "The Conspiracy to Erect an Electronic Iron Curtain," stating that any attempts at censorship will be met by what the author calls "acts of random electronic violence." The author then goes on to compare attempts at censorship to "a sort of information cleansing of the Internet" and quotes one activist as saying "I'll give up my information when they pry my cold dead fingers from the keyboard."[17]

Secondly, this notion of whiteness has a relational Other, or more accurately a gallery of "Others." Through the processes of substitution the image of alterity can take on different forms depending on local circumstances, for example, Turks in Germany or black people in America. However, representations of particular racial minorities within this international framework are commensurable with each other, in that, depending on circumstances, they can be substituted without changing the elementary structure of this translocal whiteness. In this sense the Other is designated as a *social contaminant* in both the racial body and the body politic (Zickmund, 1997). Through these figures of otherness the threat of race/cultural miscegenation ("immigrants," "slaves," "guest workers," "race mixers") and/or sexual difference ("gays," "Lesbians") is named and attributed to particular people. In addition to the coupling of *otherness* and *contamination* there is also articulation between *alterity* and *conspiracy*. This is the field in which the figure of The International Jew looms in these white looks. As Susan Zickmund points out:

> Thus the Jew is constructed as the agent which lies hidden within institutions possessing hegemonic power, structures which they then use to manipulate society. The government, the media, and even the spread of academic knowledge or ideological doctrines may emanate ultimately from this source. (Zickmund, 1997:195)

Lastly, there is the *minoritization of whiteness* within the rhetoric of white power activists. Here, whiteness is seen to be under threat, to have been superseded demographically on a global scale. This is exemplified in the white power band New Minority, whose recording "White, Straight and Proud" complains that white men have become a lesser part in "their" world. George Burdi, who signed this band to the Resistance Records label, reinforces this lament: "Look at the global population levels. Whites account for only 8 percent of the planet's population. Only 2 percent of the babies born last year [1995] were white...It's WHITE PEOPLE that are the 'new' minority" (quoted in Zickmund, 1997:198). This form of discourse is not simply confined to the digitally assisted whiteness found in the digital domain. Cindy Patton has outlined a similar process in the writing of the New Right in the United States. She outlines the specific minoritarian identity discourse expressed in periodicals like *New Dimensions* that is opposed to both the Rainbow coalition of gays/blacks/feminists and far-right white supremacists. While New Right campaigners profess a nonracialized identity as "real Americans," their claims to minority status are based on a similar set of premises to that of white power groups. Here the image of the all-pervasive ZOG is substituted with the idea that the institutions of the media and the state have been captured by black, gay, and feminist "special interest" groups (Patton 1993, 1995). Taken together these elements constitute the core ambient factors in a whiteness that is sustained in cyberspace and within which racist activists from a range of national contexts locate themselves.

While the Internet is making it possible for these forms of fascist activity to take on a new shape, the compression of time and space also brings racist activists into extreme forms of contact. This seems also to have accelerated the tendency towards factionalism that has mercifully haunted postwar fascism. The vituperative online feud between Harold A. Covington of the National Socialist White People's Party and William L. Pierce of National Alliance and both sets of their supporters is perhaps the best example of this syndrome. In March of 1998 Covington, reflecting on what he referred to as "The Future of the White Internet," wrote:

> First off, we need to look at the PRESENT of the White Internet. I do not have to tell you that a) It is a tremendously valuable tool and an immense amount of good has been worked out of the Net; while, simultaneously b) The Net is being viciously and tragically abused by a shockingly large number of either bogus or deranged "White Racists" . . . I think it is too early just yet to quantify just how the lunacy interacts with, counteracts and affects the impact of the serious political work. It is like panning for gold in a flowing sewer; both the raw, and toxic sewage and the gold are there, and the question is how much gold any individual can extract before the fumes and the corruption drive him off – or until he keels over and falls in and becomes part of the sewer system.[18]

Cyberspace offers new possibilities but it also accelerates the long-standing tendency towards attrition and division within the neofascist movement. The information age is changing the relationship between time, space, and form in racist culture. These are the new territories of whiteness that exceed the boundaries of the nation-state, while supplanting ethnocentric racisms with new translocal forms of racial narcissism and xenophobia.

Notes

1 Taken from Trad skinhead Doug Herbert's "FAQ Alt.skinheads." This joke is attributed to Dominic Green and was posted on *Alt.skinheads.* moderated newsgroup, August 1, 1998.
2 This was particularly apparent at the Harry Frank Guggenheim-sponsored conference *Brotherhoods of Race and Nation* held in New Orleans, December 1995.
3 Thanks to Keith Harris for this observation.
4 Rick Eaton telephone interview, August 20, 1998.
5 An offshoot of racist skinheads, Hammerskins take their name from the marching hammers that represented Skinheads in the Pink Floyd rock movie, *The Wall.* The branches include Confederate, Northern, Western, and Eastern Hammerskins in America and international branches have emerged including Britain Hammerskins, Charlemaigne Hammerskins in France, and the Southern Cross Hammerskins in Australia.
6 Rick Eaton telephone interview, August 20, 1998.
7 Mark Potok telephone interview, August 24, 1998.
8 Quoted in Michael Shapiro, "Skinhead is 'Out to Lunch.'" *Web Review* at: <http://webreview.com/96/04/26/news/nazi2.html.>
9 Anne Miller, "Racialist Tattoos" formerly at: <http://www.adp.fptoday.com/tattoo.htm>.
10 From *personal ads* formerly at: <http://www.adp.fptoday.com/f0090.htm>.
11 From *personal ads* formerly at: <http://www.adp.fptoday.com/f0085.htm>.
12 From *personal ads* formerly at: <http://www.adp.fptoday.com/f0085.htm>.
13 From *personal ads* formerly at: <http://www.adp.fptoday.com/m0267.htm>.

14 *Stormfront*, "Letters From the Front" at: <http://www.stormfront.org/>.
15 This is taken from a sample of 107 pieces of e-mail sent to *Stormfront* between May 26 and August 2, 1995. These letters also included examples from antifascist activists.
16 Quoted in Jon Casimir, "Hate on the Net," 1995 at: <www.mh.com.au/archive/news/950905/news6–950905.html>.
17 L. R. Beam, "The Conspiracy to Erect an Electronic Iron Curtain," 1996, at: <www.stormfront.org/stormfront/iron-cur.htm>.
18 Harold A. Covington, "The Future of the White Internet," March 19, 1998. Posted on the following newsgroups: alt.politics.white-power, alt.nswpp, alt.revisionism, alt.skinheads, alt.Revisionism, triangle.politics.

References

Anti-Defamation League of B'nai B'rith (1995) *Hate Group Recruitment on the Internet*. New York: Anti-Defamation League.

Back, Les, Keith, Michael, and Solomos, John (1996) "The new modalities of racist culture: Technology, race and neofascism in a digital age." *Patterns of Prejudice* 30,2:3–28.

Benjamin, Walter (1968) "The work of art in the age of mechanical reproduction," in Walter Benjamin *Illuminations*. London: Harcourt, Brace and World, pp.211–44.

Butler, Judith (1990) *Gender Trouble: Feminism and the Subversion of Identity*. New York: Routledge.

Capitanchik, David and Whine, Michael (1996) *The Governance of Cyberspace: The Far-Right on the Internet*. London: Institute for Jewish Policy Research.

Copilevitz, Todd (1996) "Dallas man runs skinhead site." *Dallas Morning News* April 20:1A, 19A.

Deleuze, Giles and Guattari, Felix (1986) *A Thousand Plateaus; Capitalism and Schizophrenia*. London: Athlone.

Eco, Umberto (1995) "Ur-fascism." *The New York Review of Books* June 22:14.

Escobar, Arturo (1994) "Welcome to Cyberia: Notes on the anthropology of cyber-culture." *Current Anthropology* 35,3:211–31.

Featherstone, Mike and Burrows, Roger (1995) *Cyberspace/Cyberbodies/Cyberpunk: Cultures of Technological Embodiment*. London: Sage.

Hall, Stuart and Jefferson, Tony (1976) *Resistance Through Rituals: Youth Subcultures in Post-war Britain*. Birmingham, UK: Centre for Contemporary Cultural Studies.

Haraway, Donna (1991) *Simians, Cyborgs, and Women: The Reinvention of Nature*. New York: Routledge.

Levinas, Emmanuel (1990) "Reflections on the philosophy of Hitlerism." *Critical Inquiry* 17:63–71.

Patton, Cindy (1993) "Tremble, hetero swine!" in Michael Warner (ed.) *Fear of a Queer Planet: Queer Politics and Social Theory*. Minneapolis: University of Minneapolis, pp.143–77.

Patton, Cindy (1995) "Refiguring social space," in Linda Nicholson and Steve Seidman (eds.) *Social Postmodernism: Beyond Identity Politics*. Cambridge, UK: Cambridge University Press, pp.216–49.

Plant, Sadie (1998) *Zeros and Ones*. London: Fourth Estate and Doubleday.

Simon Wiesenthal Center (1998) *Lexicon of Hate: The Changing Tactic, Language and Symbols of American Extremists*. Los Angeles: Simon Wiesenthal Centre.

Solomos, John and Back, Les (1996) *Racism and Society*. Basingstoke, UK: Macmillan.

Turkle, Sherry (1995) *Life on Screen: Identity in the Age of the Internet*. New York: Simon and Schuster.

Zickmund, Susan (1997) "Approaching the radical other: The discursive culture of cyberhate," in Steven G. Jones (ed.) *Virtual Culture: Identity & Communication in Cybersociety*. London: Sage, pp.185–205.

Culture

Introduction to Part V

David Theo Goldberg and John Solomos

Part V of the *Companion* is devoted to questions about cultural production and expression. The various papers in one way or another problematize and probe the fashioning of cultural forms and expressions by racial characterization, and the effect on racial articulation of cultural configuration.

This interplay of race and culture is exemplified by Henry A. Giroux's detailed exploration of the role of black public intellectuals within the political and intellectual environments of American society. The question of black public intellectuals has attracted much attention in recent years, particularly in relation to their growing visibility in the wider public sphere as well as in academia. Giroux's account issues a challenge to the role and impact played by this group, particularly in relation to the changing politics of racial exclusion and marginalization characteristic of American society.

During the past century or so sport has been an important arena for racial performance, and a revealing site for the articulation of racist ideologies about the black body. Douglas Hartmann suggests that the image of African-American athletes and sports personalities is representative of "golden ghettos." Scorned by racists for being black, African-American athletes are diminished by liberals for being involved with sport. Hartmann is concerned to reveal the critical importance of black sports personalities in public life in the USA, and increasingly in Europe, despite the fact that so little critical literature has been developed about the subject.

The role of racial and ethnic imagery in fashion industries across the globe has become a pervasive symbol of our times. The role of fashion in shaping our images of movement, migration, and cultural exchange has become an important mechanism for the representation of racial and ethnic otherness in contemporary societies. As Gargi Bhattacharyya argues in her contribution, however, this has not been reflected in much of the academic discourse about the meanings of race and ethnicity. Bhattacharyya undertakes to fill the gap.

In the next paper, Elvan Zabanyun engages with the role of art in the development of African-American cultural identity. Starting with the period that she considers crucial to the emergence of black American culture, namely, the 1920s, Zabanyun's analysis provides a synoptic overview of trends and processes shaping black art to the present day. She thus provides fascinating insight into the broader processes that have shaped and placed African-American culture as a specific form of cultural production and expression. In addition, she highlights the role of particular artists in broadening the boundaries and direction of art and forms of visual identity.

The final paper, by Les Back, explores the means by which questions about youth have become inextricably linked to race and ethnicity. Situating the moral concerns that underpin much public and academic debate about youth, Back's contribution suggests that the insertion of race and ethnicity into issues of youth culture has played a central role in developing accounts of racial and ethnic identity more sensitive to issues of time and place. His analysis is suggestive of the need to explore the role of multiculture within an analytic framework of youth subcultures. Back's account is sensitive to both globalized patterns of cultural change and local urban environments forming the specific contexts within which young people experience concerns about race, ethnicity, and belonging.

Chapter 26

Public Intellectuals, Race, and Public Space

Henry A. Giroux

Introduction

The significance and function of intellectuals in American society has been the source of controversy for much of the twentieth century. Questions concerning the meaning, role, and responsibilities of intellectuals are part of an often contentious tradition in scholarly work, often spilling over into the popular press. The theoretical literature is rich with commentaries about the role of the intellectual and offers a minefield of insights from writers that include Emile Durkheim, Antonio Gramsci, Michel Foucault, Alvin Gouldner, Noam Chomsky, and more recently Russell Jacoby, Jeffrey C. Goldfarb, Edward W. Said, Carol Becker, Stanley Aronowitz, and others (see Giroux, 1988, 1995a, 1995b; Aronowitz and Giroux, 1993). For many of these theorists, especially from Gramsci on, debates regarding the role of the intellectual have often functioned as part of a broader discourse about recovering the space of the political and deepening the possibilities for creating multiple, democratic public spheres. In part, the concept of the critically engaged intellectual has served as a moral referent for gauging the limits and possibilities for cultural politics within dominant social and economic formations. Derided and praised, intellectuals have occupied that in-between space of politics and culture with its ever changing demand for committed social engagement, and its simultaneous trap of cooption.

Unfortunately, while the concept of the engaged public intellectual has occupied a respectable but problematic place in progressive ideological debates, cultural workers who assume the role of critical public intellectuals have not fared so well in the popular media and everyday life. Artists, journalists, academics, and others who have been innovative and daring, willing to challenge the conventions of the dominant social and political order have too often been denounced in their role as public intellectuals, usually garnering more scorn than respect. Dismissed in their position as critics of American society, such intellectuals have frequently been the object of government prosecution, marginalized from apparatuses of power that shape public policy, and more recently targeted for censorship and denounced as subversives or un-American. They have fared equally badly in the popular media, which has a long tradition of stereotyping intellectuals as either "eggheads" or as simply irrelevant to American life. Shaped by Cold War anticommunism, a long legacy of rampant anti-intellectualism, and an ongoing hostility to intellectuals who were critical of society, public consciousness gave the stamp of approval primarily to forms of intellectual vocation engaged in the production of technical knowledge and highly specialized skills. That is, intellectuals were accepted within the public consciousness when defined primarily as technical workers. The latter category would include stockbrokers, teachers, researchers, business people, physicians, and other intellectuals who function as purveyors of culture in the limited technical sense of producing a specialized service within a narrow body of knowledge.

Given this historical legacy, it seems both odd and gratifying that academics, talk show hosts, the popular media, the national press, and a host of scholarly journals within the last decade, have heaped lavish attention on the meaning and relevance of an emerging group of black public intellectuals in the United States, though it must be noted that while the media first focused largely on progressive black public intellectuals, it soon adjusted itself to the temper of the times and largely centered on the work of conservative black intellectuals such as Shelby Steele, Randall Kennedy, and Thomas Sowell.

What is significant about this turn to black public intellectuals is that it seemed at odds with the much broader assault on political culture in which cynicism seems to reign supreme and appeared to open up a space in which to challenge the prevailing notion that the American public lives in a period of collapsed dreams, in which alternatives to the status quo don't exist. The resurgence of interest in public intellectuals also seems especially important given the assault that has been waged on all aspects of public life since the emergence of the political culture of Reaganism in the 1980s. As is well known, for quite some time we have witnessed the destruction of public school systems, public transportation, public services, the public health system, and a vast array of social services designed to protect the poor, immigrants, elderly, and young children. Given this ongoing assault on public life, the notion of the public intellectual becoming an everyday figure of speech appears puzzling, especially since the one crucial role that public intellectuals might play at the present time is to resist the withdrawal of the state from those sectors of social life that are indispensable to maintaining important social services such as education, health care, public housing, public service broadcasting, and health insurance.

After a decade of relentless attacks by neoconservatives on multiculturalism, women's studies, political correctness, public schools, funding for the arts and national public radio, the attention that has emerged surrounding public intellectuals in American society appears as both a welcome relief and an opportunity to begin a national debate about what it means to take seriously one's life as a public person in order to struggle for a society "that makes room for the richest possible self-structuring and the richest possible participation in public life" (Havel, 1998). Such a debate, theoretically at least, contains the promise of producing a vitalized language about public life and intellectual leadership. More specifically, such a discourse offers the potential for raising on a national level serious questions regarding the relevance of the university as a critical public sphere, the political significance of cultural work taking hold across an emerging number of public spheres and pedagogical sites, and the necessity of reclaiming the language of the public as part of a broader discourse for revitalizing the discourses of democracy and social justice. Of course, there is always the danger the focus on public intellectuals will fall prey to the vicissitudes of celebrity culture, as recently expressed in a *New Yorker* story on Stanley Fish, who was largely profiled because of his taste for expensive cars, his love of fancy clothes, his big salary, and his propensity to say outrageous things, such as, "Rich people are fun!". Despite the media attempt to focus on public relations intellectuals instead of publicly engaged intellectuals, it is remarkable that the social function of the intellectual is even being discussed in the media and academia. What is even more extraordinary about this debate is the way in which it has been marked by a discourse that makes race central to the discussion. In what follows, I want to situate the debate about the role of public intellectuals within a broader debate about the role of intellectuals in American society and the conditions necessary for them to function so as to expand the meaning of democratic public life. I then want to shift the terms of the debate to the way in which the media has addressed the rise of black public intellectuals and how that debate has paved the way for attempting to undermine any viable analysis of the meaning and work of progressive black public intellectuals. I want to conclude by analyzing the implications the debate on public intellectuals might have for revitalizing the culture of politics itself, and the promise it might have for reasserting the importance of political struggles within and outside of the university in shaping democratic public life.

The Rise and Fall of the Public Intellectual?[1]

In the last decade a multitude of books and articles have lamented the demise of public intellectuals in the United States. While the history of this discourse is too extensive to repeat, I plan to highlight two theoretical interventions into the debate over the current status of public intellectuals, one by Russell Jacoby and the other by Cornel West. Both positions raise important issues about the role and responsibility of intellectuals in American society, on the one hand, and the relevance of defining higher education as an essential democratic public sphere on the other.

Russell Jacoby's widely read book, *The Last Intellectuals* (1987), argued that the conditions that produced an older generation of public intellectuals in the post-World War II era had been undermined and displaced in the 1980s. The unaffiliated intellectual functioning as a social critic writing accessible prose for such journals as *The Partisan Review* offers for Jacoby an ideal of what it means to mobilize a popular audience and a model for the role of a public intellectual. Inhabiting the bohemian enclaves of Greenwich Village, these intellectuals and the public spheres that support them have become an endangered species. In Jacoby's narrative of decline, such public intellectuals as Jane Jacobs, Edmund Wilson, Dwight Macdonald, Philip Rahv, C. Wright Mills, and Irving Howe have been replaced by 1960s radicals who have forsaken the role of the independent intellectual for the safe and specialized confines of the university.

But the university, according to Jacoby, represents neither a viable public sphere nor provides the conditions for intellectuals to speak to a broader public audience. More specifically, by sanctioning the privileges of professionalism, promoting overly technical jargon, and cultivating new forms of specialization, academics have been reduced to sterile technocrats, unable, if not unwilling, to address the responsibilities of public service.[2] If we believe Jacoby, the public intellectual has been replaced by the so-called radical academic interested mainly in career advancement and the cushy rewards of tenure rather than acting as a proponent of social change.[3]

In a now famous essay first published in *Cultural Critique*, Cornel West ([1985] 1993) focused less on the demise of the public intellectual than on the emergence of a hostile climate for black intellectuals. For West, the recent shift in the broader political

385

orientation towards the right, the widening of the gap between middle-class blacks and an ever-growing black underclass, and the increasingly managerial logic of the university often intolerant of critical scholars – especially black scholars – have all hindered the development and support of black intellectuals in this country.

Retrospectively, Jacoby and West anticipated a significant set of issues that emerged late in the last decade as part of a larger debate over the role of intellectuals in the struggle for social change. Jacoby's argument that the university cannot nourish public discourse resonates strongly with the current right-wing charge that the university is too political – the unhappy result of an influx of "tenured radicals" (see Kimball, 1991). For different reasons, both sets of critics posit the university as a depoliticized site and limit pedagogy to the arid imperatives of discipline-bound professionalization and specialization.

Because of its complicity with dominant ideologies and practices, Jacoby saw the university as a conservative sphere that bought off even its most critical intellectuals.[4] On the other hand, conservatives like Roger Kimball, Charles Sykes, Lynn Cheney, David Horowitz, and William Bennett translate a contempt for critical thinking and social criticism into appropriate educational behavior and see the ideal university as an apolitical public sphere inhabited largely by a disinterested faculty engaged in an ahistorical conversation among great minds and pedagogically bound to hand down the ideas and values of the classics to a new generation of would-be thinkers.[5] The university of this latter scenario becomes in instrumental terms largely a mechanism for social and cultural reproduction and a repository for transmitting both the timeless knowledge and skills of the culture of business and the high cultural values and ideals of the dominant society see Aronowitz and Giroux, 1991, 1993. More nuanced neoconservatives such as Alan Wolfe (2001) argue a similar position but without the courage of making visible their own political convictions. Defining the most important attribute of the public intellectual as being true to oneself, Wolfe celebrates objectivity, independence, and civility as the most important elements that define the vocation of the intellectual. In this view, conventionality and disinterestedness replaces intellectual courage. Producing ideas that might be critical of existing orthodoxies or crucial to a democratic society are summarily dismissed as an expression of ideology.

In contrast, Cornel West's essay provided a theoretical service by injecting issues of politics and race into the debate over the meaning and role of public intellectuals in the United States. Expanding upon John Dewey's claim that "To form itself, the public must break existing public forms" (Dewey, 1927:31–2), West highlighted the ways in which racism operates as a structuring principle of dominant public spheres and a defining force in shaping the discourse on public intellectuals. West's argument provides a theoretical referent for challenging the context and content of much of the liberal discourse that has followed the recent discovery of black intellectuals. Accordingly, a decade later, West has both become symbolic of what it means to assume the role of a black public intellectual and he has labored to define a broader conception of the public intellectual, one that expands and deepens the responsibility of cultural workers engaged in the world of public politics. For example, he has observed that

> The fundamental role of the public intellectual – distinct from, yet building on, the indispensable work of academics, experts, analysts, and pundits – is to create and sustain high-quality public discourse addressing urgent public problems which enlightens and energizes fellow citizens, prompting them to take public action. This role requires a deep

commitment to the life of the mind – a perennial attempt to clear our minds of cant – which serves to shape the public destiny of a people. Intellectual and political leadership is neither elitist nor populist; rather it is democratic, in that each of us stands in public space, without humiliation, to put forward our best visions and views for the sake of the public interest. And these arguments are present in an atmosphere of mutual respect and civic trust (West, cited in Gates and West, 1996:71).

Implicit in West's insight is the assumption that the disappearance of political intellectuals in higher education corresponds to the passing of critical politics in public life. The effacement of progressive politics from public life is forcefully demonstrated in the response of many liberals and conservatives to the rise of a group of black public intellectuals who have challenged the notion that dominant public spheres such as the university can be called race-neutral or race-transcendent.[6] Many black academics have raised the volume of the debate on the public intellectual by reasserting the notion of racial justice into public discourse while simultaneously redefining notions of social commitment, politics, and equality.

To Be Young, Gifted, and Black

Public intellectual is by and large an excuse, the marker of a sterile, hybrid variant of "bearing witness" that, when all is said and done, is a justification for an aversion to intellectual or political heavy lifting – a pretentious name for highfalutin babble about the movie you just saw or the rhyme you just heard on the radio. (Reed, 1995:35)

Reading Jacoby's earlier attack on academics in higher education, it is clear that the lament over the decline of public intellectuals excluded black intellectuals, who appeared at the time to occupy the margins of scholarly and popular discourse. While specific individuals like Toni Morrison, Alice Walker, and Maya Angelou received attention in the national media (as artists and not intellectuals), the scholarly and popular press focused primarily on whites when it addressed the general malaise in intellectual life in America. Such writers as Robert Bellah and Benjamin Barber bemoaned the university's fall from public grace into "the quintessential institution of bureaucratic individualism" (Desruisseaux, 1996:19) and urged various public foundations to support a new generation of public intellectuals. Yet, they virtually ignored race as a crucial category within the larger context. In recent years, observations on race and democracy among a number of relatively young black intellectuals has helped to fill the lacunae, though not without prompting a great deal of criticism among both conservative and liberal intellectuals.

The discovery of the black public intellectual has nevertheless became the new American fashion – a hot topic in both scholarly publications and the popular press.[7] Expressing an historically conditioned anxiety and near manic fascination, journalists and academics seemed obsessed with probing the mystique of the "new" black public intellectual with particular attention on such African-American writers as Michael Dyson, Cornel West, Henry Gates, Gloria Watkins (bell hooks), Patricia Williams, Robin Kelley, Toni Morrison, Michele Wallace, Stanley Crouch, and Glen Loury.

But what began as a series of press releases heralding the ascendancy of black intellectuals quickly turned into a tirade of damning indictments. Heartening gestures toward the revitalization of a black public discourse soon appeared to be marked by cautious and grudging and sometimes indiscriminate criticism, mostly from white intellectuals, suggesting that African-American intellectuals were unqualified to assume the role of public intellectuals by virtue of their shoddy scholarship, their narrow focus on racial issues, and their willingness to pander to mainstream audiences.[8] In what follows, I want to briefly analyze some of these criticisms and their applicability to a thoughtful discussion of the role that black intellectuals might play in keeping alive the spirit of public criticism and practical politics, while reviving the moral and pedagogical traditions of inquiry within and beyond the university.

In 1995 a series of articles appeared in the American popular press that framed the reception of the work produced by "new" black intellectuals. These articles legitimated a particular theoretical intervention in the debate about black public intellectuals that set the stage for the counterattack to follow. In the first instance, Michael Berube argued in *The New Yorker* that the advent of a group of black intellectuals commanding significant media attention was an appropriate and welcome phenomenon given the central place of racial issues in American politics and the eruption of creative work by blacks in the realm of culture (see, e.g., Dent, 1992). Berube saw the unexpected prominence of such a group of intellectuals as particularly welcome "at a time when the idea of 'the public' has become nearly unthinkable in national politics" (Berube, 1995:80). For Berube, the new black intellectuals not only disprove the claim that "the academy has been the death of the public intellectuals...[but also] have the ability and the resources to represent themselves in public on their own terms" (p. 75).

Claiming that the arrival of the black intellectual was as important as the emergence of the New York intellectuals after World War II, Berube compared these groups less in terms of political and ideological considerations and more in terms of personalities. ("Whereas Daniel Bell was criticized for buying nice furniture in his forties, bell hooks now draws stares for driving a BMW", Berube, 1995:75). In the end, Berube said little about the substantive issues that inform the work of the black intellectuals he addressed, and especially unfortunate was his refusal to engage bell hooks's feminist politics.

But Berube did point to a series of criticisms that would be taken up more stridently by others in the popular press. For instance, he argued that the rising chorus of enthusiasm from young admirers who are taken with the black intellectuals' fluency with popular culture may divert such intellectuals as Michael Dyson from listening more attentively to "the deliberations of Senate subcommittees" (Berube, 1995:79). Implicit in this criticism is the assumption that theoretical work that critically addresses popular culture is too far removed from the "real world" of politics. While Berube did not purposely suggest, and certainly does not believe, that black intellectuals who choose to write about popular culture do a disservice to the alleged "real world" of politics, his criticism can be read as a dismissal of cultural politics as a politics of bad faith serving mainly as a "compensation for practical politics" (p. 79). In many ways, Berube's cautious critique foreshadowed a much more vicious attack on cultural politics that was to emerge in the work of Todd Gitlin, Alan Sokal, Alan Wolfe, and many others on the left (see Gitlin, 1997; Sokal and Bricmont, 1998; Wolfe, 1996).

Writing in the *Atlantic Monthly* shortly thereafter, Robert Boynton addressed a number of similar issues. Mingling his discussion of the new black intellectuals with a celebration of such earlier public intellectuals as Philip Rahv, Edmund Wilson, and Lionel Trilling, Boynton highlighted the theoretical and ideological differences between the two groups. Eulogizing the New York intellectuals, Boynton paid homage to their belief in the transformative power of high culture, their retreat from the mainstream, and their stalwart anticommunism. Measured against the history of these renowned white intellectuals, Boynton found little in the new black intellectuals to suggest the two groups had much in common.

Damning with faint praise, Boynton granted the new black intellectuals importance because "they provide a viable, if radically different, image of what a public intellectual can be" (Boynton, 1995a:56). But Boynton's sustained criticisms of the new black intellectuals more than canceled any enthusiasm for their public role. Moreover, Boynton strongly implied that the stature of the new public intellectuals shrinks considerably seen next to the likes of Edmund Wilson and Alfred Kazin and those who hung around the *Partisan Review* and the New York City bohemia after the World War. For instance, Boynton's highbrow modernism caused him some discomfort when he addressed the writing styles of the new black intellectuals. The admixture of autobiography with social criticism, along with the amalgamation of black speech, history, and experience with academic discourse found in the work (for example) of Derrick Bell and Patricia Williams signaled for Boynton the centrality of racial identity in the work of such writers, a feature that Boynton concluded "would have made the young Jewish New Yorkers squirm" (1995a:70). Such writing represents, for Boynton, an aesthetic limited by a fixation on racial identities and experiences and is "more admirable in a belleslettrist than in a wide-ranging public intellectual" (p. 70).

But more than race fixation haunts the credibility of the new black intellectuals. For Boynton, the new black intellectuals who slide easily between academia and the op-ed pages, risk substituting theoretically rigorous social criticism for celebrity punditry. Barely veiled in this criticism is Boynton's displeasure with the forms of border crossing and social negotiations that mark the discourse of many black public intellectuals. It seems inconceivable to critics like Boynton that popular cultural forms can become serious objects of social analysis.[9]

Both of these essays omit the history of black intellectuals as well as the complicated historical narratives through which emergent black public spheres arose in the twentieth century.[10] But while Berube raises a number of probing and important questions about the social functions of public intellectuals, Boynton is scornful of such intellectuals, and arrogantly offers up the cultural capital of "distinguished" white intellectuals as the legitimating trope for understanding the strengths and weaknesses of black intellectuals. This is not to suggest that Boynton indulges in a form of racism. But it does imply that the politics of whiteness offers a fundamental context for understanding how the discourse on black intellectuals is framed and addressed in the popular press. In this case, whiteness, as Toni Morrison (1992) reminds us, becomes invisible to itself and hence the all-pervasive referent for judging public intellectuals who speak and write in an effort to engage a broader public.

The politics of whiteness provides an often ignored theoretical framework for understanding why black intellectuals receive routine condemnation for speaking in a language labeled either simplistic or "too public." One cannot but wonder why white public intellectuals like Jonathan Kozol or Barbara Ehrenreich who write in accessible prose and speak plainly are not subjected to the same criticism as Michael Dyson or bell hooks receive. Eric Lott, for example, refers to Dyson's more general writings as a "troglodyte's delight." When not drawing overt parallels to cavemen, he charges Dyson with "a leftism of good manners" designed to "furnish cautious analyses of the Other half for the unknowing" (Lott, 1996:68, 54, 53).

Lott's commentary represents more than a mean-spirited misrepresentation of the complexity of Dyson's work; more often than not, it appears to be symptomatic of the elitist posturing of a white academic unaware of (or unconcerned about) his own racial privileges, who exhibits a disdain for minority intellectuals who gain public recognition as they address a variety of public cultures. For Lott, Michael Dyson's diasporic writings and public recognition suggest that he has sold out, but for lesser known black intellectuals such as cultural critic, Armand White, similar forms of border crossings become oppositional. Fame often breeds jealousy among academics, and Lott appears to have succumbed to petty sniping. But his analysis also suggests a one-dimensional response to black public intellectuals whose diasporic politics serve as a powerful critique of the white academic's often romanticized celebration of resistance as a practice confined to the margins of social and political life.[11]

One also finds a strong tendency, especially in the work of such writers as Robert Boynton and Sean Wilentz, to argue that the racialist story line of the black intellectuals represents a form of ghettoization, an overemphasis on the connectedness of black history, experience, and culture to their discourse. The notion that the history, intellectual legacies, and struggles of African Americans – along with their damning indictment of white supremacy and racial oppression – are more than mere flotsam "on capitalism's undulating surface" (cited in Hanchard, 1996:22) seems lost on many white intellectuals. Moreover, such arguments are not confined to white liberals. In a recent issue of the *National Review*, Norman Podhoretz accuses Glen Loury of abandoning his conservative ideology because Loury had the temerity to attack his fellow conservatives publicly for exhibiting a callous indifference and lack of compassion to the many problems faced by the black community (see especially Loury 1997a, 1997b). Hard pressed to account for Loury's criticism, Podhoretz suggests that it began with Loury's objection to a favorable endorsement of *The Bell Curve* that ran in the journal, *Commentary*, while Podhoretz was editor-in-chief. Oddly, Podhoretz doesn't mention Loury's resignation from the American Enterprise Institute because of its support for Dinesh D'Souza's execrable book, *The End of Racism*. For Podhoretz, Loury's criticism of the widespread endorsement by conservatives of such a racist tract has little to do with the viability of Loury's position. On the contrary, Loury is disparaged because he has taken the route of James Baldwin and leaped into the "loyalty trap," defined as a "duty in standing with 'his people'" (Podhoretz, 1999:36) But, of course, Loury found himself standing with a number of white progressives as well who also condemned *The Bell Curve*. In order to address this additional shift of loyalty, Podhoretz pulls out the final punch and accuses Loury and his cohorts of repressed racism. The implication is that any black conservative who even thinks about moving beyond the Booker T. Washington credo of self-help – urging blacks to engage in social criticism and collective struggles in the name of racial justice – does nothing less than unleash their own repressed self-hatred and racism. Podhoretz is quite clear on this issue, Moreover, the racism that informs his own position is so beyond the edge of reason that it bears repeating in order to be believed. He writes:

> But I suspect that a dirty little secret was at work here: that, deep down, many of *The Bell Curve*'s antagonists of both races secretly believe that blacks really are by genetic endowment less intelligent than whites or Asians, and that what unleashed the hysterical assault on the

book was that it seemed to confirm dread fears that have been severely repressed. (Podhoretz, 1999:36)

More appears in this critique of black intellectuals than just an impoverished version of political and social history or a deep-seated, racist contempt for critical black intellectuals. One also finds a notion of the public intellectual that disregards the enduring formation and influence of racial injustice in national public discourse.[12] In addition, those scholars who reject the constitutive role that black intellectuals play in grounding their scholarship in African-American history and discourse arrogantly assume that the moral, aesthetic, political, and social lessons of such work apply only to the interests of the black community, hence the charge that such work constitutes a "veritable ghettoization."[13]

Moreover, intellectual pundits such as Robert Boynton, Sean Wilentz, and Leon Wieseltier assume that when black intellectuals focus on race they ignore not only broader issues but also a range of questions relevant to democracy. This appears to be a catch-22 argument. If black intellectuals move beyond race as a central discourse in their work, they both lose their "authenticity," as some of their critics claim, and invalidate the very notion of the black public intellectual. But, if black intellectuals focus on racial issues, they risk accusations of either pandering to the perils of celebrity writing or ghettoizing themselves along the borders of racial politics. Each position cancels out the other and conveniently disavows the complexities, struggles, and value of the hybridized discourses black intellectuals contribute to the national debate about racism, education, politics, and popular culture.

Equally important, neither position addresses the difficulties black intellectuals face engaging in social criticism within dominant cultural formations. The main casualty of such reasoning, however, appears to be a notion of democracy attentive to the legacy and contributions of black intellectuals and the vital role they play in their struggles to deepen the critical faculties of public memory and expand the imperatives of freedom and racial justice.[14]

Toni Morrison forcefully challenges the claim that black intellectuals are fixated on racial reasoning, defending racial politics as a pedagogy and practice for democracy and social responsibility rather than a position limited to the narrow confines of identity politics:

> ... the questions black intellectuals put to themselves, and to African American students, are not limited and confined to our own community. For the major crises in politics, in government, in practically any social issue in this country, the axis turns on the issue of race. Is this country willing to sabotage its cities and school systems if they're occupied mostly by black people? It seems so. When we take on these issues and problems as black intellectuals, what we are doing is not merely the primary work of enlightening and producing a generation of young black intellectuals. Whatever the flash points are, they frequently have to do with amelioration, enhancement or identification of the problems of the entire country. So this is not parochial; it is not marginal; it is not even primarily self-interest. (Morrison, cited in James, 1995:220)

Morrison's comments unmask the racist logic that often invokes "the racial story line" as a critique of black intellectuals, and she also affirms the critical capacities of black public intellectuals who as border crossers address diverse and multiple audiences, publics, racial formations, and discourses.

The assumption that intellectuals who speak to multiple audiences become *ipso facto* sellouts has gained considerable currency in the broader discussion of public intellectuals and black intellectuals in particular. While the dangers of celebrity are real, cautious voices like David Theo Goldberg's argue that when intellectuals intervene at the level of civic debate and speak to large audiences, they face enormous constraints regarding what they can say and how they represent themselves. Paraded as media stars, such intellectuals risk speaking in sound bites, substituting glibness for analysis, and compromising their role as critical intellectuals. Of course, black intellectuals are no less immune to aligning themselves with the ideology of professionalization or the cult of expertise than are their white counterparts in the academy, and conservative black public intellectuals appear to actually relish the role. For instance, Randall Kennedy's emergence as a pre-eminent black public intellectual dispensing his expertise on racial profiling, crime, critical race theory, youth, and racial pride in all of the major media suggest less the demise of what Edward Said calls the dominant discourse of professionalism than new indices to measure the shifting breadth and scope of academic professionalization and the willingness of its often high-profile, Ivy League inhabitants to increasingly become apologists for a color-blind discourse of accommodation.[15] Kennedy's apologies for racist practices, along with his ongoing attempts to comfort whites, reassuring them of the legitimacy of "rightful forms of discrimination" and urging blacks to adopt a "politics of respectability" appear endlessly in dominant media outlets. For instance, Kennedy recently reassured his white audiences and fellow black conservatives that they need not worry about statistics affirming that "half of prison inmates are black; [or that] almost half of the women in state prison are black; [or that] nationally near one third of young black men are either in prison, on probation or parole, or awaiting trail; [or that] more young black men are in prison than in college" (Butler, 1998:1270). For Kennedy, such statistics have little to do with racial discrimination within the criminal justice system and simply signal that blacks break the law and commit criminal offenses more than whites (Kennedy, 1997b). Joining the ranks of fellow conservatives such as Shelby Steele, Thomas Sowell, and Ward Connerly, Kennedy has traded in the courage to attack racial injustice for the kind of celebrity status that comes with arguing that "any attempts to do anything specifically in behalf of nonwhites or women are self-defeating, debilitating, and unjust" (Reed, 1997:18).

Cornel West has challenged such reactionary positions, arguing that black public intellectuals need to be vigorously engaged rather than simply dismissed or uncritically celebrated. For West, progressive, black public intellectuals must exercise a critical "self-inventory," manifest as a "sense of critique and resistance applicable to the black community, American society and Western civilization as a whole" (West, 1993:85), a sentiment that resonates with Karl Marx's call for a practical politics that he described enigmatically as the "poetry of the future" (Marx, 1963:18).

Given the initial recognition of Henry Gates and Cornel West in the popular press as the most prominent black public intellectuals in the United States, it is not surprising that in the first wave of analysis about black public intellectuals, they served as measuring rods against which to judge the vision, politics, and influence of such intellectuals. For West and Gates, such a role became all the more difficult because they willingly took on the responsibility of speaking for an entire generation of black intellectuals.[16] For many critics on both the left and the right, both Gates and West exemplified less the rise of a much needed oppositional discourse from the black community than an indication that the spirit of oppositional discourse that keeps alive the radical thrust of being a public intellectual was being compromised as both appeared to be increasingly positioned, though unfairly in my mind, as "public relations" or "celebrity intellectuals." Gates refused to act like a democratic socialist, and seemed to be more at home writing for Tina Brown, the editor of *The New Yorker*, at the time and recruiting high-profile black intellectuals, such as William Julius Wilson, to join his "dream team" at Harvard University. Gates's response to such criticism appears sincere but facile: "My whole life is a commitment to the black community. That's the truth and that's what I respond to. My work is in African American Studies. Who else is that for if not primarily the black community?" (Gates, cited in Bentsen, 1998:71)

If Gates's recent work appeared to be moving dangerously close to the type of clever, safe prose typical of the Harvard Club, Cornel West's most popular work did little to provide a more oppositional discourse. West's *Race Matters* appeared to many critics to be smug and insensitive. While claiming that black public intellectuals needed to pay attention to the younger generation, West barely acknowledged an up and coming generation of black public intellectuals, except to berate them for wearing sloppy attire. Moreover, in his initial work, West ignored the centrality of public education as a site of political struggle, and harshly dismisses the important work waged by black cultural critics "independent of the academy – journalists, artists, writers, feminist groups – as 'mediocre,' thereby offering no independent support to sustain black intellectual culture" (Goldberg, 1994:5). West has since been more generous with his support of the younger generation of black public intellectuals, but it is precisely because of his and Gates's role as gatekeepers for such a generation that much animosity has been waged at the way in which the media has created media stars out of a very small number of black intellectuals, and in doing so has limited the attention given to the work of more political intellectuals such as Robin Kelley, Angela Davis, Manning Marable, Armond White, Hazel Carby, bell hooks, Joy James, Michelle Wallace, Michael Dyson, Lewis Gordon, Houston Baker, Jr., and others.

What appears missing in the current work of many celebrity black public intellectuals is a model of leadership embraced by W. E. B. Du Bois later in his life, which was posited as a principle of self-critique and strategy for practical politics. Du Bois recognized that the allegedly "best" educated people, offering advice from the Olympian heights of ruling-class private institutions, are not necessarily those who are most enlightened ethically or politically. We can draw two conclusions from Du Bois's insight. First, public intellectuals, especially those whose pedagogical journeys are largely fashioned in elite Ivy League institutions, must use their scholarship as tools in order to address the most pressing social issues of the time; but they also must be attentive to those ideas, values, and practices that they need to unlearn given their formative sojourns among the rich and the powerful. Second, such intellectuals must do more than cross those borders that separate the university from the commanding heights of the dominant media; they must also cross those boundaries that separate academically based, public intellectuals from the politics of "hopeful hope"[17] often exhibited among cultural workers struggling in the public schools, community arts programs, social service centers, shelters for battered women, and other spheres where such intellectuals toil without the fanfare of media hype or celebrity status. Moreover, the work of being a public intellectual suggests more than offering sound bites on talk radio and television news programs; it suggests refusing the lure of self-promotion and the need to attract public attention. At best it

393

means enlarging the spheres of oppositional discourse, linking moral authority with intellectual competence, and, as Pierre Bourdieu suggests, "fulfill [the] function of public service and sometimes of public salvation" by fighting to expand the possibilities of democracy, associated with the rights and services of public life, that is, health care, education, research art, work, health insurance, and so forth.[18]

The contradictions that attend various appearances of both white and black intellectuals do not automatically suggest that public intellectuals are sellouts. On the contrary, such contradictions register the challenges that public intellectuals must face to avoid cooption either within or outside the university while assuming the challenge of addressing multiple and often broad audiences. It means that public intellectuals, especially those in higher education, must avoid an uncritical romance with American culture. For public intellectuals, critical independence and strategic autonomy must include a willingness to contest the cult of professional expertise and specialization with its emphases on hierarchy, competitiveness, and objective, dispassionate research. This suggests demystifying the dominant politics of professionalism while simultaneously creating institutional spaces for hybridized zones of intellectual work in which faculty can create the conditions for new forms of solidarity consistent with defending the university as a "public sphere, one of the few to remain in the post-Fordist moment, in which many citizens can address and debate public issues" (Williams, 1995:406).

This position, along with Goldberg's, may be far too dialectical for many theorists who air their views on black public intellectuals in the popular media. For example, Adolph Reed argues that black public intellectuals who speak to diverse white and black audiences are little more than modern-day versions of Booker T. Washington, rewriting or explaining the mysteries of black America to please white audiences. According to Reed, such intellectuals turn their backs on a black constituency by refusing to address the collective capabilities of African-Americans. Moreover, they gush over each other's fame, and produce second-rate scholarly work. In the end, Reed dismisses black public intellectuals because they "are able to skirt the practical requirements of... avoiding both rigorous, careful intellectual work and protracted committed political action."[19]

Whereas David Goldberg supports the notion of the black public intellectual but rightly notes the dangers attendant upon any role that requires one to engage a massive public audience, Adolph Reed simply dismisses intellectuals as sellouts. Reed echoes the sentiments of many liberal critics who fail to grasp the political and pedagogical value of black and white intellectuals who locate themselves in the border zones that connect diverse groups, contexts, and public spheres. Cut loose from the ideological moorings of separatism and assimilation, black critical intellectuals, in particular, must renegotiate their place from the experience of "uprooting, disjuncture, and metamorphosis... that is, a migrant condition,... from which can be derived a metaphor for all humanity" (Rushdie, 1991:394).

As a dynamic discourse between scattered hegemonies and diverse social struggles, the hybrid rhetoric of the new progressive, black public intellectual is one that opens up new forms of enunciation, asks new questions, and incites new forms of shared antagonisms on either side of the racial divide. Homi Bhabha correctly argues that writers like Boynton, Reed, and Wieseltier fail to grasp the provocation of cultural hybridity, rhetorically and politically. Boynton's account doesn't quite get a hold on the scandal generated by occupying the hybrid position as a form of engaged intellectual and political address – a space of identity that Reed describes as "flimflam" and Wieseltier dismisses as, in Cornel West's case, artful dodging. (Bhabha, 1995:17)

For Bhabha, living on the boundary promises more than self-serving, celebratory posturing. Far more importantly, it offers a rhetorical and political borderline space from which to refuse the inside/outside duality, the binaristic reductionism of pure or contaminated, and the static divide between margin and center. Bhabha captures the progressive political and pedagogical possibilities of the black intellectual as a border subject critically negotiating overlapping, contradictory, and diverse public spaces while opening possibilities for new forms of solidarity:

> Communities negotiate "difference" through a borderline process that reveals the hybridity of cultural identity: they create a sense of themselves to and through an other. Reed's metaphoric boundary between black and white communities, cannot then be assumed as a binary division. And black or minority intellectuals committed to an antiseparatist politics of community have no option but to place themselves in that dangerous and incomplete position where the racial divide is forced to recognize – on either side of the color line – a shared antagonistic or abject terrain. It has become a common ground, not because it is consensual or "just," but because it is infused and inscribed with the sheer contingency of everyday coming and going, struggle and survival. (Bhabha, 1995:114)

Bhabha offers his challenge to minority intellectuals, but its larger significance expands the very meaning of the public intellectual whose work cuts across the divide of race, gender, and class. In this hybridized border area the processes of negotiation, indeterminacy, struggle, and politics provide a new set of registers for developing the conditions for transformative social engagement.

The debate over the public intellectual cannot be abstracted from a broader discourse regarding the centrality of racial justice within democratic public life. Nor can such a debate ignore how public intellectuals address the primacy of the pedagogical in providing the conditions for audiences to reconceptualize their role as active and critical citizens in shaping history and mapping the political dimensions of their economic, social, and cultural lives. The role of the public intellectual is inextricably related with mechanisms of power, politics, and ethics. Recognizing this connection offers no relief for those who deny the relevance of politics in the university, just as it demands more from those academics who reduce their role to that of the apolitical technician or neutral guardian of Western high culture. The importance of the concept of the public intellectual is that it provides a referent for rethinking the university as one of a number of crucial public spheres that offer the promise both of lending "reality to what were fundamentally moral visions" (Brenkman, 1995:8) and articulating a new vision of what education might be, who has access to it, and what opportunities might be produced by those individuals and groups who recognize and try to shape themselves in the dynamic of citizenship and public accountability.

Of course, it is now widely recognized that the definition and fate of being a prominent black public intellectual – or public intellectual in general – has as much to do with the media as it does with possessing the skills and knowledge that allows one to perform such a role. Often there is a strong inversion between those intellectuals who have access to the media and those who question, interrogate, and challenge authority rather than simply serve it. As Edward Herman and David Peterson have recently argued, the new division that appears to be emerging is between public and power intellectuals with the latter having access to the dominant media, right-wing foundation money, and the power of well-endowed institutions, and the former being those intellectuals who lack such access because "they are independent and would speak effectively to [the] public's concerns" (Herman and Peterson, 2001:5). In addition, as the culture of politics shifts into a new era of political disengagement and cynicism, progressive black intellectuals no longer seem to be the object of sustained interest by the mass media. The new black public intellectual appears in the form of conservatives such as Randall Kennedy, Thomas Sowell, Orlando Paterson, Shelby Steele, and Glen Loury, all of whom share the desire to preach the credo of color blindness, deny the central force of racism in America, and offer a voice of moderation, pointing with one hand away from how deeply racist exclusions are embedded in American institutions, the collective psyche, and its everyday relations. Being a black public intellectual is no longer synonymous with being politically progressive, just as assuming the role of a black public intellectual offers no political guarantees, particularly since such a role gains its meaning within particular social formations, historical contexts, and specific types of political action. Once fashion declines, real battles take place over the role that black and other public intellectuals might play in shaping what it means to deepen and enrich democratic public life. There is a long tradition of such struggles, and there are many individuals and groups who are refusing to participate in publicity promotions for struggles that combine theoretical rigor and social relevance, theory and practice, knowledge and commitment. In opposition to the role of public intellectual taken up by black conservatives such as Randall Kennedy, Ward Connerly, and others, I want to foreground the role of the critical public intellectual and the importance of such critical work in expanding the possibilities for democratic public life, especially as it addresses the education of youth within rather than outside of the relations of politics and culture. What exactly does this suggest?

Education and the Role of the Public Intellectual

Assuming the role of public intellectuals, educators might begin by establishing the pedagogical conditions for students to be able to develop a sense of perspective and hope in order to recognize that the way things are is not the way they have always been or must necessarily be in the future. More specifically, it suggests that educators develop educational practices informed by both a language of critique and of possibility. Within such a discourse, hope becomes anticipatory rather than compensatory and employs the language of critical imagination to enable educators and students to consider the structure, movement, and opportunities in the contemporary order of things and how they might act to resist forms of oppression and domination while developing those aspects of public life that point to its best and as yet unrealized possibilities. At the current historical moment, such hope rejects a fatalism that suggests that the only direction in which education can move is to adopt the overriding goals of the corporate culture, to prepare students at all levels of schooling in order to simply take their place in the new corporate order.[20] Hope in this context is not simply about lost possibilities, or a negative prescription to resist, but an ethical ideal rooted in the daily lives of educators, adults, students, and others who deny the machinery of corporate authoritarianism along with other forms of domination by embracing the "spark that reaches out beyond the surrounding emptiness."[21]

The discourse of educated hope and democratic possibilities insists that higher education, along with public schools, play a vital role in developing the political and moral consciousness of its citizens. As such, it is grounded in a notion of educational struggle and leadership that does not begin with the question of raising test scores or educating students to be experts, but with a moral and political vision of what it means to educate to govern, lead a humane life, and address the social welfare of those less fortunate. At stake here is the role that public intellectuals might play within and outside of the academy in linking critical knowledge to the political and social realities of people's everyday lives, or as Lawrence Grossberg points out, to the possibilities of "transforming people's lived realities and the relations of power, and . . . the absolutely vital contribution of intellectual work to the imagination and realization of such possibilities" (Grossberg, 1998:67). Educated hope points beyond the given by salvaging those dreams that call for educators to develop ethical and political projects out of the specificity of the contexts and social formations in which they undertake efforts to combat various forms of oppression (see Freire, 1998). Such intellectuals need to understand more clearly how the practices and social relations at work in particular contexts construct the mechanisms of both domination and resistance as they are lived out, experienced, and suffered, and resisted by different groups. Similarly, public intellectuals need to play a vital role in imagining how a progressive politics would address these issues so as not to reduce them to merely local struggles, and how they might be addressed within political organizations and social movements that are broad-based, international, and unified around the need to struggle against a range of social and economic injustice.

Educators who take on the role of public intellectuals can play a vital role in offering students a language of social criticism and responsibility. This is a language that refuses to treat knowledge as something to be consumed passively, taken up merely to be tested, or legitimated outside of an engaged normative discourse. Central to such a language is the goal of creating those pedagogical conditions that enable students to develop the discipline, ability, and opportunity to think in oppositional terms, to critically analyze the assumptions and interests that authorize the very questions asked within the authoritative language of the school or classroom. Such criticism cuts across disciplinary boundaries and calls for educators, students, and cultural workers to take on the role of public critics who can function as historians, archivist, pundit, social critic, bricoleur, and activist. Maurice Berger suggests that such forms of criticism create new forms of expression and practice. He writes:

> The strongest criticism today – the kind that offers the greatest hope for the vitality and future of the discipline – is capable of engaging, guiding, directing, and influencing culture, even stimulating new forms of practice and expression. The strongest criticism serves as a dynamic, critical force, rather than as an acto of boosterism. The strongest criticism uses language and rhetoric not merely for descriptive evaluative purposes but as a means of inspiration, provocation, emotional connection, and experimentation. (Berger, 1998:11)

Berger's notion of criticism affirms a notion of literacy that reveals the bankruptcy of the vocabulary of literacy associated with the discourse of both corporate culture and traditional pedagogy. Refusing both a market pragmatism and a literacy rooted in the exclusive confines of the modernist culture of print, the strongest forms of criticism emerge out of a pluralized notion of literacy that values both print and visual culture.

397

Moreover, literacy as a critical discourse provides a more complex accounting of culture, identity formation, and the materiality of power while stressing that while literacy itself guarantees nothing, it is an essential precondition for agency, self-representation, and a substantive notion of democratic public life. This suggests a discourse of criticism and literacy that unsettles common sense and engages a variety of cultural texts and public forms. It is a language that learns how to address social injustices in order to break the tyranny of the present. At the same time, an expanded notion of literacy and a willingness to take seriously the pedagogical conditions for political agency should make clear that human beings make their own history and that such histories are a matter of conditioning rather than determination. Literacy and agency within this view points to the necessity to temper any reverence for authority with a sense of critical engagement and skepticism. Moreover, within this perspective, literacy and agency are always interrelated and one's concerns as a public intellectual cannot be disengaged from what it means to be a citizen connected to the larger social and global order.

Another possible requirement for teachers who assume the position of public intellectuals is the need to develop new ways to engage history in order to develop a critical watch over the relationship between historical events and the ways in which those events are produced and recalled through the narratives in which they unfold. This suggests that educators reaffirm the pedagogical importance of educating students to be skilled in the language of public memory. Public memory rejects the notion of knowledge as merely an inheritance, with transmission as its only form of practice. In its critical form, public memory suggests that history be read not merely as an act of recovery but as a dilemma of uncertainty, a form of address and remembering that links the narratives of the past with the circumstances of its unfolding and how such an unfolding or retelling is connected to "the present relations of power" and the experience of those engaged in the rewriting of historical narratives.[22] Public memory sees knowledge as a social and historical construction that is always the object of struggle. Public memory in this instance becomes a metaphor for agency, a willingness to locate oneself within historical traditions that need to be both remembered and engaged, affirmed, mediated, and, when necessary, ruptured. As Edward Said points out, Intellectuals need to engage memory in order to make visible that which has been hidden or ignored, to make connections to the past that are often conveniently forgotten. Public memory provides a site for refusing the elimination of place, the evisceration of locality, or the traces of where we have been and what we experienced. It rejects a notion of place as provincial in favor of a diasporic cosmopolitanism. Instead, it recognizes that identities are in transit, but are made manifest within theaters of memory and place, real and abstract.

In addition, educators as public intellectuals need to expand and apply the principles of diversity, dialogue, compassion, and tolerance in their classrooms to strengthen rather than weaken the relationship between learning and empowerment on the one hand and democracy and schooling on the other. Bigotry, not difference, is the enemy of democracy, and it is difficult, if not impossible, for students to believe in democracy without recognizing cultural and political diversity as a primary condition for learning multiple literacies, experiencing the vitality of diverse public cultures, and refusing the comfort of monolithic cultures defined by racist exclusions. Differences in this instance become important not simply as rigid identity markers, but as differences marked by unequal relations of power, sites of contestation, and changing histories, experiences, and possibilities. Difference calls into question the central dynamic of power and in doing so opens up both a space of translation and the conditions for struggling to renegotiate and challenge the ideologies and machineries of power that put some subjects in place while simultaneously denying social agency to others.[23]

At the same time, public intellectuals need to recognize the limits of a politics based exclusively on theories of difference and identity. Not only does this suggest a notion of the political that engages the relations between everyday life and the state, but points to broader political categories for analyzing identity politics and its limits against the growing globalization of capital and culture. Public intellectuals need a new discourse for grasping the unity of the social, political, and global community, not so much as to shut down a proliferation of identities based on theories of differences but to engage them through relations of solidarity engaged in broader struggles that reveal both the strengths and limits of such particularities. Progressive public intellectuals need to develop a critical vocabulary that provides a purchase both on particular struggles and on what those struggles have in common in order to create a radical democratic hegemony; at stake here is the need to construct a democratic politics that affirms differences that matter but at the same time moves beyond a politics of limited interest groups. Difference in this sense becomes a marker of solidarity within and across relations of specificity and particularity. Cultural studies theorist Lawrence Grossberg is insightful on this issue:

> The real questions are: what kind of differences are effective? And where do differences make a difference? ... Such a politics would have to think about the mechanisms and modalities of belonging, affiliation and identification in order to define the places people can belong to, and the places people can find their way to. Identity becomes more of a political category to be mobilized and laid claim to, a matter of belonging to, the claim to be somewhere and hence, with someone. Challenging culture's equation with and location in the form of identity as a difference may enable us to think about the possibilities of a politics that recognizes and is organized around the positivity or singularity of the other. (Grossberg, 1998:70)

In a world marked by increasing poverty, unemployment, and diminished social opportunities, educators as public intellectuals must take a lesson from the battles critical black intellectuals have waged in protecting the social services that shape public life. This suggests struggling to vindicate the crucial connection between culture and politics in defending public and higher education as sites of democratic learning and struggle. Essential to such a task is providing students with the knowledge, skills, and values they will need to address some of the most urgent questions of our time. Educating for critical citizenship and civic courage, in part, means redefining the role of academics as engaged public intellectuals and border crossers who can come together to explore the crucial role that culture plays in revising and strengthening the fabric of public life. Culture is a strategic pedagogical and political terrian whose force as a "crucial site and weapon of power in the modern world" (Grossberg, 1996:142) can be extended to broader public discourses and practices about the meaning of democracy, citizenship, and social justice. Questions of culture in this perspective are not limited to issues of knowledge, mediation, and communication but include relations of power and institutional forms, as well as connection between meaning and the ways in which bodies are organized through particular affective investments, emotions, and desires. One of the most important functions of a vibrant democratic culture is to provide the institutional, symbolic, and emotional resources necessary for young people and adults to develop their capacity to think critically, to participate in power relations and policy decisions that affect their lives, and to transform those racial, social, and economic inequities that impede democratic social relations. This is a role that public intellectuals can take up and in doing so give concrete expression to what it means to live in a democratic society. Such intellectuals bear the burden of confronting in their work every day the issue of what kind of citizen is required in a substantive democracy, and to take up the challenge in their work of putting into place the conditions that allow students, educators, and others to actively participate in shaping the ideological visions and material relations of power that make such a democracy possible.

Notes

1 This section draws upon ideas first presented in Giroux (1997).
2 I think Michael Denning is right to argue that "the demand that all leftist intellectuals be literary journalists, writing plain English for plain people, is no less objectionable than the Old Left demand that playwrights write agitprop and novelists stick to a comprehensible social realism" (Denning, 1992:36). For sustained critical commentary on the politics of clarity, see Giroux (1992).
3 According to Jacoby, the academy undermines the oppositional role that academics might play as public intellectuals. This is especially important in light of Jacoby's belief that "Today's nonacademic intellectuals are an endangered species" coupled with his claim that "universities virtually monopolize . . . intellectual work" (Jacoby, 1987:7,8).
4 A number of books provide a far more thoughtful and optimistic view of both intellectuals and the academy as a viable public sphere. Some important examples include Robbins (1990, 1993) Ross (1989); Aronowitz and Giroux (1993); Berube (1994).
5 Conservative books on this issue are too numerous to mention, but representative examples include Bloom (1987); Sykes (1988); Kimball (1991); D'Souza (1991).
6 For a critique of this issue, see Williams (1991), especially "The Death of the Profane," pp. 44–51.
7 The "discovery" corresponds with a reality more complex than the media suggest. The category "black public intellectual" should not suggest an ideologically specific group of black intellectuals, as is generally the case in media coverage. In fact, those black intellectuals who have received the most recognition are characterized by a wide range of ideological and political positions extending from left-progressive and liberal to conservative and nationalist. Moreover, the distinctiveness of the group is taken up around the signifiers of class, race, and numbers. As Gerald Early points out, "Indeed, for the first time in African-American history there is a powerful, thoroughly credentialed and completely professionalized black intellectual class. . . . [Moreover] today's generation of black intellectuals has been well publicized; in fact, it has access to the entire machinery of intellectual self-promotion" (Early, 1996).
8 Of course, a number of black theorists also criticized the rise of the black public intellectual as a media event, see, for example, Reed (1995).
9 Boynton's modernist hangover and dislike of critical work that addresses "popular" issues is made more visible in a theoretically incompetent and politically conservative critique of cultural studies that soon followed his piece on black intellectuals. See Boynton (1995b).
10 On the black public sphere, see the wide-ranging essays in Black Public Sphere Collective (1995). For a history of black intellectual life from slavery to the present, see Banks (1996).

11 One of the worst examples of this type of critique can be found in Leon Wieseltier (1995). In a highly selective and grossly simplified reading, Wieseltier concludes that after reading all of Cornel West's work, he finds that "They are almost completely worthless" (p. 31). One can only assume that Wieseltier believes that West's popularity rests solely with the hype of the media culture and the cult of celebrity.

12 For an excellent analysis of this issue, see Brenkman (1995).

13 This position is addressed and criticized in Kilson (1996). Two of the most famous critiques of this position can be found in Harold Cruse (1967) and Richard Wright (1940).

14 On the issue of the black public sphere, see Baker (1994).

15 For a smattering of Randall Kennedy's racial apologies, see Kennedy (1997a, 1997b, 1999). For a critique of Kennedy's role as an apologist for racial injustice and a shameless defender of "black respectability," see Bell (1998).

16 It is impossible to cite all of the adulating interviews, stories, and commentaries on their publicly appointed roles as the pre-eminent black intellectuals in America, but two classic example can be found in Monroe (1996) and Bentsen (1998).

17 I take the phrase "hopeful hope" from an insightful article by Nell Irvin Painter (1996).

18 This is insightfully addressed in Bourdieu (1999). See also Bourdieu's critique of self-serving publicity intellectuals in *On Television* (1996).

19 Reed (1995:35). Reed attempts to backtrack on this attack in a more recent response to criticisms of his piece on black intellectuals. The latter commentary simply dismisses a number of black intellectuals for not taking a critical stand on Louis Farrakhan's role in the Million Man March and his recent global tour to a number of dictatorships in Africa. Reed says little about his role as a public intellectual speaking for a newspaper and readership that is largely white. He simply assumes that because other black scholars differ with him on the significance of Farrakhan's role in national politics, they do not hold themselves accountable for the positions they take as public intellectuals. Hence, Reed implicitly proclaims himself as the only black public intellectual with integrity. See Reed (1996).

20 See, for example, the attempts to reduce student learning to memorization, pedagogy to the act of transmission, and politics to the logic of accommodation in the work of E. D. Hirsch (another conservative public intellectual). For the most recent summary of Hirsch's position, see Hirsch (1999).

21 Rabinbach (1977:8). For a classic example of a critique of the utopian impulse that suggests hoping against hope, see Ilan Gur-Ze'ev (1998). Gur-Ze'ev is so utterly unreflective and self-critical that it never occurs to him to question seriously either the shortcomings of his own basic arguments or his complicity with a form of politics in which any possibility that the future can overtake the present is viewed as futile. In this diatribe against hope, now so common among educators, any notion that pedagogy, history, cultural politics, or social struggle contain the possibilities of freedom are often misrepresented and summarily derided as polemical diatribe.

22 I have appropriated this idea from Young (1998).

23 I have taken these ideas from Homi Bhabha in Olson and Worsham (1998).

References

Aronowitz, Stanley and Giroux, Henry A. (1991) *Postmodern Education*. Minneapolis: University of Minnesota Press.

Aronowitz, Stanely and Giroux, Henry A. (1993) *Education Still Under Siege*. Westport, CT: Bergin and Garvey.

Baker, Houston A. (1994) "Critical memory and the black public sphere." *Public Culture* 7,1:3–33.

Banks, William (1996) *Black Intellectuals: Race and Responsibility in American Life*. New York: Norton.

Bell, Derrick (1998) "The strange career of Randall Kennedy." *New Politics* 7,1:55–69.

Bentsen, Cheryl (1998) "Head negro in charge." *Boston Review* 90,4:64–71.

Berger, Maurice (1998) "Introduction: The crisis of criticism," in Maurice Berger (ed.) *The Crisis of Criticism*. New York: The New Press.

Berube, Michael (1994) *Public Access: Literary Theory and American Cultural Politics*. London: Verso.

Berube, Michael (1995) "Public academy." *The New Yorker* January 9:73–80.

Bhabha, Homi (1995) "Black and white and read all over." *Artforum* October:16–17, 114, 116.

Black Public Sphere Collective (1995) *The Black Public Sphere*. Chicago, University of Chicago Press.

Bloom, Allan (1987) *The Closing of the American Mind*. New York: Simon & Schuster.

Bourdieu, Pierre (1996) *On Television*. New York: New Press.

Bourdieu, Pierre (1999) *Acts of Resistance*. New York: New Press.

Boynton, Robert S. (1995a) "The new intellectuals." *The Atlantic Monthly* March: 53–70.

Boynton, Robert S. (1995b) "The Routledge revolution." *Lingua Franca* 5,3:24–32.

Brenkman, John (1995) "Race publics: Civic illiberalism, or race after Reagan." *Transition* 5,2:4–36.

Butler, Paul (1998) "(Color) blind faith: The tragedy of race, crime, and the law." *Harvard Law Review* 111:1269–78.

Cruse, Harold (1967) *The Crisis of the Negro Intellectual*. New York: Morrow.

Denning, Michael (1992) "The academic left and the rise of cultural studies." *Radical History Review* 54: p.21–47.

Dent, Gina (ed.) (1992) *Black Popular Culture*. Seattle: Bay Press.

Desruisseaux, Paul (1996) "Foundations are asked to help train and encourage new leaders." *The Chronicle of Higher Education* April 30:19.

Dewey, John (1927) *The Public and its Problems*. New York: Holt.

D'Souza, Dinesh (1991) *Illiberal Education: The Politics of Race and Sex on Campus*. New York: Free Press.

Early, Gerald (1996) "Black like them." *The New York Times Book Review* April 24:7, 9.

Freire, Paulo (1998) *Pedagogy of Freedom*. Lanham, MD: Rowman and Littlefield.

Gates, Henry Louis Jr. and West, Cornel (1996) *The Future of the Race*. New York: Knopf.

Giroux, Henry A. (1988) *Teachers as Intellectuals: Toward a Critical Pedagogy of Learning*. Westport, CT: Bergin and Garvey.

Giroux, Henry A. (1992) "Language, difference, and curriculum theory: Beyond the politics of clarity." *Theory Into Practice* 31,3:219–27.

Giroux, Henry A. (1995a) "Academics as public intellectuals: Rethinking classroom politics," in Jeff Williams (ed.) *PC Wars: Politics and Theory in the Academy*. New York: Routledge, pp. 294–307.

Giroux, Henry A. (1995b) "Beyond the ivory tower: Public intellectuals and the crisis in higher education," in Michael Berube and Cary Nelson (eds.) *Higher Education Under Fire*. New York: Routledge, pp.238–58.

Giroux, Henry A. (1997) "Black, bruised, and read all over," in Amitavar Kumar (ed.) *Class Issues: Pedagogy, Cultural Studies, and the Public Sphere*. New York: NYU Press, pp.179–95.

Gitlin, Todd (1997) "The anti-political populism of cultural studies." *Dissent* Spring: 77–82.

Goldberg, David Theo (1994) "Whither West? The making of a public intellectual." *The Review of Education/Pedagogy/Cultural Studies* 16,1:1–13.

Grossberg, Lawrence (1996) "Toward a genealogy of the state of cultural studies," in Gary Nelson and Dilip Parameshwar Gaonkar (eds.) *Disciplinarity and Dissent in Cultural Studies*. New York: Routledge, pp.131–47.

Grossberg, Lawrence (1998) "The cultural studies' crossroads blues." *European Journal of Cultural Studies* 1,1:65–82.

Gur-Ze'ev, Ilan (1998) "Toward a nonrepressive critical pedagogy." *Educational Theory* 48,4:463–86.

Hanchard, Michael (1996) "Intellectual pursuit." *The Nation* February 19:22–4.

Havel, Vaclav (1998) "The state of the republic." *The New York Review of Books* June 22:42–6.

Herman, Edward W. and Peterson, W. (2001) "Public versus power intellectuals, Part 1," in <znetcommentary-outgoings@tao.ca> May 11:1–5.

Hirsch, E. D. (1999) "Finding the answers in drills and rigor." *The New York Times* September 11:A15, A17.

Jacoby, Russell (1987) *The Last Intellectuals: American Culture in the Age of Academe*. New York: Basic Books.

James, Joy (1995) "Politicizing the spirit." *Cultural Studies* 9,2:210–25.

Kennedy, Randall (1997a) "My race problem – and ours." *The Atlantic Monthly* May: 55–66.

Kennedy, Randall (1997b) *Race, Crime, and the Law*. New York: Pantheon.

Kennedy, Randall (1999) "Suspect policy: Racial profiling isn't racist. It can help stop crime. And it should be abolished." *The New Republic* September 13/20:30–5.

Kilson, Michael (1996) "Wilentz, West, and the black intellectuals." *Dissent* Winter: 93–4.

Kimball, Roger (1991) *Tenured Radicals: How Politics Has Corrupted Our Higher Education*. New York: Harper Perennial.

Lott, Eric (1996) "Public image limited." *Transition* 68:50–65.

Loury, Glen (1997a) "Cast out by the right." *The New York Times* November 30:9.

Loury, Glen (1997b) "The conservative line on race." *The Atlantic Monthly* 280,5:144–54.

MacFarquhar, Larissa (2001) "The dean's list: The enfant terrible of English lit grows up." *The New Yorker* June 11:62–71.

Marx, Karl (1963) *The Eighteenth Brumaire of Louis Bonaparte*. New York: International Publishers.

Monroe, Sylvester (1996) "Cornel matters." *Emerge* September: 40–7.

Morrison, Toni (1992) *Playing in the Dark: Whiteness and the Literary Imagination*. Cambridge, MA: Harvard University Press.

Olson, Gary and Worsham, Lynn (1998) "Staging the politics of difference: Homi Bhabha's critical literacy." *Journal of Composition Theory* 18,3:361–91.

Painter, Nell Irvin (1996) "A different sense of time." *The Nation* May 6:38–43.

Podhoretz, Norman (1999) "The 'loyalty trap.'" *National Review* January 25:36–8.

Rabinbach, Anson (1977) "Unclaimed heritage: Ernst Bloch's heritage of our times and the theory of fascism." *New German Critique* Spring: 5–21.

Reed, Adolph (1995) "What are the drums saying, Booker? The current crisis of the black intellectual." *Village Voice* April 11:31–6.

Reed, Adolph (1996) "Defending the indefensible." *The Village Voice* XLI,17:26.

Reed, Adolph (1997) "The descent of black conservatism." *The Progressive* October:18.

Robbins, Bruce (ed.) (1990) *Intellectuals: Aesthetics, Politics, Academics*. Minneapolis: University of Minnesota Press.

Robbins, Bruce (1993) *Secular Vocations: Intellectuals, Professionalism, Culture*. London: Verso.

Ross, Andrew (1989) *No Respect: Intellectuals and Popular Culture*. New York: Routledge.

Rushdie, Salman (1991) "In good faith," in *Imaginary Homelands: Essays and Criticism 1981–1991*. London: Penguin Books.

Said, Edward W. (2001) "On defiance and taking positions," in *Reflections on Exile and Other Essays*. Cambridge, MA: Harvard University Press, pp.500–6.

Sokal, Alan and Bricmont, Jean (1998) *Fashionable Nonsense*. New York: Picador.

Sykes, Charles J. (1988) *Profscam: Professors and the Demise of Higher Education*. Washington, DC: Regnery Gateway.

West, Cornel ([1985] 1993) "The dilemma of the black intellectual," in *Keeping Faith*. New York: Routledge.

Wieseltier, Leon (1995) "All and nothing at all." *The New Republic* March 6:31–6.

Williams, Jeffrey (1995) "Edward Said's romance of the amateur intellectual." *The Review of Education/Pedagogy/Cultural Studies* 17,4:397–410.

Williams, Patricia (1991) *The Alchemy of Race and Rights*. Cambridge, MA: Harvard University Press.

Wolfe, Alan (1996) "The culture of cultural studies." *Partisan Review* 63,3:485–92.

Wolfe, Alan (2001) "The calling of the public intellectual." *The Chronicle of Higher Education* May 25: B20.

Wright, Richard (1940) *Native Son*. New York: Grossset and Dunlap.

Young, James (1998) "The holocaust as vicarious past: Art Spiegelman's *Maus* and the afterimages of history." *Critical Inquiry* 24:668–9.

Chapter 27

Sport as Contested Terrain

Douglas Hartmann

Introduction

The French sociologist Pierre Bourdieu begins his well-known "Program for a Sociology of Sport" with a parable about African-American athletes in prestigious American universities in the early 1970s. Despite their seeming public prominence and importance, Bourdieu recounts (1988), these student-athletes found themselves in "golden ghettos" of isolation where conservatives were reluctant to talk with them because they were black, while liberals were hesitant to converse with them because they were athletes. This absurd situation and the vivid image Bourdieu uses to capture it serves as an introduction to, and illustration of, the argument about race and sport that I intend to develop in this essay. In many ways, the unparalleled athletic prominence and prowess of African-American athletes is one of the most striking and seemingly progressive features of a society otherwise marked by persistent racial inequalities. Yet, at the same time, it is not clear if success in sport consistently contributes to racial progress and justice. Even more problematic, there are ways in which this sporting success actually seems to reinforce and reproduce images, ideas and social practices that are thoroughly racialized, if not simply racist.

In the pages that follow I will explore such tensions in the context of a review and critique of existing ways of understanding the relationships between race and sport in American culture.[1] These can be usefully divided into two schools of thought: those which see sport as a positive, progressive racial force and those which see sport as thoroughly implicated in the maintenance and reproduction of existing racial stereotypes and hierarchies. Rather than trying to resolve them completely, I will argue that the tensions between these two camps constitute the defining characteristic of the American sport–race nexus. More specifically, I want to suggest, borrowing from Stuart Hall (1981, see also 1996), that sport is best understood as a "contested racial terrain," a social site where racial images, ideologies, and inequalities are constructed, transformed, and constantly struggled over. It is an exercise which is intended not only to clarify our understanding of the racial significance of sport but also to reiterate the deep and multifaceted ways in which race is implicated in American culture.

This essay is compiled from two previous works: "Rethinking the relationships between sport and race in American culture: Golden ghettos and contested terrain." *Sociology of Sport Journal*, 2000, 17, 3:229–53; and "Race, culture, and the case of sport." *Culture*, 2000, 14,2:1–6. Permission to use them here is gratefully acknowledged.

My starting point is Bourdieu's insistence that sport be taken seriously *and* treated critically as a social – or in this case, racial – force. The extraordinary and highly visible success of African-American athletes I just mentioned (despite constituting only 12 percent of the American populace, African Americans comprise 80 percent of the players in professional basketball, 67 percent in football and 18 percent in baseball, Eitzen, 1999:136–7) is just one of the reasons why it is necessary to begin from this assumption. Another has to do with sport's prominent place in the public culture and the mass media. Large numbers of Americans across racial lines interact with sport and are impacted by its remarkable racial dynamics. Making the sheer demographics of these sport-based interactions even more socially significant is the passion that practices of sport inculcate among those whose lives they touch. Often in very different ways, but to a degree with few correlates in American life, sports fans (especially men[2]) tend to care deeply about sport, and feel free to express strong opinions about sport and the issues they encounter in its social space. That so many sport discussions and debates are not consciously recognized as having broader societal causes, connections, and consequences only, in my view, accentuates sport's racial power and importance further still. Sport, to redeploy Ralph Ellison's classic depiction of the African American, is at once an invisible and hypervisible racial terrain. Finally there are the obvious parallels between dominant liberal democratic ideals (and their optimistic, color-blind vision of racial harmony and justice) and sport's own culture of fairness and meritocracy. All of this is simply to insist that the interesting and important question is not *whether* sport is a significant racial force but *what kind of a racial force is sport?*

Alternative Views of Sport as a Racial Force

There are two existing ways of thinking about the racial force of sport that any serious student of the subject must take into account: one is popular or even commonsensical, the other is scholarly and deeply critical of the first. Juxtaposing these two very different visions – which I call the "popular ideology" and the "scholarly critique" – and their respective insights and shortcomings against each other is the first step toward developing a full and satisfactory understanding of the complex relationships between sport and race in the United States.

The popular ideology

Dominant cultural conceptions of sport's racial impact can be stated easily enough. Sport is seen by most Americans as a positive and progressive racial force, an avenue of racial progress and an arena of racial harmony. It is understood as a "way out of the ghetto," the great racial "equalizer," a leader in civil rights if not a literal "model" for race relations in the United States.

The notion that sport is a positive and progressive racial force has a long history in American culture. Leaders of the sporting establishment have trumpeted such claims at least since the spectacular athletic accomplishments of Joe Louis and Jesse Owens in the 1930s, and the basic empirical-intellectual foundations for the argument were laid in 1939 with the publication of Edwin Bancroft Henderson's seminal study *The Negro in Sports*. But the ideology probably reached its high point in the late 1950s and early 1960s with the fall of the color-line in professional baseball, that self-proclaimed American pastime. It was in the wake of this success that one of the most prominent African-American sportswriters of the day, a man named A. S. "Doc" Young (1963), proclaimed that Willie Mays was as important a figure for civil rights as Martin Luther King, Jr. and that Jackie Robinson ranked next to Jesus Christ among the most important and honorable men ever to have walked the earth.

Today, it is rare to hear bold and unqualified statements about sport's positive racial force (at least in part for a want of supporting empirical verification). But the relative dearth of clearly articulated and empirically supported claims that sport is a positive, progressive racial force does not mean that the notion has fallen out of favor. Quite the contrary, I believe that the absence of empirical investigation and systematic argumenta-tion is actually evidence of how deeply held and commonsensical it has come to be in American culture. The notion that sport is a positive, progressive racial force is more than just an idea, it is an ideology, an idea that has taken on a life of its own. It doesn't need to be restated or defended. It is cultural commonsense, an article of faith held by Americans, black and white, liberal and conservative, even those who don't care about sport in any other way.

A 1996 poll conducted for *U.S. News and World Report* and Bozell Worldwide found that 91 percent of Americans think that "participation in sports" helps a "person's ability to . . . get along with different ethnic or racial groups."[3] The popular frenzy that sur-rounds superstar African-American athletes such as Tiger Woods, or the fact that President Clinton chose to devote one of his three national "town-hall" meetings on race exclusively to sport, are both examples of the prominent and essentially positive racial meanings expressed in and through sport in mainstream American culture. So powerful and widely taken for granted are these ideas that commentators who want to affirm sport's general societal contributions routinely invoke racial examples to make their case. Michael Novak's (1976) and A. Barlett Giamatti's (1989) well-known celebra-tions of American sport are perfect examples. Despite the fact that neither book has much to say about race, both place Jackie Robinson's integration story prominently in their texts. Perhaps the most powerful illustration of the power of sport's progressive racial ideology came from the 1996 Centennial Olympic Games in Atlanta, Georgia. I am referring here not just to the top performances of African-American athletes such as Carl Lewis, Michael Johnson, or Jackie Joyner Kersee but more to the fact that Atlanta won the right to host the Games because the International Olympic Committee believed it would display for the peoples of the world a model of racial harmony, progress, and prosperity. These connections between sport and racial progress were drawn most forcefully in the pre-Olympic stump speeches of Andrew Young, the former mayor of Atlanta and the cochair of the Atlanta Organizing Committee who touted the Olympic Movement as the secular, global realization of his friend and mentor Martin Luther King, Jr.'s dream for a truly color-blind society.

The scholarly critique

In stark contrast to this sport-as-positive-racial force ideology stand a plethora of empirically grounded scholarly criticisms of the racial form and function of sport. Inspired by athletic activism of the late 1960s and early 1970s,[4] the primary objective and accomplishment of these works has been to demonstrate that racial inequalities and

407

injustices are not so much challenged and overcome in and through sport as they are reproduced and reinforced there. The dominant motif is captured succinctly in the subtitle of one recent (if highly controversial) contribution to the field: "How Sport has Damaged Black America and Preserved the Myth of Race" (Hoberman, 1997).

Two very different strands of research and writing contribute to this critique. One, which I refer to as an institutional approach, analyzes the racial character and organization of the sports world itself. Its primary task and preoccupation has been to demonstrate persistent patterns of racial discrimination, exploitation, and oppression in sport. This case has been made convincingly. In their 1991 review of sport sociology, the leading disciplinary home of this work, James H. Frey and D. Stanley Eitzen summarized:

> The major conclusion of this work . . . is that just as racial discrimination exists in society, [so also] it exists in sport. Blacks do not have equal opportunity; they do not receive similar rewards for equal performance when compared to whites; and their prospects for a lucrative career beyond sport participation are dismal. (Frey and Eitzen, 1991:513)

Exposing the deeply racialized character of sport has implications far beyond the world of sport. These are closely connected with the popular ideology that sport is a model of, and institutional symbol for, race relations in the United States. If even sport doesn't live up to liberal–democratic ideals, what does this suggest about their limits as defining standards for racial progress and justice?

Here it is worth noting that one of the most important and controversial claims of recent critical scholarship on whiteness is that liberal–democratic political ideologies are themselves inherently racialized owing to the inevitable social limitations (or contradictions) of their claims to abstract, universal citizenship. Racial categories are, in other words, built into the cultural structure of Western nationalism and liberal democracy. I don't know that we need to go this far. But my own work on the 1968 African American Olympic protest movement (Hartmann, 1996, forthcoming) – the movement most widely associated with the clenched-fist salute given by two African-American athletes on the Olympic victory stand in Mexico City in 1968 – has been directly influenced by such thinking. Indeed, I follow anthropologist John MacAloon (1988) in arguing that these athletes were initially received as villains, extremists, and traitors for doing little more than calling attention to their own blackness precisely because race was not an identity allowed by time-honored Olympic ritual (which itself is directly and self-consciously posited on traditional, Western conceptions of individuals, nations, and humanity and the appropriate relations among them). They were treated this way, that is, because calling attention to race exposed and threatened to disrupt the otherwise comfortable homologies among sport culture, Olympic symbolism, and liberal-democratic ideology. The point here (usually only implicit in most institutional critiques) is that the color-blind, assimilationist values at the root of liberal-democratic theory and much sport culture make it difficult to even recognize racial categories, much less provide mechanisms to address the structural inequalities that typically go along with them.

The second variation on the scholarly critique of sport builds from this notion, attending specifically to the symbolic role that sport plays in American culture with respect to race. This symbolic critique, which has emerged only in the last decade or so but already has some impressive proponents, begins from the undeniable and unparalleled success of African Americans in sport and sport's own widespread public prominence and power. But rather than seeing these social facts as a progressive political development (as the popular ideology would have it) these scholars hold that the powerful presence of African American athletes in American culture may actually perpetuate and reinforce the racial status quo. This claim derives from a deep, critical conception of the role of mass-mediated, market-based cultural forms such as sport in generating contemporary racial images and ideologies. At the core of this conception is the enormous gap between highly visible and often highly paid African Americans and those of the vast majority of African Americans – and the fact that many mainstream, middle-class Americans are unwilling or unable to recognize this disjuncture. In this context, African American athletes come to serve as what David Andrews (1996), borrowing from Derrida, calls a "floating racial signifier": dynamic, complex, and contradictory, they can be interpreted in virtually any way an audience wants.

Given the persistence of race and racism in American culture, the prominence of African-American athletes thus tends to serve one of three racializing functions. One is that attention to African American athletic success can deflect attention away from, obscure, or minimize the more general problems of racial inequality and racism. Secondly and even worse, the cultural prominence of African-American athletes can be used to legitimate existing racial inequalities by making it seem as if there are no racial barriers standing in the way of African-American mobility and assimilation. If in sport, the thinking goes, why not in other social spheres? The third point has to do with the claim that images of African-American athletes are thoroughly racialized, indelibly linked with the racial stereotypes that permeate the culture.

What is complicated about this final point is that it runs counter to many of our usual social and sociological assumptions about racism and prejudice. We tend to think of these phenomena negatively, in terms of beliefs and behaviors that exclude and privilege one racial group over another. Yet the images of African Americans in sport appear to be quite positive, even flattering and celebratory. The crucial point for critical sport scholars, however, is that what seems to be positive about these images tends to be exaggerated and one-dimensional, thus stripping African-American athletes of agency and working to reinforce imagined racial traits and characteristics. One of the most familiar strains of this argument focuses on the inherent physicality of sporting practices. The claim here, articulated most recently and controversially in John Hoberman's *Darwin's Athletes* (1997), is that because of sport's *de facto* association with bodies, and the mind/body dualisms at the core of Western culture, the athletic success of African American athletes serves to reinforce racist stereotypes by grounding them in essentialized, biological terms where athletic prowess is believed to be inversely associated with intellectual and/or moral depravity. Cheryl Cole and her associates (Cole and Denny, 1994; Cole and Andrews, 1996) develop this argument in a somewhat different fashion by examining how media portrayals and the cultural commodification of African-American athletes typically exaggerate their social differences, on the one hand, and how quickly the celebration of racial difference can turn into a condemnation of social deviance, on the other. In one of her most provocative papers, in fact, Cole (1996) argues that there is a prevailing cultural logic that links, albeit by inversion, racial images in sport and racial images about crime. Sport's racial imagery thus constitutes and contributes to a rather insidious form of "enlightened racism" (McKay 1995) in which racial stereotypes and

409

hierarchies are reproduced even as mainstream audiences believe they are being sub-verted.[5] In any case, the point is clear: that racism is a complicated, multifaceted cultural system which often ironically finds expression in the celebration and consumption of racial difference itself.

Criticism and Synthesis

As part of public discourse, these scholarly critiques provide a much-needed criticism and deconstruction of the hegemony of the sport-as-positive-racial-force ideology. They expose its empirical limitations with respect to both internal organization and broader symbolic function. Perhaps more importantly, they show how the unqualified acceptance of such an ideology can actually serve to legitimate and reproduce dominant racial meanings, practices, and hierarchies. For all of this, however, I think these critiques have often gone too far. In making these points they have too often simply exchanged one totalization (that sport is a positive force for racial change) for the other (that it is a negative, impeding one). Deconstruction, to put it even stronger, is virtually all these critiques have accomplished. And in failing to do more than deconstruct the popular ideology, these critiques have become (or at least threaten to become) a one-sided ideology of their own, an ideology which fails to appreciate the actual complexity and possibility of sport's place in the American racial order.

Stated differently, the problem with established sociological critiques is that for all the truth they contain, they see the popular ideology that sport is a progressive racial force strictly as a form of false consciousness, as *mere* ideology. The most prominent recent variation on this theme is probably John Hoberman's argument about the supposed "sports fixation" of African-American intellectuals and in the African-American com-munity in general. This cynical, dismissive attitude makes it impossible for academic critics to grasp why popular beliefs appeal so widely, especially among those they are supposed to injure the most. And, as many of Hoberman's critics suggest,[6] there are good, solid empirical reasons for the popular perception of sport as a progressive racial force.

Some are quite familiar and conventional: for example, that sport has provided an avenue of opportunity and mobility for African Americans; that these athletic successes, in turn, have much broader community impacts whether as a space for social interaction and community building or symbol of racial accomplishment and source of pride and collective identification; and that sport provides many Anglo-Americans with some of their most positive and important interactions with people of color. But that doesn't make them any less accurate. While it may not be perfect, sport is also an unparalleled institutional site of accomplishment for African Americans and remains one of the most integrated institutions in American life. In recent years, in fact, a handful of scholars have produced works that are beginning to coalesce into a serious, scholarly defense of these points. For example, Nelson George (1992) describes memorably how in the case of basketball, sport has become a crucial social space for the development of an African-American identity and aesethetic. This distinctive cultural style has obviously been useful in terms of its market value, but it is more significant still, in theoretical terms, for its capacity to inspire productive, creative labor among African-American young people living in otherwise alienating and disadvantaged circumstances (see Wacquant, 1992; Dyson, 1993; and especially Kelley, 1997).

None of this is to now conclude that the scholarly critique of sport is totally wrong and the popular ideology completely correct. Rather, it is to insist that the relationships between sport and race are more complicated and contradictory than sociological critics have usually realized. More than this, it is to suggest that instead of choosing between these one-sided, totalizing perspectives we would do better to blend their insights, to shape them into a broader theoretical synthesis. What we need, in other words, is a theory that is deeply and (once again) properly critical of the popular belief that sport is a pure and perfect arena of racial progress, but which is, at the same time, able to allow that sport may affect positive, progressive racial change under certain conditions, in certain social settings, and for certain kinds of racial concerns.

Sport as contested racial terrain

At the core of such a synthesis is the notion that sport is a kind of "double-edged sword" (Kellner, 1996) or what I will call, extending from Stuart Hall (1981), a "contested racial terrain." That is to say, sport is not just a place (or variable) whereby racial interests and meanings are *either* inhibited *or* advanced but rather a site where racial formations are constantly – and very publicly – struggled on and over. The racial dynamics of sport are both positive and negative, progressive and conservative, defined by both possibilities for agency and resistance as well as systems of domination and constraint.

Thinking of sport as a contested racial terrain requires more than just an abstract balancing act of competing racial forms and forces, much less a simple calculation of "positive" and "negative" outcomes. In addition it must begin from and be grounded in a broad, theoretically informed understanding of the American racial order and the place of sport therein as well as of the paradoxical ways in which racial resistance and change are made in the contemporary, post-Civil Rights moment. A comprehensive treatment of this theoretical framework is obviously beyond the scope of a brief conclusion but two points are crucial.

The first, which I have alluded to already, has to do with social context. It is that the racial form and function of sport cannot be properly understood unless these are situated in the context of a society marked by stark and persistent racial inequalities. If African Americans tend to see sport positively, it is not because they are fixated on sport or even that sport is inherently progressive. (Indeed, there is some evidence – Siegelman, 1998 – that African Americans are no more fixated on sport than any other group of Americans.) Rather, it is because sport offers African Americans opportunities and resources rarely found in other institutions in the society. More than this, it helps us appreciate why sport plays a privileged and particularly prominent role in American culture with respect to race.

At the same time, situating sport in the context of racial meanings and practices broadly conceived guards against bringing unrealistic, overly optimistic hopes and expectations to our thinking about the racial form and the racial function of sport in the USA. Seeing sport in context is, in other words, a way to understand the paradoxical "golden ghettos" metaphor from Bourdieu which I used to begin this paper. A similar sensibility is reflected in the title "Glory Bound" which the sports historian David K. Wiggens (1997a) gives to a collection of his seminal essays on African American sport involvement in the twentieth century. The point for these scholars – Gerald Early's brilliant essays on boxing (1994, 1989) – must also be included here is that there is tremendous possibility for those who are

411

racially oppressed, but that these possibilities are always contained within the larger structure of a thoroughly racialized if not simply racist culture.

Thinking of sport as a contested racial terrain also requires a very particular understanding of the relationship between structure and agency. Here the point involves the general theoretical insight, at the core of Bourdieu's general theory of practice; namely, that structure and agency are not opposed or mutually exclusive but in fact deeply interconnected, even mutually constitutive. This is one of the key points of my own (previously cited) work on the 1968 African American Olympic protest movement: that as much as sport has functioned to structure and reinforce dominant racial formations in the post-Civil Rights era, the dynamics of racial domination have been intimately intertwined with and revealed by attempts at activism, resistance, and challenge. Resistance and domination, as well as opportunity and constraint, thus must be taken together.

The interrelationship of resistance and domination has been a central theme for several sport scholars. Loic Wacquant (1992), for example, explains the appeal of boxing to young African-American men in Chicago by situating the sport in the socioecological context of African-American life in impoverished, inner-city Chicago. Boxing is appealing, according to Wacquant, not because it reflects the disorder and disorganized of the surrounding communities but rather because boxers and boxing coaches define themselves "in opposition to the ghetto" as "islands of stability and order," "relatively self-enclosed site(s) for a protected sociability where one can find respite from the pressures of the street and ghetto," a "buffer against the attributes and dangers of ghetto life" (1992:229). In his discussion of basketball and various other popular cultural forms in which African-American young people from the inner city invest, Robin Kelley (1997) takes these points even further to emphasize the particular possibilities for racial resistance, creativity, and enjoyment that are at the heart of popular practices and preferences such as sport. The point, for Kelley, is not just that agency is constituted in relationship to structures of racial domination in and around sport. The point, in addition, is that a popular cultural form such as sport is a particularly important site for racial resistance because it is one of the few arenas open and encouraged for African Americans in an otherwise deeply racist society.

Of course, it is one thing to point out the possibilities for individual agency, creativity, mobility, and resistance available in and through sport; it is quite another to be optimistic about the larger political implications of all this. Indeed, many scholarly critiques of sport grant the former but deny the latter (cf. Page, 1997). If resistance goes hand in hand with domination, in this view, resistance is always extremely limited, partial, and contained. There is a good deal of wisdom in this way of thinking. But however typical this outcome may be, it is important to remember that it is precisely because sporting practices are so thoroughly racialized that they present much larger scale opportunities and possibilities for social mobilization and change. This is, I think, why many of its most prominent public critics – organizations such as Lapchick's Center for the Study of Sport in Society, the NAACP, or Jesse Jackson's Operation Push – target sport: because of its prominence and the prominence of African-American athletes therein. Sport is not just a site for the reproduction of racial stereotypes and formations but also a site of potential struggle and challenge against them. It is, as I have suggested before in reappropriating Bourdieu's famous phrase, a source (or at least potential source) of cultural capital that can be directed toward larger struggles for racial justice in the USA. Again, it may not be that using sport to deliberate political effect is an easy proposition in the contemporary, post-Civil Rights era (because of the different nature of the racial structures being struggled against). But then again sport's contribution to the movement against racism in the US was never, in any case, automatic or easy. Indeed, as Jeffrey Sammons (1994) makes clear in his excellent review of the still-burgeoning historical literature, racial progress in and through sport never came easily or automatically but rather slowly and unevenly, and almost always only as the result of protracted, deliberate struggles and repressive counterresistance.

So, then, the essence of what it means to think about sport as a contested racial terrain is threefold. First, the relationships between sport and race are more complicated and indeed often contradictory than either popular audiences or sport specialists realize. Second, they are constituted within the structure of a culture that is thoroughly racialized. And third, because of sport's prominence in American culture and sport's own unique racial characteristics, these relationships have meaning and consequence far beyond the usual boundaries of the sporting world itself, meanings and consequences which can reproduce or – especially if invested with political intent – transform racial formations broadly conceived. Thinking of sport as a "contested racial terrain," therefore, not only stands as an alternative to both popular ideologies and scholarly critiques of sport's racial form and function, but is actually a theoretical synthesis of the two.

There is obviously much more that could be said here. But let me conclude simply by reiterating that thinking of sport in this way should also make clear that a full theory of sport and race interactions has as much to do with how we understand race, racism, and the complexity of struggles against them as with how we think about sport itself. If sport is golden for African Americans, it is mainly because of its unique place in and relationship to the prevailing structures of the metaphorical racial ghetto itself. This is neither a criticism nor a celebration of sport; it is simply an observation about the ironies of race and resistance in contemporary, post-Civil Rights American culture.

Notes

1   I focus on the African-American athletic experience both because this the case I know best and because it is the one from which most theories of sport and race interactions derive and depart. In any case I hope that it will have much broader applications and generalizable qualities.

2   I might also point out that what I have to say about race and sport is oriented toward, if not centered upon, males and masculinity. There are many reasons for this, but the most important ones are practical and, unfortunately, may obscure many important and consequential inter-sections (and disruptions) between race and gender in sport and in American culture. Radio stations dedicated almost exclusively to sport talk are perhaps the more recent and most obvious example of the significance of discussions and debates that take place in and around sport. See Goldberg (1998) for a recent discussion and analysis.

3   The poll, which surveyed 1000 people by telephone in a random national sample, was conducted in May of 1996 by the Tarrance Group, Lake Research, and KRC (TARR).

4   For contemporaneous descriptions of this movement, see Harry Edwards (1969) and Jack Olsen (1968). For more recent and somewhat more critical discussion and analysis see Hartmann (1996, forthcoming); Wiggens (1997b, 1988) and Spivey (1984). It is also worth recalling that Edwards, widely known as the leader of the movement, was one of the leading practitioners of and spokespersons for the race-based critique of sport. Some of his ideas can be found in *Sociology of Sport* (1973), one of the first widely used sociology of sport textbooks in the country.

5   See also Wonsek (1992); Werner (1995); Boyd (1997); Wilson (1997).

6   For discussions see Sammons (1997), Smith and Shropshire (1998), and the reviews collected in symposia in the *Social Science Quarterly* (December 1998), the *International Journal of the Sociology of Sport* (March 1998), and *Black Issues in Higher Education* (April 1998). I should also note that sports fixation thesis is not inherently liberal or conservative. Indeed, Harry Edwards has long advanced similar claims. The problem with both standard liberal and conservative formulations, in my view, is their failure to situate the African-American experience in sport within the larger context of living in and struggling against a deeply racialized culture (see Edwards, 1984).

References

Andrews, David L. (1996) "The fact(s) of Michael Jordan's blackness: Excavating a floating racial signifier." *Sociology of Sport Journal* 13:125–58.

Bourdieu, Pierre (1988) "Programme for a sociology of sport." *Sociology of Sport Journal* 5:153–61.

Boyd, Todd (1997) " . . . The day the niggaz took over: Basketball, commodity culture, and black masculinity," in Aaron Baker and Todd Boyd (eds.) *Out of Bounds: Sports, Media and the Politics of Identity*. Bloomington: Indiana University Press, pp.122–42.

Cole, Cheryl L. (1996) "American Jordan: PLAY, consensus and punishment." *Sociology of Sport Journal* 13:366–97.

Cole, Cheryl L. and Andrews, David L. (1996) "Look – it's NBA Showtime! Visions of race in the popular imagery." *Cultural Studies Annual* 1:141–81.

Cole, Cheryl L. and Denny, Harry III (1994) "Visualizing deviance in post-Reagan America: Magic Johnson, AIDS and the promiscuous world of professional sport." *Critical Sociology* 20,3:123–47.

Dyson, Eric Michael (1993) "Be like Mike? Michael Jordan and the pedagogy of desire," in *Reflecting Black African-American Cultural Criticism*. Minneapolis: University of Minnesota Press, pp.64–75.

Early, Gerald (1989) *Tuxedo Junction: Essays on American Culture*. Hopewell, NJ: Ecco Press.

Early, Gerald (1994) *The Culture of Bruising: Essays on Prizefighting, Literature and Modern American Culture*. New York: Ecco Press.

Early, Gerald (1998) "Performance and reality: Race, sports and the modern world." *The Nation* August 10/17:11–20.

Edwards, Harry (1969) *The Revolt of the Black Athlete*. New York: The Free Press.

Edwards, Harry (1973) *Sociology of Sport*. Homewood, IL: Dorsey Press.

Edwards, Harry (1984) "The black 'dumb jock': An American sports tragedy." *The College Board Review* 131:8–13.

Eitzen, D. Stanley (1999) *Fair and Foul: Beyond the Myths and Paradoxes of Sport*. Lanham, MD: Rowman and Littlefield.

Frey, James H. and Eitzen, D. Stanley (1991) "Sport and society." *Annual Review of Sociology* 17:503–22.

George, Nelson (1992) *Elevating the Game: Black Men and Basketball*. New York: HarperCollins.

Giamatti, A. Bartlett (1989) *Take Time for Paradise: Americans and Their Games*. New York: Summit Books.

Goldberg, David Theo (1998) "Call and response: Sports, talk radio and the death of democracy." *Journal of Sport and Social Issues* 22,2:212–23.

Hall, Stuart (1981) "Notes on deconstructing 'the popular,' " in Raphael Samuel (ed.) *People's History and Socialist Theory*. London: Routledge and Kegan Paul, pp.227–40.

Hall, Stuart (1996) "Gramsci's relevance for the study of race and ethnicity," in David Marley and Kuan-Hsing Chen (eds.) *Stuart Hall: Critical Dialogues in Cultural Studies*. London: Routledge, pp.411–40.

Hartmann, Douglas (1996) "The politics of race and sport: Resistance and domination in the 1968 African American Olympic protest movement." *Ethnic and Racial Studies*, 19,3:548–66.

Hartmann, Douglas (Forthcoming) *Golden Ghettos: Race, Culture and the Politics of the 1968 African American Olympic Protest Movement*. Chicago: University of Chicago Press.

Henderson, Edwin Bancroft ([1939] 1949) *The Negro in Sport*. Washington, DC: The Associated Publishers.

Hoberman, John (1997) *Darwin's Athletes: How Sport Has Damaged Black America and Preserved the Myth of Race*. New York: Houghton Mifflin.

Kelley, Robin D. G. (1997) "Playing for keeps: Pleasure and profit on the postindustrial playground," in Wahneema Lubiano (ed.) *The House that Race Built*. New York: Pantheon, pp.195–231.

Kellner, Douglas (1996) "Sports, media culture, and race – some reflections on Michael Jordan." *Sociology of Sport Journal* 13:458–67.

MacAloon, John J. (1988) "Double visions: Olympic Games and American Culture," in Jeffrey O. Segrave and Donald Chu (eds.) *The Olympic Games in Transition* Champaign, IL: Human Kinetics Books, pp.279–94.

McKay, Jim (1995) "Just do it: Corporate sports slogans and the political economy of 'enlightened racism.'" *Discourse: Studies in the Cultural Politics of Education* 16,2:191–201.

Novak, Michael (1976) *The Joy of Sports: End Zones, Bases, Baskets, Balls and the Consecration of the American Spirit*. New York: Basic Books.

Olsen, Jack (1968) *The Black Athlete: A Shameful Story*. New York: Time-Life Books.

Page, Helan E. (1997) " 'Black male' imagery and media containment of African American men." *American Anthropologist* 99,1:99–111.

Sammons, Jeffrey T. (1994) "'Race' and sport: A critical, historical examination." *Journal of Sport History*, 21, Fall: 203–98.

Sammons, Jeffrey T. (1997) "A proportionate and measured response to the provocation that is *Darwin's Athletes*." *Journal of Sport History* 24,3:378–88.

Siegelman, Lee (1998) "The American Athletic Fixation." *Social Science Quarterly*, 79, 4:892–7.

Smith, Earl and Shropshire, Kenneth (1998) "John Hoberman and his quarrels with African American athletes and intellectuals." *Journal of Sport and Social Issues* 22:103–12.

Spivey, Donald (1984) "Black consciousness and Olympic protest movement." in Donald Spivey (ed.) *Sport in America: New Historical Perspectives*. Westpoint, CT: Greenwood Press, pp.239–62.

Wacquant, Loic J. D. (1992) "The social logic of boxing in black Chicago: Toward a sociology of pugilism." *Sociology of Sport Journal* 9:221–54.

Werner, L. (1995) "The good, the bad and the ugly: Race, sport and the public eye." *Journal of Sport and Social Issues* 18:27–47.

Wiggens, David K. (1988) "The future of college athletics is at stake: Black athletes and racial turmoil on three predominantly white university campuses, 1968–1972." *Journal of Sport History* 15, Winter: 304–33.

Wiggens, David K. (1997a) *Glory Bound: Black Athletes in White America*. Syracuse, NY: Syracuse University Press.

Wiggens, David K. (1997b) "The year of awakening: Black athletes, racial unrest and the civil rights movement of 1968," in *Glory Bound: Black Athletes in White America*. Syracuse, NY: Syracuse University Press, pp.104–22.

Wilson, Brian (1997) "good blacks' and 'bad blacks': Media constructions of African-American athletes in Canadian basketball." *International Review for the Sociology of Sport* 32,2:177–89.

Wonsek, Pamela L. (1992) "College basketball on television: A study of racism in the media." *Media, Culture and Society* 14:449–61.

Young, A. S. (1963) *Negro Firsts in Sports*. Chicago: Johnson Publishing.

Chapter 28

Fashion

Gargi Bhattacharyya

Fashion is a lovely word – a promise of frippery, a distraction from everyday drudgery, the disposable pleasures of baubles and bangles and ribbons and bows. A million miles away from the nasty and often dull business of social analysis or even, heaven forbid, cultural significance. How hard to forgo the shiny dreamtime of this fantasy and do the dirty by introducing context, history, outcomes. But that is the task.

Growing up in Britain through the 1970s and 1980s, I was painfully aware that Asians were beyond fashion. The endless reinforcement of racist depictions of Asian culture and people let me know that as well as being dirty, less than human, and outside of the loop allowing respect or desire, Asians were hopelessly uncool, no matter what they wore. This was before the recent exoticisms of Asian underground and, largely, before the pre-eminence of an African-Americanized global US culture had transformed black women into mainstream objects of glamor and desire. Now I wonder if the concentrated attention which many raised-in-Britain black women bring to body care is in part a response to this childhood experience of being made monstrous – always the witch and never the princess in playground games.

Of course, now dark skin is endlessly fashionable if no more respected. White women wear the accessories of our traditional styles – bindis and headwraps meet lycra and trainers, make-up multinationals market "mehndi" body paint in my supermarket and (some) Asian and African (and Latin and Aboriginal and Native) women can even be beautiful, desirable, and the embodiment of glamor. The temptation is to read this as a mark of more substantial social changes, as if diversity in the fashion pages must lead seamlessly to diversity in all areas of living. Of course, life is never so simple and multicultural fashion glamor shifts products with little indication that the ugliness of racist oppression and violence is fading.

This is a chance to explore the role of fashion, as both an aesthetic choice and as a set of products, in our global racial and racist history. Inevitably, the following account reflects my own location in, and obsession with, Britain – I can only hope that there are suggestions here which translate to other locations.

Displaying Status and Identity

Fashion has often been disregarded or derided by those seeking to explicate our social structures and meanings – this has included inquiries into the meanings of race and

416

ethnicity. However, in recent years more attention has been given to the more ephemeral practices of everyday life and a number of writers have argued that it is these complex rituals of display and interpretation which can illuminate the meanings of our social lives. By extension, the construction of race and ethnicity can be better understood through the addition of analysis of fashion and style. This piece will suggest a number of areas in which this analysis could usefully take place – the history of textile production, migrant and minority workers and the garment industry, and everyday stylistic innovation as an arena of cultural mix and change. In different ways, these themes all illuminate the business of fashion as racialized, just as we have found many other arenas of everyday business to be racialized.

To develop these ideas, we need to set some parameters to the discussion. First, fashion should be defined as a historically specific phenomenon. The term fashion implies a particular phase in the history of clothing and a shift from an idea of clothing as determined primarily by larger constraints of necessity and fixed social status to a more open version of clothing as also a display of individual consumption. When examining this shift, it is important to distinguish between clothing and fashion. The history of costume is as long as written history itself. The story of fashion, on the other hand, is a more recent phenomenon. Fashion implies a culture of consumption which develops only with the rise of mass production. The longer history of clothing shows us that the visible markers of costume often become a means of categorizing the wearer and this categorization can include ethnic classification as well as more formalized hierarchies of status and class. With fashion, these displays of identity and status become part of a larger project of making the self through consumption.

Fashion, as opposed to clothing, has been linked to the rise of modernity and its attendant economic structures. To become fashion, clothing must take on a fiction of personal meaning, even if this is no more than the ability to consume adeptly and/or stylishly. Wilson (1985:12) has suggested that modernity creates fragmentation and dislocation and that the fear of depersonalization haunts our culture – in response, fashion develops as a means of reconciling the wish for individual identity with the mass-produced aesthetics of the industrial age.

Fashion as we understand it largely begins with the rise of mercantile capitalism and the growth of cities. Wilson describes this as the "clear distinction between all forms of traditional dress and the rapidly changing styles that had appeared in Western Europe by the fourteenth century, with the expansion in trade, the growth of city life and the increasing sophistication of the royal and aristocratic courts" (Wilson, 1985:16). Even before the growth of mass production and the development of cultures of individual consumption, fashion as rapidly changing style can be tied to the increase of available goods which came with mercantilism coupled with the more uncertain status and identity systems of city crowds and increasingly complex court structures. In these circumstances, stylistic marking through clothing becomes an important way of telling others who you are.

I want to suggest that the European rise to ascendancy, which encompasses both the development of capitalism and the elastic era of modernity, gives rise to a fiction of white subjectivity as self-authorship. The rest of the world also wishes to self-author, but we come to modernity differently. Fashion is one technique of this self-authorship, and, on occasion, is the technique most available to women. As mechanized and then mass production allow the products of fashion to become more available, the Europeanized world learns to dress up as the best display of its aspirations. For the rest of us, we learn that this is what Western culture looks like.

But long before this point, fashion has been shaping all our destinies.

The Fabric of Empire

The desire to cover and adorn the European body is a central impetus behind the bloody rise to globality of this region. Cloth is among the earliest portable luxury goods to remake the earth in the image of trade and crime.

The production of textiles is intimately tied to histories of colonial exploitation and slavery. Cotton as a product represents the tangled history of forced labor and unequal trade, while silk represents a long history of Orientalist exploration and theft. Beyond the raw materials of fashion, the production of cloth itself has been a highly imperialized affair. All in all, the advent of the levels of production required to develop "fashion" was reached only through the stolen values of colonization.

When Europe first began to appreciate the possibilities of the global and to reinvent its social organization to fit this global aspiration, cloth held a central role in the narrative of desire and possibility. The push to develop a route to the magical and wealthy East harked back to the silk route of ancient times, the promise of a direct path from West to East along which the luxuriant and foreign textures of silk could be transported back to a Europe hungry for fresh forms of ostentation.

While silk signified the promised luxury of far-off lands, cotton brought a different possibility to a Europe creeping into a new and unexpected global role. Cotton was one of those most tasty products of the mercantilist era, and, of course, everyone wanted some. Europe was still wearing wool, when it wasn't wearing animal skin – and although wool production could encompass a range of fabric weights and some diversity of color, the versatility of cotton still came as an exciting and glamorous surprise. The cotton which European traders found was richly various. It could span the heaviness of fustian and the delicacy of muslin. This cloth takes an unheard of range of colours – and in fact the riches of textiles stem from both the marvelous fiber and the dyeing techniques which developed alongside its production. In addition, "the cost of the East Indian calicoes, chintzes, and muslins allowed even the less affluent to own vivid, floral patterned, checked, or plaid clothing or soft furnishings" (Lemire, 1991:13) – so the new cottons made pattern accessible too. Rivaling the luxuriant softness of silk and offering a cheap substitute for the colors and patterns previously available only to the wealthy, cotton soon took hold of the English market. So much so, that Europe began its long history of arguing free trade for our interests, protectionism against yours in relation to the unstoppable spread of cotton fabrics.

> While Bengal was despoiled, Britain's textile industry was protected from Indian competition; a matter of importance, because Indian producers enjoyed a comparative advantage in printed cotton textile fabrics for the expanding market in England.... Parliamentary Acts of 1700 and 1720 forbade the import of printed fabrics from India, Persia, and China; all goods seized in contravention of this edict were to be confiscated, sold by auction, and re-exported.... Later, British taxes also discriminated against local cloth within India, which was forced to take inferior British textiles. (Chomsky, 1993:13–14)

Cotton was a central commodity in Britain's industrialization and, by implication, in the larger rise of capitalism. This has been discussed extensively in many other places. Eric Williams outlines the case for regarding cotton as a central commodity in the development and industrialization of Britain's economy.

> Cotton, the queen of the Industrial Revolution, responded readily to the new inventions, unhampered as it was by the traditions and guild restrictions which impeded its older rival, wool. Laissez faire became a practice in the new industry long before it penetrated the text books as orthodox economic theory. The spinning jenny, the water frame, the mule, revolutionized the industry, which, as a result, showed a continuous upward trend. Between 1700 and 1780 imports of raw cotton increased more than three times, exports of cotton goods fifteen times. The population of Manchester increased by nearly one-half between 1757 and 1773, the numbers engaged in the cotton industry quadrupled between 1750 and 1785. Not only heavy industry, cotton, too – the two industries that were to dominate the period 1783–1850 – was gathering strength for the assault on the system of monopoly which had for so long been deemed essential to the existence and prosperity of both. (Williams, 1964:106)

Williams is describing the particular role played by cotton production on the growth and transformation of the British and then the world economy. Yet the British cotton industry only came to dominate the world market after destroying the cotton industries of India. As always, the lesson is that there is nothing you have which you did not steal from us. Cotton fills a similarly central role in the economic development of the so-called New World – the globally traded cash crop around which a new economy is formed, based on the illegal expropriation of land (from Native America) and the illegal expropriation of labor (from African America).

If silk is the fabric which lures Europeans across the globe on the promise of easy money and unfamiliar opulence – in the process, transforming European aspirations so that the world becomes an entity to be charted, circumnavigated, discovered, in order that the magical alchemy of trade (meaning theft) can spread and meet its society-changing potential – then cotton is the cloth which suggests the opening into industrialization and empire. As the world hurtles through the industrial era, transforming social relations and global interdependence, we have forgotten the role of superficial whims for pretty clothing – because world history must be driven by more substantial motors than fashion.

The Rag Trade and Global Labor

In more recent times, fashion once again becomes the case study of choice through which to demonstrate the new vagaries of the global economy. No longer the archetypal product of economic development and expansion, fashion instead becomes the disparate industry which typifies the nature of work in a new international order. The production of fashion items has spanned the globe for some time, as already discussed – however, something about the structure of fashion production lends itself to exemplifying the unhappy flexibilities of globalized labor. Here we have an industry which still manufactures, but nothing heavy and very differently. The various innovations of outsourcing, home-working, moving production to cheaper labor, replacing all employment with a fiction of self-employment with the accompanying deterioration in working conditions and lengthening of the ever-flexible working day, not to mention the feminized workforce which continued to work when men could not – all of these characteristics make the fashion industry good business for sociologists of the global.

While fashion, on the one hand, takes place through systems of display and consumption which use, variously, techniques of ethnic exclusion and exotic hybridity, on the other, fashion is itself an industry with networks far beyond the moment of product display. This industry has had its own peculiar ethnic politics and, in the West, the shape of the rag trade has been deeply influenced, if not constituted, by particular histories of migration and racialization. The clothing industry, in its just mechanized form, requires limited capital and workspace. The skills of sewing and cutting are transportable, can be carried out alone, and meet a cross-cultural need. In Britain, famously, this labor-intensive market has been filled by successive waves of immigrants, most notably, East European Jewry around the turn of the nineteenth century and beyond and South Asians and Cypriots in the post-1945 period. The poor working conditions of many in the clothing industry have been linked to a variety of racialized accounts, from the tenacious myth of the immigrant small business which exploits its own (womenfolk) in sweatshops to a more widespread exploitation of migrant businesses by multinationals who know how to use the iniquities of institutional racism as an aid to the production of profit. The two explanations say that either, on the one hand, the solidified through migration patriarchy of some communities makes the women into cheap labor for community enterprise or that, on the other, the limited by racism choices of some people leave no room for more comfortable forms of paid work. Whichever explanation you choose, the main point remains – rag-trade work is still low-paid, low-status work in poor conditions and the people who do it are often those who face racism and sexism in the job market. The fashion industry relies on the hyperexploited labor of minority women and those at the higher end of the industry, the creative types, profess not to know about this at all (McRobbie, 1998:143).

Mixing, Borrowing, Stealing

In more recent times, fashion as style has become an object of study and attention as popular forms are recognized as a route to understanding everyday life. Fashion has come to be seen as another technique of displaying the self – and as such is celebrated as a popular and participatory cultural form, a way for everyone to express themselves and make their mark, regardless of income or status. In part this is a reflection of the struggles within the world of fashion, between the cultural capital world of haute couture and the alternative value system of street fashion and its commodified offshoots. Whereas in its institutionalized form fashion has been aligned to the exclusive and capital-intensive worlds of the rich, in the post-1945 period and the discovery of youth as a discrete category, fashion has increasingly sought to capitalize upon the more spontaneous and home-made dress of youth culture.

The recognition of the commercial value of youth transformed aesthetic judgments in fashion. Not only did models become younger – emerging as the precocious children of late twentieth century fashion spreads rather than the resolutely established maturity of the society ladies of earlier fashion photography – commercial fashion came to aspire to a wider aesthetic of the illicit. Part of this wish to appear dangerous is a fascination with exotic others – in the late twentieth century of Westernized global cultures this exoticism continues to be represented (most often, most lazily) through images of people of color. The outcome is that, belatedly for commodity culture, dark skin becomes beautiful, desirable, fashionable, and profitable.

In part this shift in fashion is an echo of a wider shift in cultural hegemony from a Europe of high culture and strict hierarchy to an imagined USA of egalitarian consumer cultures. In the later twentieth century, this fascination with an Americana which signifies freedom, self-discovery, and youth has been cut through with the idea that this adventure of modern living is intrinsically multicultural and, particularly, refracted through a fantasy of African America as most desirable, most urban, most contemporary of ethnic experiences. The global reach of hip-hop culture is an indication of this aesthetic. It goes almost without saying that these commodifications take place alongside a deepening inequality and violence in the USA and, despite the resilience of racist cultures old and new, in the rest of the world. The end result of this process is that the assorted antiglamor of a fashion industry in love with youth, spontaneity, and the ever elusive authenticity of street style, routinely photographs underage white girls in expensive dresses, but styled with the carefully coded accessories of multiethnic global youth culture. Who remembers now that sportswear (the new officewear for young white professionals) used to be a black thing? Or that the fashion for expensive clothes that look ordinary is the expression of a paradoxical longing for class and ethnic locations which are more "real," more authentic?

bell hooks describes this as the desire to be "down" – the desire to partake in a culture which is glamourously dangerous, streetwise, urbane in gritty everyday ways, unlike the studied urbanity of European high cultures and their commodified offshoots such as haute couture. hooks writes,

> The desire to be "down" has promoted a conservative appropriation of specific aspects of underclass black life, whose reality is dehumanized via a process of commodification wherein no correlation is made between mainstream hedonistic consumerism and the reproduction of a social system that perpetuates and maintains an underclass. (hooks, 1994:152)

So now buying glamor is about buying out of too-white cultures which have no style – the white bread connotations of being uncomfortable in your own body and not being able to dance don't fit the transformative promise of fashion. Now when we clothes-shop, we all want a little whiff of otherness, it seems.

In this weekend's newspaper supplement, and in the glossy magazines of the month, I read that yellow is the new color for the new season. Yellow is, apparently, the most unwearable of colors – a color which makes the girls in the makeovers grimace with disgust. Yellow doesn't suit the greyness of the British climate or the greyness of the British complexion and is a downright unforgiving shade all round. I think about my mother's collection of deeply yellow saris – her favorite color – and realize how little I understand about white aesthetics even now. Alongside articles that say, strangely, that yellow is the essential color this season, but is so unflattering that it should be forgotten, I see pictures of a desperately pretty and very dark-skinned girl wearing a variety of canary-colored outfits. And despite the awkward styling of fashion photography, the strange gawkiness that links designer labels to youth style, she looks truly luminescent.

One of the small consolations of frivolous fashion is that now, at last, it is the turn of the white world to be ugly.

References

Chomsky, Noam (1993) *Year 501, The Conquest Continues*. London: Verso.

Hall, Richard (1998) *Empires of the Monsoon, A History of the Indian Ocean and its Invaders*. London: HarperCollins Publishers.

Harnetty, Peter (1972) *Imperialism and Free Trade, Lancashire and India in the Mid-Nineteenth Century*. Manchester, UK: Manchester University Press.

hooks, bell (1994) *Outlaw Culture, Resisting Representations*. London: Routledge.

Lemire, Beverly (1991) *Fashion's Favourite: The Cotton Trade and the Consumer in Britain, 1660–1800*. Oxford: Oxford University Press.

McRobbie, Angela (1998) *British Fashion Design, Rag Trade or Image Industry?* London: Routledge.

Phizacklea, Annie and Wolkowitz, Carol (1995) *Homeworking Women, Gender, Racism and Class at Work*. London: Sage.

Williams, Eric (1964) *Capitalism and Slavery*. London: Andre Deutsch.

Wilson, Elizabeth (1985) *Adorned in Dreams: Fashion and Modernity*. London: Virago.

Chapter 29

Black Art: The Constitution of a Contemporary African-American Visual Identity

Elvan Zabunyan (Translation by Catherine Merlen)

How do African-American artists base their aesthetic problematics in the American society that has made them invisible because of their historical past and their skin color? How do they think out the status of visual works of art that allow them to become visible, most often through a representation of their body? And, how do they emphasize their commitment to a specific culture by appropriating the fundamental components of its history – African heritage, oral narratives, and autobiographical accounts – for the purpose of reviving a memory both individual and collective?

The point here is to study black art because it asserts its belonging to African-American culture by its technique, its historic and aesthetic references, not because it has been achieved by a black-skinned artist. At the same time, the reference to black identity, introduced by issues related to the most visible elements of this racial difference – skin color, hair texture, facial features – is widely used by a majority of visual artists as a fundamental focus of their creative process. Thus, the reflection consisting in outlining the parameters characterizing the analysis of what we call "black art" can be defined in regard to American cultural history, from which it has been and is still mostly missing.

For this purpose, we need to go back to the beginning of the twentieth century and look at the 1920s as a founding moment of African-American culture. This was the era of the Harlem Renaissance, when for the first time in its recent history (the migration of the blacks from the South to the North dates back to the 1910s), the black ghetto went through a period of unprecedented enthusiasm in African-American art. The constitution of a strictly African-American visual identity was therefore determined by its inscription at the heart of an "autonomous" cultural territory. This identity was based on a search for African origins and a will to favor the latter to the detriment of prevailing Western artistic practices. A well-known art historian and philosopher, Alain Locke, author of *The New Negro* (1925) and *The Negro in Art* (1940), was instrumental in the development of these theories.

By creating the New Negro Movement, Locke advocated the importance of Africa as an aesthetic and iconographic source of inspiration and called for the rejection of modern trends in art and the avant-garde of Paris or New York, Paris being then the world center of Western art. In the midst of this "double consciousness," the Harlem Renaissance, for the first time, allowed African-American artists and writers to think of their art according to independent criteria defined by the determination to separate themselves from the mainstream culture.

The forms of expression were narrative, and most of the time they fit into the folk traditions relating to African forebears, drawing their origins from the history of slavery. A shift in the vocabulary used is also detected: in 1922, in one of his poems, Langston Hughes was one of the first to introduce the word *black* to describe his identity.

From then on, the adjective "black" tied to racial identity makes possible the restoration of the social status of the African diaspora stemming from slavery. It labels the idea of a cultural regrouping based on skin color. Opposed to racist theories using the notion of a "black race" to diminish it, it becomes here a form of recognition for a dislocated population. On the model of the writers of the *négritude* movement (Aimé Césaire, Léopold Senghor), a new concept was developed: "blackness." This enables taking a stand in regard to cultural integration, claiming its difference in the midst of a dominant white society. Blackness also plays the role of an antidote against racial segregation.

Blackness was at the center of artistic problematics during the Civil Rights Movement of the 1960s and became a determining factor in a process of black awareness. During that time, considered as the second black revival, after the Harlem Renaissance, artists claimed the right of existence and recognition in a Eurocentric culture that has always rejected them, by placing considerable efforts into the creation of a "protest" art. The Civil Rights Movement encouraged new artistic perspectives in this manner.

Various classifications surfaced among artistic positions. These positions were linked, respectively, to three tendencies of African-American art in the early 1960s. The first, known as "the mainstream," included artists who formally carried Western art criteria into their art practice and showed their support for the "black cause" by taking a stand outside the artistic field. At the heart of the second tendency, "the blackstream," artists revealed their involvement in black identity by the skin color of the characters they represented, but without formal opposition to Western style. The third tendency was the "Black Art Movement," which claimed a complete separation from Western artistic traditions and created a radical language using codes of identification specific to the black community. African-American artists were therefore engaged in the construction of an art that was specifically black, defined in historical and political terms and not solely as a racial affiliation.

Following the experimentation in black aesthetics, the representation of black culture became, for this category of artists, a political claim characteristic of what was known, by the end of the 1960s, as the "Black Experience." In the historical continuum, and contemporaneous with nationalist political stands, there was an implementation of black nationalism in the Black Arts Movement. This also concerned issues and differences theorized at the time between black art and black artists. There is, indeed, a distinction between black artists rallying politically in and through a cultural display, and the organization of a contemporary black art exhibition. In the latter case, the undertaking is aimed explicitly at creating an artistic unity, aesthetically meaningful, while in the first case, the racial affiliation is privileged above all. The boundaries are not always well defined but motivations are clearly divergent in both perspectives. And they raise numerous issues about the legitimacy of the commitment of artists "of color" in the world of visual arts.

The Invisibility Becomes Visual

The particular issues raised take on a great number of criteria – social, economical, historical, cultural, biological – that one must take into account to understand how black artists live out their blackness, and how the racism they endure inevitably shapes the outlook they have on themselves. Visual representation takes all its meaning then from making this invisibility become visual, and determines much in the black visual arts movement (clearly suffering from a lack of acknowledgment, contrary to the African-American musical tradition).

Using means such as painting, sculpture, and photography, artists detach themselves from their own bodies to adopt an external outlook on themselves and acknowledge the "inscription of his/her race in his/her skin." This expression is borrowed from Stuart Hall (1996:16) in his essay on Frantz Fanon's *Peau noire, masques blancs* (1952), in which Fanon says:

> Effective disalienation of the black man entails an immediate recognition of social and economic realities, wrote Fanon. The dependency complex is the outcome of a double process, primarily economic... subsequently the internalization – or better, the epidermalization – of this inferiority. (Fanon [1952], 1986, p. 13)

Looking back at this last idea, Hall outlines the idea of epidermalization. Epidermis is the contact surface between the color black and the person who sees it.

This racial definition intrinsic to the historical and social development of the group can be tied to a study of African-American artistic practices. The artist introduces an aesthetic conception based on a political commitment and a historical conscience of his or her physical identity. The place of the black body and its difference is therefore difficult to deny, even though it clearly supports some racist theories. That difference also takes its meaning from a process of visual creation through the achievement of a critical distance from these so-called physical criteria. The sculptor Melvin Edwards (born in 1937), talking about his work, says:

> Sculpture was more physical than painting. It seemed to me a more direct way to deal with the inner subject. Sculpture allowed me to put in, in a more natural way, things that people were saying you weren't supposed to put in art, like race and politics. It allowed me to think more literally in those ways but have it come out in the work abstractly. (Edwards, quoted in Brenson, 1993:21)

By referring to this "interiority" of the subject, one can also ponder the words of the visual artist, Faith Ringgold (born in 1930), in an interview given in 1972. Here Ringgold accounts for the difficulty she faced in referring to the black image by stating that she painted people green or orange because she was unable to use black. Ringgold here is also experimenting with the critical and political implication in aesthetic research within the

425

visual. As early as the 1960s, in fact, artists were working to create an image different from the one imposed on them, and tried to reverse the "blackness" of the color black by transforming it into "light." In 1970, Faith Ringgold said that "Black Art must use its own color black to create its light" (Lippard, 1984:22) And the art historian Lucy Lippard adds:

> ... With humor and militancy she [Ringgold] "got rid of the white" in her art. She did this both symbolically and literally, by omitting all white pigment. Thus the Black Light Series came from a double source of blackness – formal or aesthetic and social. These were born with the death in 1967 of Ad Reinhardt, whose square Black Paintings were intended to be the "last paintings." It is particularly interesting to reflect on this transmission between a Western artist using the color black as an absence of color and an African-American artist inspired by his work of color – as one would say a woman or a man of "color" – to bring in the color black in her visual work. The inscription of the color black on the canvas becomes a form of "epidermalization" related to the desire to characterize the Blacks without specifically characterizing them. (Lippard, 1984)

This confrontation between the black and the white within visual arts, and the desire to introduce the color black – as color spread on a surface – to reveal its ethical importance beyond its aesthetic use, is particularly important at a time when visual creations have their own symbolism. This constituted in short the severing of an exclusionary relationship with the mainstream.

With visual arts raising questions about the context of their creation, essentially when the context is inherent to a racial or ethnic categorization, African–American artists are confronted by a clear-cut alternative. On one hand, there are artists determined to be part of the art world without the color of their skin being the sole condition of the existence of their work, without their work being presented only at "black" exhibitions.

On the other hand, there are those for whom the main requirement is clearly to claim the color black, and thus allow some autonomy of the creative process, without it relying on any compromise with the white artistic sphere. These artists work at the margin of the established structure, generating a critical work, and propaganda, without worrying about its approval by art professionals of the mainstream.

This contradictory outlook born from artists' accounts reveals the unstable artistic situation of black art. In the second half of the 1960s and the beginning of the 1970s, aesthetic theory is quite confusing when it comes to the description of visual arts practices of the time. And in 1971, in his introduction to *Black Dimensions in Contemporary American Art*, the artist and art historian David Driskell put forward several key elements by questioning the style, content, and reception of African–American art while trying to find in it a specificity that would allow for unity in the black aesthetic. Turning to Elsa Honig Fine's idea of a quest for identity as an ongoing process among African-American artists (1969), she states that as the black artist is endlessly engaged in that quest, an ambiguous "black" style cannot be considered as a "flaw of his/her culture." The black artist needs to start from new bases to create new forms capable of generating a "black" style. In the context of African-American art, the content is tied to a unique experience: being black in the USA. This experience has also given to itself the definition of a style, according to Honig Fine. The issue surrounding style is important, for it reveals the difficulty of supporting black art with a clearly theoretical analysis: its forms are often based on a general understanding embracing many conflicting outlooks, which are not necessarily truly constructive.

Obviously, reflecting on black art as an entity, depriving it of the possibility of aesthetic research, and forcing a style on it, is out of the question. However, black art is said to be considered in relationship to what it expresses – by its content mostly – and then categorized within a stylistic family. The disparity among styles prevents a linear analysis and leads to the contradictory attempt to "unify" through racial association. The explosion of forms is intrinsic to the critical misgivings: there are very few theorists or artists, having thought about black aesthetics in the 1960s–1970s, who managed to build a structure for the analysis. As much as it is impossible to expose a stylistic unity on the sole criterion of skin color, it is not acceptable either to concede to leniency by grouping all the African-American artists without taking into account what singles them out in the creative process. For it is the creative process that definitely allows one to determine the position occupied by the artists in regard to their status as black man or woman in the American mainstream.

It is understandable, accordingly, that the main gap comes from the split between artists attempting to create new forms by embracing a field in visual arts research that no longer refers to the content specifically, and those artists still using academic techniques to represent subjects suggesting realistically black heritage and culture.

The extent of the exclusion African-American artists have suffered is better measured when one places their works back in the context of the contemporary art of the era. By trying to build their identity from a representation of reality in itself close to a narrative (the narrative of their existence), most of the time they become estranged from the artistic reality of their time. One can see that this idea assumes completely new turns with the works of some African-American artists who, in the late 1960s (and for the 30 following years), inhabit that gap and contrast by appropriating for themselves the forms of representation of contemporary art while displaying in it elements specific to African-American culture.

Let us observe also that the aesthetic analysis of black American art is often reliant on an assimilation with black African art. Although African-American artists referring to black African art try in a way to find their roots again, they do it however from an American, rather than from an African, point of view. In the midst of this "double consciousness" (African-American), historians cannot label the black artist within an existing aesthetic category and such artists end up, for want of a label, in a complex position where they must manage to self-define themselves and their artistic work and separate the work from the black self to give it autonomy. One cannot avoid methodological errors then. Why should we, in fact, understand black art as solely rooted in life experience and overlook probable outside artistic influences?

How should we pinpoint the dichotomy between an African-American artist taking part in the mainstream and an artist (who happens to be black) producing a work meant to be shown everywhere, though it is restricted most often to black art exhibitions?

It is almost impossible to assume there is a global black culture that would allow the construction of a black aesthetic identifiable as such. And what is common to most thinkers is to find out whether or not the setting of an artistic exhibition labeled "black art" remains a sufficient step in the elaboration of an artistic identity built around a racial origin without holding it as exclusive. Then again, one is confronted by a case where the definition of a form of visual art attempts to be validated by trying to bridge an artistic void, the void of its invisibility among the world of a white art establishment.

Identities, Identifications

The role of the artists and the theorists of art and African-American culture, for this purpose, are branded by a political responsibility that gained significance following an engagement with the field without concession. However, it is necessary to observe that, despite the efforts made within the framework, for example, of a militant activity at the end of the 1960s and at the beginning of the 1970s, this did not always lead to real artistic recognition of African-American works by the world of American art, even though the latter often cited the combative stance of black artists as a model to be followed. Again, the issue illustrates a shift revealing differences within African-American artistic practices, which do not raise the same interest as their political function.

Culturally and socially, the artists tend to acquire a stature that their works do not have aesthetically. Consequently, it is necessary to consider the evolution of a history of Western art, where art, enriched by the political and social protest movement, starts to integrate new techniques of representations while trying to release itself from the academic tradition. It is in this respect that black artists bring a new outlook to visual aesthetics which also enables them to consider a creative process from a specifically contemporary point of view integrating the memory and the conscience of their black culture and identity.

At the same time, *mainstream* artists in Europe and in the United States speculate about the political scene and the ideological context in which their work was produced. The problematics specific to the creation and reception of the work, and the relationship between art and politics, fit primarily in the artistic field. On the other hand, African-American artists, largely absent from the cultural events of this period, operate primarily in a pictorial and sculptural process without confronting the forms created with a political attitude. There was, however, a common ground of protest, in 1968, with the creation of artistic and political coalitions, which stemmed from various groups – the pacifist militant artists, black artists, women artists (the AWC: Artworkers Coalition, and the BECC: Black Emergency Cultural Coalition). It was a time when many political and social events were discussed on national and international levels – the Vietnam war, the racial and sexual minorities' claims of the Civil Rights Movement and the feminist movement, the students' riots on campuses, the Latin American crisis. Their influence on contemporary artists is important. Many among them, in association with the protest movements, significantly transformed their creative process, striving for artistic practices such as conceptual art, installation art, or performance art (where the body becomes artistic material). This approach underlines the critical function of an art that protests more specifically against cultural institutions to take advantage of the rights of an often discredited artistic status.

These artists produce an art freed of academic techniques and their constraints, which redefines the concepts of space, time, form, and representation by adapting them to the process of creation itself. The inscription of artistic work in an intrinsic space within this process makes it possible to redefine the context of its diffusion and its reception and consequently produces a prospect without precedent where the artist opens up the possibility of raising the idea of art to an artistic stature that can exist without "object." This "object" stature of artwork thus leads to a reflection resting on the "dematerialization" of the artwork for the benefit of a concept.

The new artistic approaches are detached from those approaches instituted by the history of art. They build their own system of values, mainly based on freedom of creation: any material can be conceived as artistic material, any object can endorse the role of the work of art, any image (reproduced or reproducible) can become a visual reference, any action can be considered a form of artistic expression, whether or not it falls under a reduced or expanding space-time constraint, and in spite of its transitory character.

These reflections based on the issue of figurative constraints and pictorial and sculptural academic techniques are common to many American as well as European artists. The practical and theoretical approaches at the end of the 1960s often met at the level of problematics and issues dealing with the notions of the work of art, concept process, and information.

The assimilation of new forms of expression – writing, artistic installation, or urban space performance – indeed allows the freeing of African-American practices confined until then to a traditional representation. It brings to black artists the opportunity to build an artistic work in correlation with African-American social and political requirements, while integrating elements specific to their culture in a form of contemporary expression. How do black artists escape the hierarchy imposed on artistic categories, which belong to the center or the periphery, in order to make current artistic experiments their own, and to develop them by leaving the sphere of standard classifications? It is interesting on this point to note that the displacement of art territories, mentioned by Kynaston McShine in his introductory essay to *The Information Exhibition* organized in 1970 at the MOMA in New York, in some manner already has been integrated by African-American culture, which allows a natural circulation between the disciplines of music, poetry, and painting.

McShine insists on the need for a flexible movement between spaces of creation at a time of constraints and concerns caused by abrupt changes in lifestyles. He proposes a particularly significant alternative for the analysis of contemporary forms of expression based on a renewed definition of art, which is from now on formalized beyond the traditional borders – painting, sculpture, drawing, engraving, photography, film, theater, music, dance, and poetry – as the creation of new forms of representations. The artistic status is moved into a new configuration. The artists work on the concepts of mobility, of changes specific to their time, and are more interested in the possibility of exchanging ideas quickly than in seeing them "embalmed" in an "object." Thus, establishing a close connection with the environment, as well as with the problems and the events that are inherent in it, stimulated in these artists a different experimentation with their own bodies. The body is definitely not perceived in the same manner as in the self-portrait. In fact, the feelings perceived within this environment are observed and studied. We are in a process of artistic thought that poses the issue of the overtaking of art's limits close to what the German artist Joseph Beuys, one of the famous participants in *Information*, defines as "a widened concept of art."

Evoking the originality of the *Information* exhibition, Lucy Lippard notices particularly the participation of Adrian Piper. The artistic work of the African-American artist (born in 1948) undeniably reveals some of the most significant parameters of conceptual art. Her contribution to the exhibition consisted in placing a series of blank notebooks in various places in the museum, thus inviting visitors "to write, draw or otherwise indicate any response suggested by this situation (namely this project: this statement, the blank notebook and pen, the museum context, [their] immediate state of mind, etc...)" (Lippard, 1997:xix). The artist answers the issue of *Information* by reversing the question: information is no longer spreading from the museum towards the public; on the contrary, it is the viewer who is solicited to deliver his or her opinion on the very project of the demonstration. Adrian Piper's work belongs to a particular period of her artistic life when, in 1970, a reversal of her plastic activity took place, following the contemporary political events (the invasion of Kampuchea by the American army, violence on the university campus of Kent State and the emergence of the feminist movement).

This close connection between art and life (Piper's very own, set on trial through the physical performance it imposes on itself) and its visual or spatial processing make Adrian Piper one of the only black American woman artists to have been able to place her work within the mainstream art world at the time, while establishing her creative process on the basis of her racial and sexual identity and to have established a theoretical and practical experiment of its social representation. Piper's approach was built on the duality of art and life, on the involvement of the artist working out of her workshop in the constant observation of the reality of the world, and operating within the very center of urban spaces. It had a profound significance in regard to its artistic reception and its integration in the analysis proper to the process of creation. This same approach became, in an interesting manner, a significant characteristic of African-American artistic productions. It is as if the practices inherited from the art of assemblage, pop art, and conceptual art of the 1960s had enabled black artists to set free their creativity from the constraints imposed by mainstream institutions and the academic techniques of

Figure 29.1   Adrian Piper, "I Embody Everything You Most Hate and Fear," courtesy of Thomas Erben Gallery

Figure 29.2 Adrian Piper, "The Mythic Being Cruising White Women #3," 1975, courtesy of Thomas Erben Gallery

representation, and allowed them to discover a space of unlimited artistic research. This space becomes hospitable to their own urban culture, music, dance, their bodies placed in situation by the performance.

Consequently, a completely new opportunity is created to produce an artistic work defined by and for itself. Even if it remains widely ignored by the mainstream, for historical reasons similar to those that identified earlier generations, African-American art that is pointed in this new direction acquires certain independence without being categorically relegated to the margins of the artistic medium.

Adrian Piper's work is in this respect fundamental. It opens a new prospect for the history of black art by merging elements proper to the contemporaneous character of her work and her racial and sexual identity. With her writings and the visual documentation of her activity, she serves to some extent as a relay, transmitting her artistic experience to the following generation. And, in spite of the fact that her work is relatively little appreciated by her contemporaries – in particular among African-American artists who do not explicitly recognize conceptual practices – she remains essential within the historical framework of the last 30 years. The transformations that she performs in her work, by giving up conceptual art, marginalized her as a consequence. She explains that this distancing is due to her racial identity rather than her sexual identity. She decided to overcome this obstacle by directing all her artistic work towards issues of racism and its consequences on social behavior. Her skin being lighter, she is very easily considered Caucasian, and she clearly introduces this double consciousness of her identity in a dialectical approach where her actions are generated by the denunciation of racism, while being an analysis of it. She distinguishes in fact several forms of

431

racism (unaware, aware but detached, aware and engaged) and tries to contribute to an artistic and theoretical alternative prospect with her visual and intellectual work. Since the mid–1970s, a great number of her writings actually try to define racism, xenophobia, and their consequences. Her definitions take into consideration her personal experience, thus feeding her artistic practice in methods of performance and installation, placing in the scene photographic pictures and drawings. She questions the constitution of her visual identity by putting it in perspective within the intolerant American society.

Contextures

The transition carried out by Adrian Piper's practice is accompanied at the same time by artistic productions which question the role played by art within reality, the status of the artist and his or her work process, the work and its relationship with the context of its creation, from the late 1960s. A work published in 1978 makes it possible for the first time to pursue a methodical analysis of these works. Entitled *Contextures*, this is the initiative of Linda Goode-Bryant and Marcy S. Phillips. The artists involved in the movement of *Contextures* define the properties of art in terms of the objective of going beyond their limits, while consequently integrating these limits into the context of creation. Situated in the continuity of artists working within the art of assemblage and the art of installation, or developing since 1967 processes defined as "anti-form," the African-American artists center their practice not on a reproduction of the available frameworks, but adapt within their works the specific visual parameters of the time, namely, the transformations of the forms of representations such as the ones we analyzed.

Figure 29.3 Senya Nengudi, "Performance Piece," 1977, courtesy of Thomas Erben Gallery

It is thus interesting to note that the concepts of installation art, site-specific settings, and urban space production, which were until then more specific to the artistic practices of the mainstream, become in fact the essential elements of production and comprehension of these "contexturalist" artists' art. Moreover, these concepts prove to be appreciably close to their common interest for the spatial functions of dance and music, of the African-American urban or suburban culture, which are built within the actual space of the city, and the material conditions that constitute it. The appropriation of the latter and its integration in an artistic situation make it possible for black artists to carry out a significant displacement of the elements of their culture. The inscription of these objects in an artistic installation calls for both an aesthetic and a social reading representative of the African-American cultural specificities as well as for their acknowledgement and even their recognition.

From the beginning of the 1970s, Senga Nengudi (born in 1943) has engaged in visual arts through sculptural practice. She creates in particular plastic forms filled with water, and studies the phenomena of weight, volume, and extensibility of a material as well as its brittleness. She directs her investigation towards her own body, which becomes her field of experimentation. Nylon pantyhose worn by the artist is used as material for her sculptures and a feature of her performances. Her training as a dancer enables her to carry out spatial compositions, choreographing the displacements of her body and the extensions of the pantyhose stretched from the ground to the ceiling, from one wall to another, and filled with sand in order to create counterweights which distend the matter. Her use of pantyhose is linked to the human body's elasticity and reinterprets the bodily deformation of black nurses nursing child after child – theirs and those of others – until their breasts slump to

Figure 29.4 Senya Nengudi, "Studio Performance with R.S.V.P.," 1976, courtesy of Thomas Erben Gallery

their knees. "My works are abstract reflections of used bodies – visual images that serve my aesthetic decisions as well as my ideas," (the artist says). Senga Nengudi conceives her creative process like a form in becoming, centered on the movement and the transformation of the body, on the mythologies of the ancestral African or Far-Eastern cultures and the mythologies of contemporary everyday life.

Figure 29.5 David Hammons, "Fragments of the Milky Way," 1992, courtesy of Jack Tilton Gallery

The concept used as a basis for *Contextures* is consequently all the more significant since it comes after an exclusive creation of African-American art: the opening in 1974 of the first black gallery in the midst of the most prestigious and commercial white galleries of the mainstream on 57th Street in Manhattan. Linda Goode-Bryant is again at the origin of

Figure 29.6 David Hammons, "Untitled," 1990, courtesy of Jack Tilton Gallery

the initiative. At 24, she opened Just Above Midtown (JAM) where in 1975 she presented the first New York exhibition of David Hammons and, in 1976, that of Senga Nengudi.

The visual work of Hammons (born in 1943), borrowing from urban reality as well as from his daily experience by the use of common objects transfigured in "sculptures," clearly defines the concepts of *Contextures*. An essential figure in the contemporary history of black art, investigating African-American culture, David Hammons is today one of the most famous artists of his generation. Along with Adrian Piper's, his work brings the first bases of a practical and theoretical reflection to understand the transformations of the black forms of expression in the United States since the outstanding social and political events of the 1960s. While allowing an analysis which is determined by a racial identity clearly stated by the actions and the presence of the body, with constant references to black culture, these artists' works express the assimilation of new artistic concepts while being themselves the actors of these transformations.

Favoring urban space and the anonymous public of the street to the detriment of institutional spaces and the knowledgeable public, David Hammons underlines in his creative process the elements proper to African-American culture, in particular by using recovered materials of everyday life which he integrates in often transient installations. Asserting his black identity and raising political issues in his first works by referring to events that marked the late 1960s, David Hammons keeps himself from producing a political work which would refer primarily to the color of his skin. He insists on the possibility of creating a work that would not be exclusively tributary to the black "cause." At the same time, blackness enables him clearly to pose the stakes of a visual practice that borrows from African-American culture and historical heritage, and to place it in perspective on a broader artistic scale rather than to lock himself up in it.

Hammons' black identity questions the stature of contemporary black culture and the consequences of a historical heritage of slavery for African-American collective memory. By introducing a material like hair into his creative process, he fits explicitly in a visual search for his black cultural identity. For Hammons, hair is an aesthetic material of experimentation and also the symbol of a positive spirituality. Thus, he preserves its spiritual power when he uses it. Blacks' hair also has a status value insofar as it is a physical sign associated with a racial membership. "I belong to the generation which went from segregation to integration, I experienced both," said Hammons. "My approach thus reflects the good and the bad. As one of my friends says, being Black in America means to have had all these problems and to have come out of it while being conscious of one's identity," (Hammons, 1993). One notes indeed aesthetic differences within the practice of the artists who received their artistic formation in the 1950s–1960s and those of the following generation, of the 1970–1980s. The latter take a stand regarding cultural theories that had not been considered before the aesthetic transformations of the 1970s. The appropriation, within the visual arts, of forms of representation borrowed from the media and communication fields – print media, television, advertisements – and their critical alternation, cause new issues for the very definition of the concept of representation. The latter becomes the founding element of postmodern theories applied to visual arts, the artists those particular media of representation that establish a more direct confrontation with daily reality.

References

Brenson, Michael (1993) "Lynch fragments," in Melvin Edwards *Sculpture: A Thirty Year Retrospective, 1963–1993*, exhibition catalog. Purchase, NY: Neuberger Museum of Art, pp.21–33.

Dent, Gina (ed.) (1992) *Black Popular Culture*. Seattle: Bay Press.

Driskell, David C. (1970) *Two Centuries of Black American Art*. Los Angeles: Los Angeles County Museum of Art and Alfred Knopf.

Driskell, David C. (1971) "Introduction," in J. Edward Atkinson (ed.) *Black Dimensions in Contemporary American Art*. New York: Plume Books, pp.9–10.

Fanon, Frantz ([1952] 1986) *Black Skin, White Masks*. London: Pluto Press.

Ferguson, Russell, Gever, Martha, Trinh, T. Minh-ha, and West, Cornel (eds.) *Out There: Marginalization and Contemporary Cultures*. New York: The New Museum of Contemporary Art, MIT Press.

Goode-Bryant, Linda and Phillips, Marcy S. (1978) *Contextures*. New York: Just Above Midtown, Inc.

Green, Renee (1996) *Certain Miscellanies, Some Documents*. Amsterdam, Berlin: De Appel, DAAD.

Hall, Stuart (1996) "The afterlife of Frantz Fanon: Why Fanon? Why now? Why *Black Skin, White Masks?*" in *Fact of Blackness, Frantz Fanon and Visual Representation*. London: Institute of Contemporary Art.

Hammons, David (1991) *Rousing The Rubble*. Exhibition catalog. London, New York, Cambridge, MA: The Institute for Contemporary Art, P. S. 1 Museum, MIT Press.

Hammons, David (1993) "Interview with Robert Storr." *Art Press* 183:13.

Hartman, Saidiya V. (1992) "Excisions of the flesh," in Lorna Simpson *For the Sake of the Viewer*, exhibition catalog. New York, Chicago: Universe Publisher, Museum of Contemporary Art, pp.55–67.

Honig Fine, Elsa (1969) "The Afro-American artist: A Search for identity." *Art Journal* 39.1:32–5.

Honig Fine, Elsa (1982) *The Afro-American Artist: A Search for Identity*. New York: Hacker Art Books.

hooks, bell (1992) *Black Looks, Race and Representation*. Boston: South End Press.

King-Hammond, Leslie (1989) "Art as a verb: Theme and content," in *Art as a Verb: The Evolving Continuum, Installations, Performances and Videos by 13 African–American Artists*, exhibition catalog. Baltimore: Maryland Institute, College of Art.

Kirsh, Andrea (1993) "Carrie Mae Weems, Issues in black, white and color," in *Carrie Mae Weems*, exhibition catalog. Washington DC: The National Museum of Women in the Arts, pp.9–17.

Lewis, Samella (1990) *African–American Art and Artists*. Berkeley: University of California Press.

Lippard, Lucy R. (1984) "Beyond the pale: Ringgold's *Black Light Series*." Catalog exhibition, *Faith Ringgold: Twenty Years of Painting, Sculpture, Performance (1963–1983)*. New York: The Studio Museum in Harlem.

Lippard, Lucy (1990) *Mixed Blessings: New Art in Multicultural America*. New York: Pantheon Books.

Lippard, Lucy R. (1995) *The Pink Glass Swan, Selected Feminist Essays on Art*. New York: The New Press.

Lippard, Lucy (1997) *Six Years: The Dematerialization of the Art Object 1966 to 1972*. Berkeley, University of California Press.

McShine, Kynaston (1970) "Introduction." Information exhibition catalog. New York: Museum of Modern Art, p.138.

Mercer, Kobena (1994), *Welcome to the Jungle: New Positions in Black Cultural Studies*. London: Routledge.

Odita, O. Donald (1997) "The unseen, inside out: the life and art of Senga Nengudi." *NKA, Journal of Contemporary African Arts* Summer-Fall: 24–7.

Piper, Adrian (1996) *Out of Order, Out of Sight, vol. 1, Selected Writings in Meta-Art (1968–1992), vol.11, Selected Writings in Art Criticism (1967–1992)*. Cambridge, MA: MIT Press.

Powell, Richard J. (1997) *Black Art and Culture in the 20th Century*. London: Thames and Hudson.

Read, Alan (ed.) (1996) *The Fact of Blackness: Frantz Fanon and Visual Representation*. London: Institute of Contemporary Arts.

Sims, Lowery S. (1988) "Aspects of performance by black American women artists," in Arlene Raven, Cassandra L. Langer, and Joanna Fruch (eds.) *Feminist Art Criticism: An Anthology*. Ann Arbor, Michigan: UMI Press, pp.207–25.

Schmidt-Campbell, Mary (1985) "Images of a turbulent decade (1963–1973)," in *Tradition and Conflict: Images of a Turbulent Decade 1963–1973*. New York: The Studio Museum in Harlem, pp.45–67.

Tawadros, Gilaine and Dexter, Emma (eds), (1995), *Mirage: Enigmas of Race, Difference and Desire*, exhibition catalog. London: Institute of Contemporary Arts, Institute of International Visual Arts.

Willis, Deborah (ed.) (1994) *Picturing Us: African American Identity in Photography*. New York: New Press.

Chapter 30

The Fact of Hybridity: Youth, Ethnicity, and Racism

Les Back

"Wolf Children" and "Urban Villains"

Since the 1940s the category "youth" has constituted the prime icon of moral concern in Britain, the United States, and elsewhere. Under the Nazi regime a legion of spies were sent out to find out what was happening in the nightclubs where swing youth illicitly enjoyed the forbidden sounds of jazz (Peukert, 1987). Elsewhere on the streets of Los Angeles black men dressed in flamboyant "zoot suits" were stripped naked publicly and beaten up because their ostentatious style offended the patriotic austerity of wartime America (Cosgrove, 1984; see also Chibnall, 1985). Youth culture is conventionally thought of as a product of the postwar explosion of teenage consumption; however this version of cultural history obscures the connection between these "revolts in style" (Melly, 1970) and the cultural politics of race.

In postwar Britain, public forms of disquiet produced a line of youthful urban villains. The need for a more sophisticated, but empirically grounded, approach is underlined by the fact that current debates about race, youth, and urban policy are taking on a new and more complex form. In Britain anxieties about lawless masculinities (Campbell, 1993) and "yob culture" amongst a "new underclass" (Murray, 1994) certainly contain echoes of earlier debates on race, violence, and public safety in the inner city (Hall et al., 1978; Smith, 1986; Solomos, 1988). The contours of the New Right agenda (Jefferson, 1988) remain behind the veil of New Labour's crackdown on antisocial behavior, while white male working-class youth have been for some time the object of public alarm focused on the theme of "rampant racism" and/or "football hooliganism."

Youth is a cipher through which concern is articulated about the nature of a society's past, present, and future (Hebdige, 1988). Youth also becomes a focus for concern about the aftershock of immigration, that is, the destabilization of "settled" identities' patterns of cultural and economic change. Are the third generation children of immigrants identifying with the nation? Can "indigenous" white English youth carry on national customs in the face of global comsumerism? In contrast to the new pathological view of African Caribbean and white working-class cultures often mediated by concerns about crime and violence, the Asian community is often held up as "a model minority." The former Home Secretary Jack Straw commented that "traditional family values" found in Asian communities are a lesson to the whole of the nation (BBC Radio 4, The Today Programme, March 27, 2000). On the other side of this coin is the concern about the presence of world religions, particularly Islam, within British society (Modood, et al. 1994). In news reports, Orientalist representations of Asian youth focus on "Asian gangs" and religious extremism either through the guise of Islamic movements or Hindu nationalism. These are the most recent products of a re-invigorated British Orientalism. It is equally clear from recent reports that there are small sections of the British Asian population that are participating in quite extreme nationalist movements in a translocal fashion (Bhatt, 1997). All of these formations of moral concern existed alongside fears of Asian criminality and gang formation respectively. In this sense, these questions echo domestic disquiet over the settlement of postwar immigration.

Youth crime and lawlessness provides one of the key organizing themes around which moral concern is displayed. Gary L. McDowell and Jinney S. Smith (1999), in their book on juvenile delinquency, claim that youth crime is now reaching crisis proportions in Britain and the United States. The evidence garnered in this book is indeed disturbing. Crime, both against persons and property, is increasing dramatically. For some communities the likelihood of being victims of crime is disproportinate. In another study, Lawrence A. Greenfeld and Maureen A. Henneberg show that in America, black males aged 15 to 24 years old account for nearly 60 percent of the victims of homicides involving firearms while they account for just 7 percent of all persons in that age group (Greenfeld and Henneberg, 1999:28). Homicide is the leading cause of death among young black people – male and female – in the United States. There is no doubt that there are alarming levels of youth crime and violence.

The solutions proffered are perhaps predictable. The tide of juvenile delinquency is the result of a paucity of moral character. The "typical delinquents," they say, come from low income families where poor parenting and lack of socialization impels them into lives of crime and violence. The problem is "moral poverty": the solution a matter of "improving character." It is as if the debates in the 1960s and 1970s about the dangers of cultural pathology never took place. Ultimately, what is needed, they argue, are new forms of moral discipline and virtue that can govern the "wolf-children" (Tuck, 1999:185) of the "savage generation" (Smith, 1999:163). Reading these proposals for tackling youth crime is like watching someone try to lift the head of a perfectly boiled three minute egg with a pickax.

A trans-Atlantic consensus has emerged within governments of the political center concerning the position of young people. This is characterized by an authoritarian youth policy often borrowed from the United States that likes to invoke the idea of youth curfews and antisocial behavior orders in order to promote a communitarian crusade. Jonathan Sacks writes:

> We must have the courage to make judgments, to commend some ways of life and point to the shortcomings of others, however much this offends against the canons of our nonjudgmental culture. We must lead by moral vision and example, and be prepared to challenge the icons of individualism, the idolatry of our age. (Sacks, 1999:111)

Hold on a minute. The general orientation of this book and the general trend it exemplified is precisely about individualism. It's about creating very definite kinds of individual, who possess quite specific types of virtue and docility. The moral gravity engendered here is above all a matter of finding new ways to discipline and punish, or to use Edwin Meese III's telling phrase, it's about "punishing creatively" (Meese, 1999:95).

The voices that are conspicuously absent from this book are those of the "delinquents" themselves. Nowhere are they to be heard. Rather, they appear as statistical aggregates, ideal types, and social composites. There is something deeply problematic about this. The "juvenile delinquent" is not a young person, but an emblem of impending social cataclysm. They are much talked about, but they do not speak. We do not see their faces. They are present only in the shadow-like challenge they cast on public morality. More than this, young people have become the prime site for concerns about cultural continuity and change. Here "minority youth" become central to concerns about the import of foreign differences and the integrity of national culture. My starting point is that any credible discussion, both politically and sociologically, of issues of youth crime or racism or multiculturalism needs to begin by appreciating that young people can speak for themselves, and it might be worth us taking the time to listen. Equally, this is not to suggest that somehow "the kids are all right" and their only problem is the moral edifice of state power that bears down on them. Rather, it is to suggest a disruption that goes two directions. First, I am suggesting a critical evaluation of the way youth is constituted as a site of moral concern. Secondly, I want to argue for dialogue with young people in the spaces of everyday life over their aspirations, identities, and notions of belonging in societies structured by social divisions.

I want to review some of the key debates about the ways in which the cultural politics of youth have been understood. In particular, I want to discuss the contributions made within sociology and cultural studies to the understanding of youth, racism, and ethnicity. My aim here is also to point to some of the ways forward beyond the straightjacket of viewing young people as either "victims" or "problems" (Gilroy, 1987).

"Magical Solutions and Phantom Histories": Youth, Racism, and Style

Much of the early work on race and youth saw the children of migrants as somehow locked in a vice-like grip between two incommensurable cultural blocks, namely, the host society and the culture of the parental home. This literature tended to reinforce a pathological view of minority youth as "caught between" or, equally, somehow on the brink of an impending crisis. What was lost in this approach was an appreciation of what was happening in the interstices of social life where young people themselves were writing their own history of negotiation and exclusion. It was in the embryonic work of cultural studies that a more compelling version of these struggles emerged.

On the symbolic surfaces of youth culture the outline of broader social and cultural transformations could be read (Willis, 1977, 1978). Phil Cohen's influential work on the skinhead and mod youth movements suggested that their origins lay in the economic and cultural crises affecting Britain, and more specifically London, in the working-class districts to the south and the east of the capital in the mid to late 1960s (Cohen, 1972). Characterized by cropped hairstyles, braces, Doc Marten boots, and tight Levi jeans, the skinhead style utilized industrial working-class imagery to produce a conservative masculinity in a period of political, economic, and cultural upheaval. In a brilliant intuitive leap, Cohen suggested that: "the latent function of subculture is this – to express and resolve, albeit 'magically,' the contradictions which remain hidden or unresolved in the parent culture" (1972:23). Working-class racism is thus deeply embedded in the phantasm of melting class and community ties and the compensatory rise of subcultural aesthetics. Drawing heavily on Lévi-Strauss's work on myth, Cohen made the influential argument that youth culture was defined through recombination and bricolage in which the relationship between past, present, and future could be reordered. This aspect of his work was relatively neglected in Marxist-inspired work on youth that drew its theoretical framing from Anton Gramsci (see Hall and Jefferson, 1976). Reflecting on this work over 20 years later Cohen writes: "The notion of subcultural bricolage was somewhat ignored, which was perhaps a pity, given that it prefigured so much of the recent debate on postmodern identities" (Cohen, 1997:50).

The most interesting early attempts to discuss negotiations taking place between black and white young people in British cities is found in the work of Dick Hebdige and Ian Chambers (Chambers 1976; Hebdige 1974a, 1974b, 1979, 1981). Chambers saw that black cultural forms provided a resource on which white youth could draw, thus undercutting and contesting dominant cultural hegemony (Chambers 1976:160). This was particularly telling in the context of skinhead style that was built on a love for Jamaican dance music like ska and rocksteady and American sixties soul (Mercer, 1987, 1994). Hebdige argued in his seminal book *Subculture: The Meaning of Style* that in these styles were the traces of an embodied history:

> The succession of white subcultural forms can be read as a series of deep-structural forms which symbolically accommodate or expunge the black presence from the host community. It is on the plane of aesthetics: in dress, dance, music, in the whole rhetoric of style that we find the dialogue between black and white most subtly and comprehensively recorded, albeit in code. (Hebdige 1979:44–5)

Here Hebdige claims we can view a dialogue of emulation and accommodation. This turned the debate about assimilation on its head. The children of migrants played a part in changing, albeit unevenly, the cultural nature of their generation and what it meant to grow up in a metropolitan environment. Hebdige claimed that the interaction between black and white youth was encoded in youth style and could be read as a kind of "phantom history of race relations."

The question of how to read these histories has become ever more complicated. Since the mid–1980s skinhead style became increasingly popular amongst gay men in London. As mentioned previously there had been gay skinheads from the inception of the culture but during the 1980s and 1990s the style became ubiquitous in gay nightclubs. Murray Healy argues that the gay appropriation of skinhead styles is a complex combination of homoerotic desire, kitsch, and a masculinization of gay culture. The nuances of his argument are beyond the present discussion, but he claims that the pervasive gay adoption of skinhead style is starting to change the associations in London at least. He quotes a gay skinhead who is an active member of the white power music scene, *Blood and Honour*:

> When I first became a skinhead and was walking down the street, you might get a bit of hassle from people, you know, "Nazi Bastard", that sort of thing. Nowadays they say, "Batty man." It doesn't matter who you are – they've never seen you before, you could be covered in White Power tattoos – that's their first image. You get that reaction from straight blokes. For me, the gays have fucked up the Nazi skinhead image. (Healy, 1996:208)

Such combinations of sexual transgression and racial authoritarianism complicate a simple reading of the meaning of skinhead style. The important point to be stressed here is that the outward rigidity of white chauvinism often masks variegated and dissonant combinations of subjectivity. These might be carried and resolved by individual people; Healy argues that the growing public awareness of gay skins has corrupted the association between skins and a conservative, white racist straight masculinity. It is interesting that the skin quoted above invoked the association between skin style and gay London through the Creole homophobic epithet "Batty Man." The fear of being identified as gay is augmented here because these associations are being directed at white skins from a black location. As skinheadism is being globalized, its association with a hypermasculine straight image is being decoupled at "home." However, this may well be confined to London and there is little evidence to suggest that skinhead style has lost its currency as sartorial racism elsewhere in Britain (see Nayak, 1999).

During the same period racist skinheadism was exported to Germany, Czechoslovakia, Poland, Holland, Russia, Switzerland, Sweden, Brazil, Norway, and the United States (Hamm, 1993; Pilkington, 1996; Fangen, 1999). For Fangen the Norwegian white power underground is a countertrend to the fragmentation and insecurity associated with the postmodern condition. The irony here is that these movements are also the product of fragmentation, hybridity, and forms of globalization. As I have tried to argue, the politics of this culture needs to be evaluated carefully in terms of time and place.

Hybridity, New Ethnicities, and Cultural Change

The engagement with black culture also led in some circumstances to a political opening with regard to issues of multiculturalism and racism. Jones (1988) develops this approach in his analysis of white experiences of black youth culture. In his study of a section of Birmingham's youth he shows how reggae music provides a site where dialogues between black and white people can occur. He reports:

> They are visible everywhere in a whole range of cross racial affiliations and shared leisure spaces; on the streets, around the games machines, in the local chip shop, in the playgrounds and parks, the dances and blues, right through the mixed rock and reggae groups for which the area has become renowned. (Jones, 1988:xiv)

Here, the national chauvinism so prevalent in Britain during the 1980s, he argued, is simply redundant. The fact that such a phenomenon existed at all pointed to the emergence of a youthful social sphere in which racism – however fleetingly – could be organized out of social life.

It is significant that it is in sound (i.e., musical culture and language use) that the most profound forms of dialogue and transcultural production are to be found. The onotology of race is profoundly visual. In this sense sound is preontological in that it is impossible to read a human being's body from the sounds that they make. The definition of "racial types" is profoundly linked to fixing the social attributes of human beings in a visual or scopic regime. But aural cultures have different registers of demarcation because they are profoundly about the learning and mastering of codes of expression, be it in the form of learning a style of musicianship or linguistic argot. It is therefore not surprising that

443

some of the most interesting writing about youth, race, and culture have emerged from the writing on Creole language within sociolinguistics. There is a wide literature on the development of a specific British Creole spoken by the children of Afro-Caribbean migrants (Sutcliffe, 1982; Sutcliffe and Wong, 1986). But by far the most comprehensive account is Hewitt's (1986) book *White Talk, Black Talk*, an analysis of two contrasting London neighborhoods, one ethnically mixed and the other predominantly white.

Hewitt's analysis is refined and methodologically grounded in recording observed behavior. He prefigured much of the debate about youth and cultural change and showed the ways in which polycultural elements were being assembled within the mixed ethnicities of urban Britain. This completely confounded the easy reification of the division between "immigrant" and "host" and pointed to the complicated forms of cultural change happening at the micro level. What is interesting here is the complex ways in which negotiations and dialogues between particular groups (in this case between black and white young people) could coexist with the exclusion of refugees, recent migrants, or young people from south Asian communities. In Hewitt's work is the first, and perhaps most convincing account, of how popular racism works within communities of young people and the social forces that both inhibit racist responses and conversely those which exacerbate them (Hewitt, 1996).

Kelly and Cohn (1987) have shown that the concentration on black/white relations can give "interactional politics" a false significance. One of the clear lessons to be garnered from the British experience is that dialogue between Afro-Caribbean and white working-class youth may have little or no impact on the use of racist discourses that are applied by whites to other minorities. This process of triangularization in the geometry of inclusion and exclusion is one of the enduring features of the current situation. In some of London's mixed youth communities the term "Somali" has become a stigmatized form of abuse as used by black and white perpetrators. Equally, there are those, including the British National Party, who claim that "black and white" Britons get along while Bangladeshis keep "themselves to themselves" and "hang around in gangs" (Back and Keith, 1999). Indeed, one of the limits of the debate about the issue of race and youth was its prime focus being limited to the interaction between black and white youth. The result was that little appreciation was given to the way young people from south Asian communities and other ethnic minority communities are both positioned and position themselves within the cultural politics of race and racism.

This situation has begun to change with the emergence of a series of writers discussing the particularities and similarities of south Asian communities and the adequacy of the theoretical and epistemological approaches to "Asian youth" (Sharma, 1996; Kaur and Kalra, 1996; Banerjea, 2000; Gillespie, 1995). Philly Desai has pointed out that to see the involvement of young Bengali men in violent conflict with white peers as a manifestation of "poor race relations" is to miss the patterns of masculine embodied culture that they share (Desai, 1999). In this sense he argues that the process of "assimilation" has been all too effective, in that Bengali men have been integrated into cultures of conflict that both predate immigration and prefigure the experience of growing up in these urban locations. Here it is not a matter of "difference," but rather, of marking division within shared patterns of masculine culture. Violent confrontations are racialized, which in turn become a means to exclude or differentiate between groups of young men who in many respects mirror each other in terms of the forms of cultural embodiment that they perform as they move through the city.

444

One of the most significant things that has emerged from current debates is the importance of articulating the discussion of race and ethnicity with an understanding of gender relations and sexuality (hooks, 1991:77). Paul Gilroy has commented on the importance of appreciation of the ways in which "race", identity, and gender intersect within the emerging forms of black youth culture. Commenting on the controversy over the obscenity trial of Florida-based rap act 2 Live Crew, he reflected:

> An amplified and exaggerated masculinity has become a boastful centrepiece of a culture of compensation that self-consciously salves the misery of the disempowered and subordinated. This masculinity and its relational feminine counterpart become special symbols of the difference that race makes. They are lived and naturalised in the distinct patterns of family life on which the reproduction of their racial identities supposedly lies. These gender identities come to exemplify the immutable cultural differences that apparently arise from absolute ethnic difference. (Gilroy, 1993b:85)

Elsewhere he has argued that the reduction of black culture to the maintenance of a pure racialized body produces a politics that has become "subject-centred to the point of solipsism" (Gilroy, 1993a:26). The intertwining of race and gender provides a key starting point for understanding how old and new versions of blackness are realized.

While stressing the importance of the interconnection between different forms of social division it is equally important to avoid conflating their relationship. Avtar Brah makes this point succinctly when she argues:

> The search for grand theories specifying the interconnections between racism, gender and class has been less than productive. They are best construed as historically contingent and context specific relationships. (Brah, 1993:208)

She goes on to argue that it is important to understand the specific context of any articulation between race and gender if we are to appreciate how the multiple modalities of power interconnect (Brah, 1994:812).

Parminder Bhachu has argued that white feminist representations of Asian women have indulged models of multiple subordination which completely ignore their complex social and economic locations. Stressing the self-determinative qualities of Punjabi Sikh women in 1990s Britain, Bhachu has argued powerfully that these women are: "active agents [who], interpret and reinterpret, construct and reconstruct their identities and cultural locations in [the] process of continuous economic change" (Bhachu, 1991:410). This has been further developed in her most recent work on fashion and design within the south Asian diaspora (Bhachu, forthcoming). Her central argument is that within these "stitching cultures" women established a translocal economy that has achieved commercial success. Similarly, Heidi Mirza has argued that African-Caribbean women in Britain are falsely viewed as multiply subordinated underachievers. She argues that the economic success of young black women has played an important role in redefining black womanhood (Mirza, 1992). Equally, Claire Alexander shows in her book *The Art of Being Black* (1996) that black masculine identities are not an echo of unifying cultural essence but are performed and created within situational, normative, and local arenas "necessarily incomplete, in a state of constant flux and reinvention, engaged in a continual process of 'becoming' " (Alexander, 1996:199). There are two important points that emerge from these ethnographies. First, it is vitally important to understand that the interplay of ethnicity and gender does not produce mechanistic outcomes that can be easily predicted. Second, they foreground the importance of developing detailed accounts of the precise nature of this articulation.

The consequence of this work was that categories like "immigrant" and "second generation" started to be subject to critical examination. Equally, the notion that the children of migrants are somehow caught "between two cultures" was exploded. Up until this point, the debate about young people of ethnic minority backgrounds were seen as about either victims or problems (Gilroy, 1987). In the aftermath of these debates a whole series of questions were raised about the intersection of race, gender, and nation and the relationship between racism, identity, and belonging. This has led to a greater attention to the ways in which traditions are re-inscribed within postcolonial context and a focus on the issue of cultural hybridity. Homi Bhabha has pointed out the ways in which these patterns of culture have confounded the cultural order of colonialism, producing what he referred to as "hybrid displacing space" (Bhabha, 1991). Similarly, Stuart Hall called for an understanding of how notions of identity work through difference in the context of the "new ethnicities" produced in these urban metropolitan settings (Hall, 1988). Young people become the privileged bearers of cultural dynamism and change. While the emphasis on hybridity challenged earlier accounts of cultural pathology amongst "immigrant youth," its consequence is to saddle minority young people with the millstone of being the ones to deliver "newness" and transformation. Beyond this hybrid, cultural forms need not necessarily be connected with progress or any form of progressive populism. Indeed, these patterns of culture may be radical in their attention to a return to national radicalism and the concerns of roots and soil.

Chetan Bhatt has pointed to the ways in which forms of diaspora nationalism reinforce and reinscribe essentialist and exclusive forms of communal ideology. These movements operate within translocal routeways while strengthening an exclusively Hindu claim to Indian soil. The Rashtriya Swayamsevak Sangh (RSS), a semimartial organization set up in the 1920s, aims to implant Hindu supremacist ideology and encourage physical training among Hindu young men. This project has a specific youth orientated form through the RSS branches or *Shakhas* that promote Hindu education through storytelling, games, physical activities, and quizzes. He writes of this organization in the UK:

> Children's *shakhas* can be innocuous enough and can tap into the concerns of parents that their children do not speak Gujarati at home or are losing their Hindu religion of culture in Western society...Apart from basic literacy, the objective in children's *shakhas* is to emphasize Vedic heritage, what are seen as the Hindu origins of achievements in modern science and technology, to inculcate nationalism and to promote Hindu unity, self-reliance and discipline through games, stories and moral tales. Salute (*pranam*) to the saffron (*bhagawa dhwaj*) begins and ends the *shakha*. The RSS's distinctive salute cannot but invoke for the onlooker the period of the 1930s in Europe. (Bhatt, 2000:581–2).

This important work calls into question the easy coding of diaspora culture or postcolonial hydridity as progressive or transgressive. I want to return to this issue later but before that I want to first look at contemporary shifts in the cultural politics of youth, race, and nation in the United Kingdom.

Cool Britannia?: Britain between Windrush and Macpherson

With the coming to power of the Labour government in 1997 there was a pervasive hope that we might be going into a new phase in the cultural politics of race in Britain. The new government sought to brand itself by rejecting the language of race and nation that so dominated the Thatcher period and offering an image of Britain that was more inclusive and in which the management of diversity could take place. It is true to say that Blair has embarked on an ambitious program of developing government, an example of which is the opening of assemblies in Scotland and Wales, and also actively promoting a particular image of multicultural Britain under what came to be called "Cool Britainnia."

It's no surprise then that Chris Smith, the former Secretary of State for Culture, Media and Sport, highlighted British youth culture in his book *Creative Britain*:

> British bands such as Blur, Oasis, the Prodigy, Pulp and the Verve dominate much of the rest of the world. Singers such as Roni Size and Jazzie B. are putting black music on the map. And the British record and CD industry – as a result of the talent that lies behind it – is one of the great strengths of our modern economy. (Smith, 1998:7)

A small quibble here that neither Jazzy B. nor Roni Size are singers in any conventional sense. He went on to boast that the British music industry was currently worth four billion dollars to the UK economy and two billion dollars worth of this income comes from overseas sales and the record industry employs some 115,000 people. Then without a hint of selfconciousness he commented: "Its net export earnings are bigger than those of our steel industry, and our musicians' union is now bigger than our miner's union" (p. 81). The paradox here is that the lifeblood of much of the subcultural dynamism of Britain's youth was a seismic echo of the political and economic crisis that racked Britain during the 1970s and 1980s and now it has emerged as one of its most significant industries. This in itself casts a shadow over the early subcultural analysts of the "New Left" who claimed that in every "safety pin" and "Ben Sherman" shirt could be found the vestiges of youth cultural refusal and resistance.

The absurdity of this situation is captured by the fact that while New Labour has adopted the language of diversity and racial justice it has also overseen some of the most authoritarian initiatives directed against young people, and an incredibly stringent immigration policy. The tremors of moral concern about the domestic quality of "the youth question" have been in large part separated from a wider concern about the "new immigration." In recent times we have seen a tidal wave of xenophobia hit Britain surrounding the new immigration in the form of asylum seekers and refugees. What is significant about this is the degree to which domestic cultural politics of race and youth are seen as distinct to what Stephen Dobson calls the "border questions" relating to refugees and asylum seekers (Dobson, 1999). The venom and crudeness of the public outcry revolves around the image of "beggars" and "violent crime" which have become a routine reference point in the media. The general context is that asylum seekers are living below the poverty line, surviving on vouchers that can only be traded for goods, and subject to a dispersal policy that is aimed to inhibit them settling in particular areas together. Meanwhile, liberal or even left-wing politicians try to justify these draconian measures as being "fair."

All this casts a considerable shadow on exactly how "cool" is Cool Britannia under New Labour? Perhaps predictably, not all young people are benefiting from the current prosperity. Broken down into the following sectors a picture is emerging of the nature of the continued social inequality between young white people and young people from ethnic minorities backgrounds. Also, recent evidence shows that there are growing divisions within minority communities. The Labour Force survey for 1997 showed:

- The white population has higher employment rates than ethnic minority groups and lower unemployment rates for both men and women. Unemployment rates for black African (25 percent) and Bangladeshi men (20 percent) were three times more than those for white men (7 percent).
- For 16–24 year olds, the highest unemployment rate is for black youths (Caribbean, African and other) and this is true for males (41 percent) and females (36 percent). Whites have a much lower unemployment rate in comparison (15 percent for males and 11 percent for females).

In terms of income 82 percent of Bangladeshi households had below half average income (compared with 28 percent of whites and approximately 40 percent for other groups) (Modood et al., 1997). Income from self-employment formed a lower proportion of total income of households headed by a member of a black ethnic group (3 percent) and a higher proportion for those whose head of household was of Indian origin (16 percent) than those headed by members of other ethnic groups. These harsh realities lay underneath the celebration of diversity proclaimed by the Labour government.

Indeed it seems that we are witnessing the political proliferation of "diversity talk" while trading in the currency of rejuvenated national pride. Paul Gilroy has referred to this second impulse as a form of postcolonial melancholia (Gilroy, 1999), a condition that echoes the distinction made by Freud between a process of mourning that reckons with the loss of bereavement and eternal cycles of solipsism and neurosis. In Freud's reflections he talks about the ways in which the object of melancholia can sometimes be elusive: "...one cannot see clearly what it is that has been lost, and it is all the more reasonable to suppose that the patient cannot consciously perceive what he has lost either" (Freud, 1991:254). Similar things might also be said of the crisis of equally impalpable ideas like Englishness and whiteness. For Gilroy, British political life is caught like a grieving child unable to move beyond, or let go of, the death of an imperial parent. This in itself inhibits the coming of age of a truly heteroglot notion of Britishness.

Recently, Stuart Hall has argued that the future of the whole society is dependent on moving beyond the conflation of race and nation. He said in a radio interview:

> The British have a future only if they can come to terms with the fact that Britishness is not only one thing... If you think of last year, first of all there was the celebration of the Windrush arrival. Which is 50 years since the first postwar migrants. On the other hand there's the Macpherson Inquiry into the death of Stephen Lawrence. It seems to me that Britain is facing these two possibilities as an alternative future... I want the British to consciously move towards, in a more concerted and open way, a more cosmopolitan idea of themselves. (BBC Radio 4, February 12, 2000)

Anne Phoenix has pointed out that the reality of Britain today is the proliferation of complex articulations of multiple racisms and multicultures. She argues that "the contradictions and complexities of multicultures and multiracisms are a notable legacy of the Windrush" (Phoenix, 1998:96). However, the radical reconfiguration of the notion of cosmopolitanism suggested by Hall has its detractors. This is largely around the controversy surrounding the emphasis on cultural hybridity. As Kobena Mercer has commented: "the subversive potential once invested in notions of hybridity has been subjected to pre-millennial downsizing. Indeed, hybridity has spun through the fashion cycle so rapidly that it has come out the other end looking wet and soggy" (Mercer, 2000:235).

Pnina Werbner (1997), drawing on a point made by Bakhtin, suggests that "organic hybridity" is a feature of all languages and by extension all human cultures. She argued that the assimilation of difference, or new cultural influences, occur in an unconscious fashion, leaving intact a presumption of exclusive ownership in the culture of the assimilator. The diversity of cultural traces in urban life remains latent, mute and opaque (Ahmad, 1995). Others like Robert Young suggest that the emphasis on hybridity "assumes, as with the nineteenth century theorists of race, the prior existence of pure, fixed separate antecedents" (Young, 1995:25).

Young's critique, which suggests that the new cultural theory implicitly legitimates race thinking, needs to be evaluated carefully. His line of argument insists on tieing the meaning of hybridity to the legacy of race thinking. Past discourse determines present usage like some kind of embalming agent. He thus sidesteps the relationship between past, present, and future and between the places and contexts in which cultural practices are manifest. It is important to neither reduce the present to the past as does Young's analysis, nor suggest that the notion of hybridity constitutes a total break with the past. Novelty always has a relationship to its antecedence, but the impulse to read the present only through genealogy is to miss the significance of place and time. I want to argue for developing a more complex appreciation of the sites and times of hybridity. The genealogical approach to this debate never really tries to problematize the distinction in the theoretical imagination between figurative and literal meaning. When Gilles Deleuze uses the metaphor of "rhizome" to express lateral interconnection, no one with any sense should think he is suggesting that the properties of irises and human beings are somehow the same.

Others have objected to the discussions of cultural hybridity because it does not recognize the internal coherence of cultural differences, and accuse "hybridity talk" of being produced by a black intellectual elite and politically inert academics (Friedman, 1997; Hutnyk, 1997). Interestingly these "anthropological conservatives" (a phrase coined neatly by Paul Gilroy, 2000:271) can be drawn from both left and right. Their blasts of hyperpolitical posturing are little more than a vain attempt to congeal the melting foundations of anthropological authority.

Lastly, there is the charge that trying to rethink the variegations of culture and radical cosmopolitanism can be all too quickly assimilated by the desire to exploit exotica and difference commercially. These critiques often invoke an unspecified "progressive" political alternative (see Hutnyk, 1997, 2000). The idea that corporate interests assimilate cosmopolitan impulses is not new. Marx commented in 1848 that production and consumption under capitalism would take on a "cosmopolitan character" (Marx and Engels, 1998:39). No doubt this objection names an important process but the problem with it is that he *reduces* the cultural politics of hybridity to its commodified forms. Paradoxically, this line of critique is so locked in the logic of capitalism in which everything is fetish, that there is no conception of other regimes of value that are not governed by what is wrapped, bought, or sold. What is too easily taken for granted, or not grasped, is what I want to call the *fact of hybridity*.

Frantz Fanon wrote that the fact of blackness was defined by ways in which racism operated through a visual regime. In white eyes blackness is fixed as "an object in the midst of other objects" (Fanon, 1986:109). The fact of hybridity is registered in a wider range of senses, that is less tied to the maintenance of absolute boundaries of distinction and difference in human kind. What I mean by this is best illustrated by an experience rendered by Rachel Lichtenstein in the book she wrote with Iain Sinclair entitled *Rodinsky's Room*. The book is an extraordinary chronicle of her story to find out what happened to an anchorite Jewish scholar called David Rodinsky who vanished in the late 1960s from his garret above the Princelet Street Synagogue in Whitechapel, East London. As part of her search she traveled to Poland where Rodinsky and his family had lived before migrating to London. There she joins a seminar on Polish-Jewish history mostly attended by people returning to Poland in search of fragments of their own family histories. To her surprise there are also some young Poles on the course, including someone whom she describes as:

> a gentle young man called Tomek from Warsaw. "I am a Catholic but have a growing interest in Jewish life. This began when I was twelve years old and visited the Jewish cemetery in Poznan and began to ask questions. Last year I spent the summer in Israel and I am presently studying Hebrew." Tobie, an angry young fashion victim from Los Angeles, mutters, "What are you, a Jewologist?" We laugh but this is a new phenomenon, Poles who feel the loss, who see the footsteps of the former Jews embedded in their streets, hear the whispers in their music, taste the remnants in their food. (Lichtenstein and Sinclair, 1999:210–11)

This story illustrates the potential for a critical calculation with the legacy of racism and genocide to emerge from the fact of hybridity. These intertwined and overlapping (Said, 1993) histories make the total separation of self and other near impossible.

Yet, the verity of multiculture brings no guarantees. An attention to it demands some reckoning with the limits of sameness and the melancholic preoccupation with nationalism and race. These moments of critical opening cannot be reduced to a political manifesto, or some didactic call to arms of the sort that tenured revolutionaries yearn for. Rather, they point to quiet transformations and fleeting moments in which living with and through difference are realized. As Mette Andersson pointed out, in her excellent study of the experience of ethnic minority youth in Norway, young people are "constituted through difference, but through this spatially and temporally located construction, they shape new modes of subjectivity. They are creative actors, and not passive adapters to external ascriptions of identity" (Andersson, 2000:304).

It is within the urban crucible of modernity's "melting vision" (Berman, 1999) that traditions are made and invented in the present. Rendering explicit the multiple influences that resonate within metropolitan contexts like London, Amsterdam, Paris, Hamburg, Berlin, or Oslo is more than an academic enterprise; it can provide a means to make visible the threads which the discourse of race and nation have bleached from the fabric of society. However, this is of course not in itself enough. As Ali Rattansi and Ann Phoenix have pointed out: "Increasingly, the frame has to be one in which the intersections of local/global have to keep the multiplicity, relative fluidity and hybridity or syncretism of youth identities also in focus, without forgetting that identificatory processes always occur in micro sites" (Rattansi and Phoenix, 1997:143). What I want to argue for is the need to engage in dialogue with young people in innovative ways in order to establish how the "fact of hybridity" is lived and coexists with racism, exclusion, and essentialized definitions of identity, belonging, and entitlement.

References

Ahmad, Aijaz (1995) "The politics of literary postcoloniality." *Race and Class* 36,3:1–20.

Alexander, C. (1996) *The Art of Being Black: The Creation of Black British Youth Identities*. Oxford: Clarendon Press.

Andersson, M. (2000) *"All Five Fingers are Not the Same": Identity Work Among Ethnic Minority Youth in an Urban Norwegian Context*. Bergen, Norway: IMER Centre for Social Science Research, University of Bergen.

Back, L. and Keith, M. (1999) "Rights and wrongs: Youth, community and narratives of racial violence," in P. Cohen (ed.) *New Ethnicities, Old Racisms?* London: Zed Books, pp.131–62.

Banerjea, K. (2000) "Sounds of whose underground? The fine tuning of diaspora in an age of mechanical reproduction." *Theory, Culture and Society* 17,3:64–79.

Barker, M. (1981) *The New Racism*. London: Junction Books.

Berman, M. (1999) *Adventurees in Marxism*. London: Verso.

Bhabha, H. K. (1991) "The postcolonial critic." *Arena* 96:47–63.

Bhabha, H. K. (1994) *The Location of Culture* London: Routledge.

Bhachu, P. (1985) *Twice Migrants: East African Settlers in Britain*. London: Tavistock.

Bhachu, P. (1991) "Culture, ethnicity and class among Punjabi Sikh women in 1990s Britain." *New Community* 17,3:401–12.

Bhachu, P. (forthcoming) *Dangerous Designs*. London: Routledge.

Bhatt, C. (1997) *Liberation and Purity: Race, New Religious Movements and the Ethics of Postmodernity*. London: UCL Press.

Bhatt, C. (2000) "Dharmo rakshati rakshitah: Hindutva movements in the UK." *Ethnic and Racial Studies* 23,3:559–93.

Brah, A. (1993) "Difference, diversity and differenciation," in J. Wrench and J. Solomos (eds.) *Racism and Migration in Western Europe*. Oxford: Berg, pp.195–214.

Brah, A. (1994) "Time, place and others: Discourses of race, nation, and ethnicity." *Sociology* 28,3:804–13.

Campbell, B. (1993) *Goliath: Britain's Dangerous Places*. London: Lawrence and Wishart.

Chambers, I. (1976) "A strategy for living": Black music and white subcultures, in S. Hall and T. Jefferson (eds.) *Resistance Through Rituals*. Birmingham, UK: Centre for Contemporary Cultural Studies, pp.157–66.

Chibnall, S. (1985) "Whistle and zoot: The changing meaning of a suit of clothes." *History Workshop* 20:56–81.

Cohen, P. (1972) *Subcultural Conflict and Working-Class Community*. CCCS Working Papers 2. Birmingham, UK: University of Birmingham, Centre for Contemporary Cultural Studies.

Cohen, P. (1997) *Rethinking the Youth Question: Education, Labour and Cultural Studies*. Basingstoke, UK: Macmillan.

Cosgrove, S. (1984) "The zoot suit and style warfare." *History Workshop* 18:77–91.

Desai, P. (1999) "Spaces of identity, cultures and conflict: The development of new British Asian masculinities," PhD thesis, Goldsmiths College, University of London.

Dobson, S. (1999) "Cultures of exile: An examination of the construction of 'Refugeeness' in Contemporary Norwegian Society." Dissertation submitted for the degree of Doctor of Philosophy in the Graduate Studies and Research in Humanities, Nottingham Trent University.

Fangen, K. (1999) *Pride and Power: A Sociological Interpretation of the Norwegian Radical Nationalist Underground Movement*. Department of Sociology and Human Geography, University of Oslo.

Fanon, F. (1986) *Black Skins, White Masks*. London: Pluto Press.

Freud, S. (1991) "Mourning and melancholia," in S. Freud *On Metaphysics: The Theory of Psychoanalysis*. London: Penguin Books, pp.251–68.

Friedman, J. (1997) "Global crises, the struggle for cultural identity and intellectual porkbarrelling: Cosmopolitans versus locals, ethnics and nationals in an era of de-hegemonisation," in P. Werbner and T. Modood (eds.) *Debating Cultural Hybridity: Multi-cultural Identities and the Politics of Anti-Racism*. London: Zed Books, pp.70–89.

Gillespie, M. (1995) *Television, Ethnicity and Cultural Change*. London: Routledge.

Gilroy, P. (1987) *There Ain't No Black in the Union Jack: The Cultural Politics of Race and Nation*. London: Hutchinson.

Gilroy, P. (1990) " 'One nation under a groove': The cultural politics of 'Race' and Racism in Britain," in D. T. Goldberg (ed.) *Anatomy of Racism*. Minnesota: University of Minnesota Press pp.263–82.

Gilroy, P. (1993a) *The Black Atlantic: Modernity and Double Consciousness*. London: Verso.

Gilroy, P. (1993b) *Small Acts: Thoughts on the Politics of Black Cultures*. London: Serpent's Tail.

Gilroy, P. (1999) *Joined Up Politics and Post-Colonial Melancholia*. London: Institute of Contemporary Arts Diversity Lecture.

Gilroy, P. (2000) *Between Camps; Nations, Cultures and the Allure of Race*. London: Allen Lane.

Greenfeld, L. A. and Henneberg, M. A. (1999) "Youth violence and the backgrounds of chronic violent offenders," in G. L. McDowell and J. S. Smith (eds.) *Juvenile Delinquency in the United States and the United Kingdom*. Basingstoke, UK: Macmillan, pp.23–44.

Hall, S. (1978) "Racism and reaction," in Commission for Racial Equality (ed.) *Five Views of Multi-racial Britain*. London: Commission for Racial Equality, pp.23–35.

Hall, S. (1980) "Race, articulation and societies structured in dominance," In UNESCO *Sociological Theories: Race and Colonialism*. Paris: UNESCO.

Hall, S. (1988) "New ethnicities," in *Institute of Contemporary Arts Documents: Black Film/ British Cinema*. London: ICA/BFI, pp.27–31.

Hall, S. and Jefferson, T. (eds.) (1976) *Resistance Through Rituals: Youth Subcultures in Post-war Britain*. Birmingham, UK: Centre for Contemporary Cultural Studies.

Hall, S., Critcher, C., Jefferson, T., and Roberts, B. (1978) *Policing the Crisis: Mugging, the State and Law and Order*. London: Macmillan.

Hamm, M. (1993) *American Skinheads: The Criminology and Control of Hate Crime*. Westport, CT: Praeger.

Healy, M. (1996) *Gay Skins: Class, Masculinity and Queer Appropriation*. London: Cassell.

Hebdige, D. (1974a) "Aspects of style in the deviant subcultures of the 1960s." MA thesis, Centre for Contemporary Cultural Studies, University of Birmingham.

Hebdige, D. (1974b) "Reggae, rastas and rudies: Style and the subversion of form." Stencilled paper 24, Centre for Contemporary Cultural Studies, University of Birmingham.

Hebdige, D. (1979) *Subculture: The Meaning of Style*. London: Methuen.

Hebdige, D. (1981) "Skinheads and the search for a white working class identity." *New Socialist*, September: 38.

Hebdige, D. (1982) "This is England! And they Don't Live Here," in Nick Knight (ed.) *Skinhead*. London: Omnibus Press, pp.26–35.

Hebdige, D. (1987) *Cut n' Mix: Culture, Identity and Caribbean Music.* London: Routledge.

Hebdige, D. (1988) *Hiding in the Light: On Images and Things.* London: Routledge.

Hewitt, R. (1982) "White adolescent Creole use and the politics of friendship." *Journal of Multilingual and Multicultural Development* 3,3:217–32.

Hewitt, R. (1986) *White Talk, Black Talk: Inter-Racial Friendship and Communication Amongst Adolescents.* Cambridge, UK: Cambridge University Press.

Hewitt, R. (1988a) *Social Context and the Ludic Elements in Adolescent Verbal Interaction*, Working Papers in Adolescent Language Use. London: Institute of Education.

Hewitt, R. (1988b) "Youth, race and language: Deconstructing ethnicity?" Paper given at the Conference on the Sociology of Youth and Childhood, Philipps University, Marburg, West Germany, November 14–15.

Hewitt, R. (1996) *Routes of Racism: the Social Basis of Racist Action.* London: Trentham Books.

hooks, b. (1991) *Yearning: Race, Gender and Cultural Politics.* London: Turnaround.

Hutnyk, J. (1997) "Adorno at Womad: South Asian crossovers and the limits of hybridity talk," in P. Werbner and T. Modood (eds.) *Debating Cultural Hybridity: Multiculturalism and the Politics of Anti-Racism.* London: Zed Books, pp.106–38.

Hutnyk, J. (2000) *Critique of Exotica: Music, Politics and the Culture Industry.* London: Pluto Press.

Jeater, D. (1992) "Roast beef and reggae music: The passing of whiteness." *New Formations*, 18, Winter: 107–21.

Jefferson, T. (1988) "Race, crime and policing." *International Journal of the Sociology of Law* 16,4:521–39.

Jones, S. (1986) "White youth and Jamaican popular culture." Ph. D. thesis, Centre of Contemporary Cultural Studies, Faculty of Arts, Birmingham: University of Birmingham.

Jones, S. (1988) *Black Youth, White Culture: The Reggae Tradition from JA to UK.* Basingstoke, UK: Macmillan.

Kaur, R. and Kalra, V. (1996) "New paths for South Asian identity and musical creativity," in Sanjay Sharma, John Hutnyk, and Ashwani Sharma (eds.) *Dis-Orienting Rhythms: The Politics of the New Asian Dance Music.* London: Zed Books, pp.217–31.

Kelly, E. and Cohn, T. (1987) *Racism in Schools: New Evidence.* Stoke-on-Trent, UK: Trentham Books.

Lichtenstein, R. and Sinclair, I. (1999) *Rodinsky's Room.* London: Granta Books.

Macpherson, W. (1999) *The Stephen Lawrence Inquiry Report by Sir William Macpherson of Cluny.* February 1999 Section 6.34.

Marx, K. and Engels, F. (1998) *The Communist Manifesto: The Modern edition.* London: Verso.

McDowell, G. L. and Smith, J. S. (eds.) (1999) *Juvenile Delinquency in the United States and the United Kingdom.* Basingstoke, UK: Macmillan.

Meese, E. (1999) "Common sense and juvenile justice in America," in G. L. McDowell and J. S. Smith (eds.) *Juvenile Delinquency in the United States and the United Kingdom.* Basingstoke, UK: Macmillan, pp.87–98.

Melly, G. (1970) *Revolt into Style: The Pop Arts in Britain.* Harmondsworth, UK: Penguin Books.

Mercer, K. (1987) "Black hair/style politics." *New Formations* 3, Winter: 33–56.

Mercer, K. (1994) *Welcome to the Jungle: New Positions in Black Cultural Studies.* London: Routledge.

Mercer, K. (2000) "A sociography of diaspora," in P. Gilroy, L. Grossberg and A. McRobbie (eds.) *Without Guarantees: In Honor of Stuart Hall.* London: Verso, pp.233–44.

Miles, R. (1989) *Racism.* London: Routledge.

Mirza, H. (1992) *Young, Female and Black.* London: Routledge.

Modood, T., Beishon, S., and Virdee, S. (1994) *Changing Ethnic Identities.* London: Policy Studies Institute.

Modood, T., Berthoud, R., Lakey, J., Nazoo, J., Smith, P., Virdee, S., and Beishow S. (1997) *Ethnic Minorities in Britain: Diversity and Disadvantage.* London: Policy Studies Institute.

Murray, C. (1994) *The Underclass: The Crisis Deepens*. London: Inner London Education Authority Health and Welfare Unit.

Nayak, A. (1999) "Pale warriors: Skinhead culture and the embodiment of white masculinities," in A. Brah. M. J. Hickman, and Máirtín Mac an Ghaill (eds.) *Thinking Identities: Ethnicity, Racism and Culture*. Basingstoke, UK: Macmillan, pp.71–99.

Peukert, D. J. K. (1987) *Inside Nazi Germany: Conformity, Opposition and Racism in Everyday Life*. London: Penguin Books.

Phoenix, A. (1998) "'Multicultures,' 'Multiracisms' and Young People." *Soundings* 10, Autumn: 86–96.

Pilkington, H. (1996) "Farewell to the Tusovka: Masculinities and feminities on the Moscow youth scene," in H. Pilkington *Gender, Generation and Identity in Contemporary Russia*. London: Routledge.

Rampton, M. B. H. (1989) *Evaluations of Black Language Crossing and the Local Sociocultural Order*, Adolescence and Language Use Working Paper, No. 3. London: Institute of Education.

Rattansi, A. and Phoenix, A. (1997) "Rethinking youth identities: Modernist and postmodernist frameworks," in J. Brynner, L. Chisholm and A. Furlong (eds.) *Youth, Citizenship and Social Change in a European Context*. Aldershot, UK: Ashgate, pp.121–50.

Sacks, J. (1999) "Law, morality and the common good," in G. L. McDowell and J. S. Smith (eds.) *Juvenile Delinquency in the United States and the United Kingdom*. Basingstoke, UK: Macmillan, pp.99–112.

Said, E. (1978) *Orientalism*. London: Penguin.

Said, E. W. (1993) *Culture and Imperialism*. London: Chatto & Windus.

Sharma, S. (1996) "Noisy Asians or 'Asian Noise' in Sanjay Sharma, John Hutnyk, Ashwani Sharma (eds.) *Dis-Orienting Rhythms: The Politics of the New Asian Dance Music*. London: Zed Books, pp.32–57.

Smith, C. (1998) *Creative Britain*. London: Faber and Faber.

Smith, S. J. (1986) *Crime, Space and Society*. Cambridge, UK: Cambridge University Press.

Smith, J. S. (1999) "Reducing delinquency by improving character," in G. L. McDowell and J. S. Smith (eds.) *Juvenile Delinquency in the United States and the United Kingdom*. Basingstoke: Macmillan.

Solomos, J. (1988) *Black Youth, Racism and the State: The Politics of Ideology and Policy*. Cambridge, UK: Cambridge University Press.

Sutcliffe, D. (1982) *British Black English*. Oxford: Blackwell.

Sutcliffe, D. and Wong, A. (1986) *The Languages of the Black Experience*. Oxford: Blackwell.

Tuck, M. (1999) "Afterword: How can young men learn virtue," in G. L. McDowell and J. S. Smith (eds.) *Juvenile Delinquency in the United States and the United Kingdom*. Basingstoke, UK: Macmillan, pp.183–88.

Werbner, P. (1997) "Introduction: The dialectics of cultural hybridity," in P. Werbner and T. Modood (eds.) *Debating Cultural Hybridity: Multi-cultural Identities and the Politics of Anti-Racism*. London: Zed Books, pp.1–28.

Willis, P. (1977) *Learning to Labour*. London: Saxon House.

Willis, P. (1978) *Profane Culture*. London: Routledge & Kegan Paul.

Wulff, H. (1988) *Twenty Girls: Growing Up, Ethnicity and Excitement in a South London Microculture*. Stockholm: Stockholm Studies in Social Anthropology.

Young, R. J. C. (1995) *Colonial Desire: Hybridity in Theory, Culture and Race*. London: Routledge.

PART VI

Between Borders

Introduction to Part VI

David Theo Goldberg and John Solomos

In this final section of the *Companion* we have brought together a series of overview papers that explore transformations in racial and ethnic configurations in specific geopolitical settings. The rationale for this part is to provide accessible accounts of the kinds of historical transformations and contemporary processes that have helped to produce contrasting understandings of race and ethnicity. In doing so we are aware that we have not been able to cover every part of the globe, but we have managed to bring together authoritative accounts that, taken together, provide an overview of important historical trends and contemporary issues.

Michel Wieviorka's paper in a sense can be seen as a return to the themes opening Part I of the *Companion*, since it takes up again the question of the development of racism in Europe. Wieviorka's analysis focuses on the articulation of contemporary forms of racism, including the emergence of relatively new expressions of cultural racism across some European societies. Wieviorka is fully aware of the dangers of assuming that socioracial conditions are identical across the whole of Europe. At the cost of a serious analysis of differences in both history and political culture, nevertheless, he argues forcefully that any rounded account of contemporary racisms has to include an analysis of the changing nature of industrial society, patterns of institutional change, forms of cultural identity, and economic crisis. He suggests that in the end it is perhaps the very idea of Europe and its transformation that lie at the heart of racist politics in European societies today.

Percy C. Hintzen takes up a part of the globe that was transformed in the aftermath of European expansion and exploitation through the system of plantation slavery. The role of race has been integral to the forging of Caribbean identity and ethnicity from its initial moments. Hintzen's account is organized around two key arguments. First, he argues that as a result of the very manner in which the populations of the Caribbean were created in the aftermath of European expansion and forms of colonial domination, construction of forms of hybridized Creole identity became a constitutive feature in the various parts of the Caribbean. Second, he suggests that the very reality of hybridity and creolization meant that ideologies of exclusion and incorporation took particular forms in the Caribbean. He touches in some detail on the differential patterns of incorporation of Afro-Creoles and East Indians in Trinidad and in Guyana, highlighting the important role of various forms of cultural nationalism in shaping much of political debate in the Caribbean.

Four papers follow on parts of the globe generally marginalized in terms of the study of race and ethnicity. The first, by Frank Dikötter, is concerned with the articulation and development of forms of racial thinking in China. Starting from a masterful overview of the history of discourses about lineage in China, his account provides an interesting comparison to the evolution of European terms for race and ethnicity. The rest of the paper is an examination of the evolution of constructions of what it meant to be "Chinese" in both the Republican period after 1911 and the Communist period after 1949. A crucial arena of debate has focused on the relation between the Han Chinese and ethnic minorities within the borders of China. Dikötter also points out, however, that contemporary Chinese discourses and ideas about race intermingle with anti-Western themes and with nationalist political ideologies.

Bill Ashcroft considers the ways in which particular conceptions of Africa have been created in the European vision and geopolitical ordering throughout modernity. These constructions of "Africa" are a product as much of cultural creations, for instance in and by literature, as of governmental practices and imposed rule. Ashcroft calls for reimagining Africa outside of these constraining parameters, arguing that this would entail three general and shared sorts of benefits. The first would be a critical disposition towards analyzing imperial power and the effects upon the world of the various modes of colonial occupation. The second would be to enable a theory of the response of the colonized. And the third would be an examination of the nature of postcolonial society. Ashcroft is thus concerned to reposition how Africa is conceived in the European imagination because of the benefits it would generate regarding Africa itself as well as for self-reflexive theoretical understanding.

Dikötter's account of China and Ashcroft's of Africa is followed by Pandeli Glavanis's analysis of the salience of ethnoreligious identities in the Middle East. This is a part of the world that does not feature very highly in studies of race and ethnicity. Glavanis locates part of the reason for this in the complex history of the region, which he sees as resulting in a commonly held view that ethnoreligious forms of identity are perhaps the key forces that shape the political institutions and socioeconomic relations in the region. Against the region's historical background, Glavanis then looks in some detail at the ways in which ethnicity has been understood in the Middle East. He distinguishes between studies of ethnicity that were produced in the 1950s and 1960s and the accounts that have followed in the aftermath of the rise of political Islam as a key political force after 1979. Covering a wide range of recent scholarship in this growing field, he suggests that there is a need for an analysis of the region that addresses both the specificities of ethnic and religious identities and the on-going transformations in political institutions and civil society.

The penultimate paper in this volume, by Jonathan Warren and France Winddance Twine, focuses on the emergence and development of critical race studies in Latin America. Questioning the assumption that Latin America has "no race problem," Warren and Twine provide an account of racial conditions in Latin America that is both historical and based on recent conceptual and political debates. Drawing on research in Brazil, Cuba, and elsewhere, they highlight both the advances made by recent scholarship and the conceptual lacunae in much recent critical antiracist scholarship. They point, for example, to the silence in most Latin American scholarship about racial attitudes among nonwhite communities or the experience of Indians in Latin America. But they also suggest that much can be gained from including Latin America more fully in scholarly debates about the salience of race and racism within a comparative context.

The concluding paper, by Stephen Castles, is concerned with the main phenomenon likely to shape the future of racial and ethnic studies in the decades to come, namely, processes of migration and movement of people across borders. Castles' account is framed around two main concerns. The first is to provide an overview of what migration means conceptually and in practice. Second, he explores the processes that led to the globalization of migration in the second part of the twentieth and the beginning of the twenty-first centuries. Both parts of his analysis are underpinned by a preoccupation not just with the processes of movement that migration involves, but with the impact of migrant and transnational communities on the economic, social, cultural, and political fabric of the societies in which they settle. Castles' account ends by pointing towards the complex forms of multiculturalism and transnational belonging that have emerged as a result of migration processes, past and present.

Chapter 31

The Development of Racism in Europe

Michel Wieviorka

Introduction

The term "racism" appeared in the interwar period, with reference to Nazism, but the ideas and practices to which it refers are much older and are not uniquely the outcome of the European experience. Thus, it is tempting to speak of racism, with no fear of anachronism, when talking about the ancient Greeks for whom the barbarians, outside the City, were human beings, of course, but distinctly inferior. Similarly, it would not be excessive to speak of the historical depth of racism in all kinds of non-European societies where phenomena which could be described as "racist" may have emerged even before the modern era.

However, in many respects, racism is a European invention and, for many specialists, historians, sociologists, anthropologists, and philosophers, it is a characteristic of the modern, individualistic societies of the type which began to develop in Western Europe at the end of the Middle Ages. Louis Dumont (1972), for example, considered that racism fulfills an old function under a new form, as if it were representing, in an egalitarian society, a resurgence of what was differently but more directly and naturally expressed in a hierarchical society. If the former modes of distinction are suppressed you have a racist ideology. From this viewpoint racism cannot be considered a characteristic of traditional – or "holistic" – societies, to use Louis Dumont's terminology; it started in Europe when Europe began to expand throughout the world with the major discoveries, colonization, and what was already in the fifteenth century a process of economic globalization.

Thus Europe has produced racist doctrines and ideologies which have considerably evolved over time during the modern era. To begin with, throughout the seventeenth and eighteenth centuries, relatively varied representations of the other, which could be described as protoracist, were predominant; for example, some writers explained the physical differences (considered in themselves as being a cause or a sign of inferiority) of Africans or American Indians, by the environment in which they lived: climate, natural environment, but also their culture and their civilizations. Then, as from the end of the eighteenth century, the ideas which are the precursors of the period of classical, scientific racism, began to circulate. This turning point, as Hannah Arendt (1966) stresses, is to a large extent due to the increasing importance assumed by the idea of the nation throughout the nineteenth century. It was then that scientific conceptions of race were established, appropriating all fields of knowledge: travelers, writers, philosophers, and scientists, professors of anatomy and physiology, historians, philologists, and theologians all make their contributions. The aim – whether in creating new knowledge or in resorting to previous knowledge – is to demonstrate the superiority of the "white" race over the other "races," and to classify human races, as well as to demonstrate that racial mix is a source of degeneration for the superior race. Amongst others, Robert Miles (1989), Michael Banton (1983), Elazar Barkan (1992) and John Solomos and Les Back (1996) have contributed a collection of arguments to this history of scientific racism showing clearly that Europe was the place where doctrines and ideologies were created which circulated thick and fast right round the world and, in particular, as the historian George M. Fredrickson (1988) has established, from the Old World to the New, as from the end of the eighteenth century.

Nazism is the culmination of this powerful movement of ideas. Very extensive use was made of all the spheres of knowledge: medicine, chemistry, genetics, as well as anthropology, psychiatry, history, archeology, law, and demography; all were appropriated in order to establish scientific definitions, lists, and classifications of certain groups as races, starting with the Jews, and in symmetrical fashion to assert both the superiority of the Aryan race and also to endow it with a historical, cultural, and natural legitimacy.

The end of World War II and the realization of what Nazi barbarianism involved, led if not to the disappearance of scientific racism, at least to an end to its legitimacy. As Jean-Paul Sartre ([1948] 1995) said of antisemitism, a special form of racism, what had previously been a matter of opinion had now moved into the realm of criminal behavior. In the 1950s, decolonization further stressed the process of delegitimizing racism, and it might then have been thought that scientific racism was condemned twice over, once by history, but also by science. Its "retreat," to use the title of Elazar Barkan's book (1992), had been prepared as from the interwar period by the intervention of left-wing political militants, Jews, and women who questioned its very foundations. It looked as if Europe in the 1950s and 1960s would continue to witness its decline.

However, this is not what happened: today, in Europe, racism is a scourge and a major concern, all the more worrying since it is on the increase and is spreading, even in countries such as Italy which, until the 1980s, were considered nonracist to all intents and purposes. But are we talking about the same phenomenon?

New Racism

In 1968 in Birmingham, in a speech which made history in the United Kingdom, Enoch Powell, a member of the Conservative Party Shadow Cabinet, predicted that there would be "rivers of blood" in the country if his version of Conservative Party policy was not adopted: strict control of immigration, encouragement of repatriation of immigrants and family reunion in the country of origin, opposition to the legislation on racial discrimination which, in his opinion would give the black British more rights than the whites. Against this background, with the emergence of an extreme right-wing party, the National Front, what is really at issue is what was analyzed a few years later as the "new racism."

In a book of the same title, Martin Barker (1981) discusses the move from biological inferiority to cultural difference – a move by which racist discourse attempts to base its legitimacy. Arguments of the type put forward in particular by Powell are no longer based on hierarchy as much as on difference, nor do they stress the natural features of the "racialized" group, but its culture, language, religion, traditions, and customs. From this point of view, "new racism" insists on the threat that the difference of the groups targeted constitutes for the identity of the dominant group. In particular, it expresses the idea of a danger threatening the national homogeneity of Great Britain, which, since the 1950s has seen the arrival of significant waves of immigration from the former Commonwealth colonies. This analysis, which demonstrates that it is possible to shift so to speak from one racism to another, from scientific racism which has lost its credibility to cultural racism, gained widespread support in Great Britain itself. This notion has been taken up by researchers who, like Paul Gilroy (1987), are following a more or less Marxist tradition or who refer to the thought of Frantz Fanon ([1952] 1986, [1961] 1990), in whose work a criticism of cultural racism can be found along lines fairly similar to the concept covered by the "new racism."

In a way, the approach developed in Great Britain by Martin Barker recalls the concept of "symbolic racism" forged in the United States in the 1970s, which refers to the less ostensible or open forms of the phenomenon, and in particular to the prejudice with respect to blacks. American racists who adopt this approach do not refer to the assumed biological, physical, or intellectual inferiority of black Americans, but state that the fact that they resort to social welfare, or tolerate the breakup of their families, shows a lack of respect for the cultural and moral values of the nation, in particular work and the sense of individual responsibility and endeavor. But above all, the idea of a "new racism" is a concept of which variations emerged in Europe in countries other than the United Kingdom throughout the 1980s. In France, a book by Pierre-André Taguieff (1988) stresses the constitution of what he calls a "differentialist" form of racism, which can be seen in the ideological publications of the GRECE of the *Club de l'Horloge*, or in the *Front National's* discourse on identity, and he stresses the opposition between this form of racism, which appeals to cultural difference, and older forms which referred in the first instance to the physical hierarchy of races. At the same time, Etienne Balibar and Immanuel Wallerstein published a book (1991) which developed a similar point of view. Likewise, parallel concepts were developed in Belgium by Felice Dassetto and Albert Bastenier (1987).

Thus, observers of racism in Europe are struck by the capacity of the phenomenon to change while remaining the same. This is why there has been discussion of two different forms of racism, one of which is classical, scientific, and unequal, based on the idea of the superiority of some races over others, and the other, recent, cultural, and differentialist, which is based on the idea of a radical incompatibility of cultures to live together. This gives rise to important theoretical debates: might it not be better, as I have suggested (Wieviorka, 1991, 1997), to consider that any experience of racism which has a degree of historical depth necessarily combines two different philosophies – one of inferiority and the other of differentiation – contradictory as this may seem? When an immigrant-origin group is particularly prone to exploitation at the workplace because it is subject to racism, and is moreover isolated in urban space, possibly even being ordered to go home, does this not imply that this group is subjected to these two forms of racism at one and the same time? Instead of confronting two forms of racism and suggesting that they follow each other in time, it does seem to me to be preferable to show that the two major schools of thought necessarily coexist, but the forms vary: today, it is the case that in Europe we see a situation in which an approach stressing difference is stronger or more visible than that referring to inferiority, in particular when unemployment is widespread and immigrant-origin populations may seem, temporarily, not to fulfil any useful function, because no employer needs them.

The Elementary Forms of Contemporary Racism in Europe

Racism in Europe today is expressed in various ways which can be usefully grouped together empirically into a number of categories which constitute the elementary forms of the phenomenon.

To this end, our first category includes prejudices, opinions, and stereotypes, as well as racist rumors, that is to say expressions which offer representations of the Other (and of oneself) which favor the ingroup at the expense of the outgroup, magnifying the differences and even going so far as nurturing discriminatory attitudes. Our second category includes forms of racism expressed as segregation behavior. The latter is sometimes directly and explicitly racial, and is sometimes the product of social and economic processes which culminate in racial separation. Segregation is based on an attitude of differentiation; discrimination, which defines a third category of forms of racism, has more to do with hierarchization. Here we are not dealing with exclusion, but with less favorable forms of treatment of the victim group and its members in access to employment, social housing, and education, for example, or in the media. A fourth category, which ranges from racial harassment to the barbarianism of genocide, includes racist violence, which is sometimes infrapolitical and sometimes political, sometimes "hot" and expressive in the first case, and "in cold blood," organized and instrumental, in the second. Finally, we would like to add two further categories, or elementary forms of racism: first, political racism, that is, racism contained in the programs of political bodies, whether it be parties, smaller organizations, or the state, and second, ideological and doctrinaire racism as it is theorized in writings whose main objective is using racist ideology in an explanation of the world.

If these categories are applied to the European experience, country by country, we observe considerable differences, which I endeavored to analyze, along with a research team, at the beginning of the 1990s (Wieviorka, 1994). In the main, racism seems to be on the rise everywhere, since the 1960s in the UK, the 1970s in France, in Germany, in Belgium and at later dates as we go towards the south of Europe. But the development does assume different forms. Thus, racist violence is a major phenomenon in the United Kingdom, in particular in the form of racial harassment, which was already noted in Liverpool in the 1950s in relation to the Jamaicans who had come to work in the factories during World War II, or in London, for example, with the white teddy boys, who sometimes claimed to be fascists of the Oswald Mosley type and who, in 1958, attacked the Trinidadian workers who had settled in their area. At the end of the 1980s, a report from the European Parliament gave the figure of some 7,000 racist attacks per year in the United Kingdom and according to a Home Office estimate (June 1992) a racist attack took place every 30 minutes in Great Britain. On the other hand, the statistics available for France, which are published annually in the report of the *Commission nationale consultative des droits de l'homme* show figures which are derisory in comparison.

The differences are equally important if we take another elementary form, political racism. Unlike France, Great Britain does not have a large racist and xenophobic party capable, like the *Front National*, of attracting on average 15 percent of the votes at

463

elections. The National Front was founded in 1967 but this party, despite some local successes, is in no way comparable to its French namesake. Some countries in Europe do have relatively powerful extreme right parties. In Austria, the *Freiheitliche Partei Oster-reichs* (FPO, Austrian Liberal Party) under the leadership of Jörg Haider, has had considerable electoral success, and a number of extraparliamentary organizations include a significant number of nationalist and racist militants and sympathizers. In Belgium, and more specifically in Flanders, the *Vlaams Blok* combines Flemish nationalism and racism against a background of separatism, while in Wallonia, *Agir* and the *Front National*, which are smaller, are predominantly the expression of economic and social crisis. In Italy, while the neofascist MSI was becoming in the main a respectable right-wing force, in the shape of the *Allianza Nazionale*, and was eliminating its racist and xenophobic references, the *Ligua del Nord*, particularly in Lombardy, under the leader-ship of Umberto Bossi, stood for separatism, demanding an independent "Padania" in the name of a nationalism which was often redolent with anti-immigrant racism. In Germany, there was a period of electoral resurgence of the extreme right, in the form of a hazy collection of a dozen or so organizations at the beginning of the 1990s, but by the end of the 1990s there was a relative decline.

The comparison is also valid if we consider the concrete expressions of racism which are obviously at the intersection of two or more of the elementary forms which we have listed. Thus, groups of skinheads, practicing racist violence at the same time as develop-ing protopolitical racism, are more numerous and visible in some countries, like the United Kingdom, Germany, Belgium, or Scandinavia, than in others – in France, for example, they are a very limited phenomenon.

In some instances, there are no fundamental theoretical or methodological obstacles to the comparison; for example, there is no doubt that the extreme right is more powerfully constituted in France than in the United Kingdom. On the other hand, there are instances in which the comparison is more difficult. Thus, we observe considerable differences between France and the United Kingdom when the question concerns the statistics for racial violence, as we saw above, or again when the issue is one of discrimin-ation in employment or in housing – Michael Banton (quoted by Bataille, 1997) notes that 2,324 complaints for racial discrimination in employment were dealt with by the British courts as compared with only a few in France, only two of which resulted in sentences, over the same period. But does that mean that there is more violence or discrimination in the United Kingdom than in France, or is there a considerable political and administrative effort in the former to counter these scourges; in other words, do the statistics inform us about the facts or do they tell us something about those who collect the statistics or who demand them? Should we not give some consideration to a third possibility, which is that the antiracist campaign and the concepts of justice differ from one country to another, and that, for example, France uses other procedures to deal with discrimination in employment than those which consist in resorting to the courts or in practicing "discrimination testing," using the procedures recommended by John Wrench (1996)?

Finally, once it has been admitted that racism expresses itself in several different ways, which are independent of one another, it becomes much more difficult to make intra-European comparisons, between countries at the same point in time, or at different periods for the same country, given that there may well be a decline in some of the basic forces of the phenomenon and an increase in others. For example, if we observe that the

Front National is losing support at some point but, at the same time, racist violence is increasing, are we to say that racism is declining or rising in France?

The Diversity of Contemporary Racism in Europe

The above remarks do not encourage us to postulate the unity of racism in Europe today, particularly as a considerable number of other factors tend to stress the differences between countries and not the points in common.

On the one hand, each country has its own political culture, which is based on its history, traditions, and even, quite simply, on general categories of thought, with the result that the approaches to racism, and even the definitions of it, differ. Some European countries have a colonial past which weighs heavily on the present – this is the case primarily for the United Kingdom, France, and Belgium; in others, this past is of less consequence, for example in Germany and Italy, or has only recently made itself felt, in particular in Spain or in Portugal; finally, others have no colonial past. Given that racism primarily targets immigrant-origin populations, there is a difference between the racism aimed at former colonial populations and the racism aimed at populations or groups which do not share a colonial past with the host society. The legal culture also has an impact, for example, whether or not there is a reference to *ius solis*, which is the case in most European countries, or to *ius sanguinis*, as in Germany, for example, where the Turks are victims of racism, as described by Gunter Wallraff in a well-known book (1986); this form of racism excludes them from civil rights, but nevertheless does not prevent them from being more socially integrated than other minorities in other countries.

Racism also varies depending on whether the philosophical values which make up the shared foundation of the society in question are open to the idea of cultural or ethnic minorities being visible in the public sphere and being recognized therein. Thus, in France, where this option is not acceptable, generally speaking it is considered desirable for cultural differences to be restricted to the private sphere; the result is that any attempt to define someone in the public sphere by his or her belonging to an ethnic, religious, or any other sort of group will be open to accusations of aiming at the ethnicization and, further, the racialization, of collective life, with the implication that those who do so, whether they realize it or not, are racists in the eyes of their critics. On the contrary, in Anglo-Saxon culture, the "color-blind" approach of those who refuse any reference to a collective ethnic, or possibly racial, identity, and who only wish to recognize individuals in the public sphere, will be suspected of racism. This is one of the reasons which explains why it is so difficult to find ground for agreement in the harmonization of national endeavors to combat racism at the European level. Furthermore, racism seems to be so much part of the approaches which are primarily characteristic of, and specific to, each country that it is superficial, if not artificial, to seek to demonstrate the existence of any form of structuring at the European level. It is true that extreme right-wing forms of racism endeavor to forge links, and to network; but experience shows that their concerns are first and foremost at the national level. Their nationalism encourages them to continue in this direction. Extreme right-wing groups do have international contacts and exchange information, ideas, and personnel; but this is all somewhat limited and there is definitely no immediate likelihood of a united

465

European racism. Given that the radical right are united in their opposition to Europe, one might even say that the net result of the phenomenon was unfavorable.

Thus the observation of racism in its various contemporary forms in Europe does not permit us, at first glance, to suggest a unified image of the phenomenon. But over and above the forms which do vary from one country to another, an in-depth analysis of the sources of contemporary racism in Europe forces us to go further.

The End of Industrial Society

After World War II, in industrialized Western societies, racism was often concomitant with development and growth, in particular the racism which concerned immigrants employed as unskilled labor in industry, as well as in the most unpleasant urban public services such as garbage collection. In some countries, immigrant labor was recruited in former colonies, but in these same countries, as for others, immigrants also came from Yugoslavia, Italy, Spain, or Portugal. In many respects, the populations of rural origin who came to work in the more industrialized areas of the same country were comparable to immigrants and were referred to as "peasants" – for example, in Italy those who had come from the South to work in the cities in the North, or in France the Bretons attracted by the steel industry in Lorraine or the car factories in the Parisian region. In these cases, racism was one of the elements in the disparagement and exploitation of workers who were, in the main, socially integrated, since they were employed, and culturally and politically excluded, as it was often a question of single men living in hostels or furnished rooms and more concerned with preparing their return home than with contemplating any form of integration in the host country.

In the 1950s in the United Kingdom, and later along a line which ran from the north and the west to the south and the east, the image of the single, male immigrant worker in transit in a society where he had no intention of living permanently, gave way to other images, the definition of which was to a large extent due both to the permanent settlement of immigrants in European countries and to the breakdown of the social relations specific to the industrial era.

Until the 1970s, the main focus of social life was the opposition between employers on one hand and the working class on the other, protagonists in a conflict which structured society as a whole. It is true that there were other social groups apart from those, and furthermore not all workers saw themselves as part of a fundamental social conflict in which their role was to undermine class domination. But industrial society could be analyzed on the basis of this central relationship which constituted the substance of major political discussions, movements of ideas, and social struggles in spheres other than industry.

Racism was part of the relations of production, even if it is difficult to apply to the European origin immigrant workers the rudimentary Marxist analysis of Oliver Cromwell Cox for whom racism – he was writing about the United States – was the outcome of capitalism, and more specifically, the outcome of the exploitation of the black working class by whites. As we have seen, while racism does target immigrants and is part of their exploitation, there is also, in all the European countries in question, primarily in France, in Great Britain, Belgium, the Netherlands, and also in Germany, support for these same immigrants from the working–class movements and their trade union and political organizations. Overall, the working-class organizations in Europe have been a sphere of integration for those workers who were nevertheless victims of racism in other areas.

As from the 1970s, the social relationships specific to industry underwent considerable transformation. Fordism was challenged, whereas productivity agreements and the relocation of factories in emerging countries culminated in massive redundancies in European industries. Europe began to experience a slowdown in growth rates and the phenomenon of dual economies characterized by unemployment, exclusion, and fragmentation for whole categories of the employed population. Each country had its own version of this development but the end result was the same everywhere: discussion now focused on the decline of the central conflict which structured society, the end of industrial society, and the exhaustion of the working-class movement. The latter, as it lost its topicality, lost its capacity to wage struggles of a universal nature involving issues far beyond those of the specific interests of the workers alone. What remained of the working-class movements appeared to be corporatist, neocorporatist, and defensive; left-wing parties had increasing difficulty in playing their role of representing of social demands, political systems were no longer clearly defined, while at the same time the intellectual climate showed less concern with discussing the working class and, temporarily, with criticizing capitalism. The issues which emerged were those of the social vacuum, the end of the grand narrative, and large-scale mobilization. In this transformation, the traditional image of the immigrant tended to stress cultural, rather than social, aspects. The stereotype of the single male worker, the incarnation of a labor force which is destined to leave the host country sooner or later, gives way to an image which is defined in terms of national or ethnic origin, religion, language, whose presence has become a permanent feature of the host society, where he is expected, along with his wife and children, to disappear culturally if the political culture is one of integration by assimilation (France), to remain forever a foreigner if the *ius sanguinis* predominates (Germany), or to become part of a minority (United Kingdom).

In this new setting, racism is structured in opposition to immigrants and their descendants, who are in any event a new category of the population. Till then, racism was linked to the exploitation of labor; it was part of and reinforced the disparagement of those who did the worst and least paid jobs, because of their origin or their appearance. Henceforth it was to contribute primarily to processes of exclusion and discrimination in relation to employment or in urban space. More specifically, the social dimensions of racism began to be molded by two major forces. In the first instance, we have the members of the dominant group who are also victims of social change and deindustrialization and who have become marginalized in society. These people are powerless, have a distinct feeling of being neglected or abandoned, are often expected to share the same conditions as the immigrant-origin populations, and are to some extent in competition with them on the labor market. These people turn against them. Here racism may take the form of verbal abuse, but a harder version may also attract skinheads and neo-Nazis; it may be sustained and provide material for the national socialist discourse of the radical right.

The second group, often characterized by more controlled forms of expression, corresponds to the well-to-do, middle- or upper-class social groups, who are mainly concerned with maintaining a distance between themselves and the other by constructing symbolic and concrete barriers of segregation: separate residential areas, the use of private schools to avoid schools in the public sector in which the number of immigrant-origin children is

467

considered to be too high, voting for the political parties which are the most opposed to immigrants, and so forth. In some cases, as the survey carried out in France by Philippe Bataille (1997) demonstrates, the trade unions and left-wing political parties have difficulty in countering the racist climate which develops, and are to some extent permeated by the themes they engender, if only because businesses wish to keep their clientele, or politicians their electorate, which they can see are attracted by the extreme right.

In some cases the extreme right may even become institutionalized by gaining ground in the trade unions or in voluntary associations, as we can see in France with the *Front National* who have endeavored to create trade unions, have penetrated the administration of public sector housing, and have been elected to numerous local, regional, and departmental councils.

The Institutional Crisis

In the age of industrialization, European societies, each in their own way, acquired institutions which were subject to crisis as the social relationships on which they were founded broke down. The crisis was first observed in the institutions which ensured the socialization and individualization of people, and in the first instance in the schools. Theoretically, schools should give children an education which will provide them with the resources necessary to participate as fully as possible in civic and national life. Now everywhere, schools seem to be having difficulty in carrying out this mission and often the difficulties are to some extent attributed to immigration and are linked with the question of racism. Examples of racism here are the accusations that the immigrant-origin populations, perhaps considered for this reason to be a minority, are the cause of the malfunctioning of the educational system. From this point of view, children of minority or immigrant origin are suspected of introducing into schools the more general problems of the social and urban crisis, of being bearers of cultures in which violence plays an important role, of being a source of deterioration or of further difficulties for teachers, or of tensions with other pupils. They may even be accused of challenging the secular nature of education, as has been observed in Belgium and in particular in France with the "headscarf affair": since 1989, when young Muslim girls went to school wearing the Islamic headscarf, there has been a passionate debate about whether or not to forbid the wearing of this headscarf in school.

The racism crisis in schools may take a less spectacular but equally important form, that of segregation. To ensure that their children have the best chances of succeeding at school, parents turn to the schools which are known for their social and possibly cultural homogeneity, and avoid schools with a high percentage of poor and immigrant-origin children. In the long run this contributes to the fragmentation of the educational system as a whole. Segregation in housing is frequently a less direct, but more widespread, way of ensuring segregation at school.

The crisis also affects the institutions which deal with social welfare and social cohesion. The bases and workings of these institutions vary considerably from one country to another in Europe, but since the 1970s they have all experienced considerable financial difficulties, including those where they seemed to be particularly strong, such as in the Scandinavian social democracies. The aging of the population, the rise in demand for health care, and the rise in unemployment have all made inroads into the welfare state and redistribution systems set up and developed in other times, in historical circumstances of economic growth and full employment. Here again, racism targets foreigners and immigrants, in the first instance accusing them of abusing and defrauding these systems, even if in reality they contribute as much to them as they receive from them. Racism may also affect the way in which benefits linked to redistribution or collective solidarity are distributed; for example, immigrants' applications are sometimes dealt with slowly and unwillingly, or they meet with hostility and contempt at the counters.

The crisis also concerns the institutions which ensure public order and national security, the police, the judiciary, and public service employees. Thus the urban riots observed in the United Kingdom, and more frequently but in a less spectacular fashion in France, have in most cases been triggered by racist behavior on the part of the police; the victims of their heavy-handed methods and "mistakes" are to a large extent young people of immigrant origin. Although the institutional crisis may have some connection with racism, it would be wrong to generalize and reduce it to the image of "good" institutions which have been affected by external circumstances as a result of the pressure of wider social difficulties, and which have a few "bad apples" in their midst who may go as far as racist remarks, attitudes, or behavior. Institutions are more likely to become racist when they are themselves in difficulty, either because they are not in a position to offer their personnel reasonable employment, pay, and career prospects, or because they are paralyzed or destabilized by excessive endeavors to modernize, or by unexpectedly being held responsible for economic constraints, and being faced with the old organizational culture, and in particular because they are incapable of clearly stating the very meaning of their own mission, the values and the norms to be respected to ensure their own legitimacy. Contexts of this type create conditions which are propitious to the spread of racism; someone has to bear the blame and the crisis is attributed to immigrants, and racist behavior on the part of the agents who ensure the working of the institutions is allowed or tolerated.

There are two further phenomena associated with deindustrialization and the crisis of the institutions. The first is of a political nature: everywhere, the political systems which were set up or renewed at the end of World War II, or later, appear to be worn out and to have great difficulty in changing and adapting to the expectations of societies which are becoming postindustrial; and in these difficulties, the themes of nationalism and immigration which are themselves close to that of racism, become issues for discussion and exert a considerable influence on possible political realignments. This is very obvious in the rise in popularity of populist or extreme right-wing parties, for whom hostility to immigrants and, more or less explicitly, racism, antisemitism, and xenophobia are key elements in the debate. Moreover, throughout the 1980s and at the beginning of the 1990s, neoliberal ideas gained considerable ground in Europe. Their popularity rose when they recommended the rolling back of the state and rapid privatization as a solution to the crisis of the institutions. Neoliberalism is not in itself racist, and some of its ideologists are convinced and sincere opponents of racism. But one effect of this ideology and its practice is to encourage the rise of racism, if only by instigating discourse close to what American psychologists and political scientists referred to as "symbolic racism" from the end of the 1970s: in its xenophobic and racist version, the neoliberal discourse questions whether it would not be preferable to end state intervention and social policies which encourage minorities and other immigrant origin populations to depend on the state and national solidarity without making any effort of their own. Would it not be

469

preferable to stop making available guarantees and support which, moreover, attract new arrivals from abroad whose only intention would appear to be to take undue advantage of the fruit of the activity and labor of the nationals? There is a contradiction here, because in other respects the neoliberal discourse is favorable to the opening of frontiers, because this enables the free play of supply and demand on the international labor market.

The Emergence of Cultural Identities

Since the end of the 1960s, throughout the world, and more particularly in Europe, we have been witnessing the rise of cultural identities which in many respects seem to challenge the nation – the dominant identity of each country – and to make a plea for more recognition in the public sphere. From our point of view, this phenomenon is important because it is not only inherently racist but is also taking shape and is therefore in a historical phase of emergence.

The first dimension of this process, which in many respects seems to be a form of cultural fragmentation, concerns the idea of the nation. The classical representation of the nation can be illustrated by the use of contrasting pairs; thus, we can compare the French version of the nation which stresses the political will to live together and is based on a "daily plebiscite" in the well-known words of Ernest Renan, and the German version, which stresses its historical and cultural identity and the organic belonging of each of its members to the same people. Or we might refer to a modern idea of the nation, civic and territorial, with its plans for economic development and political overtures, as opposed to an ethnic idea which is to some extent hostile to the modern world, with its urbanization and industry.

Throughout Europe, the period which dates from the beginning of the 1970s has been one during which the open idea of the nation has lost ground in favor of closed, nationalist, and usually racist, antisemitic, and xenophobic versions. In the first instance, this development can be explained by the changes described above, the end of the social relationships specific to the age of industry and the crisis in the institutions. It also owes a lot to international change. The globalization of the economy – even if at times there is a tendency to exaggerate the extent to which this is the source of all our present social misfortunes, treating it as a myth or an ideology – does make it difficult to conceive of the nation as the symbolical and territorial framework for the main elements of economic activity. On the contrary, there is an increasing tendency for economic activity to take place outside the nation, or from abroad, and the nation then becomes not so much a framework as a sphere, which is subject to its consequences, and is not always able to withstand or to adapt to financial movements, commercial markets, or systems of international decisions. In some cases, nationalism and its racist developments originate in globalization or the fear of it; thus, in France, the extreme right is constantly exposing economic overtures and the subordination of the country to foreign domination. In other cases, nationalism and the racism which follows in its wake tend to convey the desire of one part of the population, or of a region, to rid itself of the burden constituted by the rest of the country, to assert itself autonomously and to participate more easily in the game of international economic relations. In some ways this is the case for movements like the *Ligua del Nord* in Italy or the *Vlaams Blok* in Belgium; in Italy the North is tired of having to subsidize the Center and the South with their structural economic difficulties, and the latter wish to separate Flanders, which is relatively prosperous, from Wallonia, which is in a state of serious crisis.

The globalization of the economy is not the only international element in the retreat of the idea of the nation into a nationalism which is to some degree racist. In some cases, the construction of Europe is also experienced as a threat from without, implying for example the loss of national sovereignty in economic and cultural affairs because these are now based on a new external power which may technocratically sweep aside the aspirations of each nation to develop autonomously. Moreover, nationalism thrives on the fear of seeing Anglo-Saxon culture, under North American domination, weaken national identities by imposing cultural products, possibly even the norms of "McDonald's type" mass consumption.

A second phenomenon, the sources of which are close to those which explain the rise of nationalism, and which may conflict with it, is the rise of specific cultural identities. The origin of these identities is very varied – religious, ethnic, of national, possibly racial, or gender origin – or again, they may convey an endeavor on the part of the actors to transform a handicap, a chronic illness, or a serious physical disability into difference, identity being used as an assertion of autonomy in the name of, and at the same time despite, this difference. In Europe, these cultural identities emerged roughly speaking in two big waves, the first beginning at the end of the 1960s, the second in the 1970s and 1980s; both subsequently continued over time and developed new forms. On the one hand, at a time when there was still economic growth, full employment, and confidence in science and progress, various groups demanded public recognition within their nation-states. In some cases, this demand was something of a challenge, in particular when regional or nationalist movements challenged a nation-state; in other cases, it was more a question of their emergence or a change, for example when throughout Europe Jews broke with the universalist formulas which, in the main, advocated being Jewish in private, but not in public, and became increasingly visible, capable of asserting themselves as such, religiously and culturally, in their relationship to the State of Israel or in their active opposition to antisemitism. What most of these demands and cultural assertions which originated in the first wave share is that they were relatively neutral socially, that is they were not a characteristic of specific or homogenous social categories. Subsequently, a second wave emerged in which on the contrary the cultural question appeared to be inseparable from the social question, in so much as the groups who demanded their recognition were at the same time subject to severe forces of inequality, to social and racial discrimination, poverty, housing in deprived areas, and so forth. This wave was primarily made up of immigrant-origin populations who realized that they were now permanently settled in the host countries and that they had to come to terms with the difficulties of asserting their cultural lives at the same time as resolving social problems of employment, income, housing, access to health and to education, and so forth.

In Europe three main philosophies predominate in the making of these specific identities. The first is one of reproduction, when an old, for example regional, identity in decline resists and is reconstructed. The second is that of the host society to which a migrant group contributes its religious, culinary, and linguistic traditions, in an endeavor to perpetuate them. The third and most important is that of the production of difference. Cultural identity here is the outcome of the work of the society in question on itself, it is the outcome of change, it is invented by the participants who may even endow it with all

471

the appearances of tradition. In practice, cultural differences often appear in the public arena, claiming to be traditional or of considerable historical depth when they are in the main new and invented. Thus, the Islam of the younger generations in the forms emerging today in Europe is in many respects new in comparison to the Islam of their parents and grandparents; it is the product of a new process linked to the social situation of the populations in question, their difficulties in integrating, racism, and social exclusion. Moreover it varies from one country in Europe to another, depending on the countries from which the immigrants come, certainly, but also and primarily on the way in which the host society deals with religious difference. This third philosophy, of production of difference, and not reproduction, is important in two respects. On one hand, it is much more important than is realized when we bear in mind the groups who emerge to demand their cultural recognition and it often involves processes of reproduction of old identities. Regional cultures, for example, are in many respects contemporary inventions, "home-made" products or "*bricolage*" in Claude Lévi-Strauss's well-known words. And on the other hand, this philosophy leads us to make a clean break with evolutionism according to which societies move through stages from tradition to modernity: in fact, one of the characteristics of modern European societies is their tendency to produce cultural difference, including the invention of traditions.

Everywhere the rise of cultural identities contributes to the reinforcement and renewal of racism. The fact is that any identity can be interpreted by the bearer as being an inherent characteristic which is a natural quality and not a cultural artefact; this tendency to the naturalization of cultural and social life contributes to the racialization of social relationships which may lead rapidly to a racialization of community life. This provides an opening for racism mainly in the form of intercommunity tensions which accord considerable importance to the differentialist rejection of otherness. And when the idea of nation itself retreats into racist nationalism, the clash of the latter with all sorts of cultural identities which are themselves possibly attracted by self-racialization may fuel a genuine dialectic of racism, a vicious spiral in which passion and violence are self-sustaining – this is what happens when the racism of the majority refers to the nation, and also when the minorities oppose one another or the dominant group.

This dialectic between the dominant identity and minority identities is an indication of the challenge to, and weakening of, the dominant identity, particularly as minorities are less and less inclined to define themselves solely in terms of the nation-state. Throughout Europe, we see various types of transfrontier networks developing, which are in many ways comparable to a diaspora. The archetype – which is that of the Jewish diaspora – has itself undergone considerable changes since World War II. In some cases, the diaspora corresponds to a founding event, a major trauma (genocide, civil war, expulsion), a particularly severe form of continuous repression, forcing a population into partial or total exile. In other cases, the point of departure is the outcome of a choice, and the diaspora is a set of attitudes in which, even after several generations, the migrants maintain close economic, cultural, personal, and family links with the home country and with other communities of the same origin settled in countries other than their own. The Chinese experience is the best example here. Finally, as Paul Gilroy has shown with reference to the Black Atlantic (1993), the diaspora can be a production, an invention, without any particular reference to a founding point in time, nor to any specific historical and territorial origin, which is in a way the case for blacks, who, from the Caribbean to the United Kingdom, including possibly the United States, have developed innovative cultural practices in the artistic sphere and that of corporal expression but also construct economic networks.

Taken together, these phenomena, be it the transformation of nations, the rise of cultural specificities, or diaspora, outline the considerable changes which, since the end of the 1960s, have shaped the image of the endless process of deconstruction and reconstruction of identities. The development of racism is facilitated by the fact that these phenomena are new and the actors have difficulty in establishing intercultural communication. This brings us to the main characteristic of racism in Europe today. As we have seen, the latter is in many respects the outcome of the ending of the social relations specific to industrial society and the crisis of its institutions and, from this angle, is the outcome of the destructuring of a world we have lost. But racism also develops as a result of cultural changes which are still emerging, since their first expressions of note date from the end of the 1960s; it is an inherent part of processes which will become increasingly important; it is one of the protagonists in tomorrow's world and not uniquely a senile figure from the past.

What is true of racism in general is also true of a specific form of the phenomenon, antisemitism. On the one hand, the hatred of Jews reproduces the classic attitudes and is based on modes of thought which have historical depth and whose expression is facilitated by the rise of economic crisis and social difficulties. But on the other hand, antisemitism is taking on new forms and is also part of new social relationships. Thus it can be encountered not only amongst the extreme right-wing nationalists, which is not surprising, but also, frequently, amongst immigrant-origin populations often originating in the Arab-Muslim world, or who have discovered, or rediscovered, Islam. It is then based on the amalgam that equates all Jews with Zionists and, therefore sees them as the sworn enemies of Muslims and Arabs; at the same time, Jews are accused of having links with the world of finance, the media, and the powers that be. But the important factor here is that this antisemitism only begins to develop when the groups which are its bearers begin to express an awareness of identity, in the same way as the Black Americans who identify with Louis Farrakhan and the Nation of Islam and are no longer "blacks" but, in the first instance, "African-Americans."

In Europe there is really little left of the old scientific racism with its appeals to science as a basis for its arguments and practices; nowadays racism is much more likely to seek legitimacy in the cultural sphere. In different ways, which vary considerably from one country to another, racism is the outcome of the destructuring of social forms which are dying, of the old recipes for the integration of a structural conflict into the institutional and cultural framework of the nation-state, and the emergence of social forms which are seeking to establish themselves, in which the theme of cultural recognition plays a central role. In other words, it tends to gain momentum when the institutions and the political system are incapable of dealing democratically with social and economic difficulties, which means that racism involves a whole set of forms of behavior associated with the crisis of the old systems; it also gains ground in circumstances where cultural identities thrive but do not learn to live together and to communicate.

The common denominator of racism in Europe today is definitely not to be found in its concrete expressions, which we have seen are many and varied; it is to be found in the in-depth processes which make of Europe an entity undergoing change.

References

Arendt, H. ([1951] 1966). *The Origins of Totalitarianism*. New York: Harcourt, Brace & World.

Balibar, E. and Wallerstein, I. (1991) *Race, Nation, Class: Ambiguous Identities*. London: Verso.

Banton, M. (1983) *Racial and Ethnic Competition*. Cambridge, UK: Cambridge University Press.

Barkan, E. (1992) *The Retreat of Scientific Racism*. Cambridge, UK: Cambridge University Press.

Barker, M. (1981) *The New Racism*. London: Junction Books.

Bataille, P. (1997) *Le Racisme au travail* [Racism at the workplace]. Paris: La Découverte.

Cox, O. (1948) *Caste, Class and Race*. New York: Doubleday.

Dassetto, F. and Bastenier, A. (1987) *Medias u Akbar. Confrontations autour d'une manifestation* [Medias u Akbar: Interpretations of a demonstration]. Louvain-La-Neuve, Belgium: Ciaco.

Dumont, L. (1972) *Homo Hierarchicus. The Caste System and its Implications*. London: Paladin.

Fanon, F. ([1952] 1986) *Black Skin, White Masks*. London, Pluto Press.

Fanon, F. ([1961] 1990) *Wretched of the Earth*. London: Penguin.

Frederickson, G. M. (1988) *The Arrogance of Race*. Middletown, CT: Wesleyan University Press.

Gilroy, P. (1987) *There Ain't No Black in the Union Jack*. London: Hutchinson.

Gilroy, P. (1993) *The Black Atlantic: Modernity and Double Consciousness*. London: Verso.

Miles, R. (1989) *Racism*. London: Routledge.

Miles, R. (1993) "Racisme institutionnel et rapports de classe: une relation problématique" [Institutional racism and class relations: a difficult relationship], in M. Wieviorka (ed.) *Racisme et modernite*. Paris: La Découverte, pp.159–75.

Sartre, J.-P. ([1948] 1995) *Anti-Semite and Jew: An Exploration of the Aetiology of Hate*. New York: Schocken.

Solomos, J. and Back, L. (1996) *Racism and Society*. London: Macmillan.

Taguieff, P.-A. (1988) *La force du préjugé. Essai sur le racisme et ses doubles*. Paris: La Découverte.

Wallraff, G. (1986) *Tête de Turc* [The Scapegoat]. Paris: La Découverte.

Wieviorka, M. (1991) *The Arena of Racism*. London: Sage.

Wieviorka, M. (ed.) (1994) *Racisme et xénophobie en Europe. Une comparaison internationale*. Paris: La Découverte.

Wieviorka, M. (1997) "Is it so difficult to be anti-racist?," in P. Werbner and T. Modood (eds.) *Debating Cultural Hybridity: Multi-Cultural Identities and The Politics of Anti-Racism*. London: Zed Books, pp.139–53.

Wrench, J. (1996) *Preventing Racism at the Workplace. A Report on 16 European Countries*. Dublin: European Foundation for the Improvement of Living and Working Conditions.

Wrench, John and Taylor, P. (1992) *Manuel de recherche sur l'évaluation des activités de formation antidiscriminatoire*. Geneva: International Labour Office.

Chapter 32

The Caribbean: Race and Creole Ethnicity

Percy C. Hintzen

Caribbean Identity

The legacy of the plantation is highly implicated in every aspect of the Caribbean. It has produced and sustains a syncretic, hybrid, transitory reality characterized by a corpus of values and institutions that maintains social integrity. Such integrity is universally recognizable throughout the region. But the region was created, from the start, as a space of transitory impermanence after the almost total extinction of its indigenous population. Caribbean reality has emerged almost in opposition to this notion of impermanence. Nevertheless, at its core, it is forced to accommodate a never-ending assault by a global and international environment and a multiplicity of ever-changing cultural, social, economic, and political forces. The result is an extremely pregnable Caribbean, constantly penetrated, while struggling to maintain its own sense of integrity and the notion of a definitive character. But there is nothing "authentic" about its socioculture and very little that has not originated from abroad. Everything is "adapted, reimagined, reinvented" (Stavans, 1995:60) to suit the needs of a domestic condition, constantly buffeted by external pressures, needs, and demands. The region's character is described by one its writers and theorists as "chaos–shock, mixture, combination, alchemy" (Taylor 1989:136).

Race and ethnicity in the Caribbean need to be understood in the above terms. There is a core of understanding about Caribbean identity (i.e., who is Caribbean) that is capable of accommodating all of the region's varied and plentiful diasporic presences. Caribbean identity is produced out of myriads of peoples who settled in the region from almost every part of the world. They joined what was left of an indigenous population. This movement of people was motivated by the colonial agenda and engendered a need for multiple accommodations. At the same time, colonialism's transitory character combined with its discourse of difference and exclusiveness to locate many who may, otherwise, have had a sound claim to Caribbean identity, outside of the boundaries of Caribbean construction.

Caribbean identity occurs within the discursive space of the "Creole." To be "Caribbean" is to be "creolized" and within this space is accommodated all who, at any one time, constitute a (semi)permanent core of Caribbean society. Creolization comes with notions of organic connection across boundaries of ethnicized and racialized difference. It has been the process through which colonial discourses of difference, necessary for its

475

legitimation, were accommodated. Everyone located in the discursive space that it has created, of whatever diasporic origin, becomes transformed in a regime of identific solidarity. At the same time, out of *créolité* has emerged a discourse of exclusion that has acted, historically, to maintain a strict and rigid boundary between "Caribbean" and "non-Caribbean." This boundary separates the local from the foreign. It has functioned strategically as a mechanism for manipulation in the maintenance of order and control.

In its historical production, Creole society in the Caribbean emerged out of the representations and institutional practices of colonialism. It was forged out of a hegemonically imposed discourse of difference that allocated historically constructed and racially identified groupings to exclusive socioeconomic sectors of the political economy. The Creole continuum was fashioned from the insertion into slave society of two historically produced racialized categories that, in European imagination, existed universally at the opposite poles of civilization. *Créolité* was produced in the confluence of these two categories. The "Afro-Creole" (what is popularly considered "black" in the region) is located at one end of the continuum. As a social category, it is the embodiment of the (changing) representations and practices of descendants of enslaved populations transported from West Africa for plantation labor. Racially constituted by "pure" descendants of Africans, its creolization is the product of a syncretic mix of traditional African culture with the cultural forms of the dominant European colonial overlords. "White Creoles" or "local whites" are located at the other end of the continuum. They are descendants of plantation owners, former indentures, small-scale peasant landholders, workers, and (to a lesser degree) colonial officials with putatively "pure" European ancestry. Their creolization is the product of cultural pollution and immersion in the denigrated space of plantation society. Their history is one of development of organic ties to the colonial territory and of interests vested in colonial affairs, especially through ownership of agricultural and business enterprises. This has been particularly true of the process of white creolization in the British, French, and Dutch Caribbean colonies. It has been less true of the Spanish colonies with their substantial populations of own-account white farmers.

Creoleness has biogenetic implications. As a social construct, racial purity, once lost in the crucible of Caribbean reality, can never be regained. The assumption here is that race, as a biological phenomenon, cannot and does not exist. As such, the idea of racial purity is a social and historical product of modernity's discourse of difference, lacking any genetic or biological basis (see Molnar, 1983:182–203). Nonetheless, the distinguishing principle of racial purity has applied with particular historical force to local Creole whites. Their claims to racial purity have been abnegated through historical insertion into a plantation society tainted by the African presence. Socially exempted from the restrictive practices of white racial purity, white Creoles became free to cohabit, as acceptable social practice, with those located lower down in the color hierarchy. There is, therefore, a connection between cultural and biological creolization. One compromises the purity of the other. Thus, insertion into the bastardized space of Creole culture has biological implications. Cultural immersion (through marriage, conversion, association, style, taste, behavior, etc.) becomes biogenetically transformative. Within the Caribbean context, it has paved the way for sexual relations across racialized boundaries. In turn, the practices of marriage and cohabitation outside of the white grouping serve to reinforce notions of white Creole racial impurity.

476

Creole discourse has been the bonding agent of Caribbean society. It has functioned in the interest of the powerful, whether represented by a colonialist or nationalist elite. It is the identific glue that bonds the different, competing, and otherwise mutually exclusive interests contained within Caribbean society. It paved the way for accommodation of racialized discourses of difference upon which rested the legitimacy of colonial power and exploitation. Racial difference was rendered benign in the cognitive merger created and sustained by Creole discourse. Competing interests and relations of exploitation and privilege became socially organized in a fluid clinal system of racial and cultural hierarchy. This was the observation of Caribbean sociologist Lloyd Braithwaite (1953) in what has been called a "reticulated" color–class pattern of social stratification (Despres, 1968).

The racial and cultural hierarchy institutionalized in Creole discourse has legitimized and normalized a differential and unequal pattern of allocation of economic, cultural, symbolic, and social values. This differential and unequal pattern of allocation has come to characterize Caribbean society and political economy. With creolization functioning to normalize this pattern of differential allocation, the power interests of a colonial elite were rendered invisible.

The normalization of racialized relations of exploitation has been effected through the superimposition of ethnicity upon racial constructs of difference. By functioning as an ethnicized construct, *créolité* renders invisible the racial basis of power in colonial and postcolonial society. As a construct devoid of racial (as opposed to color) referents, it has allowed upward mobility to those who would otherwise be located lower down in the racial hierarchy. The acquisition of the cultural capital of European knowledge locates the "dark skinned" in the upper reaches of power, privilege, and authority. This hides the fundamentally racial character of Creole discourse of difference.

Creole representation and practice functioned in the Caribbean as the mechanism for inserting principles of divide and rule into colonial society. These principles were essential for the maintenance of colonial order and for colonial exploitation. *Créolité* functioned as a mechanism for the institutionalization of difference between the Creole and non-Creole, locating the latter outside the boundaries of Caribbean society. The practice of differential allocation of value, rights, and privilege between the Creole and non-Creole became uncontested. It acted to legitimize white privilege. At the same time it hid the commonalities of interests shared by the Creole and non-Creole populations of the colonized.

The historical production of difference in Caribbean society had a direct relationship to the representations and practices of groups located inside and outside the social space of Creole society. It was the fundamental pillar supporting the discourse of white supremacy by rendering white privilege unattainable to the Creole through a discourse of white purity. The symbolic capital of white purity came be located at the heart of colonial and neocolonial exploitation. For the colonizers, location outside the social space of the Creole served, historically, as the basis for colonial practices of divide and rule. These practices operated not merely as mechanisms for the obfuscation of the commonality of interests among the colonized. They served to legitimize colonial and later neocolonial exploitation.

Nonetheless, the boundaries separating the Creole and non-Creole are highly permeable. It is this permeability that has given Caribbean society its impermanence and temporality. It allows for changing notions of "West Indian" or "Caribbean" identity

477

in response to the changing influences and the changing demands of the global environment.

Creolization and Hybridity

In reality, what is "West Indian" or "Caribbean" has come to be cognitively constructed as the product of cultural and racial hybridization. To be "West Indian" is to be located along a continuum spanning from the "pure" European at one pole to the "pure" African at the other. These refer to putative notions of racial and cultural purity. However, in the hybridized reality of Creole space, racial and cultural purity cannot exist together. The Creole at the European end of the spectrum is always tainted by contact with the "uncivilized" that has emerged historically as a creation of the European discursive imagination. At the African end, the Creole is the historical product of redemption from a past rendered "savage" in the panoptic gaze of the conquering European. Such redemption is achieved in contact with Europe's civilizing influences. The extremes exist as cultural hybrids. They represent the implications of a culturally compromised racial purity. Without a compromised polluted culture, the European could not be accommodated within the social space. For the racially pure African, accommodation at the "lower" extremes of *créolité* is accomplished through cultural redemption. The combination of racial and cultural hybridity determines location in between the extremes. For the European, this pertains to the degree of cultural and racial pollution. It implies a descent from civilization. For the African, creolization implies ascent made possible by the acquisition of European cultural forms and by racial miscegenation whose extensiveness is signified by color. This, in essence, is the meaning of creolization. It is a process that stands at the center of constructs of Caribbean identity.

To be Caribbean, then, is to occupy the hierarchical, hybridized "Creole" space between two racial poles that serve as markers for civilization and savagery. It is to be constituted of various degrees of cultural and racial mixing. At the apex is the white Creole as the historical product of cultural hybridization. The Afro-Creole is located at the other end of the Creole continuum. The "creolization" of the latter derives from transformative contact with Europe's civilizing influences and from physical separation from Africa. Valorized forms of European racial and cultural purity are rendered unattainable ideals in Creole representation and practice. Distance from the ideal European phenotype and from Europe's cultural practices determines and defines the Creole's position in the social hierarchy.

Thus, the principles of hierarchization of West Indian Creole society are intimately tied to notions of European civilization and African savagery. As it applies to Europeans, creolization implies the taint of savagery. In its application to Africans, it implies a brush with civilization. The Caribbean is the location where civilization and savagery meet and where both become transformed. These have had profound implications for nationalist discourse. For the African, creolization implies a quest for European purity through cultural acquisition and miscegenation. With *créolité* as the central cultural construct of West Indian nationalism, these aspirations have become firmly embedded in the nationalist project. In this regard, nationalism becomes transformed into a quest to be fully European.

Divergence in Creole Representation and Practice

There is no uniformity and universality in Creole representation and practice in the region. Both are enframed by the centrality of notions of "territory" in West Indian self-conceptualizations. This makes sense for a number of reasons, not the least of which is the region's geomorphology and the almost unique history of each of the islands and the few mainland "territories" that together comprise Caribbean political geography. Despite Caribbean "universals" forged out of the plantation, a history of slavery and indentureship, and European colonialism, there are territorial divergences in the specifics of culture and society. In some cases, the universal European–African hybrid is modified by the incorporation of groups whose diasporic origins are located neither in Europe or Africa. There are, also, territorial differences shaped by the distinctive influences of different European colonizing powers upon the sociocultural framework. The individual impact of the colonizing powers of Britain, France, Spain, and Holland are discernible in the distinctive colonial legacies of each on the character of Creole society. Differences emerge, also, from the relative sizes of the diasporic communities amalgamated into Creole society and from the different representations and practices of racial hybridization. Finally, Creole culture, at any one time, reflects the outcome of contestations among those located along its color/class continuum as they have employed their symbolic, social, cultural, and economic power to define and contest its content.

At the broadest level, there are significant differences between the Spanish colonies and the rest of the region. These differences are related to the size of the white Creole population and the latter's socioeconomic location in the colonial political economy. In Cuba and Puerto Rico, white "*criollo*" culture has come to be understood as the "true" nationalist culture. It is contrasted with the Spanish European culture of the upper class and with the "African" culture of the black segment of the lower class. This relates directly to the historical role of white small-scale own-account campesinos (called *jíbaros* in Puerto Rico) eking out a living on small plots in the rural areas in both countries. A racialized distinction is maintained between the black population and the descendents of the latter. This distinction was fashioned by competing claims to the nationalist space. Creole nationalism came to be associated with a free European peasantry that had prior claims to the territory. These claims to the national space were made against the contestations of the descendants, an enslaved African population that had no freehold or usufruct rights to land. The nationalism of the insular Spanish Caribbean has been crafted out of the nationalist claims of the descendants of this independent peasantry linked to a history of land ownership. These claims have been combined with the aspirations of the mulatto population for upward mobility in the racial and cultural hierarchy. In the process, the latter has become absorbed in the discursive and increasingly hybridized and color-conscious space of the white Creole. In the Dominican Republic, this mulatto population has taken on the mantle of the Creole peasantry through a reconstructed history that has eviscerated its African origins. Assertions of European ancestry are combined with pre-European claims to territory forged in a constructed history of indigenous descent. This form of nationalism leaves very little possibility of black representation. Thus, in the nationalist discourse of the Dominican Republic, blackness is consigned to a Haitian identity in the cognitive construct of belonging (see contributions in Zavala and Rodriguez, 1980). Creole nationalism in the

Dominican Republic is the embodiment of the historical claims to territory by the Spanish campesinos and of a claim to prior ownership by the descendents of Africans. The latter claim has been authenticated through the social invention of descent from the indigenous population of Taino Arawaks whose presence predates European conquest. Nationalism rejects any assertions of rights of belonging by those claiming African ancestry.

Haiti exists in contradistinction to the Spanish Creole reality. There, Creole identity is firmly embodied in the representations and practices of the black lower class. This is reflected in the close association between nationalist "*noiriste*" ideology and the black Creole-speaking population. The latter comprises the overwhelming majority in the country. The black lower class has become distinguished, both linguistically and culturally, from the Francophile middle and upper classes. These latter contain both mulattos (in the vast majority) and blacks (Trouillot, 1990:109–36). The distinction between Creole and Francophile forms in representation and practice is somewhat inchoate. Middle- and upper-class Haitians traverse the boundaries between the two. The members of the Francophile elite do employ the popular cultural forms of the Creole-speaking black lower class in their everyday associations with the latter. At the same time, they reserve the more European forms, including the use of the French language, in their formal relationships and for government administration. French practices are employed to legitimize and justify the exclusion of lower-class participation in government in an identical manner that European forms were employed under colonialism. The institutionalization of French practices has become the basis of middle class-symbolic power (Trouillot, 1990:109–36).

Notwithstanding their location at opposite poles of Caribbean nationalist expression, the cases of the Dominican Republic and Haiti expose the profound European aspirations that are at the core of Caribbean territorial nationalism. These are indicated, as in the case of the Dominican Republic, in the rejection of notions of African origins. European aspirations are evident, also, in the wholehearted embrace of European forms by those with the historical charge of fashioning, orchestrating, and implementing the nationalist agenda. This embrace becomes evident, as it is in Haiti, in the institutional and cultural representations and practices of the nationalist elite.

The Spanish and Haitian colonial experiences introduce a number of complexities into the analysis of Caribbean society that serve to obfuscate the logic of Creole historical construction. The plantation stands at the center of a Creole discursive formation out of which territorial nationalism was fashioned. In the Spanish colonies, the overwhelming influence of the *criollo* peasantry subdued its significance. For Haiti, the legacy of the country's successful revolt against plantation slavery has overwhelmed its history. The trajectory of postrevolutionary Haiti deviated significantly from the logic of plantation society.

In the English-speaking territories, the plantation retained its paramountcy. It continued to do so even after the anticolonial battles were fought and won. Forced by a demise in the international sugar market, its dominance has only recently been challenged. Thus, an examination of the Anglophone former colonies offers the best opportunity for interrogating the Creole foundation of West Indian nationalism, free from the mitigations introduced by nonplantation forms. The focus of analysis will be confined hereafter to those territories under British colonial rule at the beginning of the nineteenth century.

Creole Construction in the English-speaking West Indies

Eleven island territories and the two small mainland countries have, together, organized themselves into a Caribbean Community and Common Market (CARICOM). Guyana, the largest in land area, is a mere 214,971 square kilometers (83,000 square miles) with a population of that hovers around 800,000. It is the only English-speaking country in South America. Belize, the second of the mainland territories, enjoys a similar official linguistic distinction in Central America, even though half of its population is Spanish-speaking. Its history is unique, even for Latin America. An institutionalized colonial administration was established only in the late eighteenth century in the colony. The practice of slavery was not organized around plantation production but around a pioneering timber industry of mahogany and logwood cutters. This contributed to a pattern of racial organization that was considerably more complicated than the rest of the English-speaking Caribbean. Over time, diasporic communities of Mayan and Carib Indians, whites, blacks (both slaves and free blacks liberated from slave ships), black Caribs deported from the islands, mestizos, and South Asians, established a presence in the colony. What emerged were both the black-white and the Indian-white (mestizo) versions of Creole ethnic forms (Lewis, 1968:289–91).

The island territories are diverse in size and history. Britain was the sole colonizer of Barbados from its colonial beginnings in the seventeenth century to the granting of independence in the 1960s. Most of the other territories changed hands (some more frequently than others) with the winds of historical fortune that fed the aspirations of the various European contenders for colonial possession. Jamaica, at 10,991 sq. km (4,244 sq. miles) and with its nearly two and a half million people, is the largest and most populous of the English-speaking islands. It passed from Spanish to British colonial control in the mid-seventeenth century, remaining a British colony for over 300 years. It is the only CARICOM member of the Greater Antilles group that includes Cuba, Hispaniola (Haiti and the Dominican Republic), and Puerto Rico. Distances of several hundred miles separate Jamaica from the rest of the English-speaking West Indies. Trinidad, the second largest of the islands, came under British colonial rule after capture from Spain in 1797. Its history as a slave economy began only in the mid-eighteenth century. What remains of CARICOM are single and multi-island territories with only two (Dominica and St. Lucia) exceeding 200 square miles in size. Apart from Barbados, with a population of 250,000, only St. Lucia (136,000 people) and St. Vincent (115,000 people) have populations that exceed 100,000. The populations of St. Lucia and Dominica speak, for the most part, a variant of French Creole, reflecting the influence of their colonial past. In Trinidad, on the other hand, the influence of the country's Spanish colonial heritage is everywhere, tempered by the pervasive presence of descendants of French planters and by the relative recency of its history of African slavery. The descendants of the enslaved have given the country much more of an African flavor than most other English-speaking countries of the region. The largest segment of the populations of Trinidad and Guyana are Hindu and Muslim descendants of indentured labor from South Asia (India and Pakistan).

There is considerable economic diversity among the CARICOM countries. Trinidad (with oil and gas), Guyana and Jamaica (with bauxite) are significant producers of minerals. There are also considerable differences in agricultural production, with the

481

cultivation of sugar, bananas, citrus, rice, and spices spread among the various territories. Such economic diversity, along with recent and differential emphasis on tourism, commerce, finance, and manufacturing, have all affected the reproduction of Creole discourse.

The differences above are reflected in different constructions of *créolité*. Quite important are the visibility and significance of white Creole representations and practices. Throughout the Caribbean, territorial differences have emerged in the persistence and size of this white Creole population. These have been in response to changes in the technical and social conditions of plantation production over time. The Barbadian example is located at one extreme, where the merchant/plantocracy became highly, even though differentially, amalgamated into the socialized space of Creole society. In Guyana, Creole whites disappeared as a social category, to be replaced by absentee owners based primarily in Britain.

Coloreds or "mulattos" serve as an intermediary racial and cultural bridge between the European and African poles in Caribbean Creole social construction. They are historical products of an imposed rationality of difference in colonial racial representation and practice. White males institutionalized this rationality through the exercise of gender and racial privilege over black female slaves. In turn, the offspring of these miscegenous unions were assigned positions of privilege over the black Creoles in the color/class hierarchy of colonial society. The allocation of Creole privilege was directly related to racial and cultural manifestations of the degree of separation from an African past. It was related, also, to the extent of demonstrated cultural and phenotypical similarity with the European. Creole privilege came with considerable access to cultural and economic capital.

Coloreds became the quintessential symbol of Creole society. In combination, gradations of color and the acquisition of cultural capital, particularly education and training, determined location in the social hierarchy of Creole society. As a bridging category, the boundaries between the coloreds, on the one hand, and white Creoles and Afro-Creoles on the other, were ill defined. Africans with cultural capital were able to move up in the hierarchy, while coloreds without were propelled downward. There was a similar blurring of distinctions between the coloreds and Creole whites. Coloreds with cultural and economic capital became absorbed into the social category of the latter.

The discourse of purity becomes one of the means through which disciplinary power was imposed upon Caribbean society. Under colonialism, rituals of white purity, as symbolic capital, were at the critical core of the self-representations of the colonial administrative elite. This was contrasted with the hybridized practices of the white Creole. The difference assumed institutional expression even in the arena of political representation and administration. In the English colonies different regimes of representation between colonial administrators and the white Creole merchant plantocracy were concretized in colonial political practices of the nineteenth century. In the administration of governance, white Creole practices were represented in a merchant planter-dominated Financial College. This emerged as the representative arm of the local white population. British colonial interests were publicized and represented through a Court of Policy that served, in effect, as the legislative arm of government. In addition, executive power was exercised through a colonial administration centered on the governor and comprising civil servants appointed by the crown (Daly, 1966:214). This development of different institutional bases of political representation and practice contributed significantly to the process of white creolization. It reflected the divergent material interests of the local and metropolitan capitalists. At the same time, such divergences of institutional and economic interests differed across territory, irrespective of colonial jurisdiction. They presaged differences in the presence and significance of white Creoles in the development of Creole identity across the region.

The Discourse of Purity

The hybridized reality of Creole society left little room for accommodation of claims to cultural and racial purity. It is important to emphasize here that purity, like race, is socially constructed. It emerges out of discursive regimes of representation and practice. The case of Dominica is instructive in underscoring this discursive basis of purity. There, the indigenous Caribs have had a long history of racial intermixing with blacks. Their racially mixed offspring have been immersed in Creole society and in the practices of Creole forms of social organization. Notwithstanding this history, notions of purity continue to act as legitimizing principles for excluding these putative descendants of the indigenous Caribs from Creole nationalist society.

In the Caribbean, purity has emerged as a boundary defining and maintaining principles separating Creole society from the external world. It was fashioned historically out of the discourse of difference that authenticated colonial society. Eventually, notions of purity became the basis for separating the "local" Creole white grouping from the foreign presence of the "pure" European. This distinction became quite important in assertions of cultural paramountcy made by the national elite. It allowed the accommodation of the white local elite in the nationalist construct. More importantly, it catapulted blacks and coloreds with cultural capital into a position of social ascendance over the local white descendents of the merchant plantocracy. This was symbolically important for nationalist and postcolonial contestation of white supremacy. Having demonstrated the supremacy of culture, the nationalist elite could make claims to inclusion in a new global order of North Atlantic universalism based pre-eminently on cultural grounds. By such a demonstration, they were able to reject claims to racial supremacy that historically privileged whites. Manifest demonstration of acquired European cultural forms as both symbolic capital and cultural capital (acquired knowledge, skill, and capabilities) has become the sole basis of claims to power and privilege in nationalist formation. These cultural acquisitions are at the root of the European aspirations of the contemporary nationalist elite.

A developing distinction between local and foreign within the white population of the colonial territories served as a legitimizing principle of white colonial privilege. Such legitimacy derived directly from the discursive assertions of white supremacy. Through assertions of racial privilege, it preserved colonial entitlement against claims by local whites. Such claims came with the possibility of undermining the colonial project, as was the case in the Spanish and Portuguese (Brazil) colonies of Latin America.

To be "genuinely" white in the Caribbean is to be culturally and racially pure, untainted by absorption into the society of black former slaves. This taint of impurity, forged out of cultural and sexual contact with the African, became the basis for exclusion of white Creoles from colonial power and privilege. Paradoxically, the organic connection to the "territory" which was at the root of this exclusion assured the white Creole a position of privilege in nationalist construction. The inclusion of whites in the nationalist space was quite consistent with claims to the supremacy of culture over racial bases of privilege. It legitimized the wholehearted adoption by the nationalist movement of European institutional and cultural forms after independence was achieved.

Thus, whiteness, however tainted, retained its valorized position in Creole nationalist construction. The right of white Creoles to social and economic privilege and preference was retained, and even enhanced, with the departure of the colonial power. In many instances, white Creoles became international brokers in the new regime of sovereignty. At the same time, their representation as cultural and racial hybrids, and their organic claims to the territory protected their social and economic privilege in the crucible of anticolonial nationalism. Otherwise, nationalism's challenge to white privilege might have become the basis for expulsion. Instead, their "whiteness" was rendered invisible in the face of a nationalist rejection of white supremacy. More importantly, white creolization became the mechanism for the nonproblematization of whiteness. It legitimized a postcolonial version of racial capitalism. This explains the continued domination of whites in the private sector of the postcolonial Caribbean despite nationalism's racial challenge to white supremacy.

Thus, the nationalist movement was neither antiwhite nor anti-European. Rather, it was a contestation of the claims of whites and Europeans to supremacy and superiority. The various assertions of Africanity in national expression must be understood in these terms. Their meaning continues to be the subject of debate among scholars and writers in the Francophone Caribbean. This debate is occurring under conditions where nationalist ambitions have been frustrated. Rather than a shift to sovereign independent status like their Anglophone counterparts, the French Antilles have become incorporated into the administrative and jurisdictional structure of the French state as *départements*. Frustrated nationalist ambitions have been largely responsible for the development of a *Créoliste* movement "agitating for the local culture and language of the French West Indies" (Taylor, 1989:124). The movement has supplanted earlier nationalist expressions framed around notions of Negritude. Its leading members have rejected Negritude's assertions of Africanity that became associated with the nationalism of the English-speaking West Indies. They consider claims to an African past as a replacement of the "illusion of Europe with that of Africa" (Taylor, 1989:128). These leaders have pains-takingly pointed out the contradictions in the Negritude movement manifest, particu-larly, in the support of its leadership, headed by Aimé Césaire of Martinique, for *département* status and in Césaire's firm embrace of the party politics of France. In these expressions of *créolité*, what clearly emerges is the rejection of Africa and the embrace of Europe. This pattern of rejection and embrace is firmly implanted in the nationalist aspirations of the Caribbean. It is more convincingly evident in the competing versions of nationalist expression in the French West Indies. Rejection of Africa and embrace of Europe are not so obvious in the Anglophone versions. They became camouflaged in the racial challenge to the authorial power of Britain in the campaign for independence.

Creole discourse locates all with claims to purity outside of the territorial community of the Caribbean. This is the point of the charge by the *Créolistes* of African and European illusion. Indeed, they go a step further by valorizing hybridity as "the vanguard of a world-wide movement" (Taylor, 1989:141). In other words, they see in the portent of *créolité* a future of racial and cultural hybridity for a new North Atlantic.

This hybridized future is at the forefront of neoglobalization. Such a conceptualization is essential to the European aspirations of Creole nationalism. It substantiates the self-location of the Creole at the center of a new globalization of the Europeanized North Atlantic. Thus, Patrick Chamoiseau, one of the movement's leading ideologues, describes creolization as a "great poetics of relation, which allows people to express their newfound diversity, to live it fluidly. In creolization, there never comes a time of general synthesis, with everyone beatifically at one with one another" (see Taylor, 1989:136).

Thus, claims to purity, essentialized around geographic discourses of origin, cannot be accommodated in Creole discourse. This is the basis of the *Créolistes'* discomfort with "illusions of Africa and Europe." It is why the North must first undergo a *métissage* transformation to accommodate the European aspirations of Creole nationalism. Thus, firmly imbedded in nationalist aspirations, is the goal of the conversion of Europe into the pregnable, transitory, and open space that is the Caribbean. This is very much what has occurred in the French Antilles. The assertions of *créolité* are very much declarations that the European space formerly occupied exclusively by whites has now become hybridized. Indeed, the term "Creole," before its hybridization, signified the representations and practices of white French West Indians known as *Békés*. It referred specifically to "a white person of pure race born in the Antilles" (Taylor, 1989:132).

A fluid, transitory, open accommodation has been the functional condition of the survival of Caribbean political economy from the inception. But the ensuing discourse of hybridity was also employed for symbolic exclusion. Like the white colonial population, other diasporic communities have been functionally integrated into the political economies of the region. Unlike the whites, symbolic exclusion has acted, historically, to delegitimize any claims members of these communities may make upon the benefits of territorial residence.

As indentureship replaced the system of slavery, supplies of new labor for plantation production had to be imported. Most important in terms of numbers were "East Indian" indentures brought from the subcontinent of India. Smaller but significant numbers of indentures were also imported from Portuguese territories and from China. Postemancipation indentureship imposed its own legitimating regime of exclusion. This rested upon the "racial" and cultural location of the new indentures outside of the European-African continuum of Creole society. But the new rationality of exclusion applied, also, to European and African postslavery indentures. Portuguese indentures, imported from Madeira, were unable to make immediate claims of racial affinity with the white Creoles in Trinidad and British Guiana (now Guyana). They were socially located for a time outside of Creole society. For postemancipation African indentures, the boundary maintaining distinction between African and Afro-Creole, typical of slave society, prevailed. Once inserted into plantation society, however, Portuguese and Africans became quickly amalgamated. For the African, creolization came with location at the lowest rung in the color-class hierarchy (Warner-Lewis, 1991). The Portuguese took over from coloreds in small-scale retailing. As trading minorities, their incorporation into Creole society was identical to that of the white Creole and of the "almost white coloreds (Nicolls, 1981:422–6). This was also the pattern of incorporation for the small migrant populations of Lebanese, Syrians, Jews, and postindenture Chinese. The latter, along with the Portuguese, were able to establish themselves in the retail sector, particularly in Trinidad and Jamaica.

Amalgamation has become integral to the historical reproduction of Creole identity. It calls for an abnegation of purity through sexual and cultural immersion. The Creole space "swallows everything up . . . remain[ing] permanently in motion, pushing us head-long in a movement of diversity, of change and exchange" (Taylor, 1989:142). "Blending and impurity" stand as its fundamental values (Taylor, 1989:137). With the exception of the Syrians and Lebanese whose cultural forms disappeared with creolization, immersion has acted, historically, to modify the African-European continuum in the Anglophone Caribbean.

Rituals and practices of Creole transformation can include racial immersion through miscegenation. Cultural immersion can occur through marriage, religious conversion, association, and adoption of the tastes and style of Creole society. Cohabitation has become quite important in individual practices of creolization. For the offspring of the ensuing unions, Creole parentage negates any claim to purity. It brings with it automatic location within the white–black continuum. To some degree, cohabitation with white Creoles has offered the most acceptable means of immersion into Creole society for those located outside of the European-African space. As the most "desirable" of the Creoles, cohabitation with whites serves to lessen the social opprobrium of immersion with its implications for impurity. Thus, with the exception of the whites who were pushed "downward" into Creole space, the thrust of creolization has always been upward to the European end of the racial and cultural spectrum. The quest of the nationalist movement was to penetrate the barrier of racial purity through a hybridization of European space. Indeed it was a quest for the cosmopolitanization of European social, cultural, symbolic, and political power.

Exclusion and Incorporation

Symbolic exclusion is the instrument of disciplinary power wielded historically against diasporic communities functionally integrated into Caribbean political economy. It rendered legitimate the systematic denial of any claims members of these communities might make upon the resources of Creole society. While historically pervasive, the discriminatory and exploitative consequences of symbolic exclusion were not always universal. With exclusion came the benefits of freedom from the normative strictures of Creole society. It created opportunities unavailable to those located in the color/class hierarchy of Creole social space.

The discourse of purity served historically, until well into the twentieth century, to confine East Indians to rural agriculture and to justify their semiservile status. At the same time, however, East Indians have managed to use peasant agriculture as a spring-board for upward mobility through business and the professions. In the process, they were able to eviscerate the social stigma of agricultural labor. Their agricultural back-ground did not prefigure in social evaluations of their fitness for business and higher education, as it would have for Creole subjects. As "outsiders," these standards of evaluation were rendered irrelevant.

The benefits of exclusion were evident, also, in the ability of Chinese and Portuguese (coming as nineteenth century indentures), Syrians, Lebanese and the small number of Jews (all arriving after World War I) to exploit economic opportunity. Their exclusion from Creole society freed them from the strictures of color imposed by their light complexion. As such, they were able to ignore the principles of behavior and association implicated in the color/class hierarchy of Creole society. They established themselves in petty trade by developing highly personalized relationships with customers lower down the color/class hierarchy. From here, they created a niche in small-scale retailing, particularly in Trinidad, Jamaica, and British Guiana (now Guyana). These activities, and the pattern of associations and practices they engendered, became springboards for their structural and social insertion into colonial Creole society. Once located in Creole space, they were able to combine symbolic capital (derived from their color) with economic capital to move up in the social hierarchy. Many came to occupy positions identical with or just below Creole whites. What became most evident in their upward mobility was the importance of the symbolic capital of whiteness. Thus, the over 40,000 postemancipation Africans brought to the West Indies between 1834 and 1867 for plantation labor experienced a fundamentally different pattern of amalgamation. They did not enjoy the reward of upward mobility (Asiegbu, 1969:189–90). Instead, incorporation occurred at the lowest rung of the color/class continuum of Creole society.

It is through racial and cultural incorporation that the transitory nature of Creole society is preserved. Incorporation allows Caribbean society to respond to the constantly changing pressures and demands from outside its borders. These must be accommodated for the very economic survival of the territories of the region. Practices of amalgamation have changed the racial and cultural character of Creole society. They have produced new forms of racial hybridity involving, particularly, East Indian and Chinese post-slavery additions to plantation society. Similarly, new emergent forms of cultural hybridity have become integrated into Creole practice. Thus, cultural and racial insertion has contributed to an historical reformulation of Creole identity. It has produced, over time, a modification of its racialized construction. Dark skin continues to retain the signifying power of inferiority. However, the exclusive association of dark skin with African diasporic origin is no longer a firmly entrenched principle. This explains the possibility for rejection of African origins in the Dominican Republic.

A white–black polarity based on color has replaced Europe and Africa at opposite ends of the Creole continuum. This has been particularly the case with the incorporation into Creole society of new diasporic communities with origins in Asia and the Middle East, and of the indigenous population of the region. "Blackness," however, continues, by and large, to retain its association with Africa in an ongoing counterdiscourse to Creole construction. This is quite evident in the regional spread of a Rastafarian movement that originated in Jamaica (see Chevannes, 1995), and in the Orisha religious movement in Trinidad (see Houk, 1993).

Territorial Differences in Creole Nationalism and its Contestation

Territorial differences in nationalist discourse across the region are related to differences in Creole constructions by which they are shaped, and have led to different patterns of contestation. Despite the universality of Creole identity, there is not much to cement a sense of "oneness" in the Caribbean, even among the CARICOM territories. First, historical differences have shaped the different constructions of Creole society. Second, the process of creolization has been differentially shaped by territorial differences in the form, nature, and pervasiveness of amalgamation of those outside the European-African continuum. This is particularly evident in Trinidad, Guyana, and, to a lesser degree Jamaica and Dominica. Third, the presence and significance of white Creoles vary across territory. They have virtually disappeared from Guyana, while in Barbados they comprise a significant even though numerically small presence. In Trinidad, white Creoles trace their descent to Spanish and French settlers who preceded British colonization.

For the most part, the indigenous and diasporic communities with cultural and racial origins outside Africa and Europe remain, in representation and practice, outside of Creole society. For members of these communities, amalgamation is available through individual practices of cultural and sexual immersion. For East Indians, individual practices of racial miscegenation with Afro-Creoles have been significant enough to produce a distinctive Creole variant identified as "*douglas*" in the local lexicon. As the products of Afro-Indian unions, douglas have become integral to the construction of Creole identity in Guyana and Trinidad. They have also come to symbolize the threat posed by creolization to East Indian purity. The theme of "douglarization" emerges persistently in East Indian narratives of purity. It has become emblematic of the polluting consequences of sexual contact with Africans. Douglarization, therefore, is the process of transformation of East Indians into racial Creoles through miscegenation. Another route to East Indian creolization is through cultural amalgamation. East Indians may enter the social space of Creole organization through practices of intermarriage, religious conversion, Creole association (including location of residence), and through the adoption of Creole style and tastes.

The construction of Creole society responds not merely to the relative numbers of its various components but, most importantly, to the symbolic power at their disposal. This refers to the honor and prestige attached to its various segments and to those located outside its symbolic space. There is a constant struggle to define *créolité* and constant need to redefine its character in response to the challenges from those located outside of its identific boundaries. Out of these persistent struggles have emerged territorially specific manifestations of Creole construction. These are not static but are constantly modified over time.

The case of Trinidad provides an example of the complexities and idiosyncrasies of Creole construction and its implication for nationalist discursive formation. The European cultural component of Trinidadian society has been shaped quite significantly by Spanish colonialism (the former colonial power) and by the presence of a French merchant plantocracy (via Haiti after the Haitian revolution). As "local whites," French Creoles became historically differentiated from the administrative class of the British in colonial representation and practice. Creole identity in Trinidad has, thus, become heavily infused with French and Spanish representations and with Roman Catholicism. It has been influenced, also, by the presence of East Indian, Chinese, Portuguese, Syrian, and Lebanese diasporic populations and by the various racial and cultural hybridities produced in social interaction among all these groupings. In particular, hybridized rituals and symbols of East Indian representations and practices are gaining considerable visibility in Creole construction. This is despite the latter's historical exclusion from the creolized space of Trinidadian identific discourse. At the same time, it has amalgamated the representation and practices of douglas (the products of miscegenous unions between Africans and Indians), Portuguese (by giving up their claims to whiteness), and Chinese, Syrians, and Lebanese (through cultural amalgamation and miscegenation).

At over 40 percent of the population, the size and functional integration of East Indians in Trinidad have had profound consequences for the reproduction of Creole society and for its ensuing nationalist construction. The fundamental contradiction between their structural integration and their symbolic exclusion from nationalist space has produced an increasing crescendo of conflict and contestation. Cultural and racial amalgamation has been available only to those members of the East Indian community prepared to reject representations and practices of purity. One avenue of rejection is through conversion to Christianity by Hindus. For the smaller Muslim East Indians (less than 25 percent of the East Indian population) religion poses less of a barrier to creolization, given the monotheism and common foundation of belief that it shares with Christianity. Muslims have been much more visibly included in the representation and practices of Creole nationalist expression. However, discourses of purity continue to locate the large majority of the East Indian population, as Hindus, outside of the national space. Pressures for creolization have been most evident upon the East Indian middle class. These derive from their functional insertion into Trinidad's political economy and from the postcolonial benefits of nationalism that have accrued to their Creole counterparts. This has propelled many Hindus to incorporate more Western forms into their religious practice, signaling some measure of creolization without sacrifice to their Hindu identity (see Klass, 1991).

At the same time, there is mounting resistance to creolization among the Hindu cultural elite. In their campaign, they are employing their resources of symbolic power to petition for inclusion in the nationalist space *as East Indians*. Hindu purity is being deployed as a symbolic resource by these leaders to delegitimize the representations and practices of a polluted Creole discourse. The challenge is organized around narratives of Creole cultural degradation directed, particularly, at the cultural ascendance of Afro-Creole forms in nationalist discourse. The campaign is accompanied by mounting contestation of the claim by Afro-Creoles to a central role in nation building. In their self-representations, East Indians are beginning to present themselves as the true builders of the nation and as the nation's saviors from Afro-Creole degradation (Yelvington, 1995:77). Theirs is not merely a quest for nationalist inclusion. It is an attempt to retain representations and practices of cultural purity while resisting "douglarization." It represents a claim to the nationalist space that is legitimized through a redemptive counterdiscourse to Afro-Creole nationalism. In this regard, it presents a fundamental challenge to Trinidadian *créolité* through a rejection of notions of hybridity and of "blending and impurity" as its fundamental values.

Notwithstanding these challenges, the fundamental thrust of creolization is deeply imbedded in the Trinidadian national psyche. This thrust is evident in the mythic representation of the "Spanish." It has emerged as a means of managing the complexities and conflicting pulls of disaporic identity. More importantly, it exposes the European aspirations in Creole discourse that is at the root of the country's nationalist expression. It is a narrative of a simpler time in Trinidad colonial history before the introduction of plantation slavery (and hence of the complexity of the African presence). In the "Spanish" construct is embodied all the positive elements of the various ethnic groupings that occupy the country's territorial space (creolized or otherwise). As such, it is a trope of hybridized harmony within the context of multiple and competing representations and practices of difference (Khan, 1993). But it is a harmony forged out of idealized "European" qualities, devoid of its racial exclusivity.

In Trinidad, the struggle for the nation occurs in the field of symbolic production. Representations and practices of purity are raised as challenges to Creole nationalism. In Guyana, symbolic representations of nationhood are less important than practices of institutional solidarity. The reason has, partly, to do with the historical absence of white Creoles in the color–class order of Guyanese social construction. After 1955, nationalist organization in Guyana became integrally associated with racialized practices of institutional inclusion and exclusion. These two combined to place a much more Africa-centered stamp on Guyanese nationalist Creole expression. During the 1960s the African Society for Cultural Relations with Independent Africa (ASCRIA) had become highly integrated into the structure and organization of the black nationalist Peoples National Congress (PNC) that had run the country since 1964. Its leaders enjoyed powerful positions in the government and it had become a major recruiting arm of the party. Without question, these leaders saw their role as ensuring the location of the black lower class at the center of the country's nationalist agenda. In the color–class hierarchy of Creole society, this was the class identifically tied to the representations and practices of Africa. In the process, the country's foreign relations became quite closely related to the African continent from which it adopted, almost wholeheartedly, Tanzania's version of cooperative socialism.

The emphasis on Africa conflicted with the culturally rooted aspirations and practices of the country's middle class, a significant proportion of whom were colored. By 1971, a middle-class backlash forced the ruling party to abandon its ideology of Africa-centered nationalism. In response, ASCRIA leaders resigned their government posts and began a scathing campaign against the ruling PNC. In 1975, the ruling party was firmly established in an alliance with Eastern Europe. It was also heavily reliant upon the support of the East Indian business and organized religious sectors. Thus, in Guyana, *créolité* was less integral to nationalist representation and practice than it was in Trinidad. It was replaced by a much more *institutional* conceptualization of the nation. The nationalist space was occupied by those located in the institutions of governance and the domestic interests that they represented (see Hintzen, 1989:169–73). Thus, contestations over national identity became most manifest over access to the institutional resources of power.

As in the case of Trinidad, the challenge emerged from within the East Indian population through representatives of its working-class interests. In addition to their rejection by the middle classes, Afro-Creole assertions of nationhood were rendered problematic by the presence of an East Indian population that exceeds 50 percent of the country's total. East Indians are strategically located in all the major institutional sectors of the political economy, much more so, in most cases, than the Creole population. This is true of the local private sector where ownership and control is almost exclusively East Indian. Their strategic presence in the private sector is bolstered by racially endogamous patterns of recruitment and hiring that typifies every sector of the political economy. There is, also, a significant presence of East Indians in the professional sector. They predominate in the country's agroproductive sector, almost exclusively as cash crop producers and as plantation labor. The PNC was forced to embark on a strategy of co-optation of the most strategic sectors of the East Indian political economy, particularly its businesspeople, professionals, and educated elite. This was incompatible with an Afro-Creole definition of nationhood. As a result, the Guyanese nation has come to be embodied by the governing institutions of the state and the racial affiliations of the governing elite. This has produced a racialized struggle over control of the national space, which takes place in the political arena. It is objectified in political competition for control of the governing institutions of the state among competing racial political organization, including political parties and trade unions. The struggle for the nation, therefore, is a struggle for domination of the national political space. East Indians have mounted a significant claim to this space by wresting executive and legislative power away from segments of its creolized population in 1992. Since then, the campaign for control of the nation has shifted to the bureaucratic apparatus of government (including the country's police and security apparatus) and to the judiciary. Both remain largely under Creole control (Hintzen, 1998).

East Indians in Trinidad and Guyana have employed different strategies to challenge Creole nationalist construct and to redefine national identity. Each challenge represents a specific instance of the amalgamation over time of multiple and competing claims to nationalist space. Each is a particular response to colonial and postcolonial discourses of exclusion legitimized in the historical production and reproduction of *créolité*. These responses emerge as assaults against the rituals, symbols, and institutions of Caribbean self-representation. In the final analysis, they represent counterdiscourses to the complex of cultural and racial representations and practices constitutive of Creole identity, and to the honor and prestige that, as symbolic capital, underlie Creole claims to privilege and power.

In Dominica, the Karifuna descendants of the indigenous Caribs are engaged in a struggle for autonomy. It is pitted against the representations and practices of the Creole nation-state. The struggle represents a local manifestation of a developing organization of the indigenous in Latin America and the Caribbean. It has emerged as a response to colonial and postcolonial practices of symbolic exclusion. Such practices have been maintained under conditions of structural integration of the Karifuna population into the Dominican political economy. Contestation of nationalist authority occurs within the context of a rejection of practices of marginalization and displacement objectified by historical containment in a Carib reserve. The struggle is over legal claims for exclusive rights of occupation to this "Carib territory" which occupies the symbolic center in articulations of a discourse of racial and cultural exclusivity among the Karifuna. The demand for autonomy is accompanied, periodically, by ritual acts of purification. These include expulsions of non-Caribs, particularly Afro-Creole males and their Karifuna female partners, from Carib territory (Gregoire et al. 1996). Contestation of Creole nationalist practice by groups with putative claims to indigenous identity is not confined to Dominica alone in the English-speaking Caribbean. Parallel movements have emerged among the Carib population in St. Vincent and the Grenadines.

Creole nationalism has been negotiated differently by the much larger indigenous population of Guyana. Amerindians occupy a much more ambiguous position in Guyanese nationalist space when compared with the Karifuna in Dominica. Their integration into Creole society varies with geographic location in the country. Most Amerindians have been converted to Christianity. Amerindian immersion into Creole society and into national institutions is not uniform among the various groups and is accompanied by varying degrees of cultural hybridity. This is related to the uneven pattern of economic integration of various Amerindian communities into the Guyanese political economy. Biogenetic immersion, related to practices of miscegenation, also varies with geographic location and cultural and economic integration. The Amerindian response to Guyanese nationalism is also conditioned by the institutional location of nationalist representation and practice. The struggle for participation in nationalist space occurs in the institutional arena of politics to which Amerindians have varying degrees of access. Because of this indeterminate relationship to Creole practice and to the national space, Amerindians have been less predisposed to nationalist rejection than their counterparts in Dominica. This is despite participation in international and local organizations of indigenous peoples (Fox and Danns, 1993)

In Barbados, Creole society has deviated little from its original colonial construction. It retains much of the European-African roots in its color–class hierarchical social formation. This persistence can be explained by the territorial history of uninterrupted British colonial rule. There was no importation of labor for postslavery indentureship that laid the groundwork for challenges to Creole formulations in countries like Guyana and Trinidad. A certain idiosyncrasy has emerged in the historical reproduction of Creole society in the country. Creolization was fashioned much more from cultural syncretization. Practices of cohabitation between Europeans and Africans have been significantly less than in the other territories. This is reflected in the relatively small number of persons classified as mixed. At 2.6 percent, these "coloreds" constitute an even smaller proportion of the population than Creole whites. The latter stands at around 3.3 percent. Thus, the color–class continuum is much less smooth and much more abrupt in Barbados. There is a much more discernible distinction between white and Afro-Creoles in representation and practice that is only minimally mitigated by the presence of an intermediary grouping of coloreds. The local white Creole had considerable access to power and privilege in colonial organization. White settlement and identification with the territory was fostered historically by colonial practices of governance. This was accompanied by a great degree of institutional exclusivity in economic, social, and cultural practices. The local merchant plantocracy, together with the colonial administrators, dominated the politics of the colony until the introduction of representative government in the mid-twentieth century. Since then, power has been shared with the colored and black Creole middle class.

Creole discourse has rendered almost impossible the accommodation of any diasporic community existing outside the European–African continuum in Barbados. The latter part of the twentieth century has seen immigration of a merchant class of South Asians that has grown to 0.5 percent of the population. Despite an initial period of intermarriage within the local community, they remain confined in representation and practice to a strict location outside of the Creole nationalist space. There, they retain their cultural and racial distinctiveness as "foreign." Hindu and Muslim rituals of purity are accompanied by strict practices of endogamy in marriage. Practices of seclusion are imposed upon women, and community organization is tight and closed (Hanoomansingh, 1996).

The Eurocultural aspirations of Creole nationalism are least hidden in Barbadian nationalist discourse. Anglophilia continues to be strong in Barbadian popular consciousness, evident in the generalized pride expressed in the country's designation as "Little England." There has been little challenge mounted against the economic, social, and symbolic power of the Creole whites.

Thus, the representations and practices of Creole nationalism differ significantly across the territories of the English-speaking Caribbean. These differences reflect the different diasporic compositions of colonial and postcolonial society and the different ways that the various diasporic communities have been inserted into political economy.

Ultimately, they reflect differences in the technical and social conditions of capitalist production over time and space.

Conclusion

An examination of the Caribbean raises profound conceptual questions about race, ethnicity, and nationalism. Nationalism, according to Benedict Anderson (1983:19), is to be understood in terms of "the large cultural system that preceded it, out of which – as well as against which – it came into being." And culture constitutes the representations and practices of ethnicity. From this perspective, Caribbean ethnicity is constituted by its representations and practices of *créolité*. The problem, however, is that Creole culture serves to hide a racialized division of labor and a racialized allocation of power and privilege. It renders these divisions invisible. The discourse of racial difference is shifted to distinctions between the Creole and non-Creole. Such a shift serves to hide commonalities in social practice that can form the basis of counterdiscursive challenges to power. The visualization of similarities present "new possibilities for struggle and resistance, for advancing alternative cultural possibilities" (Escobar, 1995:155). Thus, race, ethnicity, and nationalism turn out to be nothing more than the discursive products of a modern apparatus of social control. Different constructions of *créolité* have produced and reinforced virulent forms of territorial nationalisms. These have foreclosed opportunities for regional integration. Representations and practices of racial and cultural purity have prevailed in the face of hybridity. They have been at the root of endemic racial conflict in the region. Conceptualizations of white purity continue to reinforce and legitimize a system of globalized dependency. Creole nationalism continues to hide the pervasive and overarching presence of domestic racial capitalism. The way out of these dilemmas points in the direction of a new narrative of liberation to displace the representations and practices of the repressive cultural order of *créolité*.

References

Anderson, B. (1983) *Imagined Communities*. London: Verso.

Asiegbu, J. (1969) *Slavery and the Politics of Liberation, 1787–1861*. London: Longman.

Bourdieu, P. (1990) *The Logic of Practice*. Stanford, CA: Stanford University Press.

Braithwaite, L. (1953) "Social stratification in Trinidad." *Social and Economic Studies* 2:5–175.

Chevannes, B. (1995) *Rastafari: Roots and Ideology*. Syracuse, NY: Syracuse University Press.

Chude-Sokei, L. O. (1995) "The Incomprehensible Rain of Stars: Black Modernism, Black Diaspora." Dissertation submitted to the University of California, Los Angeles.

Daly, V. T. (1966) *A Short History of the Guyanese people*. Georgetown, Guyana: Daily Chronicle.

Despres L. A. (1967) *Cultural Pluralism and Nationalist Politics in British Guiana*. Chicago: Rand McNally.

Despres, L. A. (1968) "The implications of nationalist politics in British Guiana for the development of cultural theory," in R. Bendix (ed.) *State and Society*. Berkeley: University of California Press, pp.502–28.

Escobar, A. (1995) *Encountering Development*. Princeton, NJ: Princeton University Press.

Fox, D. and Danns, G. K. (1993) *The Indigenous Condition in Guyana*. Georgetown: University of Guyana.

Gilroy, P. (1993) *The Black Atlantic: Modernity and Double Consciousness*. New York: Penguin.

Gregoire, C., Henderson, P., and Kanem, N. (1996) "Karifuna: The Caribs of Dominica," in R. E. Reddock (ed.) *Ethnic Minorities in Caribbean Society*. St. Augustine, Trinidad: University of the West Indies, Institute of Social and Economic Research, pp.107–71.

Hanoomansingh, P. (1996) "Beyond profit and capital: A study of the Sindhis and Gujaratis of Barbados," in R. E. Reddock (ed.) *Ethnic Minorities in Caribbean Society*. St. Augustine, Trinidad: University of the West Indies, Institute of Social and Economic Research.

Hintzen, P. C. (1989) *The Costs of Regime Survival: Racial Mobilization. Elite Domination, and Control of the State in Guyana and Trinidad*. Cambridge, UK: Cambridge University Press.

Hintzen, P. C. (1997). "Reproducing domination: Identity and legitimacy constructs in the West Indies." *Social Identities* 3:47–76.

Hintzen, P. C. (1998) "Democracy on trial: The December 1997 elections in Guyana and its aftermath." *Caribbean Studies Newsletter* 25:13–16.

Houk, J. (1993) "Afro-Trinidadian identity and the Africanisation of the Orisha religion," in K. Yelvington (ed.) *Trinidad Ethnicity*. Knoxville: University of Tennessee Press, pp.161–79.

Khan, I. (1993) "What is 'a Spanish'?: Ambiguity and mixed ethnicity in Trinidad," in K. Yelvington (ed.) *Trinidad Ethnicity*. Knoxville: University of Tennessee Press, pp.180–207.

Klass, M. (1991) *Singing with Sai Baba*. Boulder, CO. Westview Press.

Lewis, G. K. (1968) *The Growth of the Modern West Indies*. New York: Monthly Review Press.

Mitchell, T. (1988) *Colonising Egypt*. Cambridge, UK: Cambridge University Press.

Molnar, S. (1983) *Human Variation*, 2nd ed. Englewood Cliffs, NJ: Prentice-Hall.

Nicolls, D. G. (1981) "No hawkers and peddlers." *Ethnic and Racial Studies* 34:415–31.

Rabinow, P. (1986) "Representations are social facts: Modernity and postmodernity in anthropology," in J. Clifford and G. Marcus (eds.) *Writing Culture: The Poetics and Politics of Ethnography*. Berkeley: University of California Press, pp.234–61.

Ryan, S. D. (1972) *Race and Nationalism in Trinidad and Tobago*. Toronto: University of Toronto Press.

Stavans, I. L. (1995) *The Hispanic Condition*. New York: HarperPerennial.

Taylor, L. (1989) "Créolité bites: A conversation with Patrick Chamoiseau, Raphael Confiant, and Jean Bernabé." *Transition* 74:124–61.

Trouillot, M. (1990) *Haiti: State Against Nation*. New York: Monthly Review Press.

Warner-Lewis, M. (1991) *Guinea's Other Suns*. Dover, MA: The Majority Press.

Yelvington, K. A. (1995) *Producing Power: Ethnicity, Gender, and Class in a Caribbean Workplace*. Philadelphia, PA: Temple University Press.

Zavala, I. and Rodriguez, R. (eds.) (1980) *The Intellectual Roots of Independence: An Anthology of Puerto Rican Political Essays*. New York: Monthly Review Press.

Chapter 33

Race in China

Frank Dikötter

Introduction

While over 50 different "minority nationalities" (*shaoshu minzu*) are officially recognized to exist in the People's Republic of China (PRC), well over 90 percent of the population are classified as Han, a term translated in English as "ethnic Chinese" or "Chinese of native stock." Despite the existence in China of cultural, linguistic, and regional differences which are as great as those to be found in Europe, the Han are claimed by mainland officials to be a homogeneous ethnic group (*minzu*) with common origins, a shared history and an ancestral territory. "Han" and "Chinese" have become virtually identical, not only within official rhetoric and scholarly discourse in the PRC, but also in the eyes of many foreign scholars. Eric Hobsbawm, in an influential book which highlights the extent to which nations are social constructs rather than universal givens, perpetuates the notion of a Han majority by noting that China is among "the extremely rare examples of historic states composed of a population that is ethnically almost or entirely homogeneous" (Hobsbawm, 1990:66). Only recently have some researchers started to refute the notion of an ethnic majority, and attempted to describe China as a mosaic composed of many culturally diverse groups within the so-called "Han" (Moser, 1985; Gladney, 1991). While references did exist in traditional China to the descendants of the various Han dynasties (206BCE–CE220), the representation of the "Han" as an ethnically integrated majority is a modern phenomenon intrinsically linked to the rise of nationalism at the end of the nineteenth century. The idea of a Han majority can be considered to be a modern invention used by nationalist elites to forge a sense of common identity among the various population groups of China in contradistinction to foreign powers who threatened the country and to the Manchus who ruled the Qing empire until its fall in 1911.

As in many other countries, moreover, racial theories have been essential in the construction of group identity in China throughout much of the twentieth century. As Sun Yatsen (1866–1925) – founder of the Guomindang, China's Nationalist Party, and widely accepted as the "father" of the nation in China and in Taiwan to this day – put it in his famous *Three Principles of the People*:

> The greatest force is common blood. The Chinese belong to the yellow race because they come from the blood stock of the yellow race. The blood of ancestors is transmitted by heredity down through the race, making blood kinship a powerful force. (Sun, 1927:4–5)

Sun Yatsen and other political leaders considered the Han to constitute the absolute majority in China, a distinct people with shared physical attributes and a line of blood which could be traced back to the most ancient period. If socially constructed "races" are population groups which are imagined to have boundaries based on real or imagined biological characteristics, and if they can be contrasted to socially constructed "ethnicities," which are population groups thought to be based on culturally acquired characteristics, then both were seen to be coterminous by political elites in modern China: ideas of "culture," "ethnicity," and "race," in other words, were often conflated by political and intellectual elites in order to represent cultural features as secondary to, and derivative of, an imagined racial specificity.

Politics have been an essential factor in the emergence of racial discourse in modern China: in order to legitimize control over the territory which was part of the imperial realm until 1911, the political leaders of the Republic until 1949 and the People's Republic after 1949 have reinvented subject peoples in border areas as mere subbranches of the Han. This assimilationist vision emphasizes both the organic entity of all the peoples living within the political boundaries of China and the inevitable fusion of non-Han groups into a broader Chinese nation dominated by the Han: the political boundaries of the state, in short, could be claimed to be based on a more profound biological unity between the various peoples of China. Chiang Kai-shek (1887–1975), the effective head of the Nationalist Republic from 1927 to 1949 and the leader of the Guomindang, clearly expressed this vision of the nation as a culturally diverse but racially unified entity in his important work entitled *China's Destiny*, written during the fight against Japan in World War II:

> Our various clans actually belong to the same nation, as well as to the same racial stock. Therefore, there is an inner factor closely linking the historical destiny of common existence and common sorrow and joy of the whole Chinese nation. That there are five people designated in China is not due to differences in race or blood, but to religion and geographical environment. In short, the differentiation among China's five peoples is due to regional and religious factors, and not to race or blood. This fact must be thoroughly understood by all our fellow countrymen. (Chiang, 1947:39–40)

While this assimilationist vision is closely linked to the politics of national unity, its legitimacy has primarily been based on science. Racial theories were only made possible by the advent of scientific knowledge in Europe from the late eighteenth century onwards, as science offered a whole new episteme from which a relationship between culture and biology could for the first time be systematically imagined. Racial theories, first in parts of Europe and gradually in other points of the globe, sought to explain cultural differences as natural differences and to represent social groups as biological units: racial theorists appropriated science, from craniology to genetics, in order to present the group boundaries they had constructed as objectively grounded in natural laws. In Europe, China, and many other parts of the globe, negative attitudes about the physical appearance of individuals or population groups can be found before modernity, but these attitudes rarely formed a coherent system which could provide legitimacy to social inclusions or exclusions.

The politics of nationalism and the episteme of science were both intrinsic to modernity and only appeared in China with the reform movement which gained momentum after China's defeat against Japan in 1894–5. Imperial reformers after 1895 proposed to strengthen the country in its confrontation with foreign powers by reforming the thought and behavior of all the people. The first to systematically articulate a distinctly nationalist agenda of reform in which all citizens would participate in the revival of the country, they promoted an alternative body of knowledge which derived its legitimacy independently of the official examination system, based on the Confucian classics. The new knowledge deployed by the reformers – a complex fusion of different indigenous strains of learning with foreign discursive repertoires – was marked by an appeal to "science" as a legitimizing force. It was also influenced by historical developments specific to the Qing dynasty.

The Reconfiguration of Lineage Discourse and the Emergence of Racial Taxonomies

As noted above, racial theories were dependent on the new episteme of science which appeared only from the late eighteenth century onwards in parts of Europe before emerging elsewhere across the globe. Attitudes towards outgroups in imperial China have often been described as "culturalist": lack of adherence to the cultural norms and ritual practices of Confucianism were the principal markers distinguishing outsiders, often referred to as "barbarians," from insiders. In an assimilationist vision, however, barbarians could be culturally absorbed – *laihua*, "come and be transformed," or *hanhua*, "become Chinese." The *Chunqiu*, a chronological history of the Spring and Autumn period (722–481BCE) traditionally attributed to Confucius, hinged on the idea of cultural assimilation. In his commentary on the *Gongyang*, He Xiu (129–182CE) later distinguished between the *zhuxia*, the "various people of Xia [the first Chinese empire]," and the Yi and Di barbarians, living outside the scope of the Chinese cultural sphere. In the Age of Great Peace, an allegorical concept similar to the Golden Age in the West, the barbarians would flow in and be transformed: the world would be one. Some researchers have questioned the "culturalist" thesis by drawing attention to passages from the classics of Confucianism which are apparently incompatible with the concept of cultural universalism. Most quoted is the *Zuozhuan* (fourth century BCE), a feudal chronicle: "If he is not of our race, he is sure to have a different mind" (*fei wo zulei, qi xin bi yi*). This sentence seems to support the allegation that at least some degree of "racial discrimination" existed during the early stages of Chinese civilization. Both interpretations, however, have in common the adoption of a modern conceptual framework that distinguishes sharply between "culture" and "race," a distinction which was not clearly expressed before the advent of modernity. In China and in many other parts of the globe, physical markers and cultural characteristics were rarely separated, nor were perceived bodily differences rationalized into a coherent system which might confer legitimacy to exclusionary practices. A revealing illustration of the lack of distinction between "race" and "culture" appears in a twelfth-century description of African slaves, bought from Arab merchants by rich merchants in Canton:

> Their colour is black as ink, their lips are red and their teeth white, their hair is curly and yellow. There are males and females . . . They live in the mountains (or islands) beyond the seas. They eat raw things. If, in captivity, they are fed on cooked food, after several days they get diarrhoea. This is called "changing the bowels" [*huanchang*]. For this reason they

497

sometimes fall ill and die; if they do not die one can keep them, and after having been kept a long time they begin to understand human speech [i.e., Chinese], although they themselves cannot speak it. (Duyvendak, 1949:24)

In popular Daoism, a human had to change bones (*huangu*) in order to become immortal: by analogy, African slaves were expected to change bowels (*huanchang*) to become half-human. A physical transformation, in other words, was perceived to be an intrinsic part of cultural assimilation. Even in the nineteenth century, scholar-officials like Xu Jiyu, who had extended contact with European traders and were familiar with world geography, wrote how "the hair and eyes of some [Europeans] gradually turn black when they come to China and stay for a long time. The features of such men and women half-resemble the Chinese." If it could be shown that negative representations of physical markers existed in traditional China (Dikötter, 1992), no concept of "race" nor any systematic attempt to classify population groups on the basis of such markers existed until the emergence of modernity in the 1890s.

While long-standing attitudes towards physical characteristics may have facilitated the appearance of racial identities in China after 1895, several historical factors were more directly relevant, namely (1) the social institution and cultural discourse of the lineage, (2) the search for wealth, power, and unity by the reformers after the defeat of China in the Sino-Japanese War of 1894–5 and (3) the anti-Manchu nationalism of the revolution-aries in the first decade of the twentieth century. Lineage discourse under the Qing – a dynasty founded in 1644 by the Manchus after their invasion of China – was perhaps one of the most prominent building blocks in the construction of symbolic boundaries between racially defined groups of people.

The Qing era was marked by a consolidation of the cult of patrilineal descent, center of a broad movement of social reform that had emphasized the family and the lineage (*zu*) since the collapse of the Ming. Considerable friction arose between lineages throughout the nineteenth century in response to heightened competition over natural resources, the need to control market towns, the gradual erosion of social order, and organization disorders caused by demographic pressures. Lineage feuds as well as interethnic conflicts (*fenlei xiedou*) prevailed throughout the empire, but were more common in the south-east, where lineages had grown more powerful than in the north (Lamley, 1977). The militarization of powerful lineages reinforced folk models of kinship solidarity, forcing in turn more loosely organized associations to form a unified descent group under the leadership of the gentry. At court level too, ideologies of descent became increasingly important, in particular with the erosion of a sense of cultural identity among Manchu aristocrats. Pamela Crossley has shown how ethnic identity through patrilineal descent became important in the Qianlong period (1736–95), when the court progressively turned towards a rigid taxonomy of distinct descent lines (*zu*) to distinguish between Han, Manchu, Mongol, or Tibetan (Crossley, 1990). Within three distinct social levels – popular culture, gentry society, and court politics – the common notion of patrilineal descent came to be deployed on a widespread scale in the creation and maintenance of group boundaries.

The 1898 reformers, who championed a radical transformation of imperial institutions and orthodox ideology, understood the notion of "race" on the basis of the lineage. Leading reformers like Liang Qichao (1873–1929) and Kang Youwei (1858–1927) selectively appropriated scientific knowledge from foreign discursive repertoires to invent a new sense of group identity. In search of wealth and power in the wake of the country's disastrous defeat against Japan, in need of a unifying concept capable of binding all the emperor's subjects together in a powerful nation which could resist the foreign encroachments which had started with the first Opium War (1839–42), the reformers used new evolutionary theories to present the world as a battlefield in which different races struggled for survival. They also appealed to patrilineal culture in order to represent all inhabitants of China as the descendants of the Yellow Emperor. Extrapolating from an indigenous vision of lineage feuds, which permeated the social landscape of late imperial China, the reformers constructed a racialized worldview in which "yellows" competed with "whites" over degenerate breeds of "browns," "blacks," and "reds." Thriving on its affinity with lineage discourse, the notion of "race" gradually emerged as the most common symbol of national cohesion, permanently replacing more conventional emblems of cultural identity. The threat of racial extinction (*miezhong*), a powerful message of fear based on more popular anxieties about lineage extinction (*miezu*), was often raised to bolster the reformers' message of change in the face of imperialist aggressions: "They will enslave us and hinder the development of our spirit and body . . . The brown and black races constantly waver between life and death, why not the 400 million of yellows?" (Yan, 1959:22). In the reformers' symbolic network of racialized others, the dominating "white" and "yellow" races were opposed to the "darker races," doomed to racial extinction by hereditary inadequacy. The social hierarchy which existed between different groups of people in the empire was expanded into a vision of racial hierarchy characterized by "noble" (*guizhong*) and "low" (*jianzhong*), "superior" (*youzhong*) and "inferior" (*liezhong*), "historical" and "ahistorical" races (*youlishi de zhongzu*). The distinction between "common people" (*liangmin*) and "mean people" (*jianmin*), widespread in China until the early eighteenth century, found an echo in Tang Caichang (1867–1900), who opposed "fine races" (*liangzhong*) to "mean races" (*jianzhong*). He phrased it in evenly balanced clauses reminiscent of his classical education: "Yellow and white are wise, red and black are stupid; yellow and white are rulers, red and black are slaves; yellow and white are united, red and black are scattered" (Tang, 1968:468).

Selectively appropriating social Darwinian theories, the reformers claimed that racial survival (*baozhong*) in a context of international competition was the inescapable consequence of profound evolutionary forces. Rather than appealing to Charles Darwin's emphasis on competition between individuals of the same species, however, most reformers were inspired by Herbert Spencer's focus on group selection. For reformers like Yan Fu, Liang Qichao, and Kang Youwei, processes of evolution were directed by the principle of racial grouping, in which individuals of a race should unite in order to survive in the struggle for existence much as each cell contributed to the overall health of a living organism. Apart from the individualistic basis for competition, the reformers also ignored the neo-Darwinian emphasis on the branching process of evolution. They adopted a Neo-Lamarckian theory of linear evolution, which viewed human devleopment as a single line of ascent from the apes: the embryo developed in a purposeful way towards maturity, and this process could be guided by changes to the social and political environment. Neo-Lamarckism offered a flexible vision of evolution which closely suited the political agenda of the reformers, as human progress in the realm of politics was seen to be conducive to the racial improvement of the species.

The reformers proposed a form of constitutional monarchy which would include the Manchu emperor: their notion of a "yellow race" (*huangzhong*) was broad enough to include all the people living in the Middle Kingdom. In the wake of the abortive Hundred Days Reform of 1898, which ended when the empress dowager rescinded all the reform decrees and executed several reformer officials, a number of radical intellectuals started advocating the overthrow of the Manchu dynasty: not without resonance to the 1789 and 1848 political revolutions in Europe, the anti-Manchu revolutionaries represented the ruling elites as an inferior "race" which was responsible for the disastrous policies which had led to the decline of the country, while most inhabitants of China were perceived to be part of a homogeneous Han race. In search of national unity, the very notion of a Han race emerged in a relational context of opposition both to foreign powers and to the ruling Manchus. For the revolutionaries, the notion of a "yellow race" was not entirely adequate as it included the much reviled Manchus. Whereas the reformers perceived race (*zhongzu*) as a biological extension of the lineage (*zu*), encompassing all people dwelling on the soil of the Yellow Emperor, the revolutionaries excluded the Mongols, Manchus, Tibetans, and other population groups from their definition of race, which was narrowed down to the Han, who were referred to as a *minzu*.

Minzu, a key term used interchangeably for both "ethnic group" and "nationality" after 1949, referred to a common descent group with a distinct culture and territory. During the incipient period of 1902 to 1911, moreover, *minzu* as a term was used to promote symbolic boundaries of blood and descent: "nationalities" as political units were equated with "races" as biological units. In the nationalist ideology of the first decade of the twentieth century, *minzu* was thought to be based on a quantifiable number of people called "Han," a group with clear boundaries by virtue of imagined blood and descent. Sun Yatsen (1866–1925) became one of the principal proponents of a Chinese *minzu*, which he claimed was linked primarily by "common blood." *Minzuzhuyi*, or "the doctrine of the *minzu*," became the term used to translate into Chinese the ideology of nationalism, thus clearly indicating the overlap which was envisaged between nation and race. Nationalism was the first principle of Sun Yatsen's "Three Principles of the People," and it has been adopted ever since by both the Guomindang and the Chinese Communist Party (CCP).

The myth of blood was sealed by elevating the figure of the Yellow Emperor to a national symbol. The Yellow Emperor (*Huangdi*) was a mythical figure thought to have reigned from 2697 to 2597 BCE. He was hailed as the first ancestor (*shizu*) of the Han race, and his portrait served as the frontispiece in many nationalist publications. From mid-1903, the revolutionaries started using dates based on the supposed birthday of the Yellow Emperor. Liu Shipei (1884–1919), for instance, published an article advocating the introduction of a calendar in which the foundation year corresponded to the birth of the Yellow Emperor.

> They [the reformers] see the preservation of religion [*baojiao*] as a handle, so they use the birth of Confucius as the starting date of the calendar; the purpose of our generation is the preservation of the race [*baozhong*], so we use the birth of the Yellow Emperor as a founding date. (Liu, 1904:1)

The vision of racial grouping elaborated by the revolutionaries fighting for the overthrow of the Qing dynasty is eloquently illustrated by Zou Rong, one of the more influential nationalists, who proudly proclaimed that:

When men love their race, solidarity will arise internally, and what is outside will be repelled. Hence, to begin with, lineages were united and other lineages repelled; next, lineages of villages were united and lineages of other villages repelled; next, tribes were united and other tribes were repelled; finally, the people of a country became united, and people of other countries were repelled. This is the general principle of the races of the world, and also a major reason why races engender history. I will demonstrate to my countrymen, to allow them to form their own impression, how our yellow race, the yellow race of which the Han race is part, is able to unite itself and repel intruders. (Tsou, 1968:106)

The revolutionaries constructed a new sense of identity that narrowly focused on the Han race, pictured as a perennial biological unit descended from a mythological ancestor. By 1911, culture, nation, and race had become coterminous for many revolutionaries fighting the Qing dynasty.

Racial Discourse in Republican China[1]

The Qing empire collapsed in 1911, a momentous political event which was marked by a number of important developments, for instance the rapid transformation of the traditional gentry into powerful new elites, such as factory managers, bankers, lawyers, doctors, scientists, educators, and journalists. The result of new economic opportunities created through contacts with Western traders and the closer integration of the country into a global economy, the gradual emergence of new social formations was particularly pronounced in the large metropoles of the coast. Based on a common ground of social values, a sophisticated network of relations webbed intellectuals, urban notables, and financial elites together into a modernizing avant-garde. With the collapse of the imperial system, moreover, neo-Confucian knowledge rapidly lost its credibility and authority. With the decline of conformity to the moral imperatives enshrined in a canon of Confucian texts, a growing number of people with a modern education believed "truth" to be encoded in a nature which only science could decrypt. Identity, ancestry, and meaning were buried deep inside the body: anthropology or genetics, by probing the body, could establish the "natural" differences between population groups. Modern science, in the eyes of modernizing elites, came to replace imperial cosmology as the epistemological foundation for claims about social order. These elites viewed race as a credible concept capable of promoting national unity after the collapse of the imperial system. Not only was "race" deemed to be an objective, universal, and scientifically observable given, but it also fulfilled a unifying role in the politics of the nation: it promoted unity against foreign aggressors and supressed internal divisions. Even the "peasants with weather-beaten faces and mud-caked hands and feet" could be represented as the descendants of the Yellow Emperor, as "race" was a notion which could overarch gender, lineage, class, and region to conceptually integrate the country's people into a powerful community organically linked by blood.

Racial theories were not confined to the ruling elites concerned with the unity of the nation. With the rise of a new print culture, driven by many private publishing houses and by the general growth in literacy after the fall of the empire, a vernacular press appeared which facilitated the circulation of new forms of group identity. Public consumption of new publications which heralded the demise of "primitive races" and

501

the regeneration of the "yellow race" contributed to the spread of racial theories. Racial categories of analysis, disseminated by the new print culture, were consolidated by endless references to science. Chen Yucang (1889–1947), director of the Medical College of Tongji University and a secretary to the Legislative Yuan, boldly postulated that the degree of civilization was the only indicator of cranial weight: "If we compare the cranial weights of different people, the civilised are somewhat heavier than the savages, and the Chinese brain is a bit heavier than the European brain" (Chen, 1937:180). Liang Boqiang, in an oft-quoted study on the "Chinese race" published in 1926, took the blood's "index of agglutination" as an indicator of purity, while the absence of body hair came to symbolize a biological boundary of the "Chinese race" for a popular writer like Lin Yutang (1895–1976), who even proclaimed that "on good authority from medical doctors, and from references in writing, one knows that a perfectly bare mons veneris is not uncommon in Chinese women" (Lin, 1935:26). Archeologists, on the other hand, sought evidence of human beginnings in China. Like many of his contemporaries, Lin Yan cited the discovery of Beijing Man at Zhoukoudian as evidence that the "Chinese race" had existed on the soil of the Middle Kingdom since the earliest stage of civilization (Lin, 1947:27). Excavations supported his hypothesis by demonstrating that migrations had taken place only within the empire. It was concluded that China was inhabited by "the earth's most ancient original inhabitants."

Modernizing elites were instrumental in the dissemination of racial theories among the general public by means of school textbooks, anthropology exhibitions, and travel literature. Print culture even reached the lower levels of education, spreading racial theories via the curriculum. The opening sentence of a chapter on "human races" in a 1920 textbook for middle schools declared that "among the world's races, there are strong and weak constitutions, there are black and white skins, there is hard and soft hair, there are superior and inferior cultures. A rapid overview shows that they are not of the same level" (Fu, 1914:9–15). Even in primary schools, readings on racial politics became part of the curriculum:

> Mankind is divided into five races. The yellow and white races are relatively strong and intelligent. Because the other races are feeble and stupid, they are being exterminated by the white race. Only the yellow race competes with the white race. This is so-called evolution ... Among the contemporary races that could be called superior, there are only the yellow and the white races. China is the yellow race. (Wieger, 1921:180)

Although it is clear that individual writers, political groups, and academic institutions had different ideas about the meanings of physical features, many educated people in China had come to identify themselves and others in terms of "race" by the end of the Republican period.

Some isolated voices in China openly contested the existence of a racial taxonomy: Zhang Junmai, for instance, wisely excluded "common blood" from his definition of the nation (Zhang, 1935:10, 25). Qi Sihe also criticized the use of racial categories of analysis in China, and pointed out how "race" was a declining notion in the West (Qi Sihe, 1937). Generally, however, racial discourse was a dominant practice which cut across most political positions, from the fascist core of the Guomindang to the communist theories of Li Dazhao. Its fundamental role in the construction of racialized boundaries between self and other, its powerful appeal to a sense of belonging based on presumed links of blood, its authoritative worldview in which cultural differences could be explained in terms of stable biological laws, all these aspects provided racial discourse with a singular resilience: it shaped the identity of millions of people in Republican China, as it had done for people in Europe and the United States.

Racial classifications between different population groups were so important that they often preceded and shaped real social encounters. The poet Wen Yiduo, for instance, sailed for the United States in 1922, but even on board his courage ebbed away as he felt increasingly apprehensive of racial discrimination in the West. In America he felt lonely and homesick: he described himself as the "exiled prisoner." Wen Yiduo wrote home:

> For a thoughtful young Chinese, the taste of life here in America is beyond description. When I return home for New Year, the year after next, I shall talk with you around the fire, I shall weep bitterly and shed tears to give vent to all the accumulated indignation. I have a nation, I have a history and a culture of five thousand years: how can this be inferior to the Americans? (Wen, 1968, vol. 1:40)

His resentment against "the West" culminated in a poem entitled "I am Chinese":

> I am Chinese, I am Chinese,
> I am the divine blood of the Yellow Emperor,
> I came from the highest place in the world,
> Pamir is my ancestral place,
> My race is like the Yellow River,
> We flow down the Kunlun mountain slope,
> We flow across the Asian continent,
> From us have flown exquisite customs.
> Mighty nation! Mighty nation!
>
> (Wen, 1925)

It is undeniable that some Chinese students genuinely suffered from racial discrimination abroad, although an element of self-victimization and self-humiliation undoubtedly entered into the composition of such feelings. More importantly, however, they often interpreted their social encounters abroad from a cultural repertoire which reinforced the racialization of others. Even social experiences that had the potential to destabilize their sense of identity were appropriated and integrated into a racial frame of reference. Pan Guangdan, the most outspoken proponent of eugenics in China, expressed his disappointment with the unwillingness of a book entitled *The American Negro*, edited by Donald Young in 1928, to speak in terms of racial inequality:

> But to be true to observable facts, in any given period of time sufficiently long for selection to take effect, races *as groups are* different, unequal, and there is no reason except one based upon sentiment why we cannot refer to them in terms of inferiority and superiority, when facts warrant us. It is to be suspected that the Jewish scholars, themselves belonging to a racial group which has long been unjustly discriminated against, have unwittingly developed among themselves a defensive mechanism which is influencing their judgements on racial questions. The reviewer recalls with regret that during his student days [in the United States] he had estranged some of his best Jewish friends for his candid views on the point of racial inequality. (Pan, 1930)

Racialized Identities in Contemporary China

Racial theories were attacked as tools of imperialism following the communist takeover in 1949 (Ubukata, 1953), and university departments in such fields as genetics and anthropology were subsequently closed for political reasons in the early 1950s (anthropologists, for instance, were accused of having used disrespectful anthropometric methods that insulted the minority nationalities). While the CCP appealed to the notion of "class" as a unifying concept, it did not abandon the politically vital distinction between a Han majority on the one hand and a range of minorities on the other. Not only did the CCP perpetuate the generic representation of linguistically and culturally diverse people in China as a homogeneous group called Han *minzu*, but they also swiftly proceeded to officially recognize 41 so-called "minority nationalities" (*shaoshu minzu*) who applied for nationality recognition after the founding of the People's Republic in 1949, a number which increased to 56 by the time of the 1982 census. As the political boundaries of the country recognized by the CCP corresponded largely to those of the Qing empire, minority populations in the strategically and economically vital border regions of Xinjiang and Tibet, for example, continued to be portrayed as both organically linked yet politically subordinate people in their relationship to the Han. Although the idea of equality between different *minzu* was promoted by the CCP in order to combat "Han chauvinism" (*Da Han minzuzhuyi*), the representation of the Han as an absolute majority endowed with superior political and cultural attributes and hence destined to be the vanguard of the revolution and the forefront of economic development dominated official discourse during the Maoist period. Not entirely disimilar to the racial taxonomies used by the revolutionaries at the beginning of the twentieth century, "minority nationalities" were represented as less evolved branches of people who needed the moral and political guidance of the Han in order to ascend on the scales of civilization. The representation of the Han as a politically more advanced and better endowed *minzu* pervaded the early decades of the communist regime, while assimilationist policies were also eagerly pursued. "Han" and "Chinese," in other words, were not only seen to be coterminous, but "minorities" continued to be portrayed as mere subbranches of a broader organic web destined to fuse into a single nation.

The emphasis on class struggle at the expense of economic development was reversed after the death of Mao Zedong in 1976. After the ascent to power of Deng Xiaoping in 1978, the language of science gradually started to replace communist ideology in a number of politically sensitive domains. Paleoanthropological research illustrates how the assimilationist vision was reinvigorated by scientific research in the 1980s and 1990s.[2] Prominent researchers have represented Beijing Man at Zhoukoudian as the "ancestor" of the "mongoloid race" (*Menggu renzhong*). A great number of hominid teeth, skull fragments, and fossil apes have been discovered from different sites scattered over China since 1949, and these finds have been used to support the view that the "yellow race" (*huangzhong*) today is in a direct line of descent from its hominid ancestor in China. Although paleoanthropologists in China acknowledge that the evidence from fossil material discovered so far points at Africa as the birthplace of humankind, highly regarded researchers like Jia Lanpo have repeatedly underlined that our real place of origin should be located in East Asia. Wu Rukang, also one of the most respected paleoanthropologists in China, has come very close to upholding a polygenist thesis (the idea that humankind has different origins) in mapping different geographical spaces for the "yellow race" (China), the "black race" (Africa) and the "white race" (Europe): "The fossils of homo sapiens discovered in China all prominently display the characteristics of the yellow race . . . pointing at the continuous nature between them, the yellow race and contemporary Chinese people" (Wu, 1989:205–6). Early hominids present in China since the early Middle Pleistocene (1 million years ago) are believed to be the basic stock to which all the population groups in the PRC can be traced back. Physical anthropologists have also invoked detailed craniological examinations to provide "irrefutable evidence" about a continuity in development between early hominids and the "modern mongoloid race." Detailed studies of prehistoric fossil bones have been carried out to represent the nation's racial past as characterized by the gradual emergence of a Han "majority" into which different "minorities" would have merged. As one close observer has noted,

> In the West, scientists treat the Chinese fossil evidence as part of the broad picture of human evolution world-wide; in China, it is part of national history – an ancient and fragmentary part, it is true, but none the less one that is called upon to promote a unifying concept of unique origin and continuity within the Chinese nation. (Reader, 1990:111)

Serological studies have also been carried out to highlight the biological proximity of all minorities to the Han. Mainly initiated by Professor Zhao Tongmao, estimations of genetic distance based on gene frequency are claimed to have established that the racial differences between population groups living within China – including Tibetans, Mongols, and Uyghurs – are comparatively small. Serologists have also observed that the "Negroid race" and the "Caucasian race" are closer related to each other than to the "Mongoloid race." Zhao Tongmao puts the Han at the very center of his chart, which branches out to gradually include other minority groups from China in a tree highlighting the genetic distance between "yellows" on the one hand and "whites" and "blacks" on the other hand. The author hypothesizes that the genetic differences within the "yellow race" can be divided into a "northern" and a "southern" variation, which might even have different "origins." His conclusion underlines that the Han are the main branch of the "yellow race" in China to which all the minority groups can be traced: the political boundaries of the PRC, in other words, appear to be founded on clear biological markers of genetic distance (Zhao, 1987:351–71).

In a similar vein, skulls, hair, eyes, noses, ears, entire bodies, and even penises of thousands of subjects are routinely measured, weighed, and assessed by anthropometrists who attempt to identify the "special characteristics" (*tezheng*) of minority populations. To take but one example, Zhang Zhenbiao, an eminent anthropometrist writing in the prestigious *Acta Anthropologica Sinica*, reaches the following conclusion after measurements of 145 Tibetans:

> In conclusion, as demonstrated by the results of an investigation into the special characteristics of the heads and faces of contemporary Tibetans, their heads and faces are fundamentally similar to those of various other nationalities of our country, in particular to those of our country's north and north-west (including the Han and national minorities). It is beyond doubt that the Tibetans and the other nationalities of our country descend from a common origin and belong, from the point of view of physical characteristics, to the same East-Asian type of yellow race [*huangzhongren de Dongya leixing*]. (Zhang, 1985)

505

As a theory of common descent is constructed by scientific knowledge, the dominant Han are represented as the core of a "yellow race" which encompasses in its margins all the minority populations. Within both scientific institutions and government circles, different population groups in China are increasingly represented as one relatively homogeneous descent group with a unique origin and uninterrupted line of descent which can be traced back to the Yellow Emperor. Contemporary China, in short, is not so much a "civilisation pretending to be a state," in the words of Lucien Pye (Pye, 1990:58), but rather an empire claiming to be a race.

Medical circles, on the other hand, have been instrumental in the promotion of a eugenics program. On November 25, 1988, the Standing Committee of the National People's Congress of Gansu Province passed the country's first law prohibiting "mentally retarded people" from having children. Further laws for the improvement of the "gene pool" have been enforced since June 1995: people with hereditary, venereal, or reproductive disorders as well as severe mental illness or infectious diseases (often arbitrarily defined) are mandated to undergo sterilization, abortion, or celibacy in order to prevent "inferior births." As Chen Muhua, Vice-President of the Standing Committee of the National People's Congress and President of the Women's Federation, declared a few years ago: "Eugenics not only affects the success of the state and the prosperity of the race, but also the well-being of the people and social stability." Although eugenic legislation in itself does not inevitably entail the promotion of racial categories of analysis, since it focuses on the genetic fitness of individuals within a country rather than between population groups, some publications in demography none the less make claims about the "biological fitness" of the nation and herald the twenty-first century as an era to be dominated by "biological competition" between the "white race" and the "yellow race." The mastery of reproductive technologies and genetic engineering is seen to be crucial in this future battle of the genes, and the government has given much support to medical research in human genetics. A research team was even set up in November 1993 to isolate the quintessentially "Chinese genes" of the genetic code of human DNA.

Other aspects of racial nationalism could be noted, for instance the revival of the official cult of the Yellow Emperor, although it is important to note that outside the realm of science, many different and competing approaches to nationalism often coexist, invoking territory, language, history or culture (Unger, 1996). "Race," in other words, was a far less visible component of nationalism in contemporary China by the end of the twentieth century than it was before World War II. Only occasionally is racial nationalism expressed in a fairly unambivalent way, as during the anti-African riots on university campuses (Sullivan, 1994). Far from being a manifestation of a vestigial form of xenophobia, these events belong to the racial nationalism which has been so diversely used in China since the end of the nineteenth century. Articulated in a distinct cultural site (university campuses) by a specific social group (university students) in the political context of the reforms initiated by Deng Xiaoping since 1978, campus racism demonstrated how contradictory discourses of "race" and "human rights" could be harnessed together in politicized oppositions to the state: six months after their mass demonstrations against Africans in Nanjing, who were alleged to have violated the purity of Chinese girls, students were occupying Tiananmen Square in the name of the nation.

Negative images of foreign sexuality, to a lesser extent, have contributed to the racialization of encounters between African and Chinese students, and have played a role in the spread of collective anxieties about sexually transmitted diseases (STDs) (Dikötter, 1997b). On popular levels, the myth of "international syphilis" (*guoji meidu*) has contrasted the pure blood of Chinese people to the polluted blood of outsiders, said to have become immune to syphilis after centuries of sexual promiscuity. Official discourse and popular culture have also explained AIDS as an evil from abroad, and prostitutes who offered their service to foreigners were singled out for severe punishment in the late 1980s. This official line of thought elicited a law on the mandatory testing of all foreign residents; African students in particular have been singled out for the AIDS test. From calls for the replacement of modern lavatories by Chinese-style toilets in the West, where excrement on toilet seats is claimed to be the main cause of AIDS, to pseudo-scientific studies of the "Chinese immune system" (thought to be inherently superior to the damaged bodies of Westerners), dubious theories of cultural and racial superiority articulated by some voices in the field of medical science have perpetuated a complacent attitude which does little to alert the population to the real dangers of infection. Instead of a virus which can potentially be contracted by every sexually active person, HIV/AIDS is represented as a fair retribution for sexual transgressions which mainly afflicts racial others. In their racialization of the disease, many of the publications on STDs produced by government circles and by medical institutions carry images of white and black AIDS sufferers; they interpret gay demonstrations in America as a sign of the imminent collapse of "Western capitalist society." "Primitive societies" in Africa are also criticized for their lack of moral fiber, in contrast to the virtues of socialism with Chinese characteristics.

Besides student demonstrations, even opponents to the regime have occasionally been eager to deploy racial categories of analysis as a unifying concept against the threat of "Western culture." To take but one example, Yuan Hongbing, a lawyer at Beijing University who was briefly detained in February 1994 and has become a well-known figure in the public dissident movement, recently called for a "new heroicism" in order to save "the fate of the race" and for a "totalitarian" regime which would "fuse the weak, ignorant and selfish individuals of the race into a powerful whole." According to Yuan, only purification through blood and fire would provide a solution to China's problems: "on the battlefield of racial competition the most moving clarion call is the concept of racial superiority . . . Only the fresh blood of others can prove the strength of one race" (Barmé, 1995). Such voices, however, remain marginal, and it would be wrong to misinterpret the intense nationalism which has characterized the reform era as being exclusively "racial." As indicated in the introduction to this chapter, the notion of race is heavily dependent on the language of science, which no longer carries the same prestige and credibility as it did before World War II. Group identity in the PRC, as in many other parts of the world, including the United States and Europe, is no longer predominantly constructed on the basis of perceived phenotypical differences and legitimized by references to the presumed objectivity of "science." Outside the relatively new scientific circles which have appeared in the wake of the economic reforms, notions of race may be common among educated people but play a less explicit role in the politics of nationalism. It is precisely the lack of clear distinction between nation, ethnicity, and race, encompassed in the powerful but protean term *minzu*, which has come to distinguish nationalism in the post-Mao era on a far larger scale. Racial frames of reference have become implicit rather than explicit: as such, they are more difficult to attest and hence even harder to dispel.

Conclusion

The term "Chinese," whether referring restrictively only to the Han or more inclusively to the people of China, is a generic category comparable to the Victorian notion of "Anglo-Saxon": it is assumed to be a race, a language, and a culture, even when its members are dispersed across the globe. Symptomatic of this phenomenon is the inclusion of Taiwan in most discussions of China, despite the radically different history, politics, cultures, and languages of the island nation: it would be roughly comparable to a contemporary textbook on England which expatiated on Australia and the United States. Not only is it assumed that "Chinese" is a language shared by most inhabitants of "Greater China," despite ample evidence to the contrary, but also that all the "Chinese" are linked by virtue of descent.

It could be concluded that the racialization of identity has been central, rather than peripheral, in the politics of nationalism in China since 1895: precisely because of the extreme diversity of religious practices, family structures, spoken languages, and regional cultures of population groups that have been defined as "Chinese," ideologies of descent which play on the notion of race have emerged as very powerful and cohesive forms of identity, used by the late Qing reformers, the anti-Manchu revolutionaries, the Guomindang nationalists, or, more recently, by a number of educated circles in the PRC. The notion of race, while heavily dependent on the language of science, has undergone many reorientations since the end of the nineteenth century: its flexibility is part of its enduring appeal, as it constantly adapts to different political and social contexts, from the reformist movement in the 1890s to the eugenic policies of the CCP. It is not suggested here that race was the only significant form of identity available in China, but that notions of ethnicity, nation, and race have often been conflated in the politics of nationalism.

Since the erosion of communist authority after the Tiananmen incident in 1989, nationalist sentiments have found a wider audience both within state circles and within relatively independent intellectual spheres. Intense nationalism arising in a potentially unstable empire with an embattled Communist Party could have important consequences for regional stability in that vital part of the world, as it reinforces the portrayal of frontier countries, from Taiwan to Tibet, as "organic" parts of the sacred territory of the descendants of the Yellow Emperor that should be defended by military power if necessary. Similar to the first decades of the twentieth century, moreover, the multiplication of regional identities and the emergence of cultural diversity could prompt a number of political figures to appeal to racialized senses of belonging in order to supersede internal divisions. In contrast, multiple identities, free choice of ethnicity, and ambiguity in group membership are not likely to appear as viable alternatives to the more essentialist models of group definition which have been deployed by a one-party state in charge of an empire.

Notes

1 This section is based on Dikötter (1992).
2 The following draws on Dikötter (1998a).

References

Barmé, Geremie (1995) "To screw foreigners is patriotic: Chinas avant-garde nationalists." *The China Journal* 34, July: 229–30.

Changsha: Hunan renmin chubanshe.

Chen Tianhua (1982) *Chen Tianhua ji* [Collected works of Chen Tianhua].

Chen Yucang (1937) *Renti de yanjiu* [Research on the human body]. Shanghai: Zhengzhong shuju.

Chiang Kai-shek (1947) *China's Destiny*. New York: Roy Publishers.

Crossley, Pamela Kyle (1990) "Thinking about ethnicity in early modern China." *Late Imperial China* 11,1:1–35.

Dikötter, Frank (1992) *The Discourse of Race in Modern China*. London: and Stanford, CA: Hurst and Stanford University Press.

Dikötter, Frank (ed.) (1997a) *The Construction of Racial Identities in China and Japan: Historical and Contemporary Perspectives*. London: C. Hurst and Honolulu: University of Hawaii Press.

Dikötter, Frank (1997b) "A history of sexually transmitted diseases in China," in Scott Bamber, Milton Lewis, and Michael Waugh (eds.) *Sex, Disease, and Society: A Comparative History of Sexually Transmitted Diseases and HIV/AIDS in Asia and the Pacific*. Westport, CT: Greenwood Press, pp.67–84.

Dikötter, Frank (1998a) *Imperfect Conceptions: Medical Knowledge, Birth Defects and Eugenics in China*. London: Hurst and New York: Columbia University Press.

Dikötter, Frank (1998b) "Reading the body: Genetic knowledge and social marginalisation in the PRC." *China Information* 13, 2–3:1–13.

Duyvendak, J. J. L. (1949) *China's Discovery of Africa*. London: Arthur Probsthain.

Fu Yunsen (1914) *Renwen dili* [Human geography]. Shanghai: Shangwu yinshuguan.

Gladney, Dru C. (1991) *Muslim Chinese: Ethnic Nationalism in the People's Republic*. Cambridge, MA: Harvard University Press.

Hobsbawm, E. J. (1990) *Nations and Nationalism Since 1780: Programme, Myth, Reality*. Cambridge, UK: Cambridge University Press.

Lamley, H. J. (1977) "Hsieh-tou: The pathology of violence in south-eastern China." *Ch'ing-shih Wen-t'i* 3,7:1–39.

Liang Boqiang (1926) "Yixueshang Zhongguo minzu zhi yanjiu" [Medical research on the Chinese race]. *Dongfang zazhi* [Eastern Miscellanea] 13:87–100.

Lin Yan (1947) *Zhongguo minzu de youlai* [Origins of the Chinese race]. Shanghai: Yongxiang yinshuguan.

Lin Yutang (1935) *My Country and my People*. New York: John Ray.

Liu Shipei ([1904] 1968) "Huangdi jinian shuo" [About a calendar based on the Yellow Emperor], in *Huangdi hun* [The soul of the Yellow Emperor]. Taipei: Zhonghua minguo shiliao congbian.

Moser, Leo J. (1985) *The Chinese Mosaic: The Peoples and Provinces of China*. Boulder, CO: Westview Press.

Pan Guangdan (1930) "Review of Donald Young (ed.) *The American Negro* (1928)." *The China Critic* August 28:838.

Pye, Lucien W. (1990) "China: Erratic state, frustrated society." *Foreign Affairs* 69, no. 4:56–74.

Qi Sihe (1937) "Zhongzu yu minzu" [Race and nationality]. *Yugong* 7, 1–2–3:25–34.

Reader, John (1990) *Missing Links: The Hunt for Earliest Man*. London: Penguin Books.

Sullivan, Michael J. (1994) "The 1988–89 Nanjing anti-African protests: Racial nationalism or national racism?," *The China Quarterly* 138, June: 404–47.

Sun Wen (Sun Yatsen) (1927) *Sanminzhuyi* [The three principles]. Shanghai: Shangwu yinshuguan.

Tang Caichang (1968) Juedianmingzhai neiyan [Essays on political and historical matters]. Taipei: Wenhai chubanshe.

Tsou Jung (1968) *The Revolutionary Army: A Chinese Nationalist Tract of 1903*, intro. and transl. J. Lust. Paris: Mouton.

Ubukata Naokichi (1953) "Chugoku ni okeru jinshu sabetsu no kinshi" [On the prohibition of racial discrimination in China]. *Hikakuho kenkyu* 6, April: 40–6.

Unger, Jonathan (ed.) (1996) *Chinese Nationalism*. Armonk, NY: M. E. Sharpe.

Wen Yiduo (1925) "Wo shi Zhongguoren" [I am Chinese]. *Xiandai pinglun* 33,2:136–7.

Wen Yiduo (1968) *Wen Yiduo quanji* [Complete works of Wen Yiduo]. Hong Kong: Yuandong tushu gongsi.

Wu Rukang (1989) *Guren leixue* [Paleoanthropology]. Beijing: Wenwu chubanshe.

Wieger, Léon (1921) *Moralisme officiel des écoles, en 1920*. Hien-hien.

Yan Fu (1959) *Yan Fu shiwen xuan* [Selected poems and writings of Yan Fu]. Beijing: Renmin wenxue chubanshe.

Zhang Junmai (1935) *Minzu fuxing zhi xueshu jichu* [The scientific foundations for national revival]. Beijing: Zaishengshe.

Zhang Zhenbiao (1985) "Zangzu de tizhi tezheng" [The physical characteristics of the Tibetan nationality]. *Renleixue xuebao* 4,3:250–7.

Zhao Tongmao (1987) *Renlei xuexing yichuanxue* [Genetics of human blood groups]. Beijing: Kexue chubanshe.

Chapter 34

Globalism, Postcolonialism, and African Studies

Bill Ashcroft

Let me begin with two questions: "What are we doing when we study something called Africa?" and "What am I doing when I discuss something called African literature?" How useful really is the concept "Africa" – a concept through which we approach those writing practices coming out of this huge and diverse continent? We don't for instance normally include Mahfouz or writers from Morocco, Tunisia, or Libya. So already our Africa is a particular kind of idea of Africa. But where does that idea come from?

It is no secret that that idea comes from Europe. For centuries, Africa has represented the Other of Europe. Indeed, the homogenization implicit in the term "Africa" exists precisely to signify the concept of Europe's other. Surrounding that term is the penumbral space of prejudice and stereotyping by which the various projects of European imperialism can justify and explain several centuries of violent annexation. Whereas Orientalism is the discourse of knowing that controls the "Orient," it is the "discourse of the unknown" that generates the idea of Africa, for it is the unknown into which knowledge must advance. Thus, the *idea* of Africa precedes and justifies colonialism; and this *idea* persists to the present. The importance of this lies in the fact that it is the power of representation rather than the force of arms or even of economics which is the real key to European hegemony. The representation of Africa has been central to the imperial construction of the colonial Other in general – primitive, cannibalistic, barbaric, abject. The concept of Africa, as the Dark Continent, the geographical space which signified the limits of subjectivity itself, became the centerpiece of the entire process of racial othering by which British imperialism proceeded to inscribe the globe.

In *Heart of Darkness*, Africa is, for Marlowe, no longer the blank space on the map which had intrigued him as a boy. The blank spaces were becoming filled "with rivers and lakes and names." But "it had become a place of darkness" (Conrad, [1902] 1983:33). The increasing darkness of Africa is proportional to the growth of exploration and colonization rather than the reverse, because the perpetuation and entrenchment of the *idea* of Africa was integral to the processes of colonial control. So Africa is an invention of the West. This is something we all know. But it is not just a political invention of the Berlin conference of 1884–5. It is an invention of the European imagination, a defining trope of the relentless binarism of imperial discourse.

The question which must be asked, then, is this: "Can we really deny that this monolithic, yet particularized view of Africa as a subtropical region of mystery and darkness, of emotional primitivism and protean energy, still informs, even at some

511

subconscious level, our use of the word "Africa" in the term "African Studies?" Now I ask this question also of myself, because when I first became interested in postcolonial theory 20 years ago, it was always Africa which seemed to provide the best examples of language appropriation, of cultural diversity, racial difference, and the sheer energy of creative production. Where the Caribbean provided the most developed theoretical ideas of postcolonial production and subjectivity, it was to Africa I kept returning for examples of the material reality of colonialism and its creative political responses. Africa seemed to represent a swirling pool of material and discursive energy which could not be contained by any geographical, political, or even cultural formulation.

But the question I ask myself is this: "Would that personal sense of Africa as a field of energy have existed were it not for the name's genealogy deeply embedded in the imperial imagination?" Are we still constructing African creative work in the gaze of the West because we cannot escape the overwhelming formulation of the word "Africa" itself? Are we locked into a history of representation so powerful that even the most reflexive intellect practice cannot resist it?

The question is a significant one for African Studies because the *idea* of Africa appended to the word "Africa" haunts all discussion of Africa no matter who you are. For the historian or political scientist, the situation seems relatively simple. There is a history to the emergence of Africa in European consciousness and there are identifiable moments of occupation, annexation, acts of resistance, and independence which can be examined and discussed. We think we can inscribe this political history in its place and proceed to examine Africa objectively, with coolness and detachment. But what we generally fail to examine, indeed, appear unable to examine, is the discourse within which we ourselves are located, the discourse within which our talk about something called Africa circulates entirely within the imagination of Europe, and in this I include African intellectuals. Many studies of African writing have adopted a monolithic conception of the Africa and its cultures – Jahn (1961), Wauthier (1966), Larson (1971) – simply putting into practice the centuries of the European construction of Africa. But this is not what I am talking about. What is much more interesting is the containment of African subjects themselves and the strategies for discursive reclamation they can use.

The issue, for me, is one of language, because the signifier "Africa" has no final signified. We don't need to be post-structuralists to see that the meaning of the signifier Africa has always been endlessly deferred, and more than this, that the signifying chain "Africa" has always adumbrated affect more than articulation. This is true, of course, for all names on the map, including those such as Australia (or even Adelaide), for names become the most powerful signification of imperial spatial power, and of the power to inscribe a cultural dominance on an erased and negated colonial space. But with Africa this is more concentrated and more powerful simply because of the depth of its history and the breadth of its connotations. It is no accident that among the first images the word "Africa" may evoke is a shape on a map, for the map is the metonymy of the Eurocentric construction of the world which became entrenched in the disciplinary projects of history and literary studies and continues to be entrenched in academic analysis to the present day. The word "Africa" can never entirely escape its bondage to the *idea* of Africa in the European imagination.

But how does the postcolonial subject reimagine itself? How does the African (or the Africanist for that matter) disrupt the discourse within which he or she is constructed? To understand how difficult this is, we must understand the protean nature of the binary logic which constructs the colonial other. The binary logic of imperialism is a development of that tendency of Western thought in general to see the world in terms of binary oppositions which establish a relation of dominance. A simple distinction between center/margin; colonizer/colonized; metropolis/empire; civilized/primitive represents very efficiently the violent hierarchy on which imperialism is based and which it actively perpetuates. Binary oppositions are structurally related to one another and in colonial discourse there is a transformation of one underlying binary.

The binary constructs a scandalous category between the two terms which will be the domain of taboo, so that what might be called the "imperial gothic" emerges from such a blurring of distinctions – the colonizer going native, or barbarism encroaching on the space of civilization, or the scandalous ambivalence of colonial mimicry itself. But equally importantly, if we compile a list of such binaries, the structure can be read downwards as well as across, so that "colonizer, white, human, beautiful" are collectively opposed to "colonized, black, bestial, ugly." Clearly the binary is very important in constructing ideological meanings in general and extremely useful in imperial ideology. The transformations occurring in the binary structure accommodate a fundamental contradiction in imperialism itself, that is, its function both to exploit and "civilize." Thus we may also find that "colonizer, civilized, teacher, doctor" may be opposed to "colonized, primitive, pupil, patient," as a comparatively effortless extension of the binary structure of domination.

This binary works in a particularly powerful way in the construction of Africa because the crudest and most effective binary established by imperialism is that of black and white. It is no accident that one of the first images evoked to me by the term "African" is of a black man. The relatively recent construction of the concept of race in the eighteenth century itself is coterminous with the emergence of imperial desire. But the power of the racial binary can be seen in the readiness with which such essentialist representations can be taken over by African writers and theorists themselves. Many people of varying ethnicity were born in Africa, but are they all "African"? They demonstrate to us that hybridity may not simply mean racial or cultural mixture but a more profound dispersal of the stereotype of identity. In this respect, Africa may well provide us with a deeper and more complex concept of the hybridity of social life than we may find in other more obviously heterogeneous societies.

The "protean" nature of this binary is seen in its capacity to absorb all opposition. Thus, one response to the question "how can the postcolonial subject reimagine itself?" might be to simply reject Europe and replace it with a militant Afrocentrism. But this merely leaves the binary logic in place; the African subject is the other of Europe. In literary terms, it usually triggers a conceptual spiral in which only literatures written in "African" languages can qualify as "African literature" and only people called "Africans" can read it. So even if African literature is Africans speaking to themselves, they are still doing it as the other of Europe; the binary logic is still present in the term "Africa" itself.

The best known demonstration of the acceptance of the racial binary is of course *negritude*, and Soyinka's response to the phenomenon is instructive:

Sartre . . . classified (*negritude*) as springing from the intellectual conditioning of the mother culture; he rightly assumed that any movement founded on an antithesis which responded to the Cartesian "I think, therefore I am" with "I feel, therefore I am" must be subject to a dialectical determinism which made all those who "are" obedient to laws formulated on the European historical experience. How was he to know, if the proponents of the universal vision of Negritude did not, that the African world did not and need not share the history of civilisations trapped in political Manicheisms. (Soyinka, 1976:135–6)

Some of the most vigorous and sophisticated African theory simply reinstates such Manicheisms, confirming the African as both unitary and other. JanMohamed's concept of the Manichean allegory of colonialist discourse (1983, 1985) articulates the binary itself very well but his criticism of those texts which he calls "symbolic" and "imaginary" (after Lacan) actually reproduces the binary rather than offers a way to disrupt it.

Another method for reimagining oneself might be by way of colonial nationalism, for nationalism seems to involve the most vigorous rejection of empire. One of the most interesting aspects of Benedict Anderson's very well-known analysis of nationalism, *Imagined Communities* (1983), is the contention that nationalism is actually invented in the Creole societies of the empire and recirculates back to European society; perhaps the earliest and most politically potent example of transculturation. But what purchase on freedom does an African nation have? Certainly we have, as yet, found no alternative to the state, but can a nation exist without a centripetal, exclusionary, and monolithic mythology of identity? It would appear not. Nations merely take over the role of empire and reinstate the centrality of imperial power in the already created colonial elites. As Fanon says:

> National consciousness, instead of being the all-embracing crystallization of the innermost hopes of the whole people . . . will be in any case only an empty shell, a crude and fragile travesty of what it might have been. (Fanon, 1968:148)

Fanon describes the way the newly created middle class "constantly demands the nationalization of the economy and of the trading sectors," which to them means "the transfer into native hands of those unfair advantages which are the legacy of the colonial period" (1968:152). This cements and perpetuates the structural reality installed by colonialism. The issue has only recently been revealed in Rwanda in all its material horror. That this is an evidence of the reinstating of empire is pointed out again by Soyinka:

> One hundred years ago, at the Berlin Conference, the colonial powers that ruled Africa met to divvy up their interests into states, lumping various peoples and tribes together in some places, or slicing them apart in others like some demented tailor who paid no attention to the fabric, colour or pattern of the quilt he was patching together. One of the biggest disappointments of the OAU when it came into being more than 20 years ago was that it failed to address the issue. Instead, one of its cardinal principles was noninterference and the sacrosancticity of the boundaries inherited from the colonial situation. And now we see in Rwanda what that absence of African self-redefinition has wrought. If we fail to understand that all this stems from the colonial nation-state map imposed upon us, there will be little chance to correct the situation over the long term. (Soyinka, 1994:1)

So the task of reimagining oneself, a task which I take to be a central one for creative writers, seems to be stubbornly difficult even to engage, much less successfully to achieve.

Globalism

What of the possibility of reimagining oneself into a world community? What then of internationalism? Much recent criticism urges the construction of a theory of the global. Could the most promising avenue for the African analysis be to see Africa as part of a global system of capital, of profit, and of exploitation? Might globalism loosen the ties to a map inherited from the century of colonialism? In some respects, this makes sense. The detection of a global system of capital may put the destiny of Africa and the African nations in a different light. Globalism may reveal that Africa is not a political island. Discussing Africa in terms of the global circulation of capital may help extract Africa from the essentialist politics of nationalism, racialism, and pan-Africanism.

But the capacity of globalism to have any real effect on African Studies would lie in its ability to disrupt the *idea* of Africa inherited from the history of European imperialism. Not only does it not disrupt this notion, it entrenches it in notions of the "Third World." Just as global capital is the new diffused center, so the doctrine of internationalism is the new cultural imperialism. We no longer look to London or Paris or even New York but to an amorphous circulation of power to which we want to belong. This we call the international.

I was in South Africa recently at a conference billed prominently as "an International Conference." Now certainly South Africa has a particular need to rejoice at its acceptance back into the world. But who uses the term "international conference"? You won't find it at Harvard or Oxford, the Sorbonne or Yale. You won't find it used anywhere but by those who want to be considered "international": that is, those who dwell at the margins of the empire of knowledge; marginalized societies like South Africa or Australia, or peripheral disciplines, or marginalized fields within disciplines. Now this is, of course, overgeneralized, but the point remains the same: the "international," whether it be international opinion, the international community, even the international reputation, is not simply the sign of a new imperial dominance, but a continuation of the old imperialism in new clothes.

After all, what is imperialism? We can use it in a general sense to describe the discourse of empire over several centuries as does Said (1993). But "imperialism" as a term came to prominence surprisingly recently. It was not until the late nineteenth century that a crisis of capital occurred in Europe: as production exceeded the growth in consumption, more goods were produced than could be sold at a profit, and more capital existed than could be profitably invested. "It is this economic condition of affairs that forms the taproot of imperialism," said J. A. Hobson ([1902] 1996:71–93). Imperialism as an enthusiastically advocated policy thus accompanies the stagnation of European capital and motivates its expatriation to the colonies to generate markets, cheap resources, and cheap labor.

However, while the *mode* of imperialism as a policy is economic, its historical *energy* is profoundly cultural. The link between internationalism and the imperial dominance of subject nations can be traced back to Adam Smith. Smith is perhaps the first internationalist and his view of the role of commodities in distinguishing the civilized from the barbarous is embedded deeply in the ideology of empire. For him, the social body is a body composed of things, a web of commodities circulating in an exchange that connects people who do not see or know each other. These things make it a "civilized" body. Having an abundance of "objects of comfort" is the litmus test that distinguishes

515

"civilized and thriving nations" from "savage" ones, "so miserably poor" they are reduced to "mere want" ([1776] 1994:1x). It is trade that has caused certain parts of the world to progress, leaving others (such as Africa) in a "barbarous and uncivilized state".

Compare this with Teddy Roosevelt's speech on the eve of his election to the Presidency in 1901:

> It is our duty toward the people living in barbarism to see that they are freed from their chains ... and we can free them only by destroying barbarism itself. Exactly as it is the duty of a civilized power to scrupulously respect the rights of weaker civilized powers ... so it is its duty to put down savagery and barbarism. (Beale, 1956:32,34)

This speech, which perhaps marks the apex of imperialism and the beginning of the USA's serious appropriation of the concept as a policy, confirms the effortless way in which the ideology of imperialism, with its huge contradiction of nurture and exploitation, transfers into the twentieth century global economy. For destroying savagery and barbarism means creating consumption, and this is achieved by creating what Adam Smith calls desire:

> I come to desire the pleasure of desire itself. In fact it could not be otherwise. If desire were satiated, if it were not deflected onto a demand for commodities, the fashionable replacement of which knows no limits, then not only would the growth of wealth come to a halt but the whole social nexus of civilization would fall apart. (Buck-Morss 1995:452)

So, as capitalism is central to civilization, desire is central to capitalism and becomes its most resilient and captivating export.

But more importantly, the "benign opacity" of the global economic system, which seems to lie beyond the functioning and therefore the power of the state, is a system whose very operation relies upon the continual depiction of the abject limits of the civilized social body, the barbarous and uncivilized, which both justify and motivate the operation of capital. The ideology of global capitalism reveals itself as an almost seamless extension of the rhetoric of empire.

Ironically, this becomes reflected in even such a staunch critic of global capital as Frederic Jameson, as we see in Ahmad's criticism (1987) of his universalizing essay, "Third world literature in the era of multinational capitalism" (Jameson, 1986). Once we accept the existence of global capitalism, we are inexorably drawn, it would seem, to a global version of imperial binary logic, in which the West is continually distinguished from the Third World. Ahmad's specific objection is to Jameson's contention that, "all Third World texts are necessarily national allegories." This shows how the logic of globalism works: first, there is a monolithic thing called Third World literature; second, the only access such literature has to liberation, the only way it can escape globalism, is by means of that residue of empire, the nation; (and perhaps third, the only way the Third World subject can be understood is within the international academy).

A possible way out of essentialism for African writers could be to see their position within something called "international writing." But what does this entail? Within this formulation, the troublesome word Africa disappears, but so does the local, the cultural; gone are the dynamics of place, of linguistic inheritance and heterogeneity. Rather than engagement with power, there is merely absorption into a monolithic structure much more invidious than Africa (and like "World Music" it is still a formulation of the other). If the African subject reimagines itself back into the global economy, or into "international writing" it imagines itself straight into a position of inescapable subalterneity, a specious universalism in which it is no longer a child of empire but has become a featureless consumer.

Postcolonialism

It may come as no surprise that I have a recommendation. My suggestion does not involve an escape from the world, nor an escape from the map, nor a retirement into one's native language. Fundamentally it does not even involve an escape from power. Power is as much a part of our cultural life as the air we breathe. The postcolonial option distinguishes itself in its view of the way the writing subject engages that power; the way it engages the dominant discourse; the way it engages even the term Africa itself.

First let us be clear that "postcolonial" does not mean "after colonialism." The postcolonial is the discourse of the colonized. It begins when the colonizers arrive and doesn't finish when they go home. In that sense, postcolonial analysis examines the full range of responses to colonialism, from absolute complicity to violent rebellion and all variations in between. All of these may exist in a single society, so the term "postcolonial society" does not mean an historical leftover of colonialism, but a society continuously responding in all its myriad ways to the experience of colonial contact. There is no monolithic "postcolonialism" except the one you don't like; the one you need to invent if you want to attack the notion of postcoloniality. There are many ways of theorizing and analyzing the range of subject positions stimulated by the colonial experience, so there are many postcolonial responses and many postcolonialisms. But what characterizes most postcolonial points of view is a simple conviction of the continuing material and discursive impact of colonialism on the millions of lives it has affected.

In as much as my own theory has a goal or a project, inasmuch as it is something identifiable, it is a theory designed to assess and promote the culturally and politically transformative power of writing. I hold to the naive belief that writing can change the world, because what can be imagined can be achieved. This is not to deny the presence of oppression and injustice – quite the opposite. For the power of transformation can emerge only out of the intense desire of the colonized for justice.

Postcolonial theory has the dubious privilege of being consistently accused of two quite opposite sins: on one hand it homogenizes postcolonial experience by lumping all postcolonial societies together; and on the other is an insufficient theory of the global; that is, it is both too homogenizing and not homogenizing enough. Both of these criticisms require the invention of a spurious postcolonial monolith which takes no interest in the many different things postcolonial analysis does. For every postcolonial theorist accepts the vast variation between different experiences of colonialism and the very great differences between colonized societies. The detection of certain shared counterdiscursive strategies is not a denial of the great variety of local implementations of those strategies. Indeed these strategies cannot operate any other way than with the tools that are to hand.

More recently, postcolonial theory has been accused of being an *insufficient* theory of the global compared to other theories such as world systems theory (see During, 1992). Arif Dirlik (1994) in particular makes this claim in the desperate assumption that yet another grand theory exists around the corner to solve the world's problems. Dirlik begins by differentiating a number of positions within the postcolonial, recognizing astutely that the term covers a range of practices. But in order to advance his argument he collapses all postcolonial theory into the colonial discourse theory associated with Bhabha and Spivak, whom he finds unable to construct any radical oppositionality to modern transnational late capitalism. The first problem with this criticism is that Dirlik assumes that the only way in which cultural power operates in the world is through global capitalism; the second problem is that he assumes that only theories which operate globally can form effective resistances to the operations of such systems; the third problem is that in critiquing postcoloniality he fails to recognize, along with many others, that postcolonial discourse operates *transversely* to the globalist division of the world into "the West and the rest." Colonialism itself is a process which works through as well as upon people, and though it helps us to understand something about contemporary forms of global capitalism it is not synonymous with those forms.

But in terms of African practice, as I have suggested, the construction of globalism is particularly disempowering for writers *because* it robs them of the energy of the local. To suggest the possibility of some grand theory at the heart of every intellectual enterprise is to fall into the binary logic of imperialism, which underlies the practice of what we might call "globalist critics." On the contrary, it is only by directing criticism to the level of the local and the cultural that the effect of global formations can be adequately addressed. Global capital draws its ideological energy from imperial rhetoric. In the end it is the power of representation which operates as the sharpest tool of hegemony and it is the discursive reclamation of this power which stands as the postcolonial writer's most potent form of resistance.

There are a range of discursive practices and forms of representation the African writer must decide to engage, practices which seem to define his or her identity. There is the term Africa itself, there is the language of the colonizer, there are the literary forms of the colonizer and the concept of literature itself, not to mention the strategies of production and distribution in general. These things may either be rejected or accepted – or they may be used as tools on the understanding that the worker is not defined by the tools.

The first benefit of postcolonial analysis lies in the way it treats the name "Africa." For the name is there and we can't get rid of it. But in postcolonial analysis Africa becomes a nonidentarian geographical situation of local practices. That is, Africa, like Australia or India or Canada, is appropriated to the business of criticism in a way that dispenses with its investment in identity. In this sense we stop talking about "African literature" in any definitional way because this term can never escape the imputation of the monolithic. A term such as "the African novel" is a nomination of a certain kind of desire, yet all desire is itself a metonymy of the desire to be. So often in the postcolonial world the desire for some oppositional precolonial essence comes to take the place of reality. It is a desire which locks the hope for the future together with the fantasy of the past while forgetting the present, and the present is the only site of transformative action.

Postcoloniality then, suggests an appropriation by individual African writers of the term "Africa" itself, just as they have appropriated language, literary forms, and the whole range of creative techniques and discourses from their colonial inheritance. The term, like the colonial language, can be reflexively appropriated and used in a way which gives the writing subject a voice to be heard by the widest audience. So the African subject reimagines itself by confirming the very porous borders of Africa as a discourse of geography, history, culture, nation, and identity. It looks beyond Africa to see that African cultures share something crucial with many other cultures around the world; they share a history of colonial contact with its inevitable material effects, its conflicts, its complicities and oppositions, its filiations and affiliations. They share these things regardless of the radical specificity and differences between local cultures themselves.

Once Africa itself is reimagined, the benefits of postcolonial analysis fall into three general areas, all of which derive their particular potency from the fact that they are shared. These are: an analysis of the action of imperial power upon the world and the various modes of colonial occupation, a theory of the response of the colonized, and an examination of the nature of postcolonial society.

The analysis of imperial ideology and practice sees quite readily that Africa has always had a special place in the European imagination, that the stereotypes of the Dark Continent provided a focus for the energies of imperial annexation and oppression around the world (Brantlinger, 1988). It also reveals the extent to which the present system of global capital has a cultural base in the marginalizing rhetoric of imperialism; its constant need to invent an abject other for the civilized world in order to justify the circulation of commodities and growth of profit. In economic terms this other is assumed to have "need" for commodities, for the need for commodities is universal. But in ideological terms the supply of these commodities must be buttressed by the hegemonic distinction of the civilized and the barbarous; the spread of capitalism becomes synonymous with the destruction of barbarism.

A theory of postcolonial creative response rests firstly on the recognition that the colonizing process triggers a wide range of responses in all colonized societies. So the postcolonial response is never simply unitary, either in object or design. But for me, by far the most interesting aspect of this shared response are those strategies of transformation, by which the dominant discourse itself is invaded, appropriated, and used, by which various postcolonial subjects construct a voice that can be heard by the widest audience. This is, by the very nature of the exercise, first achieved by creative artists, as they seize control of representation, and in this respect it is the postcolonial artists who may be leading the way for other forms of postcolonial social transformation.

The examination of the nature of postcolonial society is perhaps most interesting because it uncovers elements which then redefine or reappraise all social organization. Hybridity, marginality, the rhizomic operation of imperial power and its contestation, are all principles which apply more widely than the postcolonial. But most importantly it is an examination which releases the subject from the essentialist and identarian. This reimagining of postcolonial society suggests the possibility for the kind of political redefinition which Soyinka castigates the OAU for failing to accomplish. While every writing is simply a tributary of something called international literature it will see no need to redefine the geography and nature of the African state. If one writes from a position of engagement, recognizing that no part of life is free from the transformative energy of the postcolonial, even those most precious and unique aspects of one's indigenous mythology, then change may be achievable. This is not another grand theory: we need to recognize that change occurs at the level of the local, at the level of the struggle over representation, and that political and cultural change occur first in the minds of those who imagine a different kind of world.

References

Ahmad, Aijaz (1987) "Jameson's rhetoric of otherness and the 'national allegory.'" *Social Text* 17:3–25.

Anderson, Benedict (1983) *Imagined Communities: Reflections on the Origin and Spread of Nationalism*. London: Verso.

Beale, Howard (1956) *Theodore Roosevelt and the Rise of America to World Power*. Baltimore, MD: Johns Hopkins University Press.

Brantlinger, Patrick (1988) *Rule of Darkness: British Literature and Imperialism, 1830–1914*. Ithaca, NY: Cornell University Press.

Buck-Morss, Susan (1995) "Envisioning capital: Political economy on display." *Critical Inquiry* 21, Winter: 434–67.

Conrad, Joseph ([1902] 1983) *Heart of Darkness*. Paul O'Prey (ed.). Harmondsworth, UK: Penguin.

Dirlik, Arif (1994) "The postcolonial aura: Third world criticism in the age of global capitalism." *Critical Inquiry*, Winter: 328–56.

During, Simon (1992) "Postcolonalism and globalization." *Meanjin*, 51,2:339–53.

Fanon, Frantz (1968) *The Wretched of the Earth*, trans. Constance Farrington. New York: Grove Press.

Hobson, J. A. ([1902] 1996) *Imperialism: A Study*. Ann Arbor: University of Michigan.

Jahn, Jahnheinz (1961) *Muntu: An Outline of Neo-African Culture*. London: Faber.

Jameson, Frederic (1986) "Third world literature in the era of multinational capitalism." *Social Text* 15, Fall: 65–88.

JanMohamed, Abdul R. (1983) *Manichean Aesthetics: The Politics of Literature in Colonial Africa*. Amherst: University of Massachusetts Press.

JanMohamed, Abdul R. (1985) "The economy of Manichean allegory: The function of racial difference in colonialist literature." *Critical Inquiry* 12,1:59–87.

Larson, Charles (1971) *The Emergence of African Fiction*. Bloomington: Indiana University Press.

Said, Edward (1993) *Culture and Imperialism*. London: Chatto and Windus.

Smith, Adam ([1776] 1994) *An Inquiry into the Nature and Causes of the Wealth of Nations*. Edwin Cannan (ed.). New York: Modern Library.

Soyinka, Wole (1976) *Myth, Literature, and the African World*. Cambridge, UK: Cambridge University Press.

Soyinka, Wole (1994) "Interview with Nathan Gardels, "Bloodsoaked quilt of Africa." *Weekly Mail and Guardian* (South Africa) May 20–26:31.

Wauthier, Claude (1966) *The Literature and Thought of Modern Africa*. London: Pall Mall.

Chapter 35

The Salience of Ethnoreligious Identities in the Middle East: An Interpretation

Pandeli Glavanis

In the recent publication of *Ethnic and Racial Studies Today*, the two editors, Martin Bulmer and John Solomos, note that a distinctive feature of the late 1990s is the "...much wider recognition of the theoretical centrality of race and ethnicity, [and] the spread of this recognition well beyond the triumvirate of sociology, social anthropology and history into many other disciplines" (Bulmer and Solomos, 1999:2). Similarly, in another recent collection entitled *Thinking Identities: Ethnicity, Racism and Culture*, the editors note that "the fragmentation of social relations attributed to globalising processes is reflected in the increasing range of competing sociological attempts to respond to perceived major transformations" and in particular to the increasingly recognized centrality of "...identity at a time of rapid social and cultural change" (Brah et al. 1999:1) Furthermore, the editors go on to argue that "at the present time the concept of culture has become a central theme in a wide range of debates concerning social change within social and human sciences [and] there has been a shift away from the study of structure as the privileged feature of social relations" (Brah et al. 1999:1).

In distinct contrast, most conventional scholarly accounts of the Middle East have argued for decades for the analytical priority of ethnicity (albeit sometimes religious identity) and the centrality of a cultural interpretation of socioeconomic and political developments. This derives primarily from the analytical paradigm, which has prevailed within Middle East studies, since the dissolution of the Ottoman Empire at the turn of the twentieth century, and consists of an articulation of a traditional functionalist ethnography (microstudies of communities and minorities) and Orientalism (macrohistory of political order) (Asad, 1973; Glavanis, 1975, 1990). The former had its roots in conventional studies and accounts of the logic of social reproduction of the Ottoman Empire, which had ruled the region for over four centuries. It was an account which highlighted the fact that "though the Ottoman Turks were the hegemonic people and Sunni (orthodox) Islam was the state religion, ethnic communities were tolerated and even protected as long as they complied with the authority of the state" (Esman and Rabinovich, 1988:4). In fact, Ottoman scholars had noted that "the idea of community was pervasive in Ottoman thought, and even the various social classes and groups were conceived of as 'communities'" (Karpat, 1988:37). Ottoman hegemony, therefore, was seen to be mediated via a variety of ethnoreligious communities/minorities (*millets*) which administered their own affairs and paid tribute to the Ottoman State. Thus, the relationship and tension between the various ethnoreligious communities/minorities and the central state was seen to constitute the logic of social reproduction, and was highlighted by Ottoman scholars as a central analytical concern (Karpat, 1988). It was a concern, of course, which gave primacy to ethnicity and highlighted the cultural dimension in the analysis.

The fragmentation of the Ottoman Empire, following the encroachments of European powers at the turn of the twentieth century, generated new research questions for modern Middle East studies. Following World War I, the Ottoman Empire was replaced by a variety of political entities "... who adopted the European model of the sovereign state and the European ideology of nationalism – that the state should be the homeland and incorporate the aspirations of a single people or nation" (Esman and Rabinovich, 1988:4). This, of course, posed a threat to the various ethnoreligious minorities, which had enjoyed a degree of autonomy and recognition of their different sociocultural and religious identities under Ottoman rule. Furthermore, practically all the new political entities came under some form of European colonial control, which also favored the implementation of a nation-state model of political authority. It is not surprising, therefore, that in the post-Ottoman era scholars recorded an exacerbation of "... tensions among the various ethnic communities in the Middle East and between those communities and the new states" (Esman and Rabinovich, 1988:4). Thus, ethnopolitics, ethnic conflict, and in particular the relationship between ethnic (religious) minorities and the newly established nation-states, emerged as a central analytical paradigm for modern Middle East studies (Karpat, 1988; Kedourie, 1988).

Ethnopolitics may have been inherited from Ottoman scholarship, but it quickly acquired the status of a central analytical concept in modern Middle East studies. This was reinforced by the prevailing sociopolitical situation, even after many of these new political entities had acquired formal independence in the 1950s and 1960s. The variety of political systems that had replaced the singular Ottoman administration continued to be confronted by diverse and competing ethnic, religious, and communal identities seeking to gain advantages and/or rights within the new political (colonial) boundaries. This was exemplified in a classic collection of essays, which reviewed the sociopolitical situation in the Middle East during the postindependence era. In *The Political Role of Minority Groups in the Middle East*, the editor argues forcefully that these diverse minorities constituted a threat to the political integrity, regime stability, political order, and dominant group values in these newly established nation-states (McLaurin, 1979:9–10). Almost a decade later another classic edited collection, which reviewed the relationship between ethnic pluralism and the state in the region, presented similar arguments. The editors of *Ethnicity, Pluralism and the State* noted that during most of the twentieth century, political discourse and the exercise of political power in the modern Middle East studies has been shaped and structured by ethnic pluralism (Esman and Rabinovich, 1988).

It is the prevalence of such accounts in modern Middle East studies, which has given analytical primacy to ethnicity and the cultural dimension in most interpretations of sociopolitical reality. This also differentiated it from conventional Western social science, which had assumed that the assimilation of cultural and religious identities into a national society was a necessary precondition for socioeconomic and political development. Furthermore, modern Middle East studies has adopted an analytical paradigm, which gives primacy to the salience of ethnicity in sociopolitical developments throughout the region and questions the various regional attempts to impose the Western model of the nation-state (Kedourie, 1988; Ben-Dor, 1988; Vatikiotis, 1988) This is also in distinct contrast to the classic Western social science paradigm, which has perceived ethnic and religious identities as inimical to rational social planning and economic development. In fact, until the recent recognition of the theoretical centrality of ethnicity and race, the classical European social science model had assumed that modernity would erode communal identities in favor of citizenship and loyalty to the state (Bulmer and Solomos, 1999). It is appropriate, therefore, at this stage, to present a schematic account of the modern history of the region from which Middle East studies has derived its analytical paradigm. This will allow both an evaluation of the paradigm itself and a comparison with the new theoretical developments in Western social sciences that were noted in the introductory paragraph.

A Schematic History of the Middle East

During the four centuries of Ottoman rule the *millet* system exemplified the manner by which the Ottoman State related to the various ethnic and religious minorities within its borders and allowed each *millet* a degree of self-rule within Ottoman economic and political hegemony. In fact, "Ottoman principles of social and political organization were diametrically opposed to the ideas of the territorial state and ethnic nationality" (Karpat, 1988:35). Thus, *millets* were formally recognized as constituting religious groups that differed from the Islamic identity of the Ottomans, but they did in fact also represent a variety of ethnic (religious) collectivities with no claim to any territory as such. This is highlighted by Kemal Karpat, who notes " . . . that the sense of identity and solidarity in all Middle Eastern 'national' states derives to a large extent from their sense of religious identity and communality instead of from feelings of ethnic and/or linguistic group solidarity" (Karpat 1988:37). Thus the Greek Orthodox *millet* included ethnic Greeks, but they were not the sole ethnic group to be administered by this *millet*. Other Christian denominations were organized in other *millets*, as were other religious groups such as the Jews. Nevertheless, Karpat himself also notes that the

> . . . outstanding characteristics of the Christian groups . . . was the strong coincidence of ethnicity and, sometimes, language – either spoken at home or used purely liturgically – with the faith. [Thus] the establishment of religion as the chief identifying characteristic of both Muslims and non-Muslims, . . . did not destroy the ethnic sense but in fact strengthened it as well as the religious identity from which it became inseparable. (Karpat, 1988:41–3)

It is not surprising, therefore, that with the European encroachment into the Ottoman territories during the nineteenth century, and the prominence and perceived power of the European model of the nation-state, many of the ethnoreligious communities/minorities moved towards a "national" identity model of social organization. The case of the Jewish *millet* presented the least difficulty, as ethnicity, religion, and community already coincided.

It was the Greek Revolution of 1821, however, which is accepted as being the turning point for the classical Ottoman *millet* system of sociopolitical organization. The Greek Revolution rejected the authority of the Greek Orthodox Patriarch as leader of all the Greek Orthodox subjects of the Ottoman Empire, and instead adopted the European model of the nation-state for the newly independent Greek state. Thus, towards the end of the Ottoman Empire several other *millets* took advantage of European (British and French) encroachments into the sovereignty of the Ottoman State and started to highlight their national/ethnic identities as compared to their religious affiliations. The manner, degree, and nature of other developments differed depending on the location of the community/minority and the nature of the European encroachment. Thus, Egyptian Nationalism (Urabi Revolution of 1882), at the turn of the twentieth century, had a distinctly Islamic dimension and a very visible anti-British ideology. This was primarily due to the fact that the British who had already "ruled" Egypt since 1875, landed troops in 1882 and occupied this part of the Ottoman Empire (Glavanis, 1975). On the other hand, in Lebanon the demographic "balance" between Christians and Muslims gave rise to a situation where some Christians (Maronites) openly sought protection from European states (primarily France), while the Muslim and the Christian Orthodox communities advocated a secular nationalism in opposition both to Ottoman control and European encroachments. Similarly, the early Zionist attempts to establish a Jewish homeland in Palestine, under British protection, led the Palestinian Arabs to suppress religious differences in favor of a Palestinian nationalism aimed against British and European Jewish encroachments on their land.

Following the breakup of the Ottoman Empire, at the end of World War I, the region saw the emergence of several new political entities, but this time under the tutelage/protectorate or outright colonial control of European powers. Algeria, for example, had been colonized since 1830 and was considered to be an outright French territory, while Egypt was nominally an independent state within which Britain had a very visible military and administrative presence. Similarly, Libya had been colonized by Italy, while Iran was technically an independent state where British interests held sway with the Pahlavi monarchy. Under the British mandate in Palestine, Jewish and Arab (Christians and Muslims) developed separate autonomous administrative and ethnic structures, while the Lebanese communities, under French tutelage, evolved a full confessional system. Thus, during the period in between the two world wars the Middle East region exemplified a tremendous variety of ethnic, religious, and other forms of identity, but in only one state, the Turkish Republic, was the classical model of the European nation-state adopted. The precise nature of each of the other sociocultural and political movements derived to a large extent from local relations of power and the nature of the European presence.

The newly established Republic of Turkey, for example, attempted to affirm its "Turkishness" at the end of World War I and emphasized constitutionally its secular status as a way of distancing itself from the Islamic identity that it had acquired during the era of the Ottoman Empire. The emphasis on the "Turkish" identity almost immediately accentuated the problem with its Greek minority, which led to the transfer of populations in the early 1920s, and of course generated the Kurdish "problem" which is currently not far from a civil war situation in certain parts of the Republic. Similarly, the emphasis on the secular dimension of "Turkishness" did not carry favor with the vast majority of rural and urban Turkish population, whose cohesion, solidarity, and identity had been formed under the Ottoman sociopolitical principles of the centrality of the community. Even Ziya Gokalp, the Turkish ideologue of modern Turkey, relied upon the historical and religious cultural identities derived from the Ottoman era; the *Sunni* (Orthodox) Muslim *millet* (Karpat, 1988:51–2). It is not surprising, therefore, that Turkish citizens responded to the appeals of a variety of Islamisist political organizations that challenged the secular nature of the new Republic. The assumed secularism of the new Turkish Republic and its hegemony over the state has been challenged repeatedly and saved only by the interference of the military. During the late 1990s the Islamist challenge to the hegemony of the secular state was successful and they in fact took over power for a few short months.

In Iran the Pahlevi monarchy tried to forge a modern secular nation-state by abandoning its recent Islamic heritage in favor of an ideological retreat to the assumed splendor of the pre-Islamic Achaemenid dynasty of 529–330 BCE. The failure of the Pahlevi experiment at the hands of the Islamic revolution in 1979 is so ingrained in our consciousness that it barely needs mentioning. Nevertheless, it should be noted that Islamic Iran also has to contend with a Kurdish minority within its borders.

Following World War II, movements for formal independence from European control dominated the region. The Zionist movement in Palestine was one of the earliest to declare the independent Jewish State of Israel in 1948, on part of the historic land of Palestine, and Egypt followed in 1952 with the Nasisrist Revolution which aimed at expelling British troops. Both of these adopted the classical European model of the nation-state as a form of political organization, and this was also adopted by the other states in the region as they gained formal independence during the late 1950s and the decade of the 1960s. The adoption of the nation-state model, however, did not eliminate ethnic and/or religious differences overnight. In fact in some instances it exacerbated them. Thus, in Palestine the emergence of Israel immediately created an ethnic Arab Palestinian issue, both as a minority within the new State of Israel and as refugees in a variety of other Arab states. Furthermore, the new Israeli State also faced an internal "ethnic" problem between the hegemonic control of the European (and later American) Jewish immigrants and those of Asian and African origin. Thus, by 1975, when the Asian and African Jews represented 55 percent of the Israeli Jewish population, "ethnic lists" had already become a major feature of Israeli politics. By the early 1980s, and after 54 "ethnic lists" in successive election campaigns, it became accepted that Asian and African Jews voted for the Likud (right) while European Jews voted for the Labour Party (Herzog, 1988; Kalekin-Fishman, 1994). Similarly the declaration of Algerian independence in 1965 almost immediately created the Berber problem where a non-Arab minority saw its rights, which they had acquired under French colonial rule, eroded overnight in the new constitution. During the 1990s, Algeria faced a significant and militant challenge from political Islamisists, with significant loss of life and a major dislocation of the political fabric of the state. Egypt has also experienced serious and militant challenges from Islamisist groups, and recently the intensity of the rejection of its secular political system has significantly undermined its tourist industry and its national economy. Furthermore, Egypt also stands accused in the international arena of human rights as oppressing its Christian minority (Copts), who continue to claim ethnoreligious rights and representation. Of course the Kurds, who have been denied any form of autonomy in all the states where they were present as significant minorities (Iraq, Iran, and Turkey), continue their struggle for autonomy and/or independence.

The brief narrative above can be extended to several pages in order to include the great variety of sociocultural, religious, and political forces, which have rejected the Western secular nation-state model. These movements constitute a serious challenge to the hegemonic power and control of most of the States in the Middle East region, and exemplify the salience of the ethnic and religious dimension in sociopolitical developments. Such accounts will also provide the appropriate evidence for the centrality of "ethnonationalism" and/or "ethnopolitics" as central analytical categories for the study of sociopolitical developments in this region (McLaurin, 1979:8). In this respect, therefore, the analytical paradigm that prevails within modern Middle East studies is practically diametrically opposed to that favored by conventional Western social sciences. Whereas modern Middle East studies has highlighted the primacy of the ethnoreligious dimension in its analysis of sociopolitical reality, conventional Western social science has assumed its assimilation into the private sphere of social reality and thus away from the arena of nation-state politics. Thus, it would appear that modern Middle East studies has for several decades been at the forefront of what is acknowledged as being a new and distinctive feature of the late 1990s Western social sciences: the theoretical recognition of the centrality of race and ethnicity. A fuller appreciation of such a claim, however, also requires a more detailed discussion of the methodological, conceptual, and analytical dimensions of the centrality of the ethnoreligious dimension in the modern Middle East paradigm. This is the focus of the next section.

Ethnicity and Middle East Scholarship

It is widely accepted within modern Middle East studies that certain sociocultural and political features have prevailed throughout the region in the postcolonial period and they need to be highlighted. All the newly independent states adopted some form of the nation-state model for political organization, and practically none of them declared themselves as theocratic states. In this sense it could be argued that secular forms of political organization, approximating the classical European model of the nation-state, predominated throughout the region, after formal political independence in the 1950s and 1960s. Nevertheless, this does not also imply that these formally independent states did not face challenges to their hegemonic control over their territory. On the contrary, the schematic history above indicated that in practically all of the countries in the region several forms of ethnic and/or religious sociocultural and political movements did challenge the legitimacy of these regional states. The Kurdish and Palestinian movements for national self-determination challenged the adopted and assumed political identities of the states within which they existed. Similarly, other ethnic and religious minorities, and in some cases majorities, mobilized for more rights and access to power. Thus, "ethnonationalism," although expected to recede during the postcolonial period, had not been removed from the analytical and political agenda.

Within this analytical paradigm, however, two assumptions have occupied a focal position within Middle East scholarship. First, the "mosaic" view of the region which argues that in distinct contrast to the popular image which "envisages a region with many homogeneous Arab, Muslim countries and a single Jewish state, Israel, the Middle East is in fact peopled by numerous minorities" (McLaurin, 1979:7). Second, the assumption that "conflicts among peoples in the region have existed since time immemorial and are motivated not by logic or history but by deep-seated primordial attachments" (Middle East Report, 1996:1). It is not surprising, therefore, that "national, ethnic and sectarian differences make conflict the most popular idiom of sociopolitical analysis in studies about the Middle East" (Middle East Report, 1996:1). Let me elaborate.

It was UK-based Middle East scholars who initiated the serious and systematic study of ethnopolitics and considered the role of ethnicity in the sociopolitical developments of the region in the post-Ottoman period. This was a scholarship which intended to break away from the prevailing Orientalist paradigm, with its philological approach to the study of society, and instead make use of contemporary social science methodologies and analytical concepts to study the region. Albert Hourani, based at St. Antony's College, Oxford, and considered to be the doyen of modern Middle East studies in the UK, led the way with the publication of his seminal text entitled *Minorities in the Arab World* (1947). Several essays and books followed this publication, by other prominent Middle East scholars such as Elie Kedourie, Gabriel Baer, and Bernard Lewis, which were published in the 1950s and early 1960s. This scholarship provided both quantitative and qualitative data on the various minorities, and in particular located them within the wider sociopolitical context of the new nation-states that now prevailed in the region. Furthermore, these publications theorized the relationship between religion and politics and also raised questions related to nationhood and citizenship (Esman and Rabinovich, 1988). It should be noted, however, that although these scholars did exemplify modern Middle East studies, they had all been trained as historians in the Orientalist tradition and would have been very familiar with Ottoman scholarship and the analytical centrality of the *millet* in the study of the region.

It should be noted, however, that the two classic studies that were published during the same period and which failed to focus on the centrality of ethnicity were by two scholars who had no Orientalist training. Daniel Lerner's *Passing of Traditional Society* (1958) and Manfred Halpern's *Politics of Social Change in the Middle East and North Africa* (1963), exemplified the methodology of the modernization school, and failed to give ethnicity any analytical space in their accounts of sociopolitical developments in the region. Lerner and Halpern were social scientists who had an academic interest in the Middle East, as part of a wider comparative study of developing societies, and they both applied the prevailing methodology of their discipline to the analysis of developments in this region. One account for this apparent paradox is provided by Esman and Rabinovich, who as social scientists and writing more than two decades later, edited one of the classic collections on the salience of ethnicity as an analytical concept. Given the current prominence of their edited collection it is worth quoting them in some detail.

> Several factors seem to account for this difference between the historians and the social scientists. The latter tended to view the region through conceptual lenses – modernization, empathy, the rise of the new middle class – which, while affirming important new insights, served to conceal part of the social and political reality. Some social scientists, working through questionnaires and research assistants, lost or failed to acquire contact with that reality. They were influenced in part by the apparent decline of the ethnic factor in the 1950s. They may also have been influenced by the manifest reluctance of Middle Easterners, particularly intellectuals, to admit the lingering importance of traditional (not to say archaic) loyalties that modernity should have swept aside.

> The dichotomy between historians and social scientists faded gradually in the 1960s and 1970s as works published by social scientists tended increasingly to address the region's

social and political realities more squarely . . . For a student of Syrian and Iraqi politics of the middle and late 1960s, it was clearly easier to recognize the importance of ethnicity than it had been a decade earlier. (Esman and Rabinovitch, 1988:9–10)

Esman and Rabinovich were right in noting that in distinct contrast to Lerner and Halpern, social scientists writing after the second half of the 1960s gave analytical priority to the salience of ethnoreligious identities in their respective accounts of sociopolitical developments in the Middle East. What they did fail to note, however, was that during this period the nature of the political relationship between the Middle East and the West was dramatically transformed. Whereas in the 1950s and early 1960s Western and primarily US influence was prevalent in most Middle East States, that was not the case from the mid-1960s on. In 1963, the date of the publication of Halpern's book, Egypt officially declared itself an Arab Socialist State and Nasirism became a radical Arab ideology, which was directed primarily against Western and Israeli interests in the region. This was followed by other equally radical political ideologies in Syria and Iraq and by 1967 the region witnessed the first major Arab–Israeli war in the postcolonial period. Furthermore, from the mid-1960s much of the Middle East had established close ties with the USSR, and Soviet influence in the region was growing. It is unwise to suggest any form of intellectual conspiracy, but the coincidence of international power politics in the region and the changing nature of the analytical paradigm favored by social scientists has to be noted. For although modernization theory still prevailed in Western social sciences, scholars writing on the Middle East turned to the analytical paradigm developed by the historians in the early 1950s.

Leonard Binder, a prominent political scientist from the Chicago school of political theory, exemplified the new direction adopted by social scientists writing on the Middle East. Binder's classic text, *Ideological Revolution in the Middle East* (1964), and his edited volume, *Politics in Lebanon* (1966), recognized the centrality of ethnoreligious identities and the primacy of ethnopolitics in an analysis of the sociopolitical developments in the region. The centrality of ethnicity as an analytical concept had moved from the traditional academic concerns of Middle East historians to the research agenda of modern Middle East social scientists. By the late 1970s R. D. McLaurin's (1979) edited collection finally replaced Albert Hourani's classic study (1947). Furthermore, and of particular interest here, is the fact that by the 1970s a number of doctoral studies by Middle Easterners who had studied in Western universities were also published. Many of these accepted the centrality of ethnicity as an analytical concept and provided detailed empirical case studies of its salience in contemporary sociopolitical developments in the region. Hanna Batatu's *Old Social Classes and the Revolutionary Movements in Iraq* (1978), Abbas Kelidar's *The Integration of Modern Iraq* (1979), and Fouad Ajami's *The Arab Predicament* (1981) are some examples of works which gave analytical primacy to ethnopolitics. The analytical primacy of ethnicity had completed the transition from Orientalism to modern Middle East studies. The question that has yet to be answered, however, is the extent to which modern Middle East studies was informed by sociopolitical developments in the region or by an analytical paradigm that had evolved within an Orientalist tradition. This is a question that may be partially answered by reference to academic and sociopolitical developments in the 1980s and 1990s, and will thus constitute the focus of the final section of this essay.

The Challenge of Political Islam

The publication of R. D. McLaurin's edited collection in 1979 coincided with another major event in the Middle East: the Islamic Revolution in Iran and the downfall of the Pahlevi dynasty, which had attempted to establish a secular nation-state model and had been the West's principal political ally in the region. In some respects the success of the Islamic Revolution in Iran, and in particular the subsequent emergence of political Islam as a major political actor on the global scene, introduced new, and unexpected, elements in the analysis of Middle Eastern social reality. The initial academic and political response emerged in the West and in particular among social science scholars who concerned themselves with immigrant and settler communities. Middle East ethno-politics exploded practically overnight within Western societies as many of the settler communities engaged with the ideological call of political Islam and responded to the Islamisist movements that emerged in different European States. This increased visibility of political Islam within Europe forced a number of scholars to rethink the long-standing theoretical and conceptual models regarding the relationship between ethnic identities and citizenship/nationhood (Glavanis, 1998). As Jorgen Nielsen has pointed out, however, it was the Muslim settler communities themselves that played a central role in the emergence of a new analytical paradigm:

> so dominated by the secular assumptions of academic sociology was the field, that well into the 1970s there seemed to be an expectation that communities of immigrant origin would quickly follow a course characterised by the privatisation of religion...It was partly due to the refusal of a substantial proportion of the Muslim immigrants and their children to adhere to this model that the attitude of parts of the academic community began to alter during the mid-1980s. (Nielsen, 1992:vii)

Thus in Western social science the increased visibility of political Islam, along with other forms of the politics of difference, combined with the emergence of race and ethnicity as primary analytical categories to contribute to the introduction of new analytical paradigms for the study of modernity itself, paradigms, of course, which moved a considerable distance from the classic modernisation theories. This is clearly seen, for example, in the writings of a prominent French social scientist, Gilles Kepel, who notes that:

> With the fall of the Berlin Wall in November 1989, an entire way of conceptualising the twentieth century world disappeared. At a stroke not only the confrontation between east and west, but also conflicts between social classes expressed politically in the left–right opposition became obsolete...However, along with the end of the old order symbolised by the wall, 1989 also brought events which signalled new dimensions reflecting some of the contradictions of the world to come...in Britain's rundown inner cities working-class Pakistanis burnt copies of *The Satanic Verses* [and] France, instead of uniting in celebration of the bicentenary of the 1789 Revolution and the values it proclaimed, was rent by divisions as it had not been since the Dreyfus affair, over an apparently trifling incident: could French society allow three Muslim girls (living in an underprivileged city suburb) to wear an Islamic veil to attend state school? (Kepel, 1997:1)

In distinct contrast, modern Middle East studies interpreted the emergence of political Islam as a global sociopolitical force in the 1980s as confirmation of the conventional

Orientalist paradigm, which gave primacy to traditional religious (Islamic) identities. Thus, Middle East studies, which failed to recognize that the politics of difference is socially constructed, mediated, and politicized in specific historical contexts, also appears to have acted as a mediator for the re-emergence of the Orientalist paradigm (Glavanis, 1998). This is clearly seen in the writings of a prominent Middle East scholar, Ernest Gellner (see e.g., Gellner, 1983) who has also achieved both intellectual and policy prominence in the West. As Sami Zubaida has pointed out, Gellner's account:

> occupies a privileged position. He is a renowned philosopher, social theorist and anthropologist with field-work studies in Morocco to his credit. He writes on Muslim societies against a wide canvas of philosophical and cross-historical references, making the subject more familiar and absorbing to the Western reader. Above all he advances a coherent model of "Muslim society" which allows the reader a clear conceptual hold on the subject. (Zubaida, 1995:152)

In his model, Gellner argues that modernization and urbanization in the last few decades " . . . have reinforced the religion-based urban ethos and its challenge to secular power, which explains the current surge of Islamism in politics" (Zubaida, 1995:151). Sami Zubaida, among others, has presented a critical account of Gellner's model in which he highlights the fact that although

> there are certain cultural themes common to most Muslim lands and epochs which derive from religion and common historical reference, it would be a mistake to think that the concepts and entities specified by these themes are sociologically or politically constants: they are assigned different meanings and roles by sociopolitical contexts. Modern Islamism is a political ideology quite distinct from anything in Muslim history, which in recent years, has become a dominant idiom for expression of various and sometimes contradictory interests, aspirations, and frustrations. In this it has replaced the previously dominant secular nationalism and Marxism's. (Zubaida, 1995:151)

Zubaida's alternative account is reinforced by other recent research, which also highlight the analytical centrality of interpreting political Islam *within* modernity. Haldun Gulalp, for example, considers the rise of political Islam in contemporary Turkey and dismisses the suggestion that it can be " . . . associated with anti-Western sentiment and interpreted as a continuation of the traditional conflict between Christian and Islamic civilisations" (Gulalp, 1995:15) Instead, Gulalp argues that

> Islamic radicalism is not a traditionalist plea to return to the premodern era. Quite the contrary, it is a product of the contradictions of Third World modernization and represents a post-modern reaction to the specific form of modernization experienced by the Islamic Third World. In the Islamic countries, the response to the contradictions of modernization has taken the form of a "politics of identity." (Gulalp, 1995:15)

The limitation of space prevents a further elaboration of the neo-Orientalist paradigm, or for that matter the alternative account of the rise of political Islam – that of Gulalp and Zubaida. What needs to be noted, however, is that the emergence of political Islam on the global stage has not deterred some social scientists who still favor the classical modernization approach introduced into the study of the Middle East by Lerner and Halpern in the 1950s and early 1960s. Fred Halliday, a prominent LSE social scientist, for example, states categorically in the introduction to his recent book that

> As far as "Islam" as a social and political system – it should become evident that I do not believe there is much to be gained by regarding the many sociopolitical realities that the term applies to as part of a single phenomenon. As an object of social and political analysis, or as a force in international affairs, there is little that can be explained, praised or denounced by reference to a unitary "Islam." (Halliday, 1996:2)

Halliday continues his dismissal of "Islam" as an analytical category when he goes on to note that "political argument about the 'West' versus 'the rest' turns out, on closer examination, to be a conflict between two different interpretations and variants of the Western political tradition itself" (Halliday, 1996:5). Instead, Halliday appears to favor the conventional Eurocentric modernization paradigm which highlights the centrality of the Western secular nation-state model for rational political development. This is abundantly clear when he notes that

> underlying all discussions of religion and sociopolitical matters there is the issue of secular-ism and the question of whether any attempt to reconcile the claims of religion over the social and political sphere is not bound to fail because the rights appropriate to this sphere can only be established and guaranteed in a context where religion is excluded from public life. Secularism is no guarantee of liberty or the protection of rights . . . However, it remains a precondition, because it enables the rights of the individual to be invoked against authority and because it is associated with a broader "culture" of individualism and toleration, which are themselves prerequisites for the respect of human rights . . . The only response is to promote and await – no doubt for many years to come – the secularisation of Muslim societies. (Halliday, 1996:140)

In this respect Halliday represents the strength and vitality of the Eurocentric modernization paradigm which attributes to the West analytical priority in any analysis of contemporary social, economic, and political issues. When and if an alternative voice is acknowledged within this paradigm, it is interpreted as nothing more than the " . . . agendas and interests of those who claim to speak for the silenced" (Halliday, 1996:5). This, of course, may be due to the fact that Halliday and other social scientists who favor the Western model of secular nation-state, fear the abuse of the vocabulary of the oppressed by opportunistic leaders. This is clear from Halliday's account when he notes that "one of the sharpest lessons of the twentieth century is that projects of emancipation, or the discourses associated with them, may in the hands of self-appointed leaders lead to alternative forms of oppression and denial" (Halliday, 1996:5). In this respect this essay fully endorses Halliday's concerns, for it is clear that a variety of populist and other political leaders have used the process of constructing myths and narratives, on behalf of oppressed ethnoreligious communities and minorities, solely for the purpose of advancing their own agendas. This, however, does not preclude the existence of alternative analytical paradigms or alternative narratives to that of the Eurocentric nation-state model. It is for the critical and analytical social scientists to distinguish between "opportunistic" and "alternative" narratives, which give expression to identities and collectivities at particular historical conjunctures.

531

Talal Asad is one of the few Middle East scholars who has engaged with the phenomenon of political Islam and has suggested some valuable insights. Asad engages with the phenomenon of religious (Islamic) criticism of the state within the Middle East and rejects the thesis which suggests that the "*ulema* [religious leaders], being traditional, reject any change in the status quo, because refusal to change is the essence of tradition" (Asad, 1993:209). As Asad goes on to note, the *ulema* did not mobilize when a variety of fundamental changes were introduced – "new forms of transport, new modes of building and printing, electricity, new medicines and types of medical treatment" (Asad, 1993:210). Political Islam, therefore, represents something much more fundamental than simple traditional rejection of modernization. In fact, Asad argues forcefully that it does represent a modern form of political criticism of the state, which is part of a tradition of social criticism that finds expression in the Friday sermons delivered in the larger mosques (Asad, 1993:213). Thus, Asad concludes his analysis of political Islam by noting that

> The religious criticism in this chapter is an undeniably vigorous expression of political opposition to the Saudi ruling elite... I have aimed to provide an account that suggests the limitations are due not to a permanent incapacity to contemplate change, still less to an intrinsic contradiction between religion and reason. The limitations are part of the way a particular discursive tradition, and its associated disciplines, are articulated at a particular point in time. (Asad, 1993:232)

It is from such a perspective, acknowledging the role of religion within a particular articulation of socioeconomic and political structures, that Asad is able to present an impressive critique of the account favored by Halliday that Western secularization is the only mode forward. In fact, Asad engages in such a debate with Clifford Geertz, another proponent of the "West is Best" paradigm, and rejects the notion that "the existence of ideological (religious) politics within a given society indicates that it is not yet fully modern" (Asad, 1993:233). Thus, Asad is able to argue forcefully that

> the assumption is surely mistaken that modern liberal politics precludes any direct commitment to particular moral norms, or any space for ideological based criticism. To the extent that modern politics employs the language of rights (individual or collective), ideological principles are central to it. Civil rights and human rights (including civil liberties and material entitlements) are not merely neutral legal facts, they are profoundly moralistic values constantly invoked to guide and criticise modern politics – in the domestic setting of the nation-state and beyond it in international relations. (Asad, 1993:234)

Following Asad's insights it is possible to note that in practice there is little that divides the neo-Orientalist paradigm (Gellner and Geertz) from the accounts of the modernization school as reflected in the writings of such scholars as Fred Halliday. Whereas neo-Orientalists ascribe to Islam an ever-present essence which is antagonistic to modernity (i.e., the West), the modernization scholars analytically contrast the Islamic alternative with secularization (the West). In both paradigms the Eurocentric "West is Best" thesis prevails, albeit sometimes explicitly and sometimes implicitly. It is for this reason that in the final analysis Gellner, Geertz, and Halliday inadvertently act as advocates of a Western secular model of sociocultural and political organization as the only guarantee for civil and human rights. In this respect Asad's view on the appropriateness of Western secularism as the sole model for sociopolitical organization is worth quoting at some length.

> Perhaps the feeling that secular arguments are rationally superior to religious ones is based on the belief that religious convictions are the more rigid. But there is no decisive evidence for thinking this... Fanatics come in all shapes and sizes among sceptics and believers alike – as do individuals of tolerant disposition. As for the claim that among the religious, coercion replaces persuasive argument, it should not be forgotten that we owe the most terrible examples of coercion in modern times to secular totalitarian regimes – Nazism and Stalinism. The point that matters in the end, surely, is not the justification that is used (whether it be supernatural or worldly) but the behaviour that is justified. On this point, it must be said that the ruthlessness of secular practice yields nothing to the ferocity of religious. (Asad, 1993:235–6)

Following from the above, it is possible to suggest that in distinct contrast to European social scientists (e.g., Nielsen and Kepel), Middle East studies failed to respond to the challenge of political Islam in the 1990s. At one level this is due to the nature of the analytical paradigm that has prevailed within Middle East studies. This was a paradigm which was inherited from Ottoman scholarship and, although it gave analytical primacy to ethnicity, it failed to grasp the complex nature and context within which ethnicities emerge as exemplifications of sociopolitical collectivities at particular historical conjunctures. Thus, although the "cultural and ethnic account" of sociopolitical dynamics has prevailed for decades in Middle East studies, it is an account which differs significantly from the more recent "cultural turn" in Western social sciences. As race and ethnicity moved from the margins of academic discourse to become central in contemporary social research, current scholarship also highlighted the different ways in which the politics of difference and identity formation are socially constructed, mediated, and politicized *within* modernity (Brah et al., 1999; Bulmer and Solomos, 1999). The recent "cultural turn" in social and human sciences, therefore, has also implicitly challenged conventional Western social science and especially the modernization paradigm, which sees modernity as inherently antithetical and inimical to communal and collective identities. In this respect the salience of ethnicity as an organizing principle for political action *within* modernity has gained academic credibility. Most conventional Middle East scholarship (e.g., Gellner), on the other hand, is still primarily concerned with the salience of traditional ethnoreligious identities and primordial loyalties (Asad, 1973, 1993; Glavanis, 1990). With the revival and global spread of political Islam, these Middle East scholars have reaffirmed the essentialist and primordial nature of ethnoreligious identities.

At another level, this failure may derive from the fact that Middle East studies accounts of political Islam have failed to take account of the radical nature of the Islamic challenge. This can be seen in the way in which the challenge from political Islam appears to problematize the category of nation-state, whereas most Middle East scholars (e.g., Halliday) have accepted it. The idea of the nation-state is linked to the idea of citizenship in which the citizen's highest loyalties are to the nation-state, in other words the nation-state incarnates the popular sovereignty. Political Islam apparently rejects the idea of popular sovereignty and instead places faith above any loyalty to the nation-state. Thus, conventional Middle East scholarship, which operates with an *a priori* acceptance of the tradition of the classical European nation-state, can but see political Islam as a disruptive element as it seeks to renegotiate what had been considered to be part of

533

political common sense. Furthermore, at the international level, Islamisists make claims for projects that do not respect nation–state boundaries, arguing that the current division of the world into nation-states is unjust. This challenge to the primacy of the sovereign state is not simply political or cultural but is also theoretical. Since most Middle East scholarship continues to take the classical European experience as a universal template, this has the effect of trying to read the Islamisist phenomenon in terms of apparent past European developments: hence, the belief that religious practices will diminish with the introduction of modernity (Sayyid, 1994).

Nevertheless, as Jorgen Nielsen argues, there is still a paucity of analytical and critical research which can account for the manner in which Islam as a global ethnic/religious identity motivates and structures political action, and thus postulates a new relationship between ethnic (religious) identity and the nation-state project (Nielsen, 1992). Instead, there is a plethora of often contradictory and in some cases polemic accounts of the "disruptive" potential of "Islamic fundamentalism." In fact, it could be argued that the media and Middle East studies have already defined political Islam as primarily responsible for the sharpening "cultural" confrontation between Europe and the Islamic world. Thus, it is not surprising that Islam is currently seen as the dangerous and threatening "other."

Despite several decades of scholarly output there are still many misconceptions about Islam as a global religion and civilization, and especially a high degree of ignorance about the various Muslim communities that reside in different parts of the Middle East and have chosen the vocabulary of Islam to express their identities (Asad, 1993; Glavanis, 1998; Sayyid, 1994). In part this is due to the absence of studies which can account for these various communities for whom Islam is more than just a privatized religion. Of greater significance, however, are events in the Middle East region itself, where Islam has become a potent political force with some "disruptive" potential, as perceived from a Eurocentric Middle East studies discourse. It was the politics of political Islam in the region that challenged the existing status quo, and in particular the Islamic Revolution in Iran and the militant Islamic groups in such areas as Egypt and Palestine. These events quickly moved political Islam to the top of the political and media agendas. As a consequence the second half of the 1980s and the early 1990s saw an increase in academic research and publications that dealt specifically with political Islam in the Middle East. Nevertheless, this increased attention to different identities, albeit religious in this case, did not signal any departure from the conventional Middle East studies paradigm. On the contrary it appears to have reaffirmed the validity and adequacy of such paradigms and allowed the conventional Middle East studies account to re-emerge in a new guise.

Thus, one of the intentions of this essay was to engage with the prevalent Middle East studies paradigm from the perspective of the changing relationship between power and the politics of difference. In other words, this essay has tried to locate Middle East studies social research within the broader intellectual agenda and debates relating to the formation of identity *within* modernity. This can be accomplished by locating the study of different ethnic and religious identities in the Middle East in an analytical framework which attempts to distance itself from the commonly held assumption that the classical European modernization narrative has an overriding importance in the analysis of modernity (Asad, 1993). Thus, in the first instance it is important to highlight the broader canvas on which these identities have made their mark. For although such identities should not be subsumed analytically into the Western and European narrative, their analysis cannot also be located outside the path of the modern juggernaut of global capitalism (Asad, 1993:5). In other words, we need to highlight the economic, social, and political structures within which Middle Easterners, irrespective of "citizenship," have adopted the vocabulary of different ethnicities as a means of expressing their identities, and bring attention to their narratives.

In this respect the study of ethnicity, ethnoreligious identities, and ethnopolitics in the Middle East has to be located within a broader analytical framework, a framework which accepts that the increasing globalization of economic, social, and cultural processes raises questions of national and supranational interests and in particular how these are expressed and managed. The speed with which economic and political globalization is taking place also raises issues of people's changing values and identities and their attitudes towards the Western and secular nation-state model, and especially the mechanisms and state structures by which individuals, social groups, and communities are integrated into the national project. This rapid social change on a global scale, the disruption of traditional political, cultural, and societal allegiances, and changing forms of governance and political participation, is a central concern to those responsible for constructing and maintaining political communities. This is particularly the case as the above changes have serious implications for central concerns such as the future of democracy, citizenship, nationalism, and especially civil society. Within the Middle East these are central concerns which have yet to appear as analytical priorities on the Middle East studies research agenda. Furthermore, dramatic changes in such areas as technology and employment patterns (flexibility) have accentuated and transformed divisions within societies through the creation of social categories with neither access to, nor understanding of, the new developments. This, in turn, has led to the emergence of new definitions of supranational, national, and regional political identities that reflect the increasing marginalization and social exclusion of particular social groups and communities.

Political Islam may well constitute one of the most important sociopolitical forces that has repeatedly challenged the hegemony of the newly established secular nation-states in the region. It may also be the one that has continued to attract the attention of the West: scholars, media, and politicians. Similarly, a variety of other ethnic minorities, such as the Armenians, Kurds, Palestinians, and the Berbers, to mention but the most important ones, have waged significant struggles for autonomy and/or independence in various parts of the region. Middle East studies has both documented their struggles and highlighted their marginalization. Nevertheless, they are not by any means the only sociopolitical movement to challenge the legitimacy of the secular nation-state in the region and to demand civil rights and/or citizenship rights. The migrant workers in the Arab Gulf States (numbering several millions), have demanded civil and labor rights since the early 1970s (Glavanis, 1996). On a smaller scale the *bidun* (those without nationality in the border areas between Kuwait, Saudi Arabia, and Iraq) and the *zabaliin* (rubbish collectors in Cairo) have also demanded civil rights and their recognition as legitimate social groups within these states. Of course numerous women's and feminist movements have also challenged the legitimacy of many of these nation-states for having failed to give women equal rights. Thus, the problem of identifying the causes which appear to challenge traditional social order, stability, and security in this region, is far more complex than simply the reaffirmation of primordial ethnic and/or religious identities and loyalties. There is now a clear sense of urgency for Middle East studies to benefit from recent theoretical developments in Western social science, noted above, and evolve a new analytical paradigm that can account for the complex nature of the salience of ethnic and religious identities in the region.

References

Ajami, F. (1981) *The Arab Predicament*. New York: Cambridge University Press.

Asad, T. (1973) "Two European images of non-European rule," in T. Asad (ed.) *Anthropology and the Colonial Encounter*. London: Ithaca Press, pp.103–18.

Asad, T. (1993) *Genealogies of Religion*. Baltimore, MD: The Johns Hopkins University Press.

Batatu, H. (1978) *Old Social Classes and the Revolutionary Movements in Iraq*. Princeton, NJ: Princeton University Press.

Ben-Dor, G. (1988) "Ethnopolitics and the Middle Eastern State," in M. J. Esman and I. Rabinovich (eds.) *Ethnicity, Pluralism, and the State in the Middle East*. Ithaca, NY: Cornell University Press.

Binder, L. (1964) *Ideological Revolution in the Middle East*. New York: Wiley.

Binder, L. (ed.) (1966) *Politics in Lebanon*. New York: Wiley.

Brah, A., Hickman, M. J. and Mac an Ghaill, M. (eds.) (1999) *Thinking Identities: Ethnicity, Racism and Culture*. Basingstoke: Macmillan.

Bulmer, M. and Solomos, J. (eds.) (1999) *Ethnic and Racial Studies Today*. London: Routledge.

Esman, M. J. and Rabinovich, I. (eds.) (1988) *Ethnicity, Pluralism, and the State in the Middle East*. Ithaca, NY: Cornell University Press.

Gellner, E. (1983) *Muslim Society*. Cambridge, UK: Cambridge University Press.

Glavanis, P. (1975) "Historical interpretation or political apologia?" *Review of Middle East Studies* 1:63–77.

Glavanis, P. (1990) *The Rural Middle East: Peasant Lives and Modes of Production*. London: Zed Books.

Glavanis, P. (1996) "Global labour in the Arab Gulf States." *Competition and Change*, 1,3:233–57.

Glavanis, P. (1998) " 'Race,' racism and the politics of identity," in H. Beynon and P. Glavanis (eds.) *Patterns of Social Inequality*. London: Longman, pp.54–73.

Glavanis, P. (1999) "Political Islam within Europe: A contribution to the analytical framework." *Innovation* 11,4:391–410.

Gulalp, H. (1995) "A postmodern reaction to dependent modernization." in *New Perspectives on Turkey* 8, Fall.

Halliday, F. (1996) *Islam and the Myth of Confrontation*. London: I. B. Tauris.

Halpern, M. (1963) *Politics of Social Change in the Middle East and North Africa*. Princeton, NJ: Princeton University Press.

Herzog, H. (1988) "Political ethnicity as a socially constructed reality: The case of Jews in Israel," in M. J. Esman and I. Rabinovich (eds.) *Ethnicity, Pluralism, and the State in the Middle East*. Ithaca, NY: Cornell University Press.

Hourani, A. (1947) *Minorities in the Arab World*. London: Oxford University Press.

Kalekin-Fishman, D. (1994) "Community and ethnicity in Israel: Interrelationships of theory and practice," in P. Ratcliffe (ed.) *"Race," Ethnicity and Nation*. London: UCL Press.

Karpat, K. (1988) "The Ottoman ethnic and confessional legacy in the Middle East," in M. J. Esman and I. Rabinovich (eds.) *Ethnicity, Pluralism, and the State in the Middle East*. Ithaca, NY: Cornell University Press.

Kedourie, E. (1988) "Ethnicity, majority and minority in the Middle East," in M. J. Esman and I. Rabinovich (eds.) *Ethnicity, Pluralism, and the State in the Middle East*. Ithaca, NY: Cornell University Press.

Kelidar, A. (1979) *The Integration of Modern Iraq*. New York: St. Martin's Press.

Kepel, G. (1997) *Allah in the West: Islamic Movements in America and Europe*. Cambridge, UK: Polity.

Lerner, D. (1958) *Passing of Traditional Society*. Ithaca, NY: Cornell University Press.

McLaurin, R. D. (ed.) (1979) *The Political Role of Minority Groups in the Middle East*. New York: Praeger.

Middle East Report (1996) "Minorities in the Middle East: Power and the politics of difference." *Middle East Report*, 26, 3, 1.

Nielsen, J. (1992) *Muslims in Western Europe*. Edinburgh: Edinburgh University Press.

Sayyid, B. (1994) "Sign o'times: Kaffirs and infidels fighting the ninth crusade," in E. Laclau (ed.) *The Maturing of Political Identities*. London: Verso.

Vatikiotis, P. J. (1988) "Non-Muslims in Muslim society: A preliminary consideration of the problem on the basis of recent published works by Muslim authors," in M. J. Esman and I. Rabinovich (eds.) *Ethnicity, Pluralism, and the State in the Middle East*. Ithaca, NY: Cornell University Press.

Zubaida, S. (1995) "Is there a Muslim society?" *Economy and Society* 24, 2:51–88.

Chapter 36

Critical Race Studies in Latin America: Recent Advances, Recurrent Weaknesses

Jonathan W. Warren and France Winddance Twine

Introduction

Critical race studies has made several advances in Latin America in the past decade. One of the most significant achievements has been an increase in the number and range of scholars focused on dismantling white supremacy in this region. Antiracist scholarship is no longer restricted to a handful of individuals or a few institutions, nor limited to a few national contexts such as Brazil or Cuba, traditional strongholds of critical race studies in Latin America.[1] In addition to increasing demographically and expanding geographically, this cohort of researchers has made several important theoretical and empirical inroads. They have augmented the ever-needed quantitative and qualitative documentation of the multiple dimensions of white supremacy.[2] Moreover, considerable progress has been made in the analysis of the discursive and material underpinnings of racism and the identification of sites for effective antiracist interventions.[3]

Although this intellectual movement has grown in size, amassed more data, and developed theoretically, its broader impact remains limited. For instance, antiracist scholars have yet to significantly affect the field of Latin American studies. One indicator of this is the dearth of articles published in most Latin American studies journals that directly address the issues of race and racism. Furthermore we are aware of only a single academic periodical, the Brazilian journal *Estudos Afro-Asiáticos*, devoted specifically to the study of race in Latin America. It would appear, then, that most researchers in this region continue to operate with the assumption that racism is not a particularly relevant matter in Latin America and therefore not worthy of sustained reflection. As a result, Latin Americanists have not adequately explored the significance of white supremacy for a range of social, political, and economic issues.

In this chapter our goal is to contribute to the development of antiracist scholarship in Latin America. To this end, we will highlight the empirical findings that have resulted from the recent focus in critical race studies on people of color and then discuss two shortcomings of this research: the avoidance of subaltern racism and the failure to adequately address indigenous peoples and movements.

Racial Cordiality and its Meanings

It is ironic that critical race studies emerged in Latin America, in part because of the belief that this region had "no race problem." In the aftermath of the devastating consequences racism had in Europe during World War II, the United Nations Educational, Scientific, and Cultural Organization (UNESCO) financed research on race relations in Latin America, especially in Brazil, in the hopes that its "tradition of racial equality" might provide lessons that could be utilized in other national contexts (Wagley, 1952:8). However, instead of finding a racial paradise, these scholars (most of them anthropologists) documented pervasive material and symbolic racism. For instance, in Brazil they found that the racialization of political and economic power had changed little since the abolition of slavery. Describing a municipality near Salvador, Bahia, Harry Hutchinson observed that:

> Many patterns and attitudes formed [during slavery] persist even today...There is the aristocratic group of white descendants of the *senhores de engenho* – who form almost a caste, marrying among themselves and living out their own social life apart from the Negro and racially mixed population of the community. Just as the slave owners in the past,...they depend upon the Negro and the *mestiço* for labour. A Negro cannot became a member of the aristocracy,...Negro ancestry is without doubt a grave disadvantage in economic and social mobility,...[O]nly a few Negroes have moved into high political or economic positions. There is only one plantation owner who is a Negro, and Negroes and *mestiços* hold only minor bureaucratic and political positions in the community. (Hutchinson, 1952:44–5)

Researchers also encountered a plethora of antiblack stereotypes. Below are a few of the numerous "defamatory sentiments" which Marvin Harris discovered to be "current and widespread" in Minas Velhas – a former mining town in Bahia.

- [The negro] is very foul-smelling....
- The negro isn't human. God has nothing to do with him....
- The negro has an ugly face.
- A good girl would commit mortal sin if she went with a negro. No saint would excuse her if she yielded to a negro without being first shot.
- The negro is always unsafe. What he doesn't steal he takes when no one's looking. To help a negro is a great mistake.
- If all the negros were to die, I would be happy. The negro in Brazil is like a plague on the wind.
- The negro is an ass and a brute. He's the cousin of the orangoutang, the monkey, and the chimpanzee. He isn't a person.
- The mainstay of the negro is the sickle, the axe, and the hoe, and a whip in the small of his back. (Harris, 1952:55–6)

Paradoxically, given these findings, many of these scholars argued that there was "no race problem" in the towns and regions they studied (Hutchinson, 1952:45). In the words of Charles Wagley:

> It almost might be said that "race relations" do not exist in Brazilian society. This nation of people born of marriages between three racial stocks, and formed out of slaves and their masters, has developed a society in which in the relationships between people "race" is subordinate to human and social values. (Wagley, 1952:14)

Some of the reasons scholars arrived at these conclusions, despite their empirical data, was their class reductionism (see Winant, 1994) as well as their referent of racism, the Jim Crow segregation in the United States (see Twine, 1998; Warren, 2000). Another factor was the use of *racial conflict*, rather than racial sentiments, disparities, or discrimination, as the principal measure of the "race problem." This is evidenced in the following comments made by Charles Wagley in the introduction to *Race and Class in Rural Brazil*, whose evaluation of the Brazilian racial terrain is heavily influenced by the degree to which interracial relations are peaceful or conflict-free.

> Brazilians who are aware of social realities in their country [will not] deny that race prejudice is entirely lacking, or that a mild form of racial discrimination exists and is growing in certain areas. There are well-known stereotypes and attitudes, traditional in Brazil, which indicate dispraisal of the Negro and of the mulatto. There are also well-known barriers to the social ascension of "people of colour" who are the descendants of slaves.... Yet most Brazilians are proud of their tradition of racial equality and of the racial heterogeneity of their people. They feel that Brazil has a great advantage over most Western nations in the *essentially peaceful relations which exist between the people of various racial groups in their country*. Industrial, technological and even educational backwardness may be overcome more easily than in areas of the world where racial cleavages divide the population. *Brazilians have an important tradition to cherish in their patterns of interracial relations. The world has much to learn from a study of race relations in Brazil.* (Wagley, 1952:8; our emphasis)

For contemporary scholars of race relations in Latin America, racial harmony is still considered to be a primary distinction between the United States and Latin America. However, this politeness or cordiality no longer tends to be interpreted as an indicator that race is less significant in this region than in other parts of the world. When the question is posed, "Why has there been no social movement generated by Afro-Brazilians in the post-World War II period that corresponds to social movements in the United States, sub-Saharan Africa and the Caribbean?" (Hanchard, 1994:6), it is not based on the assumption that there is no race problem in Brazil and therefore no need to mobilize. Instead the lack of dissent is regarded as an indicator of the degree to which racial hierarchies are naturalized and depoliticized. The low level of racial contestation and dearth of viable antiracist projects are viewed as signs of how hegemonic white supremacy is in Latin America. Thus contemporary critical race scholars do not consider the absence of racialized tensions, resistance, and conflict as an ideal to be modeled elsewhere but rather as a chief paradox to be explained and overcome.

Racial Hegemony

Until recently most explanations of the paucity of antiracist activism have tended to "demonize or grant inordinate powers to the elite" and erase (or at least not adequately address) the agency of nonelites (Winant, 1994:49). Making a similar observation in *Blacks and Whites in São Paulo, Brazil*, George Reid Andrews writes that:

> Surprisingly little attention is paid to the role of the subordinate racial group, perhaps on the grounds that it is whites who create and maintain racial hierarchy. But as a rich and growing historical literature makes clear, the dominated always participate in that process of creation, and not just as helpless victims and objects. Even when they act from a position of weakness and disadvantage, their actions and decisions play a central role in determining the course of historical change. (Andrews, 1991:15)

The elite-centered analyses that dominated critical race studies well into the 1980s reflect in part the degree to which analyses of white supremacy have been informed by race relations in the United States, South Africa, and the "old" Commonwealth. For example, under apartheid it was a white controlled government that ensured through violence white domination in South Africa. In the United States, it has been principally whites, and not the descendants of slaves nor American Indians, who have actively resisted antiracist political projects. Thus drawing upon a theoretical repertoire heavily influenced by these sorts of national contexts, it is understandable why initial inquiries into the weaknesses of antiracist mobilization focused primarily on the lighter-skinned segments of society (in particular, the political and economic elite) and white controlled institutions such as schools and the media.

As critical race scholars have begun to more vigorously interrogate the behaviors and perspectives of racial subalterns, a different model of white supremacy has emerged – one that is sustained not only by the more privileged sectors of society but also by nonwhites. That is, the image of race relations that the latest empirical data suggests is *not* one of a white elite that is either successfully duping racial subalterns or outmaneuvering an overpowered, yet ever resistant, population of color. The portrait that has come into focus is that of racially stratified societies in which persons of color are actively participating in the naturalization and reproduction of the racial order.

For example, rather than resisting or challenging symbolic hierarchies that esteem whiteness and denigrate blackness, researchers have discovered that the majority of nonwhites in Latin America share and embrace many of the same stereotypes and preferences as whites. The results of Figueira's (1988) study of Rio de Janeiro schoolage children and adolescents, most of whom were black, are typical of recent ethnographic and survey data:

> Of 309 students interviewed, 82.9 percent responded by identifying black figures as stupid, as for only 17.1 percent who linked a white figure with stupidity. Only 14.3 percent considered white figures ugly, while 85 percent labelled black figures as such; 5.8 percent identified black figures as people of wealth, whereas 94.2 percent of white figures were identified this way. (Hanchard, 1994:61)

Given these antiblack sentiments, it is not surprising that researchers are also learning that many, if not most, nonwhites discriminate against persons of colour, prefer white political representatives, and energetically pursue practices of whitening (i.e., the attempt to whiten oneself and one's offspring socially, culturally and biologically) (Burdick, 1998b; Dandara, 1992; McGarrity, 1992; Purcell and Sawyers, 1993; Simpson, 1993; Twine, 1998; Wade, 1993; Warren, in press). The following excerpts, taken from

Antonio Alarcón's research in the Dominican Republic, offer a glimpse of what this scholarship has uncovered.

> Only a few black intellectuals value the African heritage and propose a different concept of aesthetics. In the United States or in South Africa, a large proportion of blacks value their African heritage and try to fight racism and discrimination. In the Dominican Republic blacks call other blacks "*negro*" in a pejorative form. One can often hear a black person calling "*negro feo*" [ugly black] to a black person who did something that he or she disliked, or remarks such as "*no puedes negar que eres negro*" [you can not deny that you are black]...Dominican blacks negate themselves, and accept the values of those who are not black, rejecting their own physical appearance.

> In fact, most of the population adopt a discriminatory position toward black African physiognomy: to avoid the mix if white, to avoid darkening if mulatto, and "to improve the race" if black.

> The effort that people undertake to eliminate as much as they can their Negroid traits is enormous.

> What is particularly striking is that a substantial number of those who do not wish to have a black president or minister are black themselves....In fact, a considerable proportion of blacks have traditionally voted for the most racist and reactionary candidates.... (Alarcón, 1994:312, 308, 311, 312)

The focus on racial subalterns also indicates that people of color typically have very restricted notions of racism. In southeastern Brazil, France Winddance Twine found that both the whites and nonwhites she interviewed tended to conceptualize racism in terms of "practices of exclusion in the social and sexual spheres, while not considering racial disparities in the socio–economic, semiotic, educational and political spheres" (1998:63; see also Twine, 1997). Similarly, John Burdick observed that even those individuals who think of Brazil as a racist country, certainly not a mainstream position in Brazil, "have difficulty identifying racism in their own experiences, speak mainly of individual rather than institutional racism, and do nothing to stop either" (1998b:3) In *Orpheus and Power*, Michael Hanchard speculates that this limited interpretive framework may be a principal factor inhibiting antiracist mobilization. He argues that

> [the] processes of socialization that promote racial discrimination while simultaneously denying its existence, assists in the reproduction of social inequalities between whites and nonwhites while simultaneously promoting a false premise of racial equality between them. The specific consequences for blacks... are the overall inability of Afro–Brazilians activists to mobilize people on the basis of racial identity, *due to the general inability of Brazilians to identify patterns of violence and discrimination that are racially specific*" (Hanchard 1994:6; our emphasis)

Likely linked to this inability to recognize racism, it is emerging that Latin Americans of color engage in what Jennifer Simpson (1996:377) refers to as "white talk": the active attempt to ignore, forget or deny racism through "selective hearing," "creative interpreting," and "complicitous forgetting" (see Warren, 2000). In Colombia, Peter Wade discovered that blacks frequently report simply ignoring racism or "turning their back on the matter" (Wade, 1993:256). One "survey study, done in 1987, in the predominantly black, poor municipalities of Volta Redonda and Nova Iguaçu in Rio de Janeiro revealed that ... 63.7 percent said they had never experienced racism. Of those who said they experienced racism, 57.9 percent said they did nothing in response ... " (Hanchard, 1994:63). In *Racism in a Racial Democracy*, Twine also documented that the preferred response of nonwhites to perceived racism is silence. She theorizes that this may in turn account for the limited ability to detect, evaluate, and negotiate racism.

> The Afro-Brazilians I interviewed all reported that they had *never* discussed their experiences of racism with their family members or friends. I lived with a working-class Afro-Brazilian family for ten months. During the entire time of my field research I never heard them mention racism or engage in serious discussions of racial inequality.... *none* reported having ever discussed racism with any of their family members or friends. What is surprising is that even in their homes ... they still do not engage in discussions that could assist their family members and themselves in collectively coping with racism. (Twine, 1998:139; emphasis in original)

Some scholars have postulated that one of the motivations for racism evasiveness might be that it contradicts nonwhites' conviction that they inhabit racially meritocratic societies. That is, rather than acknowledge racial discrimination that might then call into question their belief in the racial democracy, individuals would rather deny, reinterpret, or ignore manifestations of racism. Making this linkage, Trevor Purcell and Kathleen Sawyers write, "Accepting the ideology [of equal opportunity and racial democracy] as 'truth', blacks [in Costa Rica] denied the existence of racism, preferring to interpret incidents of discrimination as social rather than racial ..." (1993:307; see also Purcell, 1993). Both Twine in Brazil and Wade in Colombia discovered that some blacks even prefer to invoke essentialized notions of black cultural and biological inferiority rather than accept the idea that racism exists in their communities (Twine, 1998:77; Wade, 1993:256).

The above illustrates some of the survey and ethnographic data that has emerged from the recent focus on nonelites of color. It needs to be underscored that many of these findings require refinement given the general dearth of quantitative and qualitative research on racial subalterns in Latin America. In fact, Carlos Hasenbalg considers the paucity of empirical detail the principal barrier to dismantling white supremacy. In his summary of the literature on race and ethnicity in the region he asserts that:

> The main barrier to development of strategies and policies designed to combat racial discrimination against nonwhite Latin Americans is the absence of information on these groups. Indeed data are lacking in several domains. Most significant is the deficiency of up-to-date official statistics regarding the demographic and socioeconomic situations of racial and ethnic groups in most Latin American countries.... The lack of official information is exacerbated by the inadequacy and scarcity of academic research on the contemporary situation of black populations in Latin America. (Hasenbalg, 1996:172)

Despite the scarcity of information regarding the material and interpretative worlds of nonwhites, enough evidence is currently available to assert with confidence that white supremacy in Latin America represents an instance of rule by consent rather than rule by force. The majority of racial subalterns, with some important exceptions such as Indians in Guatemala, are not being held in check by a white electorate or a white police state, but rather via their own sensibilities, values, visions, and voting patterns. Racial alterity has, in general, not produced hidden transcripts or critical consciousness vis-à-vis race and racism. Separate subcultures, cultural frames of reference, or ethnicities have not tended to form around racial categories in Latin America (Alarcón, 1994:310; Safa, 1998:5; Warren, 1997:109). As a result, whites and people of color often share a similar set of white supremacist aesthetics, prejudices, expectations, and memories, as well as the same limited understandings of racism.

Minimizing the Racism of Subalterns

Although the empirical data suggests that Latin America represents an instance of racial hegemony, there have been undercurrents of resistance to this portrayal within the antiracist community. More specifically, there has been a tendency to avoid or ignore those facets of nonwhite practices which might implicate them as racist agents. Thus, as critical race scholars have increasingly interrogated and analysed racial subalterns, they have simultaneously demonstrated a bias toward preserving nonwhites' innocence with regard to racism.

One of the manners in which subaltern's racism has been averted by contemporary antiracist scholars is via a regression to an antiquated, more structuralist, model of power. Consider Jorge Duany's portrayal of the negation of blackness in Puerto Rico:

> In any case study after study has shown that blacks are a stigmatised minority on the island, that they suffer from persistent prejudice and discrimination; that they tend to occupy the lower rungs of the class structure, and that *they are subject to an ideology of progressive whitening* (*blanqueamiento*) through intermarriage with lighter-skinned groups, and a denial of their cultural heritage and physical characteristics. (Duany, 1998:153; our emphasis)

Notice that Duany describes blacks as "subject to" whitening. He implies that blacks are simply passive repositories of these ideologies. The notion that blacks may articulate, sustain, and aggressively encourage whitening is side-stepped. In fact, who or what is subjecting them to these ideologies is not addressed. Instead power is portrayed as free-floating and abstracted from actors. The crucial questions about the source of racist values and discourses as well as how individuals are negotiating this cultural terrain are left unexamined.

Related to the above, a number of practices which are considered linked to white domination continue to be referred to as "white" or "dominant." For example, John Burdick indicates in the following that white supremacist points of view originate and are produced exclusively among the dominant classes.

> The Gramscian view does not help us to understand *why dominant points of view develop such persuasive power among subordinated classes*. Certainly there is no denying the influence of powerful institutions like schools and churches to teach people to accept illusions and lies. But there is something peculiarly unsatisfying about such an account [because] it [denies] subordinate classes the ability to exercise a critical faculty... A more respectful view in my opinion recognizes that powerful ideologies – such as the claim that Brazil is a racial

democracy – derive some of their power from being partly true. (Burdick, 1998b:12; our emphasis)

Is it accurate to refer to particular ideologies as "dominant points of view" if people of color embrace, develop, and modify them? It seems appropriate to refer to them as "racist" but erroneous to speak of "white practices" if they are, at least in part, the cultural products of nonwhites. An effect of this language is that the idea of subordinate classes collaborating with these discursive practices is not invited. The impression is created that these "lies" and "illusions" are simply foisted onto them. Besides furthering a notion of people of color as racism-free, this model of racist ideologies can leave scholars with unsatisfactory understandings of why it is that particular points of view resonate with subalterns, which in turn prompted Burdick to make the dubious assertion that there must be some validity to the racial democracy.

Probably one of the reasons for the mischaracterization of these ideologies is that it is still conventional wisdom that they owe their genesis to the white elite. In his overview of the literature on race in Cuba, Alejandro de la Fuente notes that "Recent scholarship has stressed . . . [that] 'the myth of racial equality' was an ideological construction of the elite that masked the objective structural subordination of Afro-Cubans in society" (1998:45). Hanchard argues that "racial exceptionalism and racial democracy were first generated by white elite in Brazil" (1994:57). In *Black into White*, Thomas Skidmore (1993) asserts that the Brazilian elite created the "whitening ideal" as a means of reconciling their belief in scientific racism with the demographic reality of a majority population of color. Given how embedded whitening and the myth of racial equality are in popular thought throughout much of Latin America, it seems plausible that the elite appropriated elements of nonelite discourses when formulating these ideologies. Thus the historical development of racist ideologies advanced in the literature, that of elite discourses trickling down or being imposed on the masses, is likely too unidirectional. Such a causal narrative overstates the determinant power of the elite. To assume, as Gramsci himself did, that "common sense" is the "sedimentation of philosophical currents," is probably a misreading of the genealogy of racial consciousness in Latin America. And as a result, scholars fail to appreciate precisely how organic these ideologies actually are and therefore misdiagnose, as in the case of Burdick above, the reasons why they resound so profoundly with non-elites.

Antiracist scholars sometimes go to considerable lengths to elide the issue of subaltern racism. An example of this is Nadine Fernandez's article on interracial relationships in Cuba. Noting that "the total picture of race in Cuba has been left half-painted by neglecting the crucial realm of lived, subjective, quotidian experience" (1996:101), Fernandez proceeds to provide invaluable documentation of antiblack racism as it emerges in her interviews with whites or is evidenced in the white-controlled media. For instance, she details a poignant story of how a white father's antiblack racism led him to beat his white daughter and threaten to kill her black lover when he discovered their relationship. However, when Cubans of color are potentially implicated, Fernandez's ethnographic richness disappears. That is, when antiblack racism among racial subalterns is indicated, Fernandez uses only general terms. She writes, in one example, that "Entrenched racial ideologies of black inferiority and notions of biologically based racial differences are prevalent in commonsense thinking" (1996:109). Thus unlike her portrayal of white racism, no thick description of nonwhites' antiblack racism is ever provided. Instead it is only referred to with unspecific expressions such as "prevalent in commonsense thinking."

In addition to being vague and lacking in empirical richness, inferences to the racism of nonwhites are often subverted. Fernandez details what is common throughout Latin America: there is a virtual absence of people of color in the media or when they are portrayed it is in a very racist fashion. She adds that "this type of representation of the familiar stereotypes becomes layered along with other negative views of blacks in forming commonsense ideologies" (Fernandez, 1996:111). What is of interest here is that immediately after this important discussion, Fernandez writes that "With these prevalent disparaging images of blacks, when blacks are accepted by whites it is often on an individual basis..." (p. 111). Thus she quickly recenters racist commonsense ideologies in white subjectivities. At the moment when one might consider both whites' and nonwhites' views of blacks and the impact that such images may have for these sectors of Cuban society, Fernandez gestures the reader away from considering nonwhites' attitudes and behaviors toward an exclusive focus on white racism.

Fernandez further dodges the issue of subaltern racism via the barometer she employs to measure and identify racism. Deciding to use interracial relations as a window into racial prejudice in Cuba, she settles on a rather narrow conceptualization of racism. She defines racism as resistance to interracial relationships. Thus precluded is the consideration of how the pursuit of interracial relations could be motivated by racism. This is problematic given that scholars have found that interracial relationships are frequently premised on racist notions of "mulattos" or "blacks" as sexually promiscuous (see Gilliam and Gilliam, 1999:65; Kutzinski, 1993; Twine, 1996, 1998). Within Fernandez's framework, an interracial relationship based on these terms would not be considered racist and a person of color's resistance to such a relationship would be defined as racist. Furthermore, the matter of whitening is not taken into account. As was discussed above, common expressions of racial prejudice in Latin America are people of colors' efforts to become romantically involved with lighter skin partners because, among other things, they see blackness as ugly and whiteness as more beautiful. In reducing racism to resistance to "mixed" relationships, Fernandez is able to avoid a discussion of white supremacist aesthetics and concomitantly avert subaltern racism vis-à-vis interracial relationships.

In an even more questionable move than simply ignoring the issue of whitening, Fernandez intimates that efforts to "improve the race" are a phenomenon of the past:

> [F]rom interviews with numerous interracial couples in Havana I discovered that these romances provoke...a fury within the white family and occasionally among white friends. At times, black friends and family reject the relationship as well. Although there has been *a historical tendency* for blacks to attempt to *adelantar la raza* (advance the [black] race) through whitening, some black families see mixed couples as a kind of betrayal of family loyalty and an affront to individual dignity. (Fernandez, 1996:104; our emphasis)

Besides insinuating that whitening is a not a contemporary practice, black resistance to "mixed couples" is misread. It is suggested that a rejection of interracial relationships is also a rejection of whitening. However, in the examples Fernandez provides of black resistance to an interracial relationship, the individuals involved do not appear to be motivated by a critique of efforts to "advance the race."

In some cases, black or mulatto families also rejected the interracial pairing of their children. Aliana [a white woman] felt that Rafael's family [who was black] didn't treat her well, "because they said that I would always humiliate their son, and that my family would always humiliate him." . . . Luis [a black man] commented that, in general, his family got along well with Irena [a white woman]. However, he noted that at the start his mother had had reservations about the relationship. "My mother said that when a black man is with a white woman, the black man makes a fool of himself. He is very jealous and is always running after the white girl, and so he lowers himself to be with her." (Fernandez, 1996:105–6)

This form of resistance hardly represents a rejection of whitening or a revaluation of blackness. On the contrary, it is a recognition of the power differential likely to exist in a relationship in which both whites *and people of color* evaluate physical beauty and cultural superiority on the basis of traits that reflect predominant European descent. Thus the parents of both Rafael and Luis were resistant to their sons' relationship with white women because they recognized that the racial hierarchies involved in interracial relationships in Cuba were so powerful that they trumped patriarchy. They realized that their sons' white partner would be able to use her racial privilege as a weapon against them (see Burdick, 1998b:29; Twine, 1998:96). Such a position does not constitute a rejection of whitening, as Fernandez implies, but rather represents a recognition of blacks' shared valuation of whiteness.

Exaggerating resistance or misinterpreting particular practices are common ways in which antiracists avoid or minimize nonwhite racism. As in the above case, a rejection of interracial relationships is misconstrued as antiracist. In other instances, silence is justified as a necessary response (Hanchard, 1994:63) or generously defined as a form of strategic resistance (see Sheriff, 1997). Silence is certainly a response to racism, but to define as resistance Afro-Brazilians' refusal to talk about racism, even in private settings, is unconvincing.

Another example of overstating resistance surfaces in Burdick's article, "The Myth of Racial Democracy." Burdick opens the essay describing a conversation he had with Manuel, a Brazilian who declares that:

"There's no racism in Brazil! Here we're all equal! How could there be racism when people of all colors intermarry and have children?" Pointing to his brown skin and short, frizzy hair, he said, "I have the blood of all races in me – white, black, Indian. How could we be racists?" (Burdick, 1992a:40)

Burdick then moves on to compare the political orientations of mulattos in Brazil and Cuba. His principal argument is that mulattos have historically allied with whites in Brazil, whereas they have tended to side with blacks in Cuba. To conclude, Burdick returns to Manuel who we learn once said the following:

There is a saying in Brazil: "If you're not white you're black." That's not really true, you know. Here, you can be other things, like me, I'm a *moreno*. But to a white man, I'm a *moreno* only if he likes me; if he doesn't like me, I'm a mulatto, or I'm even a *preto*. They play that game, you know? I guess the real saying should be, "If you're not white, you lose." (Burdick, 1992a:44)

In his analysis of this conversation, Burdick notes that "Herein lies a glimmer of the consciousness that has led an entire generation of mulattos to become activists in black

547

consciousness movements, a process which has begun to undermine the hold of the myth of racial democracy" (p. 44).

Given Manuel's overall interpretative framework, such a conclusion is certainly presumptuous. Clearly Manuel's tentative recognition, at least at moments, that the principal racial divide is between whites and nonwhites, did not lead him to question a faith in the racial democracy or his belief in the superiority of whiteness. In fact, it is evident that he considers being referred to as black as derogatory. Perhaps, then, Burdick is suggesting that this "glimmer of consciousness" has been more salient or at least more transformative for other mulattos? However, to this point in the essay Burdick's principal contention was that in contrast to Cuba there have been elements of truth to the mulatto escape-hatch in Brazil which has led Brazilian mulattos, unlike Cuban mulattos, to identify "their ultimate interest as incorporation into, rather than rejection of, the established system of race relations" (p. 44). Thus in order to allege a changed consciousness among Brazilian mulattos and remain logically consistent, Burdick needed to argue that Brazilian society had somehow become less open to mulatto social mobility. Given that he does not make this argument, Burdick's contention that "an entire generation of mulattos" has become antiracist activists comes across as wishful thinking, and is certainly misleading because it implies a groundswell of activism that is fictive. For instance, several years later, Burdick himself states that "the actual number of participants in [antiracist organizations] is not very large ... [and the] organizations remain fragmented and small. [T]he leadership and social base of the movement are mainly limited to urban, middle-class and professional *negros...*" (Burdick 1998b:4).

One of the problems with these particular allusions is that they distort the level of resistance and mobilization. They create the false sense that antiracist movements are stronger than they actually are. In comparing the black movement in Costa Rica to Brazil, Purcell and Sawyers were clearly under the erroneous impression that the Afro-Brazilian movement enjoyed a large measure of popular support. They explicitly state that, in contrast to the black movement in Costa Rica, "the Brazilian Movimento Unificado ... involved widespread grassroots' participation" (1993:313). It seems reasonable to suspect, then, that the various inferences in the literature that, intentionally or not, misconstrue the degree of antiracist activism are at least partially responsible for such blatantly inaccurate characterizations of popular mobilization.

Another way in which nonwhite resistance has been overstated within critical race studies is the emphasis placed on the future – on an emerging antiracist movement. Such a belief has been predominant in race studies in Latin America for several decades. For example, the UNESCO researchers of the 1950s predicted an upsurge in subaltern contestation. Hutchinson wrote that "in the town [Vila Recôncavo] and among the mill workers, 'people of colour' are beginning to show independence, and unwillingness always to occupy a subservient and lowly position" (1952:45). And Marvin Harris advised, "Serious attention should be devoted to the possibility that the future may bring more militant and widespread racial tension to Minas Velhas" (1952:80). In the 1980s several observers of Brazilian race relations, who were inspired by the return to democracy and the commemorations of the centennial of the abolition of slavery, made similar predictions which proved equally wrong. Reflecting on his own thoughts during this time period, Howard Winant confessed that "Many people have professed to see the movement on the horizon many times. Indeed, I freely admit that I am among that number; . . ." (1994:149).

Peter Wade's *Blackness and Race Mixture* may illustrate another instance of unwarranted optimism. In the final chapters of this work, Wade concludes that the possibility of a black movement is low:

[For] blacks in the United States . . . there have been notable instances of solidarity based on a struggle for civil rights and on an attempt to redefine the value and meaning of blackness – "black is beautiful" – both movements that are only nascent in Colombia and have received little support from blacks there. Even in a region such as the Choco, which is virtually entirely black, political, as opposed to kin-based, solidarity is a distant goal, whether this be in order to protest about the Choco as a region or about the position of blacks in Colombia in general. . . . [T]here is no overall solidarity of the Chocoanos which might raise a collective voice in protest about racial discrimination, the situation of the Choco, or the negative stereotypes and images surrounding black culture. (Wade, 1993:326)

In the epilogue we learn that Wade has returned to Colombia since the completion of his book. It is here that Wade changes course and tempers the above assessment. He argues that the possibility of mobilization is now much more promising since his last visit to the region four years earlier. "What we are witnessing, then, is the emergence of a more solid ethnic identity than previously existed. . . . Now, there is a definite element claiming that blacks are an ethnic group, and does so in privileged encounters with the state. Thus, an imagined community of blacks is emerging, . . ." (Wade, 1993:356).

Much of the evidence that Wade offers to support his claim that there has recently emerged a more assertive antiracist movement grounded in black identities is unpersuasive. For example, he notes that "the present politicization relies heavily on a regional" rather than a racial "focus" (Wade, 1993:355). He adds that "much of the recent organization has been promoted by the Church," and that many of the black activists acknowledged that there were a number of " 'black' people who refused to admit it and mulattos who wanted to reject their black heritage" (p. 355). The final piece of information provided to illustrate this alleged new political moment is also less than compelling. Wade describes a conversation he had with Amir Smith-Cordoba – a person "who is notorious for his habit of approaching people in the street whom he considers black and saying 'Hola negro!' " According to Wade, Amir recounted "that his victims (classified by him with more North than Latin American definitions of black) tend to react with less surprise or hostility today than they would have ten or fifteen years ago" (p. 356).

Perhaps, as Wade asserts, Afro-Colombians have suddenly inched closer to antiracist subjectivities and organizations. However, given the pattern of other unrealized forecasts in literature, one cannot but wonder whether such an encouraging portrait of the state of antiracist mobilization is an astute reading of a changed racial terrain or a trope which effectively directs attention away from nonwhite racism. And one's doubts are further heightened when the reader is asked to accept this analysis in the epilogue that runs counter to the conclusion reached in the previous 350-page, well-researched book and is supported by rather flimsy evidence such as the belief of a lifelong activist (certainly not the most unpartisan observer) that Afro-Colombians act with less hostility to being called black.

In closing this section we can only speculate why there seems to be an urge to deflect attention away from the racism of people of color. One of the most convincing explanations is that antiracists in Latin America have "placed a myth of whiteness at the centre of their discourse," like antiracists have, according to Alistair Bonnett, in the United Kingdom, the United States, and Canada.

> This myth views "being white" as an immutable condition with clear and distinct moral attributes. These attributes often include: being racist; not experiencing racism; being an oppressor; not experiencing oppression; silencing; not being silenced. People of colour are defined via their relation to this myth. They are defined, then, as "non-whites"; as people whose identity is formed through their resistance to others' oppressive agency; as experiencing racism; as nonracist (if not anti-racist). (Bonnett, 1996:100)

If in fact antiracists in Latin America share this myth, this would certainly account for why it is difficult for these scholars and activists to fully appreciate what the empirical evidence is clearly indicating: nonwhites tend *not* to perceive racism, are deeply racist, and thus are central to the maintenance of white supremacy. Burdick's statement hints that it may not only be difficult in a cognitive sense but emotionally as well. "There is much left out of the view that all is resistance. *The poor and oppressed sometimes say things... that are embarrassing* to an ideology that prizes agency and collective action" (Burdick, 1998b:11–12; our emphasis). Thus it would appear that the recent antiracist research, with its intensified focus on "the oppressed," is requiring scholars to come to terms with some fundamental assumptions and emotional investments about racial subalterns and the foundations of white supremacy. We should, then, probably not be surprised to find that a number of antiracists are avoiding, however unwittingly, the racism of people of color.

Whatever the reasons, the consequences of minimizing racial subalterns' racism are significant. If antiracists suppose that people of color are, in general, rejecting whitening, critical of white supremacist values and the racial democracy myth, and for the most part, sympathetic to antiracist political projects, then this prompts a particular set of research and political questions. With such an image of the racial terrain in mind, the absence of antiracist activism becomes construed as a problem with movement organizations and their leadership. It presupposes a more advanced moment of mobilization than exists. It is assumed that there is an audience waiting to be captured, when in fact an audience needs to be created. Consequently, it is not appreciated how steep an uphill battle antiracist activists face, which increases the likelihood of unfair aspersions being cast their way. Moreover a number of matters that should be rigorously investigated are likely to be ignored. To take one example, if scholars are under the impression that most nonwhites have a sophisticated understanding of white supremacy, then researchers are less inclined to explore the reasons why persons of color have restricted notions of racism, and therefore the search for effective means of increasing racial literacy will be inhibited.

Indians and Antiracism

In addition to avoiding subaltern racism, critical race scholars have all but ignored Indians. Thus, much like the broader academic community in Latin America, antiracists have not considered Indians germane to race matters. As Peter Wade observed in *Race and Ethnicity in Latin America*, there prevails "the virtually unquestioned assumption that the study of blacks is one of racism and race relations, while the study of Indians is that of ethnicity and ethnic groups" (1997:37). Facing a similar sentiment in the Brazilian academic community, Jonathan Warren writes that whenever he encounters "this often unstated, yet palpable attitude that 'race' means 'black,' it brings to mind a story a Mexican colleague once told [him]:"

> [This colleague] was from an elite family in Mexico and he looked white according to somatic constructions of whiteness in the United States. Apparently he had one grand-mother who had been Indian. When he was ten or eleven years old his peers somehow discovered this and they subsequently began to ostracize and harass him. As an outgrowth of these experiences, he decided to study issues of race and racism when he was ready to attend college. However, upon inquiring with several Mexican universities as to where and with whom he could best pursue his interests, the common response was that "We [Mexicans] don't have that problem here because we have no blacks. You will have to go to the United States if you want to study race and racism. They have blacks there." (Warren, in press)

Wade suggests that the principal idea underlying this widely held belief that race and Indians are separate and inconsequential matters "is that the category 'Indian' does not depend on phenotypical signifiers. . . . In contrast, 'black' is often seen as a category defined by more fixed phenotypical criteria that cannot be manipulated in the same way" (1997:37). It is, of course, incorrect to use race to talk of black identity, and ethnicity to talk about Indian identity, as if blackness were only about phenotype and Indianness just about culture. "Such an opposition separates phenotype from culture, as if the former was not itself culturally constructed" (Wade, 1997:39). Furthermore the category "Indian" is very dependent upon bodily signifiers in Latin America. This is one of the reasons a number of "mixed-race" Indians are viewed as racial charlatans in the region. Their African and European features mark them as inauthentic – as not "real Indians" (see Warren, in press) Conversely blackness is often contingent upon nonphysical markers.

> The Latin American material shows that, for example, the same individual dressed shabbily and smartly will be identified with different color terms that locate the person on a scale between black and white. These terms are not dependent on phenotype alone, because the context of somatic features alters people's classification – and even perhaps perception – of these features. (Wade, 1997:38)

In conversations with anthropologists in Brazil, Warren observed that none of them explicitly stated that Indianness was about culture (and not phenotype) and that this was the reason why they did not explore the relevance of Indians to the politics of race. Instead, when they defended their analytical position they did so on the grounds that this was putatively how racial subalterns conceptualized their social world. For instance, one anthropologist at the Museu Nacional in Rio de Janeiro told Warren that:

> When blacks refer to whites they mean another race, but Indians don't mean this. When Indians speak of whites, of the white man [sic], they are referring to a civilized man [sic] and to his system of life, to a different cosmology, to a different mode of thinking and seeing oneself and the world. To the Indian, the white man could be of the white, black or Asian race. The point here is that he is not an Indian and therefore is an Other. This is the only

551

reason that scholars don't think of Indian discourses as radicalized discourses. (Warren, in press)

Thus, rather than claiming that Indianness is a matter of ethnicity (i.e., culture) and not race (i.e., phenotype/biology), this person justifies the failure of Indian scholars to deal with race by claiming that Indians imagine the differences between themselves and others in exclusively cultural terms. Although it is certainly true that Indians imagine differences in cultural terms, they also tend to think in terms of biological and phenotypical differences (Warren, in press). More importantly, even if Indians meant simply "ethnic" difference, this would not necessarily put them "beyond race." As Warren (in press) argues "regardless of what they mean by 'white,' Indians are touching into being aesthetic hierarchies, national narratives, symbolic orders, discursive repertoires, political practices, and so on which ... have radicalized meanings. And so even if Indians do not conceptualize differences in 'racial terms,' this would not therefore mean that their practices were inconsequential to race matters."

Whatever the reasons for the failure to situate Indians within the study of race, the irony is that Indians may prove to be an epicenter of antiracism in Latin America. In a number of countries, the empirical evidence suggests that Indians – more so than mestizos, blacks, or whites – are consistently and aggressively challenging the ideologies of whitening and racial democracy, producing antiracist narratives of the nation, expanding and developing sophisticated definitions of racism, fighting for representation in institutions and political office and even pushing for the formation of multiracial states.[4] In Chiapas, for instance, the Zapatistas have centered the issue of racism and call for the formation of indigenous schools and political institutions – a clear resistance to the white supremacist project of *mestizaje* (Harvey, 1998). In Bolivia and Ecuador, Indians have built formidable movements which are demanding the return of their lands, greater political representation, redefinitions of national histories, and an official valuation of indigenous peoples and cultures (Field, 1991; Riveira Cusicanqui, 1991). Indians in Colombia have spearheaded a critique of the mestizo nation and have served as a model for black mobilization (Arocha, 1998; Wade 1995). In Guatemala, the Mayan people have survived the US-sponsored war and are now on the verge of creating the first nation-state in the hemisphere that is politically controlled by indigenous people (Smith, 1991; K. Warren, 1998). Even in Brazil, where Indians are a small percentage of the population, the indigenous people have created an antiracist movement that enjoys the support of the majority of Indians, whereas the black movement, as we have seen, is restricted primarily to a small number of urban intellectuals and middle-class Afro-Brazilians (Warren, in press).

Unfortunately this groundswell of antiracism has been taking place under the noses of most scholars of race who have, as outlined above, been virtually silent on this matter. And only very recently, and usually extremely tentatively, are Indian scholars beginning to conceptualize Indian communities, movements, and cultural practices in terms of racism and antiracism (see Gould, 1998; Harvey, 1998; K. Warren, 1998; Warren, in press). Thus much more cross-fertilization of critical race studies and Indian studies is in order. Just as black subjectivities and communities have been the principal catalyst for antiracist activism in the United States, Indians may prove to be the community where the greatest chance exists for upsetting white supremacy in Latin America. Given this potential, it is imperative that critical race scholars direct more energies, for example, toward theorizing the ways in which indigenous peoples and movements may offer invaluable lessons of how to disrupt white supremacy in the Latin American context (Varese, 1991; Warren, in press).

Latin American Lessons for Other Regions

In conclusion we would like to briefly comment upon how recent developments in the subfield of antiracist studies in Latin America may prove useful to antiracists working in other regions. In our own research we have borrowed insights generated in the whiteness studies literature to help explain the subjectivities and worldviews of Latin Americans of color as well as clarify how such discursive and material practices are linked to white supremacy (see Twine, 1998; Warren, 2000). This was possible because the racial thinking of nonwhites in Latin America strongly parallels that of whites in North America and the old Commonwealth. The implications of this are potentially vast for whiteness studies. For instance, within whiteness studies it is frequently assumed that "white talk" and racial illiteracy are a consequence of racial privilege. But if the same languages of race predominate in Latin America among racial subalterns, then this calls into question such an assumption. A full appreciation of this could prompt reconceptualizations of what is presently considered the basis for particular racial discourses and identities, and point to new strategies for transforming those practices which are seen as sustaining racial injustices.

Lessons gleaned from the study of race in Latin America could also illuminate the implications that nascent "multiracial" movements may have for countries outside of Latin America. For example, a number of individuals in the United States who promote "mixed-race" identities or favor the creation of "multiracial" categories on official documents often presume, with much certitude, that they are pursuing an antiracist agenda (see Root, 1996). In Latin America, the hallmark of racial formation has been the racialization of nations and regions as "mixed-race." Moreover, most people of color self-identify as racially mixed. Yet, despite the privileging of racial "hybridity," racist stereotypes and racial inequalities are equal to, if not greater, in Latin America than in the United States (see Hanchard, 1994:5). Thus Latin America offers a case study that should caution scholars and activists to carefully consider how efforts to encourage "mestizoness" do not necessarily constitute an antiracist position but rather may work to effectively sustain racial disparities.

Notes

1   For contemporary research on race and racism in Bolivia, see Abercrombie (1991), Riveira Cusicanqui (1991); Colombia, see Arocha (1992, 1998), Streicker (1995), Wade (1993, 1995); Costa Rica, see Bourgois (1989, 1998), Purcell (1993), Purcell and Sawyers (1993); the Dominican Republic, see Alarcón (1994), Baud (1996), Márquez (1992), Torres-Saillant (1998); Ecuador, see Field (1991), Hendricks (1991), Radcliffe and Westwood (1996), Stutzman (1981), Whitten and Quiroga (1998); Guatemala, see Adams (1991, 1994), Casaus Arzù (1992), Smith (1990, 1991, 1996), K. Warren (1998). Honduras, see Bateman (1998); Mexico, see Harvey (1998), Hernandez-Díaz (1994), Knight (1990), Nash (1995), Rubin (1997); Nicar-

agua, see Freeland (1995), Gould (1998), Hale (1991, 1994), Lancaster (1991); Panama, see Howe (1998); Peru, see Manrique (1995), Radcliffe, (1990); Puerto Rico, see Duany (1998), Santiago (1992); Venezuela, see Guss (1993), Pérez (1998), Wright (1990); and Latin American more broadly considered, see Hale (1996), Safa (1998), Smith (1997), Stepan (1991), Varese (1991), Wade (1997), Whitten and Torres (1998).

2   The following references represent some of the recent studies that offer primary empirical data of white supremacy and its effects on employment and the workplace: Andrews (1991), Bento (1995), Bourgois (1989), Burdick (1998), Castro and Guimarães (1993), Dweyer and Lovell (1988), Hasenbalg (1991), Lovell (1992), Lovell and Wood (1998), Queriroz (1994), Silva (1991), Silva and Hasenbalg (1992), Twine (1998), Wade (1993); education and textbooks: da Silva (1993), Figueira (1990, 1998), Pinto (1987), Queriroz (1994), Radcliffe (1990), Radcliffe and Westwood (1996) Rosemberg (1990), Rosemberg and Pinto (1987), Telles (1994), Twine (1998), Wade (1993), Warren (1997); the media and popular culture: Burdick (1998b), Fernandez (1996), Radcliffe and Westwood (1996), Simpson (1993), Wade (1993); literature: Almánzar (1987), Rappaport (1992); museums: Radcliffe and Westwood (1996); policing and the criminal justice system: Adorno (1995), Guimarães (1996), Mitchell and Wood (1999); housing and residential patterns: Santiago (1992), Telles (1992), Twine (1998), Wade (1993); interracial relationships: Burdick (1998b), Dandara (1992), Fernandez (1996), Gilliam and Gilliam (1999), Radcliffe (1990), Scalon (1992), Telles (1993), Twine (1996, 1998), Wade (1993); politics: Andrews (1991), Domingues (1988), Hanchard (1994), Radcliffe and Westwood (1996), Twine (1998), Wade (1993, 1995); aesthetics: Burdick (1998b), Figueiredo (1994), Gilliam and Gilliam (1999), Twine (1998), Wade (1993); physical and symbolic violence: Burdick (1998b), Manrique (1995), Taussig (1987), Twine (1998), Wade (1993), J. Warren (1998); and the environment: Arocha (1998), Wade (1993), Radcliffe and Westwood (1996), Warren (1999).

3   Some of the scholars who emphasize the legal, elite, or national discourses that underpin white supremacy are Arocha (1998), Baud (1996), Fuente (1998), Gould (1998), Guimarães (1995), Graham (1990), Hanchard (1994), Hasenbalg (1979), Nascimento (1989), Stutzman (1981), Moore (1988), Skidmore ([1974] 1993), and Wade (1993, 1995). Antiracist scholarship that focuses more on popular thought and everyday practices include Gould (1998), Bourgois (1989), Burdick (1998b), Wade (1993), Sherriff (1997), Twine (1996, 1997, 1998), Warren (1997, in press). Finally there are a number of studies which center on analysis of antiracist movements and activists: Field (1991), Hanchard (1994), Harvey (1998), Helg (1995), Riveira Cusicanqui (1991), Smith (1991), Wade (1993, 1995), Varese (1991), K. Warren (1998), Warren (in press).

4   See Abán Gómez et al. (1993), Abercrombie (1991), Adams (1991), Almeida et al. (1992), Arocha (1998), Berdichensky (1986), Field (1991, 1994, 1996), Hale (1991, 1994, 1996), Harvey (1998), Hendricks (1991), Hernandez-Díaz (1994), Howe (1998), Kicza (1993), Radcliffe and Westwood (1996), Riveira Cusicanqui (1991), Smith (1990, 1991, 1996, 1997), Urban (1991), Varese (1988, 1991), Wade (1995), K. Warren (1998), Warren (in press).

References

Abán Gómez, E. Andrango, A., and Bustamente, T. (eds.) (1993) *Los Indios y el Estado-Pais Pluriculturadidad y Multi-Ethnicidad en el Ecuador: Contribuciones al Debate*. Quito: Abya-Yala.

Abercrombie, T. (1991) "To be Indian, to be Bolivian: Ethnic and national discourses of identity," in J. Sherzer and G. Urban (eds.) *Indians and Nation-States in Latin America*. Austin: University of Texas Press, pp.95–130.

Abreu, A. R. de P., Jorge, A. F., and Sorj, B. (1994) "Desigualdade de gênero e raça: O informal no Brasil em 1990." *Estudos Feministas* 2,2:153–78.

Adams, R. N. (1991) "Strategies of ethnic survival in Central America," in G. Urban and J. Sherzer (eds.) *Nation-States and Indians in Latin America*. Austin: University of Texas Press, pp.181–206.

Adams, R. N. (1994) "A report on the political status of the Guatemala Maya," in D. L. Van Cott (ed.) *Indigenous Peoples and Democracy in Latin America*. New York: St. Martin's Press, pp.155–86.

Adorno, S. (1995) "Discriminação racial e justiça criminal em São Paulo." *Novos Estudos CEBRAP* 43, November: 45–63.

Alarcón, A. V. M. (1994) "Racial prejudice: A Latin American case." *Research in Race and Ethnic Relations* 7:299–319.

Almada, S. (1995) *Damas Negras: Sucesso, Lutas, Discriminação*. Rio de Janeiro: Mauad.

Almánzar, J. A. (1987) "Black images in Dominican literature." *New West Indian Guide* 61, 3–4:161–73.

Almeida, I., Almeida, T., and Bustamente, S. (eds.) (1992) *Indios: Una Reflexión Sobre el Levantamiento Indígena de 1990*. Quito: ILDIS/Abya-Yala.

Alvarado Ramos, J. A. (1996) "Relaciones raciales en Cuba: Notas de investigación." *Temas* 7, 37–43.

Andrews, G. R. (1991) *Blacks and Whites in São Paulo, Brazil: 1888–1988*. Madison: University of Wisconsin Press.

Arocha, J. (1992) "Afro-Colombia denied." *NACLA Report on the Americas* 25, 4:28–31, 46, 47.

Arocha, J. (1998) "Inclusion of Afro-Colombians: Unreachable national goal?" *Latin American Perspectives*, 25,3:70–89.

Bateman, R. (1998) "Africans and Indians: A comparative study of the black Carib and black Seminole [Honduras, Belize, Florida]," in N. E. Whitten, J. and A. Torres (eds.) *Blackness in Latin America and the Caribbean*, vol. I. Bloomington: Indiana University Press, pp.200–21.

Baud, M. (1996) "'Constitutionally white': The forging of a national identity in the Dominican Republic," in G. Oostindie (ed.) *Ethnicity in the Caribbean: Essays in Honor of Harry Hoetink*. London: Macmillan Caribbean, pp.121–51.

Bento, M. A. S. (1995) "A mulher negra no mercado de trabalho." *Estudos Feministas* 3,2:479–88.

Berdichensky, B. (1986) "Del indigenismo a la Indianidad y el surgimiento de un a ideologia indígena en andino América." *América Indígena* 45,1:643–55.

Bonnett, A. (1996) "Anti-racism and the critique of 'white' identities." *New Community: Journal of the European Research Centre on Migration and Ethnic Relations*, 22,1:97–110.

Bourgois, P. (1989) *Ethnicity at Work: Divided Labor on a Central American Banana Plantation*. Baltimore, MD: The Johns Hopkins University Press.

Bourgois, P. (1998) "The black diaspora in Costa Rica: Upward mobility and ethnic discrimination," in N. E. Whitten, J. and A. Torres (eds.) *Blackness in Latin America and the Caribbean*, vol. I. Bloomington: Indiana University Press, pp.119–32.

Burdick, J. (1992a) "The myth of racial democracy." *NACLA Report on the Americas*, 24,4:40–4.

Burdick, J. (1992b) "Brazil's black consciousness movement." *NACLA Report on the Americas*, 24,4:23–7.

Burdick, J. (1998a) "The lost constituency of Brazil's black movements." *Latin American Perspectives*, 25,1:136–55.

Burdick, J. (1998b) *Blessed Anastácia: Women, Race, and Popular Christianity in Brazil*. New York: Routledge.

Casaus Arzú, M. E. (1992) *Guatemala: Linaje y Racismo*. San José, Costa Rica: FLASCO.

Castro, N. G. and Guimarães, J. A. (1993) "Desigualdades raciais no mercado e nos locais de trabalho." *Estudos Afro-Asiáticos* 22:23–60.

Dandara, C. (1992) *O Triunfo da Ideologia de Embranquecimento: O Homen Negro e a Rejeição d a Mulher Negra*. Belo Horizonte, Brazil: Projeto Cidadania do Povo.

da Silva. A. L. (ed.) (1993) *A Questão Indígena na Sala de Aula: Subsídios para Professores de Primeiro e Segundo Graus*. São Paulo: Editora Brasiliense.

555

Domingues, R. (1988) "The color of a majority without citizenship." *Politicas Govermentais*, 7, 85. Rio de Janeiro: Instituto Brasileiro de Análises Sociais e Economicas.

Duany, J. (1998) "Reconstructing racial identity: Ethnicity, color, and class among Domincans in the United States and Puerto Rico." *Latin American Perspectives* 25,3:147–72.

Duharte Jiménez, R. (1996) "Tres mujeres Cubanas hablan de prejuicios raciales." *América Negra* 12, December: 163–74.

Dweyer, J. and Lovell, P. (1988) "The cost of being nonwhite in Brazil." *Sociology and Social Research*, 72:136–42.

Dzidzienyo, A. (1979) *The Position of Blacks in Brazilian Society*. London: Minority Rights Group.

Fernandez, N. T. (1996) "The color of love: Young interracial couples in Cuba." *Latin American Perspectives* 23,1:99–117.

Field, L. (1991) "Ecuador's pan-Indian uprising." *NACLA Report on the Americas* 25,3:39–44.

Field, L. (1994) "Who are the Indians? Reconceptualizing indigenous identity, resistance, and the role of social science in Latin America." *Latin American Research Review* 29,3:237–48.

Field, L. (1996) "Mired positionings: Moving beyond metropolitan authority and indigenous authenticity." *Identities* 3,102:137–54.

Figueira, V. M. (1990) "O preconceito racial na escola." *Estudos Afro-Asiáticos* 18:63–72.

Figueira, V. M. (1998) "O preconceito racial: diffusão e manutenção na escola." *Intercambio* 1,1:37–46.

Figueiredo, A. (1994) "O mercado da boa aparência: As cabelerias negras." *Bahia: Analise e Dados* 3/4, (March): 33–6.

Freeland, J. (1995) "Nicaragua," in Minority Rights Group (ed.) *No Longer Invisible: Afro-Latin Americans Today*. London: Minority Rights Group, pp.181–201.

Friedemann, N. S. de (1992) "Negros en Colombia: Identitad e invisibilidad." *América Negra* 3, June: 25–38.

Friedemann, N. S. de and Arocha, J. (1995) "Colombia," in M. Litvinoff (ed.) *No Longer Invisible: Afro-Latin Americans Today*. London: Minority Rights Group.

Fuente, A. de L. (1998) "Race, national discourse and politics in Cuba: An overview." *Latin American Perspectives* 25,3:43–69.

Gilliam, A. and Gilliam, O. (1999) "Odyssey: Negotiating the subjectivity of *Mulata* identity in Brazil." *Latin American Perspectives* 26,3:60–84.

Gould, J. L. (1998) *To Die in This Way: Nicaraguan Indians and the Myth of Mestizaje, 1880–1965*. Durham, NC: Duke University Press.

Graham, R. (ed.) (1990) *The Idea of Race in Latin America, 1870–1940*. Austin: University of Texas Press.

Guanche, J. (1996) "Etnicidade y racialidade en la Cuba Atual." *Temas* 7, July–September: 51–7.

Guimarães, A. S. A. (1995) "Racism and anti-racism in Brazil: A postmodern perspective," in B. Bowser (ed.) *Racism and Anti-Racism in World Perspective*. London: Sage, pp.208–26.

Guimarães, A. S. A. (1996) "O recente anti-racismo Brasileiro: O que dizem os jornais diarios." *Revista USP* 28, December–February: 84–95.

Guss, D. M. (1993) "The selling of San Juan: The performance of history in an Afro-Venezuelan community." *American Ethnologist* 20, 3:451–73.

Hale, C. R. (1991) "Miskitu: Revolution in the revolution." *NACLA Report on the Americas*, 25,3:24–8.

Hale, C. R. (1994) *Resistance and Contradiction: Miskitu Indians and the Nicaraguan State, 1894–1987*. Palo Alto, CA: Stanford University Press.

Hale, C. R. (1996) "Mestizaje, hybridity, and the cultural politics of difference in postrevolutionary Central America." *Journal of Latin American Anthropology* 2:34–61.

Hanchard, M. G. (1994) *Orpheus and Power: The Movimento Negro of Rio de Janeiro and São Paulo, Brazil, 1945–1988*. Princeton, NJ: Princeton University Press.

Harris, M. (1952) "Race relations in Minas Velhas, a community in the mountain region of Central Brazil," in C. Wagley (ed.) *Race and Class in Rural Brazil*. Paris: UNESCO, pp.47–81.

Harrison, F. V. (1995) "The persistent power of 'Race' in the cultural and political economy of racism." *Annual Review of Anthropology* 24:47–74.

Harvey, N. (1998) *The Chiapas Rebellion: The Struggle for Land and Democracy*. Durham, NC: Duke University Press.

Hasenbalg, C. (1979) *Discriminação e Desigualdades no Brasil*. Rio de Janeiro: Ediçoes Graal.

Hasenbalg, C. (1991) "Race and socioeconomic inequalities in Brazil," in P. Fontaine (ed.) *Race, Class and Power in Brazil*. Los Angeles: Center for Afro-American Studies, University of California, pp.25–41.

Hasenbalg, C. (1996) "Racial inequalities in Brazil and throughout Latin America: Timid responses to disguised racism," in E. Jelin and E. Hershberg (eds.) *Constructing Democracy: Human Rights, Citizenship, and Society in Latin America*. Boulder, CO: Westview Press, pp. 161–75.

Helg, A. (1995) *Our Rightful Share: The Afro-Cuban Struggle for Equality, 1886–1912*. Chapel Hill: University of North Carolina.

Hellwig, D. J. (ed.) (1992) *African American Reflections on Brazil's Racial Paradise*. Philadelphia, PA: Temple University Press.

Hendricks, J. (1991) "Symbolic counterhegemony among the Ecuadorian Shuar," in G. Urban and J. Sherzer (eds.) *Nation-States and Indians in Latin America*. Austin: University of Texas Press, pp.53–71.

Heringer, R. (1995) "Introduction to the analysis of racism and anti-racism in Brazil," in B. P. Bowser (ed.) *Racism and Anti-Racism in World Perspective*. Thousand Oaks, CA: Sage, pp.203–7.

Hernandez-Díaz, J. (1994) "National identity and indigenous ethnicity in Mexico." *Canadian Review of Studies in Nationalism*. 21, 1–2:71–81.

Hoetink, H. (1995) "Some notes on ethnic boundaries and culture with a glance at Brazil." *Luso-Brazilian Review* 32,2:79–87.

Hoffman, E. and Hoffman, J. A. (1993) "Race relating in Cuba." *Crossroads* 35, October: 25–8.

Howe, J. (1998) *A People Who Would Not Kneel: Panama, the United States, and the San Blas Kuna*. Washington, DC: Smithsonian Institution Press.

Hutchinson, H. (1952) "Race relations in a rural community of the Bahian reconcavo," in C. Wagley (ed.), *Race and Class in Rural Brazil*. Paris: UNESCO, pp.16–46.

Kicza, J. (1993) *The Indian in Latin American History: Resistance, Resilience and Acculturation*. Wilmington, DE: Scholarly Resources.

Knight, A. (1990) "Racism, revolution, and indigenismo: Mexico 1910–1940," in R. Graham (ed.) *The Idea of Race in Latin America, 1870–1940*. Austin: University of Texas, pp.71–113.

Kutzinski, V. (1993) *Sugar's Secret: Race and the Erotics of Cuban Nationalism*. Charlottesville: University Press of Virginia.

Lancaster, R. N. (1991) "Skin color, race and racism in Nicaragua." *Ethnology*, 30,4:339–54.

Lovell, P. (1992) "Raça, classe genero e discriminação salarial no Brasil." *Estudos Afro-Asiáticos* 22:85–98.

Lovell, P. A. and Wood, C. H. (1998) "Skin color, racial identity, and life chances in Brazil." *Latin American Perspectives* 25,3:90–109.

Manrique, N. (1995) "Political violence, ethnicity and racism in Peru in time of war." *Journal of Latin American Cultural Studies*, 4,1:5–18.

Marcia, L. (1995) "Trajectória educational e realização socioeconômica da mulheres negras." *Estudos Feministas* 3,2:489–505.

Márquez, R. (1992) "An anatomy of racism." *NACLA: Report on the Americas* 24,4:32–3.

McGarrity, G. (1992) "Race, culture, and social change in contemporary Cuba," in S. Halebsky and J. Kirk (eds.) *Cuba in Transition*. Boulder, CO: Westview Press, pp.193–205.

Mitchell, M. J. and Wood, C. H. (1999) "Ironies of citizenship: Skin color, police brutality and the challenge to democracy in Brazil." *Social Forces* 77,3:1001–2.

Moore, C. (1988) *Castro, the Blacks and Africa*. Los Angeles: Center for Afro-American Studies, University of California.

Nascimento, A. do (1989) *Brazil, Mixture or Massacre? Essays in the Genocide of a Black People*. Dover, MA.: The Majority Press.

Nash, J. (1995) *The Explosion of Communities in Chiapas*. Copenhagen: International Work Group for Indian Affairs.

Oliveira, N. dos S. (1996) "Favelas and ghettos: Race and class in Rio de Janeiro and New York City". *Latin American Perspectives* 23,4:71–89.

Penha-Lopes, V. (1996) "What next? On race and assimilation in the United States and Brazil." *Journal of Black Studies* 26,6:809–26.

Pérez, B. (1998) "Pantera Negra: A messianic future of historical resistance and cultural survival among maroon descendants in Southern Venezuela," in N. E. Whitten, J. and A. Torres (eds.) *Blackness in Latin America and the Caribbean*, vol I. Bloomington: Indiana University Press, pp.223–43.

Pinto, R. P. (1987) "A representação do negro em livros didáticos de leitura." *Cadernos de Pesquisa* 63:88–92.

Pinto, R. P. (1993) "Movimento negro e educação do negro: A ênfase na identidade". *Cadernos de Pesquisasa* 86:25–38.

Portillo, L. (writer, producer, director) (1993) "Mirrors of the heart," in J. Vecchione (executive producer) *Americas, Volume 4*. A Production of WGBH Boston and Central Television Enterprises for Channel 4, UK. South Burlington, VT: Annenberg/CPB Collection.

Purcell, T. W. (1993) *Banana Fallout: Class, Color and Culture among West Indians in Costa Rica*. Los Angeles: University of California, Center for Afro-American Studies Publications.

Purcell, T. W. and Sawyers, K. (1993) "Democracy and ethnic conflict: Blacks in Costa Rica." *Ethnic and Racial Studies* 16,2:298–322.

Queriroz, A. M. (1994) "Mulheres negras, educação e mercado de trabalho." *Bahia: Análise e Dados: O Negro*, 3/4:78–81.

Radcliffe, S. (1990) "Ethnicity, patriarchy and incorporation into the nation: Female migrants as domestic servants in Southern Peru." *Environment and Planning D: Society and Space* 8:379–93.

Radcliffe, S. and Westwood, S. (1996) *Remaking the Nation: Place, Identity, and Politics in Latin America*. New York: Routledge.

Rappaport, J. (1992) "Fictive foundations: National romances and subaltern ethnicity in Latin America." *History Workshop Journal* 34:119–31.

Reichmann, R. (1995) "Brazil's denial of race." *NACLA Report on the Americas*, 28,6:35–45.

Riveira Cusicanqui, S. (1991) "Aymara past, Aymara future." *NACLA Report on the Americas*, 25,3:18–23.

Root, M. P. P. (ed.) (1996) *The Multiracial Experience: Racial Border as the New Frontier*. Thousand Oaks, CA: Sage.

Rosemberg, F. (1990) "Segregação espacial na Escola Paulista." *Estudos Afro-Asiáticos* 19:97–106.

Rosemberg, F. and Pinto, R. P. (1987) "Raça negra e educação." *Cadernos de Pesquisa* 63.

Rubin, Jeffrey W. (1997) *Decentering the Regime: Ethnicity, Radicalism and Democracy in Juchitau, Mexico*. Durham, NC: Duke University Press.

Safa, H. I. (1998) "Introduction." *Latin American Perspectives* 25,3:3–20.

Santiago, A. M. (1992) "Patterns of Puerto Rican segregation and mobility." *Hispanic Journal of Behavioral Sciences* 14,1:107–33.

Scalon, M. (1992) "Côr e seletividade conjugal no Brasil." *Estudos Afro-Asiáticos* 23:17–36.

Sheriff, R. (1997) "Negro is a nickname that whites call blacks." Ph.D. dissertation, Department of Anthropology, City University of New York.

Silva, N. (1991) "Updating the cost of not being white in Brazil," in P. Fontaine (ed.) *Race, Class and Power in Brazil*. Los Angeles: Center for Afro-American Studies, University of California, pp.42–55.

Silva, N. and Hasenbalg, C. (1992) *Relações Raciais no Brasil Contempôraneo*. Rio de Janeiro: Rio Fundo Editora.

Simpson, A. (1993) *Xuxa: The Mega-Marketing of Gender, Race and Modernity*. Philadelphia, PA: Temple University Press.

Simpson, J. S. (1996) "Easy talk, white talk, back talk: Some reflections on the meanings of our words." *Journal of Contemporary Ethnography* 25,3:372–89.

Skidmore, T. ([1974] 1993). *Black into White: Race and Nationality in Brazilian Thought*. Durham, NC: Duke University Press.

Smith, C. (1990) *Guatemalan Indians and the State, 1540–1988*. Austin: University of Texas Press.

Smith, C. (1991) "Maya nationalism." *NACLA Report on the Americas*, 25,3:29–33.

Smith, C. (1996) "Race/class/gender ideology in Guatemala: Modern and anti-modern forms," in B. F. Williams (ed.) *Women Out of Place: The Gender of Agency and the Race of Nationality*. New York: Routledge, pp.50–78.

Smith, C. (1997) "The symbolics of blood: Mestizaje in the Americas." *Identities* 3,4:495–521.

Stepan, N. (1991) *"The Hour of Eugenics": Race, Class, and Nation in Latin America*. Ithaca, NY: Cornell University Press.

Streicker, J. (1995) "Policing boundaries: Race, class, and gender in Cartagena, Colombia." *American Ethnologist* 22,1:54–74.

Stutzman, R. (1981) "El mestizaje: An all-inclusive ideology of exclusion," in N. E. Whitten (ed.) *Cultural Transformations and Ethnicity in Modern Ecuador*. Urbana: University of Illinois Press, pp.45–94.

Taussig, M. (1987) *Shamanism, Colonialism, and the Wild Man: A Study in Terror and Healing*. Chicago: Chicago University Press.

Telles, E. (1992) "Residential segregation by skin color in Brazil." *American Sociological Review* 57:186–97.

Telles, E. (1993) "Racial distance and region in marriage: The case of marriage among color groups." *Latin American Research Review* 28:141–62.

Telles, E. (1994) "Industrialização e desigualidade racial no emprego: O exemplo Brasileiro." *Estudos Afro-Asiáticos* 26:21–51.

Torres-Saillant, S. (1998) "The tribulations of blackness: Stages in Dominican racial identity." *Latin American Perspectives* 25,3:126–46.

Twine, F. W. (1996) "O hiato de genero nas percepções de racismo: O caso dos Afro-Brasileiros socialmente ascendentes." *Estudos Afro-Asiáticos* 29:37–54.

Twine, F. W. (1997) "Mapping the terrain of Brazilian racism." *Race and Class* 38,3:49–61.

Twine, F. W. (1998) *Racism in a Racial Democracy: The Maintenance of White Supremacy in Brazil*. New Brunswick, NJ: Rutgers University Press.

Urban, G. (1991) "The semiotics of state–Indian relationships: Peru, Paraguay, and Brazil" in G. Urban and C. Scherzer (eds.) *Nation-States and Indians in Latin America*. Austin: University of Texas, pp.307–30.

Varese, S. (1988) "Multiethnicity and hegemonic construction: Indian plans and the future," in R. Guidiere, F. Pellizi, and S. J. Tambiah (eds.) *Ethnicities and Nations: Processes of Interethnic Relations in Latin America, South East Asia and the Pacific*. Austin: Texas University Press, pp. 55–77.

Varese, S. (1991) "Think locally, act globally." *NACLA Report on the Americas*, 25,3:13–17.

Wade, P. (1993) *Blackness and Race Mixture: The Dynamics of Racial Identity in Colombia*. Baltimore: Johns Hopkins University Press.

Wade, P. (1995) "The cultural politics of blackness in Colombia." *American Ethnologist* 22,2:342–58.

Wade, P. (1997) *Race and Ethnicity in Latin America*. Chicago: Pluto Press.

Wagley, C. (1952) *Race and Class in Rural Brazil*. Paris: UNESCO.

Warren, K. B. (1998) *Indigenous Movements and their Critics: Pan-Maya Activism in Guatemala*. Princeton, NJ: Princeton University Press.

Warren, J. W. (1997) "O fardo de não ser negro: Uma análise comparativa do desempenho escolar de alunos Afro- Brasileiros e Afro-Norte-Americanos." *Estudos Afro-Asiáticos* 31:103–24.

Warren, J. W. (1998) "The state of Indian exorcism: Violence and racial formation in Eastern Brazil." *Journal of Historical Sociology* 11,4:492–518.

Warren, J. W. (1999) "The Brazilian geography of Indianness." *Wicazo Sa Review* 14,1:61–86.

Warren, J. W. (2000) "Masters in the field: White talk, white privilege, white biases," in F. W. Twine and J. W. Warren *Racing Research/Researching Race*. New York: New York University Press, pp. 135–64.

Warren, J. W. (in press) *Racial Revolutions: Antiracism and Indian Resurgence in Brazil*. Durham, NC: Duke University Press.

Winant, H. (1994) *Racial Conditions: Politics, Theory, Comparisons*. Minneapolis: University of Minnesota Press.

Whitten, Jr. N. E. and Quiroga, D. (1998) " 'To rescue national dignity': Blackness as a quality of nationalist creativity in Ecuador," in N. E, Whitten, J. and A. Torres (eds.) *Blackness in Latin America and the Caribbean*, vol. I. Bloomington: Indiana University Press, pp.75–99.

Whitten, Jr. N. E. and Torres, A. (1992) Blackness in the Americas. *NACLA: Report on the Americas*. 25, 4 (February): 16–22.

Whitten, Jr. N. E. and Torres, A. (1998) "General introduction: To forge the future in the fires of the past: An interpretive essay on racism, domination, resistance, and liberation," in N. E. Whitten, J. and A. Torres (eds.) *Blackness in Latin America and the Caribbean*, vol. 1. Bloomington: Indiana University Press, pp.3–33.

Wright, W. R. (1990) *Café con Leche: Race, Class and National Image in Venezuela*. Austin: University of Texas Press.

Chapter 37

Migration

Stephen Castles

In the contemporary world, migration has become a major factor in social change. Globalization involves cross-border flows of capital, commodities, people, and ideas. The first two are generally welcomed: all sorts of frameworks have been established to encourage economic integration at the regional and global levels. But the latter pair is viewed with suspicion: immigration and cultural difference are seen as potential threats to national sovereignty and identity, and many governments and political movements seek to restrict them. Yet the reality is that population mobility is inextricably bound up with economic and political internationalization. Migration is both a result of the integration of ever-greater areas into global markets and the culture of modernity, and a cause of further social transformations in both migrant-sending and migrant-receiving countries.

Migration probably affects the majority of the world's population today. Few people spend their whole life in their native village or urban neighborhood: many experience internal migration, while a substantial minority move across national borders. Yet even those who have lived in one place all their lives are affected: they may be descendants of migrants, or their friends or relatives may have migrated in recent times, or they may have seen changes in their neighborhood through departure of locals or arrival of newcomers. Migration – along with other globalizing forces such as the information-technology revolution and electronic media – is a major factor in the erosion of traditional boundaries between languages, cultures, ethnic groups, and nation-states. Encounters between ethnic groups are often the result of migration, so that understanding migration is a crucial aspect of racial and ethnic studies.

Definitions, Types, and Numbers

Migration is a word that people often use without thinking about its precise meaning. In fact, definitions vary from country to country and between social-scientific disciplines. There is no single "correct" definition: it is important to examine what others mean when they use the term, and to be precise in one's own usage. Any definition of migration requires specification in both space and time of the phenomenon to be examined (Boyle et al., 1998: chapter 2).

With regard to space, migration refers to crossing the boundary of a geographical or administrative area. *Internal migration* means moving from one administrative area (a country, district, or municipality) to another within one country. *International migration* means crossing the frontiers which separate one of the world's 200-odd states from another. Some scholars argue that internal and international migration are part of the same process, and should be analyzed together (Skeldon, 1997:9–10). However, this chapter will mainly be concerned with international migration, because of its significance in creating multiethnic societies and undermining myths of national homogeneity. The increasing political saliency of migration issues in recent times has mainly concerned international migration. Yet rigid distinctions may be misleading: international migration may be over short distances and between culturally similar people (e.g., between Austria and southern Germany), while internal migration can span great distances and bring together very different people (e.g., movements of Uigar "national minority" people from the Western provinces of China to Shanghai, Beijing, and Shenzhen in the East). Sometimes the frontiers "migrate," rather than the people, making internal migrants into international ones. For instance, the breakup of the former Soviet Union turned millions of former internal migrants into foreigners in the successor states.

Specification in time is needed because the great majority of border crossings do not imply migration: most travelers are tourists or business visitors who have no intention of staying for long. Migration means taking up residence for a certain minimum period – say six months or a year. Most countries have a number of categories in their migration policies and statistics. For instance, Australia distinguishes between permanent immigrants who are allowed to remain for good (85,800 entrants in 1996–7); long-term temporary immigrants who stay at least 12 months, usually for work, business, or education (95,100 in 1996–7); and short-term temporary visitors (4.2 million in 1996–7) (Castles et al., 1998:4). Yet Australia is seen as a "classical country of immigration" because of its tradition of nation-building through immigration, and nearly all public debate is focused on permanent immigration. Other countries prefer to see immigration as essentially temporary and set up categories permitting varying lengths of stay. When the German Federal Republic started to recruit so-called "guestworkers" in the 1960s, some were allowed in for a few months only as "seasonal workers" while others received one-year permits. In time, it became difficult to limit residence so tightly: people who had been resident for a certain time obtained two-year, then five-year, and finally unlimited permits.

Such variations highlight the fact that there is nothing objective about definitions of migration: they are the result of state policies, introduced in response to political and economic goals and public attitudes. International migration arises in a world divided up into nation-states, in which remaining in the country of birth is still seen as a norm and moving to another country as a deviation. That is why migration tends to be regarded as problematic: something to be controlled and even curbed, because it may impinge on state sovereignty. Problems of comparison arise not just because statistical categories differ, but because such differences reflect real variations in the social meaning of migration in differing contexts. One way in which states seek to improve control is by dividing up international migrants into categories based on personal characteristics, social and cultural backgrounds, and the purpose of migration. The most frequent categories are:

- Temporary labor migrants (also known as guestworkers or overseas contract workers): men and women who migrate for a limited period (from a few months to several years) in order to take up employment and send money home (remittances).

- Highly skilled migrants: people with qualifications as managers, executives, professionals, technicians, or similar, who move within the internal labor markets of transnational corporations and international organizations, or who seek employment through international labor markets for scarce skills. Many countries welcome such migrants and have special "skilled and business migration" programs to encourage them to come.
- Undocumented migrants (also known as irregular or illegal migrants): people who enter a country, usually in search of employment, without the necessary documents and permits. Many labor migration flows consist predominantly of undocumented migrants. In some cases immigration countries tacitly permit such migration since it allows mobilization of labor in response to employer demands without social costs or measures for protection of migrants.
- Refugees: according to the 1951 United Nations Convention relating to the Status of Refugees, a refugee is a person residing outside his or her country of nationality, who is unable or unwilling to return because of a well-founded fear of persecution on account of race, religion, nationality, membership in a particular social group, or political opinion. Signatories to the Convention undertake to protect refugees by allowing them to enter and granting temporary or permanent residence status. Although refugee organizations, in particular the United Nations High Commission for Refugees (UNHCR), seek to draw a strict line between refugees and migrants, they do share many common characteristics with regard to social needs and cultural impacts in their place of settlement (UNHCR, 1997).
- Asylum seekers: people who move across borders in search of protection, but who may not fulfill the strict criteria laid down by the 1951 Convention. In many contemporary conflict situations in less developed countries it is difficult to distinguish between flight because of personal persecution and departure caused by the destruction of the economic and social infrastructure needed for survival. Both political and economic motivations for migration are linked to the generalized and persistent violence that has resulted from rapid processes of decolonization and globalization under conditions determined by the developed countries (Zolberg et al., 1989).
- Family members (also known as family reunion or family reunification migrants): migration to join people who have already entered an immigration country under one of the above categories. Many countries, including the USA, Canada, Australia, and most EU member states recognize in principle the right to family reunion for legal immigrants, although this right may be limited by a range of conditions. In such countries, family members may make up the majority of immigrants. Other countries, especially those with contract labor systems, deny the right to family reunion. In such cases, family members may enter illegally.
- Return migrants: people who return to their countries of origin after a period in another country. Return migrants are often looked on favorably as they may bring with them capital, skills, and experience useful for economic development. Many countries have special schemes to make use of this "development potential." However, some governments view returnees with suspicion since they may act as agents of cultural or political change.

None of these categories are explicitly based on the race, ethnicity, or origins of migrants, and, indeed, there are few countries today which admit to discriminating on the basis of such criteria. The exceptions are countries which give preference to people considered to be returning to an ancestral homeland: "patrials" to Britain, "ethnic Germans" to Germany, Jews to Israel, and so forth. This situation contrasts with the quite recent past, in which race was seen as a legitimate criterion for selection of immigrants. The "White Australia policy" was not fully abolished until 1972, and other countries, such as Canada and the USA, had openly racist selection policies until the 1960s. However, selection policies ostensibly based on economic, social, and humanitarian criteria may have covert or unconscious racial and ethnic biases built into them. Using skills, language knowledge, possession of capital, or assumptions of "settlement capability" may favor people from certain countries or backgrounds over others. Similarly, administrative measures, such as visa fees or choice of where to site immigration offices, can lead to bias.

How many international migrants are there, and do the numbers justify the notion that we live in an "age of migration" (Castles and Miller, 1998)? The most comprehensive and recent figures are provided by a study carried out by the United Nations Population Division (see table 37.1).

The UN figures show that the global migrant stock (the number of people resident outside their country of birth) grew from 75 million in 1965 to 120 million in 1990. The latter figure was roughly equal to 2 percent of the world's population at the time. Although the number of migrants grew slightly faster than the population as a whole, the annual growth rate (1.9 percent for the whole period but increasing to 2.6 percent from 1985 to 1990) was not dramatic if taken as a global average. By the late 1990s, the number of international migrants was estimated to be 135–40 million, including some 13 million UNHCR-recognized refugees. International migration thus remains an exception, with most of the world's people remaining in their country of origin. Internal migration by contrast is much larger: for instance, the number of internal migrants in India in 1981 was some 200 million, more than double the number of international migrants in the whole world at the time (Zlotnik, 1998). Overall, in the second half of the 1980s between 750 million and one billion people migrated – that is about one in six of the world's population (Skeldon, 1997:4).

The significance of migration as a major factor in societal change lies in the fact that it is concentrated in certain countries and regions. The UN study showed that 90 percent of the world's migrants were living in just 55 countries. In absolute terms, most migration is between less-developed countries: in 1990, 55 percent of all migrants were to be found in less developed countries. But in relative terms, the developed world has been far more affected by immigration: 4.6 percent of the population of the developed countries were migrants in 1990, compared with 1.6 percent in developing countries. An examination by geographical regions confirms this concentration: the 1990 immigrant share was highest in Oceania (17.8 per cent) followed by North America (8.6 percent) and "other Europe" (i.e., Europe without the former Eastern Bloc countries) 6.1 percent. The immigrant share in population was far lower in Asia (1.4 percent), Latin America and the Caribbean (1.7 percent), and Africa (2.5 percent) (Zlotnik, 1998). However, these very broad regional statistics conceal important changes: recent years have seen very large flows of labor migrants from the least developed countries of the South to the newly industrializing countries (NICs).

Moreover, migration affects certain areas within both sending and receiving countries more than others. As migratory chains develop, large proportions of the young men and

Table 37.1 Immigrant population by region, 1965 and 1990

	Estimated foreign-born population					
	Thousands		As percentage of total population of region		As percentage of migrant stock world total	
Region	1965	1990	1965	1990	1965	1990
World total	75 214	119 761	2.3	2.3	100.0	100.0
Developed countries	30 401	54 231	3.1	4.5	40.4	45.3
Developing countries	44 813	65 530	1.9	1.6	59.6	54.7
Africa	7 952	15 361	2.5	2.5	10.6	13.1
Northern Africa	1 016	1 982	1.4	1.4	1.4	1.7
Sub-Saharan Africa	6 936	13 649	2.9	2.8	9.2	11.4
Asia	31 429	43 018	1.7	1.4	41.8	35.9
Eastern & South-eastern Asia	8 136	7 931	0.7	0.4	10.8	6.6
China	266	346	0.0	0.0	0.4	0.3
Other Eastern & South-eastern Asia	7 870	7 586	1.9	1.2	10.5	6.3
South-central Asia	18 610	20 782	2.8	1.8	24.7	17.4
Western Asia	4 683	14 304	7.4	10.9	6.2	11.9
Latin America & the Caribbean	5 907	7 475	2.4	1.7	7.9	6.2
Caribbean	532	959	2.4	2.9	0.7	0.8
Central America	445	2 047	0.8	1.8	0.6	1.7
South America	4 930	4 469	3.0	1.5	6.6	3.7
Northern America	12 695	23 895	6.0	8.6	16.9	20.0
Europe & former USSR	14 728	25 068	2.2	3.2	19.6	20.9
Countries with economies in transition	2 835	2 055	2.4	1.7	3.8	1.7
Former USSR	140	159	0.1	0.1	0.2	0.1
Other Europe	11 753	22 853	3.6	6.1	15.6	19.1
Oceania	2 502	4 675	14.4	17.8	3.3	3.9

Source: Zlotnik, 1998: Table 1.

women of specific villages or neighborhoods leave, which may lead to local labor shortages as well as major changes in family and community life. In immigration countries, newcomers become concentrated in industrial areas and urban centers where there are chances of employment and where previous migrants can provide help with settlement. In Europe for instance, virtually all major cities have immigrant numbers higher than the average for the whole country. Typically, certain neighborhoods become centers of immigrant settlement, marked by distinctive businesses, associations, social facilities, and places of worship. Such neighborhoods are the basis for ethnic community formation and cultural and linguistic maintenance.

Another recent trend has been the feminization of migration. Although women have always formed a large proportion of migrants, their share has gradually increased: by 1995 about 48 percent of all international migrants were women, and they outnumbered male migrants in about a quarter of receiving countries (Zlotnik, 1998). More important was the shift in the character of female migration with a trend away from movement as family members of male workers or refugees and an increase in the number of women who moved independently or as heads of households. However, such changes were not always reflected in public perceptions, nor in migration regulations, which tended to automatically treat women as dependents (Lutz et al., 1995).

Understanding Migration

Migration is not a simple individual action, but rather a long drawn-out process which will be played out for the rest of the migrant's life and affect subsequent generations too. The action of crossing a border is the culmination of a complex process of migration decision making shaped by a wide range of factors. In turn, the border crossing marks the beginning of a settlement process, involving all sorts of economic, social, cultural, psychological, and political changes. Migration arises as a result of social change and in turn affects whole communities and societies in both sending and receiving areas. The experience of migration and settlement often leads to modification of the original plans, so that migrants' intentions at the time of departure are poor predictors of actual behavior. Migration can only be adequately understood through an interdisciplinary perspective: sociology, anthropology, political science, philosophy, history, economics, geography, demography, psychology, law, and cultural studies are all relevant. Most of the major social-scientific paradigms have been applied to migration research, leading to a variety of theoretical and methodological approaches (Massey et al., 1993; Boyle et al., 1998; chapter 3; Castles and Miller, 1998: chapter 2).

In terms of its influence on policy makers, the dominant approach in explaining why migration takes place has been neoclassical economic theory and its derivatives such as human capital theory. Essentially, migration is seen as being caused by differences in supply of and demand for labor in different places. People tend to move from countries where wages are low and labor is plentiful relative to capital to those where the opposite is the case. Emphasis is put on the individual decisions to migrate based on rational comparisons of the costs and benefits involved. Migrants are seen as free agents who make choices in a "migration market." People migrate if they believe that they can maximize their income by moving to another place (Todaro, 1976; Borjas, 1990). Over time, neoclassical theory assumes that a combination of labor migration and international capital flows will even out differences between countries, leading to equilibrium and a decline in migration. Constraining factors, such as government restrictions on migration, are seen as market distortions that should be eliminated.

Critics argue that the usefulness of neoclassical approaches is limited by their heavy reliance on quantitative modeling techniques, which require statistical data of an accuracy rarely available in international migration research. Moreover, neoclassical approaches seem to have little ability to predict or explain specific migratory flows. This is due to their focus on individual economic decisions, and their neglect of historical factors and collective actors including both the family and the state. A number of alternative economic approaches have been put forward. Dual labor market theory focuses on structural demand for low-skilled labor in developed economies. Labor markets become segmented, with local workers in highly developed economies gaining the education and skills needed for qualified jobs, and being unwilling to do unrewarding, monotonous, and poorly paid work. The result is recruitment of unskilled immigrant workers by employers and governments. This intensifies labor market segmentation, since ethnicity, race, national origins, and gender are used as labels to assign workers to certain jobs. Migration is seen as "demand-driven" by powerful groups in the receiving countries, rather than "supply-driven" by the income-maximizing behavior of migrants (Piore, 1980).

By contrast, a second alternative economic approach, the new economics of labor migration (Stark, 1991), concentrates on decision-making processes in areas of origin, while criticizing the individualistic assumptions of neoclassical theory. Research shows that migration decision making is often a family and community process: in situations of rapid change, a family may decide that one or more members should migrate, in order to minimize risk and maximize family income and survival chances (Hugo, 1994). Families may use migration to diversify their earning opportunities and to provide against the risk of crop failure or of loss of employment in local labor markets. Management of risk may be more significant than income maximization, so that migratory movements may continue even where earning differentials between sending and receiving areas are small. Capital accumulated through migrant remittances can be used to improve earning opportunities at home (e.g., by acquiring land or equipment), so that there is no necessary contradiction between migration and local development. From this it follows that governments can influence migration behavior through measures to reduce risk (e.g., social insurance schemes), and can also encourage use of migration and remittances to assist economic development.

Since the 1970s, some migration theorists have argued for the need to go beyond economics and use broader interdisciplinary approaches to explain migration. Historical-structural theories had their intellectual roots in Marxist political economy and world systems theory. Migration was seen as a consequence of the unequal distribution of economic and political power in the world economy. Labor surpluses in the Third World were a legacy of colonialism and Western military intervention which had brought about underdevelopment and dependency on foreign capital. Labor surpluses in backward parts of the European periphery were the result of war and regional inequalities. Migration was a way of mobilizing cheap labor in the interests of capital owners in the rich countries. Migration was as important as military hegemony and control of world trade and investment in keeping the Third World dependent on the First. In turn, labor market segmentation in developed countries divided the working class and weakened labor movements. Migration was an essential part of globalization, contributing to the growth of ethnically and socially fragmented "global cities" as centers of economic and political control (Castles and Kosack, 1985; Cohen, 1987; Sassen, 1988).

But historical-structuralist theory was in turn criticized by many migration scholars: if the logic of capital and the interests of Western states were so dominant, how could the frequent breakdown of migration policies be explained, such as the unplanned shift from

567

labor migration to permanent settlement in Western Europe after 1974 (see below)'? Both the neoclassical perspective and the historical-structuralist approach seemed too one-sided to adequately analyze the great complexity of contemporary migrations. The neoclassical approach neglected historical causes of movements, and downplayed the role of the state, while the historical-functional approach seemed to see the interests of capital as all-determining, and paid inadequate attention to the motivations and actions of the individuals and groups involved. Moreover, as migratory processes matured, it became evident that they developed their own social networks and dynamics. Migration and settlement seemed to become self-sustaining processes, which continued often in unexpected ways even if their original causes disappeared.

Out of such critiques emerged a new approach, migration systems theory, which is increasingly influential in comparative research (Fawcett, 1989; Kritz et al., 1992). An international migration system is constituted by a receiving area consisting of one or more countries and a set of sending countries linked by large flows of migrants. These may be regional migration systems, such as the South Pacific, West Africa, or the Southern Cone of Latin America. However, distant regions may be interlinked, such as the migration system embracing the Caribbean, Western Europe, and North America; or that linking North and West Africa with France. Migration systems theory suggests that migratory movements generally arise from the existence of prior links between sending and receiving countries based on colonization, political influence, trade, investment, or cultural ties. Thus migration from Mexico to the USA originated in the south-westward expansion of the USA in the nineteenth century, and the deliberate recruitment of Mexican workers by US employers in the twentieth (Portes and Rumbaut, 1990). Similarly, both Korean and the Vietnamese migrations to America were the long-term consequence of US military involvement. The migrations from India, Pakistan, and Bangladesh to Britain were linked to the British colonial presence on the Indian subcontinent. The Algerian migration to France (and not to Germany) was due to the French colonial presence in Algeria, while the Turkish presence in Germany was the result of direct labor recruitment by Germany in the 1960s and early 1970s.

According to migrations systems theory, any migratory movement can be seen as the result of interacting macrostructures and microstructures. Macrostructures include large-scale institutional factors such as global markets, interstate relationships, and the migration laws and policies of both sending and receiving countries. The evolution of an increasingly integrated world economy has clearly been a major determinant not only of labor migration but also of nation-building migrations and refugee flows. International relations and security considerations in both sending and receiving states are also increasingly significant (Weiner, 1993; Cornelius et al., 1994). The single main determinant of migration, however, is probably still the laws and regulations imposed by states of receiving countries, in response to a wide range of economic, social, and political factors. Although international cooperation is increasingly important in migration policy, domestic considerations still play a dominant role.

Microstructures refer to the informal social networks developed by migrants, in order to provide the information and cultural capital (such as knowledge of other countries, capabilities for organizing travel, finding work, and adapting to a new environment) needed to start and sustain migratory movements. Informal networks include friendships and personal relationships, families and households, and communities of various kinds. Informal networks bind "migrants and nonmigrants together in a complex web of social roles and interpersonal relationships" (Boyd, 1989:639). These bonds are double-sided: they link migrants with nonmigrants in their areas of origin, but also connect settlers with the receiving populations in relationships of cooperation, competition, and conflict. Such networks are dynamic cultural responses, which encourage ethnic community formation and are conducive to the maintenance of transnational family and group ties.

Typically migratory chains are started by an external factor, such as recruitment or military service, or by an initial movement of young (usually male) pioneers. Once a movement is established, the migrants mainly follow "beaten paths" (Stahl, 1993) and are helped by relatives and friends already in the area of immigration. Networks based on family or on common place of origin help provide shelter, work, assistance in coping with bureaucratic procedures, and support in personal difficulties. These social networks make the migratory process safer and more manageable for the migrants and their families. However, certain people (both migrants and nonmigrants) become facilitators of migration. A migration industry emerges, consisting of recruitment organizations, lawyers, agents, smugglers, and other intermediaries (Harris, 1996:132–6). Such people can be both helpers and exploiters of migrants. Especially in situations of illegal migration or of oversupply of potential migrants, the exploitative role may predominate: many migrants have been swindled out of their savings and found themselves marooned without work or resources in a strange country. The emergence of a migration industry with a strong interest in the continuation of migration has often confounded government efforts to control or stop movements.

Migration networks provide the basis for processes of settlement and community formation in the immigration area. This is linked to family reunion: as length of stay increases, the original migrants (whether workers or refugees) begin to bring in their spouses and children, or found new families. People start to see their life perspectives in the new country. This process is especially related to the situation of migrants' children: once they go to school in the new country, learn the language, form peer group relationships, and develop bicultural or transcultural identities, it becomes more and more difficult for the parents to return to their homelands. Migrant groups become a permanent part of the population of the receiving country – yet without necessarily giving up their original languages and cultures, nor their links with their countries of origin. Thus most international migratory movements lead to settlement of a proportion of the migrants (whatever their original intentions). This in turn often results in the formation of new ethnic groups and to the emergence of new types of ethnocultural diversity.

It is apparent therefore that no rigid distinction can be drawn between migration studies and the study of ethnic and racial relations. There is a strong measure of interdependence between the two areas. Migration theories which focus narrowly on one aspect of the migratory process (such as individual migration decision making) do little to advance our knowledge. Rather there is a need for a holistic approach which contextualizes any particular topic of study as just one part of a much larger process of social transformation.

Migration in History

Population movements in response to demographic growth, climatic change, and economic needs have always been part of human history. Warfare and formation of nations, states, and empires have all led to migrations, both voluntary and forced. However, from the fifteenth century, the development of European nation-states and their colonization of the rest of the world provided a new impetus: modernity involved not only the diffusion of new cultural values and the emergence of new technologies, but also the development of new types of migration (Cohen, 1987, 1995: parts 1–5; Castles and Miller, 1998: chapter 3). In Western Europe, migration played a vital role in the development of trade and industry in the early modern period (Moch, 1992), leading to an intermingling of European peoples which contradicts later nationalist myths of ethnic homogeneity. Colonialism involved overseas emigration (both temporary and permanent) of Europeans as sailors, soldiers, farmers, traders, priests, and administrators. Mortality through shipwreck, warfare, and tropical illnesses was very high, but service in the colonies was often the only chance to escape from poverty.

Another type of colonial labor migration was slavery: an estimated 15 million Africans were forcibly taken to the Americas from the fifteenth to the nineteenth centuries. The production of sugar, tobacco, coffee, cotton, and gold by slave labor was crucial to the economic and political power of Britain, France, and other European countries. Despite slave rebellions and the abolition of the Atlantic traffic by the great powers in 1815, the number of slaves in the Americas doubled from three million in 1800 to six million in 1860. Slavery had existed in precapitalist societies, but the colonial system was new in character. Its motive force was the emergence of global empires, which began to construct a world market, dominated by merchant capital. Slaves were transported great distances by specialized traders, and bought and sold as commodities. Slaves were economic property and were subjected to harsh forms of control to maximize their output. The great majority were exploited in plantations which produced for export, as part of an internationally integrated agricultural and manufacturing system (Fox-Genovese and Genovese, 1983; Blackburn, 1988).

In the late nineteenth century, slaves were replaced by indentured workers as the main source of colonial labor. British authorities recruited workers from India and China for plantations, mines, and railway construction in the Caribbean, Malaya, East Africa, and Fiji. The Dutch used Chinese labor on construction projects in the East Indies. Up to one million indentured workers were recruited in Japan, mainly for work in Hawaii, the USA, Brazil, and Peru. Indentured workers were used in 40 countries by all the colonial powers, with estimates of their numbers ranging from 12 to 37 million between 1834 and 1941 (Potts, 1990). Indentured workers were bound by strict labor contracts for a period of several years. Wages and conditions were poor, and breaches of contract were severely punished. On the other hand, work overseas offered an opportunity to escape poverty and repressive situations, such as the Indian caste system. Many workers remained as free settlers in East Africa, the Caribbean, Fiji, and elsewhere, where they could obtain land or set up businesses.

The wealth accumulated in Western Europe through colonial exploitation provided capital for the industrial revolutions of the eighteenth and nineteenth centuries. In turn, the social dislocation caused by industrialization led to mass emigration to North and South America and Australia. The USA is generally seen as the most important of all immigration countries, with an estimated 30 million people entering in the peak period from 1861 to 1920. At first migration was unregulated: anyone who could afford the ocean passage could seek a new life in America. Racist campaigns led to exclusionary laws to keep out Chinese and other Asians from the 1880s. By 1920 there were 13.9 million foreign-born people in the USA (13.2 percent of the total population). Patterns of settlement were closely linked to the emerging industrial economy. Labor recruitment by canal and railway companies led to settlements of Irish and Italians along the construction routes. Some groups of Irish, Italians, and Jews settled in the East coast ports of arrival, where work was available in construction, transport, and factories. The same was true of the Chinese on the West coast. Some Central and Eastern Europeans became concentrated in the Midwest, where the development of heavy industry at the turn of the century provided jobs. The American working class developed through processes of chain migration which led to patterns of ethnic segmentation (Portes and Rumbaut, 1990).

As Western Europeans went overseas in the (often vain) attempt to escape proletarianization, workers from peripheral areas, like Ireland, Poland, and Italy, were drawn in as replacement labor. Britain's new factory towns quickly absorbed labor surpluses from the countryside. Atrocious working and living conditions led to poor health, high infant mortality, and short life expectancy. Natural increase was inadequate to meet labor needs, so Britain's closest colony, Ireland, became a labor source. The devastation of Irish peasant agriculture and domestic industry under British rule had led to widespread poverty and periodic famines. By 1851 there were over 700,000 Irish in Britain - 3 percent of the population of England and Wales and 7 percent of the population of Scotland (Jackson, 1963). They were concentrated in the industrial cities, especially in textile factories and the building trades. Their social conditions were extremely poor and their situation was marked by hostility and discrimination right into the twentieth century.

German industrialization in the late nineteenth century led to strong demand for Polish immigrant workers. However there was fear that settlement of Poles might weaken German control of the Eastern provinces of the *Reich*. By 1890, a system of rigid control had been devised. Poles were recruited as temporary seasonal workers only, not allowed to bring dependants and forced to leave German territory for several months each year. Their work contracts provided pay and conditions inferior to those of German workers. Special police sections were established to deal with workers leaving for better-paid jobs, through forcible return of workers to their employers, imprisonment, or deportation. The status of foreigner was used to keep wages low and to create a split labor market. Foreign labor played a major role in Germany's rise to the status of a major power in the lead up to World War I, with Italian, Belgian, and Dutch workers alongside the Poles.

France had over one million migrant workers by 1881. Most carried out unskilled manual work in agriculture, mines, and factories. The peculiarity of the French case lies in the reasons for the shortage of labor: birth rates fell sharply after 1860, as peasants, shopkeepers, and artisans adopted birth control. Keeping the family small meant that property could be passed on intact from generation to generation. France therefore saw relatively little overseas emigration during industrialization, and rural–urban migration was also limited. Labor immigration played a vital role in the emergence of modern industry. It was also seen as important for military reasons. The Nationality Law of 1889 was designed to turn immigrants and their sons into conscripts for the impending conflict with Germany (Schnapper, 1994). From the mid-nineteenth century to the present, the labor market has been regularly fed by foreign immigration, making up, on average, 10–15 percent of the working class. Noiriel estimates that without immigration the French population today would be only 35 million (instead of over 50 million) (Noiriel, 1988:308–18).

The period from 1918 to 1945 was one of reduced international migrations – partly because of economic conditions, and partly because of hostility towards immigrants in many countries. In the USA, "nativist" groups claimed that Southern and Eastern Europeans were "unassimilable" and presented threats to public order and American values. Congress enacted a national origins quota system that stopped large-scale immigration until the 1960s. France was the only country to recruit foreign workers in this period, due to its substantial war losses. Migrant workers were controlled through a system of identity cards and work contracts, and were channeled into jobs in farming, construction, and heavy industry. By 1931, there were 2.7 million foreigners in France (6.6 percent of the total population). Large colonies of Italians and Poles sprang up in the mining and heavy industrial towns of the North and East of France. There were Spanish and Italian agricultural settlements in the Southwest. In the depression of the 1930s, many migrants were deported and the foreign population fell half a million by 1936 (Cross, 1983).

The Nazi regime recruited enormous numbers of foreign workers – mainly by force – to replace German men conscripted for military service. By the end of the war, there were 7.5 million foreign workers in the Reich, of whom 1.8 million were prisoners of war. It is estimated that a quarter of industrial production was carried out by foreign workers in 1944. The Nazi war machine would have collapsed far earlier without foreign labor. The basic principle for treating foreign workers was that "All the men must be fed, sheltered and treated in such a way as to exploit them to the highest possible extent at the lowest conceivable degree of expenditure" (Homze, 1967:119). This meant housing workers in barracks under military control, the lowest possible wages (or none at all), appalling social and health conditions, and complete deprivation of civil rights. Many foreign workers died through harsh treatment and cruel punishments. The Nazis took exploitation of rightless migrants to an extreme which can only be compared with slavery, yet its legal core – the sharp division between the status of national and foreigner – was to be found both in earlier and later foreign labor systems (Castles and Miller, 1998:65).

The Globalization of Migration Since 1945

After World War II, international migration expanded in volume and geographical scope. More and more countries were affected by migration, while the diversity of migrants increased, so most immigration countries received entrants from a broad spectrum of economic, social, and cultural backgrounds. Two main phases can be distinguished. The first lasted from 1945 to 1973: the long boom stimulated large-scale labor migration to Western Europe, North America, and Oceania from less-developed areas. This phase ended around 1973, with the "oil crisis," which triggered a major recession. In a second phase from the mid-1970s, capital investment shifted away from the old centers, and transnational forms of production and distribution reshaped the world economy. Migratory flows at first declined and were partly reversed, then grew again. The older industrial countries experienced new types of inflows, while new immigration countries emerged in Southern Europe, the Gulf oil countries, Latin America, Africa, and Asia. The late 1980s and early 1990s were a period of unprecedented migration. The timing of movements and their specific characteristics vary from country to country, and it is only possible to give a cursory overview here (for more detailed accounts see Stalker, 1994; Cohen, 1995; OECD, 1997; Castles and Miller, 1998).

Europe

Postwar Europe experienced several types of migration. At first, large numbers of people emigrated, mainly to North and South America and Oceania. At the same time, millions of "displaced persons" had to be absorbed, especially some 12 million who entered West Germany from the former Eastern areas lost in the War. The independence of former colonies led to the return of many colonists to Europe. By the 1950s, strong economic growth was leading to labor shortages, and employers and governments began to encourage labor migration. This was of two main types. Most Western European countries recruited foreign workers, from the less-developed periphery: Southern Europe, North Africa, Turkey, Finland, and Ireland. Some labor-recruiting countries, such as Germany and Switzerland, went to great lengths to prevent settlement through "guestworker" systems which controlled the recruitment, working conditions, and rights of the migrants. The second type of labor migration was from colonies or former colonies: from the Caribbean and the Indian subcontinent to Britain, from North and West Africa to France, and from the Caribbean and Indonesia to the Netherlands.

Colonized peoples had been granted citizenship as a form of ideological integration. Now this facilitated the entry of labor, but it also meant that the colonial workers could bring in dependents and settle. By the 1960s, the authorities began introducing laws to stop colonial immigration. There was a convergence in status between "guestworkers" and colonial workers. But by 1970 there were over 12 million immigrants in Western Europe and the process of ethnic minority formation had become irreversible.

The 1973 oil crisis led to a halt in labor recruitment. Governments expected the "guestworkers" to depart, but instead a phase of family reunion and settlement set in. Lower immigration rates allowed a demographic normalization: family reunion took place, new families were formed, and the original immigrants aged. Community formation took place, and education and welfare authorities slowly began to respond to new needs (Castles et al., 1984). But this phase of consolidation was not to last. In the mid-1980s immigration accelerated through the influx of asylum seekers and illegal workers. At the same time Southern European countries experienced a "migration transition" from migrant-sending to migrant-receiving countries. Economic growth, combined with a sharp fall in birthrates, led to labor shortages. By the late 1980s, Italy, Spain, Portugal, and Greece were using labor from Eastern Europe, North Africa, and even Asia to bring in their harvests and sweep their streets. Most of the immigrants came spontaneously and without documents (King and Black, 1997).

Refugees and asylum seekers from Eastern Europe, Africa, Asia, and the Middle East became a main type of population inflow to Western Europe. Their annual number increased from 116,000 in 1981 to 695,000 in 1992, with nearly two thirds going to Germany (OECD, 1995). A migration panic gripped Western Europe in the early 1990s: following the collapse of the Soviet bloc, influxes of up to 50 million East–West migrants were predicted. Indeed, a general reshuffle of ethnic groups in Central and Eastern Europe did take place. *Aussiedler*, persons of German descent from Eastern European countries, moved to Germany, where they had a right to entry and citizenship. Jews left the former Soviet Union for Israel and the USA. There were movements of ethnic Greeks from Albania to Greece, of ethnic Poles from Russia to Poland, of Muslim Bulgarians to Turkey and so on. Millions of people moved between the successor states of the former Soviet Union, in response to wars, ethnic persecution, environmental disasters, and economic change (UNHCR, 1995). The disintegration of Yugoslavia and the wars in Croatia and Bosnia led to mass refugee exoduses, with hundreds of thousands seeking protection abroad.

One consequence was an upsurge in racist violence and extreme-right mobilization. Another was the politicization of migration issues. Refugee-receiving countries like Germany and Sweden tightened up their entry rules. A series of intergovernmental meetings were held to find ways of controlling migration. The most important was the Schengen Agreement through which Belgium, France, Germany, Italy, Luxembourg, Netherlands, Portugal, and Spain dismantled border controls for people moving between these countries, but set up tougher control measures at the external borders of the "Schengen area." By the mid-1990s it was clear that the "human floods" from the East would not come. A new debate began in Western Europe about the future need for immigrants, due to low fertility and aging populations. The high fertility and young underemployed populations of North Africa and Turkey appear to many Europeans as both a threat and a potential benefit. Who else will provide labor for the factories and building sites, or careers for the aged, if present trends continue?

North America and Australia

The USA had restrictive immigration policies until 1965. About 250,000 persons per year were admitted in the 1950s – mainly Western Europeans and refugees. Cold War politics ensured a warm welcome for anyone from Eastern Europe and later from Cuba. However, US agricultural employers also recruited large numbers of temporary workers from Mexico and the Caribbean. At times this migration was regulated by temporary labor systems, while at other times it was illegal, but tacitly tolerated. The turning point in US policies came in 1965 with changes to the Immigration and Nationality Act, which abolished the discriminatory national-origins quota system. No one envisaged the consequences: rapid growth in intakes and a diversification of areas of origin. Immigration escalated, averaging 450,000 per year in the 1970s and 600,000 per year in the 1980s. From 1986 to 1995 about 12 million immigrants were legally admitted to the USA. Australia and Canada also experienced high immigration.

Canadian intakes grew from 89,000 in 1983 to a peak of 255,000 in 1993, and then fell to 212,000 in 1995. Australia's permanent immigration level fluctuated according to economic conditions, rising from 70,000 in 1983 to 145,000 in 1989, then declining to 70,000 again in the recession year of 1994, before starting to increase again. The main feature was the change in areas of origin, following the removal of racial discrimination in entry policy in the 1970s. Increasing shares of immigrants to Australia came from Asia; and to Canada from Asia, the Caribbean, and Latin America (OECD, 1997).

As in Europe, the early 1990s saw public panics about being "swamped" by refugees and illegal migrants from less-developed countries. Anti-immigration campaigns evoked nineteenth century fears of the "yellow peril." But there were new factors, such as reactions against economic restructuring and globalization, and competition between old and new minorities, In the USA, anti-immigration groups sought the proclamation of English as the "official language," and lobbied for the restriction of welfare payments to illegal immigrants and their children. Refugee quotas were cut, since Cold War imperatives no longer applied. The stopping of refugee boats from Haiti and Cuba by the US

Coast Guard in 1992 and again in 1994 was part of the trend towards greater restriction. The US-led invasion of Haiti in 1994 set a precedent for military action to stop mass migration. In September 1996, the US Congress passed anti-immigration legislation, designed to double the number of border guards on the frontier with Mexico. The new law also denied welfare and education to illegal immigrants and restricted eligibility of legals.

New migrations in less developed regions

In the 1980s and 1990s, huge new population movements affected Africa, Asia, and Latin America. Such migrations were not without precedent: as pointed out above, colonialism and the rise of capitalism had led to the emergence of a world labor market long before the era of globalization. But economic and political conditions had led to a relative lull in migration in the first half of the twentieth century. From the 1950s, new movements emerged, linked to decolonization, globalization, and the emergence of new industrial economies. The migration systems of the South have become closely interlinked with those of the North, making efforts by Western countries to exclude the postcolonial Other even more futile. It is impossible here to deal with the new migrations affecting the South. Instead a brief summary of migratory flows in Asia is given as an example.

Early postwar migration from Asia to European countries took place in the context of decolonization. Western penetration through trade, aid, and investment had created the material means, the cultural capital, and the communicative networks necessary for migration. Labor migration from the Indian subcontinent to Britain in the 1950s was soon followed by family reunion and settlement. Movements from Indo-China to France and from Indonesia to the Netherlands had both political and economic motivations. From the late 1960s, as racist exclusion clauses were removed in the USA, Australia, and Canada, large-scale migrations developed. They were very diverse, including unskilled workers, highly skilled personnel and refugees.

Labor migration from Asia to the Middle East developed after the oil price rise of 1973. The main labor-sending countries were Bangladesh, India, Pakistan, Sri Lanka, the Philippines, Indonesia, Thailand, and South Korea. Migration took place within rigid contract labor frameworks: workers were not allowed to settle nor bring in dependents, and lacked civil or political rights. They were generally segregated in barracks, and could be deported for misconduct. Women domestic workers were vulnerable to exploitation and sexual abuse.

From the 1980s, there was an upsurge in labor migration within Asia. The international movements were often linked to internal migrations, such as the huge rural–urban movements in China. The dislocation of rural production and social structures through industrialization, the "Green Revolution," and warfare forced people to leave the countryside. Rapid industrial and urban growth in the NICs created an enormous demand for labor. Improved living standards in these countries were generally followed by declines in fertility, creating both economic and demographic need for immigrants. Men were wanted in construction and heavy manufacturing, while women workers were in heavy demand in textile and garment industries, as well as in precision assembly processes in the electronics industry.

The estimated annual number of documented migrant workers going abroad to work from Asian countries was about one million in 1990, but had risen to 2.1 million by 1994.

575

Most still went to the Gulf, but about a quarter moved within Asia. It is impossible to estimate the numbers moving illegally, but they probably exceed the documented migrants. There was strong demand for migrant labor in fast-growing economies, including Japan, Taiwan, Singapore, Brunei, South Korea, Hong Kong, Malaysia, and Thailand. Countries with slower economic growth rates became labor reserves. These included Indonesia, China, and the South Asian countries. The Philippines is a particularly significant case, with its high birthrate, relatively good education system, and lagging development. By the mid-1990s there were an estimated 4.2 million Filipino workers, of whom 1.8 million are undocumented in 130 countries (Huguet, 1995).

Another growing movement is that of professionals, executives, technicians, and other highly skilled personnel. One form this takes is the "brain drain": university-trained people moving between highly developed countries – a great economic loss for less developed countries. Another form is executives and professionals sent by their companies to work in overseas branches or joint ventures, or experts sent by international organizations to work in aid programs. Skilled migrants are agents not only of economic change, but also bearers of new cultural values which affect the countries they work in. When they return home they also bring new experiences with them, which may stimulate change in previously monocultural countries such as Japan.

Asia has also experienced large-scale refugee movements. In the 1970s, over two million people fled from Indo-China due to the Vietnam War. Over a million were resettled in the United States, with smaller numbers in Australia, Canada, and Western Europe. Six million people (a third of the population) fled Afghanistan following the Soviet military intervention in 1979. Most went to Pakistan and Iran. There have been a multitude of smaller movements, involving for instance East Timor, Burma, Fiji, and China. In 1997, 4.8 million of the world's estimated 13.1 million refugees were in Asia (UNHCR, 1997:287).

The Asian Crisis of 1997–98 caused significant changes in migratory patterns. Labor-importing countries tried to reduce dependence on foreign workers through nonrenewal of contracts and expulsion of undocumented workers. In Malaysia, for example, the government announced that up to a million workers would be sent home and there were mass roundups of illegals, who were confined in special camps before being sent back to Indonesia and the Philippines. However, there was great pressure for emigration from countries like Indonesia, where the crisis led to soaring unemployment. In any case, Malaysian plantation owners soon found that they could not manage without foreign workers. Even unemployed Malaysians were not prepared to do this type of work. The plantation owners lobbied for a halt to the expulsion policy. In fact the number of migrant workers deported was quite small, and new recruitment started again fairly rapidly. By 1999 Asian economies were recovering and migration resumed. In the long run the crisis actually exacerbated the income differential between the least developed countries and the better-off economies. The result has been new waves of illegal migrations, together with attempts by governments to control these. It seems likely that, rather than causing a halt to labor migration, the crisis will prove to be a turning point leading to new forms of migration and settlement. The potential for growth in population mobility in Asia and other less developed regions remains enormous.

Migration, Multicultural Societies and Transnational Belonging

Migration is a large and multifaceted area of study, and this chapter has merely touched on a few themes, while omitting many others of equal significance, such as migration and development, the psychology of migration, legal aspects, migration and citizenship, and many others. In the context of this volume, the main importance of migration lies in the way that it helps increase cultural diversity in many societies, creating the conditions for new forms of ethnic relations. Historically, nation-states have been based on the idea that a people with a common culture should form a political community within fixed geographical boundaries. In reality, nearly all nation-states have incorporated groups with diverse cultures through expansion, conquest, or migration. Creating a common culture has therefore involved lengthy (and often oppressive) processes of integration or assimilation. Globalization doubly undermines the conditions for consolidation of nation-states. First, national boundaries are becoming increasingly porous, so that the national society ceases to be the exclusive (or even the principal) focus for economic, social, and political life. Secondly, the growth of migration and the increasing diversity of migrants in terms of origins, culture, and economic and social characteristics lead to ever more rapid formation of new minorities. Thus virtually all countries of immigration are becoming multicultural societies, in which a range of ethnic groups tend to cluster together and maintain their own languages, cultures, and religions over generations.

However, multicultural societies are not to be equated with multiculturalism, which refers to a policy decision by receiving societies to recognize cultural difference and take measures to ensure social justice for minorities. Indeed, there are clear signs of a backlash against multiculturalism at present in many countries, including Australia, Canada, the USA, and Sweden. The combination of economic restructuring, erosion of national cultures, and immigration – all facets of globalization – leads to reactive movements to try to rescue myths of autonomous national communities and unitary identity. Unfortunately such movements often take on racist characteristics and nurture violence against minorities. One product of this current backlash has been attempts to severely curtail international migration, especially from South to North. Similar anti-immigrant movements have arisen in Asian immigration countries, partly in response to the economic crisis. Typically such movements pose the alternatives: stay out or assimilate. Neither is realistic. As long as there are huge disparities in income, welfare, and security between poor and rich countries, migration will continue. Control measures can affect migration – for instance, by redirecting flows or turning them from legal into illegal ones – but are unlikely to stop movements permanently.

As for assimilation, it is becoming increasingly illusory in view of rapid advances in transport and communications, which make it easier to maintain transcultural identities and communities. The links between migrant community and area of origin may persist over generations. Remittances may fall off and visits home decline in frequency, but familial and cultural links remain. Once established, migration chains persist and can be reactivated at a time of crisis, as shown in the early 1990s by the mass refugee movement of former Yugoslavs to Germany, where they joined compatriots who had migrated as workers 20 years earlier. Economic relations may start with import of homeland foods and other products to the immigration area, and continue with export of manufactured goods in the other direction, leading to international business networks. Cultural linkages

577

persist as two-way connections: migrants' linguistic and cultural roots are maintained, while influences from the immigration country encourage change in the area of origin. In the long run, migration may lead to international communicative networks, which affect economic relations, social and political institutions, and the culture and national identity of all the countries concerned (Basch et al., 1994). In the past, migration, especially over long distances to countries like the USA or Australia, was seen as a one-way process leading to permanent settlement. Today, people can move frequently between countries, and be members of more than one society. This emerging transnational belonging throws up all sort of problems for ideas of unitary national identity and citizenship of a single nation-state (Baubock and Rundell, 1998). If global migration continues to grow, transnational belonging and multiple citizenship may become much more common in the future.

References

Basch, L., Glick-Schiller, N., and Blanc, C. S. (1994) *Nations Unbound: Transnational Projects, Post-Colonial Predicaments and Deterritorialized Nation-States*. New York: Gordon and Breach.

Baubock, R. and Rundell, J. (eds.) (1998) *Blurred Boundaries: Migration, Ethnicity, Citizenship*. Aldershot: Ashgate.

Blackburn, R. (1988) *The Overthrow of Colonial Slavery 1776–1848*. London: Verso.

Borjas, G. J. (1990) *Friends or Strangers: The Impact of Immigration on the US Economy*. New York: Basic Books.

Boyd, M. (1989) "Family and personal networks in migration." *International Migration Review, Special Silver Anniversary Issue, 23*, 3:638–70.

Boyle, P., Halfacree, K., and Robinson, V. (1998) *Exploring Contemporary Migration*. Harlow, UK: Longman.

Castles, S., Booth, H., and Wallace, T. (1984) *Here for Good: Western Europe's New Ethnic Minorities*. London: Pluto Press.

Castles, S., Foster, W., Iredale, R., and Withers, G. (1998) *Immigration and Australia: Myths and Realities*. Sydney: Allen & Unwin.

Castles, S. and Kosack, G. (1985). *Immigrant Workers and Class Structure in Western Europe*, 2nd edn. London: Oxford University Press.

Castles, S. and Miller, M. J. (1998) *The Age of Migration: International Population Movements in the Modern World*. London: Macmillan.

Cohen, R. (1987) *The New Helots: Migrants in the International Division of Labour*. Aldershot, UK: Avebury.

Cohen, R. (ed.) (1995) *The Cambridge Survey of World Migration*. Cambridge, UK: Cambridge University Press.

Cornelius, W., Martin, P., and Hollifield, J. (1994) *Controlling Migration: A Global Perspective*. Stanford, CA: Stanford University Press.

Cross, G. S. (1983) *Immigrant Workers in Industrial France: The Making of a New Laboring Class*. Philadelphia, PA: Temple University Press.

Fawcett, J. T. (1989) "Networks, linkages and migration systems." *International Migration Review* 23,3:671–80.

Fox-Genovese, E. and Genovese, E. D. (1983) *Fruits of Merchant Capital: Slavery and Bourgeois Property in the Rise and Expansion of Capitalism*. New York: Oxford University Press.

Harris, N. (1996) *The New Untouchables: Immigration and the New World Worker*. London: Penguin.

Homze, E. L. (1967) *Foreign Labor in Nazi Germany*. Princeton, NJ: Princeton University Press.

Hugo, G. (1994) *Migration and the Family*. Vienna: United Nations.

Huguet, J. W. (1995) "Data on international migration in Asia: 1990–94." *Asian and Pacific Migration Journal* 4,4:517–29.

Jackson, J. A. (1963) *The Irish in Britain*. London: Routledge and Kegan Paul.

King, R. and Black, R. (eds.) (1997) *Southern Europe and the New Immigrations*. London: Belhaven.

Kritz, M. M., Lin, L. L., and Zlotnik, H. (eds.) (1992) *International Migration Systems: A Global Approach*. Oxford: Clarendon Press.

Lutz, H., Phoenix, A., and Yuval-Davis, N. (eds.) (1995) *Crossfires: Nationalism, Racism and Gender in Europe*. London: Pluto Press.

Massey, D. S., Arango, J., Hugo, G., Kouaouci, A., Pellegrino, A., and Taylor, J. E. (1993) "Theories of international migration: A review and appraisal." *Population and Development Review*, 19,3:431–66.

Moch, L. P. (1992) *Moving Europeans: Migration in Western Europe since 1650*. Bloomington: Indiana University Press.

Noiriel, G. (1988) *Le creuset français: Histoire de l'immigration XIXe–XXe siecles*. Paris: Seuil.

OECD (1995) *Trends in International Migration: Annual Report 1994*. Paris: OECD.

OECD (1997) *Trends in International Migration: Annual Report 1996*. Paris: OECD.

Piore, M. (1980) *Birds of Passage: Migrant Labor and Industrial Societies*. Cambridge, UK: Cambridge University Press.

Portes, A. and Rumbaut, R. G. (1990) *Immigrant America: A Portrait*. Los Angeles: University of California Press.

Potts, L. (1990) *The World Labour Market: A History of Migration*. London: Zed Books.

Sassen, S. (1988) *The Mobility of Labour and Capital*. Cambridge, UK: Cambridge University Press.

Schnapper, D. (1994) *La Communaute des Citoyens*. Paris: Gallimard.

Skeldon, R. (1997) *Migration and Development: A Global Perspective*. Harlow, UK: Addison Wesley Longman.

Stahl, C. (1993) "Explaining international migration," in C. Stahl, R. Ball, C. Inglis, and P. Gutman *Global Population Movements and their Implications for Australia*. Canberra, Australian Government Publishing Service.

Stalker, P. (1994) *The Work of Strangers: A Survey of International Labour Migration*. Geneva: International Labour Office.

Stark, O. (1991) *The Migration of Labour*. Oxford: Blackwell.

Todaro, M. (1976) *Internal Migration in Developing Countries*. Geneva: International Labour Office.

UNHCR (United Nations High Commissioner for Refugees) (1995) *The State of the World's Refugees: In Search of Solutions*. Oxford: Oxford University Press.

UNHCR (United Nations High Commissioner for Refugees) (1997) *The State of the World's Refugees 1997–98: A Humanitarian Agenda*. Oxford: Oxford University Press.

Weiner, M. (1993) *International Migration and Security*. Boulder, CO: Westview Press.

Zlotnik, H. (1998) *The Dimensions of International Migration: International Migration Levels, Trends and What Existing Data Systems Reveal*. Technical Symposium on International Migration and Development, The Hague, Netherlands.

Zolberg, A. R., Suhrke, A., and Aguayo, S. (1989) *Escape from Violence*. New York: Oxford University Press.

Index